United Nations Conference on Trade and Development

World Investment Report 1998:
Trends and Determinants

United Nations
New York and Geneva, 1998

Note

UNCTAD serves as the focal point within the United Nations Secretariat for all matters related to foreign direct investment and transnational corporations. In the past, the Programme on Transnational Corporations was carried out by the United Nations Centre on Transnational Corporations (1975-1992) and the Transnational Corporations and Management Division of the United Nations Department of Economic and Social Development (1992-1993). In 1993, the Programme was transferred to the United Nations Conference on Trade and Development. UNCTAD seeks to further the understanding of the nature of transnational corporations and their contribution to development and to create an enabling environment for international investment and enterprise development. UNCTAD's work is carried out through intergovernmental deliberations, technical assistance activities, seminars, workshops and conferences.

The term "country" as used in this study also refers, as appropriate, to territories or areas; the designations employed and the presentation of the material do not imply the expression of any opinion whatsoever on the part of the Secretariat of the United Nations concerning the legal status of any country, territory, city or area or of its authorities, or concerning the delimitation of its frontiers or boundaries. In addition, the designations of country groups are intended solely for statistical or analytical convenience and do not necessarily express a judgement about the stage of development reached by a particular country or area in the development process.

The following symbols have been used in the tables:

Two dots (..) indicate that data are not available or are not separately reported. Rows in tables have been omitted in those cases where no data are available for any of the elements in the row;

A dash (-) indicates that the item is equal to zero or its value is negligible;

A blank in a table indicates that the item is not applicable;

A slash (/) between dates representing years, e.g., 1994/95, indicates a financial year;

Use of a hyphen (-) between dates representing years, e.g., 1994-1995, signifies the full period involved, including the beginning and end years.

Reference to "dollars" ($) means United States dollars, unless otherwise indicated.

Annual rates of growth or change, unless otherwise stated, refer to annual compound rates.

Details and percentages in tables do not necessarily add to totals because of rounding.

The material contained in this study may be freely quoted with appropriate acknowledgement.

UNITED NATIONS PUBLICATION

Sales No. E.98.II.D.5

ISBN 92-1-112426-3

Preface

The eighth annual *World Investment Report* is issued at a time when the process of globalization is under close scrutiny. Even as countries continue to forge stronger economic links with one another, in the past year unexpected financial shocks have interrupted the economic progress of a group of previously fast developing countries in Asia. This has provoked renewed interest, especially from a policy perspective, in the modes of internationalization, including through foreign direct investment.

The *World Investment Report 1998 (WIR98)* explores the implications of the Asian financial crisis for foreign direct investment in and from the affected Asian economies. As usual, it provides an analysis of current trends in foreign direct investment and international production by transnational corporations, examining key aspects of the world's largest transnational corporations, and noting major regulatory changes at the national and international levels. It provides a breakdown of regional FDI trends, and examines specific issues related to the role and impact of foreign direct investment in various parts of the world.

WIR98 also reviews the locational factors that determine the flows of foreign direct investment to host countries, and the evolving nature of those determinants as transnational corporations adjust their strategies to the pressures of increased international competition. Among other issues, it addresses the influence of regional and multilateral frameworks on the location of international production and foreign direct investment flows.

In discussing these trends and issues, *WIR98* contributes to an improved understanding of the role of foreign direct investment in the world economy and to the ongoing discussion in all quarters on globalization. It will also help stimulate the debate on financing for development that the General Assembly of the United Nations will consider in 1999.

Kofi A. Annan
Secretary-General of the United Nations

New York, August 1998

Acknowledgements

The *World Investment Report 1998* was prepared by a team led by Karl P. Sauvant and comprising Victoria Aranda, Persephone Economou, Wilfried Engelke, Masataka Fujita, Kálmán Kalotay, Padma Mallampally, Ludger Odenthal, Assad Omer, Jörg Weber, James Xiaoning Zhan and Zbigniew Zimny. Specific inputs were received from Bijit Bora, Sew Sam Chan Tung, Anna Joubin-Bret, Mina Dowlatchahi, Gabriele Koehler, Menelea Masin, Anne Miroux, Marko Stanovic and Anh Nga Tran-Nguyen. The work was carried out under the overall direction of Lynn K. Mytelka.

Principal research assistance was provided by Mohamed Chiraz Baly, Lizanne Martinez and Bradley Boicourt. Research assistance was provided by Rohan Patel, Katja Weigl, Makameh Bahrami and Paul Baker. A number of interns assisted with the *WIR98* at various stages: Maria Giovanna Bosco, Ozavize Lawani, Ju-Young Lee, Bruno Le Feuvre, Jennifer Lynn McDonald, Alain-Christian Pandzou and David Pritchett. The production of the *WIR98* was carried out by Jenifer Tacardon, Christiane Defrancisco, Medarde Almario, Florence Hudry, Hélène Dufays, Atsedeweyn Abate and Bartolomeo D'Addario. Graphics were done by Diego Oyarzun-Reyes. It was desktop-published by Teresita Sabico. The *Report* was edited by Vishwas Govitrikar and copy-edited by Frederick Glover.

Experts from within and outside the United Nations provided inputs for *WIR98*. Major inputs were received from Thomas L. Brewer, Jaime Crispi, Robert E. Lipsey, Michael Mortimore, Peter Nunnenkamp and Terutomo Ozawa. Inputs were also received from Rakesh Basant, Christian J. Bellak, Alvaro Calderón, Pankaj Chandra, Daniel Chudnovsky, Michel Delapierre, E.S. Dussell Peters, Frank Dutman, Reinaldo Gonçalves, Anabel Gonzalez, Edward M. Graham, Fabrice Hatem, Eduardo Hecker, Katharina Helmstedt, Grazia Ietto-Gillies, Yong-Hwan Lee, Mark Mason, Sheila Page, Nipon Poapongsakorn, Jason Praetorius, Eric D. Ramstetter, Jacques Sasseville, Marjan Svetlicic, Douglas van den Berghe, Rob van Tulder, Lise Weis, Obie G. Whichard, Guoming Xian and Yew Siew Young.

A number of experts were consulted on various chapters. Comments were received during various stages of preparation (including expert meetings) from Jamuna Prasad Agarwal, Manuel R. Agosín, Charles Arden-Clarke, Octavio Barros, Atchaka Brimble, Luz Curiel Beaty, Paul Bennell, Michael Blank, Susan C. Borkowski, Dali Bouzoraa, Eva Bursvik, John A. Cantwell, Jenny Cargill, Andrew Cornford, Dieter Ernst, Arghyrios A. Fatouros, Jarko Fidrmuc, Gunnar Fors, John Gara, Michael Gestrin, Jan Huner, Gábor Hunya, J. Jegathesan, Rolf Jungnickel, June-Dong Kim, John M. Kline, Masamichi Kono, Mark Koulen, Sanjaya Lall, Ngo Van Lam, Robert Ley, Nick Mabey, Raymond Mataloni, Klaus E. Meyer, Manuel B. Montes, Peter Muchlinski, Lucia Piscitello, Sylvain Plasschaert, Maryse Robert, Pedro Roffe, Matija Rojec, Alan M. Rugman, Mitsuharu Sawaji, Sara Sievers, Carrie Smith, John M. Stopford, Simon Teitel, Shigeki Tejima, Raymond Vernon, Wee Kee Hwee, Ganeshan Wignaraja and Stephen Young.

Numerous officials of central banks, statistical offices, investment-promotion agencies and other government offices, as well as executives of a number of companies, also contributed to *WIR98,* especially through the provision of data and other information.

The *Report* benefited from overall advice from John H. Dunning, Senior Economic Adviser.

The financial support of the Government of Norway is gratefully acknowledged.

Contents

Page

Boxes

Figures

Page

Page

Page

Page

Tables

Page

Page

OVERVIEW

Foreign direct investment set a new record in 1997, expanding and strengthening international production worldwide...

Worldwide foreign direct investment (FDI) inflows continued their upward climb in 1997 for the seventh consecutive year. Seemingly unaffected by the Asian financial crisis, they increased by 19 per cent to a new record level of $400 billion, while outflows reached $424 billion. The capital base of international production in 1997, including capital for direct investment purposes drawn from sources other than transnational corporations (TNCs), is estimated to have increased by $1.6 trillion in 1997.

The upward trend in investment flows supported further the expansion in international production. In 1997, the value of international production, attributed to some 53,000 TNCs and their 450,000 foreign affiliates, was $3.5 trillion as measured by the accumulated stock of FDI, and $9.5 trillion as measured by the estimated global sales of foreign affiliates. Other indicators also point in the same direction: global exports by foreign affiliates are now some $2 trillion, their global assets $13 trillion, and the global value added by them more than $2 trillion. These figures are also impressive when related to the size of the global economy: the ratio of inward plus outward FDI stocks to global GDP is now 21 per cent; foreign affiliate exports are one-third of world exports; and GDP attributed to foreign affiliates accounts for 7 per cent of global GDP. Sales of foreign affiliates have grown faster than world exports of goods and services, and the ratio of the volume of world inward plus outward FDI stocks to world GDP has grown twice as fast as the ratio of world imports and exports to world GDP, suggesting that the expansion of international production has deepened the interdependence of the world economy beyond that achieved by international trade alone.

... with the 100 largest TNCs in the world having become highly transnationalized and the 50 largest developing country TNCs catching up.

The world's 100 largest TNCs show a high degree of transnationality as measured by the shares of foreign assets, foreign sales and foreign employment in their total assets, sales and employment. The top 50 TNCs headquartered in developing countries are catching up rapidly. The composite index that combines all three shares bears this out: the top 50 TNCs headquartered in developing countries have built up their foreign assets almost seven times faster than the world's top 100 TNCs between 1993 and 1996 in their efforts to transnationalize. The transnationality index of the former was 35 per cent in 1996, while that of the latter was 55 per cent. While the value of the index for the top 100 TNCs is higher, it did not change significantly between 1990 and 1995. In contrast, the value of the index for the top 50 developing country TNCs has been increasing steadily throughout the 1990s. Naturally, there are significant differences by type of industry, with telecommunications, transport, construction and trading being the most transnational in the case of the top 50 developing country TNCs, while food and beverages, chemicals and pharmaceuticals, and electronics and electrical equipment were the most transnational among the world's top 100. The ranking of TNCs by the different transnationality indexes also differs: although General Electric tops the list of the largest 100 TNCs ranked by the size of foreign assets, Seagram ranks first in the composite index of transnationality. Likewise, Daewoo Corporation topped the list of the 50 largest developing country TNCs by foreign assets, but Orient Overseas International ranked first in the composite index of transnationality. Not surprisingly, firms at the top of the composite transnationality index are from countries with small domestic markets.

Developing countries continue to be major players in FDI inflows...

The impressive numbers documenting the growth of international production disguise considerable variation across and within regions. There is no doubt that the developed countries, with more than two-thirds of the world inward FDI stock and 90 per cent of the outward stock, dominate the global picture, but their dominance is being eroded. Developing countries accounted for nearly a third of the global inward FDI stock in 1997, increasing from one-fifth in 1990. It is in flows of inward FDI that developing countries have made the biggest gains over the 1990s, with their values as well as shares of global inflows increasing markedly: from $34 billion in 1990 (17 per cent of global inflows) to $149 billion in 1997 (37 per cent of global inflows).

...despite the strong investment performance of developed countries in 1997.

Continued strong economic growth in the United States, improved economic performance in many Western European countries, and the mergers-and-acquisitions (M&As) boom are the principal reasons for the acceleration of inflows to developed countries in 1997 (an increase of almost a fifth over 1996, to $233 billion). The United States received $91 billion in inflows, accounting for more than one-fifth of global inflows, and invested $115 billion abroad during the year. Among the countries of the European Union, the United Kingdom received $37 billion (just under a tenth per cent of global inflows) in 1997; in contrast, for the second successive year, Germany registered net FDI withdrawals. Outflows from the European Union were $180 billion in 1997, and a renewed interest in European integration prompted by the expected advent of the Euro in 1999 led to a spurt in the share of investment directed to member countries. Japan received $3 billion in 1997, a record figure, though still low compared to other developed economies, and invested $26 billion abroad.

Worldwide cross-border M&As, mostly in banking, insurance, chemicals, pharmaceuticals and telecommunications, were aimed at the global restructuring or strategic positioning of firms in these industries and experienced another surge in 1997. Valued at $236 billion, majority-owned M&As represented nearly three-fifths of global FDI inflows in 1997, increasing from almost a half in 1996. Many of the 1997 M&A deals have been large and 58 of them were each worth more than $1 billion. The United States, followed by the United Kingdom, France and Germany, accounted for the biggest share of the large M&A deals. Together, developed countries accounted for about 90 per cent of the worldwide majority-owned M&A purchases. These deals are not only a major driver of FDI flows for developed countries, but also shed light on the prevailing strategies of TNCs: divesting non-core activities and strengthening competitive advantages through acquisitions in core activities. These strategies have been made possible by liberalization (including the WTO's financial services agreement in 1997) and deregulation (e.g. in telecommunications). One outcome is a greater industrial concentration in the hands of a few firms in each industry, usually TNCs.

TNCs are achieving their goals of strategic positioning or restructuring not only through M&As but also through inter-firm agreements. A subset of such agreements involves technology-related activities and is a response to the increased knowledge-intensity of production, the shortening of product cycles and the need to keep up with the constantly advancing technological frontier. Such agreements are particularly important for enhancing the technological competitiveness of firms and their number has increased from an annual average of less than 300 in the early 1980s to over 600 in the mid-1990s. An estimated 8,260 inter-firm agreements in technology-intensive activities have been concluded between 1980 and 1996. Given their emphasis on technology or joint R&D development, it is not surprising that inter-firm agreements are prominent in knowledge-intensive industries, such as the information industry and pharmaceuticals and, more recently, in automobiles.

Countries are continuing their efforts to create favourable conditions for FDI, with bilateral treaties and regional initiatives gaining momentum, ...

During 1997, 151 changes in FDI regulatory regimes were made by 76 countries, 89 per cent of them in the direction of creating a more favourable environment for FDI. New liberalization measures were particularly evident in industries like telecommunications, broadcasting and energy that used to be closed to foreign investors. New promotional measures included streamlining approval procedures and developing special trade and investment zones (adding to the many such zones already in existence). During 1997 alone, 36 countries introduced new investment incentives, or strengthened existing ones. The network of bilateral investment treaties (BITs) is expanding as well, totalling 1,513 at the end of 1997. In that year one BIT was concluded, on the average, every two-and-a-half days. The number of double taxation treaties also increased, numbering 1,794 at the end of 1997, with 108 concluded in 1997 alone. The common thread that runs through the proliferation of both types of treaties is that they reflect the growing role of FDI in the world economy and the desire of countries to facilitate it.

Discussions of regional initiatives are taking place in most regions in the context of new or existing agreements. On the American continent, negotiations on the Free Trade Agreement of the Americas (FTAA), intended to incorporate a comprehensive framework of rights and obligations with respect to investment, have been launched. If successful, the FTAA will consolidate and integrate the various free trade and investment areas already present in the region. In Asia, the ASEAN Investment Area is scheduled to be established later this year. However, the approach of the ASEAN Investment Area is different from that of other regional initiatives in that it emphasizes policy flexibility, cooperative endeavours and strategic alliances and avoids, at least for now, legally binding commitments. In Africa, there are preliminary discussions on new regional initiatives on investment in the context of the Southern African Development Community (SADC) and the Organization of African States.

...as governments engage in broad-based and wide-ranging discussions on international investment agreements and their development implications.

The ongoing negotiations on a Multilateral Agreement on Investment at the OECD reached a critical point in 1998 after two years of negotiations, when pressures grew to make them more transparent and to initiate a broad-based public debate on FDI issues. Partly reflecting this situation, a pause for reflection until October 1998 was agreed to by the OECD ministers.

Wide-ranging discussions at the multilateral level have, meanwhile, been taking place mainly in the WTO and UNCTAD. The work of the WTO Working Group on the Relationship between Trade and Investment is focusing on the economic relationship between trade and investment; the implications of the relationship for development and economic growth; existing international arrangements and initiatives on trade and investment; and issues relevant to assessing the need for possible future initiatives. UNCTAD, on the other hand, is seeking to help developing countries participate effectively in international discussions and negotiations on FDI, be it at the bilateral, regional or multilateral level. In pursuing this objective, UNCTAD is paying special attention to identifying the interests of developing countries and ensuring that the development dimension is understood and adequately addressed in international investment agreements.

Foreign direct investment has remained a source of relative stability in capital flows to developing countries, ...

Although smaller than those of developed countries, the increases in 1997 in FDI flows into developing countries are noteworthy because they took place in an environment that presented a complex mix of adverse changes. Unlike other net resource flows such as official development assistance or some other types of private capital, such as portfolio equity investment, FDI inflows increased in 1997, with no developing region experiencing a decline in the level of inflows.

... showing resilience in the face of the financial crisis in Asia and the Pacific, ...

A new record level of $45 billion in FDI flows received by China contributed to the 9 per cent increase in total FDI flows to Asia and the Pacific in 1997. With $87 billion in 1997, Asia and the Pacific accounts for nearly three-fifths of the FDI inflows received by all developing countries, and for over a half of the developing-country FDI stock. East and

South-East Asia, the subregion most affected by the financial crisis in Asia during the second half of the year, also saw a small increase of 6 per cent to $82.4 billion in 1997 but this trend is unlikely to continue in 1998. The five Asian economies most affected by the crisis saw their combined FDI inflows remain at a level almost unchanged from that in 1996. With inflows totalling $2.6 billion in 1997, largely concentrated in oil-producing Kazakhstan and Azerbaijan, Central Asia has become a more important destination for FDI than West Asia, which received $1.9 billion in 1997.

China's current FDI boom, now in its sixth consecutive year, is showing signs of coming to an end. The rate of increase of FDI inflows declined to 11 per cent in 1997 from an average of 147 per cent between 1992 and 1993. Furthermore, FDI approvals have fallen from $111 billion in 1993 to $52 billion in 1997. The expectation of a decline is based on several aspects of the national and regional economy: a slowdown in economic growth from its exceptional performance of the past few years; excess capacity in several industries due to over-investment or weaker demand conditions; wage increases in the coastal areas that are eroding its locational advantage in low-cost labour-intensive investments; poor infrastructure in the interior provinces that hinders investment in low-wage activities; currency depreciations in other economies that are eroding the price competitiveness of foreign affiliate exports; and adverse economic conditions in its biggest FDI source economies in Asia (Hong Kong, China, Japan, the Republic of Korea, Malaysia and Thailand), which constrict their outward flows to China. While these considerations suggest an impending decline in FDI flows to China, ongoing FDI liberalization, massive infrastructure building, foreign-investor participation in the restructuring of state-owned enterprises and a continued strong growth performance compared with other countries in the region could yet mitigate the expected drop.

FDI outflows from Asia and the Pacific increased by 9 per cent in 1997 to $50.7 billion. The biggest investor is Hong Kong, China, with an outward stock of $137.5 billion in 1997. China and Indonesia experienced large increases in outflows, with big projects in natural-resource-seeking investments, while firms from Singapore and Taiwan Province of China were actively involved in acquisitions of firms in crisis-afflicted countries. TNCs from the Republic of Korea, Malaysia and Thailand had a much lower profile, as a number of their FDI expansion projects were scaled down or put on hold.

The FDI pattern emerging in Asia and the Pacific is characterized by a decline in intra-regional investment, as many of the region's TNCs grapple with mounting debts and other difficulties. On the other hand, European TNCs, having largely neglected Asia until recently, are now taking an active interest in the region. The region's FDI pattern is also characterized by an increasing share of FDI received by the services sector, partly because of liberalization but also in direct response to efforts by some host countries to become regional investment hubs. Finally, M&As are gaining in importance as a mode of investment in Asia and the Pacific, partly in response to corporate restructuring in the countries directly affected by the financial crisis.

... although the implications of the crisis for FDI in the most affected countries are a matter for concern.

For Asia, and especially the five Asian countries -- Indonesia, Malaysia, Philippines, Thailand and the Republic of Korea -- stricken by the financial crisis in the second half of 1997, the most important question relating to foreign investment is how the crisis and its economic consequences will affect inward FDI in the short and medium term. FDI plays an important role in the region and could thus assist the countries in the process of their economic recovery. FDI flows to the region have been quite resilient in the face of the crisis, remaining positive and continuing to add to the capital stock of the affected countries while other capital flows, including bank lending and portfolio equity investment, fell sharply and even turned negative in 1997 as a whole. This is not surprising given that FDI is investment made with a long-term interest in production in host countries, in order to enhance the competitive positions of TNCs. Nevertheless, neither FDI flows nor the activities of foreign affiliates in the region, in particular in the five most affected countries, can remain impervious to the changes that the crisis has set in motion.

While some effects of the crisis are conducive to increasing inward FDI, ...

Indeed, the crisis and its aftermath have changed a number of factors that influence FDI and TNC operations in the affected countries, at least in the short and medium term. Some of the changes are actually conducive to increasing FDI flows to the affected countries. One is the decrease for foreign investors in the costs of acquiring assets whose prices have fallen. In addition, the availability of firms seeking capital and the liberalization of policy with respect to M&As makes the entry of foreign investors through the acquisition of assets easier than before. All this makes it easier for TNCs to enter or expand their operations at the present time, if they can afford to take a long-term view of the market prospects in the region or if they produce for export rather than domestic or regional markets. Firms interested in strategic positioning in Asia and the Pacific or seeking created assets to complement their worldwide portfolio of locational assets might find it attractive to establish or expand operations in these countries at the present time. There is evidence that firms from the United States, Western Europe and less affected economies in the region have taken the opportunity to invest in the crisis-affected countries, especially in Thailand and the Republic of Korea. The increasing importance of M&As as a mode of entry may, however, give rise to concerns over the loss of national control over enterprises; these need to be taken seriously, so as to avoid a backlash.

A second factor conducive to increasing FDI in the most affected Asian countries is the improvement in their international cost competitiveness due to devaluations. This is especially relevant for export-oriented FDI and there are already signs that investors are responding to the changes in the relative costs of production. FDI in export-oriented industries (such as electrical and electronics manufacturing) has risen in Thailand -- as it had in Mexico after the Peso crisis -- while production for export by foreign affiliates already well established in both Thailand and Malaysia seems to be increasing. TNCs in the affected Asian economies, which are already highly export-oriented in certain industries, can take advantage of their corporate systems of integrated international production to strengthen their export orientation substantially, especially in the short and medium term.

The potential positive impact of both lower asset prices and decreased operational costs on inward FDI could be enhanced by the liberalization moves and promotional efforts that are being made by the affected countries. Governments in the countries most affected by the crisis, most of which already have fairly liberal frameworks for FDI, have further liberalized their FDI regimes, opening new areas and relaxing rules, including in the context of IMF adjustment programmes. They have also intensified their efforts to attract FDI both individually and collectively.

... others will affect it adversely.

On the other hand, some consequences of the crisis will affect FDI adversely in the short and medium term. For firms focused on domestic or regional markets, reduced demand and slower growth can be expected to lead to some cancelling, scaling down or postponement of FDI in the most affected countries. However, the impact on domestically-oriented foreign affiliates varies among industries. Foreign affiliates in the services sector are particularly susceptible to local demand conditions, because of the non-tradability of most services. Affiliates producing goods and services that depend mainly on imported raw materials and intermediate inputs would be more seriously affected than those relying on domestic sources. The automotive industry, in which TNCs figure prominently in the region, is a good example of the impact of the crisis and the range of responses: a number of automotive TNCs have scaled down, postponed or even cancelled investment projects in some of these countries; firms have also adopted various other measures to cope with the crisis, including injecting funds to help their financially distressed affiliates and subcontractors, relocating parts production, boosting exports and increasing domestic sourcing.

FDI to countries not seriously caught up in the crisis may also decline, ...

The implications of the financial crisis for inward FDI are also likely to extend to other, less seriously affected, developing countries in Asia. For one thing, some countries, especially those with close economic links to the countries most affected by the crisis, are likely to experience lower economic growth; some countries may also lose export competitiveness vis-à-vis the countries that have devalued. These factors could reduce their attractiveness as host countries, at least in the short run.

....mainly because of decreased outward FDI from some Asian home countries, ...

Furthermore, and most importantly, many Asian developing countries, including China, Viet Nam and the least developed countries of the region, depend heavily on FDI from other developing Asian countries and inward FDI flows to them could decrease because of a decrease in outward FDI from the countries affected by the crisis. In 1997, overall outward FDI from developing Asian economies rose, but flows decreased from all the five crisis-affected countries except Indonesia. The crisis is likely to reduce the financial capacities of Asian TNCs (including TNCs from Japan) to undertake FDI on account of valuation losses, increased debt burdens on foreign-currency denominated loans, and reduced profitability of operations due to contraction of demand. The impact of these factors is further compounded for some TNCs by a credit crunch at home and difficulties in raising funds abroad.

...making it difficult to predict the overall impact on FDI in the region in the short and medium term, although long-term prospects remain sound.

It is difficult to predict how the various factors set in motion by the crisis will affect, on balance, inward FDI to the crisis-stricken countries and to the region as a whole in the short and medium term. Despite their overall resilience, flows to the affected countries and to the region as a whole may well fall in 1998, but much depends on the extent to which the financial crisis spills over into the real sector. Aside from that, given that the FDI determinants proper -- regulatory frameworks, business facilitation and, most importantly, economic determinants of long-term growth -- are attractive, and that the changes resulting from the crisis have positive as well as negative implications for FDI, there is room for cautious optimism. However, the extent to which these various factors translate into actual flows will depend on the assessment by TNCs of the long-term prospects of the region in the context of their own strategies for enhancing competitiveness. If their assessment is negative, TNCs will be reluctant to invest, especially as far as market-seeking FDI is concerned, and cautious in acquiring assets in the region. If they take a positive view and take advantage of the crisis to position themselves strategically in the region, FDI flows to Asia will continue on their upward trend without serious interruption. The rationale for the latter view is that the fundamental features of the region as a destination for FDI remain sound. These same features suggest not only that longer-term FDI prospects for the region remain positive, but that they may even improve as countries strengthen certain aspects of their economies in response to the crisis.

Latin America now tops developing regions in inward FDI growth, due to economic stability, growth, liberalization and privatization, ...

The turnaround in FDI flows to Latin America and the Caribbean that occurred in the early 1990s was further strengthened in 1997: the region received $56 billion -- an increase of 28 per cent over 1996 -- and invested a record $9 billion abroad. The increase in inflows accounted for two-thirds of the overall increase in inflows to all developing countries. Apart from sustained economic growth and good macroeconomic performance, key factors in the region's FDI boom were trade liberalization, wide-ranging privatization, deregulation and regionalization. With more than $16 billion in inflows, Brazil emerged as the region's champion in 1997, surpassing Mexico with $12 billion and Argentina with $6 billion. Despite the growing role of Asian and intraregional FDI, the United States is still the largest investor in Latin America and the Caribbean, with its investment in the region reaching $24 billion in 1997, mostly in automobiles, electronics, apparel and other manufacturing.

MERCOSUR has given a boost to both intraregional and extraregional FDI. Global competition and market expansion are prompting TNCs from Europe, the United States and Asia to invest in the growing MERCOSUR market, particularly in automobiles and chemicals. In contrast, most of the manufacturing FDI in Mexico and the Caribbean Basin has been efficiency-seeking, with the United States market being the final destination of exports. In the services and primary sectors, privatization programmes have provided opportunities for expansion for both market-seeking and resource-seeking TNCs. Government policy has also played a crucial role in generating the conditions under which the current FDI boom in Latin America and the Caribbean has occurred.

Latin America's strong FDI performance has been accompanied by changes in the nature of the investment it receives. First, there are some signs that TNC activities in Latin America have become more export-oriented, as witnessed by the sizeable contributions of TNCs to the region's exports and by increases in the export propensity of United States manufacturing affiliates. Structural reforms, macroeconomic stabilization and adequate macroeconomic management have also contributed to the export performance of foreign affiliates and domestic firms. Primary-sector FDI, still important in a number of countries, is almost exclusively geared to international markets. Services FDI, mostly geared to national markets, has given rise to some exports in certain tradable services and may have increased exports indirectly through services-related activities of manufacturing operations. The lion's share of export creation by foreign affiliates has taken place in manufacturing, in response to the trend towards integrating manufacturing affiliates into global production networks, which can be most clearly observed in Mexico and the Caribbean Basin.

The recent FDI boom in Latin America has also been accompanied by large and rising current-account deficits, reviving concerns over a negative balance-of-payments impact. The immediate effects of trade liberalization on the balance of payments may well be negative because FDI tends to generate higher imports not only of capital and intermediate goods, but also of final consumer goods, if TNCs begin by establishing sales affiliates and distribution networks. In the longer run, however, the strengthened export orientation of foreign affiliates should help to improve current account imbalances, especially as import growth normalizes once the adjustment of foreign investors to the new policy environment is completed, and if complementary policies to strengthen domestic capabilities and linkages are also pursued.

...but Africa's performance has remained unremarkable – with some exceptions.

FDI flows to Africa have stabilized at a significantly higher level than at the beginning of the 1990s: an average of $5.2 billion during 1994-1996 compared to an average of $3.2 billion during 1991-1993. In 1997, inflows were $4.7 billion, almost the same as in 1996. Judging by data for United States and Japanese affiliates in Africa, the continent remains a highly profitable investment location as companies receive rates of return on their investments that by far exceed those in other developing regions. In addition, almost three-fifths of FDI flows from the major home countries of TNCs in Africa -- France, Germany, the United Kingdom and the United States -- have gone into manufacturing and services since 1989, suggesting that the widely held assumption that Africa receives FDI only on the basis of natural resources is mistaken.

While Africa trails other developing regions in attracting FDI, a group of seven countries -- Botswana, Equatorial Guinea, Ghana, Mozambique, Namibia, Tunisia and Uganda -- stand out in terms of relative FDI inflows and their growth during 1992-1996, not only in comparison to other African countries but also to developing countries as a whole. While natural resources are an important determinant for FDI flows into most of these countries, they are by no means the only explanation for their relative success in attracting FDI. A number of other factors, including fast-growing national markets, access to large regional markets, significant privatization programmes and -- in the case of Tunisia -- conditions encouraging the location of export-oriented, efficiency-seeking FDI in the country also play a role. What all these "frontrunner" countries have in common is significant progress in improving their regulatory FDI frameworks as well as significant progress in strengthening political and macroeconomic stability. Most of them have also stepped up efforts to create an FDI-friendly business climate, particularly through investment promotion activities.

FDI in Central and Eastern Europe has bounced back.

Central and Eastern European economies broke their stagnating FDI trend in 1997 -- the first year the region as a whole registered a positive GDP growth rate in recent years -- by receiving record FDI flows of $19 billion, 44 per cent more than in 1996. This turnaround took place after a decline of 10 per cent in 1996. The Russian Federation was the leading recipient, mainly in natural resources and infrastructure development. In the other Central and Eastern European economies, most of the FDI growth occurred in manufacturing and services. The FDI pattern, however, remains uneven, reflecting the diverse experiences of countries in the transition to market-based economies, the strengthening of regulatory and institutional frameworks relevant for TNC operations, and privatization efforts. As for outflows, with the Russian Federation as the leading outward investor, outflows from Central and Eastern Europe more than tripled in 1997.

Despite this turnaround, Central and Eastern Europe's share in world inward FDI stock is still low: 1.8 per cent in 1997. To a large extent, this is explained by the fact that the majority of the countries opened up to inward FDI fairly recently; their accumulated FDI stocks are therefore small. The small stock also reflects the influence of various obstacles such as problems in the legal and regulatory frameworks, a long transition-related recession and a lack of experience in FDI facilitation measures.

The principal determinants of the location of FDI are the policy framework, business facilitation measures and economic factors.

To explain the differences in FDI performance among countries and to ascertain why firms invest where they do, it is necessary to understand how TNCs choose investment locations. In general, FDI takes place when firms combine their ownership-specific advantages with the location-specific advantages of host countries through internalization, i.e. through intra-firm rather than arm's-length transactions. Three broad factors determine where TNCs invest: the policies of host countries, the proactive measures countries adopt to promote and facilitate investment, and the characteristics of their economies. The relative importance of different location-specific FDI determinants depends on the motive and type of investment, the industry in question, and the size and strategy of the investor. Different motives, for example, can translate into different location patterns depending on the investor's strategy.

The FDI policy framework, a necessary but not sufficient determinant of FDI location is becoming relatively less important with liberalization and globalization ...

The core enabling framework for FDI consists of rules and regulations governing entry and operations of foreign investors, standards of treatment of foreign affiliates and the functioning of markets. Complementing core FDI policies are other policies that affect foreign investors' locational decisions directly or indirectly, by influencing the effectiveness of FDI policies. These include trade policy and privatization policy. Policies designed to influence the location of FDI constitute the "inner ring" of the policy framework. Policies that affect FDI but have not been designed for that purpose constitute the "outer ring" of the policy framework. The contents of both rings differ from country to country, as well as over time.

Core FDI policies are important because FDI will simply not take place where it is forbidden. However, changes in FDI policies have an asymmetric impact on the location of FDI: changes in the direction of greater openness may allow firms to establish themselves in a particular location, but they do not guarantee this. In contrast, changes in the direction of less openness, especially if radical (e.g. nationalizations), will pretty much ensure a reduction in FDI.

Since the mid-1980s, an overwhelming majority of countries have introduced measures to liberalize FDI frameworks, with positive effects on inward investment. Globalization and FDI liberalization have exerted mutually reinforcing pressures on each other and the momentum for neither has subsided. This has provided TNCs with an ever-increasing choice of locations and has made them more selective and demanding as regards other locational determinants. One outcome is a relative loss in effectiveness of FDI policies in the competition for investment: adequate core FDI policies are now simply taken for granted.

Another outcome is that countries are increasingly paying more attention to the inner and outer rings of the policy framework for FDI. The key issue for inner-ring policies is policy coherence, especially the joint coherence of FDI and trade policies. This is particularly important for efficiency-seeking FDI as firms integrate their foreign affiliates into international corporate networks. At the same time, the boundary line between inner- and outer-ring policies becomes more difficult to draw as the requirements of international production make higher demands on the efficacy of the policy and organizational framework within which FDI policies are implemented. Thus, macroeconomic policies (which include monetary, fiscal and exchange-rate policies) as well as a variety of macro-organizational policies become increasingly relevant. As the core FDI policies become similar across countries as part of the global trend towards investment liberalization, the inner and outer rings of policies gains more influence. Foreign investors assess a country's investment climate not only in terms of FDI policies per se but also in terms of macroeconomic and macro-organizational policies.

Among the policy measures that can have a direct effect on FDI is membership in regional integration frameworks, as these can change a key economic determinant: market size and perhaps market growth. In fact, because of this effect, such membership can be regarded as an economic determinant in its own right. Regional integration frameworks may cover a wide spectrum of integration measures, ranging from tariff reduction among members to policy harmonization on many fronts. The inner rings for both inward and outward FDI tend to become similar; in the case of developed countries, this may happen even before regional integration becomes a fact. With developing countries, membership in a regional integration scheme usually requires at least some degree of FDI (or capital movement) policy harmonization.

A multilateral framework on investment (MFI) -- if it were to be negotiated and if it were to lead to more similar FDI policy frameworks -- would underscore the importance of the principal economic determinants and business facilitation measures in influencing location in a globalizing world economy. Even on the policy front, however, the precise impact of a possible MFI would depend on the form it takes, and particularly whether it would merely lock in the FDI liberalization process or further encourage it. Since an MFI is a hypothetical policy determinant, assessments of its possible impact on the actual quantity, quality and geographical pattern of FDI flows must be tentative and could range from scenarios that see no or very little impact, to a negative or positive impact; it must, moreover, be understood that the implications of the various scenarios would vary from country to country in accordance with specific economic and developmental conditions and specific national stances vis-à-vis FDI. If a possible MFI should lock in unilateral liberalization measures, assure greater protection, transparency, stability and predictability, and create pressures for (or even lead to) further liberalization, it would enhance the FDI enabling policy framework and could lead to more investment -- *if* the other FDI determinants were in place. However, it is also conceivable that if an MFI was of a "stand-still" type, it would not create a more liberal policy framework than the one that already exists, and hence, its impact on FDI determinants and flows would be difficult to detect, if there were to be one. Expectations about the impact of a possible MFI -- if indeed it were to be negotiated -- on FDI flows in comparison to the current regulatory framework and the direction in which it is developing, should therefore not be exaggerated. There are, of course, other issues that would need to be considered in connection with a possible MFI -- especially the possible role of such an agreement in providing a framework for intergovernmental cooperation in the area of investment -- but these fall outside the scope of the present analysis which is specifically focussed on the determinants of FDI.

... while business facilitation measures are becoming relatively more important.

It is in the context of a greater similarity of investment policies at all levels that business facilitation measures enter the picture. They include investment promotion, incentives, after-investment services, improvements in amenities and measures that reduce the "hassle costs" of doing business. While these measures are not new, they have proliferated as a means of competing for FDI as FDI policies converge towards greater openness. Furthermore, business facilitation measures have become more sophisticated, increasingly targeting individual investors, even though this involves high human capital and other costs. Among these measures, after-investment services can be singled out because of the importance of reinvested earnings in overall investment flows and because satisfied investors are the best advertisement of a country's business climate. Financial or fiscal incentives are also used to attract investors even though they typically only enter location-decision processes when other principal determinants are in place.

The relative importance of economic determinants, the most important category of determinants, ...

Once an enabling FDI policy framework is in place, economic factors assert themselves as locational determinants. They fall into three clusters, corresponding to the principal motives for investing abroad: resource (or-asset)-seeking, market-seeking and efficiency-seeking.

In the past, it was relatively easy to distinguish the type of FDI corresponding to each of these motives. Historically, the availability of natural resources has been the most important FDI determinant for countries lacking the capital, skills, know-how and infrastructure required for their extraction and sale to the rest of the world. The importance of this determinant per se has not declined but the importance of the primary sector in world output has declined. In addition, large indigenous, often state-owned, enterprises have emerged in developing countries with the capital and skills to extract and trade natural resources. These changes mean that TNC participation in natural resource extraction is taking place more through non-equity arrangements and less through FDI, although the value of FDI in natural resources has far from declined.

National market size, in absolute terms or relative to the size and income of the population, has been another important traditional determinant, leading to market-seeking investment. Large markets can accommodate more firms and allow each of them to reap the benefits of scale and scope economies -- one of the principal reasons why regional integration frameworks can lead to more FDI. High market growth rates stimulate investment by foreign as well as domestic investors. Much of the inward FDI of the 1960s and 1970s was drawn by large national markets for manufacturing products, which were sheltered from international competition by tariff barriers and quotas. Large national markets were also important for those services whose non-tradability made FDI the only mode of delivery to consumers. Such investment, however, was initially small because FDI frameworks for services were typically restrictive, excluding foreign investors in many fields such as banking, insurance and most infrastructural services. Largely immobile low-cost labour was another traditional economic determinant of FDI location, particularly important for efficiency-seeking investment.

...is changing under the impact of liberalization and globalization, as TNCs increasingly pursue competitiveness-enhancing strategies relying on a portfolio of locational assets, ...

The forces driving globalization are also changing the ways in which TNCs pursue their objectives for investing abroad. Technology and innovation have become critical to competitiveness. Openness to trade, FDI and technology flows, combined with deregulation and privatization, have improved firms' access to markets for goods and services and to immobile factors of production and have increased competitive pressures in previously protected home markets, forcing firms to seek new markets and resources overseas. At the same time, technological advances have enhanced the ability of firms to coordinate their expanded international production networks in their quest for increased competitiveness. More and more firms are therefore developing a portfolio of locational assets to complement their own competitive strengths when they engage in FDI, as witnessed by the growing number of firms that are becoming transnational.

All of these factors are changing the relative importance of different economic determinants of FDI location. The traditional determinants have not disappeared; rather, they are becoming relatively less important in FDI location decisions. The traditional motives for FDI have not disappeared either; they are being incorporated into different strategies pursued by firms in their transnationalization process. These have evolved from the traditional stand-alone strategies, based on largely autonomous foreign affiliates, to simple integration strategies, characterized by strong links between foreign affiliates and parent firms, especially for labour-intensive activities, as well as links between TNCs and unrelated firms via non-equity arrangements. Under simple integration strategies, unskilled labour becomes the principal locational determinant. Complementing it are other determinants, such as the reliability of the labour supply and adequate physical infrastructure for the export of final products. Costs feature prominently, but host country markets do not: it is access to international markets, privileged or otherwise, that matters.

Although this type of FDI is not new, it began to prosper under the conditions of globalization. Much of the investment in export processing zones and labour-intensive industries has been in response to simple integration strategies, driven by cost-price competition and, more importantly, the removal of trade (and FDI) barriers in an increasing number of countries and technological advances that permit quick changes in product specifications in response to changes in demand. However, as labour costs declined in relation to total production costs and as FDI in response to simple integration strategies became more mobile, countries had to offer additional locational advantages over and above the availability of low-cost unskilled labour to attract FDI. Productivity and some level of skill, as well as good infrastructure facilities, gained in importance as locational determinants for this type of investment. Access to international markets also became more important. Losing such access could mean losing this type of investment. This contributed to the efforts of many developing countries seeking to gain permanent access to the markets of developed countries through trade agreements or regional integration arrangements. As services became more tradable, particularly in their labour-intensive intermediate production stages such as data entry, they too began to relocate abroad in response to simple integration strategies. The locational advantages sought by such service TNCs included computer literacy and a reliable telecommunication infrastructure. Again, this contributed to the upgrading of the locational advantages that countries could offer to TNCs pursuing simple integration strategies, in their efforts to attract the more sophisticated activities that TNCs were now locating abroad.

With more and more TNC intermediate products and functions becoming amenable to FDI, TNCs strategies are evolving from simple to complex integration. Complex integration strategies can involve, where profitable, splitting up the production process into specific activities or functions and carrying out each of them in the most suitable, cost-competitive location. More than ever in the past, complex integration strategies allow TNCs that pursue them to maximize the competitiveness of their corporate systems as a whole on international portfolio of location assets. In the process, the dividing line between is becoming increasingly blurred.

... which strategies give rise to a new configuration of locational determinants, with a growing emphasis on "created assets".

To attract such competitiveness-enhancing FDI, it is no longer sufficient for host countries to possess a single locational determinant. TNCs undertaking such FDI take for granted the presence of state-of-the-art FDI frameworks that provide them with the freedom to operate internationally, that are complemented by the relevant bilateral and international agreements, and that are further enhanced by a range of business facilitation measures. When it comes to the economic determinants, firms that undertake competitiveness-enhancing FDI seek not only cost reduction and bigger market shares, but also access to technology and innovative capacity. These resources, as distinct from natural resources, are people-made, they are "created assets". Possessing such assets is critical for firms' competitiveness in a globalizing economy. Consequently, countries that develop such assets become more attractive to TNCs. It is precisely the rise in the importance of created assets that is the single most important shift among the economic determinants of FDI location in a liberalizing and globalizing world economy. In addition, the new configuration also includes agglomeration economies arising from the clustering of economic activity, infrastructure facilities, access to regional markets and, finally, competitive pricing of relevant resources and facilities.

One implication for host countries wishing to attract TNCs undertaking competitiveness-enhancing FDI is that created assets can be developed by host countries and influenced by governments. The challenge is precisely to develop a well-calibrated and preferably unique combination of determinants of FDI location, and to seek to match those determinants with the strategies pursued by competitiveness-enhancing TNCs. It must be remembered too that created assets also enhance the competitiveness of *national* firms. Thus, policies aimed at strengthening innovation systems and encouraging the diffusion of technology are central because they underpin the ability to create assets. Also important are other policies that encourage the strengthening of created assets and the development of clusters based on them as well as policies that stimulate partnering and networking among domestic and foreign firms and allow national firms to upgrade themselves in the interest of national growth and development.

* * *

All in all, the trend towards increased flows of FDI world-wide and the creation of a more hospitable environment for FDI continues. Even the Asian financial crisis does not seem, thus far, to have greatly affected either FDI inflows to, or the further liberalization of FDI policies in developing countries. Liberalization has proceeded at the international level through the proliferation of bilateral treaties and the creation of new regional markets and investment areas. One of the peculiar consequences of recent developments in the FDI area is that, by becoming commonplace, liberal national policy frameworks have lost some of their traditional power to attract foreign investment. What is more likely to be critical in the years to come is the distinctive combination of locational advantages -- including human resources, infrastructure, market access and the created assets of technology and innovative capacity -- that a country or region can offer potential investors.

Rubens Ricupero
Secretary-General of UNCTAD

Geneva, August 1998

CHAPTER I

GLOBAL TRENDS

International production by transnational corporations (TNCs) continues to grow in importance for both developed and developing countries. This chapter examines trends and developments with respect to various aspects of this phenomenon. It begins by focusing on trends in the size and pattern of international production as indicated by world foreign-direct-investment (FDI) stock, measures of foreign-affiliate operations, and the flows of FDI that contribute to the building up of international production capacity. It then examines recent trends in inter-firm agreements as these are assuming increasing importance in certain industries. Subsequent chapters deal with the largest TNCs undertaking FDI (chapter II), developments in the policy framework within which they operate (chapter III) and the host country characteristics that determine where they invest (chapter IV). Subsequent chapters also contain more detailed analyses of the regional trends that are only sketched here (chapters V-IX).

A. Overall trends

1. International production

The size and distribution of international production by TNCs -- and hence their role in the world economy -- can be gauged from estimates of the worldwide FDI stock, assets, sales, gross product and exports of these firms.[1] Indeed, all major indicators (table I.1) related to FDI and TNC activities showed higher rates of growth in 1997 (as in 1996) than did GDP and exports, compensating for the decline in growth during 1991-1995 that reflected the recession of the early 1990s (UNCTAD, 1996a). More specifically, world FDI stock, which constitutes the capital base for TNC operations, rose by over 10 per cent in 1997, to reach an estimated $3.5 trillion (annex tables B.3 and B.4).[2] It is held by a minimum of 53,000 TNCs -- large and small (table I.2). The regional distribution of outward FDI stock is heavily skewed towards developed countries, reflecting the fact that, in the past, most FDI originated and stayed in developed countries, though there are some noticeable recent increases in the stock of developing countries (table I.3). The regional distribution of inward FDI stock is approaching that of FDI inflows, with 30 per cent of the total being in developing countries in 1997. The share of South, East and South-East Asia in world inward FDI stock nearly doubled during the past decade (table I.3).

There are at least 448,000 foreign affiliates in the world and in all likelihood many more (table I.2). The role that they play in host countries has become more and more important. Assets held by all foreign affiliates in 1997 were 3.5 times as large as FDI stocks because a good part of them are financed by local loans and local shareholders as well as by finance raised in third markets (table I.1). These assets indicate the capacity of foreign affiliates to produce goods and services, as they refer to fixed assets and intangible assets that are used for production purposes and to financial assets that entitle the firms to receive income. Judging by available data, the average size of assets owned by foreign affiliates worldwide in the mid-1990s was about $28 million, almost comparable to their size at the beginning of the 1990s; however, this could be an overestimation of the size of foreign affiliates in terms of assets, because the number of foreign affiliates worldwide is probably understated considerably by available data (table I.2). But even if the number of foreign affiliates (large and small) should be close to 1 million, the average size of foreign affiliates would still be $12 million. The average assets of large foreign affiliates of United States TNCs were $132 million for 1995, up from $88 million in 1990 (United States, Department of Commerce, 1993b and 1997a).[3] The relative stagnation in the average size of assets owned by foreign affiliates worldwide suggests that more and more firms, including small and medium-sized enterprises and firms from developing countries, are establishing foreign affiliates of modest size.

Table I.1. Selected indicators of FDI and international production, 1986-1997

(Billions of dollars and percentage)

Item	Value at current prices (Billion dollars)		Annual growth rate (Per cent)			
	1996	1997	1986-1990	1991-1995	1996	1997
FDI inflows	338	400	23.6	20.1	1.9	18.6
FDI outflows	333	424	27.1	15.1	-0.5	27.1
FDI inward stock	3 065	3 456	18.2	9.7	12.2	12.7
FDI outward stock	3 115	3 541	21.0	10.3	11.5	13.7
Cross-border M&As [a]	163	236	21.0[b]	30.2	15.5	45.2
Sales of foreign affiliates	8 851 [c]	9 500 [c]	16.3	13.4	6.0[c]	7.3[c]
Gross product of foreign affiliates	1 950 [c]	2 100 [c]	16.6	6.2	7.7[c]	7.7[c]
Total assets of foreign affiliates	11 156 [c]	12 606 [c]	18.3	24.4	12.0[c]	13.0[c]
Memorandum:						
GDP at factor cost	28 822	30551 [d]	12.1	5.5	0.8	6.0[d]
Gross fixed capital formation	5 136	5393 [d]	12.5	2.6	-0.1	5.0[d]
Royalties and fees receipts	53	61 [d]	21.9	12.4	8.2	15.0[d]
Exports of goods and non-factor services	6 245	6432 [d]	14.6	8.9	2.9	3.0[d]

Source: UNCTAD, based on FDI/TNC database and UNCTAD estimates.

[a] Majority-held investments only.
[b] 1987-1990 only.
[c] Projection on the basis of 1995 figures.
[d] Estimates.

Note: not included in this table are the values of worldwide sales by foreign affiliates associated with their parent firms through non-equity relationships and the sales of the parent firms themselves. Worldwide sales, gross product and total assets of foreign affiliates are estimated by extrapolating the worldwide data of foreign affiliates of TNCs from France, Germany, Italy, Japan and the United States (for sales), those from the United States (for gross product) and those from Germany and the United States (for assets) on the basis of the shares of those countries in the worldwide inward FDI stock.

Table I.2. Number of parent corporations and foreign affiliates, by area and economy, latest available year
(Number)

Area/economy	Year	Parent corporations based in economy[a]	Foreign affiliates located in economy[a]
Developed economies		**43 442** [b]	**96 620**
Western Europe		**33 302**	**63 789**
European Union		**27 846** [b]	**54 875**
Austria	1996	897	2 362
Belgium	1996	1 110	2 000 [c]
Denmark	1997	5 000 [d]	2 012 [e]
Finland	1996	1 200	1 200
France	1996	2 078	9 351
Germany	1996	7 569 [f]	11 445 [g]
Greece	1991	..	798
Ireland	1994	39	1 040
Italy	1995	966	1 630
Netherlands	1993	1 608 [h]	2 259 [h]
Portugal	1997	1 350	5 809
Spain	1997	822 [i]	6 809
Sweden	1997	4 148	5 551
United Kingdom[j]	1996	1 059 [k]	2 609 [l]
Other Western Europe		**5 456** [b]	**8 914**
Iceland	1995	50	40
Norway	1996	900	3 100
Switzerland	1995	4 506	5 774
Japan	1996	4 231 [m]	3 014 [n]
United States	1995	3 379 [o]	18 901 [p]
Other developed		**2 530**	**10 916**
Australia	1997	485	2 371
Canada	1996	1 695	4 541
New Zealand	1997	232 [q]	1 949 [q]
South Africa	1996	118	2 055
Developing economies		**9 323** [b]	**230 696**
Africa		**32**	**330**
Ethiopia	1998	..	21 [r]
Swaziland	1996	30	134
Zambia	1997	2	175
Latin America and the Caribbean		**1 109** [b]	**21 174**
Bolivia	1996	..	257
Brazil	1995	797 [s]	6 322
Chile	1995	..	2 028 [t]
Colombia	1995	302	2220
El Salvador	1990	..	225
Guatemala	1985	..	287
Mexico	1993	..	8 420
Paraguay	1995	..	109
Peru	1997	10 [u]	1 183 [v]
Uruguay	1997	..	123
Developing Europe		**1 482**	**6 045**
Croatia	1997	70	353
Slovenia	1996	1 300	1 792
Former Yugoslavia	1991	112	3 900
South, East and South-East Asia		**6 242** [b]	**199 469**
China	1997	379 [w]	145 000
Hong Kong, China	1997	500 [x]	5 067
India	1995	187 [x]	1 416
Indonesia	1995	313 [y]	3 472 [z]
Korea, Republic of	1996	4 806	3 878
Pakistan	1993	57	758
Philippines	1995	..	14 802 [aa]
Singapore	1995	..	18 154
Sri Lanka [ab]	1995	..	139
Taiwan Province of China	1990	..	5 733
Thailand	1992	..	1 050

/...

Table I.2. Number of parent corporations and foreign affiliates, by area and economy, latest available year (continued)
(Number)

Area/economy	Year	Parent corporations based in economy[a]	Foreign affiliates located in economy[a]
West Asia		**449** [b]	**2 486**
Bahrain	1995	..	538
Oman	1995	92 [z]	351 [z]
Saudi Arabia	1989	..	1 461
Turkey	1995	357	136
Central Asia		**9**	**1 041**
Kyrgyzstan	1997	9 [ac]	1 041 [ad]
The Pacific		-	**151**
Fiji	1997	-	151
Central and Eastern Europe		**842** [b]	**12 1601**
Albania	1997	..	1 280
Belarus	1994	..	393
Bulgaria	1994	26	918
Czech Republic	1997	660	44 062 [ae]
Estonia	1998	..	3 170 [af]
Hungary	1994	66	15 205
Lithuania	1997	12	1 624
Poland	1997	58 [s]	32 889 [ag]
Romania	1998	20 [s]	6 193 [ah]
Russian Federation	1994	..	7 793
Slovakia	1997	..	5 560 [ai]
Ukraine	1994	..	2 514
World		**53 607**	**448 917**

Source: UNCTAD estimates.

a Represents the number of parent companies/foreign affiliates in the economy shown, as defined by that economy. Deviations from the definition adopted in the *World Investment Report* (see section on "definitions and sources" in annex B of this *Report)* are noted below.
b Includes data for only the countries shown below.
c Estimated by Banque Nationale de Belgique.
d Includes both Danish and foreign parent corporations in Denmark.
e Of this number, 1,517 are majority-owned foreign affiliates.
f Does not include holding companies abroad that are dependent on German-owned capital and that, in turn, hold participating interests of more than 20 per cent abroad (indirect German participating interests).
g Does not include the number of foreign-owned holding companies in Germany which, in turn, hold participating interests in Germany (indirect foreign participating interests).
h As of October 1993.
i Includes firms controlled by a foreign direct investor.
j Data on the number of parent companies based in the United Kingdom, and the number of foreign affiliates in the United Kingdom, are based on the register of companies held for inquiries on United Kingdom FDI abroad, and FDI into the United Kingdom conducted by the Central Statistical Office. The numbers are probably understated because of the lags in identifying investment in greenfield sites and because some companies with a small presence in the United Kingdom and abroad have not yet been identified.
k Represents a total of 25 bank parent companies and 1,034 non-bank parent companies.
l Represents 448 foreign affiliates in banking and 2,161 non-bank foreign affiliates.
m The number of parent companies not including finance, insurance and real estate industries in March 1996 (3,959) plus the number of parent companies in finance, insurance and real estate industries in December 1992 (272).
n The number of foreign affiliates not including finance, insurance and real estate industries in March 1996 (2,730) plus the number of foreign affiliates in insurance and real estate industries in November 1995 (284).
o Represents a total of 2,610 non-bank parent companies in 1995 and 60 bank parent companies in 1994 with at least one foreign affiliate whose assets, sales or net income exceeded $3 million, and 709 non-bank and bank parent companies in 1994 whose affiliate(s) had assets, sales and net income under $3 million. Each parent company represents a fully consolidated United States business enterprise, which may consist of a number of individual companies.
p Represents a total of 12,816 bank and non-bank affiliates in 1994 whose assets, sales or net income exceeded $1 million, and 5,551 bank and non-bank affiliates in 1992 with assets, sales and net income under $1 million, and 534 United States affiliates that are depositary institutions. Each affiliate represents a fully consolidated United States business enterprise, which may consist of a number of individual companies.
q As of March 1997.
r Represents the number of foreign affiliates that received permission to invest during 1992-May 1998.
s As of 1994.
t Number of foreign companies registred under DL600.
u Less than 10.
v Of this number, 811 are majority-owned foreign affiliates , while 159 affiliates have less than 10 per cent equity share.
w As of 1989.
x As of 1991.
y As of October 1993.
z As of May 1995.
aa This number covers all firms with foreign equity, i.e. equity ownership by non-resident corporations and/or non-resident individuals, registered with the Securities Exchange Commission from 1989 to 1995.
ab Data are for the number of investment projects.
ac The number of firms that are registered with the National Bank of Kyrgyz Republic. The actual number of firms that are in operation was 3.
ad The number of firms that are registered with the National Bank of Kyrgyz Republic. The actual number of firms that are in operation was 387.
ae Of this number 21,679 are are fully owned foreign affiliates. Includes joint ventures.
af As of May 1998. Only registered affiliates with the Estonian Commercial Register.
ag Number of firms with foreign capital.
ah The number of affiliates established during December 1990-Feburary 1998.
ai Includes joint ventures with local firms.

Note: the data can vary significantly from preceding years, as data become available for countries that had not been covered before, as definitions change, or as older data are updated.

Table I.3. Regional distribution of inward and outward FDI stock, 1985, 1990, 1995 and 1997

(Percentage)

Region/country	Inward FDI stock 1985	1990	1995	1997	Outward FDI stock 1985	1990	1995	1997
Developed countries	72.3	79.3	70.6	68.0	95.7	95.6	91.5	90.2
Western Europe	33.6	44.1	39.1	36.9	44.4	50.8	51.1	50.4
European Union	31.2	41.5	36.3	34.6	40.6	46.3	45.1	45.1
Other Western Europe	2.3	2.7	2.8	2.3	3.8	4.5	5.9	5.3
United States	24.4	22.7	20.5	20.9	36.4	25.5	25.6	25.6
Japan	0.6	0.6	1.2	1.0	6.4	11.8	8.5	8.0
Developing countries	27.7	20.6	28.1	30.2	4.3	4.4	8.4	9.7
Africa	3.1	2.2	2.1	1.9	0.9	0.7	0.5	0.5
Latin America and the Caribbean	10.1	7.1	10.2	10.9	1.1	0.7	0.9	1.0
Developing Europe	0.1	0.1	0.1	0.1	-	-	-	-
Asia	14.3	11.1	15.6	17.2	2.3	2.9	6.9	8.2
West Asia	5.7	2.8	2.1	1.7	0.3	0.4	0.3	0.3
Central Asia	..	..	0.1	0.2	-	-	-	-
South, East and South-East Asia	8.6	8.3	13.4	15.3	2.0	2.6	6.4	7.9
The Pacific	0.2	0.1	0.1	0.1	-	-	-	-
Central and Eastern Europe	-	0.1	1.3	1.8	-	-	0.1	0.2
World	100	100	100	100	100	100	100	100

Source: UNCTAD, based on annex tables B.3 and B.4.

If assets indicate the potential level of production, turnover or sales indicate the use to which assets have been put. Sales of goods and services by foreign affiliates -- an estimated $9.5 trillion in 1997 -- are growing at a faster rate than worldwide exports of goods and services, which amounted to $6.4 trillion in the same year (tables I.1 and I.4). Thus, firms use FDI more than they use exports -- by a factor of 1.5 -- to service foreign markets. Indeed, the importance of sales by foreign affiliates relative to world exports is increasing: during the early 1980s the ratio of sales of foreign affiliates to world exports was 1.1, and in 1990 it was 1.2. Sales per affiliate worldwide are about $20 million, although there is considerable variation in size of sales by home country. Thus, for example, sales per affiliate in 1995 were $100 million for United States foreign affiliates and $110 million for Japanese foreign affiliates (United States, Department of Commerce, 1997a; Japan, Ministry of International Trade and Industry, 1998a).[4]

Table I.4. Indicators of production by foreign affiliates, 1982-1997

(Billions of dollars)

Year	Assets	Sales	Gross product (Value added)	Exports of foreign affiliates
1982	1 869	2 440	559	..
1983	1 885	2 395	547	569
1984	1 965	2 632	573	680
1985	2 272	2 533	604	698
1986	2 878	2 842	755	694
1987	3 403	3 519	846	740
1988	4 027	4 180	1 017	891
1989	4 520	4 788	1 160	947
1990	5 625	5 204	1 394	1 149
1991	4 162	5 052	1 422	977
1992	6 300	5 325	1 411	1 241
1993	7 132	5 975	1 371	1 278
1994	8 361	6 624	1 574	1 455
1995	9 957	8 346	1 810	1 961
1996[a]	11 156	8 851	1 950	..
1997[a]	12 606	9 500	2 100	..

Source: UNCTAD estimates.

[a] Projection on the basis of the 1995 figures.

Note: worldwide production-related data are estimated by extrapolating the worldwide data of foreign affiliates of TNCs from Germany and the United States (for assets), those from France, Germany, Italy, Japan and the United States (for sales), those from the United States (for gross product) and those from Japan and the United States (for exports) on the basis of the shares of these countries in the worldwide inward FDI stock.

The real contribution of enterprises to an economy can be measured by gross product or value added, as it is distributed in the form of wages (income of employees), profits (income of firms) and taxes (income of governments). Foreign affiliates worldwide generated more than $2 trillion in value added in 1997 (table I.4). They also accounted for an increasing share in world GDP: close to 7 per cent in 1997, as compared to 5 per cent in the mid-1980s (table I.5).

Foreign affiliates can also contribute to the host economy through exports. They are estimated to have accounted for some one-third of world exports in 1995 (table I.5), compared to about one-quarter during the latter half of the 1980s.[5] Since the mid-1980s, the export propensity of foreign affiliates (i.e. the ratio of exports to total sales) has remained close to one-quarter in 1995 (table I.5).

Table I.5. Importance of production by foreign affiliates, 1982-1997

(Percentage)

Year	Value added of all foreign affiliates as percentage of world GDP[a]	Exports of all foreign affiliates as percentage of world exports[b]	Export propensity of foreign affiliates[c]
1982	5.3	..	..
1983	5.0	27.7	23.7
1984	5.1	31.5	25.8
1985	5.2	31.9	27.5
1986	5.5	28.6	24.4
1987	4.3	25.6	21.0
1988	5.7	26.9	21.3
1989	6.2	26.3	19.8
1990	6.4	27.5	22.1
1991	6.2	22.7	19.3
1992	5.8	26.6	23.3
1993	5.7	27.7	21.4
1994	6.1	28.3	22.0
1995	6.3	32.3	23.5
1996	6.8	..	..
1997	6.9	..	..

Source: UNCTAD estimates.

[a] Worldwide value added is estimated by extrapolating the worldwide value added of foreign affiliates of TNCs from the United States on the basis of the share of the United States in the worldwide inward FDI stock.

[b] Worldwide exports are estimated by extrapolating the worldwide exports of foreign affiliates of TNCs from Japan and the United States on the basis of the shares of these countries in the worldwide inward FDI stock. In calculating exports of Japanese affiliates, export data are adjusted to exclude those of wholesale affiliates to avoid possible double counting.

[c] Share of exports of foreign affiliates in total sales of foreign affiliates.

Technology transfers are another aspect of the cross-border activities of TNCs. Receipts and payments of royalties and licence fees are a measure -- however imperfect -- of the volume of technology flows by TNCs. Their value is increasing at double-digit rates (table I.1) and intra-firm transactions are predominant,[6] accounting for between 52 per cent for Japan to 95 per cent for Germany (table I.6). Transnational linkages between firms have become more important in acquiring and upgrading technology over the years because foreign affiliates have, at least in principle, access to their parent companies' R&D facilities and indeed to those of their entire corporate networks. Technology can also be acquired through the import of capital goods. In the case of China, for example, foreign affiliates -- and especially joint ventures -- performed quite well in this respect compared with domestic firms as a group, although in all cases the proportion of capital goods in total imports has declined (table I.7).

Table I.6. Germany, Japan and United States: receipts from patents, royalties and licence fees, 1986 and 1996

(Millions of dollars)

Region	1986			1996		
	Germany	Japan	United States	Germany	Japan[a]	United States
World	778	1 230	7 927	2 453	6 443	29 974
of which intra-firm (per cent)	92	58	76	95	52	79
Developed countries, of which	671	..	6 861	1 971	3 525	23 246
intra-firm (per cent)	92	..	78	94	..	82
Developing countries, of which	74	..	647	415	2 908	5 051
intra-firm (per cent)	93	..	55	97	..	68
Central and Eastern Europe	33	..	13	68	8	127
of which intra-firm (per cent)	94	..	-	94	..	74

Source: UNCTAD, based on Japan, Bank of Japan, 1987 and 1997 and Ministry of International Trade and Industry, 1989 and 1998a; Deutsche Bundesbank, 1988 and 1998; and United States, Department of Commerce, 1992 and 1997d.

[a] Fiscal year 1995.

While the degree of economic integration among countries has traditionally been measured by the relative importance of international trade at the national, regional or global levels, it can now also be measured by FDI flows and stocks. For the world as a whole, the ratio of FDI stock (inward plus outward) to GDP has increased steadily since 1980; the ratio of world FDI flows (inflows plus outflows) to GDP has also risen, but not steadily (figure I.1). The ratio of world trade (imports plus exports) to world GDP has remained relatively constant during the same period (figure I.1). Thus, during the past decade and a half, global integration seems to have proceeded faster through FDI than through trade. There are, of course, noteworthy differences in the pace of integration among regions and countries (figure I.2).

Table I.7. China: Machinery imports and their share in total imports, by type of enterprise, 1993 and 1997

(Millions of dollars and percentage)

	1993		1997	
Enterprise	Value of imports	Share in total imports	Value of imports	Share in total imports
Foreign affiliates	8 988	26	9 679	14
Fully foreign-owned firms	1 607	18	3 383	12
Equity joint ventures	7 381	29	6 296	16
Non-equity joint ventures	1 803	26	883	10
Domestic firms	7 491	12	4 694	7
State-owned enterprises	7 184	12	4 589	8
Collective enterprises	42	8	91	4
Private enterprises	1	14	6	6
Other	264	13	8	1
Total	18 282	18	15 255	11

Source: UNCTAD, based on International Trade Centre UNCTAD/WTO ChinaTraders database, provided by China, Statistics Department of the Customs General Administration.

2. FDI flows

The year 1997 witnessed a complex mix of economic changes around the world (UNCTAD, 1998a): the financial crisis in Asia and the halting of high economic growth in East and South-East Asia; the worst economic recession in Japan since the mid-1970s; continued high economic growth in the United States; strong economic recovery in the European Union and Latin America; weak commodity and petroleum prices that affected the economies of Africa and West Asia; and the reversal of economic decline in Central and Eastern Europe for the first time since the end of central planning. Despite different and divergent performances in different regions reflecting these developments, FDI continued to grow in all regions (figure I.3 and table I.8), with some changes in the relative importance of different host countries (table I.9) as well as in the pace at which FDI is growing.

Figure I.1. The degree of internationalization through FDI and through trade, 1980-1996

(Percentage of GDP)

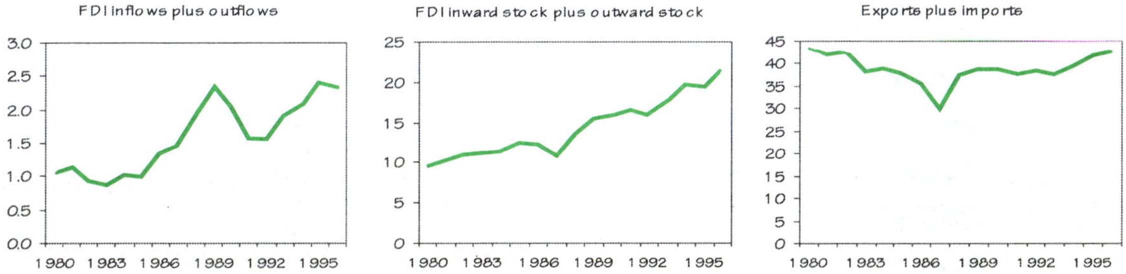

Source: UNCTAD, FDI/TNC database.

Note: the scales used for the three panels are different.

Figure I.2. Internationalization through FDI and through trade in selected countries and regions
(Percentage of GDP)

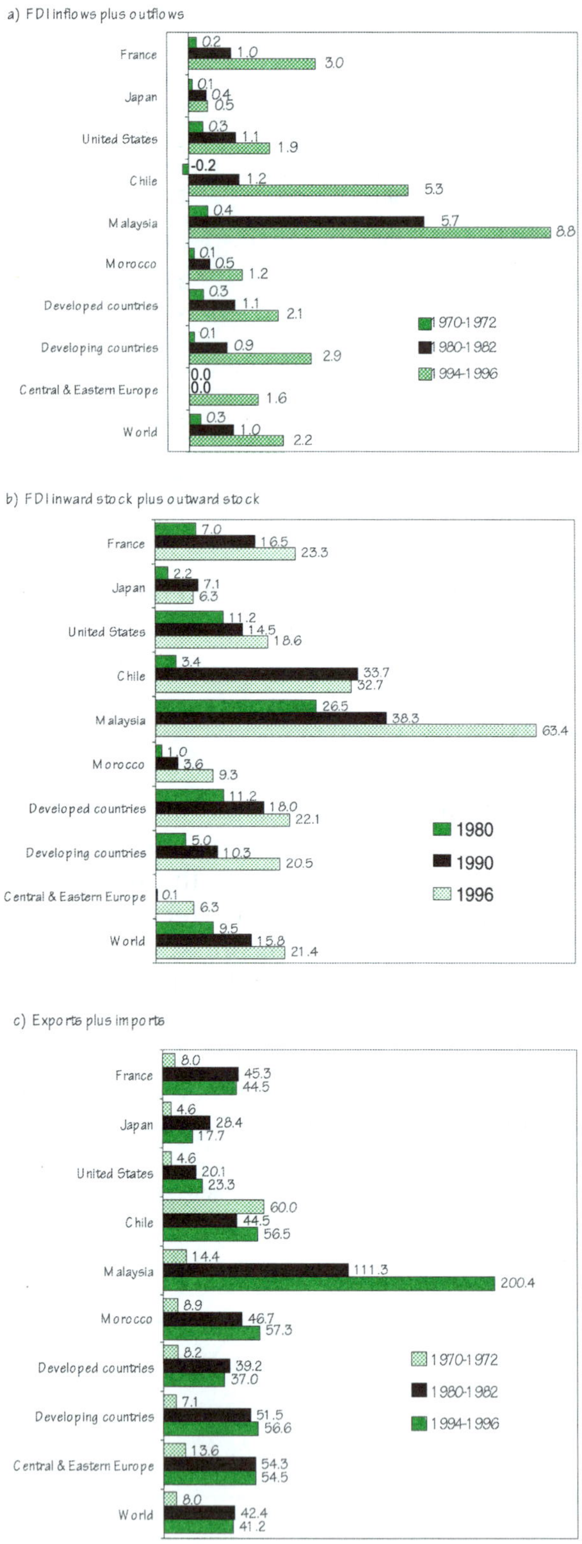

Source: UNCTAD, FDI/TNC database.

Indeed, the upward trend in world FDI flows set a new record in 1997: inflows grew by 19 per cent, to $400 billion, while outflows, after a decline in 1996, rose by 27 per cent, to reach $424 billion (table I.1),[7] the first time that the $400 billion mark had been reached and passed. World FDI flows today are nearly twice what they had been in 1990, and some sevenfold their volume in 1980. It should be noted, however, that the definition of FDI underestimates the real size of investment by TNCs because it does not cover investment financed by funds raised in domestic or international markets (UNCTAD, 1997a);[8] if funds from these sources are included, the total addition to the capital base of international production in 1997 may well have been $1.6 trillion. The definition also obscures, to some extent, the true identity of foreign investors, because foreign affiliates themselves also make direct investments abroad (see box V.2 for details).

In 1998, FDI flows are expected to increase as well, to reach a projected level of around $430-440 billion for both inflows and outflows,[9] despite lower global economic growth,[10] and decreases in FDI flows to some countries expected in 1998.[11] A major factor behind the FDI growth is the continued trend towards large-scale cross-border M&As, as well as privatizations and further liberalization. Most of the increase in FDI will probably be concentrated in developed countries, as well as Latin America and the Caribbean and Central and Eastern Europe. FDI flows into Asia and the Pacific may at best remain the same as in 1997, which would be the first time since the beginning of the 1980s that FDI flows into that region did not increase.

The outstanding positions of the United States and Western Europe in FDI inflows in absolute values are obvious. However, FDI comparisons among regions corrected for market and population-size show a somewhat different picture from that based on absolute values of FDI flows. The United States and

Western Europe become less important compared to others if values of FDI relative to market size (GDP) are considered (figure I.4). In contrast, all developing regions (except for West Asia) become more important as recipients of FDI if judged by FDI flows per $1,000 GDP, simply because many of these regions have such small GDPs. In terms of FDI inflows per capita, however, developing countries do not receive as much FDI as developed countries. In the case of FDI outflows, developed countries continue to be dominant both in absolute and relative terms. Among developing countries, South, East and South-East Asia -- already relatively important as a home region in terms of the absolute size of outward FDI -- becomes more important even than the United States if FDI as a percentage of GDP is considered.

Figure I.3. FDI inflows, by major region, 1980-1997

(Billions of dollars)

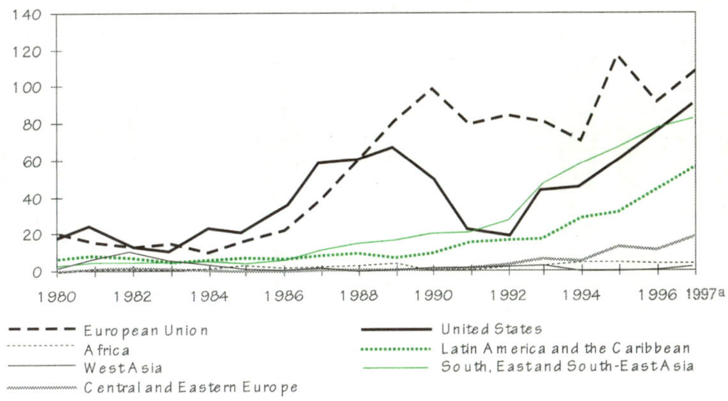

Source: UNCTAD, based on annex table B.1 and UNCTAD FDI/TNC database.

[a] Estimates.

Similarly, country rankings in terms of absolute flows of FDI and relative flows of FDI yield different results (table I.9). Not a single developed country figures among the top 30 recipients of FDI per $1,000 GDP and almost a half of the top 30 outward investors are developing economies. If FDI flows are adjusted for population size, half of the top 30 host countries are developing economies, as are the top three outward investors. There is also considerable change

Table I.8. Regional distribution of FDI inflows and outflows, 1994-1997

(Percentage)

	Inflows				Outflows			
Region/country	1994	1995	1996	1997	1994	1995	1996	1997
Developed countries	58.2	63.9	57.9	58.2	85.0	86.9	85.1	84.8
Western Europe	32.3	37.1	29.6	28.7	47.0	49.4	50.6	46.2
European Union	29.5	35.3	27.4	27.0	42.4	45.2	45.3	42.4
Other Western Europe	2.8	1.8	2.2	1.7	4.6	4.3	5.3	3.7
United States	18.6	17.7	22.6	22.7	25.8	26.1	22.5	27.0
Japan	0.4	-	0.1	0.8	6.4	6.4	7.0	6.1
Developing countries	39.3	31.9	38.5	37.2	15.0	12.9	14.8	14.4
Africa	2.3	1.6	1.4	1.2	0.2	0.2	0.1	0.3
Latin America and the Caribbean	11.8	9.6	13.0	14.0	1.8	0.7	0.7	2.1
Developing Europe	0.2	0.1	0.3	0.2	-	-	-	0.1
Asia	25.0	20.3	23.7	21.7	12.9	12.1	14.0	12.0
West Asia	0.6	-0.2	0.1	0.5	0.4	0.2	-0.3	0.1
Central Asia	0.4	0.5	0.6	0.7	-	-	-	-
South, East and South-East Asia	24.0	20.1	23.0	20.6	12.5	11.9	14.2	11.8
The Pacific	-	0.2	0.1	0.1	-	-	-	-
Central and Eastern Europe	2.4	4.3	3.7	4.6	0.1	0.1	0.2	0.8
World	100	100	100	100	100	100	100	100

Source: UNCTAD, based on annex tables B.1 and B.2.

Figure I.4. FDI flows, relative to market size and population,[a] by region, 1996

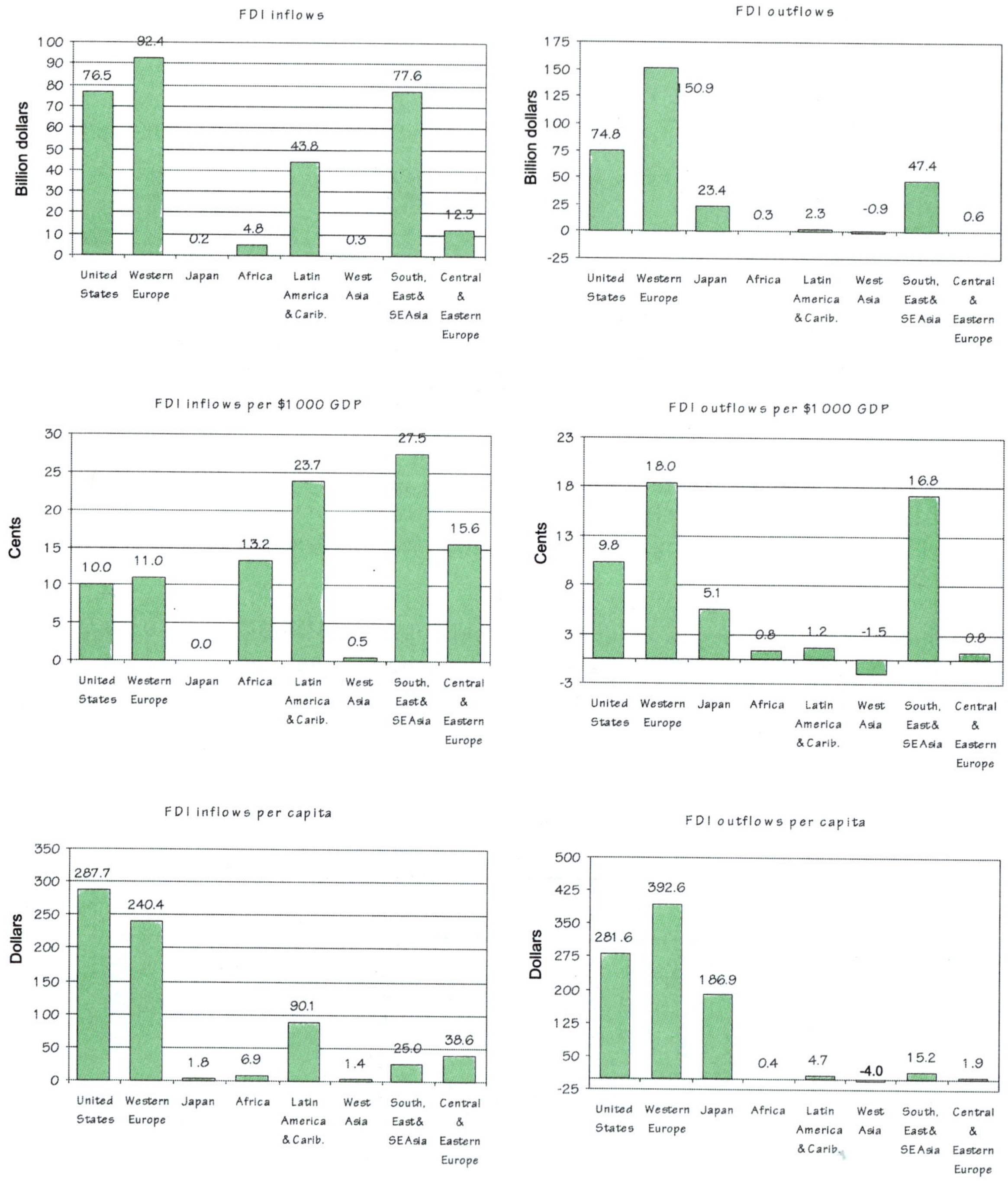

Source: UNCTAD, FDI/TNC database.

[a] As measured by GDP.

Table I.9: The world's largest host and home economies for FDI flows, FDI flows per $1,000 GDP and FDI flows per capita, 1996

	FDI inflows						FDI outflows					
	Absolute value		Per $1,000 GDP		Per capita		Absolute value		Per $1,000 GDP		Per capita	
Rank	**Economy**	($billion)	**Economy**	(Dollars)	**Economy**	(Dollars)	**Economy**	($billion)	**Economy**	(Dollars)	**Economy**	(Dollars)
1	United States	76.5	Equatorial Guinea	23.66	Bermuda	32812.5	United States	74.8	Hong Kong, China	0.17	Hong Kong, China	4474.7
2	China	40.8	Bermuda	12.80	Cayman Islands	15937.5	United Kingdom	34.1	Panama	0.11	Bermuda	2718.8
3	United Kingdom	26.0	Azerbaijan	3.84	US Virgin Islands	3867.9	France	30.4	Bermuda	0.11	Singapore	1671.9
4	France	22.0	US Virgin Islands	3.46	Singapore	3284.6	Germany	29.5	Netherlands	0.59	Switzerland	1595.7
5	Belgium & Luxem.	14.1	Guyana	1.50	Belgium & Luxem.	1338.4	Hong Kong, China	26.4	Singapore	0.51	Netherlands	1480.1
6	Brazil	11.1	Viet Nam	1.39	Aruba	1190.1	Japan	23.4	Malaysia	0.43	Norway	1346.9
7	Singapore	9.4	Cambodia	1.26	New Zealand	1019.2	Netherlands	23.1	Switzerland	0.39	Belgium & Luxem.	793.1
8	Mexico	8.2	Vanuatu	1.18	Equatorial Guinea	917.6	Switzerland	11.6	Norway	0.37	Finland	701.0
9	Netherlands	7.8	Singapore	1.00	Norway	909.2	Canada	8.5	United Kingdom	0.30	United Kingdom	583.8
10	Spain	6.5	Malta	0.93	Malta	813.9	Belgium & Luxem.	8.4	Belgium & Luxem.	0.29	Sweden	579.5
11	Canada	6.4	Kazakhstan	0.90	Ireland	688.8	Italy	6.2	Finland	0.29	France	521.6
12	Indonesia	6.2	Lao PDR	0.86	Sweden	622.5	Australia	6.2	Seychelles	0.28	Denmark	483.8
13	Sweden	5.5	Solomon Islands	0.83	Netherlands	497.3	Norway	5.9	Botswana	0.27	Germany	361.0
14	Australia	5.5	Saint Kitts & Nevis	0.82	Switzerland	483.1	Spain	5.2	Sweden	0.20	New Zealand	347.4
15	Argentina	5.1	Dominica	0.81	Austria	477.4	Sweden	5.1	France	0.20	Australia	337.6
16	Malaysia	4.7	Latvia	0.76	United Kingdom	445.2	Singapore	4.8	New Zealand	0.20	Panama	320.5
17	Poland	4.5	St. Vincent & Gren.	0.70	Hong Kong, China	424.4	Rep. of Korea	4.7	Malta	0.19	Canada	285.9
18	Chile	4.1	Grenada	0.69	Israel	424.0	Taiwan Prov. of China	3.8	Taiwan Prov. of China	0.16	United States	281.6
19	Norway	4.0	Bolivia	0.68	Saint Kitts & Nevis	404.8	Malaysia	3.7	Australia	0.16	Iceland	244.7
20	Austria	3.8	Seychelles	0.64	Seychelles	402.7	Finland	3.6	Chile	0.15	Ireland	203.9
21	New Zealand	3.7	Trinidad & Tobago	0.62	France	377.5	Denmark	2.5	Canada	0.15	Japan	186.9
22	Peru	3.6	Botswana	0.62	Bahamas	311.1	China	2.1	Denmark	0.14	Malaysia	179.8
23	Switzerland	3.5	Peru	0.59	Iceland	302.7	Austria	1.4	Germany	0.13	Taiwan Prov. of China	179.4
24	Italy	3.4	China	0.59	Australia	298.7	New Zealand	1.3	Zimbabwe	0.11	Seychelles	177.0
25	Colombia	3.3	Angola	0.58	United States	287.7	Chile	1.1	Nigeria	0.11	Austria	173.6
26	Hong Kong, China	2.5	New Zealand	0.58	Antigua & Barbuda	284.8	Thailand	0.9	Ireland	0.11	Malta	170.9
27	Russian Fed.	2.5	Chile	0.57	Chile	282.6	Panama	0.9	United States	0.10	Spain	131.3
28	Ireland	2.5	Malaysia	0.55	Dominica	253.5	Portugal	0.8	Rep. of Korea	0.10	Israel	129.0
29	Israel	2.4	Belgium & Luxem.	0.50	Trinidad & Tobago	242.4	Israel	0.7	Estonia	0.09	Italy	108.1
30	India	2.4	Namibia	0.49	Malaysia	227.0	Ireland	0.7	Iceland	0.09	Rep. of Korea	102.8

Source: UNCTAD, based on FDI/TNC database.

in the ranking of individual countries with respect to inward and outward FDI if relative indicators are used. All this implies that one has to look beyond absolute levels of FDI in order to understand the significance of FDI for different regions and countries.

As FDI inflows constitute a part of total capital investment in host countries, the ratio of FDI to gross fixed capital formation provides a closer indication of the role of TNCs in a given economy. The magnitude of this role varies from country to country, ranging from small (e.g. Bangladesh, Japan, Rwanda) to more than 30 per cent (Botswana, Nigeria, Singapore) of the share of FDI in domestic gross fixed capital formation. There are 63 countries that fall below the level of the world average of 5.3 per cent (figure I.5), most of them developing countries (51).[12] On a regional basis, however, all developing regions (except West Asia) receive more FDI in relation to gross fixed capital formation than do developed regions (figure I.5).[13]

Figure I.5. FDI inflows as percentage of gross fixed capital formation, 1994-1996

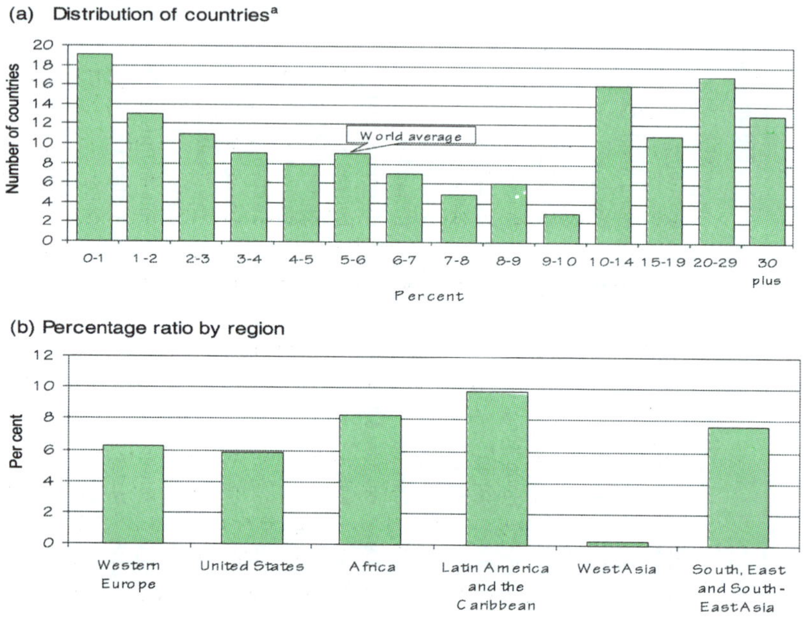

Source: UNCTAD, FDI/TNC database.

a Number of countries with percentage ratios of the level or range specified. In addition there are 8 countries that have ratios below 0 per cent due to negative FDI inflows. Does not include countries (34 in all) for which data on gross fixed capital formation are not available.

(a) Inflows

i. Developed countries and Central and Eastern Europe

Developed countries, including the countries of Western Europe, North America (Canada and the United States), Japan and several other countries (Australia, Israel, New Zealand and South Africa) continued to absorb nearly three-fifths of world inflows. Flows into developed countries have risen substantially between 1996 and 1997, to reach $233 billion in 1997 from $195 billion in 1996. While the United States has been increasing its share in world FDI since 1996, due to large inflows through large-scale M&As, Western Europe saw its share decline noticeably in 1996 and has not yet regained it (table I.8). Although there was a significant increase in FDI inflows into Japan in 1997, Japan's share in world FDI inflows, which had been minuscule during the preceding four decades, did not surpass 1 per cent in that year. Central and Eastern Europe's share in world FDI inflows remained below 5 per cent in 1997. More specifically (table I.8 and figure I.3; see also chapters V and IX):

- *United States.* With macroeconomic indicators such as the GDP growth rate, inflation and employment showing their best performance in decades, FDI flows into the United States exceeded $90 billion in 1997, accounting for more than one-fifth of world FDI inflows. Flows into the United States were, by far, the largest to any individual country, leaving the second largest host country (United Kingdom) behind by more than $50 billion. M&As were the principal modes of entry of FDI to the United States, reflecting especially an M&As boom in United States high technology (including informatics) industries. In 1997, some 90 per cent of investment outlays in foreign affiliates were made through acquisition of United States businesses, compared to 84 per cent in 1990 and 82 per cent in 1995.[14]

- *Western Europe.* Investment flows into the European Union reached $108 billion in 1997, surpassing their level of 1995, after a dip in 1996. Foreign investors responded favourably to improvements in the European Union's economic performance and the strengthening of its macroeconomic indicators in time for the introduction of the Euro in 1999. TNCs were also beginning to respond to the impending single currency in the European Union.[15] The United Kingdom continued to be the largest host country for FDI inflows in 1997. In Germany, new FDI was again (as in 1996) exceeded by FDI withdrawals.

- *Other developed countries.* FDI in Japan amounted to more than $3 billion in 1997 -- a record level of inflows for that country, but no more than about half the flows into, for example, the Netherlands. Inflows rose due to, among other reasons, the response of foreign firms to the ongoing liberalization measures in the retail and financial industries; the absence of large divestments, unlike 1996; and low asset prices, particularly inducing M&As by foreign firms. It should be noted that, because of a change in the coverage of FDI statistics since 1996, FDI data for Japan now include reinvested earnings, which were 10 per cent of inflows in 1997. Australia continued to receive large-scale investments, as during the previous three years.

- *Central and Eastern Europe.* FDI flows into Central and Eastern Europe -- a group of economies in transition -- had more than doubled in 1995. After a decline in 1996, inflows rose by one half in 1997, to $19 billion, a level comparable to that achieved by Latin America and the Caribbean in the early 1990s.

ii. Developing countries

Developing countries are recipients of both official and private capital flows. The former, however, have declined in relative importance: at the beginning of the 1990s, official finance accounted for more than a half of the flows to developing countries (World Bank, 1998);[16] by 1997, that share was barely 15 per cent (figure I.6). While the volume of overall flows grew on average by 16 per cent annually in nominal terms over the period 1990-1997, official finance declined by 3 per cent annually (World Bank, 1998). Official development assistance (ODA) to the least developed countries (LDCs) -- the group of

Figure I.6. Capital flows to all developing countries, 1990-1997

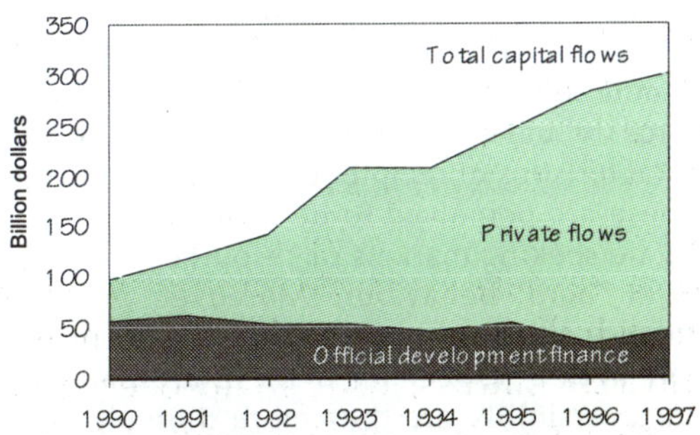

Source: UNCTAD, based on World Bank, 1998 and UNCTAD.

countries most in need of such flows, as reflected by the fact that ODA accounts for the major share of their net capital inflows -- remained stagnant from 1990-1995, and declined by 14 per cent in nominal terms (11 per cent in real terms) in 1996.

The LDCs apart, the picture indeed looks different for private flows (figure I.7). The growing importance of private flows reflects the trend towards liberalization and globalization in the areas of investment and finance. Barriers to capital movements have been abolished in many countries and investment decisions are increasingly made on a regional or global scale. Among private foreign capital flows, portfolio investment is more volatile than FDI since, unlike FDI, it is attracted not so much by the prospect of long-term growth as by the prospect of immediate gain (box I.1). Commercial bank loans accounted, on average, for roughly one-tenth of private capital flows to developing countries over the period 1990-1997, portfolio investment for about a third (box I.2) and FDI for about a half of such flows.

Figure I.7. Total private flows to developing countries, by type of flow, 1990-1997

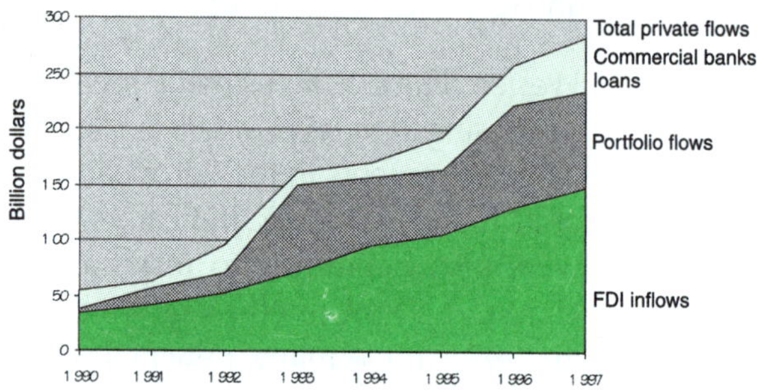

Source: UNCTAD, based on World Bank, 1998, and UNCTAD FDI/TNC database.

Box I.1. The volatility of foreign portfolio investment and FDI flows into developing countries

Repeated episodes of financial turmoil have focused international attention on the problem of volatility of private foreign capital flows and the extent to which that volatility creates an unstable environment detrimental to economic development. During the period 1992-1997, commercial bank loans displayed the highest volatility (0.71), as measured by the coefficient of variation, followed by total portfolio investment (0.43)[a] and FDI (0.35) (box table).

An analysis for 12 major developing economies and economies in transition shows that, in most of the cases, the coefficient of variation based on annual data has been higher for foreign portfolio investment than for FDI during 1992-1997 (box table).[b] For most countries, it has shown greater volatility than FDI (box table). Mexico is a case in point: even when portfolio investment fell sharply in Mexico in 1994-1995 during the peso crisis, FDI was more or less sustained (see chapter VIII). For a few countries, including Brazil, Chile and the Republic of Korea, volatility coefficients were higher for FDI than for portfolio investment during the period under consideration.

The greater overall stability of FDI flows in comparison with portfolio investment flows can be attributed to several factors. TNCs are normally more interested in longer-term profits from the production of goods and services, while portfolio investors are normally more interested in quick financial returns on their investments (UNCTAD, 1997a). The motivation to invest in the case of FDI is typically based on longer-term views of the market, the growth potential and the structural characteristics of recipient countries, and is thus less prone to reversals in response to adverse situations if these are perceived to be short term. Direct investors may also have a variety of motives -- i.e. they may be seeking markets or resources or efficiencies -- and this variety might be expected to reduce the risk of "herd" behaviour. Moreover, as FDI is made through the establishment of production facilities, or the acquisition of existing facilities in recipient countries, it is difficult to dissolve or sell them at short notice, especially if these are parts of integrated international production systems. Divestment and reversibility are thus more difficult for FDI than for portfolio investment, which can be disposed of easily by selling in financial markets.

/...

(Box I.1, continued)

Portfolio investment is not unrelated to the growth of the corporate sector of recipient countries, but it is more affected by short-term fluctuations in financial markets that influence investors' expectations of capital gains. Portfolio investors' strategies combine with the problems of asymmetrical information and the inherent volatility of emerging markets and make portfolio investment more prone to "herd" behaviour.[c] Some channels through which portfolio investment takes place enforce greater stability than others because of their specific structural and regulatory characteristics. For example, investments made by venture capital funds tend to have a long-term duration. Closed-end funds are not required to meet redemption and do not, therefore, need to liquidate their investments at short notice. Depositary receipts are traded in foreign markets, thus allowing some insulation of domestic

Box table. Volatility of foreign portfolio investment and FDI flows in selected developing countries and economies in transition, 1992-1997

Region/country	Average flows (Billion dollars)	Coefficient of variation [a]
All developing countries		
FDI	100.2	0.35
FPI	63.3	0.43
Equity	33.2	0.38
Bond	31.8	0.51
Commercial bank loans	21.6	0.71
Argentina		
FDI	4.3	0.36
FPI	10.0	0.51
Brazil		
FDI	6.3	0.96
FPI	11.9	0.46
Chile		
FDI	2.4	0.71
FPI	0.8	0.68
China [b]		
FDI	29.8	0.38
FPI	2.4	0.71
Hungary [c]		
FDI	2.3	0.57
FPI	1.6	1.25
Indonesia		
FDI	3.6	0.52
FPI	2.9	0.63
Korea, Rep. of		
FDI	1.4	0.57
FPI	11.9	0.47
Mexico		
FDI	8.2	0.40
FPI	10.7	1.22
Philippines		
FDI	1.2	0.41
FPI	0.7	1.31
Singapore [b]		
FDI	6.6	0.46
FPI	1.1	1.01
Thailand [b]		
FDI	1.9	0.19
FPI	3.3	0.52
Uruguay [b]		
FDI	0.1	0.33
FPI	0.1	0.65

Source: UNCTAD, based on official national sources, data provided by IMF and UNCTAD, FDI/TNC database.

[a] Defined as the standard deviation divided by the mean.
[b] 1992-1996.
[c] For 1997, January through August only.
Note: FPI = foreign portfolio investment.

/...

Box I.1 (concluded)

markets from external turbulence. On the whole, however, portfolio investors have a greater tendency to take concerted action, leading both to massive withdrawals in a crisis as well as to rapid recovery once confidence is restored.[d]

As noted, the analysis indicated that, for Brazil, Chile and the Republic of Korea, the volatility of portfolio investment was lower than that of FDI. This could be due to various factors. For Chile, the low volatility of portfolio investment can be explained by controls imposed on short-term capital inflows. Until 1997, the Republic of Korea applied limiting regulations to foreign equity participation in companies listed in the stock market, which minimized the volatility of portfolio equity investment.[e] In Brazil, a higher variation coefficient for FDI is likely to have been caused by recent increases in FDI through privatizations.

Nevertheless, it should be noted that FDI as currently measured contains elements of financial flows that can be affected by movements in interest rates and exchange rates in both source and recipient countries. For example, high interest rates in the United States during the 1980s encouraged United States firms to finance their capital expansions abroad by borrowing in recipient countries, rather than through equity or intra-company loans, two common components of FDI outflows. Changes in exchange rates can also affect the way in which international production is financed and hence the size of FDI flows at any given time. Examples include the expansion of Japanese international production financed through FDI in the latter half of the 1980s when the yen had appreciated. Moreover, in an environment where exchange rates or interest rates are volatile, TNCs might simply postpone their decision to invest.

Source: UNCTAD.

[a] Foreign portfolio investment refers, in principle, to investment that provides financial capital to an enterprise in a country other than that of the investor, but does not involve any management control in the enterprise (UNCTAD, 1997a, p.108). It can be channelled to recipient countries through venture capital funds, investment funds (mutual funds and closed-end funds), American depositary receipts and global depositary receipts (UNCTAD, 1997a).

[b] A similar analysis comparing the volatility of FDI and foreign portfolio equity investment, one component of total portfolio flows to emerging markets during 1986-1995, showed that the latter fluctuated more widely, with a relative variance four times that of FDI flows (UNCTAD, 1997a).

[c] For a detailed analysis of portfolio investors' behaviour and strategies, see UNCTAD, 1998c.

[d] In Mexico, for example, substantial outflows of portfolio investment during the last quarter of 1994 and the first quarter of 1995 were followed by substantial inflows in the first half of 1997.

[e] This percentage was gradually lifted from 10 per cent to 26 per cent in November 1997, and to 55 per cent in April 1998, and will be abolished by the end of 1998. (For details on regulations on foreign portfolio investment in the Republic of Korea as well as 24 other emerging market economies, see UNCTAD, 1998d.)

Developing countries have, indeed, become increasingly attractive for foreign investors. In 1997, they accounted for close to two-fifths or $149 billion of world FDI inflows, twice the level they received in 1993 and tenfold the level in 1985. (Both in 1996 and 1997, FDI flows into developing countries were larger than those into Western Europe, by about $30 billion.) However, there have been significant changes in the pattern of FDI flows into developing countries. Developing Asia -- a region that had continuously claimed an increasing share of FDI among developing countries since the early 1980s and had received the largest share among the developing regions in 1996 -- lost in relative importance in 1997. There was a corresponding increase in the share of Latin America. Major trends in various developing regions are as follows (table I.8, figure I.3 and chapters VI-VIII):

- *Asia and the Pacific.* Flows into South, East and South-East Asia -- the subregion which has accounted for the dominant share of FDI in developing regions in the past decade or so -- increased slightly in 1997, despite the financial crisis that hit several East and South-East Asian economies during the second half of the year. Even though there was a modest decline in inward investment in the five countries most affected by the financial crisis, investment in China compensated for that decline, partly as a result of the reinstatement of special fiscal incentives to foreign investors in 1997. Flows into India also increased. FDI in West Asia has been lagging because of low demand for oil -- the magnet for FDI in the region -- despite some remarkable efforts by countries in that region to improve their FDI climate (UNCTAD, 1997c). With new investments in Saudi Arabia and low but constant flows of FDI to other countries, inflows in 1997 increased over those of 1996, but did not reach the levels of the early 1990s. Central Asia -- another oil-producing subregion -- began to attract large-scale oil-related FDI in 1995 and is now a larger FDI recipient than West Asia. Flows into the Pacific remain at a low level.

- *Latin America and the Caribbean.* This region was the star performer among the developing country regions in 1997, attracting an additional $12 billion over 1996. With only a negligible impact of the financial crisis in Asia on the region, the continuation of the integration process in MERCOSUR, and privatization programmes on stream in many countries, the region re-emerged as an important host for FDI, rivalling and even surpassing South, East and South-East Asia in FDI per capita (figure I.4).

Box I.2. Foreign portfolio investment: recent trends

The importance of foreign portfolio investment in developing countries has increased since the early 1990s (text figure I.7). Recent trends are, however, characterized by large year-to-year fluctuations. In particular, there was a marked slowdown in portfolio flows to developing countries in 1995, following the onset of the Mexican crisis. However, flows increased strongly the following year, as emerging market economies, and particularly Mexico, regained access to international capital markets.[a] In 1997, there was again a reduction of about 6 per cent in portfolio flows to developing countries, because of the onset of the financial crisis in Asia.

The number and net asset values of emerging market equity funds decreased from 1,521 and $139 billion to 1,453 and $122 billion between 1996 and October 1997. Reflecting the impact of the financial crisis, the decline was due almost entirely to a fall in the value of Asian funds -- from $68 billion to $38 billion. In fact, most equity funds targeting countries in other developing regions increased in value in 1997.[b]

Despite the decline in value in 1997, South, East and South-East Asia still held (at least until October 1997) the lion's share of total regional and country funds (58 per cent), followed by Latin America (24 per cent), Central and Eastern Europe (15 per cent), and Africa and West Asia (3 per cent). In Asia, five economies held the largest amounts of equity funds (China, India, Republic of Korea, Taiwan Province of China and Thailand); in Latin America, the largest funds were concentrated in three countries (Brazil, Chile and Mexico); in Central and Eastern Europe, the Russian Federation dominated; and in Africa, South Africa was the dominant country in terms of size of equity funds held.[c]

Based on detailed data for 13 countries,[d] it appears that countries in Latin America (except Chile) generally rely more on foreign portfolio investment than on FDI: on average, their inward portfolio investment flows have by far exceeded their inward FDI flows since 1992. Among the six Asian countries in the list, only the Republic of Korea and Thailand attracted more portfolio investment than direct investment. Argentina, Brazil, Mexico, Thailand, the Republic of Korea and Indonesia also relied increasingly on bonds and notes, which were mainly allocated to the corporate sector.[e]

[a] This can be contrasted with the debt crisis of developing countries in the 1980s: it took seven or eight years for the countries affected, mostly in Latin America, and protracted debt negotiations with their commercial creditors before they were again able to tap international capital markets. These contrasting outcomes partially reflect the more serious systemic risk that emanated from the 1980s crisis.

[b] All data in this paragraph are calculated by UNCTAD, based on information provided by Micropal.

[c] ibid.

[d] Data were collected from national and international sources for the following countries: Argentina, Brazil, Chile, China, Czech Republic, Hungary, Indonesia, Republic of Korea, Mexico, Philippines, Singapore, Thailand and Uruguay.

[e] UNCTAD, based on information provided by Micropal.

- *Africa.* Continued weak demand and low prices for commodities served to dampen FDI in the primary sector, still the key sector influencing the level and composition of FDI in Africa. Recent macroeconomic improvements in the continent bode well for FDI in the region but they have not yet led to significantly increased flows.

- *The LDCs.* The group of 48 LDCs received FDI inflows amounting to just $1.8 billion, or 0.5 per cent of world FDI inflows in 1997. This is low even relative to their market size as measured by their GDP, which was 0.8 per cent of world GDP. Because of relatively large increases in FDI flows into a few countries, the LDCs as a group could maintain almost the same level of FDI in 1997 as in 1996 (a record year), despite a decline of FDI to Asian LDCs from neighbouring countries affected by the financial crisis. LDCs that received higher inflows in 1997 included Bangladesh, because of recent discoveries of natural gas; Uganda and the United Republic of Tanzania, on account of improved economic performance; and Angola, on account of its oil deposits.

(b) Outflows

Developed countries still account for the bulk of world outflows. As with inflows, the importance of developing countries with respect to outflows decreased somewhat in 1997, mainly due to decreased FDI by investors originating in South, East and South-East Asia. On the other hand, Latin American TNCs gained in importance as foreign investors. Noteworthy aspects of FDI outflows in 1997 from major regions are as follows (table I.8 and figure I.8):

- *United States.* The dominant position of the United States in outward FDI was further strengthened in 1997, sustained by higher economic growth at home as well as in the major host regions of United States FDI. In particular, flows into Latin America and to the European Union, the two major traditional host regions of United States FDI, increased significantly. Although more than a half of United States outflows of FDI are financed by reinvested earnings, the record FDI flows in 1997 were mainly caused by significant increases in equity investments, mainly made through M&As.

- *European Union.* European Union FDI outflows in 1997 were also affected by the growth of the main host regions for the Union's FDI -- the United States and its own region. In fact, all of the member states in the European Union recorded growth rates in 1997 that were equal to or higher than those in 1996. Because of this, as well as increased interest by member states in the single market in the

Figure I.8. FDI outflows by major region, 1980-1997

(Billions of dollars)

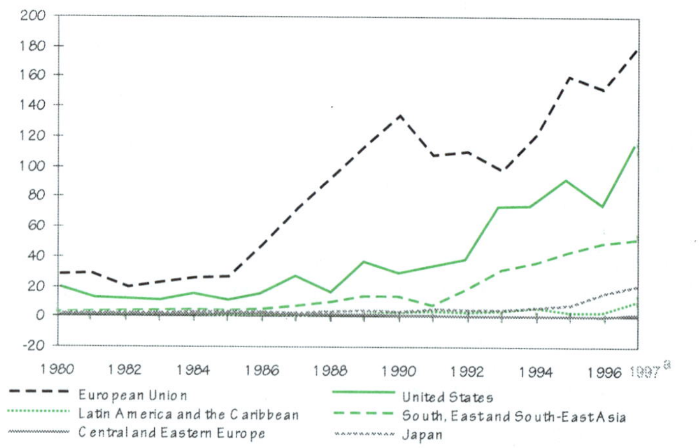

Source: UNCTAD, based on annex table B.1 and UNCTAD FDI/TNC database.

[a] Figures for 1997 are estimated.

light of the introduction of the Euro in 1999, European Union TNCs directed more FDI flows to countries within the region in 1997 than in recent years. Thus, the share of intraregional flows increased in 1997, as had happened several years before, following the announcement of the date of completion of the single market in 1987.[17]

- *Japan.* The economic recession and the financial problems of major Japanese banks did not start affecting FDI outflows from Japan seriously in 1997. Indeed, investment outflows from Japan increased in 1997; they are, however, very likely to decline in 1998. Reinvested earnings accounted for about one-fifth of total FDI outflows from Japan. Equity investment increased in 1997, following a decline in 1996.[18]

- *Asia and the Pacific.* In the principal outward investor subregion of East and South-East Asia, outflows from the Republic of Korea, having risen for the past several years, declined for the first time since 1988 as a result of the problems faced by Korean firms caught in the Asian financial turmoil. Outward FDI from other countries affected by the financial crisis, such as Thailand and Malaysia (relatively large investors within the region), also decreased significantly. Thus FDI inflows into the major host countries of intraregional investments by TNCs based in these countries such as Viet Nam and Myanmar declined. On the other hand, Taiwan Province of China, relatively unscathed by the crisis, is emerging as a large investor in the region. Hong Kong Special Administrative Region of China (hereinafter "Hong Kong, China") continued to invest mainly in China, the largest host country in the region, which absorbs the bulk of FDI from that economy.

- *Latin America.* Liberalization, privatization and regionalization have encouraged Latin America's TNCs to increase investments abroad, particularly within the region. Coupled with high regional economic growth, FDI outflows reached a record $9 billion. FDI by firms from Brazil, Chile and Mexico (as well as some tax-haven economies) surpassed one billion dollars per country. Some of the firms based in this region are global players (e.g. Cemex of Mexico) but most are still regional firms (e.g. Companhia Cervejaria Brahma of Brazil).

3. Mergers and acquisitions

In 1997, total cross-border M&A transactions worldwide amounted to some $342 billion, pushing the record level of the annual value of cross-border M&As beyond that of 1996. Cross-border M&As accounted for the bulk of the increase in FDI flows; their value in relation to total FDI inflows rose from 49 per cent in 1996 to 58 per cent in 1997, representing the highest share attained in the 1990s (figure I.9). Cross-border M&As accounted for about one-quarter of all M&As worldwide (figure I.10).

Figure I.9. The relationship between cross-border M&As and FDI flows, 1985-1997

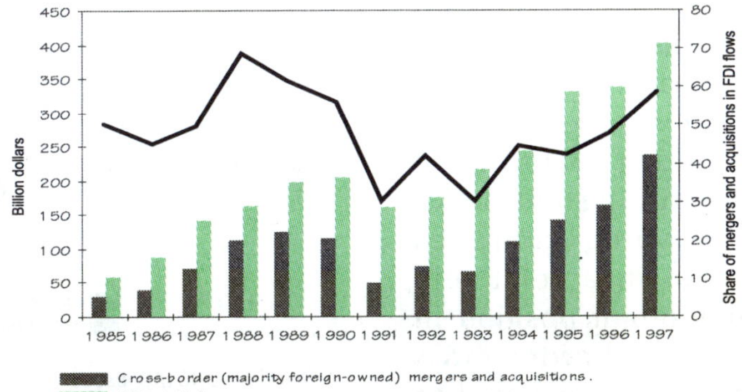

Source: UNCTAD, based on annex table B.7 and UNCTAD FDI/TNC database.

Most of the increase in the value of M&As was due to large-scale cross-border M&A deals. The number of such deals worth more than $1 billion increased from 35 in 1995 to 45 in 1996 and to 58 in 1997, and their value, respectively, from $59 billion to $86 billion and $161 billion. The largest cross-border deal in 1997, between Zurich Versicherungs GmbH and BAT Industries PLC-Financial, was valued at $18.4 billion (annex table A.I.1). During 1995-1997, the average size of large-scale cross-border M&As increased from $1.7 billion in 1995 to $2.8 billion in 1997. In fact, these mega deals accounted for about a half of global M&A transaction values in 1997, compared to one-quarter in 1995. Large-scale M&As were concluded mainly among developed country TNCs. While firms from the United States continue to account for the single largest share of large-scale cross-border M&As, other countries (especially the United Kingdom, France and Germany) also play an important role (figure I.11). In addition, the growth of large-scale cross-border M&As by firms based in Switzerland is impressive. Large cross-border M&As are concentrated in the banking and insurance, chemical and pharmaceutical, and telecommunication and media industries (figure I.12), in all of which companies face severe competitive pressures in global markets. In 1997, banking and insurance became the dominant industry for large M&As.

Figure I.10. Cross-border and all M&As in the world

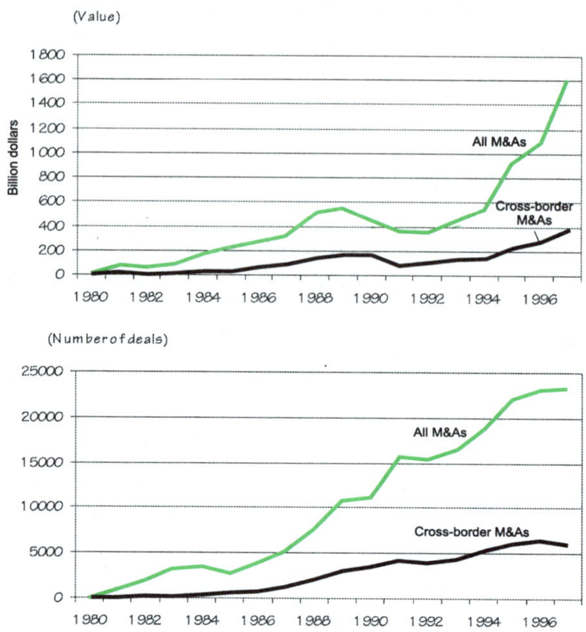

Source: UNCTAD, based on data provided by Securities Data Company, Inc. (New York).

Developed countries continued to account for about 80 per cent of all cross-border M&A sales, and about 90 per cent of cross-border majority purchases, totalling $236 billion in 1997. (Majority purchases are transactions in which the foreign investor acquires more than half the voting securities of the resulting business.) Developing countries remain in a relatively unimportant position in the cross-border M&A market, as compared to their position in FDI flows (figure I.13). The

Figure I.11. Principal home countries of firms engaged in large cross-border M&As,[a] 1995-1997
(Percentage of total value)

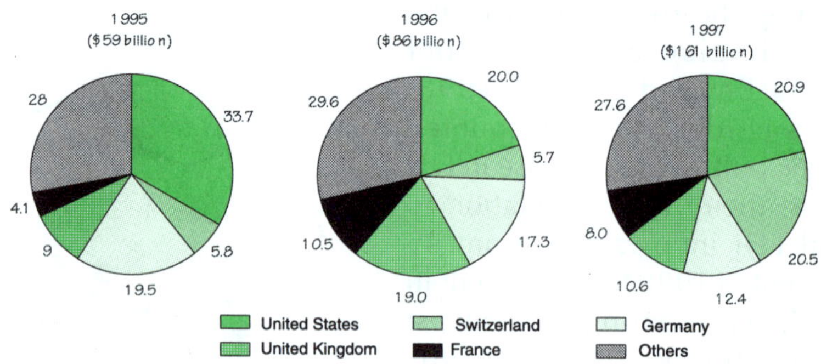

Source: UNCTAD, based on data provided by Securities Data Company, Inc. (New York) and UNCTAD 1996a and 1997a.

[a] Acquisitions exceeding $1 billion.

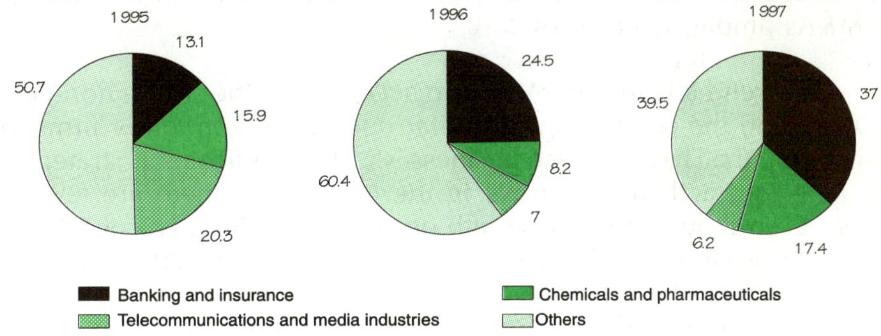

Figure I.12. Major targeted industries in large cross-border M&As,[a] 1995-1997

(Percentage of total value)

Source: UNCTAD, based on data provided by Securities Data Company, Inc. (New York) and UNCTAD 1996a and 1997a.

[a] Acquisitions exceeding $1 billion.

relatively low share of developing countries in majority M&A purchases -- about 8 per cent (annex table B.8) in 1997 or only a half of their share in FDI outflows -- suggests that TNCs from developing countries prefer the greenfield mode, or acquisition of minority shareholding, in entering markets through FDI.[19] Indeed, considering all cross-border M&A purchases including minority deals, developing countries accounted for a share almost equal to their share in FDI outflows. As in the case of outflows, South, East and South-East Asia accounts for the bulk of developing-country cross-border M&A purchases.

On the sales side of majority M&As (figure I.13 and annex table B.7), developing countries again account for less than they do in world FDI inflows. However, an upward trend in M&A sales by developing countries and countries in transition is noticeable. Among developing countries, majority M&A sales in South, East and South-East Asia have been increasing recently, in particular after the 1997 financial crisis. Significant increases in M&A sales in Latin America and in Central and Eastern Europe were also recorded in 1997, mainly on account of privatization. For example, the doubling or tripling of M&A sales in Brazil and the Russian Federation is clearly linked to privatization.

One recent feature is that M&As among large or dominant TNCs, resulting in even larger TNCs, seem to impel other major TNCs to move towards restructuring or making similar deals with other TNCs. The pharmaceutical, automobile, telecommunications and financial industries are typical examples of industries in which such a concentration trend can be observed (see figure I.14 for capital links in the automobile industry). The result is a change in industry structure. In the automobile industry, for example, the total number of major automobile makers may well decline to 5-10 by 2010, from its current

Figure I.13. Cross-border M&A sales and purchases,[a] by group of countries, 1993-1997

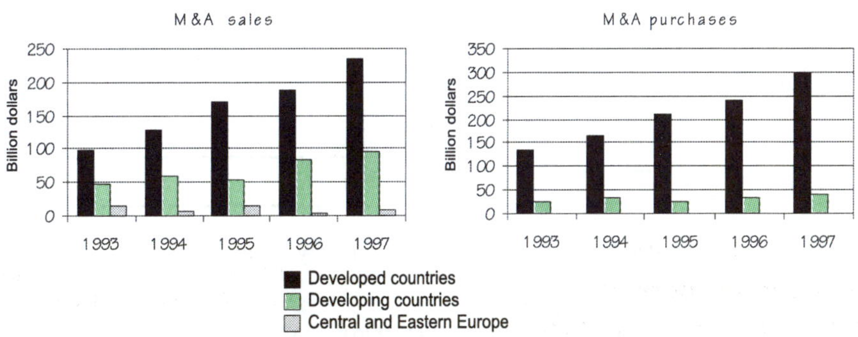

Source: UNCTAD, based on data provided by KPMG Corporate Finance.

[a] Only M&As in which the foreign investor acquires more than a half of the voting securties are included.

number of 15.[20] In the pharmaceutical industry, many markets are now controlled by a small number of firms, with seven firms having sales of over $10 billion each,[21] accounting for about a quarter of the $300 billion market.[22] In both industries, there has been a string of M&As among large firms.

The trend towards M&As is also accelerating the sale of non-core operations or affiliates by firms and the acquisition of similar operations from other firms (of divisions or affiliates, or of firms that have similar businesses). This indicates a strategic shift by TNCs to focus on their core activities. Unlike in the late 1980s, there are fewer deals among unrelated firms. Even though about one-fifth of the largest deals (13 of 58 cases) in 1997 were made among firms whose businesses were unrelated (annex table A.I.1), most of these transactions were concluded by investment bankers or brokers whose purpose is to seek capital gains rather than to expand into unrelated business areas.

In addition to the strategic considerations of firms, liberalization and deregulation are the other main factors behind the dramatic increases in M&As in both developed and developing countries. Increasing M&As in the services sector in general and in financial industries in particular reflect ongoing liberalization exemplified, among others, by the conclusion of WTO's financial services pact in December 1997 (see chapter III). The value of cross-border M&As in the services sector has been larger than in the manufacturing sector every year since 1995 (figure I.15). Banking, finance and insurance industries accounted for

Figure I.14. Cross-border links among major TNCs in the automobile industry,[a] 1998

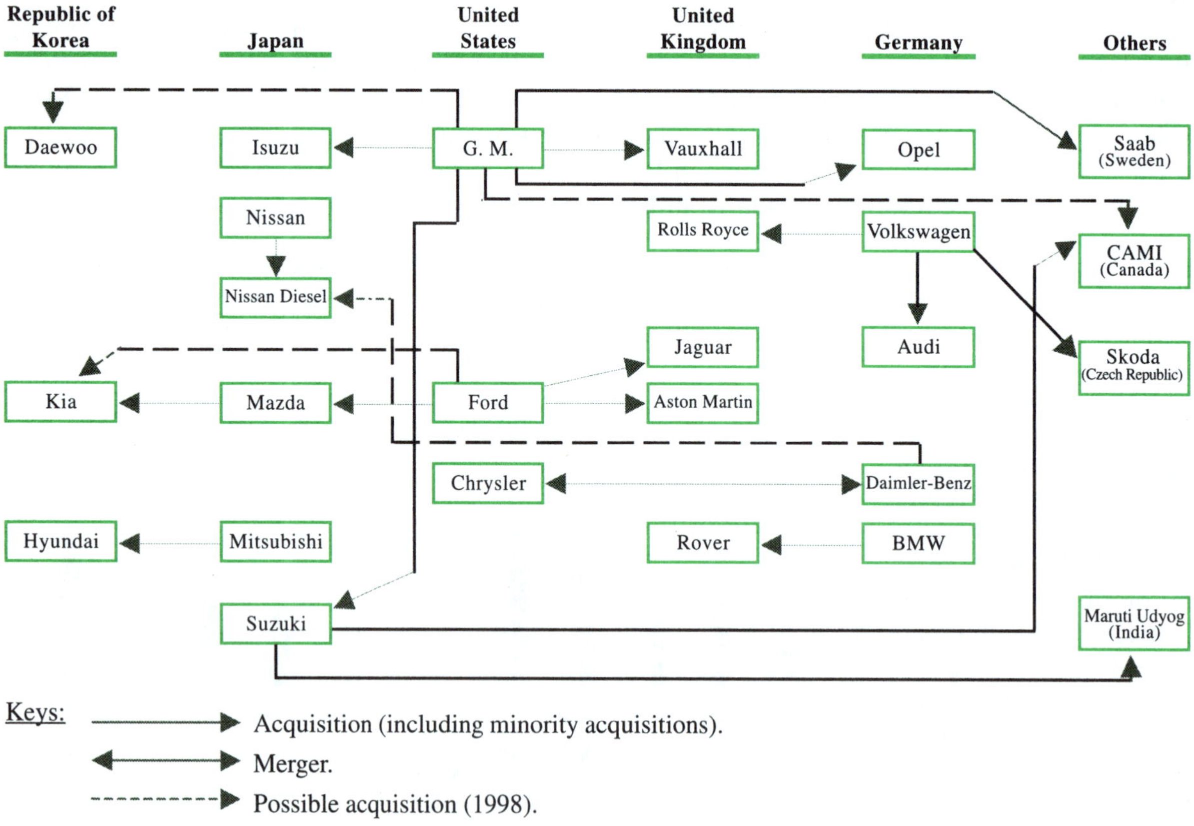

Source: UNCTAD, based on information provided by Gendai Advanced Studies Research Organization (Tokyo).

[a] Lists only the automobile TNC that have cross-border capital links. Does not include technology agreements.

about one-quarter of the value of majority cross-border M&As in 1997 (annex table B.9). Telecommunication is another industry that has been significantly liberalized; because of its importance for other industries and the large market for its services, it has attracted substantial FDI, including FDI from other industries (such as the software industry and the construction industry). Prospects for cross-border M&As in telecommunications are still high. For example, it is expected that all leading telecommunication firms will be privatized in Latin America by the year 2000.[23] It is interesting to note, however, that since full or majority ownership by foreign firms is not normally allowed in this industry, majority M&As do not figure as highly as in total M&A transactions.

Figure I.15. Sectoral distribution of cross-border M&As,[a] 1989-1997
(Percentage of total value)

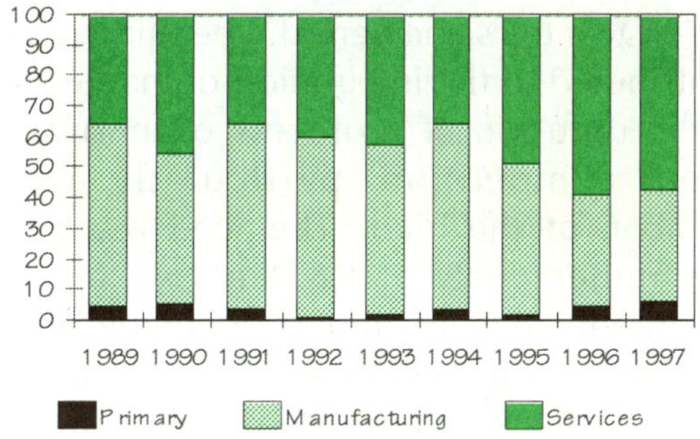

Source: UNCTAD, based on annex table B.9.

[a] Includes only M&As in which the foreign investor acquires more than a half of the voting securties.

In some industries such as transport, and in aviation in particular, deregulation has led to inter-firm agreements -- for example, code sharing -- rather than outright mergers. The value of cross-border M&As is therefore small. The production and distribution of electricity -- an industry that is beginning to be opened up to foreign firms in many countries -- is another area in which large-scale M&As have taken place recently; it has become the second largest industry, after banking and finance, in M&A transaction values (annex table B.9). In fact, five of the top 58 largest cross-border M&As were in this field in 1997 (annex table A.I.1).

B. Inter-firm technology agreements

Inter-firm agreements include a wide variety of arrangements between firms for R&D as well as for the production and distribution of goods and services. A subset of these agreements involve technology-related activities (UNCTAD, 1997a, p. 14). Over the period 1980-1996, a total of 8,254 inter-firm technology agreements were recorded in the MERIT/ UNCTAD database,[24] with the number of such agreements rising from a yearly average of less than 300 in the early 1980s to over 600 in the mid-1990s (figure I.16). Some 650 such agreements were recorded in 1996.

Underlying the upsurge in inter-firm technology agreements are a number of changes in the pattern of production and competition. During the 1980s and 1990s, production became more knowledge-intensive across a wider range of industries. This in turn has led to increases in R&D expenditures and the speed with which new products are developed and moved to market. Product life cycles have thus shortened and the costs, risks and uncertainties of keeping up with the technological frontier or moving beyond it have increased. To respond to these new

Figure I.16. The growth of inter-firm technology agreements, 1980-1996
(Number)

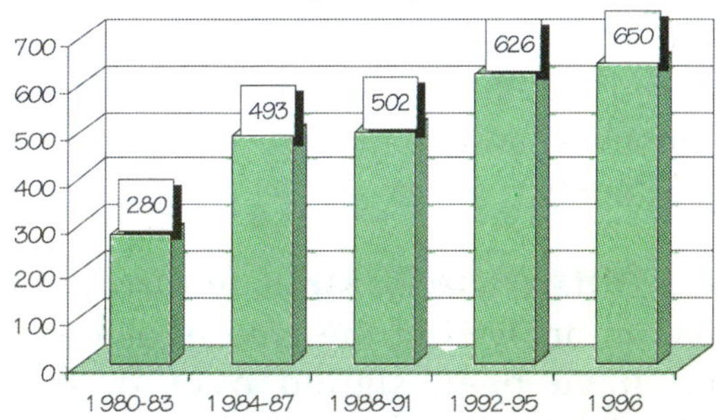

Source: MERIT/UNCTAD database.

competitive conditions, firms have sought to increase their flexibility and leverage their R&D investments through inter-firm agreements.

Over the same period, liberalization has contributed to the integration of markets and to the diffusion of a process of innovation-based competition, particularly among members of the Triad. The need to amortize the higher costs of R&D across a wider geographical space and the opening of new markets to competition have accelerated the pace of M&As within the overall process of both foreign and domestic investment. Driven by these underlying processes, the trends in inter-firm technology agreements have thus largely parallelled those in M&As (figure I.17).

Figure I.17. Inter-firm technology agreements, and M&As,[a] 1985-1996

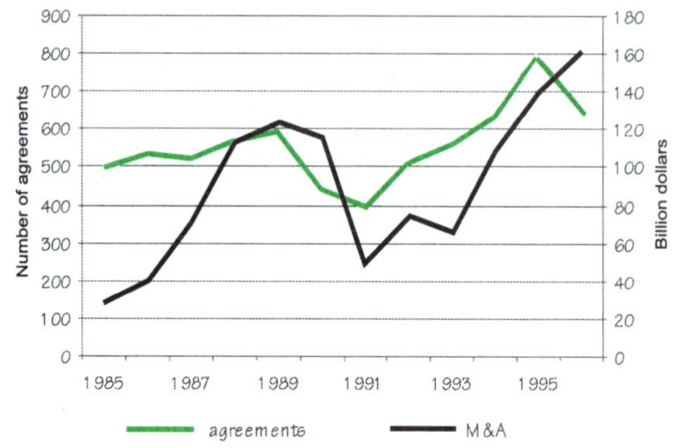

Source: MERIT/UNCTAD database.

[a] Majority foreign-owned M&As only.

1. Developed countries

Behind the aggregate figures, however, lie major differences in the strategies that firms adopt in their relationships with other companies. They emerge in the choices firms make between the acquisition of assets and the use of arm's-length inter-firm technology agreements, as well as among different types of inter-firm agreements.

More internationalized firms, for example, are not necessarily those that are most involved in inter-firm technology agreements. A rank-order correlation of the assets abroad (UNCTAD, 1997a, pp. 29-31) and the number of inter-firm technology agreements of the top 100 TNCs (ranked by foreign assets) in 1995 provides evidence for this.[25] The Spearman's rank-order correlation coefficient of .3072 and its significance at the .002 level in a one-tailed test show a very weak relationship between these two variables.[26] Nor does large size alone predict a continuously high involvement in arm's-length technology agreements. Large firms have certainly been active players in inter-firm technology agreements, but their share of the total number of such agreements has varied considerably over time (figure I.18). Throughout much of the 1980s, it hovered around 30 per cent, rising to over 40 per cent in 1991, but steeply declining to just over 20 per cent in 1995 and 1996. As M&As rose sharply in 1996 and 1997 (figure I.10), this decline may reflect a trade-off between M&As and inter-firm technology agreements.

Figure I.18. The share of the world's largest 100 firms in total inter-firm technology agreements,[a] 1980-1996

(Percentage)

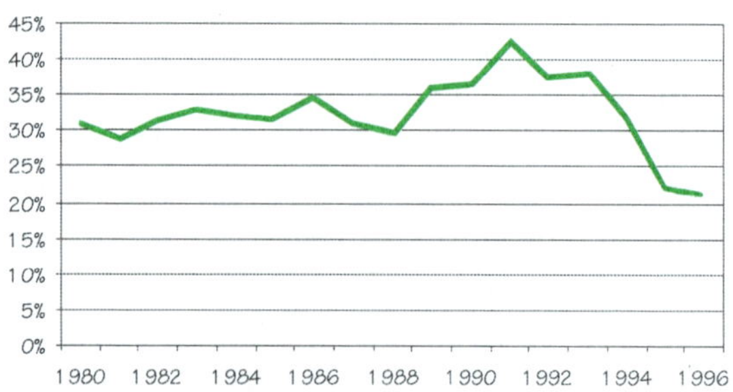

Source: MERIT/UNCTAD database.

[a] Based on the "Fortune 500" listing for 1995 (*Fortune*, 29 April 1996).

Differences in strategy also emerge from an analysis of the type of agreements that have been signed over time. In particular, two types of inter-firm agreements can be distinguished (UNCTAD, 1997a, p.

14): those that involve a one-way relationship in which the flow of technology is from licensor to licensee or from one joint-venture partner to the other; and two-way relationships involving joint research and/ or development agreements and the creation of joint R&D ventures with specific research programmes. During the 1980s, both one-way agreements and two-way partnerships followed similar rising trends (figure I.19). The preference for one-way agreements shifted to two-way partnerships towards the middle of the decade, but the trend lines remained parallel. Beginning in 1990, the slope of the two curves radically changed: whereas, during the 1988-1991 period, an average number of 223 one-way and 279 two-way agreements were being signed each year, the average annual number of one-way agreements being signed in 1992-1995 fell to 158, while the number of two-way partnerships rose to 468. These diverging trends have continued in 1996 when only 109 one-way agreements were signed as compared with 541 two-way partnerships.

Figure I.19. The evolution in the type of inter-firm technology agreements,1980-1996
(Number)

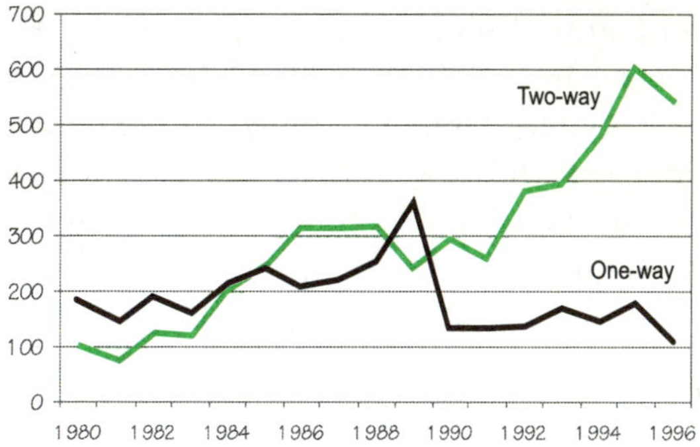

Source: MERIT/UNCTAD database.

To a large extent, the strategic choices of firms with regard to inter-firm technology agreements are shaped by industry-specific characteristics. Industries that are highly knowledge-intensive have the largest number of inter-firm agreements. Data covering the period 1980-1996 show that information technology remains the top industry in which technology agreements are being signed; it alone accounted for 37 per cent of all agreements (figure I.20). Their number has also increased dramatically over time, from an annual average of 74 during the period 1980-1983 to 248 during 1992-1995. Some 254 technology agreements were signed in that industry in 1996. Pharmaceuticals and, particularly, bio-pharmaceuticals, show a similar rising trend; their share in total agreements doubled from 14 per cent during 1980-1983 to 28 per cent in 1996. Far less knowledge-intensive are the automotive and food industries, although R&D, design, engineering and marketing are increasingly important inputs in new product development in each of these industries (figure I.20). In both cases, the number of agreements peaked in the mid-1980s. In the food industry, agreements have declined since then. In the automobile industry, however, there is a rising trend that began in the early 1990s and has continued through 1996.

Figure I.20. Number of inter-firm technology agreements, by selected industry, 1980-1996

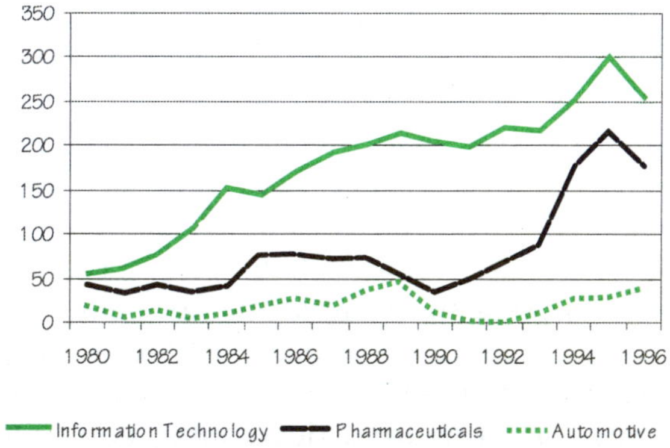

Source: MERIT/UNCTAD database.

Sector-specific patterns of competition and industry structure have also been important in shaping the partnering strategies of firms over time. The automobile industry is illustrative. The entry of newcomers from Japan during the 1960s and 1970s brought with it a fundamental restructuring of the global industry. Strategies of vertical disintegration and the use of new forms of supplier-client relationships represented a significant break with existing organizational technology in United States and European automobile firms, which had been based largely upon the mass production of standardized products and vertical integration. By 1996, only Ford and Volvo manufactured more than 60 per cent of their parts in-house. Figures for supplies of parts by vertically integrated units for other companies were as follows: 43 per cent for Volkswagen; 38 per cent for Mercedes-Benz; 37 per cent for GM, 33 per cent for BMW, Renault and Peugeot; 30 per cent for Fiat and 25 per cent for Honda, Nissan and Toyota (Kurylko, 1996). Over time, a set of preferred first-tier parts suppliers emerged with whom new forms of partnerships for the design of principal components and subsystems were entered into by companies. Joint development agreements with suppliers of manufacturing technology also became important as factory automation advanced.

By the mid-1980s, the global automobile industry gave every sign of great stability and growing concentration. The top four firms have been virtually identical since the mid-1980s, with Nissan and Volkswagen changing places in 1991. As to concentration ratios, GM's share of the world market declined slightly, but the four-firm ratio increased from 40.9 to 44.6 per cent and the ten-firm ratio from 63.9 to 71.2 per cent over the period 1985-1995 (Mytelka and Delapierre, 1997), as every assembler sought to cover the full range of vehicles.[27] With the acquisition of Rolls Royce by Volkswagen in 1998 (see figure I.14), no major luxury-car manufacturer remains independent.

Despite the role that M&As have played, partnerships have begun to increase in the 1990s, as the major automobile manufacturers sought to develop a new generation of cars to meet more stringent environmental and performance standards. Research into the use of ceramic materials and the development of fuel cells, navigational systems and other technologies have led to a variety of partnerships with suppliers of parts and components as well as with other automobile manufacturers.

A look at the portfolio of inter-firm technology agreements held by Ford (figure I.21) and Toyota (figure I.22) provides evidence of the differing ways in which companies have met these new competitive challenges. Both companies draw on an international group of manufacturing technology firms as partners; but in its relationships with parts suppliers Toyota works mainly with Japanese firms, whereas Ford engages in partnerships with a worldwide network of parts suppliers. Ford, however, is much more focused on the United States market in its partnerships with upstream suppliers of inputs for parts and components. More recently they have also developed a large number of technology partnerships with rival automobile manufacturers, many of which are geared to developing the car of the future. In contrast, Japanese technology partnerships with automobile manufacturers are far fewer and focused less on the development of a new generation of automobiles than on parts and components for such a vehicle.

For firms in developed countries, inter-firm technology agreements remain a critical means of maintaining flexibility, expanding access to a range of possible technologies from other industries, and setting standards early in the process of new product development -- thus ensuring more rapid market penetration. As agreements with rivals illustrate, they can also become a means of controlling the direction of technological change, thus strengthening their market power in the future (Mytelka and Delapierre, 1997). As discussed below, for firms from developing countries, inter-firm technology agreements provide a different array of benefits.

2. Developing countries

Although inter-firm technology agreements involving firms from developing countries account for only 455 agreements in the MERIT/UNCTAD database, their number is on the rise, from an average of 10 agreements per year in the early 1980s to nearly 40 per year in the mid-1990s. Their share has also increased from 4.9 per cent of the 4,270 agreements concluded during the 1980s to 6.2 per cent of the 3,984 agreements recorded in the 1990s (figure I.23).

Over the period 1980-1996, United States firms have been the major partners of developing country firms, accounting for over two-fifths of agreements involving the latter (figure I.24). Sixty per cent of the 191 agreements signed in this period between firms based in the United States and those based in developing countries were concluded in the 1990s. While firms from the European Union were also major technology partners for developing country firms and accounted for over one-third of the total, firms from other developed countries were far less involved in technology partnerships with the developing world. Japanese firms, for example, were partners in only 11 per cent of the agreements and firms from other developed countries accounted for barely 4 per cent of the total.

Figure I.21. The portfolio of technology agreements of Ford, 1983-1996

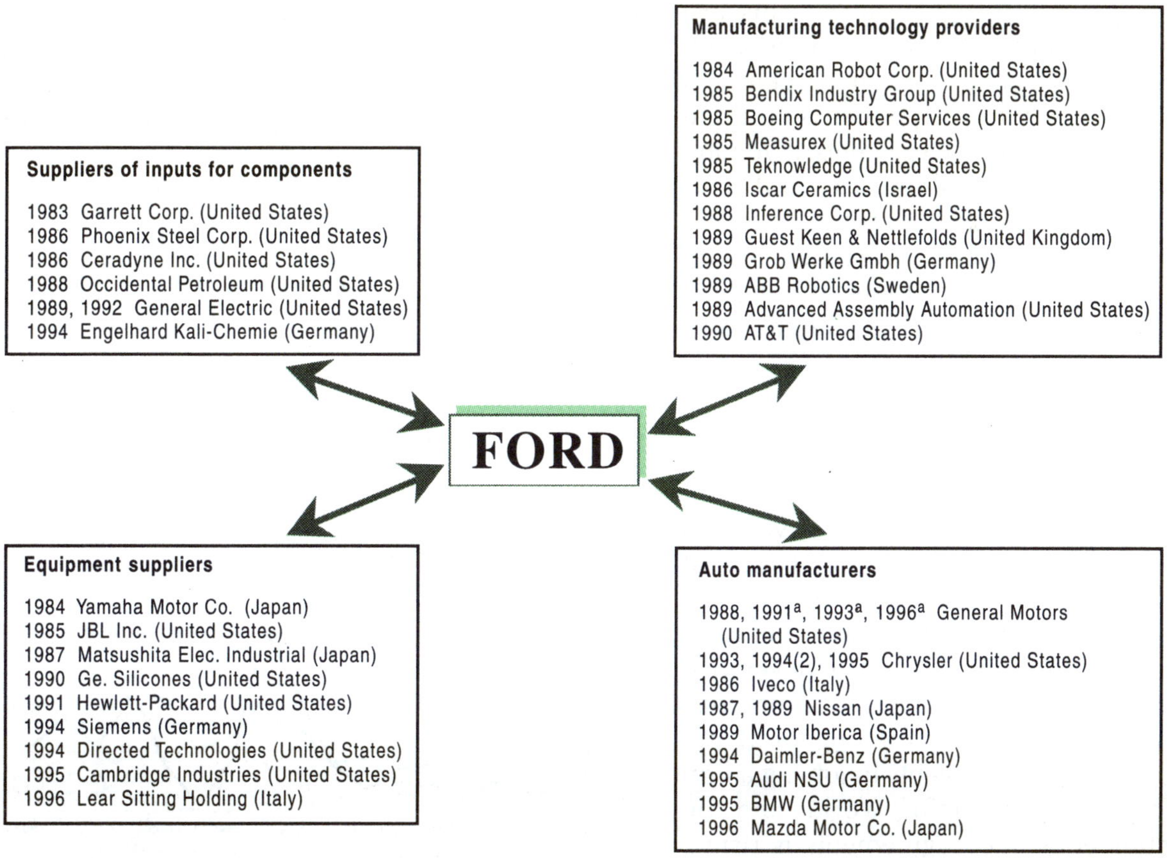

Source: MERIT/UNCTAD database.

[a] Signed 2 technology agreements that year.

Figure I.22. The portfolio of technology agreements of Toyota, 1982-1996

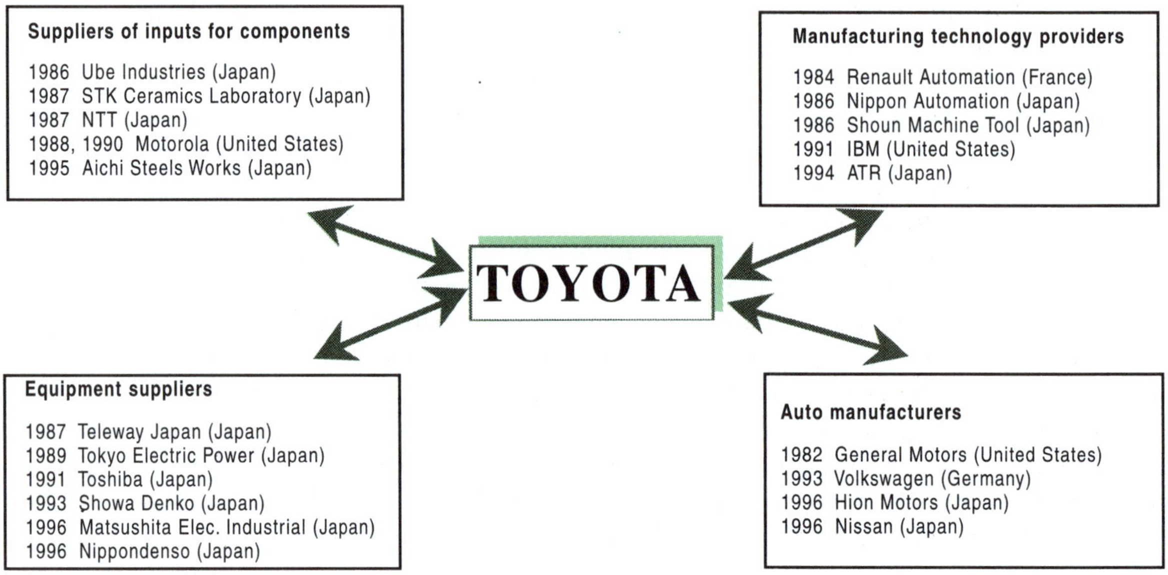

Source: MERIT/UNCTAD database.

Developing country firms are also beginning to partner more often with each other. Such agreements accounted for nearly 7 per cent of the 455 technology agreements involving a developing country firm, and their number is rising. Nearly half of the 31 agreements involving developing country firms in partnership with one another were signed in the past four years (figure 1.24).

The industry profile of partnering activity by developing country firms is significantly different from that of firms in the developed world (figure I.25), but it suggests that developing country firms are becoming viable partners in joint R&D activities. As in the case of developed country firms, information technology ranks at the top, accounting for 27 per cent of the agreements involving a firm from the developing world, and the number of such agreements is rising. From an annual average of four per year during the 1980s, it reached 13 in

Figure I.23. Developing countries: number of inter-firm technology agreements, 1980-1996
(Number)

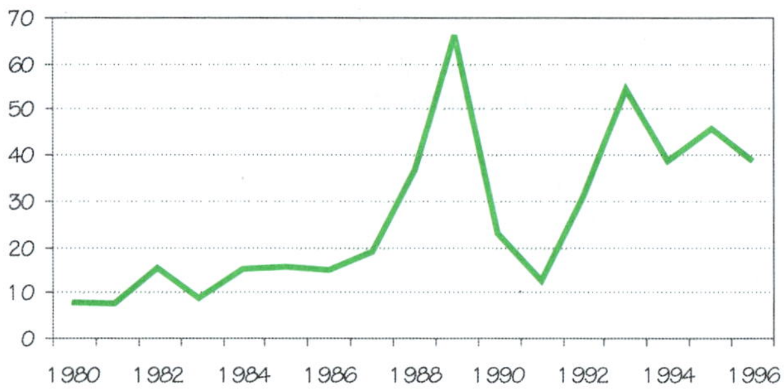

Source: MERIT/UNCTAD database.

Figure I.24. Developing country firms and their partners in inter-firm technology agreements, 1980-1996
(Number)

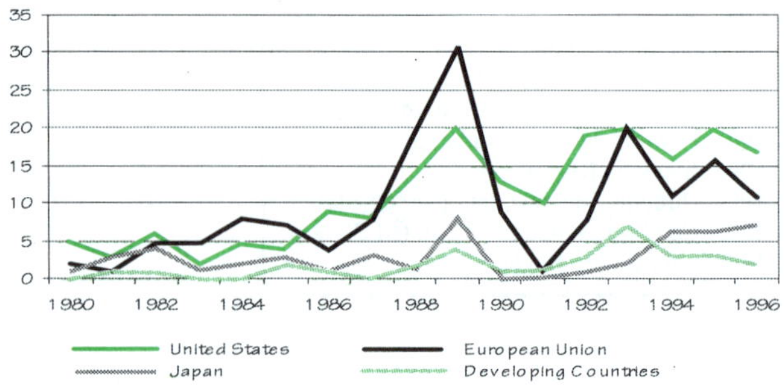

Source: MERIT/UNCTAD database.

the 1990s, with 21 alone being signed in 1996. Korean firms are the most active here, with Samsung at the top of the list. But a number of information technology firms from other Asian countries are also forming partnerships, especially with firms from the developed world (box I.3).

Pharmaceuticals constitute the second most important industry for partnering activity by firms from developed countries, but account for less than 6 per cent of the agreements involving a developing country firm. For developing country firms, technology agreements in the chemical and automotive industries are far more important and account for 19 per cent and 9 per cent of the total, respectively.

A second indicator of the extent to which firms in developing countries are becoming viable technology partners is the growing importance of two-way partnerships. This is most pronounced in knowledge-intensive industries such as information technology. In the 1980s, one-way agreements were the norm, accounting for 78 per cent of the information technology agreements involving a developing country. In the 1990s, the share of two-way agreements had risen to 55 per cent. Many technology agreements in industries such as information technology began as one-way arrangements, but have slowly transformed themselves into two-way partnerships. The Nortel Network, which links Northern Telecom (Nortel) to four Indian software companies, is a case in point (box I.3).

For developing country firms, the new two-way partnerships are a bridge to knowledge bases abroad. By providing windows on the world, they serve as a way of keeping up with a rapidly moving frontier. They also enable developing country firms to leverage their own R&D resources and to build the kind of credibility that attracts other partners and new customers at home and abroad.

Figure I.25. Industry profile of partnering activity in inter-firm technology agreements, by developing country firms and all firms, 1980-1996

(Percentage)

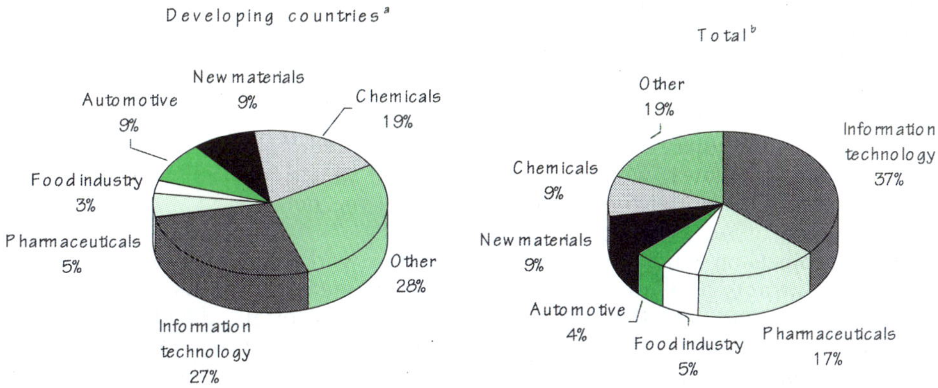

Source: MERIT/UNCTAD database.

[a] Based on 455 agreements.

[b] Based on 8,254 agreements.

Box I.3. The Nortel network

Nortel is a leading telecommunications firm from Canada which specializes in developing technology for digital networks. Its revenues in 1997 were $15.5 billion, 37 per cent of which emanated from outside North America. Software is increasingly substituting for a variety of tasks that were previously performed by telecom hardware. For firms in North America, software development has become very expensive, due in part to the shortage of skilled manpower. (Nortel alone annually absorbs more than a quarter of Canada's total output of software engineers and programmers.) As a result, it has moved to establish R&D activities abroad. Currently, it has 38 R&D collaboration sites in different parts of the world and has developed strong non-equity R&D-based relationships with four of the leading software firms in India (Basant, Chandra and Mytelka, 1998).

In 1989, the International R&D Group of Nortel entered into global software outsourcing arrangements with two Indian software development companies, Silicon Automation Systems (SAS) in Bangalore and Tata Consultancy Services (TCS) with headquarters in Mumbai. Infosys Technologies (Infosys) and Wipro Systems (Wipro), both of which are located in Bangalore, were added to this arrangement in 1992. These firms are well-established companies and compete with each other in domestic and international markets:

* TCS was set up over 30 years ago and is Asia's largest consulting group with activities that range from management consulting to information-technology solutions, offshore development and branded software products. This firm employs 9,800 people and had a turnover of $201 million in 1996-1997, of which about 8 per cent was invested in R&D.

* Infosys, founded in 1981, is a software development company with a focus on software services in the areas of distribution, finance, retailing, telecommunications, insurance, Internet and engineering and bank automation. Its turnover in 1996-1997 was $37.8 million, of which 5 per cent was spent on R&D.

* Wipro Systems, a division of Wipro Infotech, was set up in 1984 as a unit focusing on global software outsourcing. In 1993-1994 it had over 2,500 employees and a turnover of $14.3 million.

* SAS is the smallest of the four firms. Established in 1989, it develops tools and services for the design of semiconductors, telecommunications, computing and networking equipment. The firm employs 300 people, of whom 250 are engineers. Its annual turnover in 1996-1997 was $4.6 million.

The Nortel network is not equity-based, although Nortel has invested in training and in the installation of state-of-the-art telecom hardware, such as digital switches and large-capacity (2 gigabytes) dedicated lines for communication between Nortel and its Indian partners. The contractual relationship between Nortel and each of its partners is structured individually. The allocation of projects to each partner by Nortel is governed by Nortel's overall strategy to map disciplines across partners and avoid overlap. Each partner in India has specializations and, collectively, the four Indian partners duplicate Nortel's lab in Ottawa, which works on a broad spectrum of telecom products. Since the firms do not work together, Nortel remains the director of the network.

Initially projects on which Nortel's Indian partners worked were based on hierarchical, arm's-length technical contracts and involved low-skill assignments (such as programme testing and computer-aided design) and very limited interaction between Nortel's development teams and the Indian firms. The relationship evolved as the Indian partners gained experience with the successful completion of many of these projects. Learning opportunities arose especially through exchanges of experts between Nortel's research facilities in Canada and partner sites in India, and through the use of new telecommunications-related software. Gradually, Nortel began to commission larger and more complex development projects requiring more sophisticated hardware and communication infrastructure along with enhanced interaction between Nortel and Indian teams. Both Nortel and its partners hope that the relationship will evolve into a full two-way partnership.

/...

(Box I.3, concluded)

With one of these firms, the shift from a one-way to a two-way partnership is well advanced. Initially contracted for computer-aided design services, SAS has redefined its core competence as digital signal processing. This has enabled it to develop solutions for digital communications, with specific emphasis on multimedia technologies. SAS has thus moved to the development and design of prototypes of their own to meet future development needs at Nortel.

Nortel's interest in India also grew from its search for opportunities to adapt its technology for the Asia-Pacific market. Its principal international competitors -- Siemens, Alcatel, AT&T and Ericsson -- are already present in India. Nortel's alliance with the four Indian firms thus provides Nortel with access to the inexpensive software development resources of India at the same time as it allows it to enter the Indian market with products specially designed for India.

Through their relationship with Nortel, credibility in the telecommunications area has been enhanced for Nortel's Indian partners and with it their ability to attract new customers. In addition, the Indian partners have rapidly gained experience and knowledge in the design of telecommunications software, the market for which is expected to grow dramatically in India in the immediate future.

Notes

1 These estimates are obtained by using data on these variables available for the foreign affiliates of a limited number of countries (France, Germany, Italy, Japan and the United States) or a combination of one or more of the countries depending on the variable and extrapolating them on the basis of the relative share of these countries in the worldwide FDI stock. Although there are a number of problems in this methodology, the *World Investment Report* continues to use it in the absence of a better alternative. Its use implies the following assumptions: first, that all TNCs, regardless of nationality, broadly behave in a similar manner no matter where their foreign production takes place, implying that one unit of FDI produces the same size of value added, sales and exports everywhere in the world; and second, that the effects of FDI are uniform in all regions as no host-country differences are considered.

2 FDI stock measures the value of share capital and reserves attributable to direct investors, though there are several evaluation methods for deriving the values. It also includes retained dividends and loans, trade credit and debt securities due to direct investors. The OECD recommends that the FDI stock be measured in market value rather than in book value from the balance sheets of investors reported on a historical cost basis (OECD, 1996). Re-evaluation of FDI stock by various methods results in different stock figures that may lead to different and sometimes misleading interpretations of FDI situations (for example, see Gray and Rugman, 1994; and Bellak and Cantwell, 1996).

3 The figures are based on firms in *all* industries. It should be noted that the average size of foreign affiliates is different from industry to industry. In the case of foreign affiliates of United States TNCs, the average size of assets was $298 million in motor vehicles, $93 million in chemicals, $37 million in textiles and $24 million in agriculture (United States, Department of Commerce, 1997a). Average asset size also differs in keeping with the size of the parent company. For the world's largest 100 TNCs (see chapter II), the average size of foreign affiliate assets amounts to $180 billion, while United States small and medium-sized TNCs own $34 million in assets per foreign affiliate (Fujita, 1998). It should be noted that the United States survey data exclude foreign affiliates whose assets, sales or net income are less than $3 million. If these omitted affiliates are included the average size of (non-bank) foreign affiliates was $83 million, compared to $111 million for surveyed (non-bank) foreign affiliates in 1994 (United States, Department of Commerce, 1998).

4 Data from Japan's Ministry of International Trade and Industry on Japanese TNCs and their foreign affiliates suffer from a range of problems (Ramstetter, 1996). One of the problems is that data on sales (as well as other operational variables) are considerably inflated by the inclusion of sales by wholesale affiliates

whose data may be double-counted. Sales through wholesalers of goods produced by other affiliates are likely to be included in sales of wholesale affiliates. If only manufacturing affiliates are considered, the average value of sales was $84 million (Japan, Ministry of International Trade and Industry, 1998a).

5 Of course, foreign affiliates also import. In fact, the import propensity of foreign affiliates is relatively high. Data are available only for Japanese foreign affiliates: they imported more than they exported in manufacturing, by a margin of $10 billion in 1995 (Japan, Ministry of International Trade and Industry, 1998a, tables 2-21-13 and 2-22-13). In terms of contribution to GDP and the balance of payments, net exports (exports less imports), rather than total exports should be considered.

6 Payments for royalties, licence fees, patents etc. between affiliated enterprises could be influenced by profit and tax considerations; in addition, it is not always possible to distinguish between FDI-related payments and payments for technological services.

7 In principle, inflows and outflows of FDI should balance but, in reality, they do not. There are several reasons for this discrepancy, including different treatment of reinvested earnings by home and host countries, and different methods of data collection and reporting between home and host countries. Due to the fact that a number of developed home countries (which account for the bulk of FDI outflows) have better FDI data collection systems, outflows of FDI may reflect worldwide trends more accurately (United Nations, Department of Economic and Social Development, 1992a). The decline in FDI outflows in 1996 (which had not been reported in *World Investment Report 1997* (UNCTAD, 1997a), was caused mainly by the revision of the United States outflows data to exclude (non-permanent) FDI in financial intermediaries in the Netherlands Antilles and other economies. (For further details, see "definitions and sources" in annex B of this *Report.*)

8 See "definitions and sources" in annex B of this *Report.*

9 Information on FDI in 1998 is still limited. Inflows into the United States, the largest host country in the world, are most likely to rise, due to at least one large acquisition -- of Chrysler by Daimler-Benz worth $38 billion -- despite the fact that inflows in the first quarter of 1998 declined by 12 per cent over the previous period on a seasonally adjusted basis and by 3 per cent over the same period in 1997. United States outflows in the first quarter of 1998 decreased by 13 per cent over the previous period (seasonally adjusted) and declined by 4 per cent over the same period in the previous year. (Data are provided by the United States, Department of Commerce, Bureau of Economic Analysis.) Cross-border M&As by United States firms in the first half of 1998 reached half the size of the total in 1997 (William Lewis, "US mergers and takeovers set record in first 6 months", *Financial Times*, 30 June 1998, p. 18).

10 The real GDP growth rate of the world economy is expected to fall from 3.2 per cent in 1997 to 2.1 per cent in 1998. A significant decline is forecast for Asia, including Japan, while a small decrease is also expected in the United States and Latin America (UNCTAD, 1998a).

11 Small decreases in FDI outflows are expected to be recorded in the Republic of Korea and Japan, while inflows are expected to decline in Indonesia, Malaysia and the Republic of Korea in 1998, based on FDI reported for certain months of 1998.

12 These numbers do not include the countries that have negative inflows and for which the data on gross fixed capital formation are not available.

13 Direct investors take profitability into account when making the locational decisions that influence the pattern of FDI inflows. The relative importance of FDI in terms of gross fixed capital formation may also reflect, therefore, the relative level of income generated in each region. According to the data on foreign affiliates of United States TNCs, affiliates in all developing regions (including West Asia) show a higher income-sales ratio than do those in developed regions (United States, Department of Commerce, 1997a).

14 "Foreign investors' spending to acquire or establish U.S. businesses continued at high level in 1997", *BEA News Release*, 10 June 1998, from the Web site of United States, Department of Commerce, Bureau of Economic Analysis (www.bea.doc.gov/bea/newsrel/ fdi97.htm).

15 The reduction of transaction costs inside the single currency area and greater price transparency may facilitate and accelerate capital flows and cross-border M&As. (See "Birth of the Euro", *Financial Times Survey*, 30 April 1998.) The stabilization of exchange rates in this area is one of the reasons Japanese firms are increasing their FDI in the European Union (Japan, Export-Import Bank, 1998).

16 The World Bank includes, in the group of developing countries, the countries in transition of Central and

Eastern Europe.

17 As of mid-1998, only some European Union member states had reported outward FDI data for 1997 by destination. Judging by outflow data for Belgium, Denmark, Italy, Germany, Portugal and the United Kingdom for 1997, the share of FDI going to the European Union increased from 48 per cent in 1996 to 50 per cent in 1997. In particular, Belgium and Portugal showed significant increases in the share of intra-European-Union FDI: for the former, the share of FDI outflows to the European Union rose from 41 per cent in 1996 to 84 per cent in 1997 and for the latter, from 30 per cent to 49 per cent (based on UNCTAD FDI/TNC database).

18 The year 1996 showed an increase of nearly 20 per cent in FDI, but this was mainly caused by the inclusion, for the first time, of reinvested earnings; growth of outflows excluding this component was only 10 per cent.

19 Japanese firms too prefer greenfield projects or minority M&As: only 12 per cent of Japanese affiliates abroad had been established through M&As as of 1995 (Japan, Ministry of International Trade and Industry, 1998a, table 2-27-13).

20 Information provided by Gendai Advanced Studies Research Organization (Tokyo). Currently, the major 15 are: Chrysler, Ford and General Motors (United States); Honda, Nissan and Toyota (Japan); BMW, Daimler-Benz and Volkswagen (Germany); PSA and Renault (France); Fiat (Italy); Volvo (Sweden); and Daewoo and Hyundai (Republic of Korea). With the expected merger between Chrysler and Daimler-Benz, the number will be 14 in 1998.

21 They are Merck (United States), Glaxo Wellcome (United Kingdom), Novartis (Switzerland), Bristol Myers Squibb (United States), Pfizer (United States), Roche (Switzerland) and American Home Products (United States). "Global business outlook", *Financial Times Survey*, 13 January 1998, p. IV.

22 "Pharmaceuticals", *Financial Times Survey*, 16 March 1998.

23 "Global business outlook", op. cit.

24 The MERIT/UNCTAD database includes only strategic inter-firm technology agreements, that is, those that involve the long-term position of firms or products. It was developed at the Maastricht Economic Research Institute on Innovation and Technology (MERIT) of the University of Maastricht and modified by UNCTAD.

25 Derived from the MERIT/UNCTAD database.

26 Spearman's rank-order coefficient is a nonparametric version of the Pearson correlation coefficient based on a rank ordering of the data rather than on actual values. The coefficient range is from -1 to +1. The absolute value of the correlation coefficient shows the strength of the relationship between foreign assets and inter-firm technology agreements, and the sign of the coefficient indicates the direction of this relationship. The analysis excludes 15 cases for which no alliances were found in the MERIT/UNCTAD database.

27 Mass market assemblers bought up-market companies (figure I.14): Volkswagen acquired Audi and Porsche and Ford took over Aston Martin and Jaguar. At the same time, luxury car manufacturers spread their own range towards lower-end vehicles of the market: BMW bought Rover, and Daimler-Benz merged with Chrysler and also established a joint venture with Swatch.

CHAPTER II

THE LARGEST TRANSNATIONAL CORPORATIONS

A. The world's 100 largest TNCs

1. Highlights

In 1996, the top position in the list of the world's 100 largest non-financial TNCs ranked by foreign assets changed for the first time in six years when General Electric Company (United States) moved from third into first position, pushing Royal Dutch Shell (United Kingdom/Netherlands) into second place (table II.1). The rankings otherwise remained fairly stable among the top ten in the list. The only major change was Nestlé (Switzerland) moving from ninth to eleventh place, being replaced by Mobil Corporation (United States). The 1996 list of the top 100 TNCs includes ten new entrants (table II.2) and ten exits (table II.3).

Movement at the bottom of the list is also limited. Most of the 1996 entrants already occupied a position in the vicinity of the top 100 in 1995, and most of the firms no longer included in the list are now ranked between positions 100 and 120. However, special situations arise when M&As involve firms with large foreign assets, as in the case of Novartis (Switzerland), which was formed through the merger of Sandoz and Ciba-Geigy; Crown Cork & Seal Company (United States), which took over Carnauld Metalbox (France); and Kvaerner (Norway), which acquired Trafalgar Plc. (United Kingdom). In 1995, the list of the top 100 TNCs had included for the first time two TNCs from developing countries -- Petróleos de Venezuela S.A. (Venezuela) and Daewoo Corporation (Republic of Korea); in 1996, these companies strengthened their respective positions by moving up from 88 to 73 and from 52 to 43, though no other developing country firm has yet joined them.

Table II.1. The world's top 100 TNCs, ranked by foreign assets, 1996

(Billions of dollars and number of employees)

Ranking by					Assets		Sales		Employment		Transnationality index[a] (Per cent)
Foreign assets	Transnationality index[a]	Corporation	Country	Industry[b]	Foreign	Total	Foreign	Total	Foreign	Total	
1	83	General Electric	United States	Electronics	82.8	272.4	21.1	79.2	84000	239000	30.7
2	32	Shell, Royal Dutch[c]	United Kingdom/Netherlands	Petroleum expl./ref./dist.	82.1	124.1	71.1	128.3	79000	101000	66.6
3	75	Ford Motor Company	United States	Automotive	79.1	258.0	65.8	147.0	..[e]	371702	37.7
4	22	Exxon Corporation	United States	Petroleum expl./ref./dist.	55.6	95.5	102.0	117.0	..[e]	79000	72.7
5	85	General Motors	United States	Automotive	55.4	222.1	50.0	158.0	221313	647000	30.3
6	52	IBM	United States	Computers	41.4	81.1	46.6	75.9	121655	240615	54.3
7	79	Toyota	Japan	Automotive	39.2	113.4	51.7	109.3	34837	150736	35.0
8	49	Volkswagen Group	Germany	Automotive	..[d]	60.8	41.0	64.4	123042	260811	55.3
9	71	Mitsubishi Corporation	Japan	Diversified	..[d]	77.9	50.2	127.4	3819	8794	41.4
10	38	Mobil Corporation	United States	Petroleum expl./ref./dist.	31.3	46.4	53.1	80.4	22900	43000	62.3
11	3	Nestlé SA	Switzerland	Food	30.9	34.0	42.0	42.8	206125	212687	95.3
12	2	Asea Brown Boveri (ABB)	Switzerland/Sweden	Electrical equipment	..[d]	30.9	32.9	33.8	203541	214894	96.1
13	47	Elf Aquitaine SA	France	Petroleum expl./ref./dist.	29.3	47.5	26.6	44.8	41600	85400	56.6
14	14	Bayer AG	Germany	Chemicals	29.1	32.0	25.8	31.4	94375	142200	79.9
15	34	Hoechst AG	Germany	Chemicals	28.0	35.5	18.4	33.8	93708	147862	65.6
16	57	Nissan Motor Co., Ltd.	Japan	Automotive	27.0	58.1	29.2	53.8	..[e]	135331	50.4
17	74	FIAT Spa	Italy	Automotive	26.9	70.6	19.8	51.3	90390	237865	38.2
18	8	Unilever[f]	Netherlands/United Kingdom	Food	26.4	31.0	45.0	52.2	273000	304000	87.1
19	70	Daimler-Benz AG	Germany	Automotive	..[d]	65.7	44.4	70.6	67208	290029	41.9
20	11	Philips Electronics N.V.	Netherlands	Electronics	24.5	31.7	38.9	40.9	216000	262500	84.9
21	9	Roche Holding AG	Switzerland	Pharmaceuticals	24.5	29.5	12.6	12.9	39074	48972	87.0
22	56	Siemens AG	Germany	Electronics	24.4	56.3	38.4	62.6	176000	379000	50.4
23	36	Alcatel Alsthom Cie	France	Electronics	23.5	48.4	24.6	31.6	118820	190600	62.9
24	40	Sony Corporation	Japan	Electronics	23.5	45.8	32.8	45.7	95000	163000	60.5
25	19	Total SA	France	Petroleum expl./ref./dist.	..[d]	30.3	25.8	34.0	..[e]	57555	75.8
26	20	Novartis	Switzerland	Pharmaceuticals/chemicals	21.4	43.4	28.6	29.2	91192	116178	75.2
27	35	British Petroleum (BP)	United Kingdom	Petroleum expl./ref./dist.	20.7	31.8	39.2	69.8	37750	53700	63.8
28	62	Philip Morris	United States	Food/tobacco	20.6	54.9	30.7	69.2	94659	154000	47.8
29	81	ENI Group	Italy	Petroleum expl./ref./dist.	..[d]	59.5	13.2	39.3	..[e]	83424	33.5
30	69	Renault SA	France	Automotive	19.0	42.2	19.4	36.0	43381	140905	43.2
31	31	B.A.T. Industries Plc	United Kingdom	Food/tobacco	18.9	63.5	30.8	38.2	149217	163854	67.2
32	68	Du Pont (E.I.)	United States	Chemicals	18.4	38.0	20.8	43.8	34000	97000	43.7
33	30	Rhone-Poulenc SA	France	Chemicals/pharmaceuticals	..[d]	27.1	13.3	16.8	41818	75250	67.4
34	1	Seagram Company	Canada	Beverages	18.2	18.6	12.2	12.6	..[e]	31000	97.3
35	42	BASF AG	Germany	Chemicals	17.9	28.2	23.8	32.4	42339	103406	59.2
36	46	Honda Motor Co., Ltd.	Japan	Automotive	17.8	33.5	26.4	42.3	..[e]	101100	56.6
37	43	BMW AG	Germany	Automotive	..[d]	29.1	25.5	34.8	51900	116112	59.1
38	77	Mitsui & Co., Ltd.	Japan	Diversified	17.1	61.2	56.6	132.0	..[e]	11250	35.4
39	82	Nissho Iwai Corporation	Japan	Trading	..[d]	47.2	28.8	89.1	1997	6684	32.4

/...

Table II.1. The world's top 100 TNCs, ranked by foreign assets, 1996 (continued)

(Billions of dollars and number of employees)

Ranking by					Assets		Sales		Employment		Transnationality index[a]
Foreign assets	Transnationality index[a]	Corporation	Country	Industry[b]	Foreign	Total	Foreign	Total	Foreign	Total	(Per cent)
40	93	Itochu Corporation	Japan	Trading	15.2	66.1	40.2	153.5	2584	9766	25.2
41	58	Hewlett-Packard	United States	Electronics	15.2	27.7	21.4	38.4	48200	122000	50.0
42	28	Ferruzzi/Montedison	Italy	Chemicals/agribusiness	..[d]	21.6	11.8	15.5	17570	29564	68.3
43	51	Daewoo Corporation	Korea, Republic of	Diversified	14.9	32.5	10.2	26.4	37501	47609	54.5
44	27	News Corporation	Australia	Media	14.5	24.2	8.6	9.9	17212	26513	70.6
45	78	Chevron Corporation	United States	Petroleum expl./ref./dist.	14.4	34.9	14.9	42.8	12095	40820	35.3
46	48	Dow Chemical	United States	Chemicals	14.4	24.7	11.3	20.1	21039	40300	55.6
47	37	Robert Bosch GmbH	Germany	Automotive	..[d]	21.3	16.7	26.7	..[e]	172359	62.4
48	86	Marubeni Corporation	Japan	Trading	13.1	60.8	43.9	113.0	..[e]	9282	30.1
49	15	Cable And Wireless Plc	United Kingdom	Telecommunication	13.0	15.5	7.0	9.7	29613	37448	78.1
50	4	Thomson Corporation	Canada	Printing and publishing	12.8	13.2	7.3	7.7	47200	50500	94.9
51	66	Texaco Incorporated	United States	Petroleum expl./ref./dist.	12.7	27.0	21.2	44.6	11323	28957	44.6
52	10	Michelin	France	Rubber & plastics	..[d]	14.7	11.7	13.7	..[e]	119780	84.9
53	88	Matsushita Electric	Japan	Electronics	12.3	67.8	23.8	62.0	..[e]	270651	28.3
54	61	Xerox Corporation	United States	Photo equipment	12.1	26.8	8.8	17.4	..[e]	86700	47.8
55	23	Ericsson LM	Sweden	Electronics	..[d]	16.9	17.4	18.7	50053	93949	72.5
56	6	Holderbank Financiere	Switzerland	Construction materials	11.7	12.7	6.9	8.0	39122	42970	89.8
57	64	BCE Inc.	Canada	Telecommunication	11.5	30.1	13.3	20.6	46000	121000	46.9
58	39	Saint-Gobain SA	France	Industrial material	11.5	21.6	10.2	15.7	74467	111701	61.6
59	76	Broken Hill (BHP)	Australia	Metal	11.4	28.1	5.6	15.3	20400	60100	37.1
60	97	Hitachi, Ltd.	Japan	Electronics	11.4	80.4	19.8	68.7	56400	330100	20.0
61	87	Sumitomo Corporation	Japan	Trading/machinery	11.4	43.5	29.9	108.4	2873	9129	28.4
62	7	Electrolux AB	Sweden	Electrical appliances	10.7	12.5	15.2	16.4	98220	112140	88.7
63	98	AT&T Corp.	United States	Telecomm./electronics	..[d]	55.6	8.8	52.2	..[e]	130400	18.1
64	67	Procter & Gamble	United States	Chemicals/cosmetics	10.7	27.5	17.5	35.8	..[e]	106000	43.7
65	80	International Paper	United States	Paper	10.4	28.3	6.0	20.1	31000	87000	34.2
66	91	AMOCO Corporation	United States	Petroleum expl./ref./dist.	10.3	32.1	8.0	36.1	9290	41723	25.5
67	45	Volvo AB	Sweden	Automotive	10.2	20.5	20.7	23.3	26435	71905	58.5
68	44	McDonald's Corporation	United States	Restaurants	9.6	17.4	6.1	10.7	153000	237000	58.9
69	18	Grand Metropolitan	United Kingdom	Food/beverages	..[d]	17.5	12.7	14.0	55000	65699	76.2
70	16	Glaxo Wellcome Plc	United Kingdom	Pharmaceuticals	9.4	14.2	12.0	13.0	40209	53460	77.9
71	26	BTR Plc	United Kingdom	Plastics and foam	9.4	14.1	10.9	14.4	..[e]	115805	70.9
72	59	Johnson & Johnson	United States	Chemicals/pharmaceuticals	9.2	20.0	10.7	21.6	47600	89300	49.5
73	65	Petróleos de Venezuela S.A.	Venezuela	Diversified/trading	8.9	45.4	31.7	33.9	12756	59318	44.9
74	89	Fujitsu Limited	Japan	Electronics	8.9	38.1	10.8	36.3	53000	167000	28.3
75	25	Hanson Plc	United Kingdom	Building material	8.6	14.9	18.4	19.5	35000	56000	71.6
76	63	Motorola, Inc.	United States	Electronics	8.6	24.1	16.9	28.0	63738	139000	47.3
77	92	Générale des Eaux	France	Diversified/utility	8.5	45.9	10.0	32.4	57433	217300	25.3
78	96	Nippon Steel	Japan	Metal	..[d]	36.3	5.8	24.7	..[e]	24527	23.4

/...

Table II.1. The world's top 100 TNCs, ranked by foreign assets, 1996 (continued)

(Billions of dollars and number of employees)

Ranking by: Foreign assets	Ranking by: Transnationality index[a]	Corporation	Country	Industry[b]	Assets: Foreign	Assets: Total	Sales: Foreign	Sales: Total	Employment: Foreign	Employment: Total	Transnationality index[a] (Per cent)
79	21	Akzo Nobel N.V.	Netherlands	Chemicals	8.3	11.7	9.8	13.3	52900	70700	73.2
80	99	Chrysler Corporation	United States	Motor vehicles	8.3	56.2	8.2	61.4	26000	126000	16.3
81	55	Canon Electronics Inc.	Japan	Electronics	8.3	22.6	14.9	22.1	38197	75628	51.6
82	29	Coca-Cola	United States	Beverages	8.2	12.0	12.6	18.7	20000	30000	67.5
83	5	Solvay SA	Belgium	Chemicals/pharmaceuticals	..[d]	8.8	8.4	8.8	31413	35400	92.2
84	90	Mitsubishi Motors	Japan	Automotive	8.0	26.1	8.5	29.6	18900	74700	28.3
85	13	Northern Telecom	Canada	Telecommunication	7.9	10.9	11.4	12.8	..[e]	67584	80.6
86	24	Petrofina SA	Belgium	Petroleum expl./ref./dist.	7.8	11.6	15.9	19.8	9217	13588	71.8
87	53	Bridgestone	Japan	Rubber and plastics	7.8	15.2	10.0	18.0	..[e]	92458	53.5
88	84	Pepsico, Inc.	United States	Beverages/food	7.8	24.5	9.2	31.6	..[e]	486000	30.4
89	50	Danone Groupe SA	France	Food	7.8	19.4	9.2	16.4	55987	81579	54.9
90	41	Crown Cork & Seal	United States	Packaging	7.6	12.6	5.0	8.3	..[e]	44611	60.2
91	94	Toshiba Corporation	Japan	Electronics	7.6	46.8	14.0	44.0	..[e]	186000	24.0
92	12	Kvaerner ASA	Norway	Shipbuilding/ engineering	..[d]	9.1	7.0	9.1	69303	80199	81.7
93	95	Atlantic Richfield	United States	Petroleum expl./ref./dist.	7.4	25.7	3.4	18.6	..[e]	22800	23.4
94	54	RTZ CRA[g]	United Kingdom/Australia	Mining	7.3	15.8	4.7	9.3	31616	51492	52.5
95	73	Mannesmann AG	Germany	Engineering/telecom.	7.3	15.5	8.2	23.0	41689	119703	39.1
96	33	Pharmacia & Upjohn	United States	Pharmaceuticals	7.3	11.2	4.9	7.2	..[e]	31700	66.4
97	100	GTE Corporation	United States	Telecommunication	7.1	38.4	2.8	21.3	..[e]	102000	15.8
98	72	American Home Products	United States	Pharmaceuticals	7.1	20.8	5.8	14.1	28300	59746	40.7
99	17	Eridania Beghin-Say SA	France	Food	6.9	9.2	8.0	10.2	14617	19340	76.4
100	60	Société au Bon Marché	France	Beverages/luxury products	6.8	21.9	4.2	6.5	..[e]	22862	47.9

Source: UNCTAD/Erasmus University database.

[a] The index of transnationality is calculated as the average of three ratios: foreign assets to total assets, foreign sales to total sales and foreign employment to toal employment.

[b] Industry classification for companies follows the United States Standard Industrial Classification as used by the United States Securities and Exchange Commission (SEC).

[c] Foreign sales are outside Europe whereas foreign employment is outside United Kingdom and the Netherlands.

[d] Data on foreign assets are either suppressed to avoid disclosure or they are not available. In case of non-availability, they are estimated on the basis of the ratio of foreign to total sales, foreign to total employment or similar ratios.

[e] Data on foreign employment are either suppressed to avoid disclosure or they are not available. In case of non-availability, they are estimated on the basis of the ratio of foreign to total sales, foreign to total assets or similar ratios.

[f] Foreign assets, sales and employment are outside the United Kingdom and the Netherlands.

[g] Foreign assets, sales and employment are outside the United Kingdom and Australia.

Table II. 2. Newcomers to the world's top 100 TNCs,[a] ranked by foreign assets, 1996

Ranked by foreign assets	Corporation[a]	Country
26	Novartis[b]	Switzerland
42	Ferruzzi/Montedison	Italy
55	Ericsson L.M.	Sweden
77	Générale des Eaux	France
79	Akzo Nobel	Netherlands
87	Bridgestone Corporation	Japan
90	Crown Cork & Seal	United States
92	Kvaerner ASA	Norway
99	Eridania Beghin-Say	France
100	Société au Bon Marché	France

Source: UNCTAD/Erasmus University database.

a This includes companies that could not be considered in 1997 because of the late arrival of a response to UNCTAD's questionnaire.
b The merger of Sandoz and Ciba-Geigy resulted in the new TNC Novartis.

Table II. 3. Departures from the world's top 100 TNCs,[a] ranked by foreign assets, 1996

Ranked by foreign assets in 1995	Corporation	Country
38	Ciba-Geigy AG[b]	Switzerland
84	Carrefour	France
85	SCA	Sweden
90	Sara Lee	United States
93	NEC Corporation	Japan
94	Thomson SA	France
97	Imperial Chemical Industries (ICI)	United Kingdom
98	United Technologies	United States
99	RJR Nabisco	United States
100	Pechiney SA	France

Source: UNCTAD/Erasmus University database.

a This includes companies which could not be considered in 1997 because of late arrival of a response to UNCTAD's questionnaire.
b The merger of Sandoz and Ciba-Geigy resulted in the new TNC Novartis.

Overall, a snapshot (table II.4) of the world's 100 largest TNCs shows a continuous trend towards greater transnationality -- in terms of foreign assets, sales, and employment, and thus in the overall transnationality index. More specifically, these were the principal developments:

Table II. 4. Snapshot of the world's 100 largest TNCs,[a] 1996

(Billions of dollars, percentage and number of employees)

Variable	Total	Change 1996 vs. 1995
Foreign assets	1 808	6.3
Foreign sales	2 149	7.4
Foreign employees	5 939 470	2.4
Median index of transnationality[b]	54.8	3.8

Source: UNCTAD/Erasmus University database.

a Measured by foreign assets.
b In per cent, as defined in footnote a) of table II.1. The change between 1995 and 1996 is expressed in percentage points.

- *Country composition*. Since the list of the top 100 TNCs was first published in 1990, it has remained dominated by firms from the Triad (European Union, United States and Japan; figure II.1; see also in the annex tables A.II.1 and A.II.2). In 1996, 85 of the top 100 TNCs were headquartered in the Triad, compared to 86 in 1990. The United States, Japan, the United Kingdom, France and Germany alone accounted for three-quarters of the entries in both years. Their dominance has remained roughly unchanged since 1990, regardless of whether one considers number of firms, foreign assets, foreign sales or foreign employment. Within the Triad, the number of firms from the European Union declined between 1990 and 1996 (mostly from France and the United Kingdom), although they still account for the largest number (39) in the top 100 list. European Union firms have also seen their share of foreign assets and foreign employment decline, whereas Japanese firms increased their share of foreign activities, doubling it in

Figure II.1. The world's 100 largest TNCs: the five most important home countries, 1996

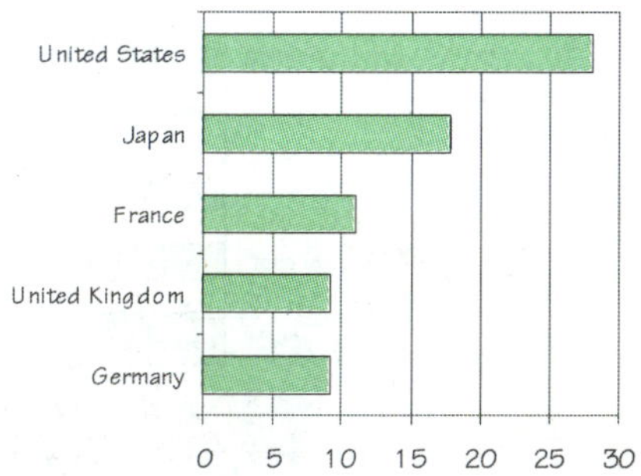

Source: UNCTAD/Erasmus University

employment. The number of Japanese firms in the list rose by 50 per cent between 1990 and 1996, from 12 to 18.

- *Foreign assets*. Total foreign assets of the top 100 TNCs amounted to $1.8 trillion in 1996 (table II.4). Between 1993 and 1995, they had risen by around 30 per cent, followed by a slower growth of six per cent between 1995 and 1996. A number of individual firms, however, have grown much faster (figure II.2). For example, TOTAL's (France) foreign assets rose by an outstanding 53 per cent between 1995 and 1996, and another three firms saw increases of 40 per cent or more. Conversely, other firms saw their foreign assets shrink (figure II.3). This shrinking group is led by Volkswagen whose foreign assets fell by about a third between 1995 and 1996. Another three firms lost more than a fifth. For all of the 100 TNCs, the ratio of foreign assets to total assets increased marginally from 41 per cent in 1995 to 43 per cent in 1996.

Figure II.2. Top 5 increases in foreign assets among the world's top 100 TNCs, 1995-1996
(Percentage)

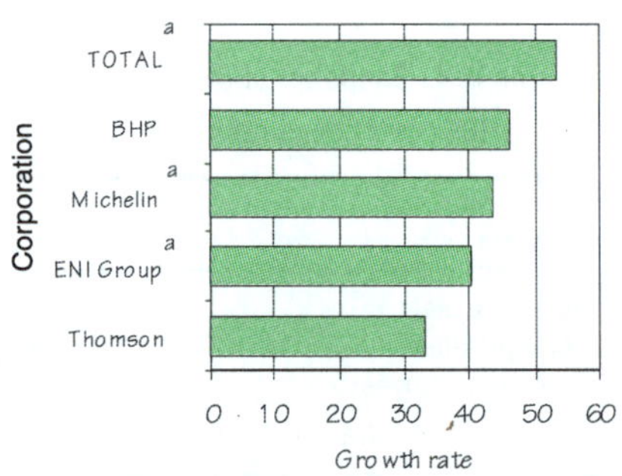

Source: UNCTAD/Erasmus University database.

Figure II.3. Top 5 decreases in foreign assets among the world's top 100 TNCs, 1995-1996
(Percentage)

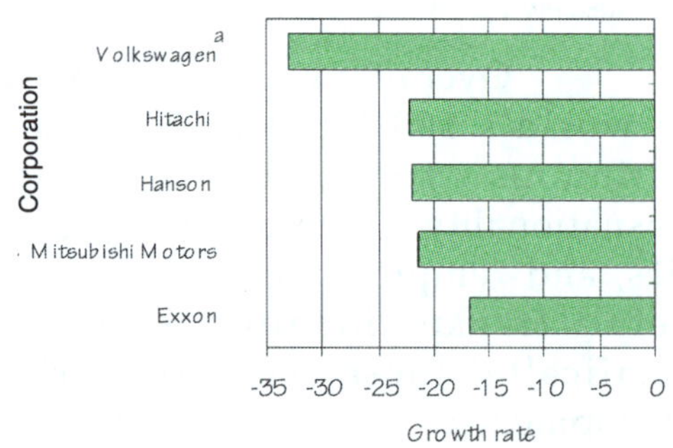

Source: UNCTAD/Erasmus University database.

- *Foreign sales*. Total foreign sales of the top 100 TNCs amounted to $2.1 trillion in 1996 (table II.4), an increase of seven per cent from 1995. This rise, and a relatively slower rise in total sales, resulted in an increase in the ratio of foreign sales to total sales, from 48 per cent in 1995 to 52 per cent in 1996. The firm experiencing the largest increase in foreign sales was Hanson (United Kingdom) (figure II.4), whereas FIAT (Italy) experienced the largest fall in foreign sales (figure II.5).

Figure II.4. Top 5 increases in foreign sales among the world's top 100 TNCs, 1995-1996
(Percentage)

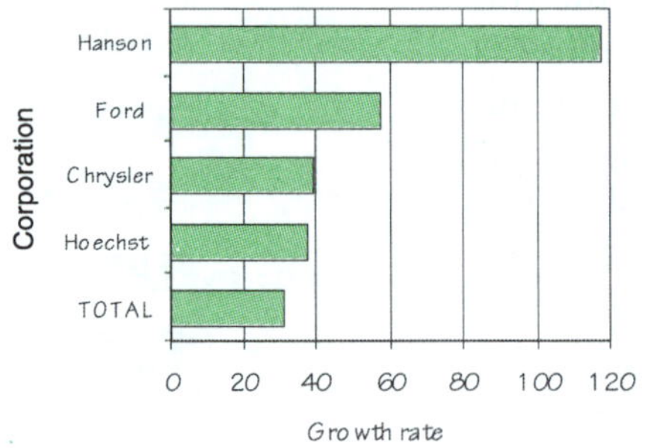

Source: UNCTAD/Erasmus University

Figure II.5. Top 5 decreases in foreign sales among the world's top 100 TNCs, 1995-1996
(Percentage)

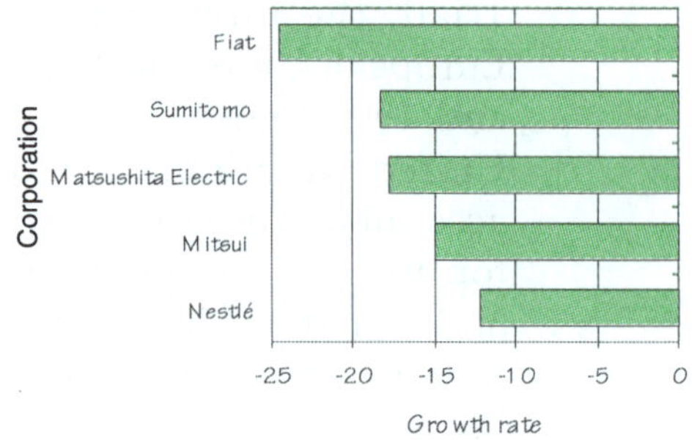

Source: UNCTAD/Erasmus University

Foreign sales of the top 100 TNCs grew faster than their foreign assets; on a global level, the reverse was true (table I.1). This suggests that, as far as assets are concerned, smaller companies are expanding abroad faster than large ones.

- *Foreign employment*. Total foreign employment of the top 100 TNCs amounted to some 5.9 million in 1996 (table II.4), an increase of 2 per cent over 1995. During the same year, total employment decreased by 3.5 per cent, from 12.1 million to 11.8 million employees. Consequently, the ratio of foreign-to-total-employment rose from 48 per cent to 51 per cent. This pattern continued the trend of declining overall employment and rising foreign employment since the list was first published for 1990. The companies with the largest increase in foreign employment are led by Michelin (France) (figure II.6). Two other firms registered increases of over 100 per cent. On the other hand, five TNCs reduced their foreign employment by between 25 per cent to 57 per cent (figure II.7). No particular patterns in terms of home countries or industries appear to explain this performance, even if all TNCs are considered.

Figure II.6. Top 5 increases in foreign employment among the world's top 100 TNCs, 1995-1996

(Percentage)

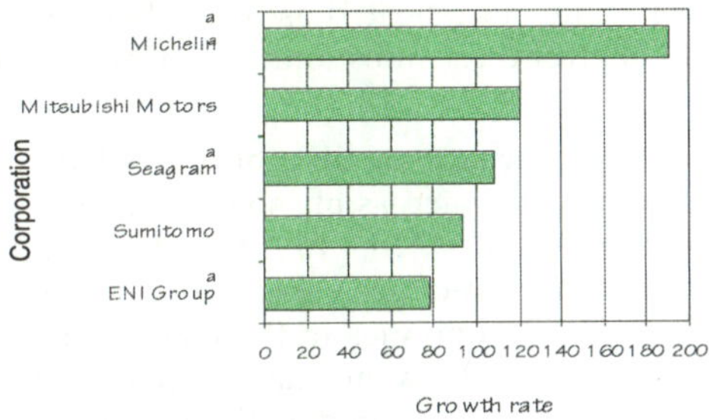

Source: UNCTAD/Erasmus University database.

Figure II.7. Top 5 decreases in foreign employment among the world's top 100 TNCs, 1995-1996

(Percentage)

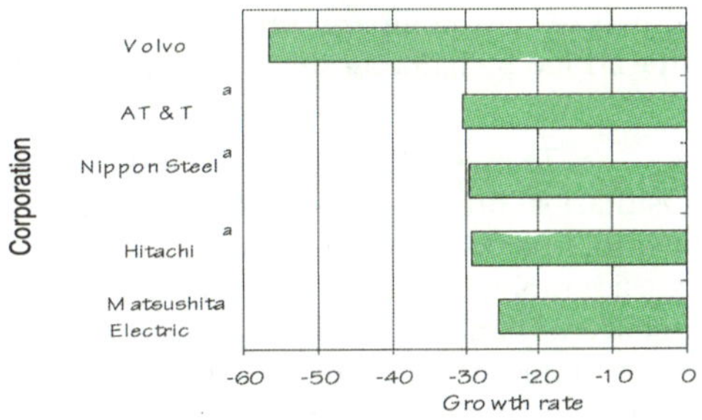

Source: UNCTAD/Erasmus University database.

- *Industry composition*. Firms operating in the electronic/electrical industry make up the largest group in the top 100 (table II.5). They are followed closely by TNCs from the pharmaceutical/chemical, automotive, petroleum and mining, and food/beverages industries -- most of which are highly concentrated industries. The top 10 TNCs among the top 100 have been dominated by TNCs from the automobile and the petroleum industry. They constitute usually half of the entries in this top group since the list for 1990 was first

Table II.5. Industry composition of top 100 TNCs, 1990 and 1996

(Number of entries)

Industry	1990	1996
Electronics/electrical equipment	14	17
Chemicals and pharmaceuticals[a]	18	16
Automotive	13	14
Petroleum refining/distribution and mining	13	14
Food and beverages[b]	9	12
Diversified	2	4
Telecommunication	2	5
Trading	7	4
Machinery & engineering	3	2
Metals	6	3
Construction	4	3
Media	2	2
Other	7	4
Total	100	100

Source: UNCTAD/Erasmus University database.

[a] Chemicals also includes Ferruzzi/Montedison.
[b] Food and beverages also includes B.A.T. Industries (tobacco) and McDonalds.

published. All other industries are represented with at most five entries in the list. This distribution by industry of the top 100 has not changed significantly since 1990. The principal exceptions are the electronics/electrical industry (which increased the number of its entries from 14 to 17), while the food and beverages firms increased their number of entries from 9 to 12 . Conversely, the number of firms from the chemical/pharmaceutical industry was reduced from 18 to 16, following the trend of concentration particularly in the pharmaceutical industry. The metal industry reduced its entries in the list from six to three for, amongst others, similar reasons. It should be noted that the list of the top 100 is dominated by manufacturing and primary sector firms. Services are under-represented, and financial services are not included, although the latter are transnationalizing as well (box II.1), and indeed have been doing so for some time (Fujita, 1989).

Box II.1. The international spread of banking

The transnationalization of manufacturing firms is captured by the lists of the top 100 TNCs and top 50 TNCs based in developing countries. These lists also contain a number of services firms. But financial services firms do not easily lend themselves to inclusion in such lists. In the case of banks, for example, their balance sheets show exclusively *financial* assets, whereas assets of manufacturing firms are largely of a *real* nature. The comparability of sales figures is even more complicated as it touches the question of the value added by banking services. Statistics that could answer these questions are only beginning to emerge.

To assess the spread of banking, statistics on the international distribution of banking entities (i.e. subsidiaries, branches, representative offices) based on publicly accessible sources have been used. They show that banks of selected (major) OECD countries (annex tables A.II.4 to A.II.7) have banking entities in a considerable number of developing and transition economies, and vice versa. Not surprisingly, the largest presence of banks from developing countries and transition economies in the OECD area is found in the United States and the United Kingdom -- 171 and 153, respectively (annex table A.II.4). However, the scale of this presence in relation to that in France, Germany and Japan is inflated by the availability for the United Kingdom and the United States of figures for representative offices (and, for the latter, figures for agencies as well [a]). Amongst the developing and transition economies, banks from the Republic of Korea have the largest number of entities in the OECD countries covered (76), but banks from Brazil are represented in the largest number of OECD countries (10) (annex table A.II.5).

Not unexpectedly, two financial centres -- Hong Kong, China; and Singapore -- are host to the largest number of banking entities from the OECD countries: 108 and 87, respectively (annex table A.II.6). But there are also large presences from OECD countries in the Czech Republic and the Russian Federation -- for which, however, as well as for other transition economies, the figures are inflated in relation to those of Asia and Latin America by the inclusion of representative offices -- as well as in the Republic of Korea. The region with the smallest presence of OECD banks is Latin America, but this impression may at least partly reflect the incompleteness of data for that region. Japan and the United States have the largest presence of banking entities in developing and transition economies: 116 and 113, respectively (annex table A.II.7).

The data, although incomplete and no more than partially illuminating about the transnationalization of the banking industry, suggest that, at least with regard to the number of banking entities in major markets, those from developing economies as well as from economies in transition have already achieved a considerable international presence, even when compared with the foreign presence of banking entities from OECD countries. Of course, if data were available on the transnationalization of banking assets and the sizes of the assets of different banks, one might well arrive at a different picture.

Source: Cornford and Brandon, forthcoming.

[a] In the United States International Banking Act of 1978, an "agency" is defined as "any office or any place of business of a foreign bank located in any State of the United States at which credit balances are maintained incidental to or arising out of the exercise of banking powers, checks are paid, or money is lent but at which deposits may not be accepted from citizens or residents of the United States" (sections 3101 to 3107). The principal use of agencies is for the financing of, and provision of other services related to, international trade between the host country of the agencies and the country of their parent banks.

Below the surface of a slowly progressive transnationalization of the top 100 TNCs a diverse picture emerges, with home countries, industries and individual firms performing often in quite different ways. This diversity is also visible when it comes to the degree of transnationality of firms and industries.

2. Degree of transnationality

The degree of international involvement of a firm can be measured in various ways (box II.2). The index of transnationalization used here is a composite of three ratios -- foreign assets/total assets, foreign sales/total sales and foreign employment/total employment. The value of this index for the top 100 as a group was 55 per cent in 1996 (table II.4). While this represents an increase of 4 percentage points over 1995, until then it had not changed significantly since 1990 (figure II.8); in fact between 1990 and 1993, the value of that index had even decreased. The growing internationalization of assets has contributed the most to the increase in the transnationalization index (TNI).

Figure II.8. Average transnationality index of the world's 100 largest TNCs, 1990-1996

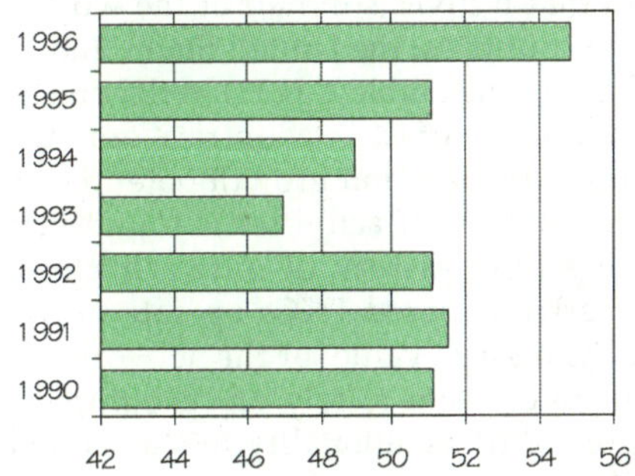

Source: UNCTAD/Erasmus University

The overall index hides a number of variations. For the top 100 TNCs as a whole, the transnationalization index ranged from 97 per cent for Seagram to 16 per cent for GTE in 1996; this is quite similar to 1990, when the range was 97 for Nestlé to 15 for General Electric. In 1996, Nestlé

Box II. 2. Measurement of transnationality

Transnationality is a function of the extent to which a firm's activities are located abroad. A transnationality *index*, however, can be compiled in different ways, e.g. by choosing a single key variable (like assets) or by combining several variables (assets, employment and sales). The *WIR* uses the latter method (approach I, annex table A.II.8). The conceptual framework underlying this index (and other similar indices) is based on the dichotomy between foreign versus home country activities, and helps to assess the degree to which the activities and interests of TNCs are embedded in their home economy or in economies abroad. A high value of this index, even for the individual corporation, under certain circumstances, may raise questions about a home country's locational advantages, particularly if accompanied by low levels of inward investment. However, a high value could also indicate strong international competitiveness on the part of the home country firms. A drawback of this index is that it does not take into account the size of the home country and does not distinguish between TNCs whose foreign activities are concentrated in a few foreign countries, and TNCs whose activities are spread across numerous host countries.

An approach that measures this dimension of transnationality is captured in the network-spread index, which is constructed precisely to reflect the number of host countries in which a firm is established.[a] At the level of a corporation, a high network-spread index can be an indicator of both negative and positive elements. For a TNC, a high network-spread index may be accompanied by higher costs of managing far-flung operations (transaction costs), but it may also indicate high levels of ownership advantages as well as high levels of knowledge of market conditions in many countries, or a combination of ownership and internalization advantages with a broader portfolio of locational assets. The main drawback of this approach is that the index does not take account of the magnitude of a company's activity in a given host country: each host country is counted once, independently of the amount of assets, sales and employment located in it. This drawback cannot easily be remedied, as corporations do not regularly report assets, sales and employment for each host country.

/...

(Box II. 2, concluded)

A correlation analysis of the transnationalization index and the network-spread index for the top 100 TNCs yields a rather low rank-correlation coefficient (0.40; annex table A.II.9). This underlines the fact that TNCs can transnationalize considerably without having to spread their foreign assets extensively (see annex table A.II.8., examples are firms such as Seagram, Exxon, Volkswagen, Nissan and McDonald's). At the industry level, the average transnationality index ranges from 81 per cent for construction and construction materials to 35 per cent for services and trading (annex table A.II.10). The average number of countries in which the top 100 TNCs in a particular industry operate ranges from 54 for food and beverages (including tobacco) to 31 for trading and construction. The corresponding value of the network-spread index for services and trading is 30 per cent and for construction and construction material is 17 per cent. In no industry is the network-spread index higher than the transnationality index. Given that TNCs investing abroad typically direct their investments towards major markets and not necessarily at *every* market, it is more likely that a TNC reaches significant shares of foreign assets, sales and employment, and thereby a significant degree of transnationality, than that it reaches a high value in the network-spread index.

In other words, it is more likely that a firm reaches, say, 50 per cent on the transnationality index than that it invests in half of the world's economies. Furthermore, TNCs from two of the most important home countries, the United States and Japan, rank very low on both the transnational and network-spread indices (annex table A.II.11), reflecting a phenomen also observed at the aggregate level. Such suggests that the large size of these countries' domestic economies may have allowed their TNCs to realize some of their competitiveness and growth potential at home. Conversely, the highest degree of transnationality and the widest spread of activities is found in TNCs originating in smaller economies and/or in economies that have a long history of outward FDI (the Netherlands, United Kingdom, Switzerland and Sweden). Netherlands-based TNCs operate in the highest number of countries and, correspondingly, that country has the highest value for the network-spread index (annex table A.II.11). More generally, firms from smaller economies seem to rely on geographically more diversified corporate networks, as well as on a higher degree of transnationality to stay competitive and to compensate for smaller home markets. This might well be an advantage in the age of globalization.

It should be noted that both the transnationalization index and the network-spread index provide only for an imperfect and broad indication of the "depth" of a TNC's involvement abroad. For instance, a company could have warehouses in each of the world's economies amounting to half of its assets. Accordingly, it would score very high (100 per cent) on the network-spread index and quite well (50 per cent) on the transnationalization index. At the same time, its degree of integration into the host economy is -- in this case -- quite limited. To capture the depth of the transnationalization process requires the development of additional indices.[b]

In sum, the transnational index and the network-spread index capture different aspects of a corporation's transnationalization. The importance of foreign assets, sales and employment captured by the transnationalization index is complemented by the extent of geographical diversity captured by the network-spread index. The differences in the values of the two indices suggest that, while the top 100 TNCs are quite transnationalized, they do not exhibit a broad geographical spread. Both indices are, in a sense, approximations of the importance of taking advantage of a portfolio of locational assets -- an important source of the competitiveness of firms in a globalizing world economy (UNCTAD, 1995a) -- for the international competitiveness of firms; therefore they provide information about the comparative international competitiveness of firms.

Source: Ietto-Gillies, forthcoming.

[a] The number of countries in which a company has foreign affiliates is denoted as "N". An index in percentage terms (and thus comparable to the transnational index) is derived by taking N as a percentage of N*, the number of foreign countries in which, potentially, the company could have located affiliates. N* is chosen to be the number of countries in the world that have inward FDI. In practice, N* is estimated as the number of countries that are in receipt of inward stock of FDI minus 1 (to exclude the home country of the TNC); on the basis of the data in the *WIR 97*, N* is equal to 178. The index N/N* is the network-spread index.

[b] One indicator that has been used in this respect is R & D. On an index developed for this purpose, 144 TNCs ranked 23 per cent in 1993 (Dunning, 1996, p.5). It should also be noted that the actual values in the indices used are also influenced by a number of factors that are not taken into account in their calculation, e.g. the size of the home market; the age and experience of firms in foreign markets; the extent and pattern of regional integration and liberalized entry provisions for FDI; and the extent to which firms take advantage of economies of scale and scope and can substitute trade for FDI. In addition, indices calculated on a regional basis -- assuming data availability -- would probably capture the geography of a firm's expansion more accurately.

lost its leading position in transnationality to Seagram (table II.6), a Canadian beverages company with interests increasingly geared to the entertainment and publishing industries. The ten TNCs with the highest transnationalization index show values of between 85 and 97 per cent. A number of firms (led by Hanson of United Kingdom) saw considerable rises in transnationalization (figure II.9), while others (led by Volvo of Sweden) experienced declines of up to 15 percentage points (figure II.10).

Table II.6. The world's top 10 TNCs in terms of degree of transnationality, 1996

Ranking by Transnationality index[a]	Ranking by Foreign assets	Corporation	Country	Industry	Transnationality index[a] (Per cent)
1	34	Seagram Company	Canada	Beverages	97.3
2	12	Asea Brown Boveri (ABB)	Switzerland/Sweden	Electrical equipment	96.1
3	11	Nestlé SA	Switzerland	Food	95.3
4	50	Thomson Corporation	Canada	Printing and publishing	94.9
5	83	Solvay SA	Belgium	Chemicals/pharmaceuticals	92.2
6	56	Holderbank Financiere	Switzerland	Construction	89.8
7	62	Electrolux AB	Sweden	Electrical appliances	88.7
8	18	Unilever	Netherlands/United Kingdom	Food	87.1
9	21	Roche Holding AG	Switzerland	Pharmaceuticals	87.0
10	52	Michelin	France	Rubber & Plastics	84.9

Source: UNCTAD/Erasmus University database.

a The index of transnationality is calculated as the average of the ratios: foreign assets to total assets, foreign sales to total sales and foreign employment to total employment.

Figure II.9. The top 5 rises in transnationality among the world's largest TNCs, 1995-1996
(Percentage points)

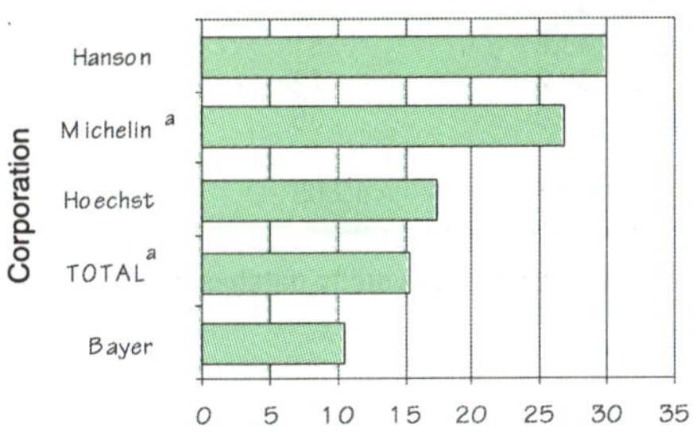

Source: UNCTAD/Erasmus University database.

Figure II.10. The top 5 falls in transnationality among the world's largest TNCs, 1995-1996
(Percentage points)

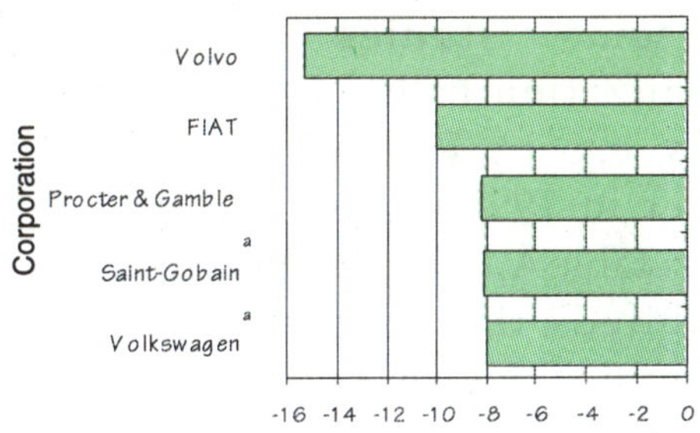

Source: UNCTAD/Erasmus University database.

The list of the leading ten TNCs by degree of transnationality (table II.6) is dominated by firms from small industrial countries, i.e. countries with a GDP of less than $ 500 billion in 1996. This is representative of a wider phenomenon (table II.7): firms with the highest transnationality index, such as ABB, Nestlé, Solvay, Electrolux, Unilever and Roche come from small countries, such as Switzerland, Belgium, Sweden and the Netherlands. Over the 1990-1996 period, the average transnationality index of the top ten firms from small countries increased from an already high 77 per cent to an even higher 79 per cent. During the same period, the average transnationality index for the top ten firms located in larger countries decreased from around 54 per cent to around 49 per cent (table II.7). Companies whose transnationality index changed very little during 1990-1996 include Saint-Gobain (France),

Daimler-Benz (Germany), Nissho Iwai (Japan) and Hoechst (Germany).

The industry picture, too, shows great variations (table II.8). Food and beverages (67 per cent) tops the list, trading (29 per cent) is at the bottom. For some industries, the foreign assets' share of total assets is very low (for five of them, below ten per cent), implying that the higher transnationalization-index ratings are mostly reached by foreign sales and employment shares.

The degree of transnationality of the top five firms in all industries that are represented by at least five firms in the lists of 1990 and 1996 increased over the 1990-1996 period, albeit unevenly and more modestly than has been suggested in some studies on the globalization of industries and firms, e.g. by Ruigrok and van Tulder in 1995 (figure II.11 and annex table A.II.3). Chemical firms exhibited the largest gains, electronics the smallest. The top five trading companies remain amongst the least internationalized, whereas the top five petroleum firms (closely followed by chemical firms) have the highest transnationality index of all industries. The transnationality index of the top five electronics and pharmaceutical firms hardly changed.

All indications are that the forces of globalization will lead to an increase in the degree of transnationality of firms (box II.3).

Table II.7. Transnationality index for small and large home economies, 1990 and 1996

(Percentage and number of entries)

	1990			1996		
	Number of entries	Average TNI	Top 10 average	Number of entries	Average TNI	Top 10 average
Small[a]	21	70.7	77.0	20	74.0	79.0
Large[b]	81	46.3	53.6	83	50.7	48.6
Totals	102[c]	51	-	103c	54.8	-

Source: UNCTAD/Erasmus University database and OECD.

a Small (GDP of less than $ 500 billion in 1996): Australia, Belgium, Republic of Korea (there was no entry in 1990), the Netherlands, New Zealand (was no entry in 1996), Norway, Sweden, Switzerland and Venezuela (no entry in 1990).

b Large (GDP of more than $ 600 billion in 1996): Canada, France, Germany, Italy, Japan, United Kingdom, United States.

c Unilever, Royal Dutch Shell are included in both catagories for the years 1990 and 1996. RTZ CRA is included in both catagories only for the year 1996.

Table II.8. Averages in transnationality and foreign assets, by industry, 1996

Industry	Average transnationality (Per cent)	Foreign assets (Billion dollars)	Foreign assets as per cent of top 100 foreign assets
Food and beverages	67.2	171	9.5
Chemicals and pharmaceuticals	65.3	247	13.7
Miscellaneous	62.4	141	7.8
Electronics and electrical equipment	52.8	357	19.7
Oil, petroleum and mining	52.1	331	18.3
Telecommunications	47.9	50	2.8
Automotive	43.8	381	21.1
Diversified	39.2	73	4.0
Trading	29.0	56	3.1
TOTAL	54.8[a]	1,808	100

Source: UNCTAD/Erasmus University database.

a Average.

Figure II.11. Average in transnationality index of the top 5 TNCs in each industry,[a] 1990 and 1996

(In percentage of top 100 total)

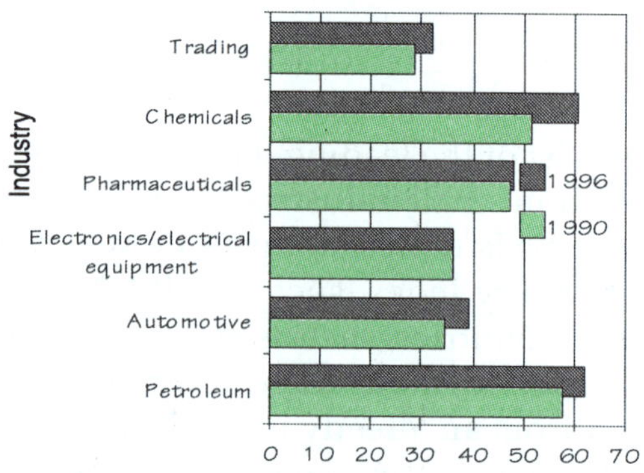

Source: UNCTAD/Erasmus University database.

a Only industries that have at least five entries and in which the same 5 top TNCs featured in the lists of the top 100 TNCs in 1990 and 1996.

Box II.3. Transnationalization in the medium term

A survey carried out between July and November 1997 among 300 managers of TNCs and international experts around the world, supplemented by about 100 direct interviews, suggests that the trend towards a further transnationalization of firms will continue in the medium term, independently of the size, sector and location of the TNCs. More specifically, between 1996 and 2002, the contribution of foreign activities to respondents' business is expected to rise from an average of 47 per cent to 56 per cent in sales, from 35 per cent to 45 per cent in production, from 34 per cent to 42 per cent in employment, from 36 per cent to 42 per cent in gross investment, and from 32 per cent to 41 per cent in assets (box figure 1). As a result, a rising number of companies will establish genuine transnational production and sales networks, compared with a minority in the early 1990s. Only 33 per cent of the respondents to the survey considered their companies "completely global" or "highly coordinated internationally" in 1990; this proportion had risen to 56 per cent in 1996 and could reach 78 per cent in 2002, while the proportion of those considered "little coordinated internationally" had fallen from 67 to 22 per cent between 1990 and 1996 (box figure 2).

Box figure 1. Transnationalization indicators
(Percentage of responses received)

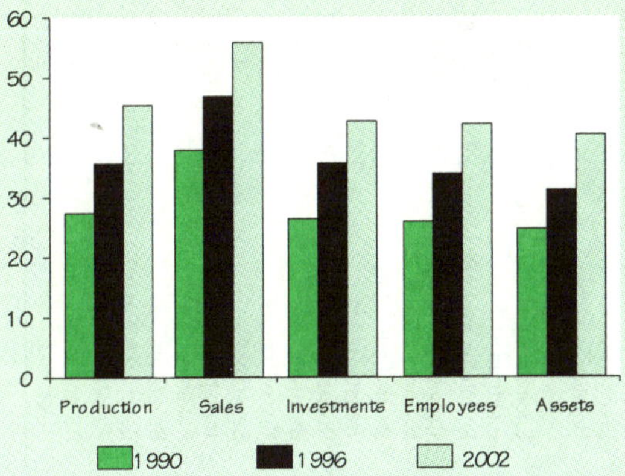

Source: Invest in France Mission, Arthur Andersen and United Nations, 1998.

Box figure 2. Transnational integratiion
(Percentage of responses received)

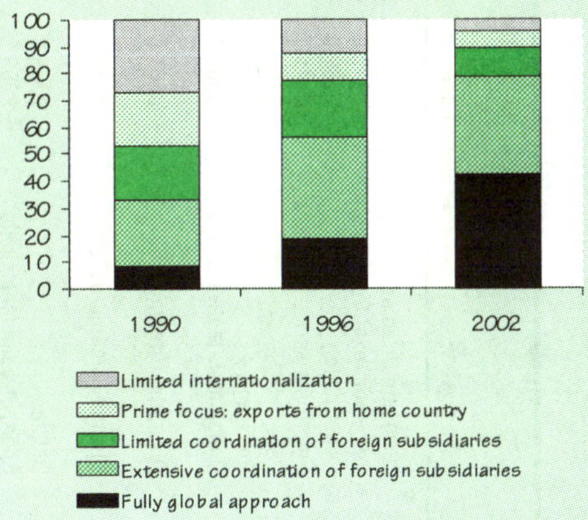

Source: Invest in France Mission, Arthur Andersen and United Nations, 1998.

B. The largest TNCs from developing countries

The top two positions in the list of the largest 50 TNCs headquartered in developing countries, ranked by foreign assets did not change in 1996: as in 1995, Daewoo (Republic of Korea) leads the list (table II.9), followed by Petróleos de Venezuela (PDVSA) (Venezuela). Further below, however, LG Electronics (Republic of Korea) fell to rank 18 from 5 and was replaced by Sappi Limited (South Africa). In the transnationality index, a company from Hong Kong, China, topped the list in 1996: Orient Overseas International. Panamerican Beverages (Mexico), the company holding the top position last year, ranked second in 1996 (table II.10). The 1996 top 50 TNC list includes twelve new entrants (table II.11), replacing twelve exits (table II.12). As with the top 100 TNC list, changes in positions at the lower end of the list are also few. But, overall, mobility on the top 50 TNC list appears to be higher than on the top 100 TNC list.

Table II.9. The top 50 TNCs from developing countries ranked by foreign assets, 1996

(Millions of dollars and numbers of employees)

Ranking by: Foreign assets	Ranking by: Transnationality index[a]	Corporation	Country	Industry[b]	Assets: Foreign	Assets: Total	Sales: Foreign	Sales: Total	Employment: Foreign	Employment: Total	Transnationality index[a] (Per cent)
1	9	Daewoo Corporation[c]	Republic of Korea	Diversified/trading	14933.0	32504.0	10238.0	26370.0	37501	47609	54.5
2	15	Petróleos de Venezuela S.A.	Venezuela	Petroleum expl./refin./distribution	8912.0	45402.0	31659.0	33854.5	12756	59318	44.9
3	11	Cemex S.A.	Mexico	Construction	5259.0	9941.0	2027.0	3365.0	9783	20527	53.6
4	4	First Pacific Company	Hong Kong, China	Electronic parts	4645.7	8491.8	6317.5	7025.7	37393	52880	71.8
5	5	Sappi Limited	South Africa[g]	Paper	3760.3	4846.1	2248.6	3438.2	8744	21055	61.5
6	22	Acer Group	Taiwan Province of China	Electronics	..[d]	16076.0	..[e]	6100.0	..[f]	44000	36.1
7	6	Jardine Matheson Holdings	Bermuda	Conglomerate/diversified	3380.2	7788.0	8187.4	11605.0	140000	200000	61.3
8	21	China National Chemicals, Imp. & Exp. Corp.	China	Diversified/trading	3201.6	6166.8	7965.6	17955.0	828	6466	36.4
9	17	China State Construction Engineering Corp.	China	Diversifies/construction	2810.0	5730.0	1590.0	5080.0	..[f]	2500	40.2
10	7	Compãnia de Telecomuni-caciones de Chile S.A. (CTC)	Chile	Utilities	2735.6	4406.3	768.8	1274.0	4997	8982	59.4
11	45	Sunkyong Group	Republic of Korea	Energy/trading/chemicals	2693.0	30793.0	10302.0	42094.0	2500	33299	13.6
12	36	YPF S.A.	Argentina	Petroleum expl./refin./distribution	2650.0	12084.0	864.0	5937.0	2139	9762	19.5
13	50	Petróleo Brasileiro S/A - Petrobras	Brazil	Petroleum expl./refin./distribution	2583.1	33736.3	1508.0	26758.7	22	43468	4.4
14	23	Cathay Pacific Airways	Hong Kong, China	Transportation	2555.0	7968.0	2023.0	4151.0	4038	15757	35.5
15	39	Samsung Electronics	Republic of Korea	Electronics	..[d]	25837.0	..[e]	23456.0	..[f]	59086	16.3
16	20	New World Development	Hong Kong, China	Hotel/construction	2321.2	12413.5	471.6	2162.4	31440	45000	36.8
17	19	Hyundai Engineering & Construction Co.	Republic of Korea	Engineering/construction	2287.0	8404.0	1461.0	5116.0	15950	28000	37.6
18	32	LG Electronics	Republic of Korea	Electronics	2083.2	16662.1	2429.2	14070.0	30889	65284	25.7
19	31	Petroliam Nasional Berhad	Malaysia	Petroleum expl./refin./distribution	1876.6	23219.9	6134.1	8901.4	72	13640	25.8
20	13	Citic Pacific Ltd.	Hong Kong, China	Trading/distr./motor vehicles/supplies	1678.6	6456.3	890.8	1648.9	8100	11750	49.7
21	47	Companhia Vale do Rio Doce	Brazil	Mining	1599.0	17891.0	1342.0	4938.0	86	15483	12.2
22	43	China Shougang Group	China	Diversified/metals	1582.6	6630.0	1032.7	4385.3	1623	221961	16.1
23	18	Singapore Airlines	Singapore	Transportation	1574.0	8584.4	3978.9	5122.4	2818	12966	39.2
24	28	Hutchinson Whampoa	Hong Kong, China	Diversified	..[d]	8174.0	1400.0	4743.0	10500	27733	28.6
25	2	Panamerican Beverages	Mexico/Panama	Beverages	1436.0	1705.0	1567.0	1993.0	..[f]	31400	81.4
26	3	Guangdong Investment	Hong Kong, China	Miscellaneous	1392.9	2316.4	628.8	836.5	12122	13531	75.0
27	8	Fraser & Neave Limited	Singapore	Beverages	1357.0	4532.0	1178.0	2008.0	10213	11955	58.0
28	1	Orient Overseas Intern.	Hong Kong, China	Transportation	1255.8	1306.1	1718.4	1882.3	3396	4030	90.6
29	14	Dairy Farm International	Hong Kong, China	Retailers	..[d]	3124.0	..[e]	6967.0	..[f]	49900	46.5
30	46	Comp. Cervejaria Brahma	Brazil	Beverages	985.6	3699.8	124.6	2468.7	573	8769	12.7
31	40	South African Breweries	South Africa[g]	Beverages/hotels	959.0	5271.0	1327.0	8002.0	15006	106900	16.3
32	29	Tatung Co.	Taiwan Province of China	Electrical equipment	..[d]	3652.0	..[e]	3010.0	..[f]	27250	28.1
33	42	San Miguel Corporation	Philippines	Beverages	903.1	3761.6	329.9	3241.8	3994	28544	16.1
34	38	Keppel Corporation	Singapore	Diversified	887.8	13478.5	329.2	2061.2	4057	14320	17.0

/...

Table II.9. The top 50 TNCs from developing countries ranked by foreign assets, 1996 (continued)

(Millions of dollars and numbers of employees)

Ranking by: Foreign assets	Ranking by: Transnationality index[a]	Corporation	Country	Industry[b]	Assets: Foreign	Assets: Total	Sales: Foreign	Sales: Total	Employment: Foreign	Employment: Total	Transnationality index[a] (Per cent)
35	33	China National Metals & Minerals Import & Export Corp.	China	Diversified/trading	884.6	2388.1	1282.4	4950.4	182	1288	25.7
36	30	Sime Darby Berhad	Malaysia	Diversified	833.0	10611.0	2072.2	4312.0	8132	36421	26.1
37	24	Dong-Ah Construction Ind.	Republic of Korea	Construction	..[d]	5120.0	..[e]	3086.0	..[f]	6583	34.8
38	25	Wing On Company	Hong Kong, China	Retailers	804.0	1591.5	47.6	392.6	1449	4083	32.7
39	49	Reliance Industries	India	Chemicals	801.7	5440.0	18.5	2431.0	1300	16778	7.7
40	41	Sadia Concordia S.A.	Brazil	Food	626.0	2123.0	554.0	2997.0	140	29975	16.1
41	26	Hongkong And Shanghai Hotels	Hong Kong, China	Hotel/property	625.0	3523.0	64.0	343.0	3126	5957	29.6
42	34	Souza Cruz S.A.	Brazil	Diversified	609.4	2198.8	560.1	1766.8	109	9876	20.2
43	48	Compãnia de Petróleos de Chile	Chile	Petroleum expl./refin./distribution	602.0	5705.0	79.4	2958.0	891	8389	8.0
44	12	Malaysian Airline Berhad	Malaysia	Transportation	559.0	5294.3	1045.9	1386.5	..[f]	13788	51.2
45	16	Gruma S.A. de C.V.	Mexico	Food	552.0	1557.0	726.0	1607.0	6222	12160	43.9
46	27	Barlow Limited	South Africa[g]	Diversified	522.2	2136.8	1449.2	3937.9	7932	30740	29.0
47	44	Vitro S.A.	Mexico	Miscellaneous	477.0	3386.0	451.0	2128.0	4274	33428	16.0
48	37	Bavaria S.A.	Colombia	Beverages	472.0	6746.0	421.0	1752.0	2972	13031	17.9
49	35	Empresas CMPC S.A.	Chile	Pulp & paper	390.9	2891.0	311.2	1174.3	2002	10294	19.8
50	10	Plate Glass & Shatterprufe Ind.	South Africa[g]	Building, automotive & furniture	372.0	758.5	773.1	1328.3	10533	19300	53.9

Source: UNCTAD/Erasmus University database.

a The index of transnationality is calculated as the average of the three ratios: foreign assets to total assets, foreign sales to total sales and foreign employment to total employment.

b Industry classification for companies follows the U.S. Standard Industrial Classification which is used by the United States Securities and Exchange Commission (SEC).

c Consolidated data are provided.

d Data on foreign assets are either suppressed to avoid disclosure or they are not available. In case of non-availability, they are estimated on the basis of the ratio of foreign to total sales, foreign to total employment and similar ratios for the transnationality index.

e Data on foreign sales are either suppressed to avoid disclosure or or they are not available. In case of non-availability, they are estimated on the basis of the ratio of foreign to total assets, foreign to total employment and similar ratios for the transnationality index.

f Data on foreign employment are either suppressed to avoid disclosure or they are not available. In case of non-availability, they are estimated on the basis of foreign to total sales, foreign to total assets and similar ratios for the transnationality index.

g Within the context of this list South Africa is treated as a developing country. Data for some important mining companies were not available.

Table II.10. The top 5 TNCs from developing countries in terms of degree of transnationality, 1996

Ranking by Transnationality Index[a]	Ranking by Foreign assets	Corporation	Country	Industry[b]	Transnationality index[a] (Per cent)
1	28	Orient Overseas Intern.	Hong Kong, China	Transportation	90.6
2	25	Panamerican Beverages	Mexico/Panama	Beverages	81.4
3	26	Guangdong Investment	Hong Kong, China	Miscellaneous	75.0
4	4	First Pacific Company	Hong Kong, China	Electronic parts	71.8
5	5	Sappi Limited	South Africa[c]	Paper	61.5

Source: UNCTAD database.

a The index of transnationality is calculated as the average of the three ratios: foreign assets to total assets, foreign sales to total sales, and foreign employment to total employment.

b Industry classification for companies follows the U.S. Standard Industrial Classification which is used by the United States Securities and Exchange Commission (SEC).

c Within the context of this list South Africa is treated as a developing country.

Table II.11. Newcomers to the top 50 TNCs from developing countries,[a] 1996

Ranked by foreign asset[s]	Corporation	Country
5	Sappi Limited	South Africa[b]
10	Compãnia de Telecomunicaciones de Chile	Chile
17	Hyundai Engineering & Construction Co.	Republic of Korea
19	Petroliam Nasional Berhad	Malaysia
23	Singapore Airlines	Singapore
28	Orient Overseas Intern.	Hong Kong, China
39	Reliance Industries	India
42	Souza Cruz S.A.	Brazil
43	Compania de Petroleos de Chile	Chile
44	Malaysian Airline Berhad	Malaysia
48	Bavaria S.A.	Colombia
50	Plate Glass & Shatterprufe Ind.	South Africa[b]

Source: UNCTAD database.

a This includes companies that could not be considered last year because of late arrival of a response to UNCTAD's questionnaire.

b Within the context of this list South Africa is treated as a developing country.

Table II.12. Departures from the top 50 list of TNCs from developing countries,[a] 1996

Ranking by foreign assets	Corporation	Country
9	China State Construction Engeneering Corp.	China
13	China Chemicals, Imp. & Exp., Corp.	China
15	Singapore Telecommunications Ltd.	Singapore
18	Grupo Televisa S.A. de C.V.	Mexico
33	China Metals and Minerals	China
35	Genting Berhad	Malaysia
40	China Shougang Group	China
43	Creative Technology Ltd.	Singapore
45	Chinese Petroleum	Taiwan Province of China
46	Grupo Celanese SA	Mexico
47	Formosa Plastic Group	Taiwan Province of China
50	Ssangyong Cement Industrial Co., Ltd.	Republic of Korea

Source: UNCTAD database.

a This includes companies that could not be considered because of late arrival of a response to UNCTAD's questionnaire.

As in the case of the world's top 100 TNCs, a snapshot (table II.13) of the 50 largest TNCs from developing countries shows a continuous trend towards greater transnationalization:

- *Country composition.* Since the top 50 TNCs list was first published in 1993, it has been dominated by firms from a few countries, mainly Hong Kong, China; the Republic of Korea; and, to a lesser degree, by Mexico and Brazil. Their relative dominance has remained largely unchanged since 1993. For the first two economies -- Hong Kong,

Table II.13. Snapshot of the top 50 TNCs from developing countries,[a] 1996

(Billions of dollars, percentage and number of employees)

Variable	Total	Change 1996 vs. 1995
Foreign assets	104	31.1
Foreign sales	338	14.2
Foreign employees	1,615,216	16.5
Median index of transnationality[b]	35.1	3.1

Source: UNCTAD database.

a Measured by foreign assets.

b As defined in footnote a) of table II.9. Change is measured in percentage points.

Figure II.12. Country breakdown of the top 50 TNCs from developing countries by number of entries for 1993 and 1996

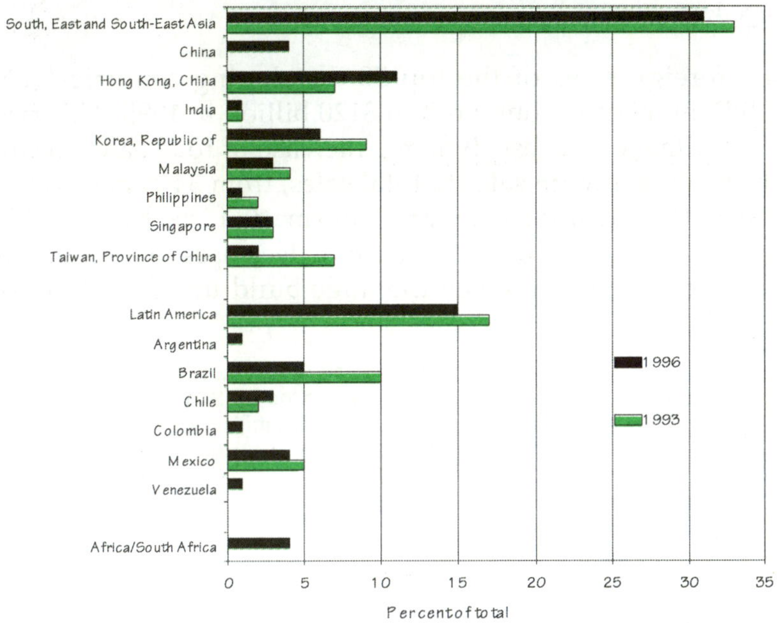

Source: UNCTAD database.

China and the Republic of Korea -- the dominance remains regardless of whether the absolute numbers of firms, foreign assets, foreign sales or foreign employment are considered (figure II.12, see also annex table A.II.12).

- *Foreign assets.* Total foreign assets of the top 50 developing countries' TNCs amounted to $103 billion in 1996. Between 1993 and 1995, they increased by around 280 per cent, and by a further 31 per cent between 1995 and 1996, from $79 billion to $104 billion. The latter increase, although considerable, represents a relative slowdown compared with the overall increase between 1993 and 1995. The overall ratio of foreign assets to total assets increased from 17 per cent in 1995 to 22 per cent in 1996. Figure II.13 shows the top five TNCs from developing countries with the largest increases in foreign assets; figure II.14 shows the top five TNCs with the largest decreases. Even though the ratio of foreign to total assets is about half of the ratio of the top 100, the top 50 developing countries' TNCs have built up their foreign assets almost seven times faster during the period from 1993 to 1996 than the top 100 TNCs did (see also *foreign employment* below). This trend partially reflects a catching-up effect, as the top 50 developing countries' TNCs implement strategies to exploit their

Figure II.13. Top 5 increases in foreign assets among the top 50 TNCs from developing countries, 1995-1996
(Percentage)

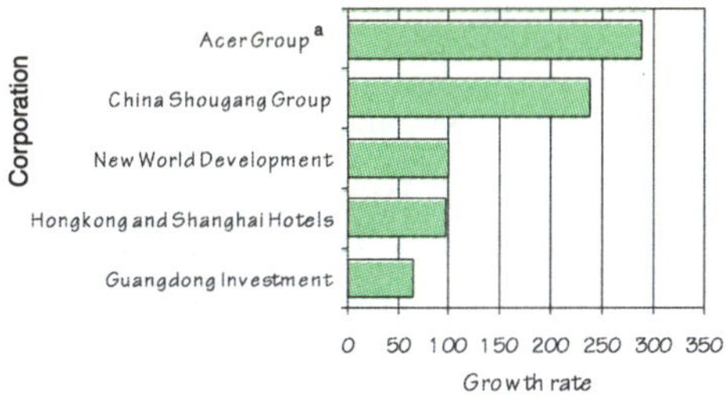

Source: UNCTAD database.

[a] Estimated growth rate.

Figure II.14. Top 4 decreases in foreign assets among the top 50 TNCs from developing countries,[a] 1995-1996
(Percentage)

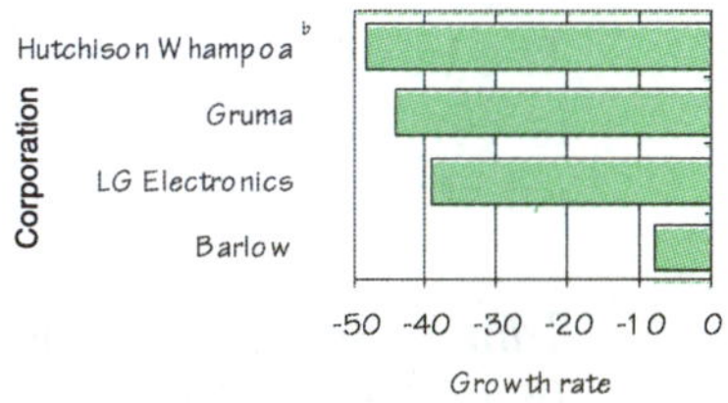

Source: UNCTAD database.

[a] The foreign assets of only 4 TNCs declined in the period.
[b] Estimated growth rate.

growth potential and competitiveness through increased transnationalization and the acquisition of a portfolio of locational assets, similar to the trend displayed by the top 100 TNCs.[1]

- *Foreign sales.* Total foreign sales of the top 50 developing countries' TNCs amounted to $137 billion in 1996, compared to $120 billion in 1995. This rise of 14 per cent, and a simultaneously less dynamic increase of total sales, resulted in an increase in the ratio of foreign sales to total sales, from 34 per cent in 1995 to 41 per cent in 1996. (For detailed company information, see figure II.15 for the top five increases and figure II.16 for the top five decreases in foreign sales.) This large increase is not surprising given the huge build-up of foreign assets between 1993 and 1995.

Figure II.15. Top 5 increases in foreign sales among the top 50 TNCs from developing countries, 1995-1996
(Percentage)

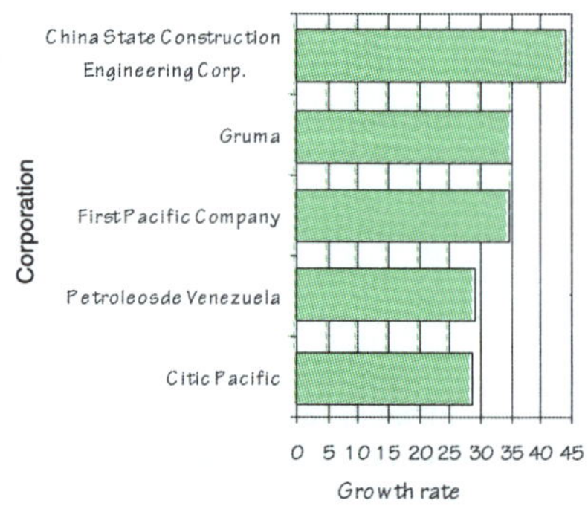

Source: UNCTAD database.

Figure II.16. Top 5 decreases in foreign sales among the top 50 TNCs from developing countries, 1995-1996
(Percentage)

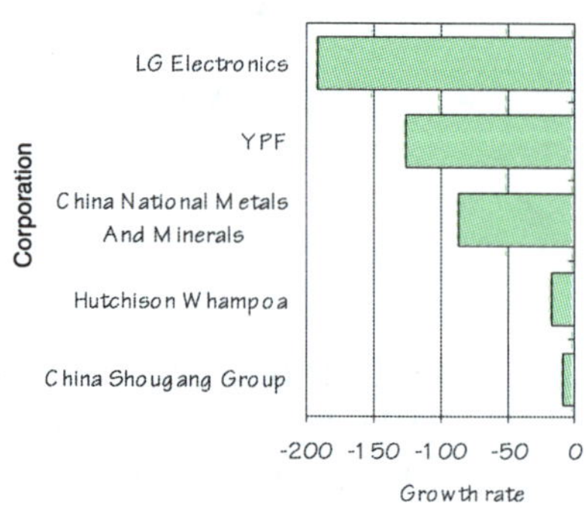

Source: UNCTAD database.

- *Foreign employment.* Total foreign employment of the top 50 developing countries' TNCs rose by almost 17 per cent between 1995 and 1996, to about 1,240,000, while in 1993, that figure was about 548,000. During the period 1993-1996, total employment increased by only three per cent. Consequently, the ratio of foreign-to-total-employment rose from 11 per cent in 1993 to 34 per cent in 1996. These trends of declining or stagnating overall employment and simultaneously increasing foreign employment are common to the top 50 TNCs and the top 100 TNCs. Figure II.17 shows the five TNCs with the largest increases in foreign employment, and figure II.18 shows the five TNCs with the largest decreases in foreign employment. The build-up of foreign employment is very much in line with the build-up of foreign assets and foreign sales.

Figure II.17. Top 5 increases in foreign employment among the top 50 TNCs from developing countries, 1995-1996
(Percentage)

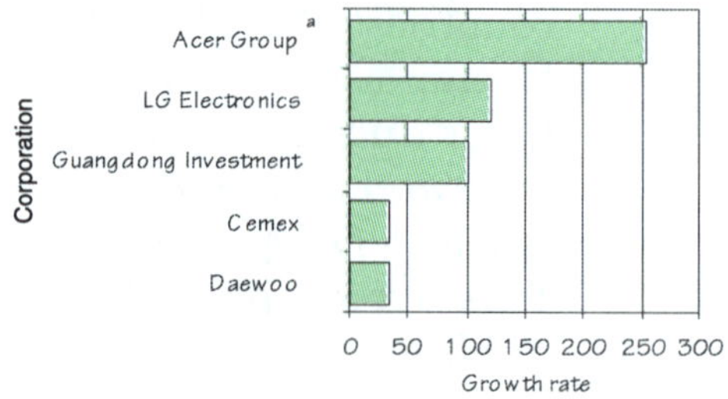

Source: UNCTAD database.

[a] Estimated growth rate.

- *Transnationality.* Wing On Company International (Hong Kong, China) enjoyed the highest rise in transnationality index between 1995

Figure II.18. Top 5 decreases in foreign employment among the top 50 TNCs from developing countries, 1995-1996
(Per cent)

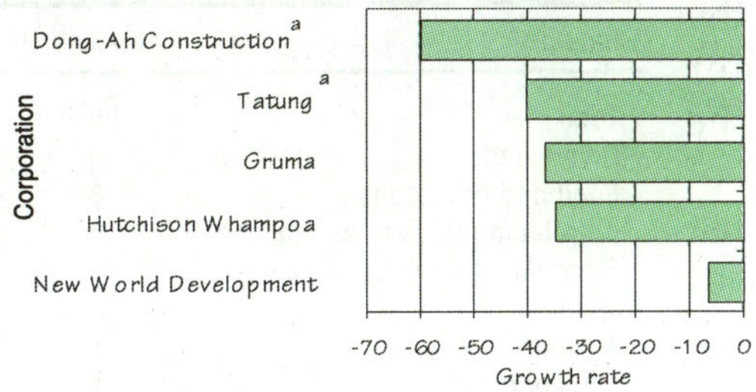

Source: UNCTAD database.

[a] Estimated growth rate.

and 1996 (figure II.19), and Gruma (Mexico) experienced the largest fall (figure II.20). The telecommunication, transportation, construction and trading industries are the most transnational industries among the top 50 TNCs, with transnationality indices of almost 60 per cent to 45 per cent (table II.14). This result contrasts with the findings for the top 100 TNCs (table II.8), where food and beverages, as well as chemicals and pharmaceuticals rank significantly higher than they do for the top 50 TNCs from developing countries. The difference between the top 50 TNCs and top 100 TNCs in their transnationalization indices of the petroleum and mining industry is also remarkable: 19 versus 52.

Figure II.19. Top 5 rises in transnationality among the top 50 TNCs from developing countries, 1995-1996
(Percentage)

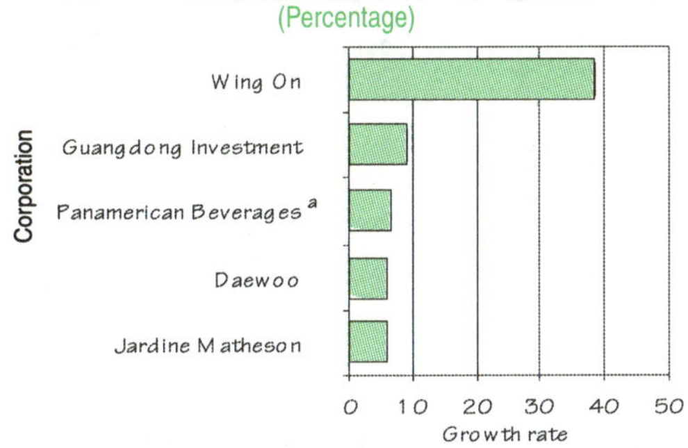

Source: UNCTAD database.

[a] Estimated growth rate.

Figure II.20. Top 5 falls in transnationality among the top 50 TNCs from developing countries, 1995-1996
(Percentage)

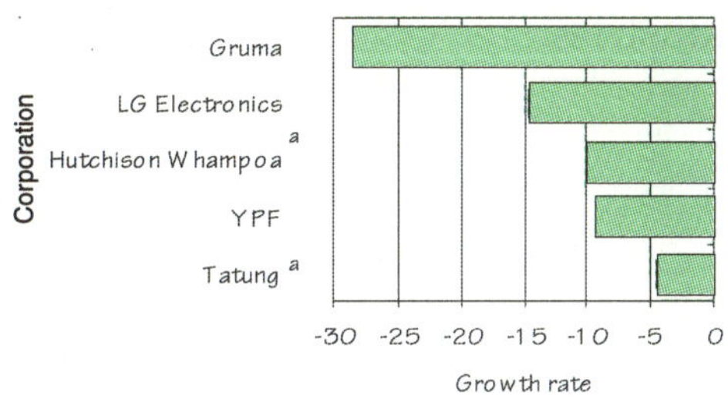

Source: UNCTAD database.

[a] Estimated growth rate.

Table II. 14. Averages among the top 50 TNCs from developing countries in transnationality, by industry, 1996

Industry	Average transnationality (Per cent)	Foreign assets (in billion dollars)	Foreign assets as per cent of top 100 foreign assets
Telecommunications	59.4	2.7	2.6
Transportation	54.1	5.9	5.7
Construction	47.4	6.3	6.2
Trading	44.6	6.3	6.2
Miscellaneous	38.1	5.6	5.4
Steel, machinery, engineering	37.6	2.3	2.2
Electronics and electrical equipment	35.6	13.6	13.2
Tourism/hotel	33.2	2.9	2.8
Food and beverages	32.8	7.3	7.0
Diversified	32.3	31.1	30.1
Oil, petroleum and mining	19.4	18.2	17.6
Chemicals and pharmaceuticals	7.7	0.8	0.8
Automotive	-	-	-
TOTAL	35.1[a]	103.3	100.0

Source: UNCTAD database.

[a] Average.

- *Industry composition*. Apart from diversified TNCs, corporations in food and beverages, petroleum and electronics/ electrical equipment industries dominate the top 50 TNCs (table II.15); all other industries have less than five entries in the list. The high proportion (22 per cent) of diversified TNCs in the top 50 TNC list contrasts with the low proportion of diversified TNCs (five per cent) in the top 100 TNC list.

As noted for the top 100 TNCs, the process of transnationalization continues gradually for the top 50 TNCs. There is no clear indication that one industry sector is leading the trend. Expansion as well as occasional retreat is rather evenly distributed over all industries.[2]

Table II.15. Industry composition of top 50 TNCs from developing countries in 1993 and 1996
(Number of entries)

Industry	1993	1996
Total	50	50
Diversified	9	11
Food and beverages	8	8
Petroleum ref./distr. and mining	2	6
Electronics/electrical equipment	7	5
Other	5	5
Trading	1	4
Transportation	1	4
Construction	6	3
Tourism/hotel	4	2
Steel, machinery & engineering	4	1
Chemicals and pharmaceuticals	1	1
Automotive	1	-
Media	1	-

Source: UNCTAD

Notes

1 On the growth of TNCs from developing countries, see United Nations, Department of Economic and Social Development, 1993.

2 Unfortunately, data available for the top 50 developing countries' TNCs do not lend themselves to the calculation of a network-spread index as was developed for the top 100 TNCs.

CHAPTER III

INVESTMENT POLICY ISSUES

A. Trends

The trend towards a liberalization of national investment regimes has been accompanied by intensified international discussions and negotiations on FDI rules, which have generally complemented trends at the national level.

1. National policies

Over the past four decades, countries in all regions have come to adopt FDI-specific regulatory frameworks to support their investment-related objectives,[1] and every year a number of existing regimes are amended. By 1997, at least 143 countries and territories had enacted FDI-specific legislation (figure III.1 and table III.1). In 1997 alone, 17 countries introduced new foreign investment laws or substantially changed existing laws, and another 59 introduced regulatory changes with respect to one or more specific items affecting FDI. Initially, many investment laws were intended to control the entry and operations of foreign investors; since the early 1980s, however,

Figure III.1. Cumulative number of countries and territories with special FDI regimes, 1953-1998

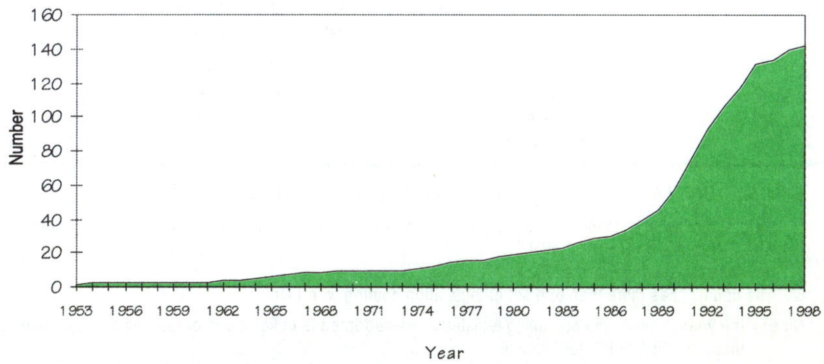

Source: chapter III, table III.1.

Table III.1. Countries and territories with special FDI regimes,[a] 1998

Developed countries	Africa	Asia and the Pacific	Latin America and the Caribbean	Central and Eastern Europe[b]
Greece (1953)	Central African Republic (1963)	Kuwait (1965)	Brazil (1962)	Hungary (1988)
Turkey (1954, 1995)[c]	Kenya (1964)	Republic of Korea (1966)	Chile (1974)	Slovenia (1988)
Australia (1975)	Seychelles (1967, 1994)c	Pakistan (1976)	Argentina (1976)	Albania (1991)
Canada (1985)	Lesotho (1969)	Cook Islands (1977)	Barbados (1981)	Belarus (1991)
New Zealand (1985)	Liberia (1973)	Tonga (1978)	Panama (1983)	Croatia (1991)
Israel (1990)	Comoros (1982, 1992)c	Maldives (1979)	El Salvador (1988)	Estonia (1991)
Spain (1992)	Morocco (1983, 1995)c	Saudi Arabia (1979)	Bahamas (1990)	Latvia (1991)
Finland (1993)	Democratic Republic of the Congo (1986)	Bangladesh (1980)	Bolivia (1990)	Poland (1991)
Ireland (1994)	Rwanda (1987)	Bahrain (1984)	Trinidad and Tobago (1990)	Romania (1991)
Portugal (1995)	Senegal (1987)	Samoa (1984)	Colombia (1991)	Russian Federation (1991)
France (1996)	Somalia (1987)	Solomon Islands (1984)	Nicaragua (1991)	Slovakia (1991)
	Botswana (1988)	Qatar (1985)	Peru (1991)	Bulgaria (1992)
	Gambia, The (1988)	Viet Nam (1987)	Honduras (1992)	Czech Republic (1992)
	Gabon (1989)	Myanmar (1988)	Paraguay (1992)	Republic of Moldova (1992)
	Mauritania (1989)	Iran, Islamic Republi of (1990)	Venezuela (1992)	Ukraine (1992)
	Niger (1989)	Sri Lanka (1990)	Ecuador (1993)	The former Yugoslav Republic of Macedonia (1993)
	Togo (1989)	Taiwan Province of China (1990)	Mexico (1993)	Lithuania (1995)
	Zimbabwe (1989)	Tuvalu (1990)	Cuba (1995)	
	Benin (1990)	Iraq (1991)	Dominican Republic (1995)	
	Burundi (1990)	Niue (1991)	Jamaica (1995)	
	Cameroon (1990, 1994)[c]	Philippines (1991)	Uruguay (1998)	
	Sudan (1990)	Syrian Arab Republic (1991)		
	Mali (1991)	Thailand (1991)		
	Uganda (1991)	Yemen (1991)		
	Burkina Faso (1992)	Azerbaijan (1992)		
	Congo (1992)	Democratic People's Republic of Korea (1992)		
	Malawi (1992)	Nepal (1992)		
	Namibia (1992)	Papua New Guinea (1992)		
	Algeria (1993)	Mongolia (1993)		
	Cape Verde (1993)	Turkmenistan (1993)		
	Mauritius (1993)	Armenia (1994)		
	Mozambique (1993)	Cambodia (1994)		
	Sierra Leone (1993)	Indonesia (1994, 1995)[c]		
	Tunisia (1993)	Lao People's Democratic Republic (1994)		
	Zambia (1993)	Malaysia (1994)		
	Angola (1994)	Oman (1994)		
	Djibouti (1994)	Afghanistan (1995)		
	Eritrea (1994)	Bangladesh (1995)		
	Ghana (1994)	China (1995)		
	Côte d'Ivoire (1995)	Georgia (1995)		
	Guinea (1995)	Jordan (1995)		
	Nigeria (1995)	Palestinian territory (1995)		
	Libyan Arab Jamahiriya (1996)	Kazakhstan (1997)		
	Madagascar (1996)	Kyrgyzstan (1997)		
	Egypt (1997)	Micronesia, Federated States of (1997)		
	Ethiopia (1997)	Uzbekistan (1998)		
	United Republic of Tanzania (1997)			

Source: UNCTAD, based on national reports and various sources.

[a] Refers to a law or decree dealing specifically with FDI. This table does not cover provisions contained in laws or regulations that do not deal specifically with FDI, but are relevant to FDI.

[b] Includes developing Europe.

[c] The country has more than one set of legislation dealing with FDI.

Note: the year in which the prevailing legislation was adopted is indicated in parenthesis. Economies are listed according to the chronological order of their adoption of FDI legislation.

most countries have adopted frameworks designed to attract investors and create a favourable investment climate.[2]

Of a total of 151 regulatory changes made in 1997 by 76 countries, 89 per cent were in the direction of creating more favourable conditions for FDI, and 11 per cent in the opposite direction, a three per cent increase in the former over the preceding year (table III.2). The favourable changes included liberalizing measures as well as new incentives; the unfavourable changes increased control or reduced incentives.[3] During the period 1991-1997 as a whole, 94 per cent of the FDI regulatory changes were in the direction of creating a more favourable environment for FDI (table III.2), continuing a trend that started in the 1980s.[4] Liberalization moves in 1997 involved in particular the removal of operational conditions and the opening up of new industries to FDI (table III.3), sometimes through the revision of negative lists of industries previously closed to FDI. This was the case in both developing and developed countries. The majority of changes concerned the telecommunication and broadcasting industries. Streamlining approval procedures was also an important feature of legislative reform, particularly in Africa.

Table III.2. National regulatory changes, 1991-1997

Item	1991	1992	1993	1994	1995	1996	1997
Number of countries that introduced changes in their investment regimes	35	43	57	49	64	65	76
Number of regulatory changes	82	79	102	110	112	114	151
Of which:							
More favourable to FDI[a]	80	79	101	108	106	98	135
Less favourable to FDI[b]	2	-	1	2	6	16	16

Source: UNCTAD, based on national sources.

[a] Including liberalizing changes or changes aimed at strengthening market functioning, as well as increased incentives.

[b] Including changes aimed at increasing control as well as reducing incentives.

The legislative activity in 1997 was partly a response to international commitments. For example, a significant number of countries revised their intellectual property frameworks, following their commitments under the WTO Agreement on Trade-related Aspects of

Table III.3. National regulatory changes and their distribution, by type, 1997

Item	1997
Number of economies that introduced changes	76
Number of changes	151
- in the direction of more favourable conditions for FDI	
more liberal entry conditions and procedures[a]	3
more liberal operational conditions[b] and frameworks[a]	61
more incentives	41
more promotion (other than incentives)[c]	8
more sectoral liberalization	17
more guarantees and protection	5
- in the direction of less favourable conditions for FDI	
less incentives	7
more control	9

Source: UNCTAD, based on national sources.

[a] Includes changes applying across the board.

[b] Includes performance requirements as well as other operational measures.

[c] Includes free-zone regulations.

Intellectual Property (TRIPS), the Madrid Protocol and the European Union's Directives on Trademarks. The entry into force of the Fourth Protocol of the General Agreement on Trade in Services (GATS) on Basic Telecommunications Services also led to the further removal of impediments to FDI entry in the telecommunication industry, while the adoption of the Fifth Protocol of GATS on Financial Services (see below) is expected to relax limitations on the presence of foreign suppliers of financial services. Pursuant to commitments under the WTO Agreement on Trade-related Investment Measures (TRIMs), certain types of performance requirements have also been notified to the WTO, i.e. have been made more transparent (table III.4).[5]

Investment promotion is an area in which government activity is particularly noticeable. Incentives are still on the rise. During 1997, 36 countries introduced new incentives or strengthened existing incentives (mostly fiscal). At the same time, seven countries introduced measures to abolish incentives, particularly tax holidays.

Measures other than incentives, such as setting up investment promotion agencies and facilities, have also been taken to promote FDI. The trend towards establishing

Table III.4. Measures notified under Article 5.1 of the TRIMs Agreement, June 1998

Country	Type of measure	Sector
Argentina	Local content and trade balancing	Automotive industry
Barbados	Local content	Pork-processing industry
Chile	Local content and trade balancing	Automotive industry
Colombia	Local content	Automotive industry
	Local content and trade balancing	Agriculture
Costa Rica	Local content	General
Cyprus	Local content	Cheese and groundnuts
Dominican Republic	Local content	General
	Trade balancing	Pork
	Trade balancing	General
Ecuador	Local content	Automotive industry
Egypt	Local content	General
India	Local content	Pharmaceutical products
	"Dividend balancing" [a]	General
Indonesia	Local content	Automotive industry,[b] utility boiler, fresh milk and soybean cake
Mexico	Local content and trade balancing	Automotive industry
Malaysia	Local content	Automotive industry
	Local content	General
Nigeria	Local content	General
Pakistan	Local content	General
Peru	Local content	Milk and milk products
Philippines	Local content and foreign exchange balancing	Automotive industry
	Local content	Certain chemicals
Poland	Local content	Cash registers [c]
Romania	Local content	General
South Africa	Local content	Automotive industry
	Local content	Telecommunication equipment
	Local content	Tea and coffee
Thailand	Local content	Various designated products
Uganda	Local content	General
Uruguay	Trade balancing	Automotive industry
Venezuela	Local content	Automotive industry

Source: based on information provided by WTO.

[a] The term "dividend balancing" used in India's TRIMS notification describes a measure applied by India in 22 consumer goods industries which provides that, during a period of seven years after the start of commercial production, the amount of dividend that can be repatriated should be covered by the export earnings of the firm.

[b] In October 1996, Indonesia withdrew the part of its notification that concerned measures in the automotive industry.

[c] Poland has informed the TRIMs Committee of the elimination of this measure as of January 1997.

specialized schemes to attract foreign investors, such as export processing zones and free-trade and investment zones, was strong in 1997: eight countries either formulated free zone regulations or established new free zones in that year, adding to the substantial number of more than 800 such zones in existence in 102 countries (table III.5).

Table III.5. Export processing zones and free zones, by region, 1996

Region	Number of zones	Selected countries [a]
North America	320	United States - 213,[b] Mexico - 107
Asia	225	China - 124, Indonesia - 26
Europe	81	Former Yugoslavia - 9, Bulgaria - 8, Slovenia - 8
Africa	47	Kenya - 14, Egypt - 6, Sudan - 4
Caribbean	43	Dominican Republic - 27
Central America	41	Honduras - 15, Costa Rica - 9
Latin America	41	Brazil - 8, Colombia - 11
Middle East	39	Turkey - 11, Jordan - 7
Pacific	2	Australia - 1
Total	839	608

Source: WEPZA, 1997.

[a] Figures show the number of zones in a given country. The 18 countries shown, along with the United States, accounted for over 70 per cent of all zones worldwide. In addition, close to 100 other countries host export processing zones or free zones.

[b] The United States also has 380 sub-zones in manufacturing plants.

2. Developments at the international level

At the bilateral level, the network of bilateral investment treaties (BITs) has expanded further, with the total number of treaties having reached 1,513 by the end of 1997 (compared to 1,360 by the end of 1996). Of these, 249 were between developing countries. In 1997 alone, 27 per cent of the 153 treaties concluded that year were between developing countries (figure III.2). The number of countries that have signed BITs has increased from 165 in 1996 to 169 in 1997. Apart from BITs, bilateral treaties for the avoidance of double taxation have also become quite numerous, and are discussed separately in the last section.

Figure III.2. BITs concluded in 1997, by country group[a]

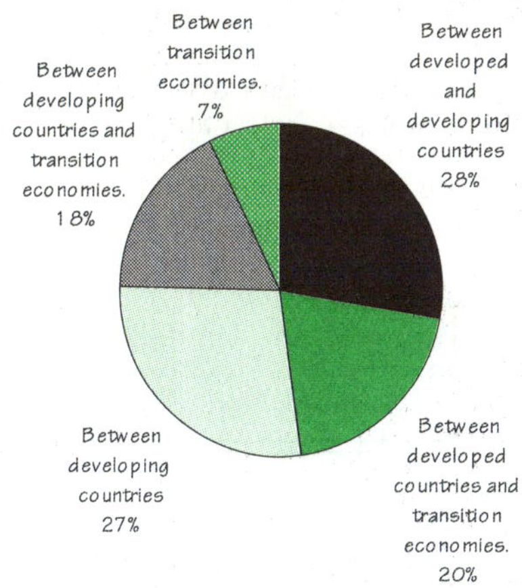

Source: UNCTAD, database on BITs.

[a] In 1997, 153 BITs were concluded.

At the regional, plurilateral and multilateral levels, discussions or negotiations on the development of investment rules have proceeded in various forums. While there are considerable differences regarding the pace, scope and depth of these discussions and negotiations, one thing they have in common is that representatives of civil society (box III.1) are increasingly paying attention to them (box III.2).

- At the Second Summit of the Americas in Santiago de Chile on 19 April 1998, the countries of the region launched negotiations for a "Free Trade Agreement of the Americas" (FTAA) which is expected to be concluded by 2005. The agreement is to be balanced, comprehensive and WTO-consistent and would constitute a single undertaking. Its negotiating process is to be transparent and to take into account the differences in levels of development and size of the economies in the region in order to create opportunities for full participation by all countries.[6] The negotiations on investment rules are to build on the efforts already initiated by

Box III.1. Defining civil society

The idea of "civil society" seeks to capture the way in which the world appears to be changing politically, at the heart of which is a shift in the relationship between the state and citizenry. While civil society can be seen as a counterbalance to the state, both are inextricably linked. Civil society is a "work in progress" which, while existing throughout much of the world in different shapes and forms, at different levels of organization, capacity and strength, is a socio-political reality whose continuing expansion demands active support if the goals of development, democracy and human rights are to be realized. In this sense, the building of civil society can be seen as an objective whose achievement must be purposefully and actively sought, in order to achieve wider economic, political and social goals.

Traditionally, the United Nations has employed the term "NGO", cited in the United Nations Charter, to define a relatively limited universe of non-state actors, particularly international (but sometimes national) non-governmental organizations active in the fields of development, disarmament, women's equality and human rights. However, civil society as a whole is made up of NGOs, community-based and grass-roots organizations, professional associations, representative bodies of the enterprise and financial communities, trade unions, the media, academic institutions, professional guilds and a range of major social interest groups, all providing an interface between citizens and the state. Until recently, civil society has been defined, and perceived, only in the national context. However, that is now changing rapidly and the civil society with which international organizations work is itself in the process of becoming globalized, reflecting the globalization of issues.

One area where there is a lack of definitional clarity is whether the private business sector should be included in the definition of civil society. Non-profit, value- and aspiration-driven organizations of civil society usually reject the notion that they belong to the same category of organizations as private enterprises driven by the profit motive. The reverse is also the case. However, some forums (including UNCTAD) have accepted that non-profit business associations and cooperatives could be treated as part of civil society. It is also necessary to consider whether trade unions created within the private sector, but with a role that takes them beyond their social origins when they seek to influence state employment policies, should be treated differently.

A case can also be made that national parliaments, and thus also their members, should be treated as a separate category, distinct from civil society, as the legislative branch of government.

Given the sheer diversity of the institutions that comprise -- and represent -- civil society and the private sector all over the world, an absolute definition that excludes business from civil society is perhaps not very helpful. However, one useful way to regard both NGOs and the business community, in whatever form the latter organizes itself, is as interest groups concerned with advancing their own agenda through the United Nations.

Source: UNCTAD (forthcoming, a).

Box III. 2. NGOs and international rules on investment

The late 1990s might come to be remembered as the time when non-governmental organizations (NGOs) first became a force in international economic policy-making and when the principles of participation, consultation and sustainable development gained increasing acceptance in shaping international debate. NGOs are likely to remain a force to be dealt with in the foreseeable future. One indicator of their influence is the role they played with regard to the negotiations of the Multilateral Agreement on Investment (MAI) in the Organisation for Economic Co-operation and Development (OECD).

Many NGOs pursue a step-by-step strategy. The first is to approach a relevant domestic ministry, e.g. the environmental ministry of a member of the European Union. Should this fail, the national legislative assembly (i.e. the parliament) may be approached. The final approach is to civil society generally at national and international levels. Some NGOs put more emphasis on lobbying via civil society from the very outset of their work on an issue.

Certain NGOs have had a long involvement in at least some international economic debates and negotiations on which they have had an impact, such as, for example, the negotiations on the draft United Nations Code of Conduct on Transnational Corporations (UNCTAD, 1996b), the Guidelines on Consumer Protection (UNCTAD, 1996b), and the Rio Earth Summit and the GATT/WTO -- all in the

/...

(Box III.2, concluded)

late 1980s and early 1990s. In more recent years, the availability of such a facility as the Internet has greatly enhanced the capacity of NGOs to share information, coordinate their efforts and connect with a global audience, including an audience in developing countries, with up-to-the-minute material. The importance of new technological tools and the increasing organization and sophistication of NGOs cannot be understimated; according to a commentator, "some think it could fundamentally alter the way in which international economic agreements are negotiated".[a]

The involvement of NGOs in international economic negotiations can be traced to at least 1988 when the United States, at the request of the Earth Island Institute in California, enforced a provision of the Mammals Protection Act (1972) relating to the high mortality rate of dolphins when tuna were caught with purse-seine nets; since tuna swim below dolphins, some dolphins were caught and drowned in the purse-seine nets. Mexico disputed this decision and brought the United States to a General Agreement on Tariffs and Trade (GATT) -- now World Trade Organization -- dispute panel (Lindert and Pugel, 1996). The GATT panel found that the United States decision was inconsistent with GATT rules. This decision upset environmentalists worldwide and suggested to many of them that the multilateral trade rules were indifferent if not inimical to environmental concerns. Some environmental NGOs took the position that a change was needed in the GATT/WTO rules to make them more "environmentally friendly"; others felt that the whole system needed to be reviewed. In the subsequent debates over the North American Free Trade Agreement (NAFTA) in 1995, some NGOs opposed NAFTA whereas others sought to modify it to take environmental and labour issues into account.

In late 1996, the focus of many NGOs already working on trade, investment and development issues shifted in part to the OECD, where the MAI was under negotiation. Concerns of NGOs in this domain have been exacerbated by a suit brought against the Government of Canada by the United States Ethyl Corporation under provisions of the NAFTA that are similar to the proposed MAI provisions. Ethyl claimed that the decision by the Government of Canada to ban the import and transport of MMT -- a petrol additive produced by Ethyl that is allegedly considered to have an adverse effect on the operation of vehicle pollution control components -- was effectively 'expropriation' since it reduced the value of the company's assets. NGOs feared that, were the Government of Canada to lose this suit, there would be major legal repercussions in the area of the environment and public health and safety.

The case in Canada, and the general situation flagged by the NGOs, falls under the rubric of a "regulatory taking": a situation where, by virtue of the implementation of a law or regulation by a government, the assets of a private party lose value. The issue is relevant because, in the draft language of the MAI, it appeared to some that a regulatory taking affecting a foreign investor might qualify as an expropriation and hence be subject to compensation. If it were so, the investor-state dispute-settlement procedure could well decide in a given case that a regulatory taking constituted an expropriation. NGOs are concerned that much environmental law and regulation might be undone if governments grow fearful of endless and costly lawsuits by foreign investors under the MAI.

Perhaps the main contribution of recent NGO campaigns has been in moving the debate on international investment rules away from narrow technical issues and towards a wide-ranging discussion of regulation and globalization. This shift was emphasized in the OECD Ministerial Statement (OECD, 1998a), which devoted much attention to the need for governments to engage in a discussion with "interested groups in their societies" over the process of globalization and the implications of the MAI.

In brief, NGOs have established themselves as a force to be reckoned with in discussions and negotiations over international rules on investment. These organizations are likely to continue to play a role in such negotiations, whether at the OECD or in some other forums. Indeed, the ongoing debate is a clear reminder that FDI issues, which by their very nature touch on the entire range of matters relating to production and the production process, raise complex questions of national policy in both developed and developing countries. If broad consensus is to be achieved, it is thus essential that international investment discussions and negotiations involve all those potentially affected. This is the logical consequence of the internationalization of the domestic policy agenda.

Source: Graham, 1998.

[a] "Network guerillas", *Financial Times*, 30 March 1998.

the FTAA Working Group on Investment (box III.3) and "aim to establish a fair and transparent normative framework to promote investment through the creation of a stable and predictable environment to protect the investor, his investment and related flows, without creating obstacles to investments from outside the hemisphere."[7] A Negotiating Group on Investment was established for this purpose. In June 1998, during the first meeting of the FTAA Negotiations Committee, it was agreed that the Negotiating Group on Investment "should develop a framework incorporating comprehensive rights and obligations on investment, taking into account the areas already identified by the FTAA Working Group on Investment and develop a methodology to consider potential reservations and exceptions to the negotiations."[8] Furthermore, the San Jose Declaration recognizes and welcomes the interests and concerns that different sectors of society have expressed in relation to the FTAA -- in particular business, labour, environmental and academic groups -- and encourages these and other sectors of civil societies to present their views on the topics under negotiation in a constructive manner. To that end, it establishes a committee of government representatives to receive inputs from civil society groups and present a range of views for the consideration of ministers.

- Also on the American continent, on 17 June 1998, the four members of MERCOSUR and Canada signed a "Trade and Investment Cooperation Arrangement" aimed at enhancing economic relations between the parties, in particular in the areas of trade and investment. The arrangement establishes a plan of action which foresees a framework for negotiating bilateral investment agreements, cooperation on customs matters, and the identification of measures distorting or hindering trade and investment. Furthermore, this plan of action provides for cooperation in the WTO and other appropriate forums on issues of common interest as well as consultations on the negotiation and implementation of the FTAA. The arrangement also establishes a council of business representatives from the member countries to advise the parties on areas of particular concern to the private sector.

Box III.3. Preparing for negotiations on investment rules in the FTAA

The Working Group on Investment met between September 1995 and March 1998. It had two objectives:

- To present to the governments of the region a precise and clear assessment of the existing normative frameworks applicable to foreign investment in the American continent, as well as a description of inward and outward investment flows in the region.
- On the basis of such an assessment and description, the Working Group was to prepare for the negotiations on a future investment chapter of the FTAA by promoting an exchange of ideas among countries on the regulatory alternatives available to them.

The Group was asked to begin by developing two inventories, one of the existing investment agreements within the region and the other of the national investment regimes in the continent. On the basis of these inventories, the Group was then to identify the areas of convergence and divergence in the national and international frameworks.

As for convergence, the Group found that practically all countries of the American continent offered constitutional protection to the basic principles of private property, freedom of enterprise,

/...

Box III.3 (concluded)

equality between foreigners and nationals, and due process of law. All investment agreements between countries in the region are based on the principles of national treatment and most-favoured-nation treatment, and many include basically the same exceptions to most-favoured-nation treatment (i.e. economic integration schemes, tax treaties and bilateral concessionary finance schemes). Most national regimes and investment agreements are committed to allowing transfers of capital related to an investment in a freely convertible currency and at the exchange rate prevailing on the day of the transaction, without prejudice to exceptions in cases of serious balance-of-payments problems. There is convergence regarding the justification of an expropriation decree and the criteria used to determine the amount of compensation, the means of payment and the due process guarantees to be followed. Finally, there is also a great similarity between the agreements with respect to settlement of disputes, not only with respect to disputes between the parties but also with respect to disputes between investors and host countries, and many of the countries of the FTAA are members of ICSID or are in the process of adhering to it.

The main areas of divergence were found to lie in the definition and scope of the concept of foreign investment, as well as in the criteria for determining the nationality of juridical persons; the processes of authorization and registration of foreign investment, including the existence of a national authority specifically responsible for these matters (different powers being held by sub-national authorities in different countries); the scope of the application of national treatment and most-favoured-nation treatment, in so far as some agreements grant national and most-favoured-nation treatment only to investments already established in accordance with national legislation, while others grant such treatment at the pre-establishment phase; and the industries that are open to foreign investment.

With respect to its second objective, the Group identified various perspectives and options for dealing with key substantive elements of an investment agreement. More specifically, it recommended the following:

- **With respect to the objectives of the negotiations**, the Group recommended that these should aim at establishing a fair and transparent legal framework conducive to a stable and predictable investment climate to protect investors, their investments and related flows, and stimulate investment opportunities while avoiding unjustifiable obstacles to extra-hemispheric investment.

- **Regarding the substance of the negotiations**, the Group recommended that the negotiation should include, at a minimum, the principles of non-discrimination, national treatment, most-favoured-nation treatment and fair and equitable treatment. In addition, the Group identified 12 substantive issues that will be subject to negotiation (without prejudice to the possibility that, during the negotiations, other relevant issues may be agreed upon): basic definitions, scope of application, national treatment and sectoral reservations, most-favoured-nation and sectoral reservations, fair and equitable treatment, expropriation and compensation, compensation for losses due to armed conflicts, admission of managerial personnel, transfers of funds, performance requirements, general exceptions and settlement of disputes.

- **On possible approaches to the negotiations**, two options were discussed. The first option was the negotiation of a chapter on investment that would establish obligations of general application, allowing for clearly defined reservations and exceptions on them. To achieve this, the chapter on investment would be divided into three areas: definitions, principles and obligations of general application; mechanisms for the settlement of investment disputes; general exceptions and specific reservations to the general obligations. The second option was to engage in three activities: to expand and deepen the statistical study on investment flows in the Hemisphere with a view to arriving at the harmonization of national statistical systems; to focus the negotiations only on the question of scope and coverage, in order to establish a transparent, comprehensive and balanced normative framework, to continue discussions on specific issues on which there is already convergence at the national level; and to continue the interaction with the private sector through seminars, conferences and workshops.

Source: Anabel Gonzalez, President, Negotiating Group on Investment, Free Trade Area of the Americas.

- At the ASEAN Bangkok Summit Meeting in 1995, members decided to enhance ASEAN's FDI attractiveness. The thrust of the work being carried out, as described in the ASEAN Plan of Action on Cooperation and Promotion of Foreign Direct Investment and Intra-ASEAN Investment, involves cooperation on programmes for the promotion of FDI and intra-ASEAN investment; consultations and exchange of information and experiences among ASEAN investment agencies on a regular basis; creation of an Investment Unit within the ASEAN Secretariat; joint training programmes for investment officials; simplification of investment procedures and enhancement of transparency in investment policies; and other measures to promote greater intra-ASEAN investment by facilitating the effective exploration of the region's comparative and complementary locational advantages. These various activities are to be consolidated in a framework agreement on the ASEAN Investment Area, which is expected to be signed later in 1998. It would be based on three pillars: cooperation and facilitation; promotion and awareness; and liberalization programmes. The investment initiative being discussed in ASEAN, for now, differs from the rule-oriented approach adopted in other regional integration frameworks by being designed to encourage investment through voluntary cooperation amongst members, while avoiding legally binding commitments and dispute settlement mechanisms. Thus, the ASEAN Investment Area proceeds mainly through an approximation of objectives, strategies and practices, while emphasizing policy flexibility and informal consultations to resolve difficulties (Bora, forthcoming).

- Work has continued in the OECD with regard to the negotiations on a Multilateral Agreement on Investment (MAI), initiated in 1995. At the April 1998 ministerial meeting, the ministers decided to allow for a period of assessment and consultations, in order to deal with outstanding difficulties (OECD, 1998a). Ministers recognized in particular that, while the agreement needed to ensure a high standard of liberalization, it also needed to take into account economic concerns and political, social and cultural sensitivities; that it needed to be consistent with the sovereign responsibility of governments to pursue domestic policies; and needed to address environmental and labour issues, among others. They also stressed their commitment to a transparent negotiating process and to active public discussions on the issues at stake. A number of non-OECD member countries were welcomed to participate as observers (box III.4).

  One of the high points in the recent MAI negotiations was the meeting of the MAI Negotiating Group with non-governmental organizations (NGOs) in October 1997,[9] after the text of the draft agreement was made public through the Internet (www.OECD.org/ daf/cmis/mai/maindex.htm). Since then, the MAI has attracted wide attention, not only among NGOs but also in a number of parliaments, including the European Parliament. The overarching concern of NGOs is that the rights bestowed upon foreign investors by the MAI be balanced by a requirement to meet environmental and social responsibilities, the latter including the right of countries and communities to manage their own development. They have stressed the need to ensure that key MAI provisions on, for example, general treatment and expropriation cannot be construed to undermine the regulatory powers of government. This was all the more important, they argued, in the light of the special treatment given to foreign

Box III.4. The OECD Multilateral Agreement on Investment: state of play as of July 1998

In April 1998, the negotiations on a Multilateral Agreement on Investment (MAI) in the OECD reached a critical stage. The negotiations had begun formally in 1995. Between September 1995 and early 1997, the negotiating process was mostly of a technical nature. Between early 1997 and the OECD ministerial meeting of April 1998, negotiators had been under increasing pressure from non-governmental organizations and others to increase transparency and seek broad-based political support. Partly as a result of these pressures, a pause for reflection was agreed to by the ministers, to last until October 1998. The following paragraphs describe the objectives, basic principles, main features and main outstanding issues as they have emerged from the negotiation process and the draft agreement so far:

The MAI is intended to provide a broad multilateral framework for international investment with high standards for the liberalization of investment regimes, the protection of investment, and effective dispute-settlement procedures. It seeks to provide predictability and security for international investors and their investments, and thus promote economic growth and efficiency, sustainable development and employment, and rising living standards for both developed and developing countries (Witherell, 1995; Engering, 1996).

Basic principles

- The MAI addresses investors and investments, including their establishment, expansion, operation and sale. Investment will be defined broadly to include enterprises, real estate, portfolio investments, other financial instruments and intangible assets.
- The MAI is meant to be a free-standing international treaty open to all OECD members and the European Community and to accession by non-members willing and able to meet its obligations. In reviewing proposals for adherence to the MAI, the parties would give full consideration to the particular circumstances of each country, including country-specific exceptions to accommodate the applicant's development interests. Eight non-members currently participate as observers.[a] In addition, there is an ongoing dialogue with non-member countries, with business and labour, and with non-governmental organizations.
- Country-specific exceptions would be an integral part of the agreement, and MAI disciplines would not apply where specific exceptions had been agreed to. Negotiators are aiming for a set of disciplines and exceptions that would achieve a high standard of liberalization and a satisfactory balance of commitments, taking full account of economic concerns and political, social and cultural sensitivities.
- There is increased convergence of views on the need for the MAI to address environmental and labour issues. There is broad support for including a strong commitment by governments not to lower environmental or labour standards in order to attract or retain investment. Furthermore, the MAI seeks to be consistent with the sovereign responsibility of governments to pursue their policy objectives. The MAI would not inhibit the normal non-discriminatory exercise of regulatory powers by governments. Investors would not be able to challenge domestic regulations as *de facto* expropriation.

Main features

Core MAI rules:

- *Transparency*: publication of laws and regulations affecting investments.
- *National treatment:* foreign investors and investments to be treated no less favourably than domestic investors and investments.
- *Most-favoured-nation treatment:* investors and investments from one MAI party to be treated no less favourably than those from another MAI party.
- *Transfer of funds:* investment-related payments (including capital, profits and dividends) must be freely permitted to go to and from the host country.

/...

(Box III.4, concluded)

- *Performance requirements:* targeted prohibitions on certain requirements imposed on investors, such as minimum export targets for goods and services, local content rules or technology transfer requirements.
- *Expropriation:* may only be undertaken for a public purpose, with prompt, adequate and effective compensation.
- *Dispute settlement:* provision for resolving disputes through consultations, with recourse, if necessary, to binding arbitration of disputes between states and between foreign investors and host states.

Exceptions to MAI rules:

- *General exceptions*: any country would be able to take measures necessary to protect its national security or to ensure the integrity and stability of its financial system.
- *Temporary safeguards:* provisions to enable countries to take measures necessary to respond to a balance-of-payments crisis.
- *Country-specific exceptions:* negotiated among MAI parties, they will permit each country to maintain non-conforming laws and regulations.

Furthermore, the MAI would not:

- mandate detailed domestic measures affecting investment, nor require member countries to adopt a uniform set of investment regulations;
- prevent parties from providing funds for domestic policy purposes; and
- require parties to accept each others' product or service quality or safety standards.

The OECD Guidelines on Multinational Enterprises -- a code of good business conduct setting out OECD members' expectations behaviour and activities of TNCs -- would be annexed to the MAI without changing their status as non-binding recommendations.

Main outstanding issues

- **Liberalization and exceptions:** proposed exceptions to most-favoured-nation treatment for regional integration schemes (REIO clause); cultural exceptions; current lists of reservations to the MAI; flexible regime of standstill on new non-confirming measures.
- **Labour standards:** whether there should be a provision prohibiting lowering labour standards to attract or retain an investment; whether the MAI should explicitly support internationally recognized core labour standards.
- **Environmental protection:** the objective is to ensure that the MAI does not stimulate "pollution havens", is consistent with multilateral environmental agreements, and does not prevent the parties from setting national environmental standards for investment, both foreign and domestic.
- **Conflicting jurisdictions:** this issue arose because of the adoption in one country of two laws that would directly affect investors from third countries. A tentative agreement reached on this issue in May 1998 between the United States and the European Union appears to contain elements for possible inclusion in the MAI.

In March 1998, the Chairperson of the Negotiating Group put forward a package proposal which included the following elements: language for the preamble; a qualification on national treatment; a binding provision on non-lowering of standards on health, safety, environment and labour measures; an interpretative note regarding the articles dealing with general treatment and expropriation aimed at making clear that the MAI would not inhibit the exercise of normal regulatory powers of government (particularly in the area of environment); and a cross-reference to the OECD Guidelines on Multinational Enterprises.

Source: OECD materials.

[a] Argentina; Brazil; Chile; Estonia; Hong Kong, China; Latvia; Lithuania; and the Slovak Republic.

investors through the investor-state dispute-settlement provisions which would allow these issues to be decided by international expert tribunals. The NGOs also called for the MAI to include provisions on labour rights and consumer and environmental standards in order to ensure that the removal of barriers to FDI did not lead to a lowering of standards in these areas. Some special interest groups such as authors and film-makers called attention to the threat that the MAI could pose for preserving cultural identity. Many of these and other concerns were also shared by the European Parliament in a "Resolution containing Parliament's recommendations to the Commission on negotiations in the framework of the OECD on a multilateral agreement on investment (MAI)" (box III. 5). Finally, NGOs believe that, as it stands, the MAI is unbalanced with respect to the rights and obligations of foreign investors and that adding non-binding guidelines for the behaviour of foreign enterprises to the MAI's legally binding provisions on investment protection would not be sufficient to rectify the balance. In fact, some NGOs (e.g. Consumer Unity and Trust Society (CUTS) and the Council of Canadians (CoC) have prepared alternative texts to those in the MAI draft (CoC, 1998; CUTS, 1998).[10]

Box III. 5. Resolution containing Parliament's recommendations to the Commission on negotiations in the framework of the OECD on a multilateral agreement on investment (MAI)

(Excerpts)

<u>The European Parliament</u>

- having regard to its resolution of 14 December 1995 on the Commission communication entitled 'A level playing field for direct investment worldwide',[a]

....

D. concerned that the draft multilateral agreement on investment (MAI) reflects an imbalance between the rights and obligations of investors, guaranteeing the latter full rights and protection while the signatory states are taking on burdensome obligations which might leave their populations unprotected,

E. whereas the MAI must not only provide benefits to the industry and the countries of origin, but should also contribute to responsible development of the country of establishment by promoting technology, sustainable economic growth, employment, healthy social relations and protection of the environment,

F. whereas the aim of an MAI should be to prevent ruinous competition between investors which would be harmful to the populations concerned in order to foster, on a global scale, environmentally and socially sustainable and regionally balanced economic development,

G. regretting the fact that the negotiations have hitherto been conducted in the utmost secrecy, with even national parliaments being excluded, although transparency and parliamentary supervision in key international economic issues are of crucial importance for the legitimacy of relevant international agreements,

H. whereas the EU has not yet supplied any studies on the impact of the MAI on trade, commerce and the labor market or intellectual property and whereas the compatibility of the MAI with existing environmental, social and cultural legislation and legislation on intellectual property rights in the EU, relations with the ACP countries and the EU's development policy, and its relationship with international environmental agreements (MEA), international conventions on intellectual property and regional agreements (REIO) have still not been clarified.

I. puts to the Commission the following recommendations:

1. Emphasizes the need for a broader public debate and ongoing parliamentary monitoring of the negotiations being conducted within the framework of the OECD, bearing in mind that the decisions to conclude an agreement are a matter for the state and national parliaments, the European Parliament and the Council;

/...

(Box III.5, continued)

2. Calls on the Commission, within a reasonable period, to carry out an independent and thorough impact assessment in the social, environmental and development fields, investigating to what extent the draft MAI is in conflict with:

(a) relevant international agreements, such as the Rio Declaration, Agenda 21, the UN Guidelines on Consumer Protection (1985), the UNCTAD Set of Multilaterally Agreed Principles for the Control of Restrictive Business Practices(1981) and the HABITAT Global Plan of Action and international commitments already entered into by the OECD;

(b) previously agreed OECD guidelines, such as the undertaking to integrate economic, social and environmental policy (May 1997), agreements on the responsibilities of multinational enterprises, as laid down in the OECD Code of Conduct of 1992, and OECD policy on development cooperation as formulated in 'Shaping the 21st century: the contribution of development cooperation' (1997);

(c) regional, national and EU legislation designed to promote sustainable development.

3. Notes that non-OECD member states, and hence developing countries in particular, may also accede to the agreement under negotiation, but regards the fact that those countries may not themselves exert any influence on the content of the agreement as a major shortcoming of the MAI, and calls on the states involved in concluding the MAI to refrain from exerting any pressure on the developing countries in order to induce them to accede to it;

...

5. Calls for the question of investment protection to be examined in a multilateral context in which all the developing countries are involved, so that UNCTAD, as well as the WTO, would be the appropriate forum for these negotiations; the WTO's consideration of this question must take full account of the results of the UN conferences, particularly with regard to the environmental and social dimensions;

6. Stresses that it is essential that the principle of partnership, which is now accepted both by the OECD and by the G8 as the basic characteristic of relations between developed and developing countries, should be respected, so that the interests of the developing countries and their national policies are taken into account as well as the interests of investors;

....

11. Considers it necessary for a derogation to be made for balance-of-payments disequilibria coupled with a provision to deter parties from abusively invoking balance-of-payments problems;

12. Is concerned that the performance requirements might curtail the right of States to implement existing industrial policies and to develop any new ones as required in future, particularly in the field of social and environmental legislation, culture and intellectual property, and fears that EU Member States may come under pressure in these areas in the next few years;

13. Calls on the Commission, therefore, in formulating prohibitions of specific performance requirements, to ensure that the latter do not conflict with the environmental social, structural and cultural policies of the EU and its Member States;

14. Insists further that reference should be made to compliance with international human rights conventions and environmental and social standards not only in the preamble of the MAI and that the MAI should contain unequivocal provisions which prevent a lowering of existing environmental and social standards by the MAI and make possible the introduction of new standards;

/...

- In 1997, the OECD adopted the Convention on Combating Bribery of Foreign Public Officials in International Business Transactions (OECD, 1997a). The Convention seeks to establish high standards for national and international measures to combat bribery by public officials in international business transactions, including foreign investment, thus avoiding the distortions that bribes can introduce in the international flow of investment.[11] Another plurilateral instrument addressing this problem is the Inter-American Convention against Corruption which was opened for signature in March 1996 (OAS, 1996). The Convention in particular prohibits -- subject to the constitutions and fundamental principles of the legal systems of the states parties -- any act of

(Box III.5, concluded)

15. Welcomes the inclusion of the OECD guidelines for multinational undertakings as a an annex to the MAI, but advocates that those guidelines should constitute a compulsory component of the MAI and calls in any case in this connection on the governments of the Member States to encourage international enterprises to draw up their own codes of conduct comprising provisions in the field of environmental protection, human rights and social matters;

....

18. ... EU legislation and preventing further harmonization of EU legislation; insists, therefore, on the insertion of a separate part of a Regional Economic Integration Organization (REIO) clause permitting new harmonized measures, e.g. environmental legislation, adopted within the framework of such an organization and replacing the measures previously applied by these States; takes the view that countries belonging to REIOs are not obliged to extend to countries not belonging to the organization concerned the more favourable treatment reserved for member countries;

....

21 Calls for the invoking of national security interests to be made subject to objective criteria which are verifiable under the disputes settlement procedure; in this connection also advocates the inclusion of an anti-abuse clause;

....

23. Considers the proposed provisions on investment protection, and in particular on expropriation, compensation and the transfer of capital and profits, to be too far-reaching; takes the view that governments must make sure that they cannot be condemned to making compensatory payments if they establish standards on the environment, labor, health and safety;

....

37. Calls on the Commission, the Council and the Member States to submit, pursuant to the procedure provided for in Article 228(6) of the EC Treaty, the definitive draft of the MAI to the Court of Justice for full examination;

....

IV. Calls on the parliaments and governments of the Member States not to accept the MAI as it stands:

....

VI. Instructs its President to forward this resolution to the Council, the Commission, the governments and parliaments of the Member States and the Secretariat of the OECD.

Source: European Parliament, 1998.

a *Official Journal of the European Commission*, 22 January 1996, p. 175.

bribery involving international economic transactions; suggests a number of preventive measures (including measures aimed at promoting accountability, transparency and the involvement of civil society); seeks to strengthen intergovernmental cooperation; and aims at fostering the progressive development and hamonization of domestic laws in this area.

- In Europe, the Energy Charter Treaty (UNCTAD, 1996b, vol. I) entered into force on 16 April 1998 and, by the end of June 1998, 38 countries had ratified it (www.ENCHARTER.ORG). Moreover, the negotiations on a Supplementary Treaty regarding investment and an amendment to the Energy Charter Treaty's trade provisions were concluded in December 1997 (www.ENCHARTER.ORG). As regards investment, the Energy Charter Treaty contains an obligation to accord non-discriminatory post-investment treatment without exceptions. In this context, non-discrimination means the better of two standards: MFN treatment and national treatment. For the pre-investment phase, however, its investment provisions contained only a best-endeavour commitment with respect to non-discrimination and provided that the Supplementary Treaty would deal with the conditions for a legally binding non-discrimination obligation for the pre-investment phase. The Supplementary Treaty, as negotiated, provides for two types of exceptions from the non-discrimination principle. First, it grandfathers existing restrictions; these exceptions are set out by each country, listing each nonconforming measure in an annex to the treaty. The text also provides an option for listed countries to reserve all or some of the state's shares or assets that are being privatized to its own nationals.

- At the multilateral level, the Fourth Protocol to the General Agreement on Trade in Services (GATS) on Basic Telecommunications Services was concluded in 1997 in the framework of the WTO. It entered into force on 5 February 1998. Among other things, it contains commitments to open market access for FDI entry in telecommunication service industries (WTO 1997a; see UNCTAD 1997a, box V.18 for a summary description).

- The WTO negotiations of schedules on financial services were concluded on 12 December 1997. The results were attached to the Fifth Protocol to the GATS on Financial Services (WTO, 1997b) which is expected to enter into force by March 1999. These negotiations led to new and expanded commitments on the liberalization of market access for financial services, including market access through commercial presence, which typically involves all forms of FDI entry. In fact, as in other service industries, a large part of commitments on financial services concern commercial presence. The new commitments relate, among other things, to the elimination or relaxation of limitations on foreign ownership and control of local financial institutions (particularly through increase of foreign equity to more than 50 per cent), limitations on the juridical form of commercial presence (branches, subsidiaries, agencies, representative offices, etc.) and limitations on the expansion of existing operations. Some commitments involve "grandfathering" of existing branches and subsidiaries of foreign financial institutions that are wholly owned or majority-owned by foreigners. Commitments were made in all of the three major financial service sectors --

banking, securities and insurance -- as well as in other services such as asset management and the provision and transfer of financial information. More countries made commitments in banking than in securities. Commitments in insurance were increased in number and depth. With five countries making commitments in financial services for the first time, the total number of WTO members with commitments in financial services will increase to 102 upon the entry into force of the Fifth Protocol. These commitments may be particularly important for some developing countries which have only recently started to adopt market reforms in financial services. Indeed, given the close interrelations between financial services and macroeconomic policy, and the strategic role of services industries in influencing the allocation of financial resources and ultimately in attaining development objectives, governments have traditionally assumed a major role, both as providers and as regulators of financial services.

Finally, financial services have unique characteristics: financial stability and investor protection are crucial policy objectives in all countries, with potential effects on all other economic activities. In the light of these, such services were provided with a prudential carve-out in the GATS Annex on Financial Services, and some countries have also chosen to schedule measures that may be characterized as prudential measures but could be challenged as limitations on market access or national treatment in the future.

- Work has also proceeded in the WTO Working Group on the Relationship between Trade and Investment on the basis of a list of issues that were identified for examination and discussion. These cover four broad areas: implications of the relationship between trade and investment for development and economic growth; the economic relationship between trade and investment; stocktaking and analysis of existing international instruments and activities regarding trade and investment; and the identification of common features and differences between the two areas, including overlaps, possible conflicts and gaps in existing international instruments (box III.6).

UNCTAD, in accordance with its mandate, is pursuing a number of activities relating to international investment agreements. Their main purpose is to help developing countries participate as effectively as possible in international discussions and negotiations on FDI in which they choose to participate, be it at the bilateral, regional, plurilateral or multilateral level (box III.7). More specifically, and with a view to consensus-building, the work programme concentrates on deepening the understanding of the issues involved in international investment instruments; exploring the range of issues that need to be considered; helping to identify the interests of developing countries; and ensuring that the development dimension is understood and adequately addressed. In this context, UNCTAD -- with the active participation of principal groups in civil society -- is paying special attention to issues related to the development friendliness of international investment agreements (box III.8).

* * *

An attempt to assess the above processes at this stage would of course be premature. But the outcomes of some of the discussions permit at least a few preliminary observations:

Box III.6. The WTO Working Group on the Relationship between Trade and Investment

The General Agreement on Tariffs and Trade (GATT) was concerned with measures affecting cross-border trade in goods. The World Trade Organization (WTO), its successor organization, is concerned with the treatment of foreign enterprises and natural persons as well. However, the treatment of foreign investment in the WTO Agreements is rather fragmented and limited in comparison with other existing international investment arrangements. In recent years, not only have FDI flows continued to increase but the pattern of these flows has changed considerably, as the proportion of FDI flowing to developing countries has increased rapidly. These developments have been supported by the liberalization of national investment laws and the proliferation of bilateral and regional investment agreements which in turn have facilitated complementary links between trade and investment. These and similar factors led to the establishment of the WTO Working Group on the Relationship between Trade and Investment at the first WTO Ministerial Conference, held in Singapore in December 1996.

The creation of the Working Group reflects a compromise between various views. The Singapore Ministerial Declaration requires the Group to examine the relationship between trade and investment, while stating *inter alia* that:

- the work in this Group shall not prejudge whether or not negotiations will be initiated in the future;
- the Group shall cooperate with UNCTAD and other appropriate international fora to make the best use of available resources and to ensure that the development dimension is taken fully into account;
- the WTO General Council will determine after two years how the work should proceed;
- future negotiations, if any, regarding multilateral disciplines will take place only after an explicit consensus decision is taken among WTO members regarding such negotiations; and
- the Working Group on the Relationship between Trade and Investment and the Working Group on the Interrelations between Trade and Competition should draw on each other's work.

Given the breadth of the mandate, a detailed work programme was adopted at the first meeting of the Working Group in June 1997, in the form of a "Checklist of issues suggested for study" ("the list") (WTO, 1997c). The list covers both economic and normative issues and reflects the varying interests of the members of the WTO as well as the complex nature of FDI:

Item I concerns the implications of the relationship between trade and investment for development and economic growth. Among the specific areas suggested for study are the examination of issues such as the effects of investment on transfer of technology, balance-of-payments equilibrium, employment creation and competition.

Item II deals with the economic relationship between trade and investment. It covers *inter alia* the determinants of FDI, the effects of trade policies and trade agreements on investment flows, and the effects of investment policies on trade flows.

Item III concerns existing international arrangements and initiatives on trade and investment. It includes a stocktaking and analysis of existing WTO provisions on investment-related matters; bilateral, regional, plurilateral and multilateral investment agreements other than those covered by the WTO; and the implications for trade and investment flows of existing international instruments.

Item IV deals with issues that are relevant to assessing the need for possible future initiatives and includes the identification of common elements and differences in existing international instruments in the area of investment, the advantages of entering into different types of investment agreements, and the rights and obligations of home and host countries and of investors.

/...

Box III.6 (concluded)

At meetings of the Working Group held in October and December 1997, the Group discussed the first three items on this checklist and, in March and June 1998, identified a number of specific subjects that require further study. It also began discussions on the fourth item.

Further meetings of the Working Group are scheduled to take place in October and November 1998. The Group will probably submit a report to the General Council at the end of 1998, on the basis of which the General Council will decide how the work should proceed.

Source: UNCTAD, based on WTO materials.

Box III.7. UNCTAD's work on a possible multilateral framework on investment

To give effect to the mandate received from UNCTAD IX which called upon UNCTAD to identify and analyse implications for development of issues relevant to a possible multilateral framework on investment (MFI) (UNCTAD, 1996c), UNCTAD has developed a work programme which comprises:

- **Substantive support to the intergovernmental process,** including the Trade and Development Board; the Commission on Investment, Technology and other Financial Flows, and its expert meetings on MFI-related issues; as well as the WTO Working Group on the Relationship between Trade and Investment (where UNCTAD has observer status). By mid-1998, two expert meetings of the Commission had been held, dealing with existing agreements on investment and their development dimensions: the first meeting (28-30 May 1997) focused on bilateral investment treaties and the second (1-3 April 1998) on regional and multilateral investment agreements.

- **Issue papers.** Preparation of a series of issue papers addressing key topics related to international investment agreements (on such issues as e.g. national treatment, right of establishment, transfer of technology and restrictive business practices). The main purpose of this series of over 20 papers is to address key concepts and issues relevant to international investment instruments, and to present them in a manner that is useful to policymakers and negotiators. Particular attention is given to the way in which the key topics have been addressed in international investment agreements so far and what their development implications are.

- **Regional symposia.** Symposia for policymakers in capitals aim at facilitating a better understanding of key issues related to international investment agreements, particularly from a development perspective. The first regional symposium for Africa took place in Fèz, Morocco, in June 1997; the second for Asia took place in July 1998, in New Delhi; further symposia are scheduled to take place during 1998 in Latin America and the Caribbean.

- **Geneva-based seminars.** Undertaken jointly with the WTO, these are meant to facilitate informal discussions among delegates in Geneva on economic and regulatory investment issues. The first such seminar took place in February 1998; the second in June 1998.

- **Dialogues with civil society.** The secretariat has invited interested groups from civil society to participate actively in a dialogue with relevant policymakers involved in international investment agreements. The first event of this kind, which took place in December 1997, was a high-level discussion, co-sponsored by UNCTAD and the European Roundtable of Industrialists, between Geneva-based ambassadors and European business leaders; a similar event, co-sponsored with NGOs, took place with a group of NGOs in June 1998; and a third event is planned for the Autumn of 1998 with trade union representatives. A seminar was also organized jointly with the Consumer Unity and Trust Society (CUTS) and the Rajiv Gandhi Institute in New Delhi in July 1998.

- **Training activities** on FDI for capacity-building purposes. Further training activities on FDI will consist of training courses for junior diplomats and a master class for negotiators.

Source: UNCTAD, 1998e.

- Whatever the fate of these various initiatives, many countries see that it is necessary for them to examine the implications and appropriateness of international investment agreements.
- As discussions and negotiations on FDI advance at various levels, it is also becoming increasingly apparent that agreements on investment, by their very nature, are difficult to negotiate, since they touch, at least in principle, on the entire range of questions relating to production and the production process and therefore involve complex issues of national policy in both developed and developing countries.
- For international investment agreements to be effective and stable, they need to take into account the interest of all parties, to incorporate a balance of interests and to allow for mutual advantage. This applies particularly to developing countries and, more generally, to agreements between countries at different levels of development. In particular, any agreement involving developing countries must incorporate the special dimension of development policies and objectives. Consequently, one of the main challenges ahead is how to ensure that the development objective is given effect and translated into the structure, contents and implementation of international investment agreements (box III.8).
- A more procedural lesson that emerges is that, if broad consensus is to be achieved, it is important that international discussions and negotiations associate, in one way or another, all those potentially affected, including representatives of civil society who have a real stake in the outcome of these processes.

B. Double taxation treaties

The evolution of investment regulations -- which includes adopting less restrictive national laws, concluding BITs and pursuing regional agreements and multilateral discussions on FDI issues -- has also been accompanied by increasing resort to bilateral treaties for the avoidance of double taxation. This section focuses on double taxation treaties, in particular on their role with respect to FDI and the recent trends in their number and distribution.

1. The role and characteristics of double taxation treaties

Reduced obstacles to FDI and the possibilities that they open up for firms to disperse production activities within integrated international production systems create new challenges for tax authorities. Since countries throughout the world are actively competing for the productive growth opportunities that accompany foreign investment, the question of possible double taxation of income from foreign affiliates -- especially those that are an integral part of a firm's globally integrated production and distribution system -- has become increasingly important and complicated (UNCTAD, 1993a, pp. 201-210). Put differently, differences in national taxation norms may entail conflicting interests among all involved (Plasschaert, 1994, p. 3). In the case of a TNC, for instance, both home and host countries may tax income from foreign affiliates. This situation results from taxation taking into account both the source of income and the residence of the taxpayer, which gives rise to overlapping assertions of jurisdiction and hence to double taxation. More generally, international double taxation is a phenomenon consisting of the concurrent exercise by two or more countries of their taxation rights, a phenomenon generally deemed not to be conducive to business transactions in general and FDI in particular (box III.9).

Box III.8. The development-friendliness of investment agreements

Development is the fundamental objective of developing country governments and of the international community as a whole. How and to what extent this objective can be served by international agreements that address investment issues is a question that is currently attracting considerable attention. If international agreements can, indeed, be helpful in this respect, an important issue is how the concerns of the principal actors in this regard -- host countries, home countries and investors -- can be addressed in a mutually beneficial manner. To a large extent, an investment-friendly environment is also a development-friendly environment. At the same time, it is important to ensure that the developmental needs and concerns of host developing countries are centrally addressed by any investment agreement so that it is development-friendly as well as investment-friendly in its orientation.

Indeed, there are various approaches that might be appropriate, and they are not necessarily mutually exclusive. The ones that are outlined below are intended to be illustrative:

- One approach is to establish a catalogue of development-friendly elements of international investment agreements. Such a catalogue could be a checklist of elements -- without a hierarchy among them -- of issues and concerns that can be consulted when negotiating international investment agreements, be they at the bilateral, regional, plurilateral or multilateral levels. Such a catalogue would be compiled to make sure that, when negotiating agreements, negotiators have indeed considered all relevant issues. Given the congruences, to a large extent, of an investment-friendly environment and a development-friendly environment, such a catalogue would therefore include virtually all issues that need to be considered in the context of investment agreements. A more elaborated version of this approach is to analyse each of these elements in greater detail and to determine how they contribute, singly or collectively, to the development objectives of host countries. Indeed, this kind of analysis may be indispensable because, in practice, it is possible that one element would counteract another.
- A second approach would be to identify a set of development objectives that international investment agreements should serve. Such objectives could include, for example, securing a stable, predictable and transparent investment climate; increasing the quantity and quality of FDI flows; strengthening domestic entrepreneurship; and recognizing the non-discriminatory exercise of governmental regulatory power in pursuing development objectives.
- A third approach begins with the recognition that not only the contents (i.e. specific treaty provisions) of investment agreements need to be development-friendly, but their very structure (i.e. overall design or plan) needs to reflect this objective, as should their implementation (i.e. specific actions by the various parties involved). The challenge is, of course, to spell out in operational detail what "structure" means beyond the statement of objectives and to transcribe it into workable formulations that can be implemented, enforced, monitored and, if disputes arise, adjudicated. On the other hand, when it comes to "content", the catalogue of development -- friendly elements, as well as the development objectives, appears relevant.

UNCTAD's efforts at identifying the development dimensions of international investment agreements draw on ideas, suggestions and feedback from governments as well as other interested parties.

Source: UNCTAD.

The principal response of governments to the challenges of double taxation presented by increased FDI is the extensive and still widening network of bilateral tax treaties which has developed over the past 30 years. There are currently around 1,700 bilateral double taxation conventions in existence (IBFD, 1998).[12] The OECD Draft Taxation Convention/ Model Tax Convention (1963/1977/1992) (OECD, 1997b), and the United Nations Model Double Taxation Convention between Developed and Developing Countries (1980) have provided the framework for the great majority of these bilateral treaties. These models are quite similar, the main difference being that the OECD model favours residence taxation while the United Nations model gives more weight to source taxation (Goldberg, 1983).

The main purpose of international taxation agreements is to deal with tax rights and thus with the allocation of revenues between countries. The contracting countries seek a balanced trade-off between their interests. With respect to developing countries, the challenge as host countries is to find a suitable balance between receiving a share of revenues from foreign affiliates operating in their territory and maintaining a climate that attracts FDI. In this respect, it is generally supposed that, having a smaller share of revenues as a result of tax concessions would in the long run be compensated for by increased inflows of FDI, associated technology and other benefits that are part of the FDI package. For capital exporting countries, as home countries, it is important, on the one hand, to keep their firms internationally competitive by allowing them to benefit from tax concessions in a host country and, on the other hand, to treat all its residents (or taxpayers) equally.

In sum, in examining international taxation with reference to FDI and corporate activity in general, and with respect to developing countries (which are by and large host rather than home countries) in particular, the following broad questions are raised:

- how to divide or share the revenues between host and home countries;
- what kinds of methods to adopt, or which types of measures to take, for the benefit of the host or source country (this is related, among other things, to the definition of "permanent establishment"); and
- what method to use in order to encourage FDI, taking into account the tax benefits,if any, granted in the source country.

From the perspective of investing firms, the binding nature of a tax treaty as an international agreement contributes to a secure basis for FDI; the certainty engendered by the inclusion of rules in a tax treaty is valuable, even in cases where this does not involve a revenue concession, especially where there is a background of unstable domestic tax legislation. By adopting a treaty, a country commits itself in cases of dispute to the objective of avoiding double taxation through a mutual-agreement procedure and adopts an internationally accepted approach to dealing with transfer-pricing issues. Firms and their employees can expect that treaties using the United Nations/OECD model frameworks will be interpreted and applied consistently with the published Commentary on the provisions of the Model Convention (United Nations, 1997). It is generally believed that although, *in form*, the countries conclude a bilateral treaty, *in substance*, by concluding a treaty using an accepted framework, they subscribe to international rules immediately familiar to taxpayers -- rules that promote stability, transparency and certainty of treatment. These features may be at least as important to firms as the particular concessions or incentives that a treaty may contain.

Double taxation treaties generally attribute the exclusive right to tax either to the country where income arises, or to the country of which the taxpayer is a resident. Alternatively, it may attribute this right to both, with an obligation imposed on the country of residence to provide relief for any resulting double taxation. Treaties are aimed not at establishing uniformity of application of taxes but at establishing tax criteria for the prevention of double taxation (Pires, 1989, p. 214).

Typically, a double taxation treaty:

- states its objective of resolving tax problems between contracting parties and determines its scope of application with regard to juridical or physical persons (*ratione personae*) and taxes (*ratione materiae*);

- sets out detailed allocation rules for different categories of income, e.g. income from real property, taxable without restriction in the source country; and interest income, subject to limited taxation in the source country;

Box III.9. Taxation principles

Double taxation can arise in the case of the transnational operations of firms if both host and home countries claim the right to tax firms' revenues. Two main principles underlie the jurisdictional basis of taxation: the first principle is related to the source of income or the site of economic activity (also known as the "territorial principle"); the second is related to the residence (or fiscal domicile) of the earning entity. According to the source principle, a country taxes all income earned from sources within its territorial jurisdiction. Under the residence principle, a country taxes the worldwide income of persons residing within its territorial jurisdiction. Varied criteria are used by countries to determine residence (e.g. for individuals, physical presence or home in a country; for corporations, place of management, head office or incorporation).

Nearly all countries apply some combination of these two jurisdictional principles. Some Latin American countries, however, have traditionally taxed solely on the basis of the source principle. This is also a feature of the tax systems of South Africa and Hong Kong, China.

Apart from these source and residence principles, the criterion of nationality is also applied by a few countries in the case of individuals. This is the case in the Philippines and the United States, whose tax systems combine that principle with the source and residence principles. Under the nationality principle, citizens of the United States, for example, are taxed on their worldwide income no matter where they reside. The United States likewise taxes aliens resident within its territory on their worldwide income and also taxes income derived by non-resident aliens from sources within its territorial jurisdiction. Firms incorporated in the United States, irrespective of the location of their head offices or seats or places of management and control, are taxed on their worldwide income, while foreign corporations are generally taxed solely on income derived from United States sources and effectively connected with a business such a corporation carries on in the United States.

According to some views, taxation only on the basis of the source principle would encourage nationals or residents to invest abroad, thus leading to a flight of capital. It has been argued that countries using only the source principle have adopted it out of necessity because of the great difficulties their tax administrators would encounter if they attempted to find out how much foreign income was accruing to their residents. On the other hand, the residence principle, although based on overall capacity to pay, has proved to be of only limited significance in countries whose residents do not have substantial investments in other countries and whose fiscal administration is not well equipped to ensure its application.

Source: United Nations, 1997.

- establishes the arm's-length principle as the standard for the adjustment of transfer prices by tax authorities in the case of transactions between associated enterprises (box III.10);

- contains rules giving exemption from tax or credit for foreign tax in the residence country, where income is taxable in the source country;

- contains rules on non-discrimination,[13] mutual assistance and the exchange of information;

- establishes procedures for mutual agreement between tax authorities to avoid double taxation in cases of dispute; and

- occasionally contains provisions on assistance in the collection of taxes.

Box III.10. Transfer pricing and double taxation treaties

Transfer prices -- the pricing of goods and services in international intra-firm transactions -- raise complex problems not only for firms engaged in cross-border production, but also for the tax authorities concerned. This is because the allocation of costs and profits between parent firms and foreign affiliates across borders is an area particularly prone to double taxation, and transfer prices determine in large part the income and expenses -- and therefore taxable profits -- of associated firms in different countries. Tax authorities are concerned about the loss of tax revenues and foreign exchange as a result of transfer-price manipulation. On the other hand, the authorities recognize the variety of business circumstances involved and the inherent difficulties of comparing intra-firm and external transactions.

Model conventions and most double taxation treaties contain a description of associated firms with a view to helping countries allocate business income in transactions between associated firms. Treaties give tax authorities the opportunity to make adjustments in the contracting country to which profits are under-reported. They treat each firm, whether parent firm or affiliate, as a separate entity, and the income of each firm is determined by treating it as though it dealt with every other firm at arm's length. The most difficult issue in applying the arm's-length principle is the policing of the prices set by associated firms for transfers of goods, services and intangible property among them. For this purpose, they describe associated firms in terms of common control, management, or capital investment, either between two entities or through a third party. Where the allocation of profits between associated firms located in different contracting countries is distorted as a result of that status, the countries to which an associated firm has underreported profit may impose an adjustment on that firm to accrue the amount underreported. In order to protect against double taxation, most of the treaties provide that, in the event that one contracting country should make an adjustment, the other contracting country should make an appropriate adjustment restoring, as a result, the aggregate profits of the associated firm to its original level.

Double taxation treaties also provide for "multilateral agreement procedures" to discuss their adjustments and correct discrepancies. This mechanism is actually used for resolving any disagreements arising out of the implementation of a treaty in the broader sense of the term. Such a mechanism is a special procedure outside the legal and judicial system of each contracting country and applies in connection with all provisions of the treaty and, in particular, to provisions on associated firms. As a consequence, if an actual allocation is considered by the tax authorities to depart from the arm's-length standard and the taxable profits are redetermined, taxpayers are entitled to invoke the mutual agreement procedure in the framework of which the action by tax authorities can be considered.

Source: Plasschaert, 1994, pp.1-3; United Nations, 1997 and OECD, 1997b.

2. Effects of tax treaties

Tax treaties have their effects through the limitation of the contracting parties' powers to tax. This is done in principle by devising methods for relieving double taxation. In existing treaties, two leading methods are followed for mitigating or eliminating double taxation (Muchlinski, 1995, p. 278). These are the exemption method and the credit method (box III.11). Tax treaties incorporating these methods adopt the following approaches. The source country exempts from taxation (or taxes at a reduced rate) certain categories of income but retains unrestricted taxation rights over other categories. Where the source country taxes at a reduced rate, the residence country gives a credit against its own tax for the tax imposed by the source country. Where the source country taxes without restriction, the residence country will either give a credit against its own tax for the tax imposed by the source country or exempt the income from its own tax.

Box III.11. Methods of relief from international double taxation

In order to avoid double taxation, tax treaties include rules for its alleviation. In this respect, two main methods have commonly been used to mitigate international double taxation.

The first is the tax-exemption method. So far as the income of firms is concerned, exemptions are confined by statute to profits of foreign permanent establishments and income from real property situated abroad. The main reason for the application of this method is that the exemption of foreign-source income from taxation by the country of residence may place the investor in a position of tax equality with residents of the source country, because the tax on that income is determined solely by the level of taxation in the source country. Thus, tax concessions granted by the source country are not reduced or cancelled by the tax of the investor's country of residence. Countries using the exemption method normally do not exempt dividends, interest and royalties from foreign sources from the domestic income tax. Many developed countries, however, grant special relief for domestic intercorporate dividends in order to eliminate or mitigate recurrent corporate taxation, first at the level of a foreign affiliate and then again at the level of the parent company. Some of these countries, either by internal law or by treaty, extend this exemption to dividends paid by a foreign affiliate to a domestic parent.

When this method is applied within the framework of a bilateral tax treaty, one of the parties is granted the exclusive right to tax certain items of income. As in the case of unilateral exemption, the exemption by one party of all or part of an item of income may be integral or may occur with progression. In the case of full exemption, a country of residence might be forbidden to take the exempted item into account in computing its residents' taxable income.

The second method of double taxation relief is the credit method. Countries using this method reduce their normal tax claims on foreign profits by the amount of tax the investor has already paid thereon to the source country. The latter could thus raise its tax rate to the level of the tax of the country of residence without imposing an additional tax burden on the investor. Correspondingly, special tax concessions granted by the source country, which reduce that country's level of tax below the level charged by the country of residence on that income, do not to that extent accrue to the investor's benefit. But this result is limited in its practical scope, since capital-exporting countries consider bona fide foreign affiliates engaged in production activities as being outside their national tax jurisdictions and do not tax their profits until they are repatriated in the form of dividends.

Differences in definitions of taxable income used by host and home country tax authorities may create some difficulties. For instance, the home country authorities may define a corporation's profit obtained in a certain country more narrowly than that country's income tax authorities do, for example, as a result of differences in depreciation allowances or investment credits. The source country's income tax may then be in excess of the tax that the home country would have assessed on that income, which is the upper limit on the tax credit allowed by the home country. Thus, even if the

/...

The essential feature of the exemption method is that the investor's country of residence exempts from taxation certain items of income from foreign sources. Exemption is mainly granted in respect of active income; passive income such as interest, royalties or dividends is generally taxed, with a credit being given for foreign taxes. The exemption-with-progression method has been used in treaties concluded by Austria, Belgium, Germany, Finland, France, Iceland, Luxembourg, the Netherlands, Spain and Switzerland.

In contrast, the main feature of the credit method is that the investor's country of residence treats the foreign tax, within certain statutory limitations, as if it were a tax paid to itself. Within the framework of a bilateral treaty, each of the contracting parties levies income taxes, but the country of residence permits income taxes paid to the source country to be deducted from its own income taxes, with certain exceptions. The treaty usually indicates which taxes qualify for the credit. A variant of this method (called "matching credit method" or "tax-sparing method") has been developed, according to which the country of residence grants a tax credit calculated at a higher rate than the tax rate currently applied in the source country. Tax-sparing clauses have been included in many bilateral treaties concluded with developing countries by most of the major home countries including Canada, France, Germany, Japan and the United Kingdom. An interesting feature found in recent treaties is reciprocal extension of tax-sparing credit. It is also indicated that the adoption of this method tends to be limited in scope (list of incentives) and in time duration.

(Box III.11, concluded)

host country statutory tax rate is less than the home country rate, it is possible that some part of the host country tax may be disallowed as a credit against home country tax. In the case of dividends in respect of minor (portfolio) holdings in foreign companies, countries applying the credit method normally deduct from their own tax only the foreign tax levied on the dividends as such. However, in order to eliminate or mitigate recurrent corporate taxation, significant capital- exporting countries adopting the credit method allow as a credit against the corporate tax due from the parent company not only the tax levied on dividends by the country where the subsidiary operates, but also the corporate tax paid by the affiliate as far as it relates to profits distributed to the parent company (so-called "indirect tax credit" or "credit for underlying tax").

According to the credit method, the tax burden on investment abroad is the same as that on domestic investment, provided that the tax in the source country does not exceed that in the residence country. This tendency towards equality of tax treatment may have serious implications for developing countries' efforts to attract FDI, since their tax incentives may be nullified. No consequences follow from the use of the credit method while profits from tax incentives are reinvested in the operating subsidiary. However, if such profits are repatriated, the benefit of incentives may pass from foreign investors to the governments of their countries of residence in the form of an increased tax yield.

A method that avoids this problem is the tax-sparing method (referred to as matching credit methods), which can be found in treaties which have been signed by many developed countries, especially European countries, with developing countries. Quite often, the country of residence has granted a credit not only for the tax actually paid in a developing country, but also for the tax spared by incentive legislation in the host country.

There is recent evidence of increasing reluctance on the part of developed countries to adopt the tax-sparing method in their tax treaties. Concerns about the effectiveness of tax incentives and the abuse of tax-sparing provisions have prompted a reconsideration of the use of the tax-sparing method in new treaties and renegotiations of existing treaties.

Source: United Nations, 1980 and 1997; and OECD, 1998b.

It is generally accepted that one of the most important effects of tax treaties is the legal certainty they provide to investors, in both the home and the host countries. Regardless of any changes affecting a host country's tax system, foreign investors cannot be taxed beyond the levels allowed by a treaty. This effect is less comprehensive in the home country. In reality, certain changes in the home country tax system can affect the investor regardless of the existence of a treaty. For example, if the treaty provides for the credit method, a general increase in the corporate tax rate in the home country will also affect a resident deriving foreign-source income, regardless of the treaty. However, the exemption method, if adopted in the treaty, could not be modified at will by the home country.

Tax treaties can have development implications and cannot, therefore, be fully separated from the context of various monetary, fiscal, social and other policies of contracting parties. When the parties are at the same or a similar level of development, the gain or loss of revenue resulting from reciprocal flows of investment does not have the same significance as when the parties are at different stages of development. The presumption of symmetries of gains and losses underlying tax treaties between countries at the same level of development is not applicable for countries at different stages of development. The loss of revenue may have a different "value" for a contracting party, depending on its level of development. For this reason, it could be argued that any eventual reduction in tax revenue from locally produced income should be offset by an increase in investment and technology flows. Since income flows are generally from developing to developed countries, a pattern of tax treaties in which the source country gives up revenue more often than not will not involve the rough symmetry of sacrifice which it might in tax treaties between developed countries. It should also be noted that developing countries, in their domestic laws, often introduce measures aimed at the alleviation of the tax burden of foreign investors, through a variety of tax incentives including income-tax exemptions, reduction or exemption of export proceeds, and reduction or exemptions of individual income taxes for foreign personnel. The benefits of these tax incentives for investors may exceed those resulting from tax treaties. These benefits are, however, offered unilaterally rather than in the context of an international agreement and it may be that foreign investors will value more highly the benefits of more modest reductions or exemptions given in the context of tax treaties with the attendant advantages of stability, transparency and certainty of treatment. From the perspective of host countries, having a smaller share of revenue, as a consequence of concessions offered either in domestic legislation or in the context of a tax treaty, could be (though it need not be) compensated for by increased flows of capital and technology into their economies as the result of an improved climate for FDI.

A number of different views have been expressed on the role that the tax factor plays in attracting or inhibiting FDI (Plasschaert, 1994, pp. 46-47). Although this factor remains subsidiary to other factors, it is also generally accepted that, with the removal of barriers to FDI, taxation may gain more importance in investors' decisions. Long-term investors may attach more importance to the general features of a country's tax system than to its temporary incentives. In considering the role of the tax factor in attracting or inhibiting FDI, it may be important to distinguish the significance of incentives from that of other features of the tax system such as stability, transparency and certainty of treatment. Still, other things being equal, the tax factor could play a determining role in the choice of an FDI location and this in turn could give rise to a tax competition for investment (OECD, 1998b) (box III.12).

Box III.12. Tax competition

The international tax environment is evolving as a result of the removal of capital controls and the continuing liberalization of financial markets, aided by the development of new communication technologies. As obstacles to the flow of capital are reduced, business decisions such as financing and investment have become more sensitive to tax differentials. As a response to these developments, governments of both developed and developing countries have become more inclined to use the tax regime to attract FDI, as evidenced by the rapid spread of preferential tax regimes.

Preferential tax regimes have in common the opening up of profit-shifting possibilities without corresponding shifts in real activities. While these regimes were typically found in tax havens in the past, they have been adopted in recent years by an increasing number of other countries. Once one country introduces such a regime, others may find it necessary to respond with similar measures, thereby triggering a "race to the bottom" in the corporate tax field. This form of tax competition is viewed by an increasing number of countries as harmful because it distorts the flows of capital and reduces the tax base, making investment decisions tax-driven rather than commercially-driven.

Recognizing that these issues can be effectively addressed only through international cooperation, both the European Union and the OECD have recently adopted non-binding instruments for dealing with harmful preferential tax regimes. These instruments, the European Union's Code of Conduct (European Union Council, 13559/97/FIS 167) and the OECD Guidelines (OECD, 1998b), take as a starting point whether a jurisdiction imposes no or low effective taxes in identifying a harmful preferential tax regime. Other criteria considered include whether a regime is "ring-fenced" (i.e. whether it is partly or fully isolated from the economy of the country providing the regime), whether its operation is non-transparent; and whether the jurisdiction operating the regime fails to exchange information with other countries. While the European Union Code and the OECD Guidelines differ in some respects (the main difference being that the OECD Guidelines are limited to financial and other service activities, while the European Union Code covers all types of business activities), the general view is that they are broadly compatible and mutually reinforcing.

Both instruments emphasize the importance of associating non-OECD countries with them. This reflects the concern that, unless the principles behind these instruments are widely accepted, the implementation of these instruments may provoke a displacement of activities to non-OECD countries.

In addition to the Guidelines, the OECD has agreed on a number of recommendations to counter the harmful effects of tax competition. One of these recommendations proposes the development of an OECD tax haven list by October 1999. The objective is to identify and list, on the basis of certain criteria, tax jurisdictions that constitute "tax havens".

Other recommendations are:

Domestic level

- that countries that do not have controlled foreign corporation rules or equivalent rules consider adopting them and that countries that have such rules ensure that they apply in a fashion consistent with the desirability of curbing harmful tax practices;
- that countries that do not have foreign investment fund rules or equivalent rules consider adopting them and that countries that have such rules consider applying them to income and entities covered by practices considered to constitute harmful tax competition;
- that countries that apply the exemption method to eliminate double taxation of foreign source income consider adopting rules that ensure that foreign income that has benefited from tax practices deemed as constituting harmful tax competition does not qualify for the application of the exemption method;
- that countries that do not have rules concerning reporting of international transactions and foreign operations of resident taxpayers consider adopting such rules;
- that countries exchange information obtained under these rules;
- that countries in which administrative decisions concerning the particular position of a taxpayer may be obtained in advance of planned transactions make public the conditions for granting, denying or revoking such decisions; and

/...

3. The universe of double taxation treaties[14]

The number of double taxation treaties (DTTs) has increased rapidly in the past four decades (figure III.3). By the end of 1997, 1,794 treaties,[15] covering 178 countries and territories, were in existence (figure III.4). This compares with 1,513 BITs involving 169 countries at the end of 1997. Between 1960 and 1997, the rate of increase for DTTs has been steady while the rate of increase for BITs rose sharply in the late 1980s.

Figure III.3. Cumulative number of DTTs and BITs, 1960-1997

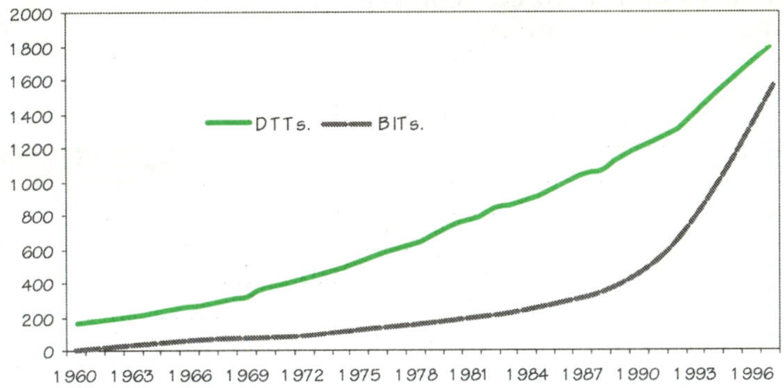

Source: UNCTAD, database on BITs and database on DTTs.

Originally, DTTs were concluded mainly between developed countries. Over the years, however, as first the developing countries and then the economies in transition became important host countries for FDI and also emerged as home countries, the universe of tax treaties expanded also to include them (figure III.4). The increased participation of

(Box III.12, concluded)

- that countries, in the context of counteracting harmful tax competition, should review their laws, regulations and practices which govern access to banking information with a view to removing impediments to accessing such information.

Tax treaty level

- that countries should undertake programmes to intensify the exchange of relevant information concerning transactions in tax havens and preferential tax regimes constituting harmful tax competition;
- that countries consider including in their tax conventions provisions aimed at restricting the entitlement to treaty benefits for entities and income covered by measures constituting harmful tax practices and consider how the existing provisions of their tax conventions can be applied for the same purpose;
- that countries consider terminating their tax conventions with tax havens and consider not entering into tax treaties with such countries in the future; and
- that countries consider undertaking coordinated enforcement programmes (such as simultaneous examinations, specific exchange-of-information projects or joint training activities) in relation to income or taxpayers benefiting from practices constituting harmful tax competition.

The recommendations also envisage that the OECD Model Tax Convention be modified to include such provisions or clarifications as are needed in respect of the earlier recommendations. To this effect, it is recommended that the Commentary on the Model Tax Convention be clarified to remove any uncertainty or ambiguity regarding the compatibility of domestic anti-abuse measures with the Model Tax Convention.

Source: OECD, 1998b.

developing countries and economies in transition has not been limited to concluding agreements with developed countries.[16] Indeed, since the 1980s, DTTs are increasingly being concluded between developing countries and between economies in transition (figure III.5).

Figure III.4. Number of countries and territories with DTTs, 1960-1997

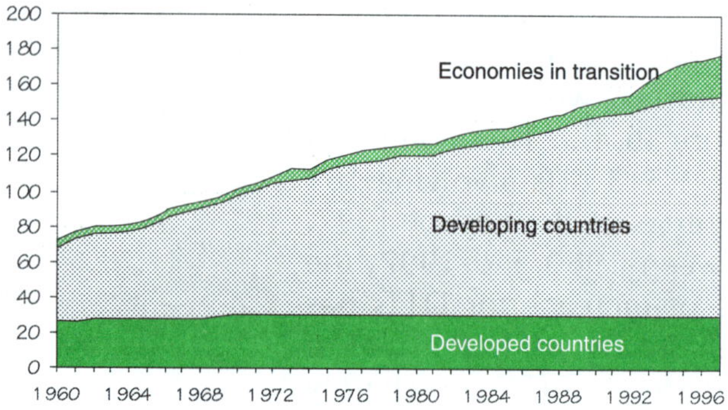

Source: UNCTAD, database on DTTs.

Other salient features of the universe of DTTs are (figures III.3-7):

* Whereas the top 10 countries with the highest number of BITs include two developing countries (China and the Republic of Korea) and two economies in transition (Romania and Poland) (UNCTAD, 1998b), *all* of the top ten countries with the highest number of DTTs concluded are developed countries.

* The most prolific countries concluding DTTs in the 1990s have been the economies in transition. The leaders are Poland and Hungary, with 59 and 53 treaties respectively. Of the economies in transition in Central Asia, Kazakhstan led with 17 treaties. The region also has the second highest number of DTTs per country and the third highest number of intraregional DTTs.

* Thirty-five African countries have signed a total of 247 DTTs. Of these, only 26 are with other African countries. The average number of DTTs per country grew rapidly for North Africa in the 1970s and 1980s, most of the growth being attributable to Egypt, Morocco and Tunisia.

* Countries in Asia and the Pacific intensified their DTT activity in the 1980s. During the 1960s they had signed only 29 tax treaties and hence had a very low average number of treaties per country in the region. Since then, 43 countries have signed a total of 560 treaties. Part of the growth in this number includes a substantial increase in the number of DTTs concluded within the region. Not surprisingly, the most active in the region were the East Asian countries.

Figure III.5. Number of intraregional DTTs, by region, 1960-1997

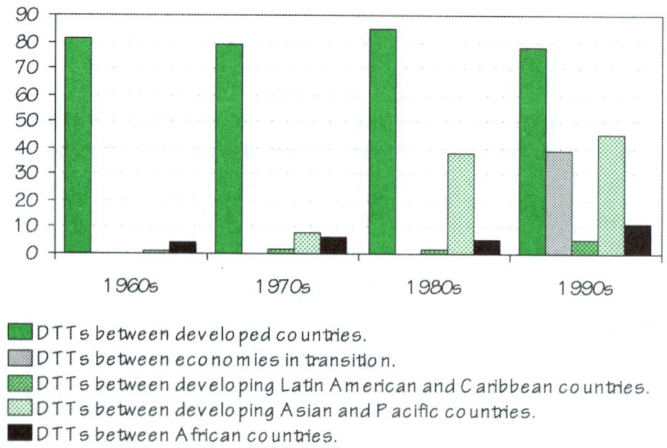

Source: UNCTAD, database on DTTs.

* Latin American and Caribbean countries have signed a total of

218 treaties, but only 9 of these are intraregional. Argentina and Brazil lead the region with 27 and 21 treaties, respectively. This region has one of the lowest number of DTTs per country.

* The United States has signed 154 DTTs, the highest number of any developed country, followed by the United Kingdom with 148 treaties.

* * *

Figure III.6. Number of DTTs concluded: top 20, 1997

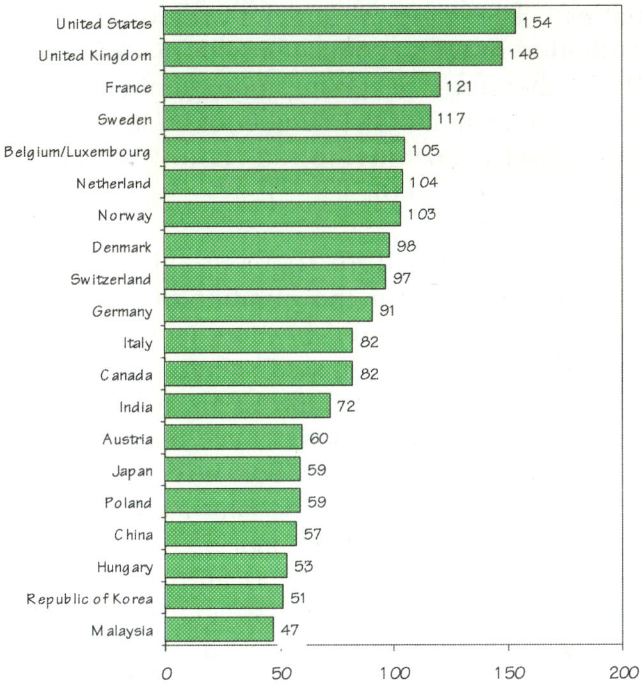

Source: UNCTAD, database on DTTs.

If the universe of DTTs is compared with the universe of BITs it needs to be kept in mind that both types of treaties have specific but distinct purposes. The principal purpose of DTTs is to deal with issues arising out of the allocation of revenues between countries; the principal purpose of BITs is to protect the investments that generate these revenues (and they do not deal with tax issues). They are therefore complementary. As developed countries were traditionally the principal home and host countries, DTT issues arose primarily between them, which is why most of the earlier DTTs were between developed countries. As developing countries were seen to involve certain risks for investors, BITs were initially concluded primarily between developed and developing countries; there are no BITs between developed countries. In the early 1960s, developed countries had signed 71 of 72 BITs with a developing country partner, whereas for DTTs the comparable number was 35 per cent. The differences in purpose have also manifested themselves at the country level. Perhaps the most significant observation in this regard is that some countries with a high propensity to sign tax treaties have a low propensity to sign BITs. For example, the United States, by the end of 1996, had signed only 39 BITs, but had signed 154 DTTs. Similarly, India had signed 72 DTTs, but only 14 BITs.

Figure III.7. Average number of DTTs per country, by region and decade, 1960s-1990s

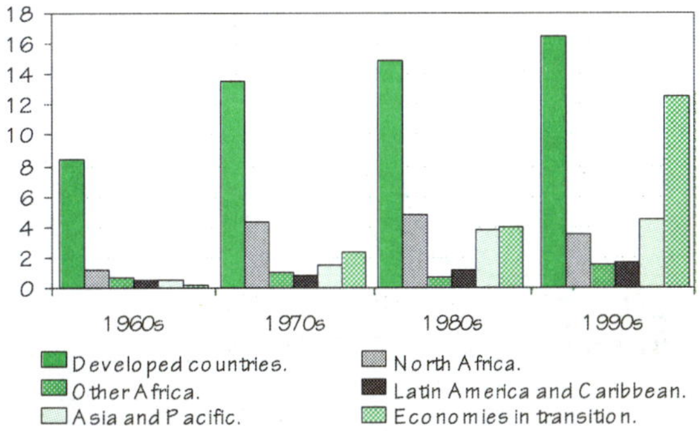

Source: UNCTAD, database on DTTs.

As developing countries became outward investors, and a good part of their investment was in other developing countries (especially in Asia), they also began to conclude both types of treaties. The regional and intraregional distribution of DTTs compared with that of BITs is, therefore, becoming more similar, with the exception of the number of treaties signed between developed countries (figures III.2 and III.8).

In general there is a positive relationship between the number of tax treaties and BITs signed by countries, a relationship that strengthened significantly in the 1980s and further in the 1990s (figure III.9).[17] Developed countries have almost the same propensity to sign both BITs and tax treaties (921 and 1,222); the same applies to countries from Africa (326 and 272), Asia and the Pacific (684 and 584) and Latin America and the Caribbean (330 and 228). Only the economies in transition have some catching up to do, having signed 770 BITs and only 299 DTTs.

Figure III.8. DTTs concluded in 1997, by country group[a]

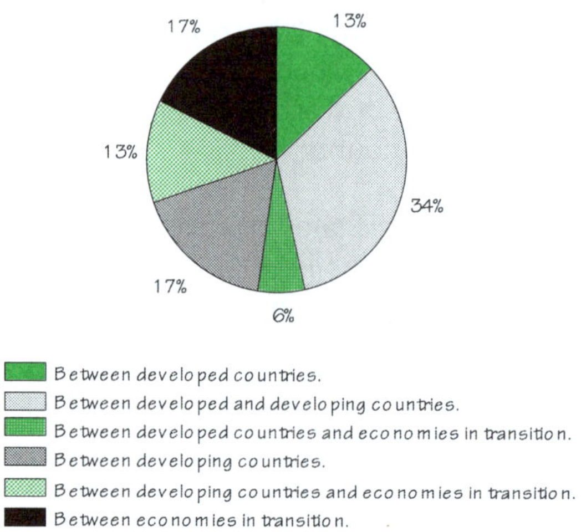

Source: UNCTAD, database on DTTs.

[a] In 1997, 108 DTTs were concluded.

Figure III.9. The correlation between DTTs and BITs signed by countries, by decade, 1960s-1990s

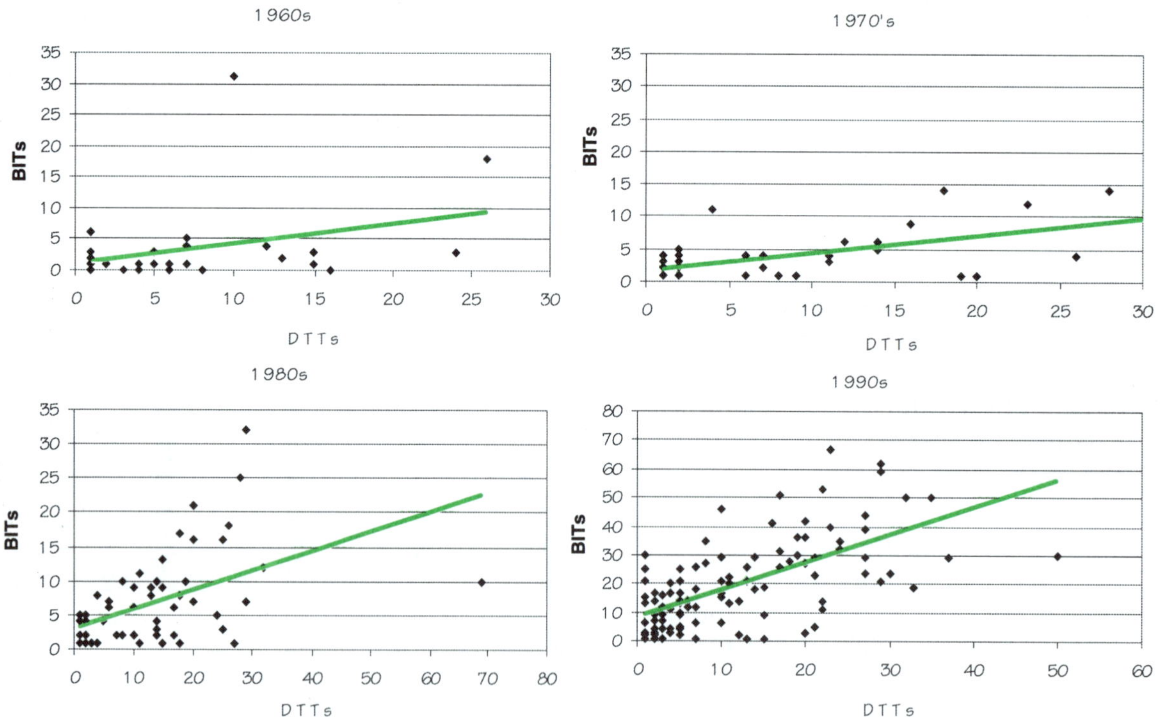

Source: UNCTAD, database on DTTs and BITs.

In sum, the universes of BITs and DTTs, although having started from different points and for different -- but complementary -- purposes, are evolving in the same direction. The propensity to sign both types of treaties has increased -- a reflection of the growing role of FDI in the world economy and the desire of countries to facilitate it.

Notes

1 The absence of a specific FDI law or code does not mean that there are no national laws bearing on FDI, in one way or another.

2 Frequent amendments of laws can cast doubts on the stability of a national legal regime, but the changes in FDI regimes referred to here are mainly in the direction of facilitating and attracting FDI and are thus contributing to improving the countries' investment climate.

3 As the granting of incentives can distort investment flows, their reduction has -- from this perspective -- a similar effect as, for example, a decrease of barriers to FDI.

4 On changes in FDI regimes before 1991, see UNCTC, 1978-1994.

5 According to article 5.1 of the TRIMs Agreement, WTO members, within 90 days of the date of entry into force of the WTO Agreement, shall notify the Council for Trade in Goods of all TRIMs they are applying that are not in conformity with the provisions of the Agreement.

6 "Declaration of Santiago", Santiago, Chile, 19 April 1998, mimeo..

7 Ministerial Declaration of San Jose, 19 March 1998, annex II.

8 "Working Programme for the FTAA Negotiating Groups" (FTAA, TNC/01), p. 5.

9 The joint statement of NGOs arising from that meeting was endorsed by over 600 development, consumer, environment, citizens, human rights and indigenous people organizations (WWF-UK, forthcoming).

10 The position of NGOs with respect to the MAI is reflected, among others, in Clarke, 1998; CI, 1996; CUTS, 1996; European Parliament, 1998; FOE-I, 1998; Korn, 1997; Oxfam, 1998; Public Citizen, 1998; WCC, 1998: WDM, 1997; WGA, 1997; WWF-International, 1996, 1997, 1998a, 1998b; WWF-UK, forthcoming.

11 These efforts build on previous initiatives in the United Nations. Indeed, as early as 1978, the United Nations Economic and Social Council negotiated an "International Agreement on Illicit Payments". In 1979, an almost complete draft of the Agreement was transmitted to the General Assembly which, however, decided to take no action on it (UNCTAD, 1996b, p .103).

12 A broad definition of double taxation treaties (apart from agreements on income and capital) would include bilateral agreements on inheritance, gifts and air or sea transport. These agreements generally contain rules with fiscal implications.

13 The non-discrimination clause is generally understood as a national treatment clause. The clause prohibits a treaty partner from granting to nationals of the other contracting party a treatment more burdensome than that granted to its own nationals, provided the former are in the same situation as the latter or a substantially similar one. It further ensures that none of the contracting parties treats companies in a differentiated way depending on whether their capital is held by its own nationals or by nationals of the other treaty partner. Mention should be made of the long-standing acceptance of the principle of non-discrimination in international fiscal relations. In fact, long before the emergence of the double taxation treaty at the end of the nineteenth century, the principle of non-discrimination in fiscal matters had been embodied in many different types of international agreements under which each contracting party granted nationals of the other contracting party the same treatment as its own nationals (consular or establishment conventions, treaties of friendship or commerce, etc.).

14 The international community has been dealing with the question of double taxation since 1928. For instance, the League of Nations was involved in the elaboration of rules governing the taxation of firms operating in two or more countries. In 1935, a draft convention was prepared.

15 This total includes 26 multilateral treaties, but neither model treaties nor the treaty between France and Quebec.

16 In this analysis, economies in transition include those in Central Asia.

17 A simple regression yields estimated positive coefficients ranging between 0.26 and 0.43, with the highest coefficient for the 1990s. All were significant at the .05 per cent level. There was a jump in the constant term in the regressions that should also be noted. In the 1960s regression it was 1.054, but in the 1980s regression for the 1960s it was 3.133.

CHAPTER IV

HOST COUNTRY DETERMINANTS OF FOREIGN DIRECT INVESTMENT

It is widely agreed that foreign direct investment (FDI) takes place when three sets of determining factors exist simultaneously (Dunning, 1993a):[1] the presence of ownership-specific competitive advantages in a transnational corporation (TNC), the presence of locational advantages in a host country, and the presence of superior commercial benefits in an intra-firm as against an arm's-length relationship between investor and recipient.

- The ownership-specific advantages (e.g. proprietary technology) of a firm -- if exploited optimally -- can compensate for the additional costs of establishing production facilities in a foreign environment and can overcome the firm's disadvantages vis-à-vis local firms.

- The ownership-specific advantages of the firm should be combined with the locational advantages of host countries (e.g. large markets or lower costs of resources or superior infrastructure).

- Finally, the firm finds greater benefits in exploiting both ownership-specific and locational advantages by internalization, i.e. through FDI rather than arm's-length transactions. This may be the case for several reasons. For one, markets for assets or production inputs (technology, knowledge or management) may be imperfect, if they exist at all, and may involve significant transaction costs or time-lags. For another, it may be in a firm's interest to retain exclusive rights to assets (e.g. knowledge) which confer upon it a significant competitive advantage (e.g. monopoly rents).

While the first and third conditions are firm-specific determinants of FDI, the second is location-specific and has a crucial influence on a host country's inflows of FDI. If only the first condition is met, firms will rely on exports, licensing or the sale of patents to service a foreign market. If the third condition is added to the first, FDI becomes the preferred mode of servicing foreign markets, but only in the presence of location-specific advantages. Within the trinity of conditions for FDI to occur, locational determinants are the only ones that host governments can influence directly.[2]

To explain differences in FDI inflows among countries and to formulate policies to capture inbound investment, it is necessary to understand how TNCs choose investment locations. This need has become all the more topical as discussions and negotiations on international investment frameworks -- whether at the bilateral, regional or multilateral levels -- have gathered momentum and the possibility of a multilateral framework on investment has raised questions as to whether, why and how international investment agreements matter for the location of FDI and the activities of TNCs. In particular, a key question (one similar to that faced by the creators of the post-Second World War multilateral trading system) is what effect, if any, a multilateral framework on investment might have for the growth and pattern of FDI.

The objective of this chapter is therefore to review the location-specific (host-country) determinants of FDI flows and stocks and to analyze how these have changed in a liberalizing and globalizing world economy. The impact of international investment frameworks on FDI is examined separately, since that is a matter of special interest to countries in the light of recent international discussions.

This review of host country determinants begins with the role of national policies and especially the liberalization of policies (a key factor in globalization) as FDI determinants. Then follows a review of business facilitation measures: as the world economy becomes more open to international business transactions, countries compete increasingly for FDI not only by improving their policy and economic determinants, but also by implementing pro-active facilitation measures that go beyond policy liberalization. While not as important as the other two sets of determinants, these measures are receiving increased attention. Economic determinants and, in particular, their changing significance in the context of liberalization and globalization are reviewed next, and the chapter ends with a review of issues related to the impact of international investment frameworks. (For a graphic overview of host country determinants of FDI, see table IV.1.)

Several caveats are required before reviewing the FDI determinants:

- Direct investment abroad is a complex venture. As distinct from trade, licensing or portfolio investment, FDI involves a long-term commitment to a business endeavour in a foreign country. It often involves the engagement of considerable assets and resources that need to be coordinated and managed across countries and to satisfy the principal requirements of successful investment, such as sustainable profitability and acceptable risk/profitability ratios. Typically, there are many host country factors involved in deciding where an FDI project should be located and it is often difficult to pinpoint the most decisive factor. Although the analysis that follows treats each of the three sets of determinants separately, the interrelationships among them must be borne in mind.

- The relative importance of different location-specific determinants depends on at least four aspects of investment: the motive for investment (e.g. resource-seeking or market-seeking FDI), the type of investment (e.g. new or sequential FDI), the sector of investment (e.g. services or manufacturing) and the size of investors (small and medium-sized TNCs or large TNCs). The relative importance of different determinants also *changes* as the economic environment evolves over time. It is therefore entirely possible that a set of host country determinants that explains FDI in a particular country at a given time changes as the structures of its domestic economy and of the international economy evolve. At the same time, there are also location-specific determinants that remain constant. In the analysis that follows, only the most important host country determinants will be examined.

- As a general principle, host countries that offer what TNCs are seeking, and/or host countries whose policies are most conducive to TNC activities, stand a good chance of attracting FDI. But firms also see locational determinants in their interaction with ownership-specific and internalization advantages in the broader context of their corporate strategies. These strategies aim, for example, at spreading or reducing risks, pursuing oligopolistic competition, and matching competitors' actions or looking for distinct sources of competitive advantage. In the context of different strategies, the same motive and the corresponding host country determinants can acquire different meanings. For example, the market-seeking motive can translate, in the case of one TNC, into the need to enter new markets to increase the benefits arising from multiplant operations; in the case of another TNC, it can translate into the desire to acquire market power; and for still another TNC, it can aim at diversifying markets as part of a risk-reducing strategy. This points to the need for host countries not only to understand the motives of potential investors but also to understand their strategies.[3]

Table IV.1. Host country determinants of FDI

Host country determinants
I. Policy framework for FDI • economic, political and social stability • rules regarding entry and operations • standards of treatment of foreign affiliates • policies on functioning and structure of markets (especially competition and M&A policies) • international agreements on FDI • privatization policy • trade policy (tariffs and NTBs) and coherence of FDI and trade policies • tax policy
II. Economic determinants
III. Business facilitation • investment promotion (including image-building and investment-generating activities and investment-facilitation services) • investment incentives • hassle costs (related to corruption, administrative efficiency, etc.) • social amenities (bilingual schools, quality of life, etc.) • after-investment services

Type of FDI classified by motives of TNCs	Principal economic determinants in host countries
A. Market-seeking	• market size and per capita income • market growth • access to regional and global markets • country-specific consumer preferences • structure of markets
B. Resource/ asset-seeking	• raw materials • low-cost unskilled labour • skilled labour • technological, innovatory and other created assets (e.g. brand names), including as embodied in individuals, firms and clusters • physical infrastructure (ports, roads, power, telecommunication)
C. Efficiency-seeking	• cost of resources and assets listed under B, adjusted for productivity for labour resources • other input costs, e.g. transport and communication costs to/from and within host economy and costs of other intermediate products • membership of a regional integration agreement conducive to the establishment of regional corporate networks

A. The national FDI policy framework

Core FDI policies consist of rules and regulations governing the entry and operations of foreign investors, the standards of treatment accorded to them, and the functioning of the markets within which they operate (UNCTAD, 1996a and 1997a). These policies can range from outright prohibition of FDI entry to non-discrimination in the treatment of foreign and domestic firms -- and even preferential treatment of foreign firms. They typically satisfy various objectives -- reducing or increasing FDI, influencing its sectoral composition or geographical origin, encouraging specific contributions to the economy and affecting ways in which these contributions are made. To achieve these objectives, FDI policies are usually accompanied by other policies that also influence investors' decisions.

Among these supplementary policies used to influence locational decisions, trade policy plays the most prominent role. For example, to attract FDI and to maximize its contributions to their import-substituting development strategies, countries in Latin America used a mix of protectionist trade policies combined with policies allowing FDI in manufacturing. Asian countries, in contrast, used both FDI and trade policies (e.g. exemptions from import duties) to encourage TNCs to contribute to their export-oriented economic strategies. For example, Hong Kong, China pursued laissez-faire trade and FDI policies. On the other hand, the FDI policies of such economies as the Republic of Korea, Taiwan Province of China and (previously) Japan were embedded in a broader set of industrial policies guiding and selectively inducing TNCs to link up with local firms to help increase local innovative and export capacities (UNCTAD, 1995a).

Other related policies may include privatization policies and policies determined by the international agreements a country has signed:

- Privatization is a special case of acquisition, as it involves purchases of firms from the state. It has two dimensions: an FDI-policy dimension and a competition-policy dimension. If privatization welcomes foreign investors, it broadens the scope of FDI. The competition-policy dimension becomes relevant if, in industries characterized as natural or near-natural monopolies, the sale of a privatized company to a domestic or foreign investor only means the transfer of a monopoly from the state to a private agent (UNCTAD, 1997a).

- International investment agreements provide an international dimension to national FDI policies. Some of them focus on insurance and protection, while others deal with broader issues (UNCTAD, 1996b).

Policies used intentionally to influence FDI and its location constitute the "inner ring" of the policy framework for FDI. The features of such a framework vary among countries and also vary over time in the same country. This has become obvious since the broad-front advance of more market-based economic policies began in the mid-1980s. Core FDI policies themselves have become more liberal and, coupled with more liberal trade policies, have contributed to a more cohesive policy framework. Globalization has led to yet further changes affecting the FDI framework which are discussed in greater detail in subsection 2 below.

The following section discusses FDI policy itself as a host country determinant. It focuses first on the role of liberalization in attracting FDI and then addresses the question of how the role of regulation has changed in a liberal global environment.

1. FDI policy as a determinant

The importance of core FDI policy as a determinant is best illustrated by the obvious fact that FDI cannot take place unless it is allowed to enter a country. Its potential relevance is also evident when policy changes sharply in the direction of more or less openness. It should be noted, however, that policy changes in the direction of openness differ in an important way from those in the direction of restriction: even when extensive, they cannot guarantee their desired results, as radically restrictive policies can pretty much guarantee theirs. Open policies are basically intended to induce FDI -- but the inducement may not be taken. Restrictive policies, on the other hand, such as sweeping nationalizations of foreign affiliates, can effectively close the door to FDI. (For the effects of more moderate restrictive policies, see the discussion of Canadian FDI policy in box IV.1.)

Box IV.1. Reviewing FDI in Canada

With the passage of the Foreign Investment Review Act (FIRA) in the early 1970s, Canada began to review inward FDI. FIRA was established as a result of rising government and popular concern with the high share of TNC sales and assets in a number of crucial industries of the Canadian economy. The Act required a review of "... most acquisitions of control by non-Canadians of existing businesses in Canada ... and the establishment of new businesses in Canada by non-Canadians who either did not already have a business in Canada or did not have a business to which the new business was or would be related" (Canada, Minister of Supply and Services, 1985, p. 3). It provided for a Foreign Investment Review Agency to advise the minister responsible for the administration of the Act to decide whether a proposed foreign investment would provide "...significant benefit to Canada..." (ibid., p.3). By the time the Act was repealed in 1985, more than 3,600 proposed foreign investments had been reviewed, of which 84 per cent were allowed and 16 per cent were either rejected or withdrawn, perhaps in anticipation of non-approval. The rate of rejections and withdrawal was much higher in resource based industries and in services than in manufacturing: 20 per cent and 19 per cent, respectively, against 8 per cent (ibid., table XXI).

Foreign-owned firms declined in importance "... as a result of changes in ownership mainly through government and private acquisitions..." (Canada, Statistics Canada, 1980, p. 19). The foreign share in Canadian output declined from the early 1970s through at least 1992, although not by a great deal, even though the restrictions on inward investment were largely removed in the 1980s. The reduction in foreign ownership resulted not only from the restrictions on new FDI contained in the Act but even more from the purchases of foreign-owned assets by Canadian public enterprises, such as the purchase of equity in Pacific Petroleums, Ltd. from the Phillips Petroleum Company of the United States by Petro-Canada at a total cost of about $1.5 billion in 1978 and 1979.[a] This single acquisition reduced the foreign share of Canadian assets by 1.6 percentage points and was accompanied at about the same time by a private purchase that caused Husky Oil limited to be reclassified from United States to Canadian control (Canada, Minister of Supply and Services, 1985, pp. 19-25). The Act and the purchases were not completely independent events: by reducing foreign firms' opportunities for growth, the Act increased the willingness of foreign parent firms to sell Canadian affiliates and lowered the prices that Canadian entities had to pay for them.

An econometric investigation of the effects of FIRA on the flow of United States direct investment into Canada found only a weak evidence of a negative impact (Kudrle, 1995). Among others, FIRA was found to have affected directly only new business cases and acquisitions, and not all FDI inflows. There was also no evidence suggesting that FIRA operated successfully as a discriminating monopsonist in its dealings with United States firms. However, FIRA might have affected FDI from other countries more unambiguously than United States FDI. The overall conclusion was that while more accurate measures of the existing variables or the addition of other variables might provide evidence of a more significant negative impact, FIRA may well have had a greater impact on Canada's popular image as a host to FDI than on either the volume or profitability of investment.

Source: UNCTAD.

[a] Another reason for the decline in foreign ownership could be the relative unattractiveness of Canada as a site for export-oriented manufacturing, given the very high exchange value of the Canadian dollar coupled with relatively low productivity.

Since the mid-1980s, the liberalization of FDI frameworks has become the dominant type of FDI policy change: of the 151 FDI policy changes that occurred during the period 1991-1997, 94 per cent contributed to creating more favourable conditions for FDI (chapter III, table III.2 and box IV.2). The most conspicuous example of the importance of FDI liberalization as a locational determinant (but by no means the only one) is the experience of Central and Eastern Europe. The stock of FDI in that region was less than $200 million in 1985 and less than $3 billion in 1990; it had risen to $66 billion by the end of 1997 (chapter IX). Perhaps the most significant change in FDI performance has occurred in China, where inward FDI stock rose from $3 billion in 1985 to $169 billion in 1997 (chapter VII). In China's Guangdong Province, the leader in FDI liberalization, the foreign-owned share of industrial production rose from 8 per cent in 1990 to 33 per cent in 1993 (Lipsey, Blomström and Ramstetter, 1998). In other countries, however, similar changes in FDI policies have not had similar effects on FDI. A case in point is Africa, where regulatory frameworks in most countries are quite open (chapter VI), but FDI inflows remain low. Other cases are furnished by some countries in Central and Eastern Europe, where the liberalization of FDI policies has had little effect on FDI flows, despite the impressive performance of the region as a whole. These examples underline the fact that open FDI policies are a necessary, but not a sufficient, host country determinant of investment.

Box IV.2. The process of liberalization of FDI policies

Defining FDI liberalization

FDI liberalization is a dynamic process that involves the following (box figure):

(a) the tempering or removal of those market distortions that result from restrictions applied specifically (and, hence, discriminatorily) to foreign investors (e.g. barriers to entry and operations) and from the granting or withholding of incentives and subsidies that discriminate in their favour or against them;

Box figure. The liberalization of FDI policies

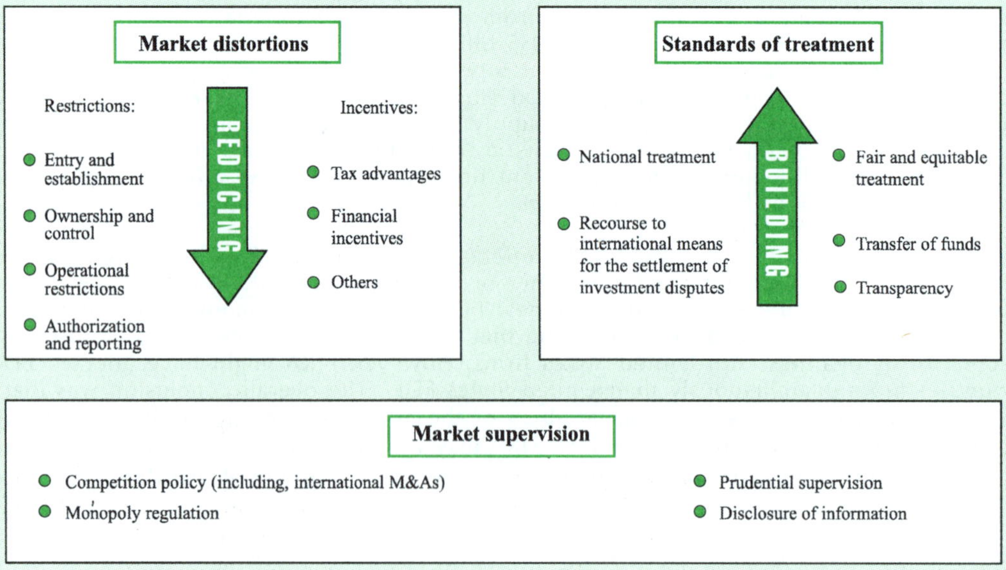

/...

(Box IV.2, continued)

(b) the strengthening of certain positive standards of treatment for foreign investors (e.g. national treatment, most-favoured-nation treatment, fair and equitable treatment); and

(c) the strenghtening of market supervision to ensure the proper functioning of the market (e.g. competition rules, disclosure of information, prudential supervision).

While the first two elements are indeed central to FDI liberalization, their overall beneficial effects depend to a considerable extent on the presence of effective supervision of the market.

A distinction must be drawn between policies aimed at liberalizing FDI and policies aimed at creating a favourable investment climate and, especially, at attracting or promoting FDI. The distinction is not an easy one in practice. The two types of policies are closely linked in a means-end relationship: the principal objective of both is to attract FDI. Liberalization, however, is not the only possible method of attracting FDI, nor is it necessarily the most effective one under all conditions; a variety of restrictive measures have also been used to attract FDI, for example, closing the market for further entry.

The broader context within which foreign affiliates operate inside a country is also relevant and, as liberalization progresses, it becomes increasingly visible. Indeed, certain aspects of the internal normative framework, such as the existence of a comprehensive legal framework for business activities, are essential to give meaning and effect to the liberalization of FDI. A properly functioning legal order, including well-functioning courts, is also required to ensure predictability and certainty of business operations. Moreover, for maximum effect, given the close interlinkages between FDI, trade and the dissemination of technology, the policy frameworks for all three would need to be consistent and moving in the same direction.

It follows from the foregoing that, overall, the liberalization of FDI regimes does not imply a weakening of the role of government, but rather a redefinition of some of its functions and the strengthening of others. Indeed, the liberalization of FDI involves difficult policy choices among desired outcomes and significant trade-offs between objectives (UNCTAD, 1994a).

How far has the liberalization of FDI gone?

Reducing restrictions

Today, all countries admit FDI in principle. On the other hand, no single country grants unrestricted right of entry to all activities. However, the number of activities in which FDI is barred or restricted has been considerably reduced, especially in the manufacturing sector but also increasingly in natural resources and services, as most countries have gradually moved to open traditionally closed industries, often in the course of their privatization programmes (e.g. telecommunications, public transport, other public utilities and the construction of public infrastructures, fishing, mining, oil and energy), although some restrictions remain. Ownership requirements and control restrictions (through, for example, "golden shares") are limited to certain strategic industries, particularly after privatization (e.g. broadcasting). Fade-out requirements have virtually disappeared. Most countries have eliminated authorization requirements for the entry of greenfield FDI, replacing them with registration, although some authorization requirements and restrictions on the number of foreign firms allowed remain in many countries (both developed and developing) for some "strategic" industries (e.g. banking and finance, air transport, broadcasting, telecommunications) and often apply to both foreign and domestic firms. There are also indications that certain operational conditions - such as performance requirements or those relating to the hiring of foreign managerial personnel - are becoming less significant. Certain types of performance requirements have been reduced or have become more transparent as a result of international commitments and transitional measures under the TRIMs Agreement (see chapter III above). Others, not covered under the TRIMs Agreement, have become more focussed and tend to be voluntary, required mainly in return for incentives. These have also become more targeted and tend to discriminate less either in favour of or against foreign investors. In a number of developed countries

/...

Similar variations in the effects on FDI flows may be found when sectoral policies are liberalized. In some industries liberalization has produced rapid and significant responses by foreign investors, in others not. In communications and public utilities, the TNC response to policy liberalization has been swift, as exemplified by the rapid increase of the share of these industries in the total outward FDI stock of the United States from below one per cent in 1990 to nearly three per cent in 1996.[4] In manufacturing industries, on the other hand, especially in industries characterized by simple technologies, standardized goods, intense competition and low transportation costs -- those producing pencils, towels or toothbrushes -- liberalization has not led to more FDI and trade and domestic production have remained the dominant modes of serving local markets. The reason for the ineffectiveness of FDI liberalization in such cases is not necessarily the absence of locational advantages but the scarcity of firms with ownership-specific advantages and, where there are advantages, lack of motive to internalize them.

In brief, the negative effects of restrictive policies are much stronger than the positive effects of liberal policies. A liberal policy framework "determines" FDI in the sense that it *enables* TNCs to invest in a host country: it allows, and may even encourage, FDI but there is no guarantee that investment will actually occur. Policy liberalization is a necessary but not a sufficient determinant of FDI and other determinants have to come into play for investment to flow into the country.

(Box IV.2, concluded)

(for example, among members of the European Union) certain types of incentives are now prohibited or subject to ceilings. Exchange restrictions on the repatriation of profits and capital have become exceptional measures reserved for cases of serious balance-of-payments difficulties in most countries. Most restrictions on outward FDI have also disappeared in developed countries and are being gradully reduced in a number of developing countries and transitional economies.

Strengthening positive standards of treatment

The standards of non-discrimination and national treatment of FDI after its entry into the host country are now reflected in the laws and international agreements of many countries (often with certain qualifications and exceptions), as are the principles of due process and fair and equitable treatment. Host countries, including many developing countries, are also granting foreign investors legal protection and guarantees against non-commercial risks. The number of developing countries that have signed bilateral, regional and multilateral agreements dealing with the treatment and protection of FDI after entry has increased dramatically in the 1990s, after most countries in Latin America and in Central and Eastern Europe took to signing them.

Strengthening market controls

An increasing number of countries in all regions have adopted or are strengthening antitrust laws. The number of countries having competition laws has increased from less than 40 in 1980 to over 70 in 1997 (UNCTAD, 1997a, figure V.1). Most have also established mechanisms to supervise international mergers and acquisitions, stock exchanges, and financial markets.

In sum, the trend towards a liberalization of FDI policies is indeed pervasive and has led to a convergence of FDI regimes, although numerous and at times significant differences remain. To the extent that FDI policy frameworks become similar, specific differences -- other things being equal -- become more important influences on the locational decisions of investment projects.

Source: UNCTAD.

2. The impact of globalization

The relationship between FDI policies and globalization runs both ways: each affects the other. Indeed, it was the liberalization of national policy frameworks that helped unleash one of the key driving forces of globalization as we know it today: increasing international production by TNCs. At the same time, progress in the liberalization of trade, as well as technological progress in telecommunications and transportation, permitted TNCs to pursue increasingly regional and global strategies, and to integrate their production structures on a regional or global basis, which in turn creates incentives to liberalize FDI policies. This mutually reinforcing process has in fact shaped international production in recent years and led to its integration at a deeper level than the shallow integration based on arm's-length trade and flows of financial capital (UNCTAD, 1993a).

The accelerating process of FDI liberalization has led countries to extend more open policies into industries long considered sensitive (e.g. telecommunications, air transportation) and to permit forms of FDI entry previously considered less desirable, such as the establishment of fully owned subsidiaries, M&As and participation in privatization programmes. This has, in turn, provided TNCs with an ever-increasing choice of locations and they have become more selective and demanding as regards other host country determinants.

The outcome of all this is that, while the liberalization of FDI frameworks has contributed to an acceleration of FDI flows by creating more "space" for them, a process of diminishing returns has set in and liberal FDI policy is increasingly losing its effectiveness as a locational determinant of FDI. Competing intensely with one another for FDI and finding that liberal policies are no longer enough, host countries have increasingly come to realize the importance of adopting proactive measures to facilitate business transactions by foreign investors and of improving the economic determinants of FDI.

The speeding up of liberalization and the simultaneous weakening of its effectiveness as a determinant of FDI has extended the scope of FDI policy frameworks. In particular, it has drawn attention to other policies that may affect FDI but that have not been specifically considered in this context in the past. These could be seen as constituting the "outer ring" of policies in the FDI context, as distinct from the core policies directly used to influence FDI, the "inner ring" of policies discussed earlier. (The dividing line between these two types of policies is increasingly being blurred, as outer-ring policies move into the inner ring.) Broadly speaking, outer-ring policies can be divided into macroeconomic and macro-organizational policies:

Macroeconomic policies. These are mainly monetary and fiscal policies, including those affecting taxes and exchange rates:

- Monetary and fiscal policies, which determine the parameters of economic stability such as the rate of inflation and the state of external and budgetary balances, influence all types of investment. Since they determine interest rates and thus the cost of capital in a host country, they directly affect one of the determinants of the investment decision, although the effects of interest rates on FDI are smaller than on domestic investment because TNCs normally have a greater choice of sources of financing.[5]

- Fiscal policies also determine general tax levels, including corporate and personal tax rates and thereby influence inward FDI. Other things being equal, a country with lower corporate tax rates should stand a greater chance of attracting an FDI project than a country with higher rates.[6] Personal tax rates may affect managers' choices as regards the location of regional headquarters and may affect the hiring of foreign personnel.

- Exchange-rate policy is related to stability and may influence FDI decisions by affecting the prices of host country assets, the value of transferred profits, and the competitiveness of foreign affiliate exports.[7]

Macro-organizational policies. These affect patterns of resource allocation as well as the structure and organization of economic activities and include the following:

- First, there are structural policies influencing the industry composition of manufacturing (e.g. policies vis-à-vis sunset and sunrise industries), the spatial composition of economic activities (e.g. regional development policies), the functional composition of activities (e.g. R&D policies), and the composition of activities by type of ownership and intensity of competition (e.g. deregulation of service industries). Some of these policies have been used in the FDI context for some time, although with different degrees of intensity. A case in point is technology policy. In the past, developing countries encouraged the transfer of technology through FDI and some also tried to control the outflow of technology payments. Recently, these policies have been oriented more towards building technological capacity. They have encouraged links, for example, between foreign investors' research and domestic industries through the provision of tax credits, or provided information and services to facilitate technological partnerships between domestic and foreign companies. The realization that almost all of these policies can affect FDI is relatively recent. It is now widely understood that environmental policies may influence FDI or that policies vis-à-vis small and medium-sized enterprises may facilitate FDI through creating a pool of potential suppliers of competitive intermediate products to foreign affiliates.

- There are also policies determining the functioning of factor markets, such as labour-market policies that may have either a discouraging or an encouraging impact on inward FDI.

- Finally, there are policies that affect the supply and quality of productive resources in a host country. Such policies can affect not only the quantity of FDI a country receives but also its quality. Thus, educational and health policies that raise the supply and quality of human capital in a country or policies that promote infrastructure development can improve a country's locational advantages substantially and give it an edge over others.

To sum up, one of the consequences of the worldwide trend towards the liberalization of FDI policies has been the realization by countries that, as their FDI policies proper become similar, the value of these policies as tools to influence locational decisions becomes less pronounced. Host countries are instead increasingly evaluated by potential foreign investors on the basis of a broader set of policies within which FDI policies are embedded. This has in turn several consequences. First, it vastly expands the *number* of policies constituting what investors consider a good investment climate. Second, it makes greater demands on the *effectiveness* of FDI-related policies: to be effective, they need to be coherent within a broader set of policies. Third, it leads to the emergence of *new policy areas* that cut across traditional policies such as those affecting the production and use of created assets, a new type of resource increasingly sought by TNCs. Finally, and most generally, it leads to the realization that an effective national FDI policy framework requires a thorough understanding of the determinants of TNC decisions regarding foreign investment, including in particular the broader corporate strategies of TNCs, and requires also the long-term improvement of the economic determinants of investment. Before discussing this most important set of determinants, the chapter takes up business facilitation measures as FDI determinants.

B. Business facilitation

From the perspective of foreign business the liberalization of core FDI policies discussed in the preceding section -- consisting of reducing barriers for inward FDI, strengthening standards of treatment for foreign investors and assuring the proper functioning of markets -- is, above all, seen as an enabling act aimed at creating a framework that establishes, by and large, a level-playing field for all investors and thus makes it possible for *them* to take action.[8] This enabling act is increasingly complemented by proactive measures, aimed at facilitating the business that foreign investors undertake in a host country (table IV.1). Business facilitation measures include promotion efforts, the provision of incentives to foreign investors, the reduction of the "hassle costs" of doing business in a host country (e.g. reducing or eliminating corruption and improving administrative efficiency), and the provision of amenities that contribute to the quality of life of expatriate personnel. Few of these measures are entirely new; what is new is that, in a globalizing world economy, such measures have proliferated rapidly and become increasingly routine, pervasive and sophisticated.

Historically, the need for promotional action arose when countries changed their attitudes and policies towards the role of FDI in their development from negative to positive, but investors did not respond to the changes or responded more weakly than desired. Such countries had to deal with an image problem vis-à-vis foreign investors, who continued to perceive them as places not friendly to FDI. Ireland and Canada, for example, at one point undertook information and advertising campaigns aimed at changing unfavourable perceptions concerning their investment climates (Wells and Wint, 1990). As many developing countries and virtually all economies in transition have faced similar problems, their liberalization efforts have been increasingly complemented by promotional programmes, typically executed by investment promotion agencies (IPAs) that were newly established or transformed from earlier screening and monitoring agencies.

With time, promotional activity has become more important. Countries that have changed their FDI policies, countries that wanted to regain investors' attention, and countries that were invisible or unattractive to investors have all begun to resort to it (UNCTAD, 1995a, p. 275). Governments have become increasingly aware that it is one thing to change a policy, and quite another to get the information to FDI decision makers -- let alone convince them to make an investment).[9] Promotional actions were also taken to shorten the delayed reactions of investors to emerging investment opportunities' or to help investors, especially small and medium-sized firms, discover new opportunities that they would not find on their own. Such actions were also aimed at shortening psychic distances between host and home countries.[10] Finally, as mentioned in the last section, the weakening impact of liberalization by itself has induced governments to "want to do more" to influence FDI location decisions. Consequently, the number of countries with investment promotion programmes -- be they developed, developing or in transition -- has increased rapidly. If membership of the World Association of Investment Promotion Agencies (WAIPA) can be taken as a proxy, at least 95 countries had such programmes in 1997 (annex table A.IV.1).[11] These programmes have become one more tool governments use to attract foreign investors,[12] together with bilateral investment treaties (box IV.3), membership in the Multilateral Investment Guarantee Agency and, perhaps, investment incentives (box IV.4).

Intensified competition for FDI has also led to more proactive policies aimed at actually bringing in FDI and servicing it when received. Investment-generating measures can consist

Box IV.3. Bilateral investment treaties: similarities and differences

An important characteristic of bilateral investment treaties (BITs) is the considerable uniformity in the broad principles underlying the agreements, coupled with numerous variations in the specific formulations employed. There is a core of provisions that is common to a large number of BITs, namely:

- the definition of investment is asset-based, broad and open-ended so that it can accommodate new forms of foreign investment; it includes tangible and intangible assets and generally applies to existing as well as new investments;
- entry and establishment of investment is encouraged, although typically subject to national laws and regulations, i.e. most BITs do not grant a right of establishment;
- most treaties provide for fair and equitable treatment, often qualified by more specific standards, such as prohibiting arbitrary or discriminatory measures or prescribing a duty to observe commitments concerning investment;
- most treaties specify that, when there are various agreements applying to the investments covered, the more favourable provision among them applies; treaties now grant national treatment, the principle also often being subject to qualifications (to take into account the different characteristics between national and foreign firms) and exceptions (relating mainly to specific industries or economic activities, or to policy measures such as incentives and taxation);
- a guarantee of most-favoured-nation (MFN) treatment, subject to some standardized exceptions, is found in virtually all BITs;
- virtually all BITs recognize the right of the host country to expropriate subject to the condition that it be for a public purpose, non-discriminatory, in accordance with due process and accompanied by compensation; the standards for determining the modalities of compensation are often described in different terms that could potentially result in similar outcomes;
- a guarantee of free transfer of payments related to investment is common to virtually all BITs, although it is often qualified by exceptions applicable in cases of balance-of-payments difficulties;
- a State-to-State dispute-settlement provision is also virtually universal; and
- an investor-to-State dispute-settlement provision has become a standard practice, with a growing number of BITs providing the investor with a choice of mechanisms.

In addition, some BITs include one or several of the following provisions:

- a requirement that the host country ensure investors access to information on national laws;
- a prohibition on imposing performance requirements - such as local content, export conditions and employment requirements - on the investor as a condition for the entry or operation of an investment;
- a commitment to permit or facilitate entry and sojourn of foreign personnel in connection with the establishment and operation of an investment; and
- a guarantee of national and most-favoured-nation treatment on entry and establishment.

Source: UNCTAD, forthcoming b.

of direct mail or telephone campaigns or industry-specific investment missions. But the most important and promising -- though at the same time difficult and costly -- activity is targeting firms that are likely to respond to promotion efforts and to invest in a given host country, especially in activities considered particularly desirable from the host country's point of view (Wells, 1993; Wint, 1993). A case study of ten IPAs from developed and developing countries, undertaken in the late 1980s, showed clearly the shift of focus of these agencies' activities from image-building to investment-generation (Wells and Wint, 1990, p. 15). And a survey conducted by UNCTAD in the mid-1990s among 81 IPAs confirmed that a great majority of them "had a system for identifying and attracting investors". When asked, however, if such a system was computerized, only 28 per cent of IPAs from developing countries and 53 per cent from developed countries answered "yes", indicating that many of these systems may be quite rudimentary (UNCTAD, 1997b, p. 30).

Investment-facilitation services are another increasingly important component of promotional activities in both developed and developing countries (Young and Hood, 1994). Initially, they were introduced to increase the efficiency of FDI liberalization, which aroused investors' interest but did not necessarily lead to investment, because bureaucratic barriers facing investors after a project was approved were frequently so high that they discouraged would-be investors. Such services consist of counselling, accelerating the various stages of the approval process and providing assistance in obtaining all the needed permits. In developing countries and some developed countries, they frequently led to the creation of "one-stop shops" -- single organizations supposed to be able to handle all matters related to FDI projects (Wells and Wint, 1991).

Under the pressures of competition for FDI in a globalizing economy, investment-facilitation services have been extended to include after-investment services, that is, services rendered to established foreign affiliates regarding day-to-day operational matters (Young and Hood, 1994, p. 54).[13] The reasons for the inclusion of these services in investment promotion efforts are twofold. One is the realization that sequential investment -- that is the reinvestment of earnings by established foreign affiliates -- can be a significant source of FDI (in the case of United States foreign affiliates it can account for up to a half of the annual outflows of FDI). Secondly, there is a growing awareness that satisfied investors are the best evidence of a good investment climate in a host country and that, therefore, they can help to attract other investors. Needless to say, if the expansion of a foreign affiliate is not possible for reasons beyond the reach of the host country (because, for example, corporate strategies have set other priorities), a no less important objective is to *retain* the existing level of FDI, i.e. to prevent divestment (UNCTAD, 1995a, p. 279). As FDI stock increases, the weight of these considerations among various factors guiding promotional decisions also increases. According to the UNCTAD survey, cited above, 78 per cent of the IPAs stated that they have tried to develop a process of encouraging foreign investors to reinvest through upstream and downstream linkage activities (UNCTAD, 1997b, p. 36). However, although after-investment services have become one of the standard functions undertaken by IPAs, there seems to be considerable room for improvement in them (Young and Hood, 1994, p. 46). But then it may be that, although countries are aware of the importance of after-investment services, IPAs face budgetary constraints which have not yet allowed them to translate this awareness into workable comprehensive programmes.

The story as regards other business facilitation measures (table IV.1) and especially as regards investment incentives is largely similar. Most of these, if not all, were known before. For example, incentives have been used to compensate foreign affiliates for additional costs related to performance requirements imposed by host country governments. In a global economy, performance requirements are used less frequently, because they are increasingly considered an unnecessary hassle which might discourage foreign investors.[14] But the use of investment incentives has proliferated. The range of incentives and the number of countries, provinces and local authorities that offer them has increased considerably since the mid-1980s (UNCTAD, 1995a, p. 290; and box IV.4). Sometimes, countries even engage in direct competition for specific investment projects with financial and other incentives, and such competition can be very costly.

Box IV.4. Incentives to attract FDI

What are incentives?

Incentives are any measurable economic advantage afforded to specific enterprises or categories of enterprises by (or at the direction of) a government, in order to encourage them to behave in a certain manner. They include measures either to increase the rate of return of a particular FDI undertaking, or to reduce (or redistribute) its costs or risks. They do not include broader non-discriminatory policies, relating to the availability of physical and business infrastructures, the general legal regime for FDI, the general regulatory and fiscal regime for business operations, free repatriation of profits or the granting of national treatment. While these policies certainly bear on the location decisions of TNCs, they are not FDI incentives per se. The main types of incentives used are fiscal incentives (e.g. reduction of the standard corporate income-tax rate, investment and reinvestment allowances, tax holidays, accelerated depreciation, exemptions from import duties), financial incentives (e.g. government grants, subsidized credits, government equity participation, government insurance at preferential rates) and market preferences (e.g. granting of monopoly rights, protection from import competition, closing the market for further entry, preferential government contracts). Other types of incentives frequently used include preferential treatment on foreign exchange and subsidized dedicated infrastructure and services.

Economic rationale for incentives

The economic rationale behind incentives is to correct the failure of markets to reflect the wider benefits arising from externalities in production -- for example, those resulting from economies of scale, the creation of widely diffused knowledge and the upgrading of skills of mobile workers. Incentives can thus be justified to cover the wedge between the private and the social returns on an investment. In a more dynamic context of growth and development, incentives can be justified to correct the failure of markets to reflect the gains that can accrue over time from declining unit costs and learning by doing -- the classic infant-industry argument used in a very different context. Incentives can also be justified to compensate investors for lost return due to other government interventions (for example, duty remissions on imports or performance requirements) or for carrying certain public costs where a government lacks the institutional capacity to bear them itself. In sum, incentives can serve a number of development purposes. However, they also have the potential to introduce economic distortions (especially when they are more than marginal) that are analogous to subsidies on trade, and they involve financial and administrative costs. It is not in the public interest that the cost of incentives granted exceed the value of the benefits to the public.

Competition for FDI with incentives

Governments use incentives to attract FDI, to steer investment into favoured industries, activities or regions, or to influence the character of an investment, as, for example, when technology-intensive investment is being sought. Today, most investment incentives are directed to domestic and foreign investors alike, although sometimes only foreign investors can access certain incentives (as when special incentive packages are geared towards large projects or specific foreign investors, or where advanced technologies are involved that can only be provided by foreign investors). The range of incentives available to foreign investors and the number of countries that offer incentives have both increased considerably since the mid-1980s, as barriers to FDI and trade have declined. In addition, many countries are experiencing increasing incentives competition among regional or even local

/...

(Box IV.4, concluded)

authorities to attract FDI. Also, incentives are becoming increasingly focused and targeted and are sometimes contingent upon certain conditions being met by the investor. In fact, countries often offer a broad array of options linked to different objectives, thus further multiplying the number of incentive programmes available to foreign investors. However, it is difficult to discern clear patterns across countries and regions on the type of industries or activities favoured by incentive programmes. An increasing number of countries target investment activity in industries involving technology and high value-added (such as electronics, robotics, computer software) and in infrastructure projects. While manufacturing industries are still the main focus of incentive programmes, some governments continue to offer incentives in agriculture, fisheries, mining and oil exploration. Some countries are also offering incentives to encourage companies to locate specific corporate functions within their territories (say, to set up regional headquarters). As a general rule, developed countries make more use of financial incentives than of fiscal ones, partly because fiscal incentives are less flexible and their adoption involves more difficult parliamentary procedures. However, this pattern is reversed in developing countries, presumably because these countries lack the resources needed to provide financial incentives. Market incentives have played an important role until recently, although market reforms and the introduction of competition policy in an increasing number of countries are narrowing the scope for these incentives.

Whatever the rationale for FDI incentives, they are ultimately successful only to the extent that they succeed in attracting investment to a country away from another; if it were otherwise, and the investment were to take place anyway, the incentive would be superfluous. In an open world economy, in which barriers to FDI are falling, many countries have increased their incentives with the intention of diverting investment away from competing host countries. Competition for FDI with incentives is pervasive not only among national governments but also among sub-national authorities. When governments compete to attract FDI, there will be a tendency to overbid, i.e. bidders may offer more than the wedge between public and private returns. The effects can be both distorting and inequitable since the costs are ultimately borne by the public and hence represent transfers from the local community to the ultimate owners of the foreign investment. In such competition for FDI, the poorer countries are relatively disadvantaged.

The effect of incentives on investment decisions

In spite of this competition, there is considerable evidence to suggest that incentives are a relatively minor factor in the locational decisions of TNCs relative to other locational advantages, such as market size and growth, production costs, skill levels, adequate infrastructure, economic stability and the quality of the general regulatory framework. For example, in a survey of 30 TNCs covering 74 investment projects in four industries -- automobile, computer, food processing and petrochemicals - many companies reported that incentives were frequently not even considered and simply made an already attractive country more attractive. Investment decisions were made mainly on the basis of economic and long-term strategic considerations concerning inputs, production costs and markets (Guisinger, 1983, 1989, and 1992). Although there has been considerable recent research on the effects of incentives on overall FDI flows, the conclusions have tended to support the research undertaken in past decades. However, as regards individual investment projects, there is increasing evidence that when the location is broadly determined, e.g. a member country of the European Union or a country with a large national market, then incentives can play a decisive role in choosing, e.g. between Scotland and Wales; Ireland and Scotland; or North of England and North of France (Bridge, 1998; Dunning, 1998c; Mytelka, forthcoming and Phelps, et al, 1998).

Foreign investors may respond differently to different types of incentives depending on their strategies. A number of studies that have analyzed incentive preferences by type of investor (Reuber et al., 1973) found that export-oriented investors seeking inexpensive labour valued fiscal incentives more highly than market protection or other incentives. Market-seeking investors, on the other hand, value market protection more than fiscal incentives. In the case of regional incentives, financial incentives, particularly grants, seem to have a greater impact on investors' decisions than fiscal incentives. In recent years, a wide variety of incentives are being offered for foreign investors to transfer advanced technologies and attract R&D facilities (including tax reductions, subsidized infrastructure and land and industrial parks); governments have also intervened through the creation of markets (with defence expenditures and government purchasing) and research funding. However, a recent study (Vallanchain and Satterthwaite, 1992) concluded that fiscal incentives and financial aid did not influence location, while the establishment of enterprise zones and research parks did.

In brief, while incentives do not rank high among the main FDI determinants, their impact on locational choices can be perceptible at the margin, especially for projects that are cost-oriented and mobile.

Source: UNCTAD, 1996a.

The proliferation of similar policies and practices is driven by demonstration effects, which are driving forces in any competition and increasingly lead to benchmarking, especially in a regional context: IPAs look at what their competitors are doing and try to catch up.[15] Even better, they try to distinguish themselves from their competitors by doing more and leaving them behind. The result is a certain trend towards a convergence of policies and practices, not only in the area of FDI liberalization but also in the area of business facilitation. Convergence is taking place as regards instruments which are inexpensive and easy to use as well as promotional measures that are expected to have an immediate effect on a country's investment climate.[16] Such measures are thus quite different from actions aimed at ensuring political and economic stability, the establishment of a sound macroeconomic framework, the upgrading of a country's human resources or the strengthening of its physical infrastructure -- all of which take time (UNCTAD, 1994a, p. 311).

With respect to the effectiveness of business facilitation measures (and especially of promotional measures and incentives) as FDI determinants, it has to be kept in mind that they can only play a supporting role and will rarely be decisive factors. If a host country does not have some basic economic determinants (discussed in the next section) in place, or if other components of the investment climate are unsatisfactory, no promotional efforts or incentives will help it to attract significant FDI.[17] Highly publicized cases of successful investment promotion activities underline this very clearly. One frequently cited case of successful investment-generating activities relates to United States FDI in the Malaysian electronics industry, which was generated through investor targeting by Malaysia's Industrial Development Authority (MIDA) including specific investment missions to capital-exporting countries, particularly focusing on the electronics sector of the United States (UNCTAD, 1995a, pp. 276-277). While this is a good example of successful investment generation by an IPA, this success was possible because of the presence of broader economic and other factors such as the availability of productive human resources at competitive costs, well-developed transportation and communication infrastructure, a stable and open economy, and the widespread use of English (UNCTAD, 1994a, p. 74). Moreover, these factors were well-grounded in a broader effort aimed at establishing a favourable investment environment and covering in a comprehensive manner all areas of importance to investors (Jegathesan, 1998). Malaysia followed the earlier example of Singapore, which had identified Apple Computers as a potential investor and persuaded it to invest there even before the company had invested elsewhere abroad (Wells, 1993, p. 51). But again, this was possible because Singapore could capitalize on its economic determinants which were being continuously upgraded. Examples from other parts of the world, such as those of Ireland and Costa Rica (which recently succeeded in attracting a $500 million FDI project by Intel), show a similar pattern: promotional efforts played a certain role (box IV.5), but this role was possible because of economic determinants that were continuously upgraded by government policies in such areas as education, infrastructure or the nurturing of small potential suppliers to foreign affiliates.

As regards incentives alone, there is much evidence that, overall, they are not an important element in the set of factors that determine inward FDI. Once, however, a decision has been *made* to undertake FDI in a given region or a given country, incentives may have an impact on influencing the precise choice of location within the region or country. If one country in a region or one locality in a country offers incentives and another does not, then, other things being equal, incentives can influence locational decisions between these countries and localities, tilting the balance in favour of the incentives provider (UNCTAD, 1995a, p. 299; and Jegathesan, 1998, p.18).

To conclude, one should not overestimate the importance of business facilitation-related FDI determinants. Applied alone, business facilitation measures are not sufficient for FDI to take place. Neither are they necessary, as is an enabling policy framework for FDI. There

Box IV.5. Ireland's FDI policy

Foreign ownership of firms operating in Ireland was not allowed between the early 1930s and the late 1950s with the exception of firms established before 1932. The objective of this policy, laid down in the Control of Manufactures Act, was to reserve the gains from infant-industry protection for locally owned firms. In the course of the 1950s, industrial policy began to reverse, with the abolition of the Control of Manufactures Act and the establishment of the Shannon Free Airport Development Company in 1959.

In the 1980s, investment promotion strategies became more focused on certain attractive sectors. The strategy had three core elements:

- selecting leading, high value-added industries, namely electronics, computer software, financial services, medical instruments, and international services;
- creating specialized industrial clusters in designated locations; and
- promoting links to domestic firms, for example, through marketing and R&D (Ruane and Görg, 1997; Price Waterhouse, 1989, p.31; Tillett, 1996).

The Industrial Development Agency (IDA) of Ireland took a central role in coordinating efforts involving both national and local authorities and developing a range of incentives and promotional efforts to approach potential foreign investors systematically (IDA, 1998; Tillett, 1996). Fiscal incentives have included fixed-asset grants designed to reduce the cost of building or refurbishing factory premises, grants for financing new machinery and equipment, and grants for establishing R&D facilities (up to 50 per cent of the costs of fixed assets and a share of other expenses of such facilities). When Ireland joined the European Economic Community in 1973, grants favouring exporters had to be extended to all newly established firms (Ruane and Görg, 1997).

With respect to regional development policy, the IDA introduced the concept of special industrial zones to generate "clusters of new activity" (Tillett, 1996, p. 7). To encourage FDI to tap these sites, IDA approaches "flagship investors" with the aim of using these leading firms to pull in other firms from the same industry. For example, after Lotus set up software operations in Ireland, other software companies also established affiliates in the vicinity (Tillett, 1996).

Finally, as the qualifications of the labour force were not a major initial attraction, Ireland made a concerted effort to increase the level of education. At the firm level, the government offers employment and training grants; for the country as a whole, it has persistently upgraded education, so that some 40 per cent of school-leavers are now engaged in tertiary education (Ruane and Görg, 1997).

The pattern of inward investment in Ireland has been visibly influenced by this policy. In 1997, some 1,100 to 1,200 foreign firms were active in Ireland. The inflow of FDI into the country since the 1950s has served to create new comparative advantages in industries such as chemicals, office machinery and electrical engineering, which had barely existed before the Second World War. Ireland has become one of the largest exporters of software, produced by 600 companies employing some 19,000 persons. The electronics industry has emerged as the second largest industry in Ireland; this industry, led by about 200 foreign-owned companies, generated over one-third of export revenues in 1997. The overall result is a "...quite phenomenal growth of export-oriented FDI in manufacturing, from a zero base in the late 1950s to a situation where almost 60 per cent of gross output and 45 per cent of employment in manufacturing is in foreign-owned export-oriented firms." (Barry and Bradley, 1997, p. 1798).

Source: UNCTAD, based on information received from the Industrial Development Agency of Ireland.

are enough examples of considerable investment inflows into countries that used neither promotional techniques nor incentives (Brazil in the 1970s and 1990s and Indonesia in the 1980s). But, even if this category of determinants is not equal in importance to the other two categories, neither should it be underestimated, because business facilitation measures can indeed make a difference -- especially in little-known investment locations or in countries implementing reforms and improving their FDI policies or with concrete individual investment projects. Above all, while the convergence of investment regimes and business facilitation practices reduces the relative effectiveness of these determinants, notable *differences* in this respect may assume greater significance when it comes to locational choices.

C. Economic determinants

The economic determinants of inward FDI can be grouped for analytical convenience into three clusters, each of them reflecting the principal motivations of TNCs for investing in foreign countries: resource-seeking, market-seeking and efficiency-seeking (table IV.1). As with the evolution of FDI regulations, these determinants have changed in response to the forces of liberalization and globalization. This section reviews the economic determinants of inward FDI, focussing on the principal ones, and analyses how they have changed over time. Wherever relevant, additional factors that facilitate FDI flows are also noted. The underlying assumption is that an enabling framework for FDI is in place unless otherwise specified.

1. Traditional economic determinants

a. Natural resources

Historically, the most important host country determinant of FDI has been the availability of natural resources. In the nineteenth century "much of the FDI by European, United States and Japanese firms was prompted by the need to secure an economic and reliable source of minerals, primary products for the (then) investing industrializing nations of Europe and North America" (Dunning, 1993a, p. 57). Up to the eve of the Second World War, about 60 per cent of the world stock of FDI was in natural resources (ibid.). After the War, especially since the 1960s and 1970s, the relative importance of natural resources as a host country FDI determinant has declined. In the case of major home countries, the share of the primary sector in their outward stock of FDI decreased from almost 25 per cent in 1970 to 11 per cent in 1990 (UNCTAD, 1993a, p. 62). During the first half of the 1990s (1991-1995), the share of this sector in the total outflows of Germany, Japan, the United Kingdom and the United States was below 5 per cent and, among major investors, France alone had a share as high as 9 per cent (UNCTAD, FDI/TNC database).

Even when it was prominent as an FDI determinant, the presence of natural resources by itself was not sufficient for FDI to take place. Comparative advantage in natural resources usually gave rise to trade rather than to FDI. Investment took place when resource-abundant countries either lacked the large amounts of capital typically required for resource extraction or did not have the technical skills needed to extract or sell raw materials to the rest of the world. In addition, infrastructure facilities for getting the raw materials out of the host country and to its final destination had to be in place or needed to be created.

While the decline in the importance of natural resources as an FDI determinant can be attributed to a decline in the importance of the primary sector in world output, a reconfiguration of conditions at both firm and country levels reflecting the changing relationship between developing host countries and natural-resource-seeking TNCs also played a role. This reconfiguration was characterized by the emergence of large indigenous enterprises in many developing countries, usually state-owned, with sufficient capital and technical skills to permit governments to rely on them for the production and distribution of raw or processed products. This meant that, in a number of cases, FDI was no longer necessary and host countries could revert to trade based on comparative advantage. In other cases, FDI gave way to joint ventures with TNCs, or non-equity arrangements. This does not mean that FDI in natural resources has declined in absolute terms. In fact, the inward FDI stock in the primary sector of developed countries increased more than fivefold during 1975-1990, while inward stock in developing countries increased more than sixfold (UNCTAD, 1996a, p.5). Though declining in relative importance, the availability of natural resources is still a determinant of FDI and continues to offer important possibilities for inward investment in resource-rich countries. Natural resources still explain much of the inward FDI in a number of countries, developing (e.g. countries in sub-Saharan Africa), developed (e.g. Australia) and countries in transition (Azerbaijan, Kazakhstan and Russian Federation).

b. National markets

An important group of traditional economic determinants of inward FDI corresponds to the need of firms, including TNCs, to grow and/or to stay competitive by gaining access to new markets at home and abroad and/or increasing existing market shares. From a host country's perspective, the relevant economic determinants for attracting market-seeking FDI include market size, in absolute terms as well as in relation to the size and income of its population, and market growth (table IV.1 and the annex to this chapter). Large markets can accommodate more firms both domestic and foreign (especially important for non-tradable services), and can help firms producing tradable products to achieve scale and scope economies. As growth is a magnet for firms, a high growth rate in a host country tends to stimulate investment by both domestic and foreign producers.

Traditionally, market size and growth as FDI determinants related to national markets for manufacturing products sheltered from international competition by high tariffs or quotas that triggered "tariff-jumping" FDI. Market access became the predominant motive for investing in the manufacturing sector of developed countries between the two world wars and of developing countries in the 1960s and 1970s, during the heyday of import-substitution industrialization. This motive was paramount, for example, in the wave of United States investments in Europe, especially in the United Kingdom, during the early post-war period (Dunning, 1998a, p. 258), and in Japanese investments in the United States after the mid-1980s, following voluntary export restrictions and the possibility of further protectionist measures in the automobile industry.

National markets were also important for many service TNCs, although the principal reason was not the existence of tariffs, but the fact that most services were not tradable and therefore the only way to deliver them to foreign markets was through establishment abroad. Theoretically, this should have made market size and growth strong host country determinants for FDI in the services sector. But the size of this investment was small compared to the size of the services sector, mostly because of restrictive FDI frameworks in both developed and developing countries. Infrastructural services, for example, were typically publicly owned monopolies and foreign ownership in financial services such as banking and insurance was either not permitted or restricted.

c. Other traditional determinants

Apart from natural resources and national markets, there are also other location-specific economic determinants of FDI reflecting other types of TNC motivations. The availability of low-cost unskilled labour, largely immobile, has been the most prominent among them. This is so especially for TNCs seeking greater efficiency in producing labour-intensive final products or for TNCs producing final products for which some stage of production, geographically separable from other stages, is intensive in the use of unskilled labour. Availability in this sense implies not only abundance but low costs relative to productivity. A low price is a natural consequence of abundance, unless it is offset by host governments' interventions to raise the price through minimum wage laws or high social insurance taxes, or the labour is made inaccessible by distance or poor infrastructure. This type of FDI began to emerge in the 1960s, but it began to flourish only under conditions of globalization and will therefore be discussed in the next section.

2. The impact of globalization

The principal forces that have driven the globalization process, alone or in combination with one another -- improvements in technology, markets more open to trade, FDI and technology flows, and the resulting competitive pressures (UNCTAD 1996a, pp. 95-97) -- have led to a reconfiguration of the ways in which TNCs pursue their resource-seeking, market-seeking and efficiency-seeking objectives. They have thereby also redefined the determinants of inward FDI. Traditional inward FDI determinants and the types of FDI associated with them have not disappeared in a globalizing economy but their importance is declining.

Improvements in technology have contributed to the deregulation of a number of important service industries (e.g. telecommunication), in many cases opening them up to FDI. As most of the technological improvements were carried out by firms, the result was a pool of companies with enhanced ownership-specific advantages that put them in a better position to become TNCs. Technology has become one of the most important tools for competition; indeed, in a number of industries, technological improvements in products including services and processes like marketing have become the key to competitiveness. This in turn underlines the importance of access to created assets, i.e. to assets that can provide a competitive edge. Technology and a capacity for continuous innovation are the key created assets. In addition, technological improvements in transportation and telecommunication technologies have also provided TNCs with the ability to coordinate and manage their assets across borders and to service markets anywhere in the world. Combined with their general management expertise, TNCs have now enhanced their internal capacity to manage global complexity, turning it into one of their ownership-specific advantages.

The opening of markets to trade, FDI and technology flows has created enlarged markets for final and intermediate goods and services, and has provided TNCs (and domestic firms) with better access not only to national, regional and international markets, but also to markets for factors of production and other resources. This has enlarged the range of choices that TNCs have regarding the modalities of serving these markets (especially FDI, trade, licensing, subcontracting, franchising); increased their access to immobile resources (unskilled labour, low-cost skilled labour, marketing expertise embodied in enterprises); and improved the efficiency of their international production systems.

With technological improvements enhancing the ability of firms to expand production and the opening of markets creating space for such an expansion, firms have sought new opportunities to improve their growth and competitive positions. Existing TNCs have responded by making the acquisition of locational assets -- and their most efficient organization -- an important part of their competitiveness-enhancing strategies. Enterprises that are not TNCs -- and no longer as protected by national protectionist regimes as in the past -- have responded by undertaking FDI so as to acquire new locational assets. This is reflected in the growing number of TNCs, large and small, from both developed and developing countries. The number of TNCs in 14 OECD countries rose from about 7,000 in 1968/1969 to about 34,000 by the mid-1990s. The total number of TNCs stood at an estimated 52,000 by the mid-1990s, many of them obviously small and medium-sized enterprises. The number of TNCs from developing countries grew from around 4,000 in 1991 to around 9,000 by the mid-1990s. By 1997, they accounted for 14 per cent of world FDI outflows, compared to 2 per cent in the late 1970s.

In the management of locational assets firms can pursue a variety of strategies, simple and complex, to integrate international production. What follows is a discussion of these strategies and their implications for host country determinants of FDI.

a. Simple integration strategies

In a world with trade barriers, limits on the movement of factors of production and overwhelmingly non-tradable services, TNCs pursued differentiated strategies based on stand-alone foreign affiliates, relatively independent from parent companies and without links to other affiliates of the same parent firm. Thus they were mostly horizontally organized enterprises with plants in a number of countries. Vertically integrated structures were limited to natural-resource TNCs. Only under conditions of globalization did TNC strategies give rise to vertically integrated TNC structures, also in other sectors, spread across the globe.

Simple integration strategies have been the first step in this direction. They are used by TNCs facing competitive pressures and aim at reducing the production costs of labour-intensive products or processes in the value-added chain (UNCTAD, 1993a). They entail the transfer of these products or processes to foreign affiliates, controlled through equity or non-equity arrangements (e.g. subcontracting), established in countries that offer the locational advantages required by these processes. The three clusters of locational economic determinants (table IV.1) are involved in different ways in these strategies:

Resources. The principal locational advantage needed to attract FDI guided by this strategy is unskilled labour. But as countries with abundant unskilled labour interested in attracting this type of FDI have never been in short supply, they typically had to offer more by way of the quality and quantity of this resource to prevail in competition with other countries, e.g. the reliability of its supply and the level of its skills. Other resources include the availability and quality of physical infrastructure for exporting the final output produced by such labour. Though the principal resource sought is labour, in practice, it is always labour *plus* other advantages: if labour alone were sufficient to attract FDI, most of this type of investment would be concentrated in countries with abundant unskilled labour, which it is not.

Efficiency. As cost reduction is the principal driver of this type of strategy, the cost and productivity of labour as well as the cost of physical infrastructure are the most important determinants of FDI. It is the loss of this advantage (in most cases due to wages rising in excess of productivity) that may lead to the relocation of a foreign affiliate to other countries offering more competitive conditions.[18]

Markets. The market of a host country is not the primary consideration here.[19] Access to international markets, or at least to markets of developed countries, is particularly important. If a host country enjoys privileged access to large developed country markets, this gives it an important locational advantage. If this access is limited by tariff or non-tariff barriers, the advantage is correspondingly limited. And if a host country loses access to international markets, in most cases it also loses foreign affiliates relying on such access.

Simple integration strategies are not new. They began to emerge on a visible scale when the first export processing zones were established in the late 1960s and 1970s. They were typically geared towards labour-intensive industries, driven by price-based competition, (e.g. textiles and clothing, shoes, toys, and sports equipment) as well as towards the labour-intensive aspects/components of otherwise capital-intensive industries (e.g. semiconductors in the electronics industry and electrical wiring in the automobile industry). Typically, foreign affiliates established within the framework of this strategy are located in developing countries and, more recently, in economies in transition. Although this type of strategy and associated FDI has limits determined by the declining share of labour costs in the total costs of manufacturing and of tradable services, it only began to prosper when barriers to trade and FDI were lowered; costs and time needed to transport goods over long distances were reduced; and communication technology permitted not only the overall coordination and management of affiliates located even in different continents, but also the immediate adjustment of design or product specifications in response to demand changes caused, for example, by sudden shifts in fashion.

At the same time, the nature of locational advantages related to this type of investment has also changed:

- As more countries compete for this type of investment, they offer locational advantages that go beyond low-cost labour. In addition to physical infrastructure and the availability of inputs like energy and water, educated and trained labour has become an important resource. While low-cost labour remains a locational advantage, the increasingly sought-after advantages are competitive combinations of wages, skills and productivity.[20] In addition, the importance of FDI policy and especially business facilitation including incentives has increased greatly, because the competition among countries for this type of investment is most intense.

- This sort of investment has always been mobile (for example, in response to wage increases, stricter labour laws or changes in quotas that affect access to final markets),[21] but this mobility has now increased dramatically and so has the risk of losing the locational advantage for this sort of FDI. Such a loss does not, however, have to be harmful to a host country; it may signal an economic restructuring process involving increasing labour productivity, and the acquisition of new skills and capabilities, in which the lower grade of FDI is replaced by a new, higher-quality and less mobile FDI. This has indeed happened in labour-intensive industries in the newly industrializing economies of Asia (UNCTAD, 1995a, chapter V).[22] TNCs undertaking this type of FDI also include firms from developing countries, as well as foreign affiliates that capitalize on their experience through indirect FDI and have moved up-market towards designing and organizing and controlling networks of suppliers of various labour-intensive goods spread over several countries, and act as intermediaries between these suppliers and client firms in developed countries.

- Some host countries with an abundant supply of low-wage unskilled and skilled labour have been able to consolidate these advantages by gaining durable or even permanent access to large markets of developed countries through regional integration schemes. Examples are NAFTA, the Caribbean Basin Initiative, the Lomé Convention and the association agreements of the European Union. While, in a number of these schemes, market access has led to increased FDI flows into labour-intensive industries, this has not always been the case and has usually occurred only if other economic determinants were favourable.

The discussion so far has focused on locational advantages related to efficiency-driven strategies in labour-intensive manufacturing processes. Technological improvements in the area of telecommunications and computers make it possible to extend these strategies to information-based services by increasing their tradability. Services that have become tradable include such simple labour-intensive activities as data entry and such skill-intensive ones as the production and servicing of software programmes. Host countries that have been able to develop locational advantages in this respect -- especially a computer-literate labour force and a reliable and competitive telecommunication infrastructure -- are able to attract FDI in industries in which it did not exist before. These improvements have permitted TNCs to pursue more sophisticated competitiveness-enhancing strategies, namely, complex integration strategies, which in turn draw on a wider range of other locational advantages of host countries.

b. Complex integration strategies

The forces of globalization have heightened the preoccupation of firms with their competitiveness, that is, their ability to survive and grow while attaining their ultimate objective of maximizing profits (UNCTAD, 1995a, p. 126). In pursuing this objective in a liberalizing and globalizing world economy, firms are increasingly pushed beyond simple integration strategies, towards complex integration[23] that permit them to benefit to the highest extent possible from the international portfolio of their locational assets. In other words, firms increasingly seek locations where they can combine their own mobile assets most efficiently with the immobile resources they need to produce goods and services for the markets they want to serve. As a consequence, firms split up the production process into various specific activities (such as finance, R&D, accounting, training, parts production, distribution), or segments of these activities, with each of them carried out by affiliates in locations best suited to the particular activity. This process creates an international intra-firm division of labour and a growing integration of international production networks. Liberalization creates the opportunities for such networks to emerge; technological progress (especially in information and communication technology) makes it possible for such networks to be operated efficiently on an international basis; and competition forces firms to take advantage of these opportunities to integrate their locational assets. Complex integration strategies thus combine the pursuit of the three factors motivating FDI -- markets, resources and efficiency -- which used to be distinct and distinguishable into a single motive: enhancing competitiveness. Complex integration strategies therefore make it increasingly difficult to point to a single locational determinant. Instead, they blur the lines between the traditional clusters of economic determinants, as the boundaries between types of FDI disappear.

What does this mean for the economic determinants of FDI? Satisfying or possessing at least *one* of the principal determinants may no longer be sufficient for a host country to be successful in the highly competitive world market for FDI. Rather, countries that offer an adequate *combination* of the principal locational determinants that are important for global corporate competitiveness, namely, conditions for efficient operations; high-quality resources/assets; and access to markets can attract TNCs that pursue integrated international production strategies.

The precise interaction of the principal locational determinants for competitiveness-enhancing FDI varies across goods and services. And, in spite of a shift in the relative importance of different economic determinants and the need for combining them effectively, the traditional determinants continue to be influential (box IV.6). For example, the availability of natural resources -- typically for export to the world market -- remains the principal determinant for natural-resource-seeking FDI. Similarly, access to local markets remains key for non-tradable services that must be produced when and where they are consumed. But there is also a growing range of goods and (tradable) services for which FDI is seen as a means of increasing competitiveness. It is for projects in this range that countries compete in the world FDI market, because these projects are flexible as far as locations are concerned. For such investments, decisions as to where to locate are based on the best possible combination of the principal locational determinants in the light of their expected contribution to the competitiveness of the corporate system as a whole.[24]

For competitiveness-enhancing investments, a stable, state-of-the-art enabling framework is taken for granted as far as FDI policies per se are concerned. Furthermore, there is a growing expectation by firms that the inner ring of policies directly related to FDI will be expanded. The implication is that TNCs pursuing integrated international production strategies will avoid locating activities in countries in which they fear a possible loss of freedom to operate internationally. Furthermore, preference would be given to locations that are open and well connected to the global economy, and characterized by stability, transparency, predictability, and coherent policies that recognize the importance of strong complementarities between trade and FDI.

Also taken for granted is that the national policy framework is complemented by BITs (box IV.3), double taxation treaties (chapter III.B), the host country's membership in MIGA, and the applicability of relevant international treaties such as the New York Convention on the Recognition and Enforcement of Foreign Arbitral Awards, the Convention on the

Settlement of Disputes between States and Nationals, and the TRIMs and TRIPS Agreements. Various business facilitation measures, while not decisive, are also expected.

But the key is the shift of importance among the economic determinants of FDI location. When firms undertake competitiveness-enhancing FDI, they seek not only cost reductions and bigger market shares, but also access to technology and innovatory capacity. These resources, as distinct from natural resources, are typically people-made, they are "created assets." Possessing such assets is central for firms' competitiveness in a globalizing economy (box IV.7).

The implications of this for locational determinants go well beyond merely increasing the number of corporate functions that countries may try to attract. Compared to natural resources, these new types of resources can be created by host countries and influenced by governments. The result is that countries that do not possess natural resources can still attract FDI by creating assets that are in demand by TNCs. For example, Costa Rica, which could do nothing to attract copper-seeking FDI, has been able to create the conditions and resources, including skilled labour, needed to attract a $500 million investment project by

Box IV.6. The continuing relevance of traditional determinants

Although the most profound shifts among FDI determinants result from integrated international strategies, especially complex strategies, the traditional economic determinants related to large markets, trade barriers and non-tradable services are still at work, and account for a large share of worldwide FDI flows. Data on the distribution of sales of foreign affiliates of United States TNCs in host countries are indicative in this regard: two-thirds of TNC activity is still of this type (UNCTAD, 1996a, p. 106). (These figures are higher in the services sector, including trading affiliates, and lower in manufacturing but they do not change the overall outcome.)

Some of the largest national markets remain unmatched in size by the largest regional markets or even by entire continents. For example, the market of the European Union during most of its existence has been smaller than the United States market; the market of the African continent (without South Africa) is smaller than that of the Republic of Korea; and the combined markets of the 14 Central and Eastern European countries are smaller than the market of Brazil. As regards trade barriers, even though the general trend has been towards the reduction or even abolition of tariffs and quotas, they continue to remain in force in several (especially developing) countries and in some industries in a much wider group of countries. These continue to generate import-substituting FDI and discourage efficiency-seeking FDI. In non-tradable services, as well as goods that are perishable or need to be adapted to consumer preferences or local standards, the market-seeking motivation, and the corresponding locational attractiveness of host countries, remain as strong as ever. In fact, there has been an explosion of FDI in the services sector as a result of the general trend towards the liberalization of FDI frameworks for services.

Still, although FDI remains strongly driven by its traditional determinants, the relative importance of different locational determinants for competitiveness-enhancing FDI is shifting. For example, again using United States data for foreign affiliates in manufacturing, though it is still true that these affiliates are predominantly oriented towards domestic markets: their domestic sales have dropped from 64 per cent in 1982 to 60 per cent in 1993. A similar trend can be observed in tradable services (e.g. computer and data-processing services) in which domestic sales declined from 85 to 81 per cent over the same period (UNCTAD, 1996a, p. 106). Perhaps more telling are data for United States foreign affiliates in the European Union, as the evolving policy framework there is more indicative of the FDI policy framework emerging globally: sales to local markets in that region declined from 76 per cent to 64 per cent between 1966 and 1993, while exports increased from 24 per cent to 36 per cent (UNCTAD, 1996a, pp. 107 - 108).

Source: UNCTAD.

the INTEL Corporation. Moreover, this type of project is unlikely to be relocated with as much ease as projects relying on a single type of easily available resource like low-cost unskilled labour.

Apart from created assets, other host country determinants relevant for competitiveness-enhancing FDI are:

- *Agglomeration economies.* TNCs seeking created assets in knowledge-intensive industries may gravitate to spatial clusters of related activities or specialized support services within a country or a region. While older clusters, as in the case of the Swiss watch industry, were largely national, the new clusters such as science and technology parks, R&D consortia and service-support centres are characterized by a strong involvement of TNCs, often as flagship firms (Dunning, 1998a, p. 58). The reason for this is that new clusters are often geared more towards external economies that help to upgrade the competitive advantage of the participating firms, such as knowledge creation and the exchange of uncodifiable knowledge, interactive learning and face-to-face discussions. To benefit from these externalities, firms have to be present in locations where such clusters exist. Once present, TNCs not only benefit from them but may also contribute to their further development.

- *Infrastructure facilities.* An indispensable condition for complex integration strategies is the ability to link specialized affiliates in mutually supporting networks of activities through adequate infrastructure facilities. Such facilities include high-quality telecommunication links and reliable transportation systems, especially for foreign

Box IV.7. Created assets

In their quest for competitiveness, TNCs assign a particularly important role to obtaining access to created (or strategic) assets: the principal wealth-creating assets and a key source of competitiveness for firms (Dunning, 1993a, pp. 60-61; 1998c, p. 47; Mytelka, 1987; and Stewart, 1997).

Created assets can be tangible like the stock of financial and physical assets such as the communication infrastructure or marketing networks, or intangible. The list of intangible assets is long, but they have a common denominator: knowledge. They include skills, attitudes (e.g. attitudes to wealth creation and business culture), capabilities (technological, innovatory, managerial and learning capabilities), competencies (e.g. to organize income-generating assets productively), relationships (such as interpersonal relationships forged by individuals or contacts with governments), as well as the stock of information, trade marks, goodwill and brainpower. These assets can be embodied in both individuals and firms and they can sometimes be enhanced by clusters of firms and economic activities.

The importance of created intangible assets in production and other economic activities has increased considerably. A large proportion of the costs of many final goods and services, ranging from simple products such as cereals through books and computers to automobiles, consists of the costs of such created assets as R&D, design, advertising, distribution and legal work. Less than 10 per cent of the production cost of automobiles now consists of labour costs; the rest relates to the contributions of various created assets. Moreover, international competition increasingly takes place through new products and processes and these are often knowledge-based. R&D activities leading to new products and processes are costly and risky. At the same time, markets for knowledge-based resources and assets are becoming more open and enterprises embodying these assets can be bought and sold. The result is that TNCs have taken advantage of these opportunities and used FDI as a major means of acquiring created assets and enhancing corporate competitiveness.

Source: UNCTAD.

affiliates that are part of "just-in-time" production systems and for regional headquarters.

- *A broad range of resources.* As potentially all parts of the production process and activities of a firm can be assigned to specialized foreign affiliates, the range of resources sought in host countries is wide and cuts across the entire value-added chain. It includes not only inputs like natural resources, low-cost labour and engineering skills, but also functions like accountancy, legal services, purchasing and marketing, and finance and R&D capabilities. Complex integration strategies are thus an extension of earlier strategies that were limited to one type of resource (e.g. natural resources) or one type of process (e.g. labour-intensive processes): the entire value-added chain is now subject to cross-border vertical integration. Locations that seek to attract a wide range of value-added TNC activities need to be able to provide a correspondingly wide range of resources.

- *Specialized resources.* Countries that cannot provide a broad range of resources may still be able to attract specialized FDI, because complex integration strategies make it possible to match specific locational advantage with the needs of a single functional activity that requires specific types of skills. Typically, however, such specialized resources have to be of high quality (e.g. a workforce with technological sophistication and adaptability).

- *Competitive pricing of resources and infrastructure.* Resources including created assets and infrastructure have to be available at internationally competitive prices, although pricing may matter less in the case of specific assets that enhance competitiveness in non-cost-related areas, such as access to new markets, products or technologies.

- *Markets.* Large markets are important for complex integration strategies based on scale and scope economies. Although successive rounds of multilateral trade liberalization have decreased the relevance of market access through FDI for many products, it continues to be important for non-tradable services, perishable goods, products that are not globally standardized and require local customization, products in which competitiveness demands a quick response to changing consumer preferences, and products requiring extensive after-sales service. Production in a market may also be desirable if the costs of production are subject to wide fluctuation derived from exchange-rate changes.

While many of the principal locational requirements needed to attract competitiveness-enhancing FDI can be found in developed countries, they also exist in developing countries and in economies in transition. It is important to emphasize, however, that it is not an entire country that needs to meet these requirements; it can also be a subregion, a municipality, a valley or a science park, as long as they are embedded in the appropriate national policy framework. The challenge is precisely to develop a well-calibrated -- and preferably unique -- combination of the principal determinants of FDI location in a liberalizing and globalizing world economy and to seek to match it with the strategies pursued by competitiveness-enhancing TNCs.

National policies have an important role to play in this respect, in two ways:

- Locational advantages do not necessarily arise spontaneously -- they may need to be created and nurtured. In particular, policies aimed at strengthening innovation systems and encouraging the diffusion of technology are central here, as these underpin the ability to create assets. Important also are all other policies that encourage the strengthening of created assets and the development of clusters based on them, as well as policies that stimulate partnering and networking among domestic and foreign firms.

- Equally, if not more importantly, created assets (like the principal locational determinants in general) are also beneficial to national firms and facilitate their growth and competitiveness, be it on their own or in partnership with foreign firms in the interest of national growth and development. That firms from developing countries are increasingly participating in cross-border R&D partnerships with firms from developed countries (chapter I.B; see also box IV.8) is an encouraging sign in this respect.

Box IV.8. Knowledge-seeking FDI in R&D operations

R&D has been a corporate function typically carried out in home countries. Under competitive pressures, R&D is increasingly undertaken abroad. For example, expenditure on R&D undertaken by foreign affiliates in the United States has been growing disproportionately faster than the size of their operations: between 1985 and 1995, it grew by a factor of 3.4, while sales increased by 2.5 and employment by 1.7 (Dunning, 1998b). One study has found that, between 1991 and 1995, 11 per cent of United States registered patents of the world's largest firms were generated by research undertaken in countries outside the home country of the parent company (Cantwell and Harding, 1997, quoted in Dunning, 1998c, p. 51).

The reasons for conducting R&D abroad include both the need to create new core products and processes and the need to acquire knowledge necessary to advance the productivity of domestic R&D (Dunning, 1998b). A study of Swedish firms, for example, found that firms located R&D in countries that specialized in their products' production so as to have access to knowledge in the host country's centres of excellence and to benefit from localized spillovers (Fors and Zejan, 1996).

FDI in R&D operations is attracted to locations that feature particular kinds of intellectual resources. Most of these are concentrated in developed economies and this is where most R&D still takes place. In 1994, for example, some 90 per cent of research by foreign affiliates of United States TNCs was conducted in developed countries (Mataloni and Fahim-Nader, 1996). Microsoft, a United States TNC, has established a research laboratory in the United Kingdom, commenting that "going to Europe gives us a way to hire people who bring new talents and new perspectives to our work that we couldn't get any other way".[a] Similarly, foreign semiconductor or computer firms have established research facilities in California, while foreign pharmaceutical and chemical firms have settled in New Jersey in order to tap industry-specific knowledge networks available in these locations. The resources include technically sophisticated workers, the exchange of information that takes place among technical staff concentrated in a given location and, more visibly, specialized university or other research laboratories.

Developing countries that have built up specialized training facilities, research centres or science and technology parks have also become host to industries intent on using high-tech inputs. Bangalore, India is one example of a district featuring a large number of government and state-supported research institutes; these were initially centred on the aeronautics industries of Karnataka State. India has also established institutes of technology, which are educational institutions designed to provide technical skills, as well as a Department of Electronics to target software development. When Texas Instruments decided to invest in the area in 1986, the availability of a large number of computer-literate technicians and researchers as well as of research centres were decisive variables. In turn, the work of Texas Instruments drew in other computer-technology TNCs. The Government of India and its Department of Electronics responded by establishing software technology parks, resulting in a virtuous R&D cycle (Lateef, 1997, pp. 13-16).

Source: UNCTAD, based on the studies cited.

[a] "Microsoft picks England as site of research lab", *New York Times*, 18 June 1997.

D. The impact of international policy frameworks

In their efforts to attract FDI and to influence its quality, countries increasingly conclude international agreements dealing with an expanding set of issues (UNCTAD, 1996a, 1996b). A number of these instruments may influence some of the FDI determinants and thus exert an impact on FDI flows. This section discusses the extent to which the most important of the existing or potential agreements -- bilateral, regional, plurilateral and multilateral -- do indeed affect FDI determinants and, if so, whether they can also influence FDI flows, either alone or together with other determinants.

1. Bilateral investment treaties

Bilateral investment treaties (BITs) were originally concluded between developed and developing countries, with a view to promoting investment between the treaty partners. Increasingly, BITs are also concluded between developed or developing countries on the one side and economies in transition on the other; they are also being concluded between developing countries. The number of these treaties increased significantly in the 1990s: about three-quarters of the over 1,500 treaties in existence at the end of 1997 date from the 1990s.

BITs exert some influence on the policy framework for FDI, by contributing to the improvement of an investment climate.[25] They do so, in particular, by strengthening the bilateral standards of protection and treatment of foreign investors and establishing mechanisms for dispute settlement (box IV.3). In this manner, they help to reduce the risk of investing in countries party to these treaties. BITs do not alter the economic determinants of FDI and they seldom provide for proactive promotion measures by governments (UNCTAD, forthcoming b).

Since FDI flows are determined by a variety of factors, it would be unreasonable to expect that any improvements in the investment climate brought about by BITs, which relate only to parts of the FDI policy framework, could exert a significant impact on FDI flows. Even such important economic determinants as large and growing markets or an abundant labour force do not work alone as FDI determinants, but only in tandem with other factors. And, just as there are cases of countries receiving substantial FDI flows without putting business facilitation measures into place, so there are examples of countries with large FDI flows and few, if any, BITs. Conversely, there are also examples of countries that have concluded many BITs but have attracted only modest amounts of FDI.

A comprehensive recent statistical analysis (UNCTAD, forthcoming b) confirmed the relative insignificance of BITs in determining FDI. Both an analysis of time-series data on bilateral FDI flows in relation to 200 BITs, and a cross-sectional analysis of 133 countries investigating the relationship between total FDI flows and stocks and the number of BITs and other independent economic variables, showed that variables such as market size and growth, exchange rates and country risk are more important than BITs as FDI determinants. At best, BITs play a minor and secondary role in influencing FDI flows and explaining differences in their size among countries. Moreover, with the rapid proliferation of BITs in the 1990s, the distinctive influence of BITs as a signal to attract additional investment may have been eroded, as compared to a period when such treaties were still comparatively rare. Indeed, BITs are increasingly regarded by foreign investors as a standard feature of the institutional structure introduced in the past decade.

None of this means that BITs do not support the existing level of investment or prevent it from declining; the analysis mentioned above focused on the impact on FDI growth. There is some evidence that foreign investors encourage governments of home countries to conclude BITs with host countries in which they already have FDI. Furthermore, BITs may matter as a protective device for small projects, undertaken by small and medium-sized enterprises, even if the amounts involved are too small to affect the total or even bilateral flows of the host countries investigated in these analyses. Finally, while it may be quite reasonable to expect the impact of a BIT on FDI flows to occur soon after its conclusion (as most of these analyses do), it cannot be ruled out that an impact may only occur many years later.[26] This may well happen if important locational determinants of FDI are not yet in place in a host or home country. This is in line with earlier conclusions concerning policy determinants, namely, that they are enabling in character: by themselves, they have little or no effect, because they have to be complemented by economic determinants and, in specific circumstances, can be helped by investment facilitation measures.

2. Regional integration frameworks

The impact of regional integration frameworks (RIFs)[27] -- which range from free-trade areas to complete economic integration -- on FDI determinants depends on a variety of factors. First and foremost is the scope and depth of the integration envisaged by a RIF, which determines the extent of policy harmonization and varies by type of RIF. At the one extreme, a shallow RIF that entails no more than tariff reductions among members and external tariffs on non-members can have an impact on FDI determinants through trade or strategic responses to competitors (static effects) and growth (dynamic effects). A deeper RIF that also allows for the movement of capital (including FDI) would be expected to have effects on the investment determinants of TNCs beyond those induced by trade liberalization or growth alone.[28] In general, as a region becomes more integrated as the result of a RIF, the influence of the RIF on FDI determinants can work through more channels. In addition, as regulatory FDI frameworks become more harmonized within a region, more importance is attached by TNCs to economic determinants in deciding their precise location. To a lesser extent, the importance of business facilitation also rises.

The credibility of RIFs, manifested in the extent to which RIF provisions are actually implemented, is another factor determining the impact of RIFs on FDI determinants. Failure to implement RIFs fully means that their impact on FDI determinants cannot be pronounced, as illustrated by the failure of numerous RIFs in the 1960s and 1970s to exert any discernible influence on TNCs.[29] More recent RIFs, such as NAFTA, MERCOSUR and earlier the European Union, have exerted greater influence on FDI determinants, especially those related to policy and economic conditions, precisely because they have been implemented more strictly than their predecessors. If member countries choose to be exempted from RIF provisions and continue to restrict access to certain industries, retain high tariffs for certain products or keep low environmental standards, such exemptions can also influence FDI determinants, even if they are temporary. They also place in doubt the member countries' commitment to adhere to a given RIF. Similarly, the speed with which a member country implements RIF provisions -- for example, abolishing tariffs -- also influences the country-specific impact of the RIF on FDI determinants.

A third factor is the prior interdependence of member countries and the established linkages among them, as indicated, for example, by the levels of trade and FDI barriers. For countries that have already established significant links, the principal influence of a RIF on FDI determinants would depend on how they address divergences in domestic policy. The Free Trade Agreement between the United States and Canada (1989), for example, had very little impact on FDI flows to Canada, partly because bilateral trade between the two countries had already been considerably liberalized prior to the Agreement, either through multilateral rounds of tariff reduction or through sectoral agreements like the Canada-United States Auto Pact (Blomström and Kokko, 1997, pp. 15-17). The Free Trade Agreement meant that cross-penetration of markets through FDI was not especially required and this was evident in a decline in Canadian outward FDI to the United States (Blomström and Kokko, 1997, p. 17).

In terms of the depth and scope of integration, most of the recent RIFs cover the middle ground: links among members are strengthened principally by reducing or abolishing tariff and non-tariff barriers. In the case of free trade areas, the movement of factors of production, particularly FDI capital, is often not addressed explicitly.[30] In the case of customs unions, a common external tariff vis-à-vis the rest of the world is also adopted, and policies including those affecting FDI, are harmonized.

A distinction needs to be drawn here between RIFs confined to developed countries and those involving developing countries. For most recent RIFs among developed countries (e.g. the case of the enlargement of the European Union), the pre-existing, largely open, FDI framework[31] remains in effect after the implementation of the RIF.[32] Not addressing the movement of capital explicitly in the RIF does not therefore necessarily detract from its impact on economic and business facilitation determinants. For most RIFs that involve developing countries, the pre-existing FDI framework is typically not open to the same degree for all members, with the restrictions often reflecting the level of development and structural characteristics of their economies. Therefore, in the case of NAFTA, MERCOSUR and the revised Andean Pact, FDI provisions are included explicitly on both the inward and the outward side, even if no provisions on the movement of other factors of production are included. In these cases, RIFs can have a direct impact on the host countries' policy frameworks for FDI, in addition to their impacts on other categories of FDI determinants. For example, NAFTA further opened Mexico's service sector to FDI.

Regardless of the depth of integration prior to the introduction of a RIF, TNCs interested in investing in a region will still have to choose where to locate among member countries, or among locations within a member country. In choosing where to invest, TNCs consider region-wide factors together with factors that apply only to individual countries or to locations within countries. Being a member of a RIF implies that some country-specific location advantages may decrease in importance as FDI determinants, while region-specific location advantages may increase (see discussion below). In the case of tradable goods and services, for example, market size is often redefined not in terms of the market of the member country that a TNC considers a potential location, but in terms of the regional market. Since the same definition of market size would apply to all RIF member countries, other determinants come to play a much more important role in the locational decisions of TNCs. The locations most successful in attracting FDI are likely to be those that provide the best opportunities for TNCs to exploit both country-specific and region-specific advantages. For example, the United Kingdom has been one of the most successful countries in the European

Union in terms of attracting FDI because its locational advantages combine access to its own locational advantages with access to the wider European Union market. Mexico has benefited from the same consideration in the framework of NAFTA.

It follows from the discussion above that, even if RIFs have a positive impact on FDI determinants for the region as a whole, not all member countries necessarily benefit to the same extent. For some countries, membership in RIFs will enhance their location-specific advantages. For small countries, the size of their domestic market will no longer deter market-seeking foreign investors in tradables since they will now have access to the region's market, and not just the host country market. For the same reason, the size of the domestic market of large countries will no longer be as attractive and, therefore, will become less of a bargaining asset for host country governments. Economic determinants specific to individual member countries or business facilitation at the local level can thus become important.

The discussion that follows looks at the ways in which RIFs influence each of the three categories of FDI determinants, namely, the policy framework for FDI, the set of economic determinants, and the factors pertaining to the facilitation of business.

a. The impact of regional integration frameworks on FDI determinants

(i) The policy framework

As mentioned earlier, the majority of RIFs do not explicitly address FDI policy,[33] although there is an increasing tendency for free trade agreements to include investment. Even RIFs postulating a high degree of integration among members, including provisions regarding the movement of capital, may not necessarily contain explicit FDI policy provisions (Brewer and Young, 1998). The overall impact of RIFs on the policy framework for FDI therefore depends on whether a RIF contains provisions liberalizing the movement of capital (including FDI capital); on how restrictive the capital movement and investment regimes of the member countries had been prior to the implementation of the RIF; and on other policy-liberalization provisions contained in the RIFs, notably trade policy.[34] Of these conditions, whether or not a RIF contains explicit FDI provisions -- for example, on national treatment, most-favoured-nation treatment, rules of origin, performance requirements, dispute settlement -- may be the least important for developed countries and most developing countries as far as inward FDI is concerned, because inward investment regimes are typically open even prior to the implementation of RIFs. The OECD member countries, for example, adopted the Code of Liberalisation of Capital Movements in 1961, though capital-movement liberalization did not accelerate until after the mid-1970s. Even in many developing countries, at least partially open FDI policies have typically been in place prior to the implementation of a RIF, as the example of Mexico prior to joining NAFTA illustrates. So the direct impact of explicit FDI provisions contained in RIFs on FDI policy determinants is likely to be small in many instances, unless they result in a *considerable* liberalization of investment regimes.

Other policy provisions contained in RIFs, especially those relevant to trade liberalization, are likely to be more important in determining FDI. In the overwhelming majority of RIFs, the central elements and the most important factors influencing market-seeking FDI are the liberalization of trade barriers and the granting of preferential market access to members. Trade liberalization and trade policy coordination among RIF members contribute to a policy framework conducive to FDI because they create favourable conditions for foreign affiliates within the region to access regional markets for final and intermediate products. They also allow TNCs to establish regionally integrated production networks to enhance their efficiency. In the case of customs unions and free-trade areas, trade discrimination against non-members in the form of tariff barriers makes the size of a regional market more appealing and encourages market-seeking FDI by TNCs not present in the region. The removal of non-tariff barriers, or their harmonization, also exerts a positive influence on market-seeking FDI.

Apart from trade liberalization, the harmonization of related policies among members can also play a role as FDI determinant. The "social charter" of the European Union, for example, seeks to ensure that working conditions, wages, social expenditures, etc. would not differ substantially among members and thus give "unfair" location-specific advantages to some member countries. Likewise, European Union environmental regulations seeks to ensure that FDI would not be diverted to members with lax environmental regimes. Such policy harmonization can act as a brake on a "race to the bottom" in competitive policy liberalization meant to attract FDI.

Finally, RIFs may also influence the *speed* of FDI (and trade) policy liberalization. The prospective NAFTA Agreement, for example, prompted Mexico to liberalize its FDI framework even before the Agreement was signed, even though the liberalization of services and parts of the primary sector accelerated only after Mexico became a signatory. In some cases, however, member countries that are ready to deregulate a particular industry (e.g. financial services in the case of the European Union) may be obliged to wait until the other members of the RIF have reached a similar point. In the European Union not all countries were ready to deregulate their financial services at the same time, and a tier system was introduced to resolve that. But the reverse may also take place: countries that are lagging behind in terms of deregulation of industries and liberalization of policies may be pressured to move faster by other RIF members.[35] For example, RIF members may be encouraged to privatize, usually with foreign-investor participation, as a means of reducing the share of the public sector in their economies. Even if (as is often the case) pressures to liberalize do not apply to FDI policies per se, they can affect the overall policy framework of a member country in a manner that encourages FDI.

More generally, RIFs can reaffirm their members' commitments to adhere to liberal policies and bring about a momentum to continue the liberalization process in both FDI and trade. To put it differently: unless RIFs substantially alter national FDI policy frameworks, they will not have a major impact on FDI policy determinants from the point of view of individual countries. Their contribution to FDI policy determinants lies in ensuring member countries' commitment to adhere to a liberal existing policy framework, or to liberalize it if is restrictive, to harmonize policies, to lock in liberalizing changes, to increase momentum to liberalize further, to strengthen standards of treatment and protection, and to encourage policies that ensure the proper functioning of markets (e.g. competition policy).

(ii) Economic determinants

Market size and growth are the FDI economic determinants that are most affected by the implementation of a RIF. Dynamic effects of RIFs in encouraging higher rates of economic growth can help boost inward FDI. Most importantly, the size of the market is redefined under a RIF as the size of the region's market. The possibility of accessing a market wider than that of a single country for tradable goods and services becomes an inducement to invest in the region. This is exemplified by United States FDI in the European Union. A part of United States affiliate sales in the European Union are geared to the regional market: their sales in the European Union in countries other than the host country itself accounted for 31 per cent of their total sales in 1995. All this is made possible by the removal of intraregional trade barriers within the region, which carries the implication that a single host country's market size is no longer as significant a determinant of market-seeking FDI as it used to be before the implementation of the RIF. The redefinition of market size from national to at least regional is encouraged if a common external tariff is imposed. This can induce at least some import-substituting (tariff-jumping) FDI, as firms previously serving the regional market through exports seek to become "insiders" and switch to FDI. The extent to which this takes place depends on how heavily protected the host (regional) market becomes after the implementation of a RIF, and whether TNCs had already invested in the national markets prior to the RIF. In a liberalizing world of falling barriers, the location advantage of a large regional market may not be what it used to be, unless the RIF also dictates some protection, say, through a common external tariff. Of course, even in the absence of a common external tariff, the regional market may still be an attractive location as long as the RIF eliminates obstacles beyond tariff barriers or facilitates business transactions. In addition, there may be advantages associated with becoming an "insider" in a regional area, such as benefiting from rules-of-origin regulations (Eden and Appel Molot, 1993).

All this means that regional integration frameworks increase the geographical scope and size of "effective" markets because they increase the ease of access within member markets through the removal of trade and other barriers. However, even if all trade and investment barriers between countries were removed, cultural, linguistic and other less obvious barriers to doing business would remain (Motta and Norman, 1996), as would the importance of proximity to local consumers. So accessing an individual member country's market, although less significant as an FDI determinant under a RIF, cannot be discounted. A survey of TNCs about the importance of different factors in attracting FDI into the United Kingdom conducted by the Department for Enterprise concluded that access to European Union markets was an important factor but access to the United Kingdom's market was more significant for all types of FDI (Bachtler and Clement, 1990).[36]

With the implementation of a RIF, the accessibility of a region's market *from* a given location becomes an important FDI locational determinant. In addition to abolishing customs-clearance procedures that help speed up border crossings, good physical infrastructure, especially in transport and communications, facilitates access to regional markets. The importance of infrastructure as an FDI determinant is therefore enhanced considerably when a RIF comes into effect, for both market-seeking and efficiency-seeking TNCs.

As the importance of market size as an FDI determinant becomes more uniform for all countries that are members of a RIF and as the removal of cross-border barriers within the region increases competitive pressures, determinants related to enhancing efficiency come to play a bigger role for all types of FDI. Increased market size -- from national to regional or global -- is in itself an efficiency-inducing determinant because it provides the demand dimension that gives rise to the possibility of exploiting economies of scale and scope in production and distribution. Indeed, one of the primary advantages of enlarged markets under RIFs is that they create the demand conditions that allow TNCs to reap economies of scale and scope in all parts of the value chain. On the production side, cost considerations are especially important for efficiency-seeking TNCs (Burgenmeier and Mucchielli, 1991; Dunning, 1993a; Robson, 1993). RIFs allow such TNCs to locate each value-added activity of the production process in the most cost-efficient location within the region in order to rationalize operations regionally by taking advantage of productivity-adjusted cost differences in labour, technology, and other resources (UNCTAD, 1993a). In sum, RIFs help to create both the demand conditions and the production conditions needed to improve efficiency in production.

RIFs also influence TNCs' access to resources. In many RIFs, TNCs can access the skills, technologies or other strategic assets available in member countries other than those in which their production operations are located. The European Union, for example, allows all foreign affiliates regardless of their location within the Union to participate in European Union-sponsored R&D projects -- subject to certain restrictions on the transfer of technology to non-member countries (Brewer and Young, 1998). When RIFs allow the movement of labour, some labour moves across borders in response to TNC employment opportunities, which may mitigate the importance of the skill-seeking motive for FDI within the region.

Furthermore, RIFs give foreign investors the opportunity to be close to clusters of companies producing similar products or having similar R&D facilities and thus to exploit regional as well as sub-national agglomeration economies and obtain access to created assets. Proximity to a cluster of companies producing similar products or having similar R&D facilities, for example, need not necessarily require that a TNC invests in the same country where these companies or facilities are physically located. It may very well invest in a bordering country in close physical proximity to the cluster of companies or R&D facilities.[37] Thus within regions, a greater concentration of FDI in a few supranational clusters may develop that allows FDI to be more dispersed in terms of *country distribution*, but more concentrated in terms of *geographical space.*

Finally, RIFs promote greater competition to capture expanded markets or increase market shares within the region. Firms may respond to the increased competition for markets by establishing a physical presence, especially if arm's-length competition through trade is hindered by a common external tariff. Increases in intraregional and extraregional cross-border acquisitions designed to access resources or defend competitive positions often accompany RIFs. About one-quarter of Japanese manufacturing affiliates in Western Europe established during the mid-1990s were established through acquisitions, compared to 10 per cent of those established in 1990 (JETRO, 1991, 1996).

(iii) Business facilitation

The primary effect of RIFs on business facilitation FDI determinants is to reduce intra-regional business transaction costs. Such costs arise directly from inadequacies of information, asymmetries in doing business in different countries, the heterogeneity of administrative procedures, and differences in business support measures. Recognizing the importance of business facilitation obstacles, some RIFs seek to harmonize efforts to remove them or replace them with comprehensive region-wide programmes for FDI facilitation. In the case of the European Union, for example, the removal of internal tariff barriers was not sufficient for creating a unified regional market because of other obstacles to intraregional transactions, especially in services. The European Economic Community identified 280 barriers to cross-border transactions in 1985, and removed about 90 per cent of them in 1993 as part of the single market programme (Yamazawa, 1997). APEC has a comprehensive programme to facilitate trade and FDI whose objectives include "smart card" visas for short-term travel; procedures for APEC-wide accreditation of standards; and minimum restrictions on arrival in a member country (Yamazawa, 1997).

Since RIFs allow a region's market or many of its resources to be more easily accessible by TNCs from any location within the regional bloc, and policy coordination and harmonization gives rise to a more level playing field, business facilitation factors become increasingly important, as they concern matters which individual member countries -- and, increasingly, sub-national authorities -- can address to distinguish themselves from one another when competing for FDI. Even if some business facilitation measures are harmonized across members, there still remain important differences among members that allow them to compete for FDI. Measures aimed at targeting specific investors, providing social amenities and marketing a country as an investment location usually fall outside the scope of RIFs, and can therefore be used by each RIF member to enhance location-specific advantages. One result is precisely a proliferation of incentives used to attract FDI (UNCTAD, 1995a).

b. *The impact of regional integration frameworks on FDI flows*

From aggregate FDI data it is difficult to determine the impact of individual FDI determinants on investment flows or stocks received by a region or by specific member countries within a RIF. This is because FDI determinants work together under RIFs as well as in combination with factors unrelated to RIFs, such as certain macroeconomic changes. The evidence presented here relates to the overall impact of RIFs on FDI flows or stocks. Only inferences can be made about the extent to which a particular determinant is responsible for that impact. Furthermore, the evidence presented below is largely static, in the sense that it describes the one-time impact of RIFs on FDI. Dynamic effects of RIFs on FDI deriving from increased growth rates or heightened competition are much more difficult to assess.[38]

This section examines three cases of RIFs: the European Union (RIF among developed countries), NAFTA (RIF among developed-developing countries) and MERCOSUR (RIF among developing countries).

Prior to 1985 (when the Single Market Programme was initiated), members of the European Economic Community (EEC) received increased FDI inflows mostly from outsiders (Dunning, 1997; UNCTC, 1993) and particularly from the United States (table IV.2). Between 1957 and 1972, the share of the EEC (6 members) in the outward stock of the United States increased from 7 per cent to 17 per cent. Accessing the EEC market in the presence of non-tariff barriers seems to have been the principal motivation of this wave of FDI (Dunning, 1997). The 1992 Single Market Programme had not only a positive quantitative impact on FDI inflows but also a qualitative one, as corporate adjustment and efficiency considerations by "insiders", foreign affiliates as well as European Union firms, took precedence over market-access considerations in the manufacturing sector, although market access continued to be important in services. In fact, the Single Market Programme led to substantial intra-European-Union FDI flows as firms sought to acquire market positions within the new framework (UNCTC, 1993). One exception was Japan: as a latecomer, it invested heavily in the European Union in the late 1980s and early 1990s in both manufacturing and services. Except in the case of services, United States TNCs did not rush to invest in the European Union to the same extent as Japanese firms, having established their desired investment positions earlier on. United States foreign affiliates in services, however, did expand their capital expenditures (Lipsey, 1990).

Table IV.2. Share of the EEC (6) in United States' outward FDI stock

(Percentages)

1950	1955	1957	1962	1967	1972
5.4	6.1	6.6	10.0	14.4	17.1

Source: UNCTAD, FDI/TNC database.

At the country level, Spain and Portugal benefited greatly from EEC membership, with both countries receiving record FDI inflows in the years before and immediately following their accession, induced by access to the regional market, policy liberalization and lower wages. Ireland, with a stable macroeconomic environment, good infrastructure, a skilled workforce and advanced business facilitation measures, experienced one of the faster growth rates in FDI among all European Union members between 1983 and 1992 (table IV.3).

Table IV.3. Growth rates of inward FDI flows, EEC (9) member countries, 1983-1992

(Percentages)

Country	Per cent
Denmark	37
France	33
Belgium-Luxembourg	27
Ireland	27
Netherlands	22
Italy	14
United Kingdom	14
Germany	5

Source: UNCTAD, FDI/TNC database.

While FDI flows to the NAFTA region increased immediately before and after its implementation, it was in Mexico that NAFTA had a noticeable impact. In the years immediately before NAFTA, FDI inflows to Mexico doubled to over $4 billion annually and in the years following NAFTA they increased even more, to over $10 billion in 1994, falling slightly to $9.5 billion in 1995. (The investment boom in the United States in the aftermath of NAFTA is largely unrelated to NAFTA.) Mexico's liberalization of FDI policy (locked in and reinforced by NAFTA provisions), proximity and guaranteed access to the United States market (as long as local content requirements were satisfied), and the availability of low-cost labour all led to substantially higher FDI inflows into Mexico, despite the peso crisis. In other words, FDI flows into Mexico in the context of NAFTA were governed by a combination of economic determinants (market size, resources and efficiency), policy considerations (the greater FDI protection awarded by NAFTA), and specific provisions at the sectoral level (Blomström and Kokko, 1997).

FDI flows into MERCOSUR as a whole increased immediately before and after its implementation in 1995 ($10 billion in 1995 and $17 billion in 1996). Market-access considerations, coupled with trade liberalization, and provisions to promote and protect FDI appear to have helped to attract investment (Blomström and Kokko, 1997). MERCOSUR provides access to a market of some 200 million people in Argentina, Brazil, Paraguay and Uruguay (as well as to Bolivia and Chile, associate members since 1996).

Nevertheless, it is difficult to attribute any FDI gains to the MERCOSUR framework alone (Blomström and Kokko, 1997). Macroeconomic reforms as well as trade and investment liberalization and, in particular, the decision to implement privatization programmes had begun before the implementation of MERCOSUR. But, as in the case of NAFTA, MERCOSUR has helped to consolidate these changes. Especially in Argentina and Brazil -- the two countries that have benefited the most in terms of FDI flows -- investment inflows have responded in part to non-RIF factors, especially to privatization and the success of national macroeconomic reforms. The availability of natural resources has also been a magnet for FDI. In sum, it is not obvious how far FDI gains have been the direct outcome of MERCOSUR.

It appears that RIFs have contributed positively, but to a varying extent, to the growth of FDI into the recipient region in all the three cases discussed above. The impact has been the greatest when the changes in any of the categories of FDI determinants brought about by the RIF have been the most profound. Within regions, however, there are disparities in the distribution of investment among member countries (and among regions within countries). In particular, RIF locations that have already attracted considerable investment (e.g. clusters) may see their locational attractiveness further enhanced. On the other hand, low-wage locations in a RIF that rate well on the principal FDI determinants may be able to attract substantial FDI flows geared towards the larger market. This suggests that successful host countries are those that possess the right combination of location-specific advantages to match the ownership and internalization advantages of the firms that have decided to invest in the region. It also suggests that governments may need to pursue active regional policies to see that the benefits of integration are shared throughout the region.

Conclusion

Under RIFs, the choice of the country in which a TNC invests still depends on its evaluation of the location-specific determinants that the country offers. In general, functioning RIFs can enhance the location-specific FDI determinants of member countries. However, some of these determinants, like market size or access to certain resources, are now assessed from a regional rather than national perspective.

With the creation of RIFs, access to the regional market supersedes access to national markets as an important FDI determinant. From the point of view of each member country, what becomes important for FDI in tradable goods and services is its ability to provide good access to the region-wide market. This depends on how well it is integrated into the regional bloc in terms of policy harmonization as well as physical accessibility. Not being left behind in the harmonization process and establishing good infrastructure facilities therefore acquire greater prominence as national FDI determinants. Sustained increases in growth rates, one of the dynamic benefits of RIFs, also help to boost FDI. Again, it is the region's growth that matters more, and not national growth. This does not mean that national markets or growth no longer matter; they remain important FDI determinants, especially for non-tradable services, but they matter less.

The greater openness that exists within RIFs gives rise to more competition among firms, domestic or foreign. The likelihood that FDI will be affected by reactions to "strategic" moves of other firms, as firms try to position themselves in the best possible situation to benefit from a RIF, also increases. It is more likely under RIFs that firms will position themselves in such ways as to exploit first-mover advantages ahead of their competitors and that they will be more inclined to engage in cross-border strategic alliances. Such strategic responses to RIFs by TNCs can be expected to boost FDI in a regional bloc.

Production-related FDI determinants, as opposed to determinants related to demand, come to play a more important role in location decisions under RIFs. In particular, asset-augmenting and asset-exploiting FDI can take advantage of location-specific immobile factors of production or resources within the region, with access to the region's market already being assured by the RIF. Many of these resources are created assets that can be accessed through formal or informal links with supranational (or sub-national) clusters of companies or research facilities giving rise to agglomeration economies. Efficiency, too, acquires a new dimension in a regional context. The existence of a greater variety of production inputs at a wider choice of prices means that TNCs can make better choices within regional blocs than in a single country alone. Regional integration frameworks also allow TNCs to take advantage of a greater number of FDI determinants without having to trade one determinant against another. Access to enlarged markets, for example, can be achieved without having to sacrifice access to location-specific resources that help to enhance efficiency. In the case of NAFTA, for example, foreign automobile manufacturers can still reap the benefits of lower costs in Mexico without losing access to the broader North American market. On the one hand, this makes regions attractive locations; on the other hand, as national locational advantages become less distinct, they give rise to more competition for FDI among member countries (or locations within countries).

On the policy front, greater uniformity of trade and other policies that influence FDI means that TNCs can expect similar treatment across the region. This does not mean that policy determinants are not important, but it does imply that their distinctiveness as country-specific location advantages diminishes for the members of a regional arrangement. For the region as a whole, RIFs can accelerate the process of trade and FDI liberalization; ensure its continuity, transparency and stability; and reaffirm the protection of foreign investors. So, at the regional level, RIFs can give policy determinants a boost in importance.

Under such conditions, business facilitation factors, less frequently addressed by RIFs, come to play a more important role in the competition for FDI. A number of proactive measures to facilitate international production can be carried out fairly rapidly by national governments. By offering after-investment services, social amenities and other business facilitation services to foreign investors, national governments or sub-national authorities can attempt to influence TNC location decisions.

In conclusion, RIFs diminish the ability of member countries to attract FDI on grounds of country-specific location advantages alone, including their ability to negotiate with foreign investors on the basis of such advantages. The regional context, and the extent to which a member country is able to tap into it in order to enhance its own location advantages, become more important for the location of FDI. Business facilitation measures, although not the most significant category of FDI determinants, become more significant as they are among the few areas on the basis of which member countries (or locations within countries) can compete for FDI. Intraregional competition for FDI through business facilitation is thus not only likely to intensify but may also take place increasingly at the sub-national level, as locations within member countries compete for FDI more fiercely than countries themselves. The challenge for RIF members (or sub-national locations) is to marry their own distinct locational advantages with the advantages that the region offers to create an environment that complements the ownership and internalization advantages of TNCs.

3. The potential impact of a possible multilateral framework on investment

In recent years, discussions on international investment frameworks have intensified, including the possibility of plurilateral and multilateral frameworks (chapter III; UNCTAD, 1996a). One of the questions that has been raised in this context concerns the extent to which a possible multilateral framework on investment (MFI) would influence investment decisions and, in particular, lead to higher FDI flows around the world.

The development of an MFI, if such a framework were to be negotiated, would represent a change in the policy-framework cluster of determinants (table IV.1). Although such a framework might also affect some elements of business facilitation (such as investment incentives), it would not involve significant and direct changes in the principal economic determinants. Indeed, by making FDI policies potentially more similar, an MFI would underline the importance of economic (and business facilitation) factors in determining FDI flows.

The precise effect of an MFI on the policy-framework cluster of determinants would depend on its content, including definitions, scope and safeguards. Because an MFI is only a hypothesis, three scenarios, based on differing assumptions, are discussed below for purely analytical purposes.[39] The discussion is thus at an abstract level and should be read with the understanding that the specific implications of each scenario would vary from country to country in accordance with specific economic and developmental conditions and specific national stances vis-à-vis FDI.

This section does not deal with the advantages or disadvantages of an MFI, but with a hypothetical question: if there were an MFI, how would it affect the volume and pattern of FDI flows? Since an MFI is only a hypothesis and not a reality -- and since there is little information about how TNCs would incorporate a variable such as an MFI into their locational decisions -- answers to this question are unavoidably tentative.[40]

One conceivable outcome of an MFI is that it would help to *increase* FDI flows -- and perhaps affect other features of such flows as well. Such an outcome is based in part on the assumption that a multilateral agreement would not only consolidate recent changes towards more liberal policies by many countries but would incorporate "rollback" provisions -- requiring countries to commit themselves to reducing or eliminating existing barriers to FDI and strengthening investment protection and the proper functioning of markets. Even in the absence of further liberalization, a multilateral framework could facilitate investment by providing stronger assurances -- as compared with unilateral or even bilateral measures -- when it comes to the protection of FDI and the stability of domestic FDI regimes. The presumably greater stability, predictability and transparency resulting from an MFI would create a generally more favourable climate for investors. The impact on inflows might be greatest for those countries that were not already signatories to bilateral, regional, plurilateral or multilateral investment agreements, and countries whose current policies, even if favourable to FDI, are not considered sufficiently predictable by investors. At the same time, whether or not FDI flows would actually increase -- and whether there would be a change in the quality and patterns of flows -- would depend on the precise content of an agreement, the nature of national commitments and exceptions to the generalized multilateral rules and, of course, the other FDI determinants that would come into play at that point.

A second conceivable outcome of an MFI is that it could actually *reduce* the quantity and quality of FDI flows, because the negotiation of an MFI would take several years, creating uncertainties about the investment climate worldwide and thereby discouraging foreign investors. Further, even if negotiations did produce an agreement, the MFI that would result could conceivably enshrine a less liberal multilateral environment than has already evolved unilaterally or regionally. (However, the extent to which a formal binding of the regulatory framework at a less liberal level would affect FDI flows is unclear.) Such an MFI could also alter the patterns of FDI flows across geographic regions and industries. In particular, an MFI might reduce FDI flows to countries that gain from the currently restrictive policies of their competitors for such investment and increase flows to otherwise desirable locations that are receiving little inward FDI because of uncertainties about policies.

A third conceivable outcome of a possible MFI is that it would have *little or no impact* on the quantity and quality of FDI flows, as it would not materially alter the policy framework for FDI. One reason why this might be the result is that there has already been significant liberalization in many countries, in particular in many developing countries and countries in transition, during the 1980s and 1990s (chapter III, table III.2); and this liberalization has contributed to a surge of FDI flows that reached a new record in 1997. Therefore, an MFI that contains, for example, standstill provisions -- requiring countries to commit themselves not to introduce new barriers to FDI, lower standards of investment treatment or measures likely to impair the proper functioning of markets -- would essentially maintain the status quo, as far as the openness of economies to FDI, their treatment of foreign affiliates and the functioning of their markets are concerned. Moreover, the extensive network of bilateral investment treaties, which numbered over 1,500 by the end of 1997 (chapter III), would provide protection for investors and could be easily extended to additional countries. Finally, on this view, there would be no significant effects on the geographic patterns of FDI flows, as they are largely influenced by other FDI determinants.

* * *

On balance, these considerations suggest that an MFI would improve the enabling environment for FDI, to the extent that it would contribute to greater security for investors and greater stability, predictability and transparency in investment policies and rules. This, in turn, could encourage higher FDI flows and potentially some redistribution of those flows, particularly to countries whose investment climates would newly reflect the multilateral framework. How much difference an MFI would make, however, in terms of the quantity, quality and patterns of *actual* FDI flows is difficult to predict because as in the case of BITs, it is precisely the function of an enabling framework to allow other determinants, and especially economic determinants, to assert their influence.

Expectations about the impact of an MFI on FDI flows (if it were indeed to be negotiated) in comparison to the current regulatory framework and the direction in which it is developing should, therefore, not be exaggerated. There are, of course, other issues that need to be considered in connection with a possible MFI -- especially the possible role of such an agreement in providing a framework for intergovernmental cooperation in the area of investment (UNCTAD, 1996a, 1997a) -- but these fall outside the scope of the present analysis, which is specifically focused on the determinants of FDI flows.[41]

Notes

1 The analytical framework on which this description is based is known as the 'OLI (ownership, location, internalization) paradigm' -- also the 'eclectic paradigm'.

2 Governments *can* influence the other two conditions but only indirectly -- for example, through the promotion of cross-border partnerships in R&D, thereby reducing the imperfect nature of technology markets and thus affecting transaction costs, degree of competition and other elements of ownership and internalization choices.

3 As TNCs increasingly seek to hone their competitive advantages, their strategies can become quite diverse, even within the same industry (UNCTAD, forthcoming a, pp. 147-148).

4 See United States, Department of Commerce, 1997c, pp. 119-148 (and earlier articles in the same series).

5 Interest rates were found to be a factor influencing flows of FDI from the European Union to the United States (chapter V).

6 On the question of tax competition, see chapter III, box III.12.

7 In general, *changes* in exchange rate levels are expected to have a greater impact on FDI than *differences* in exchange rate levels, which were found insignificant as determinants of bilateral FDI flows among Canada, Germany, Japan, the United Kingdom, and the United States (Goldberg and Kolstad, 1994). Estimates for Malaysia and Thailand (e.g. Ramstetter, 1995a and 1995b) also suggest that exchange rate levels have not generally had a statistically significant effect on FDI in these countries. For a discussion of the effects of the 1997/1998 currency devaluation in Asia on FDI, see chapter VII.

8 From the perspective of local SMEs, equality of conditions can create an imbalance that favours large foreign firms. For example, if no speical measures are put in place to facilitate loans to SMEs, equal access to short and long term borrowing will favour larger TNCs firms.

9 Brazil, always a *potentially* attractive host country because of its market size, provides a good example. In the 1970s, it was the largest recipient of FDI among developing countries. It lost this position to other countries in the 1980s, as a result of the loss of macroeconomic stability, leading to a drastic reduction of FDI inflows. In the early 1990s, it introduced policies aimed at restoring macroeconomic stability and at re-attracting FDI. While the stability was restored almost immediately, it took two to three years for FDI flows to take off again, and to begin to grow rapidly. In interviews with CEOs of TNCs conducted for a study on FDI in Brazil in spring 1996, three years after the reforms started, it was clear that many CEOs were not yet convinced that the Brazilian reforms would hold (UNCTAD, forthcoming a).

10 Known in the FDI literature to be a factor influencing locational decisions (Johanson and Wiedersheim-Paul, 1993). It is based on the premise, confirmed by evidence, that investors tend to favour what they know, and regard territories they do not know as risky, a lack of knowledge being strongly associated

with the fear of negative possibilities. This lack of knowledge is deepened by differences in language, culture, political systems, levels of education, levels of development, etc. generating a psychic distance between home and host countries. Psychic distance, however, is not constant. It is being progressively reduced by modern tools of communication, trade and travel. Promotional actions can contribute to reducing it further.

11 This number does not include such countries as the United Kingdom and France, known for strong promotional programmes, but not yet members of WAIPA, which was established in 1995. In addition, many programmes are executed at the level of regions, or states within countries; perhaps these are even more numerous than national programmes. For example, virtually all of the states in the United States have such programmes, including promotional offices abroad in large home countries, such as Japan. Increasingly, regions and large cities in Europe have similar programmes.

12 For a recent example, see the programme of the Republic of Korea, chapter VII, box VII.11.

13 The discussion here focuses on business facilitation, including after-investment services as determinants of FDI. But after-investment (or aftercare) services can also be rendered with a view towards maximizing the FDI contribution to local economic development (Young and Hood, 1994, pp. 45 and 52). It should be noted as well that daily contact with foreign investors resulting from rendering these services puts IPAs in a unique position, which could enable them to be the first to identify faulty policies and, optimally, become champions of reforms.

14 Other reasons for the less frequent use of performance requirements include the fact that the TRIMS agreement stipulates the phasing out of certain performance requirements that distort trade (e.g. export requirements).

15 Characteristic in this regard is the following statement made recently by the head of CzechInvest, the national investment promotion agency, on the occasion of introducing a new package of incentives in the Czech Republic: "Up until now the Czech Republic has been competing with Poland, Hungary and Western European countries at a disadvantage. This package [of incentives] will enable the Czech Republic to compete on equal terms for prime mobile direct investment projects looking for a low-cost, highly-skilled location in Europe" (CzechInvest, 1998) (see also chapter IX, box IX.4).

16 However, convergence has limits. First, both promotional actions and incentives cost money, and some of them cost a lot of money. Therefore, for example, developing countries and economies in transition typically do not have pockets as deep as developed countries when it comes to financial incentives, which tend to focus on fiscal incentives (UNCTAD, 1995a, pp. 291-292). Second, there is a growing awareness that promotional programmes and incentives should be carefully tailored to the needs of individual host countries and not simply copied from the programmes of other countries (UNCTAD, 1997b). Third, many of these activities are very difficult to carry out and, even if carefully planned and well executed, they take time (e.g. reducing corruption).

17 Investment promotion activities, if not well-grounded in a favourable investment environment, may be counterproductive or even harmful if they create perceptions and expectations not in line with reality.

18 This type of investment is highly mobile because non-equity forms of FDI involve control but not ownership and this reduces the cost of closing down or abandoning foreign affiliates.

19 However, as the host country develops and acquires higher standards of living, final consumer goods produced by foreign affiliates may be redirected to its own domestic market.

20 A number of econometric studies, going back to the 1960s and forward to the mid-1990s have, on the whole, failed to confirm the common-sense expectation that low wages would be an important factor in attracting FDI into a host country. Among these are a study of manufacturing affiliates of United States TNCs in 1966 (Kravis and Lipsey, 1982) and a study of FDI flows from 14 home countries to 45 host countries in 1990 and 1991 (Wei, 1997a and 1997b).

There is rather less here than meets the eye. Low wages *are* a positive determinant of FDI but only other things being equal. What matters is not wage levels as such but these levels as adjusted for the productivity of labour inputs. The other point to note is that even productivity-adjusted wages are only one factor among others and their influence on any particular investment decision depends on the context of that decision, as determined by the relevant policy framework, the size of the relevant market, and the like. Hence, studies of the determinants of location decisions taken by foreign firms in one and the same country are likely to be more useful for analyzing the relationship between wage levels and investment flows than studies covering a variety of host countries. Indeed, analyses of the location decisions of Japanese firms in the United States between 1950 and 1992 (Head, Ries and Swensson, 1994) and of foreign investment entries into the United States between 1981 and 1983 (Coughlin, Terza and Arromdae, 1991) found higher wages to have a deterrent effect on location decisions.

21 In the textile and clothing industry quotas have been determined for many years by the Multi-Fibre Arrangement. Products in this industry were subcontracted on the basis of "market niche", that is, price elasticity of demand, cost/quality ratios *and* available quota (Mytelka, 1991).

22 A good part of this type of investment has been located, as mentioned earlier, in export processing zones. Where these remained as enclaves and did not draw upon supplies from the local economy, their dynamic impact and role in the transfer of technology and in shaping local technological capacity were weaker than where these linkages were established (e.g. in the Republic of Korea). In general, the firms in these zones are less likely to upgrade rapidly. In consequence, their contribution to the development of human capital is often limited and their vulnerability to price-and-productivity-based mobility is greater.

23 For elaboration on, and documentation of, the concept of complex integration strategies, see UNCTAD, 1993a, Part Two.

24 To a certain extent this applies also to non-tradable services, as various locations may compete for the mobile assets that are required to produce them; and it even applies to natural resources, where there are alternatives to them.

25 For details see UNCTAD, forthcoming a.

26 Needless to say, this observation also applies to other components of an enabling FDI framework.

27 Regional integration frameworks -- the focus of this section -- are policy-led integration initiatives adopted by governments. Economic integration, however, can also take place in the absence of policy-led integration initiatives, through transactions that promote greater interdependence and cohesion among economies. TNCs can instigate closer integration not only through cross-border arm's-length transactions (trade), leading to "shallow integration", but also through intra-firm transactions among members of their corporate networks, leading to "deep integration" (UNCTAD, 1993a; see also Lloyd, 1996). There are also arrangements that are more partial in nature, such as regional growth triangles (Pomfret, 1996).

28 A RIF that allows the free movement of both labour and capital would also affect FDI determinants. It would presumably reduce the need for resource-seeking FDI, where the resource sought is unskilled labour, and strategic asset-seeking FDI, where the asset sought is skilled labour.

29 It must be recognized that, in many instances, TNCs were attracted by markets that were protected by tariff barriers in the period preceding efficiency-seeking and competitiveness-enhancing FDI, since this reduced competitive pressures from imports while simultaneously allowing higher earnings (see Mytelka, 1994).

30 For example, the Australia-New Zealand Closer Economic Relations Agreement covers trade in goods and services (including labour mobility), but does not cover investment.

31 Of course, this did not always hold true. In the case of the European Union, for example, the Treaty of Rome contained specific provisions on capital movements, the right of establishment et al., all of which are relevant policy determinants of FDI. But these were not enough to open various service industries to FDI, which had to wait for the 1992 Single Market Programme to come into effect.

32 Article 73 of the Maastricht Treaty "grandfathered" existing FDI restrictions, mainly at the sectoral level on the inward side; there are virtually no restrictions on the outward side (Brewer and Young, 1998, p. 182).

33 Most RIFs that do address FDI policy are common markets and economic unions that, by definition, allow the movement of capital, including FDI capital, among members. But RIFs other than common markets and economic unions may also contain explicit FDI provisions for their members. The Gulf Cooperation Council, for example, has liberalized the movement of capital among member countries (Brewer and Young, 1998), creating conditions conducive to the entry of FDI. ASEAN members have adopted safeguards against nationalization and the provision of adequate compensation against expropriation, among other things (UNCTAD, 1996a, p. 148). NAFTA contains explicit FDI provisions on standards of treatment (national treatment and most-favoured-nation clauses); procedures for the settlement of disputes; procedures for phasing out existing export-based and production-based performance requirements; and bans on new export-performance, import-substitution and domestic-content requirements (Hufbauer and Schott, 1993, chap. 4).

34 For services, the liberalization of FDI regimes alone is not enough to attract investment. Policy changes as regards deregulation, privatization, consumer protection and the like may also be required.

35 Indeed, this can be observed even before countries become members of a RIF. For example, countries wanting to join the OECD or the European Union (through the association agreements) sometimes assume FDI liberalization obligations before they become full members.

36 Other important factors included skills, costs, language and responses to competitors' strategies.

37 Dunning (1997, p. 3) estimated that roughly three-fifths of inward FDI in the core countries of the European Community prior to 1985 was within a 500-mile radius of Frankfurt. This raises the question of polarization vs. spread effects, the distribution of associated benefits and the need for regional policies.

38 It has been suggested by Blomström and Kokko (1997, p. 4) that TNCs may act as catalysts for these dynamic effects associated with RIFs.

39 For more detailed analyses of the issues involved in discussions of a possible MFI, see UNCTAD 1996a and the series of UNCTAD issue papers in progress, scheduled for publication during 1998-1999.

40 Many of the questions that are now being raised about a possible MFI were raised more than half a century ago at the time of the creation of the General Agreement on Tariffs and Trade (GATT). They have reappeared from time to time, particularly during major rounds of trade negotiations. Despite the fact that investment issues are still often referred to as being among the "new" issues on the multilateral agenda, they are in fact not new. What is new is that they are being considered more directly and more extensively, particularly in relation to rules and institutional mechanisms.

41 For a discussion of other issues, see UNCTAD, 1996a and 1997a.

Annex to chapter IV.
An econometric test of market related FDI variables

There is a long history of econometric analyses of factors determining the amount of FDI a country receives. However, it is hard to derive any conclusion from these studies as to whether the list of determinants has changed over time or whether some have gained or lost importance. One reason comparisons over time are difficult is that the measures of investment, the measures of determinants, and the range of countries examined differ from study to study.

There is some advantage, then, in performing such an econometric analysis using the same list of determinants, measured in the same way, for the same set of countries over time. The following analysis covers 142 countries over the period 1980-1995.

Several variables related to host country markets have appeared in some form in almost all of the past explanations of the extent of inward FDI. One is the size of the host country or, more precisely, of the host country's internal market. A second is the rate of growth of the host country, which can be thought of as a predictor of future market size. A third is the average income of the residents of a country, which is related to their effective demand for the kinds of goods or services produced by foreign affiliates.

Table IV.A.1 presents a version of an explanation of the inward FDI stock in each of 142 countries at intervals between 1980 and 1995, based on these national market variables. The measure of market size is nominal GDP for each year, translated into dollars by average annual exchange rates; the growth variable is growth in real GDP over the previous five years; and the average income variable is GDP per capita, measured in current purchasing power parity (PPP) terms. The nominal GDP and, in three of the four years represented in the table, the real GDP per capita, are statistically significant at the 1 per cent level, in the expected positive direction. In other words, large markets and high-income markets attract more FDI, but past growth rates are apparently not projected into the future by potential investors. More than half of the variance in the investment levels is accounted for by these

Table IV.A.1. Regression of nominal inward FDI stock on nominal GDP, past growth in real GDP, and real GDP per capita

	1980	1985	1990	1995
Nominal GDP	0.0298***	0.0414***	0.0549***	0.0524***
	(0.0025)	(0.0022)	(0.0046)	(0.0065)
Growth in real GDP - previous five years	476	-377	-5,137	11,534
	(1,950)	(2,485)	(13,404)	(25,853)
Real GDP per capita	0.226	0.564***	1.439***	1.637**
	(0.144)	(0.187)	(0.486)	(0.750)
R^2	0.591	0.780	0.682	0.579

Figures in parentheses are standard errors

** Significant at 5% level
*** Significant at 1% level

host-country market variables but the precision of the explanation reached a peak in 1985 and has been declining ever since. That decline points to the possibility that host country market variables have declined in importance relative to some other unspecified determinants of inward FDI.

If the residuals from these equations are taken as representing the effects of unspecified determinants of inward FDI levels, then the market variables and the change in real income for the current period can explain changes in investment over the ensuing five years. One possible interpretation of the residuals is that they represent transitory past events or policies that have caused some host countries to have larger investment stocks and other countries smaller investment stocks than would be the case if FDI were distributed host countries in a pattern optimal from the point of view of international investment allocation. In that case one would expect negative coefficients for the residuals. Negative coefficients could represent a catching-up to more "normal" levels by potential host countries which had been previously neglected or which had in the meantime made their policies more welcoming towards inward FDI. Alternatively, negative coefficients might indicate a relapse to more "normal" levels in those host countries that had been favoured as FDI locations in the past but had then lost their advantages, or by countries that have modified their policies to be more restrictive towards inward FDI. Positive coefficients might mean that the factors that produced high levels of inward investment relative to income and income growth were long-term in nature, and continued to produce higher than average levels of inward FDI. An alternative interpretation of positive coefficients would be that high levels of inward investment, whatever their cause, themselves created circumstances, such as agglomeration economies, that attracted further investment.

The results are shown in table IV.A.2. The coefficients of the residuals from the investment stock equations are strongly positive. Host countries that have received more inward FDI than can be explained by their domestic market characteristics in a base year continue to receive more investment in subsequent years. This result suggests that there may be permanent or at least long-term features of host countries, outside of their domestic market characteristics, that attract FDI to an exceptional degree.

Among the other variables in the equations of table IV.A.2, initial market size, represented by nominal GDP, is the most consistent influence favouring further inflows of FDI. The coefficient for the growth of the host country market during the period increases in size over time and is statistically significant at the 5 per cent level for the final period. Thus, the inward flow of FDI during a five-year period is higher if the recipient country has a larger market; if it has received more investment in the past than would be expected from its domestic market characteristics; and if its domestic market has grown more rapidly than that of competing countries during the period.

Some recent literature on the determinants of inward FDI has focused on characteristics such as the extent of corruption (Wei, 1997a, 1997b) and other aspects of the organization of the host government or, more generally, society. After considering a variety of measures for 66 countries that are potential additional explanatory variables (Mauro, 1995), two are used here for further examination: "bureaucratic efficiency" (which combines ratings for three categories: judiciary system, red tape and corruption) and "political stability".

Table IV.A.2. Regression of nominal inward FDI flow on nominal GDP, current growth in real GDP, real GDP per capita, and residuals from inward FDI stock equations

	1980-1985	1985-1990	1990-1995
Nominal GDP	0.0314*** (0.0017)	0.0473*** (0.0026)	0.0234*** (0.0023)
Growth in real GDP - current five years	-896 (2,071)	4,257 (4,572)	8,221** (3,750)
Real GDP per capita	-0.011 (0.104)	1.123*** (0.228)	0.628** (0.249)
Residuals (from reg of stock on inv on no GDP, its growth & real PC GDP)	0.103 (0.065)	1.180*** (0.106)	0.387*** (0.051)
R^2	0.771	0.827	0.684

Figures in parentheses are standard errors

** Significant at 5% level
*** Significant at 1% level

Since the additional variables are available only for a much smaller group of countries, the equations of table IV.A.2 are shown in table IV.A.3 for this smaller group. While the equations do not fit quite as well, the story they tell is much the same: nominal GDP and per capita real GDP are both positive influences, while past real GDP growth is not a significant factor. If the residuals from this equation are calculated and related to the government efficiency and political stability variables, no relationship is found. If the government efficiency and political stability variables are added to the inward FDI stock equations of table IV.A.3, they do not add anything to the explanation. The same is true if they are added to the inward flow equations (these equations are not shown here). Thus, these additional variables do not, at least for a smaller sample of countries, account for the unspecified influences incorporated in the residuals.

Table IV.A.3. Regression of nominal inward stock of FDI on nominal GDP, past growth in real GDP, and real GDP per capita for a smaller group of countries

	1980	1985	1990	1995
Nominal GDP	0.0275*** (0.0036)	0.0400*** (0.0033)	0.0540*** (0.0065)	0.0504*** (0.0086)
Growth in real GDP - previous five years	609 (7,167)	-1,367 (6,482)	-1,676 (30,834)	-7,849 (44,105)
Real GDP per capita	0.623* (0.359)	0.814** (0.370)	1.629* (0.824)	1.508 (1.172)
R^2	0.571	0.771	0.662	0.532

Figures in parentheses are standard errors
* Significant at 10 % level
** Significant at 5% level
*** Significant at 1% level

It has been argued that government-related and political variables would be more important in developing countries than in developed countries, where the range of the variables may be much smaller. Therefore the equations of table IV.A.3 have been recalculated for developing countries alone. The results are shown in table IV.A.4. They again confirm the predominant influence of host country market size, with larger coefficients than for the world as a whole. Per capita income, while a consistently positive influence, is not generally statistically significant, and the explanatory power of the equations is considerably weaker for these countries. In table IV.A.5, the political stability variable is added and here, for the first time, the equations provide evidence that an institutional characteristic of a host country has a positive influence on inward FDI.

Table IV.A.4. Regression of nominal inward stock of FDI on nominal GDP, past growth in real GDP, and real GDP per capita, developing countries

	1980	1985	1990	1995
Nominal GDP	0.0510*** (0.0092)	0.0714*** (0.0200)	0.0638*** (0.0140)	0.1279*** (0.0208)
Growth in real GDP - previous five years	3,879 (2,427)	-1,367 (3,815)	11,150 (7,307)	16,719 (20,311)
Real GDP per capita	0.019 (0.145)	0.594 (0.385)	0.737* (0.382)	0.560 (0.488)
R^2	0.472	0.254	0.452	0.604

Figures in parentheses are standard errors

* Significant at 10 % level
*** Significant at 1% level

Table IV.A.5. Regression of nominal inward stock of FDI on nominal GDP, growth in real GDP, real GDP per capita, and political stability developing countries

	1980	1985	1990	1995
Nominal GDP	0.0519*** (0.0092)	0.0785*** (0.0194)	0.0657*** (0.0136)	0.1297*** (0.0209)
Growth in real GDP - five years	2,104 (3,039)	-2,851 (3,718)	11,239 (7,038)	24,312 (21,635)
Real GDP per capita	-0.049 (0.162)	0.135 (0.429)	0.378 (0.416)	0.165 (0.624)
Political stability	511.538 (526.419)	1988.908** (953.940)	2097.259* (1133.746)	3054.675 (3010.638)
R^2	0.471	0.317	0.491	0.604

Figures in parentheses are standard errors
* Significant at 10 % level
** Significant at 5% level
*** Significant at 1% level

The residuals from the equations of table IV.A.4 are used, together with initial nominal GDP, the growth in real GDP during the period, and the initial per capita income, to explain the inflow of FDI to developing countries (table IV.A.6). Market size is again the main influence. It is followed by the residual significant in two periods; growth in real GDP, significant in only one period, and real per capita GDP which is only marginally significant. Political stability (table IV.A.7) does not contribute to the explanation of the inflow of FDI to developing countries in the equations.

Table IV.A.6. Regression of nominal inward stock of FDI on nominal GDP, current growth in real GDP, real GDP per capita, and residuals from inward FDI stock equations, developing countries

	1980-1985	1985-1990	1990-1995
Nominal GDP	0.0404** (0.0148)	0.0184** (0.0089)	0.0860*** (0.0148)
Growth in real GDP - current five years	627 (4,703)	7,179*** (2,159)	1,378 (5,997)
Real GDP per capita	0.393 (0.249)	0.579*** (0.180)	0.940*** (0.417)
Residuals	0.339 (0.254)	0.213*** (0.076)	0.553*** (0.180)
R^2	0.272	0.497	0.598

Figures in parentheses are standard errors

** Significant at 5% level
*** Significant at 1% level

Table IV.A.7. Regression of nominal inward flow of FDI on nominal GDP, current growth in real GDP, real GDP per capita, and residuals from inward FDI stock equations and political stability, developing countries

	1980-1985	1985-1990	1990-1995
Nominal GDP	0.0431*** (0.0149)	0.0216*** (0.0090)	0.0857*** (0.0151)
Growth in real GDP - current five years	-670 (4,776)	6,795*** (2,133)	992 (6,372)
Real GDP per capita	0.225 (0.281)	0.415* (0.206)	1.003* (0.520)
Residuals	0.249 (0.262)	0.179* (0.078)	0.567*** (0.196)
Political stability	833 (665)	687 (447)	-285 (1,370)
R^2	0.284	0.516	0.585

Figures in parentheses are standard errors

* Significant at 10 % level
*** Significant at 1% level

A conclusion to be drawn from the econometric analysis is that host country market-size variables remain the dominant influence on inward FDI, although they explain less of the variation across countries in more recent years than in earlier periods. Whatever factors in the past caused some countries to receive more FDI than might have been expected on the basis of their market characteristics remain influential. However, for the world as a whole, the institutional variables included in this exercise are not the explanation. A candidate for further explanation, not tested here, would be existing membership in or recent adherence to a regional arrangement, for example the European Union or NAFTA.

In developing countries, the domestic market variables, while strongly significant, explain less than half the variance among countries in inward FDI stock except in the last year examined, 1995. That contrasts with the situation for all countries, in which more than half the variation is explained in all years. One institutional variable, political stability, seems to be of some influence among developing countries, where it is positively related to a host country's attractiveness as a location for FDI and in some periods adds to the explanation of the inward investment stock. It does not, however, add to the explanation of inward FDI flows in these countries. The coefficient of the residual variable calculated from the inward investment stock equation, representing favourable and unfavourable characteristics not identified here, becomes increasingly large over time for these developing countries, despite the fact that market variables explain a large part of the variance.

All in all, national market variables do explain much of the variation in inward FDI attractiveness among countries, but the size and importance of the residuals and their predictive power is a challenge for further investigation.

Source: UNCTAD.

CHAPTER V

DEVELOPED COUNTRIES

Developed countries sent $359 billion abroad in foreign direct investment (FDI) in 1997 and received $233 billion in FDI in turn. Their share of global outflows of FDI continued to exceed 80 per cent, whereas their share of inflows was significantly lower at 58 per cent. Both outflows and inflows in 1997 were noticeably higher than in 1996, the outflows substantially so (annex tables B.1 and B.2).

The Triad (the European Union, Japan and the United States) accounted for 87 per cent of FDI flows into and 89 per cent of outflows from developed countries in 1997, slightly less than the about 90 per cent for both in 1996. The European Union led the Triad in both FDI outflows and inflows, followed by the United States and Japan (annex tables B.1 and B.2). In terms of FDI stock as well, the European Union was considerably ahead of the United States. Outside the Triad, the largest developed country recipients of FDI in 1997 were Australia and Canada (figure V.1) and the largest outward investors Canada and Switzerland (figure V.2). Flows into South Africa remained low until 1996 but doubled in 1997.[1] For the developed countries as a whole, FDI as a percentage of gross fixed capital formation is considerably higher for outflows than inflows, with both of them very low for Japan (figure V.3). As always, these figures are net figures, reflecting the fact that firms not only invest abroad, but also divest (box V.1). They do not, however, take into account that, especially in the case of developed countries, a part of outward FDI is undertaken by foreign affiliates, i.e. is indirect FDI (box V.2).

A. United States

In 1997, the United States reported $91 billion in FDI inflows and $115 billion in outflows, again far exceeding inflows and outflows of any other country. Both amounts set new records (figures V.1 and V.2). Inflows were 19 per cent higher than in 1996; outflows 53 per cent (figure V.4). As a result, the share of the United States in worldwide FDI rose to 23 per cent for inflows and 27 per cent for outflows. In terms of the regional and sectoral

Figure V.1. Developed countries: FDI inflows, 1996 and 1997[a]

(Billions of dollars)

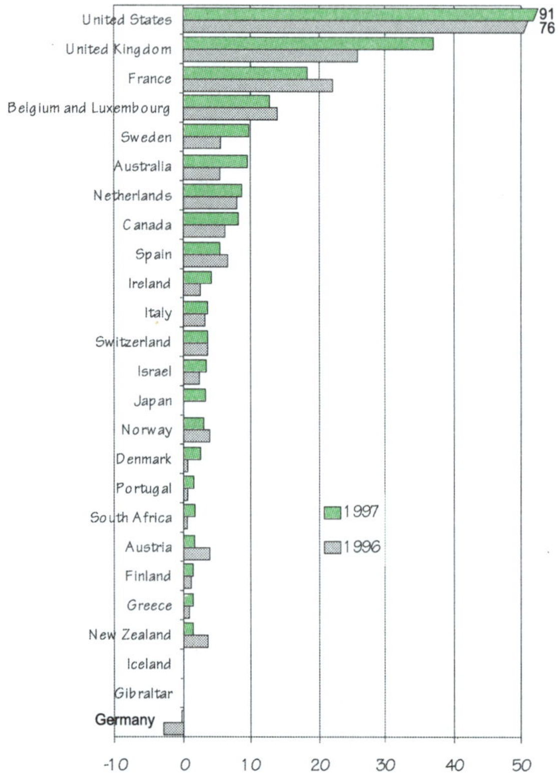

Source: UNCTAD, FDI/TNC database.

[a] Ranked on the basis of magnitude of 1997 FDI inflows.

Figure V.2. Developed countries: FDI outflows, 1996 and 1997[a]

(Billions of dollars)

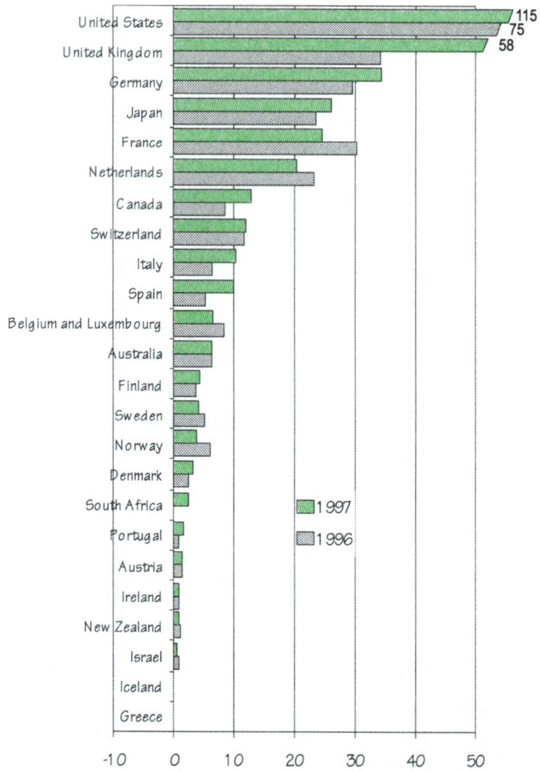

Source: UNCTAD, FDI/TNC database.

[a] Ranked on the basis of magnitude of 1997 FDI outflows.

Box V.1. Divestment

Although FDI represents investment made with a view towards a lasting interest in, and control of, enterprises located in countries other than the home countries of TNCs, divestment of foreign assets by firms engaged in FDI also takes place quite frequently. Reasons for divestment unrelated to corporate restructuring include decreased demand; mismanagement; overinvestment; and changes in the regulatory environment. (For an illustrative list of reasons for divestment, based on a survey of Japanese firms, see annex table A.V.1) It is worth noting, however, that TNCs may withdraw even when foreign affiliates are successful, as part of a deliberate, broader corporate strategy of reorganization, restructuring and downsizing in order to increase the efficiency of their corporate systems as a whole. Currently, for example, firms are generally moving towards consolidating their main activities around core competencies, splitting off non-core activities through divestments, including the divestment of assets located abroad.[a]

According to data for the countries that report statistics on divestment by foreign investors separately, divestments accounted for from 25 per cent of total Portuguese FDI to more than 70 per cent of Spanish gross investments in 1995 (box table 1). As the amount of divestment (like that of investment) fluctuates from year to year, the share of divestment in gross FDI outflows varies as well. Data for the two largest outward-investor countries -- the United Kingdom and the United States -- indicate that this share has fluctuated between 12 and 40 per cent for the former and between 14 and 66 per cent for the latter (box table 2). While it is difficult to discern any trend, the following observations may be pertinent:

/...

Figure V.3. Developed countries: FDI flows as a percentage of gross fixed capital formation, 1994-1996

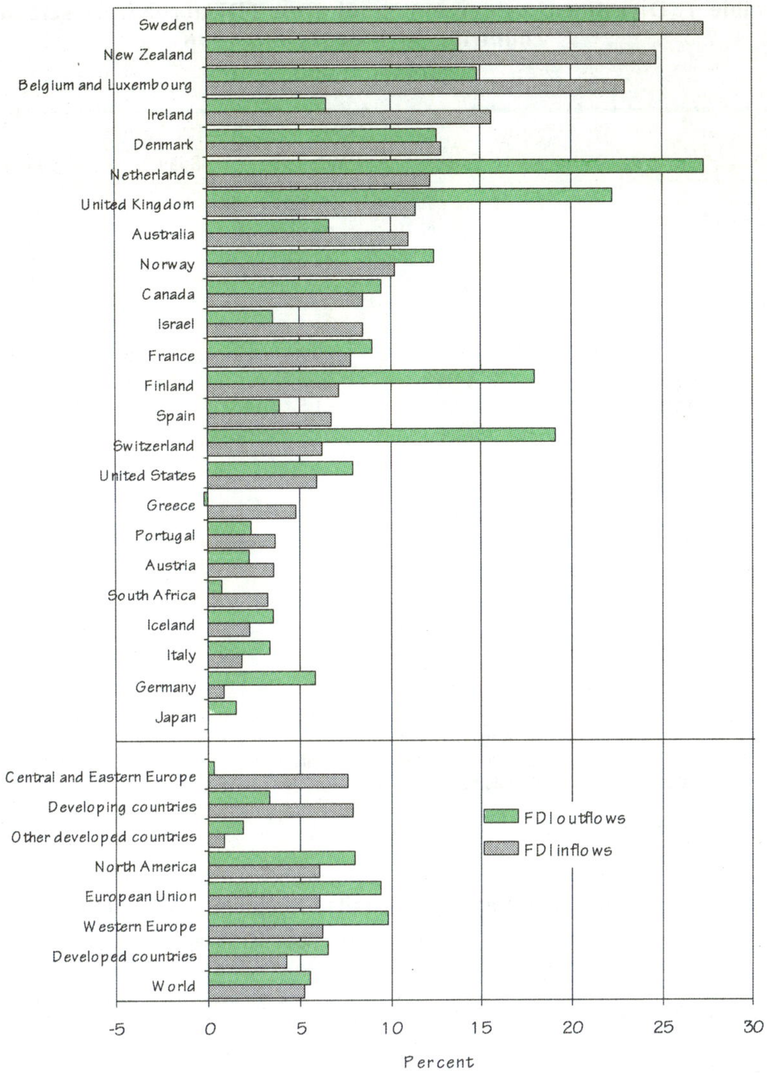

Source: UNCTAD, FDI/TNC database.

[a] Ranked on the basis of magnitude of 1997 FDI intflows as a percentage of gross fixed capital formation.

(Box V.1, continued)

- The higher the FDI flows or the number of firms investing in a country, the greater the likely amount of divestment in absolute value. A typical example concerns Japanese affiliates in the United States. Large Japanese investments made there in the latter half of the 1980s were not always successful and were therefore liquidated. In fact, the United States accounted for 30 per cent of the accumulated number of Japanese affiliates closed during the past 40 years (Toyo Keizai, 1998).

- The more competitive markets are, the more likely it is that divestments will occur. A high level of competition can lead to low levels of profit and, more generally, drive uncompetitive firms from markets. The divestment ratio for FDI is thus unsurprisingly high in the United States -- a highly competitive market in many industries.[b]

/...

(Box V.1, continued)

Box table 1. Divestment as percentage of gross FDI abroad, by selected home countries, by host region, 1996

(Percentage)

Host region/country	Home country: France	Portugal[a]	Spain[a]	United Kingdom	United States
Developed countries	76.9[b]	28.8	72.2	49.6[c]	25.2[d]
Europe	80.4[e]	28	73.7	12.5	24.9
North America	63.4	48.3	48.1	76.3	19.4[f]
United States	64.6	..	..	72.9	..
Developing countries	20.2	1.1	76	4.7	12.3
Africa	..	3.2	116.1	3.3	..
Latin America and the Caribbean	11.9[g]	0.3	76.2	3.1	16.2
South, East and South-East Asia	19.4[h]	1.5	17.5	5.6	8.3[i]
West Asia	27.9[j]	-	0.3	-	..
Central and Eastern Europe	15[k]	-	21.6	..	..
World	73	25.4	72.3	40.2	17

Source: UNCTAD, based on FDI/TNC database.

a Data are for 1995.
b Data are for OECD countries.
c Includes also Central and Eastern Europe.
d Not including Japan and developed countries in the Pacific.
e Data are for the European Union.
f Data cover only Canada.
g Data are for Argentina, Brazil, Mexico, Panama and Netherlands Antilles only.
h Data are for China; Republic of Korea; Hong Kong, China; Singapore; and Thailand.
i Includes also Japan and developed countries in the Pacific.
j Data cover only Saudi Arabia.
k Data cover only the Russian Federation.

Box table 2. Gross FDI[a] and divestment in the United Kingdom and the United States, 1983-1996

(Millions of pounds and dollars and percentages)

Year	United Kingdom: Gross FDI (Millions of pounds)	United Kingdom: Divestment (Millions of pounds)	United Kingdom: Divestment as percentage of gross FDI	United States: Gross FDI (Millions of dollars)	United States: Divestment (Millions of dollars)	United States: Divestment as percentage of gross FDI
1983	3 498	665	19.0	19 861	13 166	66.3
1984	5 814	1 226	21.1	26 773	15 186	56.7
1985	8 625	1 754	20.3	24 196	11 034	45.6
1986	11 798	1 460	12.4	23 511	4 832	20.6
1987	19 159	2 637	13.8	40 120	9 075	22.6
1988	20 916	3 323	15.9	27 047	10 829	40.0
1989	21 491	3 479	16.2	54 148	23 981	44.3
1990	10 108	3 180	31.5	51 109	16 998	33.3
1991	9 304	3 554	38.2	45 991	13 295	28.9
1992	10 107	3 747	37.1	52 724	11 137	21.1
1993	17 358	4 490	25.9	89 610	12 363	13.8
1994	21 040	5 563	26.4	86 242	17 970	20.8
1995	27 604	3 679	13.3	121 983	36 868	30.2
1996	22 014	8 855	40.2	103 091	17 531	17.0

Source: UNCTAD, based on FDI/TNC database.

a (Net) FDI flows plus divestment.

/..

(Box V.1, concluded)

- FDI in tax havens or FDI made in response to incentives is particularly vulnerable to divestment. If countries have a large share of their outward FDI in tax havens, divestment can become large relative to gross outward FDI. Spain, which had more than a tenth of its gross FDI in tax havens, divested itself of more than 70 per cent of it in 1996 (box table 1); if only Spanish investment in tax havens is considered, divestment was much higher than new investment. Such divestment generally takes the form of withdrawals of intra-company loans. Investments in financial intermediaries in tax havens, such as the Netherlands Antilles, are typically a transient feature of a country's outward FDI, as exemplified by United States FDI in these locations.[c]

Reported FDI, being a net figure, does not indicate how much new investment is made and how much divestment takes place.[d] High net figures may disguise reinvested earnings; low ones may disguise divestment. Divestment by an individual company does not necessarily imply that the operations of the foreign affiliate are in an unhealthy state. However, large or sustained divestments can signal to host countries that they are no longer attractive locations for foreign firms.

---

a This is reflected in FDI statistics which normally report flows on a net basis. OECD (OECD, 1996) and IMF (IMF, 1993) recommend that countries report gross investment, divestment and net investment (gross investment less disinvestment) separately; however, there are not many countries that report these elements of FDI separately. In the case of investments of a non-permanent nature, the IMF recommends not including such investment in FDI statistics (IMF, 1993, para. 365).

b The profitability of foreign affiliates in the United States is relatively low: in 1995, the ratio of net income to sales was a meagre 1 per cent for foreign affiliates (United States, Department of Commerce, 1997a); in Japan, this ratio was 2.6 per cent in 1995 (Japan, Ministry of International Trade and Industry, 1998b). In contrast, United States affiliates abroad earned 5.4 per cent by way of profits (United States, Department of Commerce, 1997b).

c See, for example, "U.S. international transactions, first quarter 1998", *BEA New Release*, 18 June 1998, from the Web site of United States, Department of Commerce, Bureau of Economic Analysis (www.bea.doc.gov/bea/newsrel/trans198.htm).

d Increases in parent company payables to foreign affiliates are also counted as divestment. If a foreign affiliate is established in order to supply the parent company with goods and services, the parent company payables to the affiliates tend to expand with the growth of trade between them. Although this is based on balance-of-payments accounting and is different from other reasons in nature, it should be noted that this type of transaction is recorded as divestment as well.

Box V.2. Indirect FDI

The sources of FDI are not only parent TNCs -- companies that own and operate affiliates abroad -- but their foreign affiliates as well. FDI by a foreign affiliate is *indirect* FDI, signifying that the resulting asset-stock is owned by the parent firm *via* the foreign affiliate, and that it represents, therefore, an indirect flow of FDI from the parent firm's home country (and a direct flow of FDI from the country in which the affiliate is located).[a]

Whether indirect FDI occurs or not depends on factors related to home and host country policies as well as on factors related to firms' strategies and behaviour.

- Taxation and embargoes are among the country-specific factors that might induce indirect FDI. For example, Mauritius had concluded a double-taxation treaty with India in 1982; this attracted foreign firms, especially those owned by non-resident Indians, to establish holding companies in Mauritius to invest in India. Serving as a conduit for this indirect FDI, Mauritius has become one of the largest FDI sources for India.[b] Similarly, an investment embargo by one country on another may induce TNCs to invest in the latter economy via a third economy that is not affected by the embargo. Firms based in Taiwan Province of China, for example, invest in China via their affiliates in Hong Kong, China.
- Firm-related factors conducive to indirect FDI include the type of division of labour that exists within corporate networks, which, among other things, can give a certain degree of autonomy to foreign affiliates vis-à-vis their parent firms. Regional headquarters, for example, may be able to make their own decisions as regards undertaking FDI. In the ASEAN region, nearly half of the Japanese affiliates located in Singapore have affiliates in other countries in the region (UNCTAD, 1996a).

Reported FDI, whether inward or outward, is supposed to include such investments by definition. In fact, the *Balance of Payments Manual* of the IMF and the OECD's benchmark definition of

/...

(Box V.2, continued)

FDI include investment by foreign affiliates in the definition and advise governments to include it in their FDI data, (IMF, 1993; OECD, 1996).[c] When it comes to a country that hosts a foreign affiliate engaged in FDI, the investment (an indirect investment by the affiliate's parent firm) is recorded as outward FDI from that economy, because the definition of FDI for balance-of-payments purposes is based on the location rather than on the ownership of the investing enterprise. However, such an investment is typically not recorded in the statistics of the home country of the ultimate parent firm. Tracing the ultimate beneficial owner, and hence the magnitude of the share of the ultimate home country as compared with the immediate home country from which the investment is made, is difficult and possible only for selected countries (e.g. Austria, see annex table A.V.2).[d]

The inclusion of indirect FDI in the outward FDI of countries hosting foreign affiliates engaged in FDI obscures the actual volume of FDI made by nationally-owned firms of those countries. (Interestingly, the same applies to strategic alliances many of which are made by affiliates and not recorded for the parent firm.) Information distinguishing FDI made by nationally-owned firms from that made by foreign affiliates located in a given country is also limited. According to data for some countries, the importance of indirect FDI relative to total outward FDI varies among countries (box table 1). For Canada and Switzerland[e] as well as Hong Kong (China) and Singapore -- where affiliates play an important role -- the percentage of indirect FDI is relatively high, accounting for one-fifth to one-half of outward FDI. In contrast, reflecting the domestic orientation of the operations of foreign firms in the United States, FDI by foreign affiliates located in the United States accounts for a small percentage of total United States outward FDI.

FDI originating in tax-haven economies is mostly undertaken by foreign affiliates. According to United States data (the only data available on ultimate ownership), assets in the United States owned, for example, by firms based in the Netherlands Antilles were worth $11 billion in 1995; but $8 billion of this amount was held, ultimately, by other countries (annex table A.V.3). On the other hand, the foreign assets of developing country TNCs can be underestimated. United States affiliates of firms based in Brazil, for example, had one billion dollars' worth of assets in the United States in 1995; but a reassessment of Brazilian foreign assets on the basis of data on inward FDI in the United States by

Box table 1. Indirect FDI from selected countries, various years

(Percentage)

Item	Canada 1987	Canada 1990	Canada 1993	Hong Kong, China	Singapore	Switzerland 1996	United States 1992
Share of the number of parent firms accounted for by foreign affiliates	26	28	29	..	..	..	..
Share of the number of foreign affiliates accounted for by foreign affiliates	20	21	21	..	..	..	..
Share of outward FDI stock accounted for by foreign affiliates	16	15	19	..	..	17[a]	4[b]
Share of outward FDI flows accounted for by foreign affiliates	..	..	..	30[c]	50[c]	..	..
Share of foreign sales accounted for by foreign affiliates	..	..	..	..	..	..	3
Share of foreign employment accounted for by foreign affiliates	..	..	..	..	..	..	4

Source: UNCTAD, based on unpublished data provided by Statistics Canada, United States, Department of Commerce; and UNCTAD, 1997d.

[a] FDI made by financial and holding companies in which the majority share is owned by foreign firms.
[b] Share of foreign assets.
[c] Estimates (not for a particular year).

/...

structure of United States FDI inflows and outflows, the following developments stand out (table V.1):

- For both inflows and outflows, the European Union continued to be the most important investment partner of the United States. However, the European Union's share (and notably Germany's share) in inflows declined markedly in 1997. Japan's share also declined, but this is a trend dating back to the beginning of the 1990s. On the other hand, Switzerland invested heavily in the United States in 1997: inflows from that country more than doubled, to $8.3 billion, rivalling France ($8.7 billion) and the United Kingdom ($8.6 billion). However, the biggest investors in the United States in 1997 were Germany ($10.7 billion) and the Netherlands ($10.3 billion).

- Developing countries continued to attract about one-third of United States FDI outflows (table V.1). They are, moreover, also emerging as a not unimportant source of United States FDI inflows (10 per cent). In both inflows and outflows, Latin America and the Caribbean were the dominant developing-region partner in 1997. That region's share in United States FDI outflows amounted to one-fifth of the total. But FDI flows into the United States from Latin America and

(Box V.2, concluded)

Brazilian affiliates in other countries shows that assets of United States affiliates ultimately owned by investors from Brazil amounted to $8.7 billion (annex table A.V.3). This pattern of investing in the United States through foreign affiliates in intermediate countries is not much followed by developed country firms. A British firm, say, is likely to invest in the United States directly, not through its affiliates elsewhere.

The policy implications of indirect FDI are complex. TNCs that undertake FDI from one of their host countries may do so because they regard that country as a strategic location for their regional or global operations. As far as the host countries are concerned, it may be important for them to monitor the volume and direction of indirect FDI because it may provide them with a better understanding of their own advantages for outward FDI: to the extent that outward FDI is determined by ownership advantages, the advantages underlying indirect FDI may be erroneously attributed to the immediate home country's firms. Of course, foreign affiliates -- depending on their degree of specialization and competence within a TNC network -- might also enrich the existing ownership advantages of their corporate systems by adding advantages that have been locally developed, making further FDI possible. Still, the larger the share of indirect FDI by other countries' TNCs in a country's overall outward FDI, the greater the uncertainty of the national competitiveness of outward FDI. Thus, the non-recognition of indirect FDI could lead to an overestimation of the competitiveness of a country's firms in international markets and this may detract from the need to consider policy measures to enhance competitiveness. In any event, as TNCs operate more and more globally, and their corporate networks become more and more complex, investments by foreign affiliates will become more important.

---

[a] As far as the host country is concerned, the same FDI represents foreign-controlled FDI.

[b] Mauritius has been the second largest investor in India, after the United States, since 1995. It accounted for about one-fifth of total approved FDI inflows into India in 1997 (UNCTAD, FDI/TNC database).

[c] "Statistics ... should, as a matter of principle, cover all enterprises in which the direct investor has directly or indirectly a direct investment interest" (OECD, 1996, paragraph 15), while the IMF stipulates "Direct investment enterprises comprise ... subsidiaries ..., associates ... and branches ... either directly or indirectly owned by the direct investor" (IMF, 1993, paragraph 362).

[d] This is especially so in the case of internationally owned TNCs and firms with diversified shareholdings.

[e] At the end of 1996 foreign financial and holding companies in Switzerland held outward FDI stock worth Sfr 33 billion, more than the level of FDI stock held by chemical and plastics firms (Sfr 30 billion), the second largest investor industry after insurance (Sfr 40 billion).

the Caribbean were not much larger than those from many developed countries such as France, Germany, Netherlands, Switzerland and the United Kingdom in 1997. However, flows from offshore financial centres accounted for three-quarters of United States inflows originating from the Latin American region.[2]

- Investment inflows and outflows in manufacturing as a whole continued to decline significantly in relative importance, accounting for just over a quarter of overall FDI outflows and 40 per cent of FDI inflows in 1997 (table V.1). Finance

Figure V.4. Developed countries: growth of FDI, 1996-1997[a]

(Percentage)

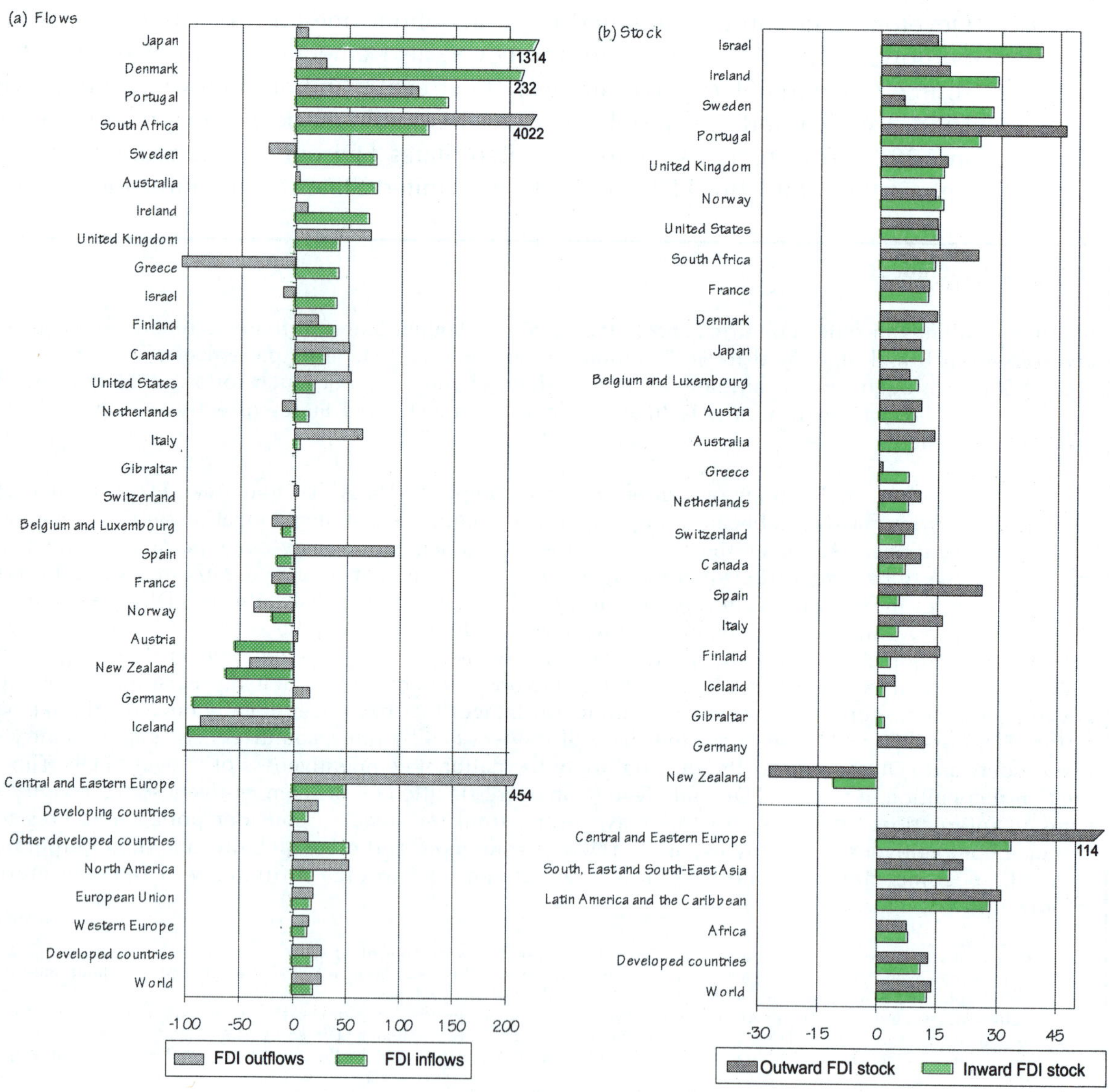

Source: UNCTAD, FDI/TNC database.

[a] Ranked on the basis of magnitude of growth of FDI inflows and inward stock.

and insurance was the dominant industry in outflows (accounting for 42 per cent of the total);[3] finance and insurance was also the dominant industry in inflows, followed by chemicals and wholesale trade.

The composition of FDI by mode of financing reveals considerable volatility over time, and was strikingly different for inflows and outflows. Equity capital continued to be the most important component of inflows to the United States in 1997. There are two major

Table V.1. United States: FDI inward and outward flows, 1995-1997

Item	Inflows			Outflows		
	1995	1996	1997	1995	1996	1997
Total, in billions of dollars.	58.8	76.5	90.7	92.1	74.8	114.5
of which (percentage):						
Equity capital	81.5	72.4	51.2	44.0	33.5	39.9
Reinvested earnings	16.0	13.1	21.8	51.3	64.6	49.8
Intra-company loans	2.5	14.4	26.9	4.7	1.9	10.3
By industry (percentage):						
Petroleum	6.6	11.6	4.9	0.7	6.8	10.0
Manufacturing	48.9	45.1	39.9	48.3	33.6	28.2
Distributive trade [a]	13.4	14.1	13.9	9.6	7.6	3.0
Finance and insurance [b c]	25.0	16.2	24.3	25.0	32.8	42.2
Other industries	6.1	13.0	17.0	16.3	19.2	16.6
By country/region (percentage):[d]						
Developed countries	92.9	96.5	89.7	75.8	62.5	65.0
Canada	8.2	10.8	10.4	9.3	9.7	9.4
European Union	59.8	62.9	55.4	53.0	43.3	46.2
Other Western Europe [e]	7.8	4.7	10.8	3.7	4.8	6.7
of which:						
Switzerland	6.9	4.0	9.1	2.0	1.1	4.4
Other developed countries	17.2	18.2	10.8	9.4	4.7	2.8
of which:						
Japan	13.8	13.4	10.4	2.5	-0.4	0.7
Developing countries	7.1	3.5	10.3	26.9	34.8	34.3
Africa	-0.2	-0.6	1.1	0.1	0.7	2.3
Latin America and the Caribbean	4.9	4.3	6.5	17.4	21.5	20.8
West Asia	-0.6	0.7	0.1	1.0	0.7	1.0
South, East and South-East Asia [f]	3.0	-0.9	1.7	6.2	11.9	10.3
of which:						
China	..	..	..	0.3	1.3	1.1
Central and Eastern Europe	..	..	..	0.1	2.0	1.3

Source: UNCTAD, based on data obtained from the United States, Department of Commerce, Bureau of Economic Analysis webpage (www.bea.doc.gov., updated on 18 June and 19 June 1998) and information provided by this office.

[a] For outflows, distributive trade includes only wholesale trade (excludes retail trade).
[b] Finance and insurance includes depositary institutions.
[c] For outflows, finance and insurance includes real estate.
[d] For outflows, totals do not necessarily add up to 100 per cent due to investments in international affiliates that are not classified under specific countries.
[e] Includes developing Europe. For inflows, includes also Central and Eastern Europe.
[f] Includes the Pacific.

reasons for this prominence. First, overall M&A activity (some of which took the form of acquisition of equity of United States firms by foreign companies) was at record levels in 1997. Second, equity capital inflows also reflected considerable funding provided by foreign companies to their existing United States affiliates to expand operations in the buoyant United States economy.

However, the share of equity capital in total flows into the United States decreased from about three quarters in 1995-1996 to about a half in 1997. Correspondingly, the share of intra-company debt nearly doubled, to 27 per cent (table V.1). This exceptionally high share can be attributed to large loans by European financial institutions to their finance affiliates located in the United States (Bach, 1998). Low interest rates in European Union countries may have induced loan financing of FDI in the United States. Prime lending rates in 1997 were about 2 percentage points lower in France, the Netherlands and the United Kingdom than in the United States (IMF, 1998a). Among major investors in the United States, only Germany reported slightly higher lending rates. The difference in lending rates was most pronounced between the United States and Switzerland (8.4 per cent versus 4.5 per cent). This may have contributed to the emergence of Switzerland as an important investor in the United States in 1997.

Consistent with this reasoning, intra-company debt played a marginal role in FDI outflows of the United States. One-half of FDI from the United States was accounted for by reinvested earnings in 1997, down from two-thirds the year before. Equity capital was the driving force of FDI outflows in 1997. United States companies acquired some large foreign businesses; significant transactions were concentrated in finance and in utilities (electric power and telecommunications) in response to new market opportunities provided by privatizations of state-owned firms in this field (Bach, 1998).

Persistent economic growth in the United States provided a strong stimulus to FDI inflows. The economy expanded for the sixth year in a row, providing a favourable environment for profitable operations. Real GDP growth of 3.8 per cent in 1997 exceeded growth in the preceding years. High corporate profitability in the United States in general went along with improved profitability of foreign affiliates located in the country, many of which reinvested a higher share of their earnings in the United States.

However, the attractiveness of the United States as a location for FDI does not derive only from its large and growing market. In addition, various structural characteristics of the economy underlie its locational advantages. The World Economic Forum's competitiveness index, which is based on various indicators and investors' perceptions, portrays the United States as one of the most attractive investment locations. Among industrial countries, the United States received the highest index value in 1997; among the complete sample of 53 countries under consideration, only Singapore and Hong Kong, China outperformed the United States.

Major competitive strengths of the United States, as identified by the World Economic Forum, include the following (WEF, 1997):

- Labour markets are much more flexible than in major European economies (except the United Kingdom) and Japan. The United States also received a favourable ranking, although lower than those of five developing economies (Hong Kong,

China; Indonesia; China; Singapore; and Taiwan Province of China), the Czech Republic and Luxembourg, with regard to productivity-adjusted wage costs (WEF, 1997, table 7.20).

- The United States is the frontrunner with respect to technological innovations. Spending on R&D amounted to 2.5 per cent of United States GDP in 1995, with just four countries showing an even higher ratio. Moreover, the United States tops the list of all countries under consideration with regard to the quality of scientific research institutions and competitive advantages stemming from indigenous innovation. Technological leadership is also reflected in the pattern of royalties and licence fees (Bach, 1998, p. 79). In 1997, the United States received $34 billion in royalties and licence fees, compared with payments of just $9 billion.

- The service sector, which is attracting an increasing share of FDI worldwide, appears to be most developed in the United States, with its share in GDP accounting for 72 per cent in 1995, compared with an average of 66 per cent for all high-income economies (World Bank, 1997a). More specifically, the sophistication of financial markets is considered more advanced in the United States than in any other country except the United Kingdom (WEF, 1997, table 3.01) and overall infrastructure is assessed to be superior only in three countries: Singapore, Germany and Switzerland (WEF, 1997, table 4.01).

- The quality of management in the United States is superior to all other countries surveyed (WEF, 1997, table 6.01). The same applies to marketing skills on which foreign investors may draw.

All this implies that the United States is well prepared to benefit from inward FDI. This is exemplified by the extent to which the United States benefits from the transnationalization of R&D activities. R&D expenditure per employee in the United States affiliates of foreign-based TNCs amounted to $3,600 in 1995, compared with $2,400 in 1990. The 1995 R&D expenditure per employee was less than the corresponding figure for United States parent companies ($5,200), but greater than the figure for their foreign affiliates ($2,200) (table V.2). Between 1990 and 1995, the R&D intensity (measured by the share of R&D expenditures in total sales) of United States affiliates of foreign-based TNCs increased from 0.1 per cent to 1.1 per cent. For foreign affiliates of United States TNCs, R&D intensity decreased somewhat from 0.08 per cent to 0.07 per cent (United States, Department of Commerce, 1993a, 1993b, 1997a and 1997b).

Table V.2. United States: R&D expenditure per employee in foreign affiliates and parent firms, 1990 and 1995[a]

(Thousands of dollars)

Item	1990	1995
Affiliates of foreign-based TNCs in the United States	2.4	3.6
Foreign affiliates of United States TNCs[b]	1.9	2.2
United States parent companies	3.5	5.2

Source: United States, Department of Commerce, 1993a, 1993b, 1997a and 1997b.

[a] Non-bank affiliates/non-bank parent companies.
[b] Majority-owned foreign affiliates only.

The United States has benefited from globalization not only by way of FDI inflows but also by way of FDI outflows, which contributed to the further transnationalization of United States companies in 1997, with one-third of outflows being directed towards developing countries (table V.1). This suggests that United States firms, while still locating the largest share of their international production in developed countries, have increasingly made use of the locational advantages of developing countries. The intensity with which United States companies are engaged in the international division of labour between developed and developing countries is in striking contrast to that of European companies. For example, the share of developing countries in total German FDI outflows was just 11 per cent in 1997, even after some increases.

Yet, as an economy, the United States does not appear to be leading the way towards globalized production. Outward orientation by means of FDI has remained fairly limited so far: despite the large and growing outflows, the outward FDI stock of the United States is considerably smaller as a percentage of United States GDP (some 10 per cent) than the ratio of outward FDI stock to GDP of most other industrial countries (figure V.5); the same applies to FDI outflows as a percentage of gross fixed capital formation (figure V.3). To a large extent, this may be the case because large economies are typically less transnationalized than smaller ones. This "large-country" bias (shared also by Japan -- see section C) renders it rather unlikely for the United States to approximate the ratios for countries such as the Netherlands and the United Kingdom, which reveal particularly high ratios of outward FDI stock to GDP (figure V.5). Those ratios remain significantly higher for these two countries even if FDI stocks held in other European Union countries are netted out: in 1995, FDI outward stocks outside the European Union accounted for about 50 per cent and 64 per cent respectively of the total outward FDI stocks of the Netherlands and the United Kingdom (EUROSTAT, 1998a). Consequently, the adjusted outward FDI stock/GDP ratio is about twice as high as the ratio for the United States. Furthermore, it is striking that the increase in the outward FDI stock/GDP ratio since 1980 has been relatively small for the United States, compared to the world as a whole.

Figure V.5. Developed countries: FDI stock as a percentage of GDP, 1996[a]

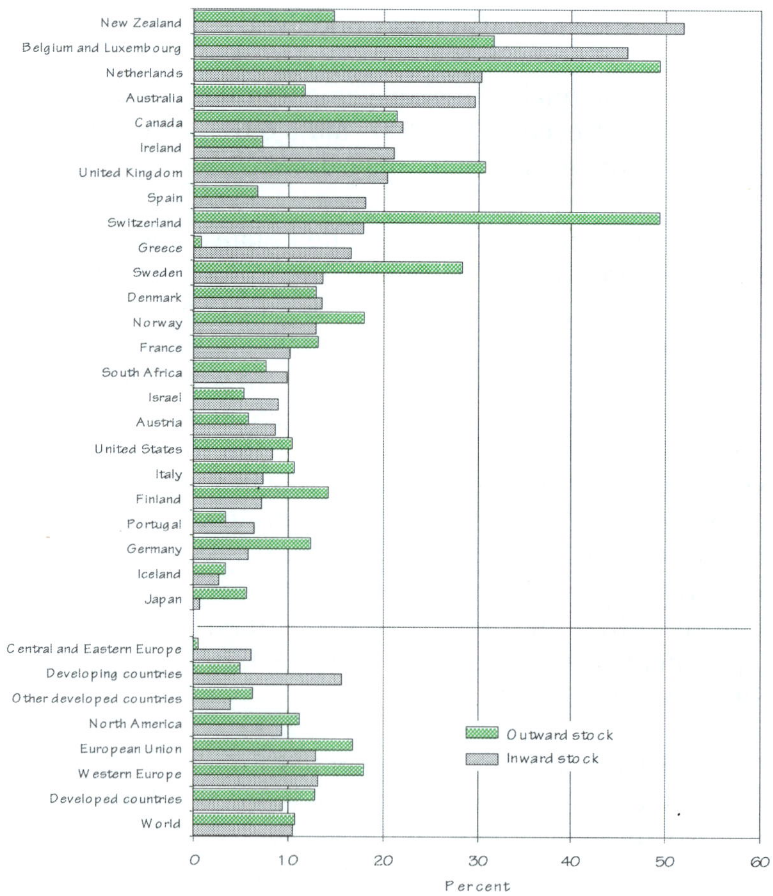

Source: UNCTAD, FDI/TNC database.

a Ranked on the basis of magnitude of FDI inward stock as a percentage of GDP.

The notion that the United States is not as globalized in terms of international production as other countries with lower (and sometimes much lower) outward FDI stock is supported by the persistently strong concentration of TNC activities and resources in parent companies within the United States. For example, United States parent companies accounted for about three-quarters, and majority-owned foreign affiliates for about one-quarter, of gross product (value added), capital expenditures and employment of United States TNCs (United States parent companies and their majority-owned foreign affiliates combined) in 1995 (table V.3). A cross-country comparison of foreign assets, foreign sales and foreign employment indicates that the concentration of TNC activities at home was stronger for United States TNCs than for TNCs based in the European Union: the average transnationalization index of the top 100 TNCs for 1996 was 65 for the European Union (41 TNCs) and 43 for the United States (28 TNCs). (See chapter II for further details). However, the contribution of parent companies in the United States to overall TNC activities has declined modestly since 1982. R&D expenditures were concentrated even more strongly in parent companies, which accounted for 88 per cent of worldwide R&D (93 per cent in 1982) by United States TNCs (Mataloni, 1997, p. 46; and United States, Department of Commerce, 1985). Finally, global sourcing was still limited in the mid-1990s: only 6 per cent of the value of United States parent companies' output was accounted for by inputs purchased from abroad.

Table V.3. United States: share of parent companies in gross product, employment and capital expenditures of United States TNCs,[a] 1982 and 1995

(Percentage)

Item	1982	1995
Gross product	78.1	74.6
Employment	78.8	75.7
Capital expenditures	80.8	76.4

Source: Mataloni, 1997, p. 45.

a Non-bank TNCs. Totals refer to data for parent companies plus majority-owned foreign affiliates, as data for other affiliates are largely missing.

It fits into this picture that the share of intra-firm trade in total United States exports and imports of goods has changed little over the past two decades (Zeile, 1997, p. 23).[4] All this reflects that firms in the United States, contrary to what might be concluded from the sheer size of the country's FDI abroad, are under less pressure to internationalize than firms in other developed countries. This is because of the size and in particular the large internal market of the country, but also, and perhaps more importantly, because of the integrated nature of its economy, the absence of barriers to competition and the maintenance of high levels of consumption.

B. Western Europe

The countries of Western Europe received $115 billion in FDI in 1997 and sent $196 billion abroad. Not surprisingly, both inflows and outflows were dominated by the European Union, which accounted for 94 per cent of the region's inflows and 92 per cent of its outflows. Switzerland was the largest investor among the non-European Union countries of Western Europe, accounting for 6 per cent of Western Europe's outflows in 1997 (figure V.2). But when outflows are related to gross fixed capital formation, Switzerland ranked fourth, in the region, behind the Netherlands, Sweden and the United Kingdom (figure V.3). In terms of absolute inflows, the United Kingdom, France and Belgium and Luxembourg were the most important recipients among European Union countries in 1997 (figure V.1). As a percentage of gross fixed capital formation, however, it was Sweden that attracted the highest FDI inflows within Western Europe as a whole during 1994-1996, followed by Belgium and

Luxembourg, and Ireland (figure V.3). Likewise, the inward FDI stock, relative to GDP, was highest in Belgium and Luxembourg in 1996, followed by the Netherlands and Ireland (figure V.5).

The importance of FDI stock relative to GDP is higher in both inward and outward FDI stock for non-European-Union countries than for European Union members. This again reflects the smaller size of these countries and the fact that the pressures to internationalize production, whether for accessing markets, obtaining resources or enhancing efficiency, are greater for firms in those countries that do not have the same access to the large European markets for goods, services and factors of production enjoyed by European Union member country firms.

Although the growth of flows into the European Union was substantial in 1997 after negative growth in 1996, the level was still lower than in 1995. With dramatic increases in flows into the United States in recent years, the United States is catching up with the European Union as the single most important investment recipient (figure V.6). In addition, if intra-European Union FDI is netted out, the United States emerges as the principal recipient of FDI during most of the years from 1980 to 1996 (figure V.6). Exchange-rate developments might have been expected to provide an incentive to FDI inflows into the European Union, as might the 1997 appreciation of the dollar by about 10 per cent in nominal terms against the ECU (IMF, 1998a) and the stability of the nominal exchange rate of the ECU against the yen. All of this suggests that the major factors in FDI developments in Europe in 1997 were country-specific.

Figure V.6. European Union, intra-European Union and United States FDI inflows, 1985-1997
(Billions of dollars)

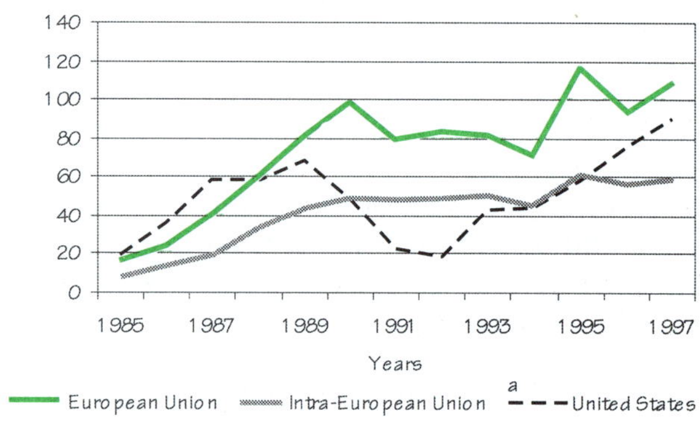

Source: UNCTAD, FDI/TNC database.

[a] Intra-European Union investment was estimated by using the share of the European Union in the total European Union investment provided in EUROSTAT, 1997 and 1998b.

The 1997 performance of the European Union as a group in attracting FDI conceals strikingly different developments in individual countries (figure V.4):

- Inflows declined most notably in France (by $ 3.7 billion), Austria (by $ 2.1 billion) and Belgium and Luxembourg (by $ 1.6 billion), Especially in the cases of Belgium and Austria, this seems to be related to perceptions of foreign investors as regards these countries' locational attractiveness: they were downgraded by 6 and 8 ranks, respectively, in the 1997 competitiveness index of the World Economic Forum (1997) and were placed in the bottom half of the group of 53 countries surveyed.

- In sharp contrast, the United Kingdom received substantially increased FDI inflows; its share in overall European Union inflows rose from 28 per cent in 1996 to 34 per cent in 1997. This is consistent with foreign investors' approval of the country's economic policies, including labour-market reforms. According to the World Economic Forum (1997), the United Kingdom ranked at the top of all

European Union countries in this respect. The United Kingdom also performed better than the European Union as a whole in GDP growth in 1997, 3.5 per cent versus 2.6 per cent.[5] However, high FDI inflows may also reflect competitive weaknesses of individual United Kingdom companies, e.g. in the automobile industry, which rendered them vulnerable to takeovers and mergers. These factors seem to have dominated two potentially depressing effects on inward FDI: the appreciation of the British pound vis-à-vis the ECU in 1997, and the decision of the Government not to participate in the European Monetary Union.

- Developments were also diverse on the European Union's periphery. Most notably, FDI flows into Ireland increased in line with an improving competitiveness record revealed in surveys and a high GDP growth of 8.3 per cent in 1997 (three times higher than GDP growth for the European Union as a whole). At the same time, Spain received less than half the FDI inflows it had received during the peak years of 1990-1992, when Spain seemed to have benefited a great deal from corporate restructuring in anticipation of the single European market.

The diverging trends of FDI inflows, both in the core countries of the European Union and on its periphery, underscore earlier findings according to which the effects of deepening integration on the intra-European Union distribution of FDI inflows are ambiguous. Whether increased integration leads to a concentration of FDI in core countries, or instead (or also) improves the chances of peripheral countries to catch up with core countries, depends critically on locational attractiveness of these countries (chapter IV.D.2).

FDI flows among the member states of the European Union have lost some of their importance. In 1996, FDI outflows from the European Union to the rest of the world were about the same as those within the European Union (EUROSTAT, 1998b), the first time since 1989 that this had occurred. This could reflect the tapering off of the effects of economic integration. There are some signs, however, that intraregional FDI is again on the rise, after the announcement of the European Monetary Union. Much of inward FDI from outside the European Union comes from the United States, Switzerland and Japan. But Japanese FDI has been declining since 1995. Instead, Norway has become a large investor. The United States, Switzerland and Norway together accounted for more than 90 per cent of inward FDI flows from outside the European Union in 1996. In 1995, the most recent year for which data are available, FDI inflows in manufacturing were almost on a par with those in services (EUROSTAT, 1998b). In the service sector, real estate, business services, and finance continue to be the dominant FDI recipients.

The European Union as a whole also remained the most important outward investor in 1997, exceeding United States FDI outflows by more than two-thirds (figure V.7). The United Kingdom maintained its position as the most important European Union investor abroad, followed by Germany, France and the Netherlands (figure V.2). Among these major investors, outflows from Germany and the United Kingdom increased in 1997; the United Kingdom's growth rate (70 per cent) was particularly dramatic (figure V.4). At the same time, some other European Union countries reported steeply rising FDI outflows (particularly Spain and Italy).

The gap in outflows between the European Union and the United States has narrowed since the 1980s. In 1985-1990, European Union outflows had exceeded United States outflows by a factor of 3.7 (UNCTAD, 1997a); in 1997, this factor was 1.6. Moreover, since 1993, the outward orientation of European Union investors has not even rivalled that of United States investors, if intra-European Union investment flows are netted out (figure V.7). This suggests that globalizing through outward FDI beyond the Union's boundaries has taken second place to regional networking and strategic positioning within the Union. The regional distribution of European Union FDI outflows provides further evidence in this respect: in comparison with Japan and the United States, European Union firms have traditionally accorded less importance to developing countries as locations for their outward investment (European Commission and UNCTAD, 1996, p. 20). In 1995, almost two-thirds of European Union outward FDI stock was held in just five industrial countries (in descending order: United States, Switzerland, Australia, Canada and Japan).[6] The strong concentration in industrialized countries has, however, declined somewhat:

- FDI from European Union countries, notably from Germany and Austria, provided the most important source of FDI inflows into Central and Eastern Europe.

- Indications are that European Union TNCs are paying increasing attention to Asia. According to an UNCTAD-ICC survey (chapter VII), 34 per cent of the respondent firms from Europe said tha they would increase FDI in the short and medium term, compared with 19 per cent each for Japanese and North American firms. They can be expected to continue to catch up with other investors in Asia (UNCTAD-ICC, 1998).

- Apart from the United States, the European Union was the second most important source of FDI in Latin America (ECLAC, 1998). The presence of European investors increased, especially from Spain, Germany and the United Kingdom. Major attractions were services and manufacturing in the MERCOSUR area.

Data on FDI outflows from selected European Union member states also suggest an increasing orientation towards developing countries: the share of developing countries in total FDI outflows increased from 10 per cent in 1991 to 14 per cent in 1993 and to 17 per cent in 1996.[7] The German case is noteworthy: the share of developing countries in German FDI outflows rose from 6 per cent to 12 per cent between 1991 and 1997. Comparing average German outflows in 1996-1997 with average outflows in 1993-1994, overall German FDI increased by a factor of 1.8 over the three-year period.[8] The increase was roughly of the same order for outflows to Central and Eastern Europe, slightly higher for outflows to Latin

Figure V.7. European Union, intra-European Union and United States FDI outflows, 1985-1997

(Billions of dollars)

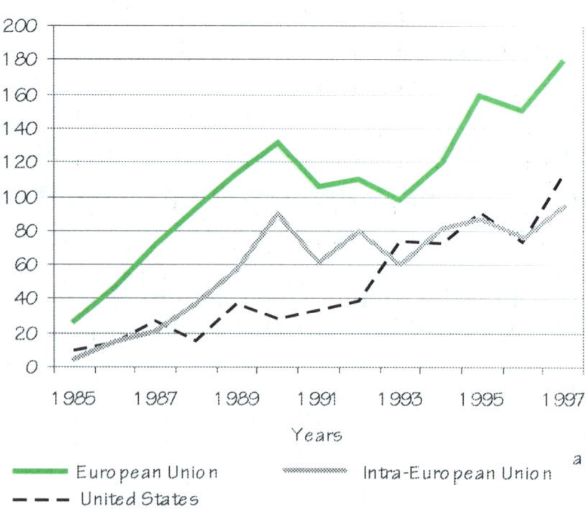

Source: UNCTAD, FDI/TNC database.

[a] Intra-European Union investment was estimated by using the share of the European Union in the total European Union investment provided in EUROSTAT, 1997 and 1998b. The share for 1997 is based on UNCTAD estimates.

America (which doubled), and considerably higher for outflows to a group of developing economies in Asia. Flows into ASEAN countries plus China; Hong Kong, China; Taiwan Province of China; and Republic of Korea increased by a factor of 2.7. Interestingly, outflows in 1997 point to an ambiguous effect of the Asian financial crisis: German FDI outflows to ASEAN countries declined by 17 per cent in 1997 from 1996; in contrast, they increased by 50 per cent to the Republic of Korea. With regard to FDI outflows to countries less affected by the financial crisis, outflows to Hong Kong, China dwindled in 1997 to one-fifth of the 1996 flows, declined modestly in the case of Taiwan Province of China, and exceeded the 1996 level in the case of China.

C. Japan

Japan ranked fourth (behind the United States, the United Kingdom and Germany) in outward FDI stock in 1997. The country's outward stock of $285 billion accounted for 8 per cent of the world FDI stock, but for no more than 6 per cent of Japan's GDP (figure V.5). With respect to outflows, Japan's relative importance has clearly declined. Average outflows during 1996-1997 were similar to those of France but lower than those of Hong Kong, China. Outflows from the latter have exceeded those from Japan every year since 1993, though in 1997 they were comparable (annex table B.2). Relative to gross fixed capital formation, Japanese outflows were much smaller than those of almost all other developed countries (figure V.3). Comparing the periods 1986-1990 and 1991-1997, Japanese outflows declined from a yearly average of $32 billion to an average of $22 billion; as a result, Japan's share in worldwide outflows was almost cut in half to 10 per cent, nearly returning it to the level of the early 1980s.

Several factors help to explain this development. The decline of Japan's importance as an investor country is mainly due to the burst of the "bubble" economy in the early 1990s, during which FDI outflows were inflated by the seemingly abundant liquidity in an overheated economy.[9] In a sense, therefore, the country is returning to its normal pattern. Something similar is true of Japanese investment in Europe. When fears of a protectionist "fortress Europe" proved to be unfounded, the incentive to undertake market-oriented investment projects in tradable goods in the European Union weakened.[10] In addition, exchange-rate developments had an effect on Japanese FDI (UNCTAD, 1994a). For example, outflows recovered in 1993-1996 when the yen appreciated in real terms. However, the increase of FDI outflows continued in 1997 at a rate of 11 per cent (23 per cent in yen terms, the highest growth in the 1990s), although the yen had weakened considerably since 1996. In January 1998, the real effective exchange rate was back to its low level of 1991 (IMF, 1998). This should have depressed FDI outflows as the international price competitiveness of producing in Japan and domestic liquidity was reduced but, so far, FDI outflows have not been affected.

It should also be noted that the growth of FDI outflows in 1997 coincided with economic stagnation in Japan, possibly resulting in a decline of the economy in 1998, the first time since 1974.[11] Depressed demand conditions at home may have induced Japanese companies to invest abroad as foreign investment seemed more profitable than domestic investment, which is expected to decline in manufacturing by 6 per cent in 1998.[12] More importantly, though, it seems that cyclical factors that should have had adverse effects on FDI outflows were overruled by longer-term strategic considerations. The need to keep up with global competition through establishing increasingly international production systems figures prominently among these.

Japanese companies can meet this need by building on existing foundations. In particular, they have clearly been the frontrunners in drawing on the comparative advantages of neighbouring countries with lower per-capita income by investing in them. In 1985, for instance, developing Asia hosted 19 per cent of total Japanese outward FDI stocks, compared with 6 per cent and 3 per cent, respectively, of the outward stocks of the United States and the European Union (European Commission and UNCTAD, 1996, table I.6). In fact, the very pattern of Japanese outward investment in Asia gave rise to the "flying geese" development paradigm (UNCTAD, 1995a, ch. V).

On the whole, however, the transnationalization of Japanese TNCs has remained weak by the standards of other developed countries:

- Japanese outward FDI stock in 1996 was low as a percentage of GDP, not only compared with most other developed countries but also with the South, East and South-East Asian countries (figure V.5).

- In 1996, FDI outflows as a percentage of gross fixed capital formation were even lower in Japan than in countries such as Portugal and Spain (figure V.3).

- As concerns the average transnationalization index of the Japanese firms in the top 100 TNCs, they ranked clearly below TNCs based in the European Union and in the United States (chapter II).

All this suggests that Japanese investors still have some way to go to adjust to global competition. The need to do so will become even more pressing if the current wave of mergers and acquisitions involving companies in Europe and the United States continues. Japanese TNCs may then attempt to further strengthen their presence in Europe and the United States, while firms from elsewhere seek access to the Japanese market.

Apart from developing Asia, which still absorbed one-quarter of Japanese FDI flows in 1997, the United States and Western Europe have traditionally figured high in Japanese FDI. The United States clearly represents the most important host country, absorbing 43 per cent of FDI outflows on a notification basis in 1991-1997. (It accounts for roughly the same share of Japan's outward FDI stock in 1997.) By contrast, Japanese FDI has remained marginal in Central and Eastern Europe, even among the prospective European Union members, although slight increases in FDI from Japan were recently observed (UNCTAD, 1996a). The shares accounted for by Latin America and Africa declined until recently. In 1997, however, with the economic recovery and improved macroeconomic fundamentals in Latin America, Japanese FDI flows to this region increased considerably on a notification basis. For example, outflows to Brazil increased by a half, and outflows to Mexico tripled (table V.4).

The need to adjust to global competition may also affect the sectoral structure of Japan's FDI. In the past, investment in the primary sector had become less and less important, a trend that is likely to continue. The manufacturing sector, too, lost slightly in importance in

Japan's FDI stocks; in particular the 1997 share of FDI stock in labour-intensive production in the textiles (including leather and clothing) and iron and steel industries was nearly half that in the mid-1980s, whereas FDI in electric and electronic equipment gathered momentum and now accounts for the largest share in the manufacturing sector. Finally, a major shift towards the services sector occurred as well and real estate, finance and insurance figured most prominently (table V.4).

It is open to question whether the shift in Japan's FDI from manufacturing to services will continue in the near term. As concerns services, a major change had occurred already

Table V.4. Japanese outward FDI on a notification basis,[a] by region and by industry, 1985-1997[b]

(Percentage)

	Flows					Stock	
Region/industry	1993	1994	1995	1996	1997	1985	1997
By region							
Developed countries[c d]	69.8	62.0	67.3	64.9	63.1	50.5	65.9
United States	40.9	42.2	44.1	45.8	38.5	30.2	40.7
Europe [d]	22.0	15.2	16.7	15.4	20.8	13.2	18.5
Developing countries	30.2	38.0	32.7	35.1	36.9	49.5	34.1
Africa[e]	1.5	0.8	0.7	0.9	0.6	4.0	1.7
Latin America and the Caribbean	9.4	12.7	7.5	9.3	11.7	18.7	12.3
Brazil	1.2	3.0	0.6	1.8	2.2	5.5	2.3
Mexico	0.1	1.5	0.4	0.2	0.6	1.6	0.7
South, East and South-East Asia	18.4	23.6	24.0	24.2	22.6	23.3	18.3
China	4.7	6.2	8.7	5.2	3.7	0.3	2.3
West Asia	0.6	0.7	0.3	0.5	0.9	3.6	1.3
By industry[f]							
Primary	3.0	2.1	2.5	3.9	5.3	15.5	6.2
Manufacturing	30.9	33.6	36.8	42.2	35.8	29.2	29.7
Food	2.5	3.1	1.6	1.5	1.1	1.3	1.5
Textiles	1.4	1.6	2.0	1.3	1.8	2.5	1.6
Chemicals	4.8	6.3	4.2	4.3	5.6	4.8	4.2
Iron and steel	2.1	2.5	3.0	5.1	2.6	6.2	3.4
General machinery	3.3	4.0	3.7	3.0	2.4	2.4	2.8
Electric machinery	7.7	6.4	10.5	13.6	12.4	4.5	7.3
Transport equipment	2.6	4.9	3.9	8.1	5.4	4.5	4.1
Others	5.5	4.5	7.2	4.1	4.0	3.5	3.9
Services	65.4	63.4	58.8	51.8	57.8	51.8	62.2
Construction	0.8	0.9	0.8	0.7	0.8	1.0	0.8
Real estate	16.8	12.5	11.7	12.9	10.3	3.0	13.3
Finance and insurance	17.8	15.8	10.6	16.2	22.2	13.0	18.1
Commerce	14.1	10.7	10.4	10.0	8.1	15.2	10.8
Transport services	6.0	6.3	4.5	3.7	4.3	7.1	5.5
Others	9.9	17.2	20.9	8.4	12.1	7.1	13.7
All regions/industries (Billion dollars)	36.0	41.1	52.7	49.7	54.7	83.6	689.8

Source: UNCTAD, FDI/TNC database.

a Detailed geographical breakdown of FDI is not available on an actual or balance-of-payments basis. There is no breakdown available at all for industry, therefore, figures reported in this table are different from those reported elsewhere.

b Fiscal year (April to March in the following year).

c Includes developing Oceania.

d Includes Central and Eastern Europe and developing Europe that together account for a negligible share.

e Includes South Africa.

f The total for the three sectors does not necessarily add up to 100 per cent because FDI made for the purpose of establishing and expanding branches is not allocated to any of these sectors.

in 1997 and early 1998, when flows in financial industries declined considerably. This reflects the need for large-scale restructuring of Japan's financial industries, which carry a large burden of non-performing debt and have to comply with stricter prudential standards. As a consequence, one-fifth of all foreign branches of Japanese banks are expected to be closed down by the year 2000 (table V.5). Likewise, some Japanese securities firms are also experiencing difficulties, with Sanyo Securities and Yamaichi Securities, the latter being one of the four largest securities firms in Japan, going bankrupt in 1997, and Kankaku Securities, a medium-sized firm, planning to close all foreign operations in 1998.

The preoccupation with financial restructuring within Japan may dampen the trend towards services in Japanese outward FDI, even though the trend will probably continue on a worldwide scale. As the importance of financial industries in Japanese FDI is most apparent in Europe, the closing down of foreign affiliates and reduced new flows in these industries would have an impact on total Japanese FDI in the region. By contrast, Japan's FDI in manufacturing does not appear to be greatly affected by its current economic problems. For example, Toyota announced a large-scale FDI project ($590 million) in France in late 1997; suppliers of parts and components for automobiles (e.g. Kansei) are planning investments in the United Kingdom in 1998; and various Japanese steel companies are interested in acquiring Korean steel producers.[13] Indeed, according to a survey by the Export-Import Bank of Japan, 90 per cent of Japanese TNCs are planning to maintain or even increase the current level of FDI in manufacturing.[14] The investment plans of these TNCs do not appear to be affected by lending constraints of debt-ridden Japanese banks, since the operations of manufacturing affiliates abroad have traditionally been financed mostly from their own resources, including loans from parent firms, and by borrowing from non-Japanese banks (Japan, MITI, 1998a, table 2-16-13).

Table V.5. Number of foreign branches of major Japanese banks, 1997 and 2000

	Number of foreign branches		Number of domestic branches	
Bank	1997	2000[a]	1997	2000[a]
Industrial Bank of Japan	22	18	28	27
Long-Term Credit Bank of Japan	13	7	24	20
Dai-Içhi Kangyo Bank	25	18	339	Less than 310
Sakura Bank	23	19	430	394
Fuji Bank	25	24	290	262
Bank of Tokyo-Mitsubishi	50	48	322	282
Asahi Bank	12	9	353	328
Sanwa Bank	25	20	299	259
Sumitomo Bank	40	23	305	283
Tokai Bank	36	32	283	250
Mitsui Trust and Banking Co.	4	3	57	51
Yasuda Trust and Banking Co.	7	-	50	50
Toyo Trust and Banking Co.	6	4	56	54
Bank of Yokohama	4	3	165	157
Ashikaga Bank	Withdrew all in 1997		140	135
Hokuriku Bank	Withdrew all in 1997		176	156
Kiyo Bank	Withdrew all in 1997		..	..
Fukui Bank	Withdrew all in 1997		..	..

Source: UNCTAD, based on *Nihon Keizai Shimbun*, 18 March 1998, and various newspaper accounts.

[a] Planned.

Notes

1 The Republic of South Africa has been classified so far by UNCTAD under "developed countries". Nevertheless, since it has many characteristics typical of developing countries, it is also discussed in chapter VI dealing with Africa.

2 The United States Department of Commerce revised its FDI flow data recently to exclude investments in financial affiliates that are more akin to portfolio investments for 1994-1997. For FDI outflows, intra-company debt transactions with finance affiliates in the Netherlands Antilles, as well as other financial intermediaries, are reclassified from FDI to portfolio investments. For other years in this *Report*, the United States FDI outflows are adjusted to exclude FDI flows to financial affiliates in the Netherlands Antilles only. For details, see "definitions and sources" in annex B of this *Report.*

3 Including depositary institutions.

4 This is because of two countervailing developments. On the one hand, the share of intra-firm trade in total trade of United States parent companies has increased markedly since 1982. On the other hand, United States parent companies have accounted for a declining share in total United States trade in goods.

5 Data from EUROSTAT, "EU annual growth quickens to 2.6%", 1 April 1998, http://www.europa.eu.int/en/comm/eurostat.

6 "EU has 472 BN ECU in foreign direct investment", 28 April 1998, http://www.europa.eu.int/en/comm/eurostat.

7 Data based on FDI outflows from Belgium and Luxembourg, Denmark, Finland, France, Germany, Netherlands, Portugal, Sweden and the United Kingdom (UNCTAD, FDI/TNC database).

8 Data from UNCTAD, FDI/TNC database. Note that the 1997 data and the total FDI outflows in 1994 do not include reinvested earnings.

9 For a detailed discussion, see UNCTAD, 1994a.

10 With adjustment to European integration almost completed and protectionist fears receding, Japanese FDI outflows to Europe as a share of its total FDI outflows on notification basis fell from their peak of 25 per cent in fiscal 1990 to 15 per cent in fiscal 1996, though they increased again to 21 per cent in fiscal 1997 (table V.4).

11 Fiscal 1997 (April 1997 to March 1998) had a negative growth rate. Although Japan announced a comprehensive economic package of some $128 billion in April 1998 to stimulate the economy, this may not be enough to restore growth.

12 *Nihon Keizai Shimbun,* 24 February 1998, p. 1.

13 *Frankfurter Allgemeine Zeitung,* 14 May 1998, p. 18.

14 The Export-Import Bank of Japan conducts a survey of the investment plans of Japanese TNCs every year. The most recent survey, covering 445 manufacturing TNCs, was conducted in October 1997. The results are reported in its periodical, *Journal of Research Institute for International Investment and Development (Kaigai Toshi Kenkyu-jo Ho),* in January 1998.

CHAPTER VI

AFRICA

A. Trends

Flows of foreign direct investment (FDI) to Africa amounted to an estimated $4.7 billion in 1997, the same level as in 1996 but over twice as high as at the beginning of the decade (figure VI.1). Nevertheless, flows into the region remain low, and the share of Africa in total FDI flows into developing countries remains a mere 3 per cent -- comparable, for example, to those of a single Asian developing economy, Malaysia -- but they have risen since the early 1990s, and some countries are doing better than previously in terms of inward FDI.

As in the past several years, the largest recipients in 1997 were Nigeria, Egypt, Morocco, Tunisia and Angola (figure VI.2), accounting together for two-thirds of FDI flows to Africa. With only a few exceptions, all of the 20 most important recipients of FDI experienced increased inflows in 1997 as compared to 1996 (figure VI.2). Investment inflows as a percentage of gross fixed capital formation (GFCF) in 1994-1996 and FDI stock as a percentage of gross domestic product (GDP) in 1996 ranged widely among African countries, with both large and small FDI recipients figuring among the highest-ranking countries in these respects (figures VI.3 and VI.4). Moreover, a number of smaller African countries (e.g. Lesotho[1] and Malawi), which received low *inflows* in absolute terms, hosted higher *stocks* per $1,000 of GDP than many of the larger

Figure VI.1. FDI inflows to Africa, 1989-1997

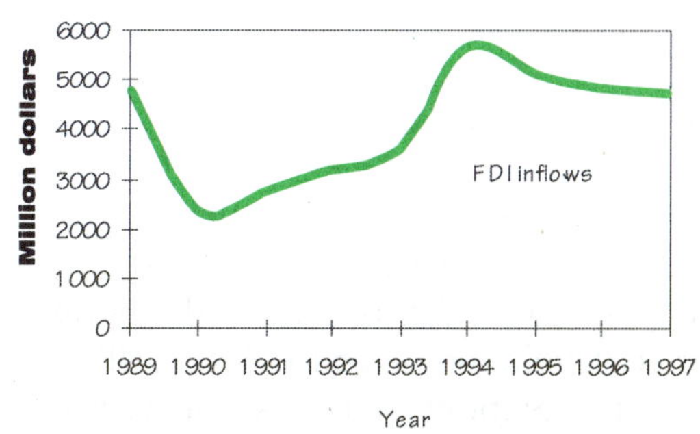

Source: UNCTAD, FDI/TNC database.

recipients in 1996, suggesting that, over a period of time, their inward FDI flows relative to their size have been comparable to or even higher than those of the larger economies (figure VI.4).

Several factors contribute to these relatively high FDI inflows for the smaller economies in Africa. Apart from the sizeable reserves of natural resources that many of them possess, some countries (like Botswana) are relatively competitive investment locations for FDI undertaken to service the markets of larger neighbouring countries, e.g. South Africa. In countries, especially landlocked ones with poor transport infrastructure, firms might find FDI a more reliable mode to service the local market than trade. In yet other small economies, high FDI inflows per dollar of GDP might mean simply that GDP growth has been slow or negative over a number of years; under such conditions, even a relatively modest foreign investment would appear large relative to GDP. However, there is no evidence of a systematic statistical bias in favour of small countries, since the majority of least developed countries (most of which are of small market size) have a low FDI-to-GDP ratio (table VI.1).[2]

Among the subregions in the continent, North Africa continued to receive increased investment inflows, raising its share in total FDI inflows to Africa from 29 per cent in 1996 to 39 per cent in 1997. Flows into sub-Saharan Africa were an estimated $2.9 billion in 1997, down from $3.3 billion in 1996; the decline of investment flows to Nigeria, mainly in the petroleum industry played a significant role in this decrease.[3] However, although sub-Saharan Africa's share in total investment flows to Africa declined by 10 per cent during 1997, it remained at 61 per cent in 1997, higher than at the beginning of this decade. The noticeable increases in FDI inflows to Angola, the United Republic of Tanzania and Uganda during 1994-1997 -- paralleled by the decrease in FDI inflows to Equatorial Guinea in 1997 and especially to Nigeria during 1995-1997 -- suggest that FDI flows within sub-Saharan Africa are less concentrated than before. However, a large number of sub-Saharan countries are still largely bypassed by foreign investors. Despite the declining flows to Equatorial Guinea and Nigeria, the share of oil-exporting countries in FDI flows into Africa remains significant, accounting for slightly more than half of the flows in 1997.

According to the South African Reserve Bank, investment inflows into South Africa (which is classified among "other developed countries" according to United Nations statistics and is not included in the ranking in the figures in this section) showed a significant

Figure VI.2. Africa: FDI flows into the top 20 recipient countries in 1997 and flows to the same countries in 1996[a]

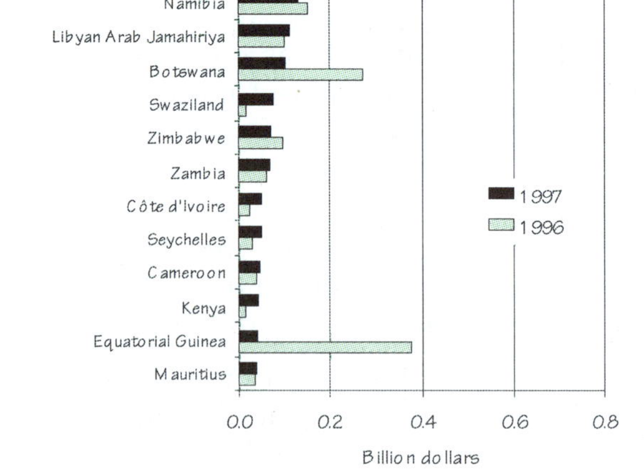

Source: UNCTAD, FDI/TNC database.

[a] Ranked on the basis of the magnitude of FDI inflows in 1997.

increase in 1997: from $760 million in 1996 to $1.7 billion in 1997 (South African Reserve Bank, unpublished data).[4] The increase in 1997 largely reflects inflows due to a limited number of privatization-related projects. After an initial surge of privatizations in the late 1980s and early 1990s, privatization slowed in South Africa as the new government established new priorities and adopted new criteria for privatization. In 1997, however, it revived with the sale of 30 per cent of Telkom to a consortium of a United States (SBC) and Malaysian investor (Telekom Malaysia), as well as sales of six radio stations, the domestic airline Sun Air, and a hotel and food group. FDI unrelated to privatization seems to have decreased between 1996 and 1997.[5] South Africa may also be seeing the trailing off of an adjustment factor, namely the return to South Africa of firms that had limited their presence or operated in neighbouring countries under the pre-1994 regime. Still, at the end of 1997, there was a buy-back of 49 per cent of the shares of the vehicle-assembler Delta Motor by General Motors, which had divested in 1989.[6] Over the past four years, four-fifths of FDI came from just five countries: the United States, Malaysia, the United Kingdom, Germany and Japan. In 1997, British and Malaysian companies in particular were the most dynamic investors.[7] Most investment (60 per cent of total flows) was undertaken in the form of mergers and acquisitions (M&A). The top target industries were telecommunication, energy and oil, motor vehicles and components, and food and beverages (Business Map, 1998, p. 16). During the first half of 1998, FDI flows continued to be driven mainly by privatization, including the purchase of a 20 per cent share in the Airport Authority by the Italian firm Aeroporti di Roma (ibid, p. 14). Some foreign investment may also have been attracted by the restructuring and "unbundling" of large South African conglomerate companies.

The principal home countries of TNCs investing in Africa in the period 1982-1996 included the United Kingdom, France, the United States, Germany, Japan and the Netherlands (table VI.2). France became the single most important investor in the region during 1992-1996, overtaking the United Kingdom which had held this position during 1987-1991. France was, moreover, the only major home country that continuously increased its investment flows to Africa during the years 1982-1986 and 1992-1996. Inflows from the United Kingdom suffered a significant dip during 1987-1991, as did those from the United States and Germany, while FDI flows from Japan fell considerably during 1992-1996. A number of smaller European countries, such as the Netherlands and Switzerland,

Figure VI.3. Africa: FDI flows as percentage of gross fixed capital formation, top 20 countries,[a] 1994-1996
(Annual average)

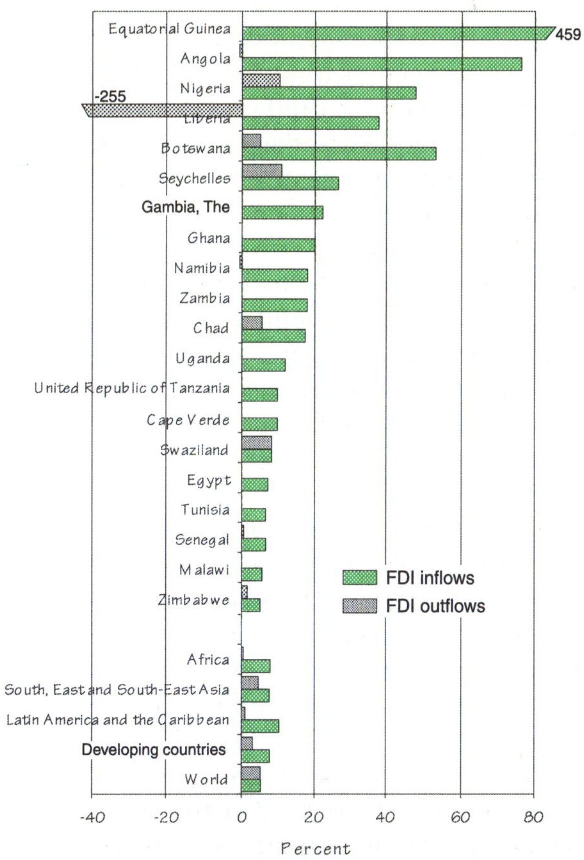

Source: UNCTAD, FDI/TNC database.

[a] Ranked on the basis of the magnitude of FDI inflows as a percentage of gross fixed capital formation in 1994-1996.

showed substantial increases in their FDI flows into Africa, with the former becoming the third most important source of FDI flows into Africa during 1992-1996.

FDI from developing Asia has increased in Africa in recent years (UNCTAD, 1997a). The principal Asian developing economies from which FDI flows originated have been the Republic of Korea and Malaysia, followed by Taiwan Province of China and China. Thus far, however, these investments have been confined to limited numbers of countries in the region, such as Egypt, Ghana, Guinea, Mauritius (box VI.1.), Seychelles, Uganda, the United Republic of Tanzania, Zimbabwe[8] and South Africa.[9] To what extent Asian FDI in Africa -- apart from the Malaysian FDI in South Africa that has already been mentioned -- might suffer a decline on account of the Asian financial crisis that began in mid-l997 is difficult to predict. The 1998 survey by UNCTAD/ICC on the effects of the Asian crisis suggests that FDI flows to Africa from Asian countries other than the Republic of Korea might be sustained at a level similar to that in 1997 (see chapter VII).

The sectoral distribution of FDI stock in Africa has remained stable between 1989 and 1996 (figure VI.5). The primary sector accounts for the largest share of FDI in Africa with around 40 per cent of total FDI stock in the period 1989 to 1996, while the importance of FDI in manufacturing has increased slightly in that period from 29 to 30 per cent and the share of FDI in services in total FDI dropped from 33 per cent in 1990 to just 27 per cent in 1996.[10] However, there are some striking changes in the sectoral composition of FDI in Africa from individual home countries and changes in it during 1989-1996. While French TNCs have tended to invest mainly in the primary sector during the past decade or so (together with increasing absolute volumes also in the other two sectors), investment from Germany and more recently the United States has been more dynamic in the secondary sector. In the case of the United States, investments in food and related products, primary and fabricated metals, and other manufacturing have led to an upward trend in FDI in manufacturing and an increased share of the secondary sector in the total FDI stock. On the other hand, the relative importance of the secondary sector has decreased for the United Kingdom's FDI in Africa (after it peaked at 37 per cent of total British

Figure VI.4. Africa: FDI stock as a percentage of gross domestic product, top 20 countries,[a] 1996

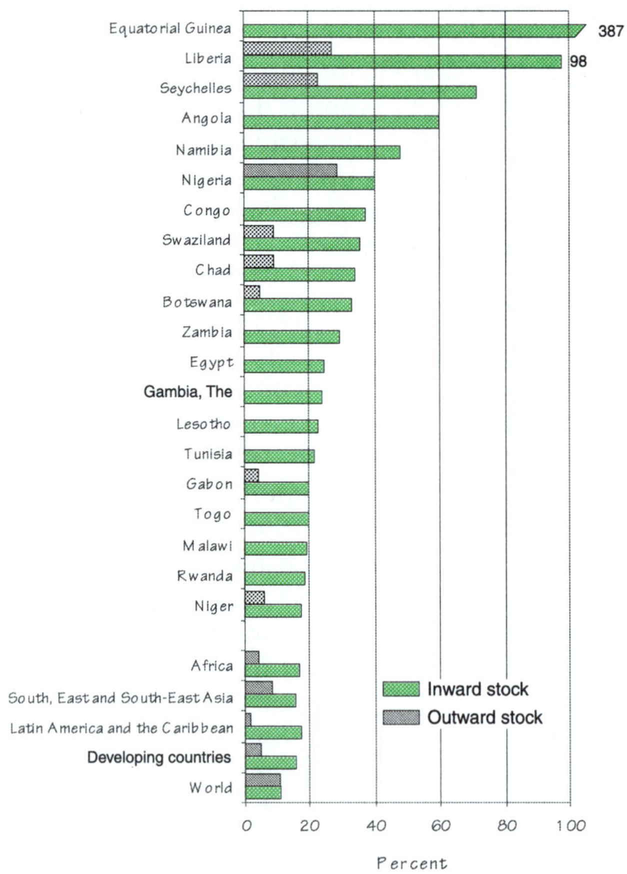

Source: UNCTAD, FDI/TNC database.

[a] Ranked on the basis of the magnitude of FDI inward stock as a percentage of gross domestic product in 1996.

investment in 1994), even though it continues to account for a larger share of United Kingdom FDI stock in Africa than of the FDI stock of any of the other three principal home countries, i.e. France, Germany and the United States. For United States' FDI, the tertiary sector gained in importance in both absolute and relative terms, mainly through FDI in banking and insurance. For FDI from Germany, this sector increased only marginally in importance.

Several factors have contributed to sustaining and increasing FDI inflows into a number of African countries during the past few years. These include changes in the economic conditions determining inflows of FDI to African economies as well as changes in the policy

Table VI.1: FDI flows into the least developed countries in Africa, selected indicators, 1987-1991 and 1992-1996

(Millions of dollars and percentage)

	FDI inward flows							
	Average		Per $ 1 000 GDP		Ratio to GFCF[b]		Per capita	
	1987-1991	1992-1996	1987-1991	1992-1996	1987-1991	1992-1996	1987-1991	1992-1996
	(Million dollars)		(Dollars)		(Per cent)		(Dollars)	
Angola	156	260	23	53	26	76	17	24
Benin	3	1	2	-	1	-	1	-
Burkina Faso	2	4	1	2	-	1	-	-
Burundi	1	1	1	1	1	1	-	-
Cape Verde	1	5	3	16	1	6	2	14
Central African Republic	1	-2	1	-2	1	-2	-	-1
Chad	9	15	8	15	8	13	2	2
Comoros	4	-	16	2	7	1	7	1
Congo, Democratic Republic of	-13	1	-2	-	-1	-	-	-
Djibouti	..	3	..	5	..	4	..	4
Equatorial Guinea	11	110	83	690	30	285	32	282
Ethiopia	1	3	-	1	-	-	-	-
Gambia, The	5	9	19	24	12	19	6	8
Guinea	20	9	7	3	5	2	3	1
Guinea-Bissau	1	1	5	4	2	2	1	1
Lesotho	13	17	25	23	4	3	7	9
Liberia	244	14	204	10	231	28	98	5
Madagascar	11	12	4	4	3	3	1	1
Malawi	19	10	12	6	7	5	2	1
Mali	1	11	1	5	-	2	-	1
Mauritania	3	8	3	7	2	3	2	3
Mozambique	9	33	7	23	1	4	1	2
Niger	16	4	7	2	5	2	2	-
Rwanda	13	2	6	2	4	1	2	-
Sierra Leone	16	-4	20	-4	23	-7	4	-1
Somalia	-3	-	-2	-	-1	-	-	-
Sudan	-3	-	-	-	-	-	-	-
Togo	11	-	7	-	4	-	3	-
Uganda	-0	78	-0	16	-	10	-	4
United Republic of Tanzania	2	70	0	14	-	6	-	2
Zambia	114	56	34	17	35	16	14	6
Memorandum:								
South Africa	-23	404	-	3	-	2	-1	10
Average for developing countries[a]	212	613	8	17	3	7	8	20
Average for Africa[a]	60	96	7	10	3	6	5	7

Source: UNCTAD, FDI/TNC database.

[a] Including South Africa.

[b] GFCF = gross fixed capital formation.

Box VI.1. FDI in Mauritius

Mauritius is one of Africa's most dynamic examples of economic growth. In the 30 years since independence, the country has successfully restructured itself from a predominantly mono-crop (sugar) economy to an export-oriented manufacturing one and has now reached the status of a middle-income country with a per capita income that exceeds by far that of most other African countries ($3.380 in 1995) .

FDI has played a pivotal role in the development of the country's economy. Following the establishment of an export processing zone, and the implementation of an export-oriented development strategy in the 1970s, FDI flows to Mauritius peaked in the early 1990s -- the same time that flows to the East Asian economies were growing rapidly. Mauritius' success in attracting FDI was largely due to its key comparative advantages: skilled, low-cost labour; a reasonably efficient physical infrastructure including cost-competitive export processing zones; preferential access to the European Union and United States markets; a sound legal system for dispute settlement and yearly accounting practices; and clearly articulated policies favourable to FDI. Also, compared to other African countries, Mauritius already had a strong business environment with a vibrant entrepreneurial culture very early in its development process. The economic advantages of the country attracted investment in labour-intensive manufacturing industries, especially in garments and textiles. Investors in such other labour-intensive manufactures as leather, rubber, fancy goods and toys were also attracted.

Box table. FDI inflows to Mauritius, 1985-1997

(Millions of dollars and percentage)

Country/group	1985-1990 Annual average	1985-1990 Annual growth rate	1991-1997 Annual average	1991-1997 Annual growth rate
Mauritius	22.0	49.5	23.0	13.9
Memorandum:				
Developing countries	24 720.0	22.0	92 181.0	23.6

Source: UNCTAD FDI/TNC database.

In the early 1990s, however, flows to Mauritius slowed and even fell for a period, this at a time when flows into developing countries as a whole continued to increase. Investments in Mauritius from three out of the five major home countries of TNCs investing in the country -- Germany, China and the United Kingdom -- have also decreased in the last few years. Manufacturing industries, especially the traditionally dominant textile and garment industries, have been the most affected, with investors moving to other lower-cost locations. The fact that low-skill activities continue to dominate FDI arrivals accounting for 98 per cent of FDI in both 1985-1989 and 1990-1997, respectively, indicates that there has been little progress in upgrading and diversification since 1985. Thus, there has been not only a slowdown in attracting FDI into the traditional industries, but the country has also not yet been very successful in attracting FDI into new high-skill and technology-intensive industries. (The recent increase was mainly due to one relatively large textile project from India.)

There are a number of challenges Mauritius has to cope with in order to safeguard its earlier success in attracting FDI:

- One challenge is posed by rising labour costs, an inevitable consequence of the rapid development process of recent years, which has led to a decline in the competitiveness of Mauritian exports. The emergence of other viable low-cost host countries in Africa such as Kenya, Madagascar and Zimbabwe has also increased competition for FDI in industries that have traditionally attracted it in Mauritius.
- Another challenge is the threat of elimination or reduction of preferential access to the European Union and United States markets, as the Lomé Convention comes up for review.

/...

environment influencing FDI in Africa. The latter include measures at the national level in host countries, especially privatization, increased liberalization of markets, and more open FDI and trade frameworks as well as business facilitation measures. Other factors are international initiatives and home country measures to encourage FDI in Africa.

Perhaps the most important factor has been Africa's macroeconomic performance which has improved significantly during the 1990s. The year 1997 was the fourth consecutive year of growth for Africa as a whole (United Nations, 1998a, p. 1) and several countries of the region achieved growth rates exceeding 5 per cent in 1997.[11] However, despite continued efforts on the part of many African countries to pursue strict monetary and fiscal policies to ensure macroeconomic stability, there is still need for further improvement of macroeconomic conditions. Thus, the average inflation rate for the continent increased from an already high 34 per cent in 1996 to 47 per cent in 1997 (United Nations, 1998a, p. 20),[12] Sudan and

(Box VI.1, concluded)

- A third challenge is posed by the combination of a limited supply of industrial skills, a lack of local suppliers of inputs, a limited technological infrastructure and a low local demand for high technology products, which together have made it difficult for Mauritius to increase the spread and quality of its FDI.

Mauritius' FDI policy regime and promotion strategy, though largely favourable to attracting export-oriented FDI, could be further improved. There have been delays in getting foreign investment approvals in Mauritius. Overlaps in the activities of the different public institutions responsible for foreign investment approval and promotion could have resulted in bureaucratic and structural bottlenecks in the approval process. Moreover, the country's investment promotion strategy might benefit from more focus on a reduced number of potential sectors and home countries for attracting FDI. Finally, fiscal incentives for foreign investment could be geared more towards promoting technological upgrading, creating linkages with local industries, increasing local value added, and facilitating research and development.

Like comparable economies in South-East and East Asia, Mauritius now faces the challenge of moving to a new phase in its economic development. Like the successful Asian economies, Mauritius needs to develop new comparative advantages in its established industries and competitive advantages in emerging industries. The loss of competitive advantage as a low-cost producer could, for example, be compensated for by developing the country's potential as a regional headquarters for TNCs. Its potential as an offshore financial centre could be realized with a more active approach to tapping new offshore business. Investment in relevant education and skills-building could be accorded priority. A re-engineering of the existing incentive package may also be needed, along with the streamlining of investment promotion activities, in order to target the desired industries.

The Government of Mauritius has recognized the challenge and has started a number of initiatives to ensure competitiveness in the future, such as a skills development programme, a reprioritizing of the education and skill-building policies, the establishment of a National Productivity and Competitiveness Council, and other initiatives to support the technological upgrading of the domestic economy and to make Mauritius a more attractive place for FDI in higher-value-added activities. Also, the Government has taken steps to reduce delays in processing and approving investment projects through the establishment of a Board of Investment that -- among other things -- will implement a fast track approval procedure for investment projects, and has introduced other measures to facilitate investment, including the issuance of multi-entry visas for foreign investors. Furthermore, the Government also supports the increasing outward investment by Mauritius-based companies in other African countries in order to strengthen the competitive edge of Mauritius-based industries.

Source: UNCTAD, based on Lall and Wignaraja (1998) and information obtained from national sources.

the Democratic Republic of the Congo being among the most seriously affected countries in recent years, while a number of other developing regions such as Latin America and the Caribbean managed to reduce their inflation rates significantly.

Privatization in Africa is becoming an increasingly important -- although far from fully explored -- avenue for foreign investment. Opportunities for FDI have been created by steadily expanding privatization programmes in countries such as Angola, Cape Verde, Cote d'Ivoire, Egypt, Ghana, Kenya, Morocco, Mozambique, Nigeria, Senegal, South Africa, Tunisia, Uganda and Zambia, and by the recent introduction of similar programmes in Botswana, Burkina Faso, Eritrea, Madagascar, Namibia and Zimbabwe (see also section VI.B). In North Africa and the Middle East, total sales of stakes in companies to private investors amounted to $1.5 billion in 1996, a 100 per cent increase as compared to 1995 (World Bank, 1998, p. 106), with $1.2 billion of the sales occurring in Egypt alone. The accelerated privatization efforts in Egypt in particular, supported by measures allowing foreign investors for the first time to purchase stakes of more than 50 per cent in public enterprises, contributed to a remarkable increase in privatization sales in that country. In Morocco, the sale of a 30 per cent stake in the Société Marocaine des Industries du Raffinage (SAMIR) to a Swedish investor contributed to the increase in privatization revenues. Nonetheless, foreign exchange earnings from privatization in North Africa and the Middle East in 1996 were less than 10 per cent of the value of total sales, suggesting that FDI through privatization was relatively low and that the domestic private sector was the main actor in the privatization process in many African countries. In sub-Saharan Africa, $299 million of a total of $623 million in privatization sales in 1996 were raised through sales to foreign investors. Ghana topped the list with $186 million, selling a $112 million share in Ashanti Goldfields to foreign investors through an international placement of shares, followed by Kenya with $137 million,

Table VI.2. The major home countries for FDI flows into Africa,[a] 1982-1996

(Millions of dollars)

Country	Cumulative flows, 1982-1986	Country	Cumulative flows, 1987-1991	Country	Cumulative flows, 1992-1996	Country	Cumulative flows, 1982-1996
United States	1200	United Kingdom	2812	France	2290	United Kingdom	4987
France	1152	France	1300	United States	1683	France	4742
United Kingdom	600	Japan	1183	United Kingdom	1575	United States	3259
Germany	507	United States	376	Netherlands	807	Germany	1401
Italy	458	Netherlands	197	Germany	714	Japan	1099
Sweden	210	Switzerland	182	Switzerland	461	Netherlands	1072
Norway	98	Germany	180	Italy	282	Italy	912
Netherlands	68	Italy	172	Canada	201	Switzerland	656
Austria	64	Belgium	152	Norway	196	Norway	318
Belgium	63	Canada	38	Portugal	194	Canada	256
Denmark	33	Finland	37	Spain	107	Sweden	226
Canada	17	Norway	24	Japan	21	Portugal	203
Switzerland	13	Austria	24	Australia	17	Spain	107
Australia	-15	Denmark	11	Denmark	13	Austria	97
Japan	-105	Portugal	10	Sweden	12	Denmark	57
		Sweden	4	Finland	10	Finland	48
		Australia	-199	Austria	10	Belgium	8
				Belgium	-207	Australia	-197
Total	**4363**		**6502**		**8387**		**19251**

Source: UNCTAD, FDI/TNC database, based on OECD.

[a] Table only includes the member countries of the OECD Development Assistance Committee (DAC).

Figure VI.5. FDI stock from France, Germany, the United Kingdom and the United States in Africa,[a] by sector, 1989-1996

(Millions of dollars)

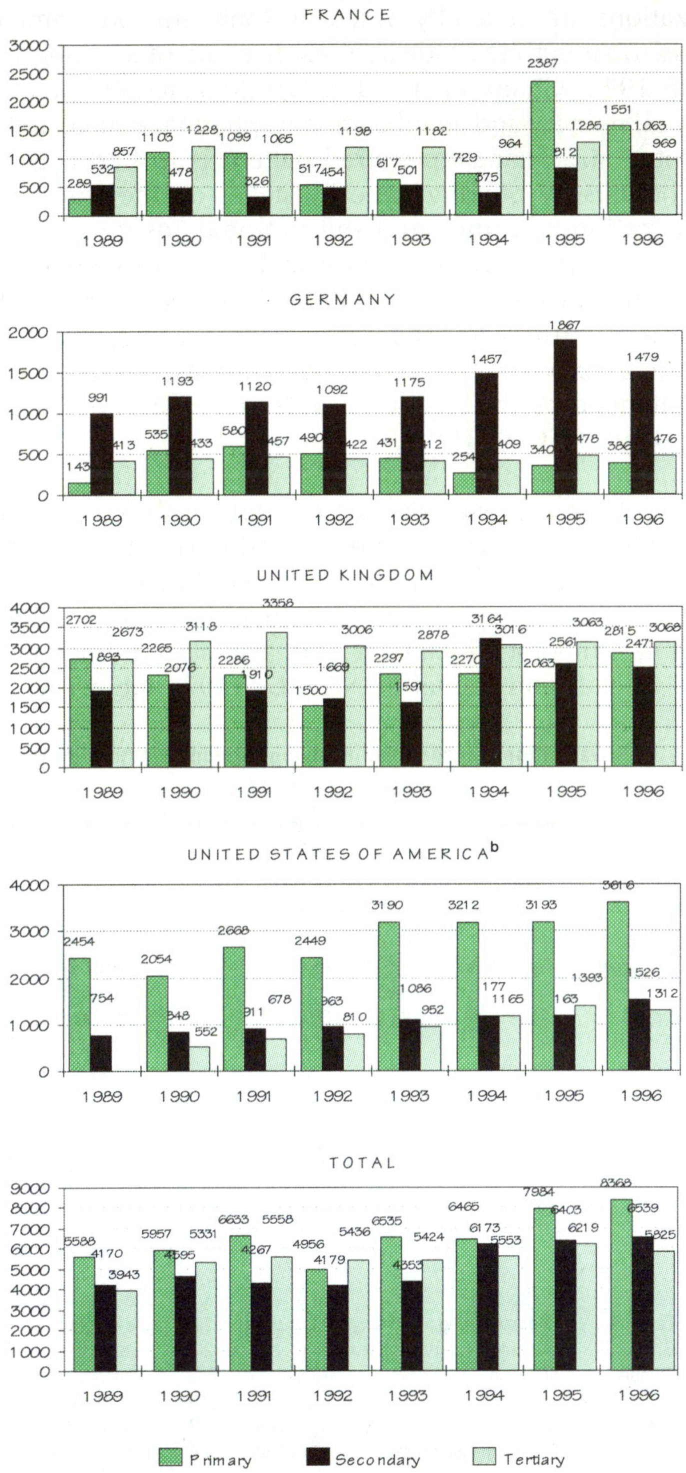

Source: UNCTAD, based on national sources.

[a] Includes South Africa.

[b] Figures for 1989 tertiary sector were not available.

which included a share of 26 per cent of Kenya Airways sold to KLM for $26 million (table VI.3).

These privatizations are generally based on long-term programmes and thus can be expected to continue to attract FDI. Mozambique has one of the oldest programmes, dating from 1987-1988. In 1998, Ghana intended to sell 20 state enterprises, including a cocoa buying company, an oil refinery and an oil company, pharmaceutical and bottling companies, and a palm oil plantation. Ghana's preferred pattern is to find a combination of foreign partners and local holders by offering minority stakes on the stock market.[13] Zambia is planning the privatization of mines and the national insurance corporation in 1998. Madagascar formed a Ministry of privatization in 1997 and plans to include the national airline and oil company and telecommunications in its programme. Botswana issued its white paper on privatization in December 1997. Namibia's strategy is first to "commercialize" state enterprises by, among other things, exposing them to competition, with privatization intended as the long-term outcome (SADC / Financial and Investment Sector Coordinating Unit (FISCU), 1998).

African countries have also made efforts to improve their national policy frameworks for FDI. Some 47 of the 53 African countries had adopted national laws governing FDI by 1997; 28 of these legal instruments having been introduced or amended in the 1990s (chapter III). According to a recent survey of least developed countries, only six of the 29 least developed countries in Africa for which data were available still had a restrictive regime for the repatriation of dividends and capital (UNCTAD, 1997f, table T.A1 and T.A2). All other

Table VI.3. Privatization transactions involving foreign investors in Africa, 1996

(Millions of dollars)

Company	Country	Industry	Equity share acquired (Per cent)	Amount	Method of sale	Purchaser(s)
Ashanti Goldfields	Ghana	Mining	5.0	112.2	Sale of shares	Institutional investors
HEVECAM	Cameroon	Agriculture	90.0	41.1	Tender	GMG Investments PTE, Panwell Group
Tomos Ghana Ltd	Ghana	Automotive services	50.0	30.2	Sale of shares	Tomos (Slovenia)
Kenya Airways	Kenya	Airlines	26.0	26.0	Direct sale	KLM (Netherlands)
Ghana Rubber Estate Ltd	Ghana	Industry	75.0	23.7	Joint venture	SIPH (France)
Northern Breweries (1995)	Zambia	Brewery	70.0	9.0	Tender	Lonrho Zambia
Portland Cement Co.	Malawi	Cement	51.0	5.6	Direct sale	CDC (United Kingdom)
Total (U) Ltd	Uganda	Petroleum	50.0	5.4	Sale of shares	Total Outre Mer (France)
Domaine Heveicole de L'Etat Cavally	Cote d'Ivoire	Agriculture	100.0	5.1	..	CDC (United Kingdom)
Tema Shipyard & Drydock	Ghana	Transport	60.0	4.2	Joint venture	PSC Terna Shipyard Ltd. (Malysia)
BP Zambia Ltd & Zamlube Refiners Ltd	Zambia	Petroleum	25.0	3.3	Pre-emptive rights	BP (United Kingdom)
Metal Fabricators of Zambia	Zambia	Manufacturing	33.0	3.2	Pre-emptive rights	Foreign investors[a]
Ghamot Motors	Ghana	Automotive services	75.0	2.8	Joint venture	Marubeni (Japan)
Pamodzi Hotel	Zambia	Tourism	70.0	2.1	Tender	Tata Zambia Ltd.
National Bicycle Co. Ltd	Tanzania	Industry	..	2.0	Sale of shares	Avon Cycles
National Engineering Co. Ltd	Tanzania	Industry	..	1.7	Sale of shares	Modern Trading Agencies
Agip (U) Ltd	Uganda	Petroleum distribution	50.0	1.6	Sale of shares	Agip Petrol International (Italy)
Kibimba Rice Co. Ltd	Uganda	Agribusiness	..	1.5	Sale of shares	Foreign investor [a]

Source: UNCTAD, based on World Bank, unpublished data.

[a] Name of company not disclosed.

countries had free or relatively free regimes that allowed the remittance of profits without major obstacles. Most countries have also enlarged the number of industries open to foreign investment and many now produce lists of the few restricted industries rather than lists of the many open to investment.

African efforts to reform FDI policy are increasingly acknowledged by both domestic and foreign investors. Thus, for instance, according to the results of a survey by the World Economic Forum, respondent companies considered that in a number of policy areas -- including trade, governance, access to finance, road infrastructure and telecommunications -- significant improvements have taken place in Africa as a whole (WEF, 1998a). Openness to trade, improvement in institutions, and the availability and affordability of telecommunication infrastructure and computers were assessed by the companies to have been the areas with the greatest progress (WEF, 1998a, p. 20). Also, almost all of the 23 African countries included in the survey received good evaluations of their dividend-remittance and investment-protection policies (see also section VI.B. and table VI.4).

In addition to the improvement of national policies related to FDI (see also section VI.B.), a large number of African countries have signed bilateral investment treaties, which numbered 326 in 1997. In addition, by 1998, the majority of African countries (41) had signed the Convention establishing the Multilateral Investment Guarantee Agency (MIGA), as well as the Convention on the Settlement of Investment Disputes between States and Nationals of Other States (42) (see also section VI.B. and annex table A.VI.1); 40 African countries have adopted the Paris Convention for the Protection of Industrial Property and 41 African countries have signed one or more agreements in the WTO relating to FDI, such as the TRIPS or TRIMS Agreements, under the umbrella of the WTO Final Act of Marrakesh (UNCTAD, 1997g), although some countries are still in the process of revising domestic laws and notifying the WTO.

Efforts on the part of many African countries to improve their FDI frameworks have reached such a level that "the perception that Africa is a risky place to invest is therefore correct only to the extent that in some African countries, obsolete laws and excessive bureaucratic practices still exist and create an unfavourable investment

Table VI.4. The investor friendliness of the FDI regulatory framework in Africa: rankings according to several indicators, 1997

Country	Ranking of exchange rate policy[a]	Ranking of FDI protection[b]	Ranking of dividend-remittance policies[c]
Botswana	6.06	4.00	6.65
Burkina Faso	4.50	5.20	5.35
Cameroon	4.25	4.92	5.69
Côte d'Ivoire	4.43	5.25	5.75
Egypt	5.03	5.59	5.59
Ethiopia	4.67	5.20	5.33
Ghana	4.89	4.94	6.09
Kenya	4.24	4.72	5.51
Malawi	4.05	3.95	5.13
Mauritius	5.09	5.13	6.58
Morocco	4.82	5.88	6.59
Mozambique	4.32	4.68	5.33
Namibia	5.84	5.61	6.00
Nigeria	4.47	4.00	5.42
South Africa	5.16	3.70	5.63
Tanzania	5.09	5.23	5.82
Tunisia	5.40	6.43	6.50
Uganda	4.79	4.96	6.04
Zambia	4.56	4.46	5.90
Zimbabwe	3.22	4.15	5.22
Average, FDI front-runner countries[d]	5.20	5.10	6.10
Average, other	4.50	4.90	5.70

Source: UNCTAD, based on World Economic Forum, 1998a.

Note: the investors in the particular countries were asked to give evaluations between 1 and 7 (1: strongly disagree and 7: strongly agree) for the following statements:

[a] The exchange-rate policy is favourable to export expansion.

[b] Investment-protection schemes are readily available for most foreign investors.

[c] Dividend-remittance policies do not impede business development.

[d] The term FDI "front-runner country" refers to Botswana, Equatorial Guinea, Ghana, Mozambique, Namibia, Tunisia and Uganda (see section VI-B).

climate" (Mutharika, 1997, p. 280). Indeed, as macroeconomic conditions improve and regulatory frameworks are becoming more liberal, measures to facilitate business, such as the reduction of bureaucracy and corruption as well as policies to promote FDI become more important. While it is true that "red tape" is a problem in many African countries and corruption is still widespread -- there are significant differences among African countries and, judging from companies' assessments, the continent as a whole does not fare much worse than other developing regions (WEF, 1998a, p. 28). African countries have now established investment promotion agencies that focus on attracting foreign investors through a variety of measures. Twenty-five African investment promotion agencies are currently members of the World Association of Investment Promotion Agencies (WAIPA) (table VI.5). Moreover, there are also signs of increased activity in joint investment promotion at the regional level. For example, the investment promotion agencies of the member countries of the Southern African Development Community (SADC)[14] held a joint meeting in Centurion, South Africa, in June 1998 to discuss possible cooperation in joint marketing missions, exchange of experiences as to promotion practices and business intelligence, and a joint staff-development programme.

The efforts by African host countries to improve their investment climate are also increasingly complemented by interregional initiatives to promote investment and trade. The steps towards better access to foreign markets for least developed countries which were announced at a high-level meeting hosted by the WTO in October 1997 improved the access of the 33 least developed countries in Africa to the United States market subject to certain conditions, and provided long-term guarantees of their present access to the European Union under the Lomé Convention. They may also gain easier access to the markets of some of the

Table VI.5. African members of the World Association of Investment Promotion Agencies (WAIPA), 1997

Country	Agency's name
Algeria	Agence de Promotion de Soutien et de suivi des Investissements (APSI)
Angola	Instituto do Investimento Estrangeiro (IIE)
Cameroon	Investment Code Management Unit (ICMU)
Cape Verde	Center for Investment, Export and Tourism Promotion (PROMEX)
Congo, Democratic Republic of	Fonds de Promotion de l'Industrie (FPI)
Cote d'Ivoire	Centre de Promotion des Investissements en Cote d'Ivoire (CEPECI)
Egypt	General Authority for Investment (GAFI)
Ethiopia	Ethiopian Investment Authority (EIA)
Gambia, The	National Investment Promotion Authority (NIPA)
Ghana	Ghana Investment Promotion Centre (GIPC)
Kenya	Investment Promotion Centre (IPC)
Lesotho	Lesotho Investment Promotion Centre (LIPC)
Mali	Centre National de Promotion des Investissements (CNPI)
Morocco	Direction des Investissements Exterieurs, Ministere des Finances et des Investissements Exterieurs
Namibia	Namibia Investment Centre
Nigeria	Nigerian Investment Promotion Commission (NIPC)
Senegal	Guichet Unique
Seychelles	Seychelles International Business Authority (SIBA)
Sierra Leone	Department of Trade, Industry and State Entreprises
Sudan	General Administration for Investment Promotion
Tanzania	Zanzibar Investment Promotion Agency
Tunisia	Foreign Investment Promotion Agency (FIPA Tunisia)
Uganda	Uganda Investment Authority (UIA)
Zambia	Zambia Investment Centre
Zimbabwe	Zimbabwe Investment Centre

Source: based on UNCTAD, 1997h.

more advanced developing countries. Improved access to developed country markets may increase the chances to attract efficiency-seeking FDI for those countries that already have the conditions for such investment in place (see section VI.B). The idea of giving FDI a more prominent role vis-à-vis official capital flows has also been discussed within the framework of the design of the forthcoming new Lomé Agreement. Within the framework of the current Lomé Convention, the European Union offers several schemes to support investment in the African, Caribbean and Pacific partner countries. The Centre for the Development of Industry, for example, promotes technical or commercial partnerships between European firms and firms from African, Caribbean and Pacific countries, e.g. through providing assistance in finding appropriate partner companies or co-financing feasibility studies. Other interregional agreements -- such as the association agreement between North African countries and the European Union that foresees the creation of a free-trade area between the European Union and Algeria, Egypt, Morocco and Tunisia -- can also significantly promote trade and investment flows, especially export-oriented FDI, if the agreements are broad enough in their coverage. Some FDI in countries such as Morocco for example, is already attributed to the fact that it will be a part of the free-trade zone with the European Union in 2010.[15] Apart from the activities of the European Union, individual member states of the European Union, along with a number of other OECD countries, have undertaken measures to promote investment in developing countries including some in Africa. These include the provision of information, the support of feasibility studies, and matchmaking programmes that bring domestic and foreign firms together.

There are also important initiatives by home countries to encourage companies to invest in Africa. Thus, the United States House of Representatives approved in March 1998 the African Growth and Opportunity Act, designed to promote private sector initiative in Africa in general and FDI in particular. The initiative includes a proposal to remove all quotas and tariffs for apparel and textile imports from Africa. In addition, the Overseas Private Investment Corporation (OPIC) has been asked to play a lead role in the initiative by establishing a $150 million fund for equity investment in Africa and by setting up a $500 million private equity fund for investment in particular infrastructure projects, with the expectation that the fund will induce private investors to participate (Mutharika, 1997, p. 279; Lang, 1997). By 1997, OPIC had provided $775 million in political risk insurance and finance for investments in about 40 African countries (Mutharika, 1997, p. 279). However, the measures under the Act are subject to conditions that countries must satisfy -- as judged by the United States administration. These include, in particular, that countries have established or are making continued progress towards establishing a market oriented economy and do not engage in gross violations of internationally recognized human rights.

At the micro-level, what is of particular interest to investors is the profitability of their investments in Africa. In the case of United States FDI (table VI.6), it is noteworthy that between 1980 and 1997 there was only one year (1986) in which the rate of return on investment was below 10 per cent. Since 1990, the rate of return in Africa has averaged 29 per cent and since 1991 it has been higher than that in any other region, including developed countries as a group, by a factor of two or more, in many years. Net income from British direct investment in Africa was reported to have increased by 60 per cent between 1989 and 1995 (Bennell, 1997a, p. 131) and, in 1995, Japanese affiliates in Africa turned more profitable than in the early 1990s and have been even more profitable than those in any other region except for Latin America and the Caribbean and West Asia (figure VI.6).

Table VI.6. Rates of return on United States FDI in Africa and selected regions,[a] 1983-1997

(Percentage)

Region	1983	1984	1985	1986	1987	1988	1989	1990	1991	1992	1993	1994	1995	1996	1997[b]
Africa[c]	17.7	23.7	17.3	5.6	15.5	13.9	17.4	24.2	30.6	28.4	25.8	24.6	35.3	34.2	25.3
Primary[d]	19.3	27.1	19.6	4.9	12.8	10.2	13.0	22.8	35.4	29.1	26.1	23.9	34.2	36.9	..
Manufacturing[d]	13.9	13.6	8.8	13.8	19.0	24.0	15.4	20.4	16.0	18.9	30.5	30.0	42.8	21.3	..
Tertiary[d]	11.9	7.1	3.4	19.5	20.6	8.7	n.a.	23.8	n.a.	22.2	23.5	21.7	21.6	23.1	..
Other	2.0	7.0	16.9	21.5	36.6	41.7	n.a.	48.0	28.4	40.8	13.5	44.1	35.0	17.4	..
Asia[e]	27.6	26.1	18.1	13.0	20.3	22.4	23.3	27.6	23.8	22.6	20.7	18.4	20.2	19.3	16.2
Latin America	7.0	9.9	9.5	10.3	9.5	14.2	15.7	13.0	12.1	14.3	14.9	15.3	13.1	12.8	12.5
Developing countries	14.9	17.3	13.4	10.9	13.2	16.5	17.8	17.2	15.9	17.2	16.9	16.5	15.8	15.3	14.0
All countries	13.0	14.3	12.6	12.2	13.4	15.5	14.8	14.3	11.6	10.4	11.1	11.7	13.3	12.5	12.3

Source: UNCTAD, based on United States, Department of Commerce, various issues.

[a] The rate of return is calculated as the net income of United States foreign affiliates in a given year divided by the average of beginning-of-year and end-of-year FDI stock.
[b] The stock data for 1997 used in the calculation are estimates by the United States Department of Commerce.
[c] Excluding South Africa.
[d] Including South Africa.
[e] Including West Asia, South, East and South-East Asia and the Pacific; excluding Australia, Israel, Japan and New Zealand.

However, the number of TNCs that enjoy these profits appears to be declining, judging from the number of foreign affiliates of United States and German TNCs in the region, which has dropped significantly between and the mid-1980s and mid-1990s. The number of the former declined from 596 in 1982 to 444 in 1994 -- although in 1995 there was an increase in this figure to 516 (United States, Department of Commerce, various issues)[16] -- and that of the latter from 669 in 1984 to 573 in 1996 (Deutsche Bundesbank, various years). The reduced number of affiliates has been attributed to divestment by some TNCs that had decided to re-focus their investment on core activities and core regions for their business and for which the reforms in Africa in the 1990s came too late to influence that decision (Bennell, 1997a, p. 136). Other reasons for divestments by TNCs include problems in remitting profits as well as a deteriorating and difficult business environment that led to significant "hassle costs" for the private sector (ibid, p.135).

Investment outflows from developing Africa increased from $ 0.3 billion in 1996 to 1.1 billion in 1997 (figure VI.7). The increase was mainly due to the rise (from $500 million in 1996 to $800 in 1997) in outflows from Nigeria and an increase of outflows from Liberia from -0.4 billions in 1996 to more than $200 million in 1997. These two countries accounted for over two-thirds of outward investment from Africa during 1994-1996.

Figure VI.6. Profitability of foreign affiliates of Japanese TNCs, by selected host region, 1995

(Percentage)

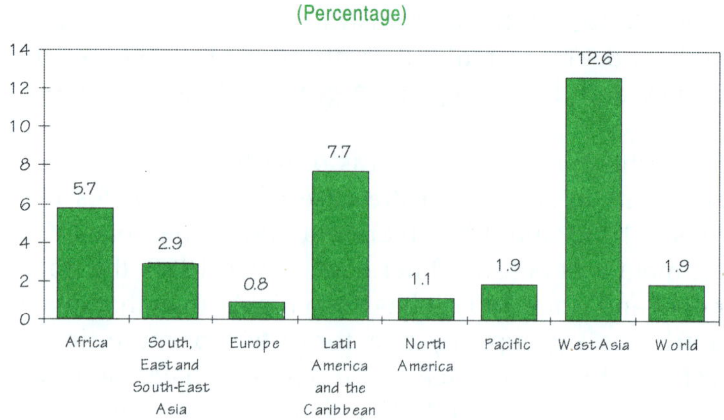

Source: UNCTAD, based on Japan, Ministry of International Trade and Industry, 1998a.

* * *

There are encouraging signs that Africa may expect rising inflows of FDI in the future. Inward FDI flows to North Africa have shown a robust positive trend in the 1990s. In sub-Saharan Africa, total annual average inflows have also risen, from $ 3.2 billion in 1991-1993 to $5.2 billion in 1994-1996. On the other hand, the decline in commodity prices, especially the prices of petroleum, gold and diamonds, could reduce the attractiveness of some of the countries that have been major recipients of FDI in the recent past, including South Africa, Angola and Nigeria. But economic fundamentals in the region are improving and enabling policy frameworks for investment are being put in place in an increasing number of countries. Indeed, the simultaneous improvement in policy initiatives both externally (such as the least-developed-country initiative by a number of international organizations and the Africa initiative of the United States) and internally augurs well for foreign investment in Africa notwithstanding the slight fall of FDI inflows into sub-Saharan Africa in 1997. Growth, economic reform and improvements in the regulatory frameworks of many countries are increasingly recognized by both domestic and foreign investors. While some countries are benefiting from increasing FDI inflows, however, others are still waiting for inward investment to take off, suggesting either that the improvements in economic prospects and the investment climate are not yet attractive enough or that they have not yet become widely apparent to potential investors. It is also possible that in some countries the change of legislation has not yet been reflected in administrative practice. This makes it important to explore what can be learned from the frontrunner countries in Africa about improving performance as well as image, to attract greater investment.

Figure VI.7. Africa: FDI flows from the top 17 outward investor countries in 1997 and flows from the same countries in 1996[a]

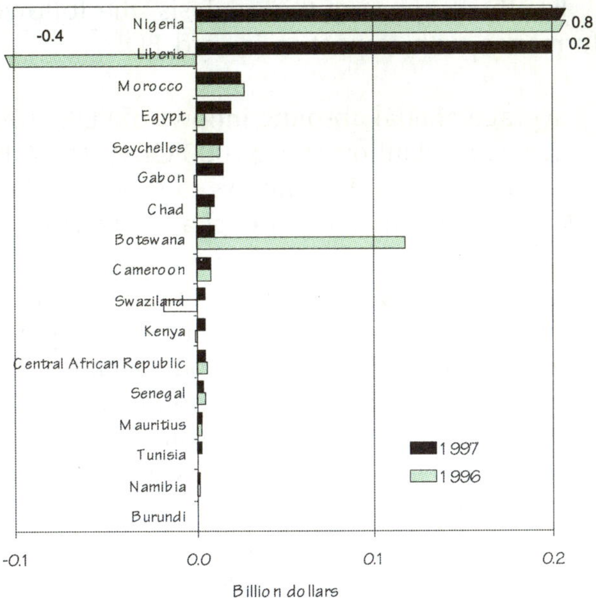

Source: UNCTAD, FDI/TNC database.

[a] Ranked on the basis of the magnitude of FDI outflows in 1997.

B. Recent country success stories

1. Which countries are they?

Africa as a whole trails other continents in attracting foreign investors. However, there are countries that stand out with an FDI-attracting performance in recent years that is not only better than the average for African developing countries but also above the average for all developing countries. These "frontrunners" demonstrate that African countries can become attractive locations for foreign investors, even in a period when reports of political unrest and economic instability prevent many investors from exploring the opportunities that the continent has to offer. This section identifies a group of recent frontrunners and examines their characteristics and the factors underlying their success.

For the purpose of this analysis, the following indicators have been used to measure performance with respect to inward FDI[17]:

- average annual absolute inflows of FDI, 1992-1996;
- average FDI inflows per $1000 GDP, 1992-1996;
- average ratio of FDI inflows to gross fixed capital formation, 1992-1996;
- average FDI inflows per capita, 1992-1996.

As the analysis does not focus on the impact of FDI, no indicators measuring the quality of the investment received have been used. The period 1992-1996 has been chosen not only to average out annual fluctuations, but because it is a period which has seen an economic recovery and a return to relative political stability in the continent and widespread policy change in the FDI area. Because the analysis focuses on recent success stories, flow indicators have been used, as opposed to stock indicators, which tend to reflect FDI performance over a longer period.

To qualify as a frontrunner, a country had, first, to receive FDI flows above the developing-country average as measured by at least one of these indicators. In other words, it needed to perform not only better than the average African country but also better than the average developing country. This filter yields the following 18 countries: Angola, Botswana, Chad, Democratic Republic of Congo, Egypt, Equatorial Guinea, the Gambia, Ghana, Lesotho, Liberia, Mozambique, Namibia, Nigeria, Seychelles, Tunisia, the United Republic of Tanzania, Uganda and Zambia.

The four indicators used capture only the level of FDI performance during a given period; they are static forms of measurement. To capture the dynamics of performance, these 18 candidates had to pass through an additional filter, namely an improvement in the performance on any of the four indicators which is above the level of improvement of developing countries as a group. Thus, for a country to be counted as a frontrunner, the increase in the value of at least one of the indicators from the period 1987-1991 to the period 1992-1996 for the country had to be higher than the increase in the same indicator for the average developing country, subject to the condition that in the case of an indicator that related absolute FDI inflows to an economic variable, the latter (the denominator) did not decline. This filter yields the following seven countries (table VI.7):[18]

- Botswana
- Equatorial Guinea
- Ghana
- Mozambique
- Namibia
- Tunisia
- Uganda

The countries represent the most dynamic countries in Africa in terms of attracting FDI flows during 1992-1996 according to the selected methodology. Together, they accounted for more than 24 per cent of FDI flows into Africa in 1996 while representing only 9 per cent of Africa's population and 8 per cent of the continent's GDP. It should be noted that two of the frontrunners (Mozambique and Uganda) received below African- average FDI flows during 1992-1996 (since either absolute or relative FDI performance above the developing country average allowed a country to enter the ranks of the frontrunners, provided the second criterion regarding an increase in one of the indicators was satisfied as well). This suggests that these two countries had only recently begun to attract FDI or resumed doing so after a break. Conversely, the frontrunner group excludes some African countries that were among the largest recipients of FDI flows during 1992-1996.[19] The frontrunner group, moreover, does not include a number of countries such as Egypt, Mauritius, Morocco and Nigeria that rank high among African countries on the basis of FDI stock indicators (annex table A.VI.1). Although some of them (e.g. Nigeria) received significant amounts of FDI flows during the period under consideration, all of these "historic" frontrunners lacked dynamism as defined by the second criterion mentioned above and are therefore not in the centre of this analysis.

The group of the selected frontrunners is heterogeneous not only in their level of development (Equatorial Guinea, Mozambique and Uganda are least developed countries (LDCs) while Botswana and Tunisia are middle-income countries), but also in their geographic location on the continent. As regards economic structure, Equatorial Guinea is an oil-based economy and attracts FDI almost exclusively with its rich endowments of offshore oil reserves, while other frontrunners such as Tunisia and Ghana, with more diversified economies, receive significant FDI in non-primary sectors. This heterogeneity underlines the need for a broad-based analysis of the determinants contributing to the relative success of the frontrunners in attracting FDI.

Table VI.7. Africa: Recent FDI frontrunners by selected indicators, 1987-1991 and 1992-1996

(Millions of dollars and percentage)

	Average FDI inflows per year			FDI inflows per $1000 GDP			Ratio of FDI inflows to GFCF[a]			FDI inflows per capita		
	1987-1991	1992-1996	Change[b]	1987-1991	1992-1996	Change[b]	1987-1991	1992-1996	Change[b]	1987-1991	1992-1996	Change[b]
	(Million dollars)		(Per cent)	(Million dollars)		(Per cent)	(Million dollars)		(Per cent)	(Million dollars)		(Per cent)
Botswana	56.7	137.9	143	18.6	33.1	78	6.5	12.9	100	46	95	108
Equatorial Guinea	11.1	109.7	888	82.9	689.8	732	30.2	285.2	845	32	282	778
Ghana	11.9	121.4	920	2.1	20.5	869	1.7	14.9	754	1	7	778
Mozambique	9.2	33.3	263	6.8	23.5	247	1.2	3.6	201	1	2	228
Namibia	29.6	108.4	267	14.3	37.5	163	8.4	16.8	99	23	72	221
Tunisia	86.4	387.3	348	7.8	23.3	197	3.5	9.0	158	11	44	306
Uganda[c]	-1.4	77.6	19 796	- 0.1	15.9	18 816	- 0.1	10.3	15 175	0	4	16 672
Average for Africa[d]	60.1	96.1	60	6.7	10.4	54	3.3	5.9	77	5	7	39
Average for all developing countries[d]	212.1	613.0	189	8.2	17.3	111	3.5	6.8	98	8	20	164

Source: UNCTAD FDI/TNC database.

[a] GFCF = gross fixed capital formation.

[b] Percentage change during the period 1987-1991 to 1992-1996.

[c] In the years 1989 and 1990, Uganda experienced negative FDI inflows of $1.8 and $5.9 million, more than offsetting the positive inflows of the other years in the period 1987-1991 and resulting in a negative sum for the FDI inflows of that period as a whole.

[d] Including South Africa.

2. Why do they perform well?

The heterogeneity of the frontrunner group of African countries identified above suggests that a variety of determinants has to be looked at in a search for the underlying reasons for their superior performance as regards inward FDI in recent years (chapter IV).

(a) The policy framework

Almost all of the countries that have been identified as frontrunners have made considerable progress in acquiring or regaining political stability in recent years. Although the threat of unrest and armed conflict has not disappeared, conditions have improved - as, for example, in Mozambique which has seen the ending of a long-standing civil war. Since political stability -- including the predictability and reliability of the regulatory framework affecting business, such as the tax system -- has been found to be the most basic factor for companies considering investment in Africa (Sachs and Sievers, 1998, p. 39), it might well be a key factor explaining the recent performance of the frontrunners. There are several examples of TNC decisions, in particular outside the primary sector, being influenced by the political situation of a country. For example, apparently, one of the reasons why Hyundai decided in 1993 to establish its car assembly plant in Botswana -- intended mainly to service the South African market -- was that it was seen as a stable country with a strong economy and fewer uncertainties than other potential locations (Corporate Location, 1994, p. 9).

With respect to economic stability, the situation is mixed. While almost all frontrunner countries show a trend towards increased macroeconomic stability, the degree of stability varies significantly and not all members of the group have performed better than the rest of Africa. Thus, six of the seven frontrunners managed to reduce their average annual inflation rate in the 1990s. However, Tunisia is the only country in the group with a relatively low rate of inflation of 5.2 per cent for the 1990s. All other FDI frontrunners had significantly higher rates, some of them exceeding an average of 20 per cent for 1990-1996. As for the government deficit as a percentage of GDP, another indicator of macroeconomic policy, the frontrunner group has also made progress. With the exception of Namibia, all the frontrunner countries for which data were available have reduced their budget deficits gradually since the beginning of the 1990s (table VI.8), although their deficit levels in the 1990s are still higher than the African average. Thus, only for a few of the frontrunners could the level of macroeconomic stability have played an important role in attracting above-average FDI, although the frontrunners' ongoing efforts to improve the macroeconomic picture could have been perceived by foreign investors as evidence of the long-term commitment of their governments to create a more stable and business-friendly environment.

As regards trade policies, another important factor influencing FDI flows to a country, there is a general trend towards more open trade regimes in Africa, but there is no evidence that the trade regimes of the frontrunners have differed significantly from those of other African countries in the 1990s. As judged from several admittedly rough indicators such as the mean tariff level applied in 1990-1993 or the proportion of all goods covered by non-tariff barriers, there appears to be no systematic difference between the front-runner group and other African countries, nor were the frontrunners necessarily more integrated into the world economy as measured by the ratio of the sum of exports and imports to GDP[20] (table VI.9).[21] However, one of the frontrunners, Tunisia, has like some other (non-frontrunner) countries including Egypt, Mauritius and Morocco, managed to attract efficiency-seeking FDI in such industries as textiles and apparel, among other things with the help of appropriate trade policies. This has involved, among other measures, offering special incentives, such as exemption from import duties for inputs into export goods manufactured in the country or other trade privileges for companies operating in export processing zones (EPZs). In most of the other frontrunner countries, the setting up of EPZs or other schemes particularly targeted at investors in efficiency-seeking, export-oriented industries is only just beginning, and there are shortcomings in areas important for the successful attraction of such investment (see subsection (c) iii below). In Mozambique, for instance, the regulation governing the Industrial Free Zones designed for investors with a minimum investment of $5 million and a required minimum export content of 85 per cent of production came into effect only in January 1998 (SADC/FISCU, 1998, p. 59).

As for the policy framework for FDI per se, all of the frontrunner countries appear to have made special efforts to improve regulations and measures concerning FDI, although with significant differences. In terms of signing international agreements governing investment protection (annex table A.VI.2), the most active countries in the group are Ghana, Tunisia and Uganda, and, to a lesser extent, Botswana.[22] These countries have signed all principal international conventions related to FDI and are members of all relevant international institutions that deal with issues related to FDI, including MIGA, the International Convention for the Settlement of Investment Disputes between States and Nationals of other States (ICSID) and the Convention on the Recognition and Enforcement of Foreign Arbitral Awards. The other countries in the group have signed only some of the existing conventions (annex table A.VI.2). The latter is particularly true for Equatorial Guinea and Namibia. However, even these countries, like other frontrunner countries, have signed the convention establishing MIGA, while in the rest of Africa only 34 of 46 countries have

Table VI.8. Africa: selected indicators of macroeconomic stability for recent FDI frontrunner countries and averages for all Africa

(Percentage)

Country	Rate of inflation 1980-1990 (I)[a]	Rate of inflation 1990- most recent year (II)[a b]	Difference (II)- (I)	Overall government deficit(-) or surplus (+) as a percentage of GDP (current prices) 1980-1990 (III)	Overall government deficit(-) or surplus (+) as a percentage of GDP (current prices) 1990-most recent year[b] (IV)	Difference (IV) - (III)
Botswana	10.9	11.8	+ 0.9	9.4	5.5	-3.9
Equatorial Guinea	17.3	11.7	- 5.6	- 14.0	- 4.9	9.1
Ghana	47.4	30.8	-16.6	- 12.0	- 6.8	5.2
Mozambique	52.3	43.2	- 9.1	- 18.2	- 5.8	12.4
Namibia	17.5	10.5	- 7.0	- 1.6	- 4.0	2.4
Tunisia	8.3	5.2	- 3.1	- 4.7	- 3.8	0.9
Uganda	103.5	16.9	- 86.6	- 9.5	-3.0	6.5
Average, all Africa[c]	16.1	30.7	+ 14.6	- 6.7	- 3.8	2.9

Source: UNCTAD, based on African Development Bank, 1998.

[a] Refers to consumer price indices (general), (1980 = 100).
[b] "Most recent" refers, in most cases, to 1996.
[c] Including South Africa.

done so. In bilateral investment agreements (BITs) also, the frontrunner group appears to have been more active than other African countries. While the frontrunners signed, on average, almost eight such treaties per country, the 41 non-frontrunners for which information was available averaged only five BITs per country. Again, as with international conventions, there are differences within the group: i.e. while Tunisia signed 41 BITs (exceeded only by the 43 signed by Egypt) and Ghana nine, the other frontrunners had all concluded less than five BITs each by the end of 1998, which was below the average for the non-frontrunners. In the conclusion of double taxation treaties (DTTs) the picture is also mixed among the frontrunners. By 1 January 1998, Tunisia had signed 23 such treaties -- more than half of the 41 treaties concluded by the whole frontrunner group and more than any other African country. All other frontrunner countries for which data are available had signed five (Namibia) or fewer such treaties. The average for the 45 African non-frontrunner countries was more than seven DTTs each -- higher than the frontrunner average of five.[23]

With respect to national policy frameworks for FDI, the national investment codes of most of the FDI frontrunner countries had been revised by the mid-1990s with the general aim of encouraging investment.[24] While there is no comprehensive comparison of investment codes of African countries based on objective criteria, the subjective perceptions of investment regulations by foreign investors provide some evidence that the frontrunner countries, by and large, had made more progress in creating a regulatory environment conducive to FDI than most other African countries (see table VI.4) Thus, in a survey of investors in 23 African countries, conducted by the World Economic Forum (WEF, 1998a),[25] the group's investment-protection schemes for foreign investors received higher average marks from respondents than the other countries included in the survey, with Namibia and Tunisia receiving the

Table VI.9. Africa: total real trade[a] as a share of GDP and indicators of trade barriers in recent FDI frontrunner countries and other African countries

(Percentage)

Country	Real trade as share of GDP: Share 1981-1993	Real trade as share of GDP: Average annual difference 1980-1983 to 1990-1993 [b]	Mean tariff rate,[c] 1990-1993	Standard deviation of tariff rates,[c] 1990-1993	Proportion covered by non-tariff barriers,[c] 1990-1993
FDI frontrunners					
Botswana	106.9	- 2.7	..	..	..
Equatorial Guinea	..	..	..	..	..
Ghana	21.0	4.5	15.0	81.3	..
Mozambique	..	..	5.0	..	..
Namibia	..	..	...	..	..
Tunisia	42.3	-0.3	30.0	11.7	32.7
Uganda	9.4	0.2	17.1	9.1	..
Other African countries					
Egypt	33.6	-1.9	28.3	28.9	45.2
Lesotho	83.3	-3.3	..	..	..
Mauritius	50.1	3.82	..	..	35.2
Morocco	24.8	0.39	24.5	13.2	..
Nigeria	55.5	- 5.6	34.3	25.0	8.8

Source: UNCTAD, based on World Bank, 1997c, tables 5.6 and 6.1.

a Real trade is the sum of exports and imports of goods and services measured in constant prices.
b Computed as the difference between the end points of the period shown, averaged over ten years.
c For all goods.

most positive evaluations (table VI.4). All of the FDI frontrunner countries also received a positive evaluation from companies when it came to dividend remittance policies, another major component of an FDI framework, with their average evaluation again higher than the others'. The countries surveyed in the *Africa Competitiveness Report* performed worse in terms of the effectiveness of antitrust policy -- another important policy that can have an impact on FDI (UNCTAD, 1997a) -- as compared to other FDI-related policies. In this case, there was no major difference between the frontrunner group and others. Still, businesses appeared by and large to have found the competition or anti-trust policy frameworks in FDI frontrunner countries acceptable, with the exception of Botswana, Mozambique and Namibia (WEF, 1998a, p.218).[26]

Compared to the slow speed of privatization at least in sub-Saharan Africa, some of the FDI frontrunners are doing much better; 32 per cent (649) of the 2,040 privatization transactions undertaken in sub-Saharan Africa before 1997 are accounted for by the six sub-Saharan frontrunner countries (World Bank, 1997b, p. 278).[27] While privatization does not necessarily imply that foreigners are allowed to purchase stakes in the privatized enterprises, its absence virtually eliminates the possibility of FDI in many industries and countries. Mozambique and Ghana were the most active in privatization in the group of FDI frontrunners, with each accounting for more than 100 privatization transactions up to 1997 (see section VI.A).[28] In the case of Mozambique, while most of the companies have been sold to Mozambican entrepreneurs, about 50 per cent of the equity capital for privatization until 1998 came from foreign sources, in particular from Portugal, South Africa and the United Kingdom (SADC / FISCU, 1998, p. 58). In Uganda, FDI flows were also significantly associated with the privatization programme (Corporate Location 1998, p.22).[29]

(b) Business facilitation

While almost all African countries have recently made efforts to facilitate business and reduce bureaucratic "red tape", the FDI frontrunners appear to have made the most progress in this respect. Survey data in the *African Competitiveness Report 1998* suggest that, on average, government regulations impose less of a burden on business competitiveness in the frontrunner countries than in other African countries. Companies doing business in frontrunner countries also confirmed more strongly that state interference in private business was minimal (WEF, 1998a, pp. 187; annex table A.VI.3). The only exception was Mozambique, that received a rather low assessment in both respects. Tunisia and Botswana received particularly high marks. Nonetheless, "red tape" remains an important obstacle for investment even in many frontrunner countries.[30] A recent study on administrative barriers to investment in Mozambique highlighted bureaucratic impediments to investment that the frontrunners share with the majority of developing --and sometimes even developed-- countries (IFC, 1996). These include:

- *Non-transparency of decision-making processes.* Bureaucratic approval processes are often non-transparent, frustrating companies as they receive little information on how and when a formal approval process regarding their investment project will end.

- *Complicated regulatory frameworks.* One consequence of the complexity and non-transparency of regulatory frameworks is that foreign companies have to hire experts (typically ex-functionaries) to deal with the regulatory processes, resulting in the payment of fees that represent additional costs for the investor.

- *Costly and time-consuming licensing procedures.* To obtain an industrial licence that allows an investor to operate in Mozambique, at least 25 separate bureaucratic steps are needed. The costs incurred by companies due to these administrative requirements can be significant.[31]

As to corruption, which constitutes -- according to the survey results in the *Africa Competitiveness Report 1998* -- one of the most important factors influencing investment decisions in Africa (Sachs and Sievers, 1998, p. 36), on average the frontrunner group appear to be less affected by this problem than the group of non-frontrunner countries featured in the *Report,* and at least some of the frontrunners have made considerable progress in the reduction of corruption. According to this *Report,* Botswana appears to have the lowest corruption level of all African countries and would even compare with the top half of the OECD countries in this respect. Tunisia also shows up well compared with OECD countries (Kaufmann, D., 1998, p. 28). Among the FDI frontrunner countries featured in the report, Mozambique and Uganda appear to have the biggest problems with corruption although Uganda in particular has made considerable improvements in recent years (ibid.)

As to investment facilitation, almost all frontrunner countries offered incentives for foreign investors, guaranteed a time limit within which local authorities are obliged to complete screening processes and had programmes in place to train officials in developing a welcoming attitude vis-à-vis foreign investors.[32]

Finally, successful investment promotion becomes a more important determinant for FDI in Africa as the countries on the continent improve with respect to the other determinants. Almost all FDI frontrunner countries had established investment promotion agencies[33] and all of the frontrunner countries that were included in UNCTAD's survey of best-practice business promotion (UNCTAD, 1997b) had also established a one-stop shop for FDI by 1996.[34] The investment promotion agencies in these countries also assist foreign investors in obtaining work permits and other licences and all have a process in place encouraging foreign investors to reinvest. Some countries (e.g. Botswana, Namibia and Uganda) have installed offices of their investment promotion agencies overseas actively to promote themselves in major home countries of TNCs. It is important to note, in this connection, that in general, countries successful in attracting FDI focus their efforts on certain TNCs and certain home countries of TNCs (UNCTAD, 1997b, p. 51). While it is difficult to compare the performance of investment-promotion activities and to judge when some of the success in attracting FDI can be attributed to a well-functioning investment promotion agency, there is some evidence that most of the best agencies of this kind in Africa were located in the frontrunner group. Thus, according to a ranking of the best investment promotion agencies in Africa and the Middle East, five of the eight frontrunner countries were represented in the top ten (Corporate Location, 1997, p.39).[35] Uganda's agency for investment promotion received an award for being the best African investment promotion agency in 1997[36] and can compare, at least in some respects, even with the top agencies in the world.[37]

(c) Economic determinants

The FDI frontrunners in Africa vary considerably as regards the economic determinants of FDI, although determinants themselves vary in importance according to type of investment.

i. Resource-seeking investment

Perhaps more than in other developing regions, natural resource extraction plays an important role in FDI in Africa and so it is not surprising that the majority of frontrunners are countries with economies dominated by primary products, especially mineral resources. Equatorial Guinea receives FDI almost exclusively to exploit its rich oil and gas reserves. Botswana and Namibia have received significant FDI in mining, particularly for diamonds. Ghana also received much of its FDI in the primary sector and even Tunisia attracted some FDI in the exploration of oilfields and the construction of a gas pipeline to export Algerian gas to Italy (El Hedi Lahouel, 1998, p. 14). Since 1994, 33 per cent of the stock of Ashanti Goldfields, the largest Ghanaian gold mine and the first and only genuinely African firm to be listed on the New York and Toronto stock exchanges, is held by the United Kingdom-based company Lonrho. However, although large endowments of oil or other natural resources are helpful to attract investment, they are not, by themselves, normally sufficient to explain success with respect to FDI in Africa. Thus, the average absolute FDI flows into the group of oil-producing African countries were, at $338 million, much lower than the average for all developing countries.[38]

The very fact that there is a large number of natural-resource rich countries in Africa -- excluding countries that have received large inflows in the past as reflected by large FDI stock-- that received much less FDI than the frontrunners during 1992-1996, highlights the fact that natural resource endowments, are conducive to, but not sufficient on their own for, attracting FDI in that sector. A survey among Australian mining companies on the ranking of different exploration and investment criteria for mining in Africa, put an "attractive geology" only in third place (Oestensson, 1997, p. 6). According to the respondents, the granting of the right to mine a successful discovery as well as the guarantee of equitable profit repatriation were more important criteria for their investment decisions.[39]

Apart from natural resources and tourism, there are few resources or assets, such as specific technological knowhow, that African developing countries possess in sufficiently large quantities to attract FDI. Also, with a few exceptions such as Egypt or South Africa, no country on the continent possesses industrial clusters of a considerable size, that is, agglomerations of companies in the same industry that could be attractive for foreign investors as providing a pool of a highly specialized experts or workers.

In sum, natural resources explain much of the FDI inflows into most of the frontrunner countries. However, acknowledging that natural resources are often not sufficient by themselves to attract FDI, most of the frontrunner countries have put particular emphasis on creating an enabling regulatory environment for FDI in this sector.

ii. Market-seeking investment

Overall, Africa has lost in attractiveness as a market, as compared to the markets of other developing regions, during the past two decades. For instance, the gross domestic product (GDP) of sub-Saharan Africa almost stagnated between 1980 ($293 billion) and 1995 ($297 billion) , while that of South, South-East and South Asia as well as Latin America and the Caribbean more than doubled. However, while recent GDP growth rates for Africa did not exceed an annual average of 2.5 per cent from 1991 to 1997, all FDI frontrunners showed a strong, above-African average growth in real GDP (table VI.10). While the increasing FDI inflows might have contributed to this positive development, the positive growth rates were at the same time a reason for the increased appeal of these emerging markets.

Table VI.10. Africa: average annual growth rates of real GDP, 1991-1997 and GDP (current prices), 1996 in recent FDI front-runner countries and all countries

Country	Average annual growth rates of real GDP, 1991-1997 (Per cent)	GDP 1996 (Millions of dollars)
Botswana	5.0	4 995.4
Equatorial Guinea	25.6	4 401.5
Ghana	4.3	159.0
Mozambique	6.0	6 179.4
Namibia	4.8	3 107.0
Tunisia	4.5	19 485.0
Uganda	6.8	6 345.0
Average, all Africa[a]	2.5	7 290.0

Sources: UNCTAD, based on African Development Bank, 1998.

[a] Including South Africa.

The positive development in GDP growth has attracted some market-seeking FDI in particular into SADC area. Botswana, Mozambique and Namibia have all received FDI in the retail sector, mainly through South African chain stores such as Shoprite Checkers, Pep Stores or McCarthy. Retail affiliates opening up in these countries are sometimes accompanied by investment in food-processing activities, for example, in dairy products (Business Map 1998, pp. 34, IDC 1997, p. 34; SADC/FISCU, 1998, p. 23)). Other TNCs specializing in food processing, in particular in beverages, have also invested in these expanding markets.[40] Services, and especially financial services, are another area in which most of the frontrunners had attracted some market-seeking FDI. In the SADC region, South African Banks such as Standard Bank have expanded their operations into SADC frontrunner countries. Ghana has received 60 per cent of its FDI inflows outside the primary sector since 1995 in services (table VI.11). While some of these are related to mining

Table VI.11. FDI inflows into Ghana by sector and industry,[a] 1995-1997[b]

(Millions of dollars and percentage)

	1995		1996		1997		1995-1997[c]	
	Value	Percentage	Value	Percentage[a]	Value	Percentage	Value	Percentage
Primary	20	11	5	2	60	10	87	8
Agriculture	20	11	5	2	60	10	87	8
Secondary	75	41	54	21	95	16	225	21
Manufacturing	75	41	54	21	95	16	225	21
Tertiary	88	48	199	77	454	75	749	71
Building and construction	14	8	39	15	7	1	62	6
Commerce	5	3	8	3	7	1	19	2
Tourism	3	1	2	1	4	1	7	1
Other services	67	36	150	58	436	72	661	62
Total	183	100	258	100	609	100	1 061	100

Source: UNCTAD, based on Ghana Investment Promotion Centre, unpublished data.

Note*:* figures are based on project approval data. Entries may not add up to totals due to rounding.

[a] Does not include mining and petroleum.

[b] 1997 data are for January - September 1997 only.

[c] Data are for September 1994-September 1997 only.

activities, the other important service industry was financial services.[41] There are also some niche-markets, particularly in services, in which the frontrunners receive FDI (box VI.2). Although market-seeking investments are common in African countries with larger markets in terms of absolute size and higher GDP per capita levels like Tunisia, Kenya or Zimbabwe, they are more noteworthy in the case of relatively small markets such as Namibia or Botswana or LDCs with a low purchasing power such as Mozambique or Uganda.

Access to a larger regional market has also been a factor in attracting FDI for some of the frontrunners. In particular, FDI in Namibia and Botswana seems to have been influenced by their membership of the Southern African Customs Union (SACU) through which they have free access to the South African markets.[42] Hyundai and Volvo, for instance, have both established their assembly plants in Botswana in order to deliver to the South African market and also to tap the emerging car markets of neighbouring Namibia and the Democratic Republic of the Congo (Corporate Location 1994, p.9) . As regional integration is less advanced in Africa outside of the SACU or even the SADC region, other (frontrunner) countries have more difficulties to capitalize on their central location among a number of other countries: an example is Ghana, in the ECOWAS region, which has still to make progress on an integration arrangement.

Box VI.2. Africa as a location for market-seeking and efficiency-seeking FDI: the case of the ABC Bücherdienst GmbH in Namibia

The ABC Bücherdienst GmbH launched its mail-order book business in 1991 in Regensburg, Germany. In 1995, the company began to sell books via the INTERNET and became Germany's biggest on-line supplier of books. In early 1996, the company had approximately 100,000 customers in more than 60 countries and employed 60 people.

In 1997, the company started to expand internationally by creating affiliates in the United States and Namibia. The most recent of these affiliates - ABC Media Investments Ltd. (which employs 9 people) was founded because Namibia and South Africa are -- given the significant number of German speakers in the population of both countries -- important markets for books sold by the company. The Namibian affiliate's main task is to service the company's customers in Africa (mainly through e-mail). However, the affiliate also helps to service the German market by processing customer requests during bank holidays in Germany and processing data related to the books offered by the company. The Namibian affiliate, therefore, not only delivers services to the local market but is also vertically integrated into the firm to reduce costs of personnel for servicing the German market.

Additional factors influencing the decision to establish an affiliate in Namibia were the availability of German-speaking personnel, an affinity for the country on the part of the management in Germany as well as incentives granted by the Government of Namibia in the framework of the country's "export-processing entity" incentives programme. In the case of the ABC Bücherdienst GmbH, these included import concessions for computer hardware as well as public subsidies of up to 75 per cent for training courses for local employees. The recent acquisition of the ABC Bücherdienst GmbH by the Seattle-based Amazon.com -- the world's largest online book-order service -- may have consequences for the Namibian affiliate. It is planned that it processes all e-mail transactions, leading eventually to a considerable investment in English-speaking staff, as the Namibian affiliate would also distribute literature in English, in particular to the South African market.

Sources: UNCTAD, based on information provided by the company and the Africa-Association in Hamburg, Germany.

iii. Efficiency-seeking FDI

Except for Tunisia, none of the frontrunner countries has received efficiency-seeking FDI on a large scale. Like some other African countries -- Mauritius, Morocco, Egypt and, to some extent, Lesotho -- Tunisia has been able to build up a comparative advantage in some industries characterized by a high labour intensity such as textiles that typically attract efficiency-seeking FDI. Tunisia, alongside the other countries mentioned, has been particularly successful in attracting export-oriented FDI into its textile and apparel industries and establishing itself as a production location for these goods in the world market. It had the highest share of manufacturing exports (more than 68 per cent) in total exports for all African countries in the period 1990-1994 and was able to increase its share in global exports in textiles and apparel (Sachs and Sievers, 1998, pp.40). Although there are no figures indicating what part of these exports is accounted for by foreign firms, the lion's share of these exports are destined for the European Union.

The combination of factors necessary to attract efficiency-seeking FDI -- infrastructure facilities, a workforce with skills levels that allow for a timely and cost-efficient production and delivery of goods to overseas markets, supported by liberal trade policies and easy access to the markets of industrialized countries -- is complex. It is thus no surprise that this type of FDI is predominantly located in Mauritius and some North African countries where a relatively favourable policy environment has prevailed over a longer period of time so that the necessary conditions have been put in place. An investment-friendly environment, conducive to investment as reflected in particular in infrastructure policies as well as in the quality of ancillary public services, is of particular importance for transaction-intensive activities such as manufacturing (as opposed to natural resource extraction and agriculture) (Collier,1997). In many African countries, including most of the frontrunners, the policy environment has not been conducive to manufacturing investment for a long time; an uncompetitive transport sector, typically coupled with unreliable infrastructure facilities and neglected and overpriced telecommunication services, has made transaction costs far greater in Africa than elsewhere in the world (Collier, 1997).[43] Infrastructure facilities in most of the frontrunners are no better than in most of the non-frontrunner countries; i.e. measured by some key indicators for infrastructure (table VI.12) only Tunisia and, to some extent, Namibia stand out with values above the African average.

These findings are supported by the results of the previously mentioned survey reported in the *Africa Competitiveness Report 1998*, to the extent that it provides no evidence to indicate that the frontrunner countries were on average significantly better regarded by foreign investors in air transport, port facilities and inland waterways (WEF, 1998a, p. 202). With respect to overall transportation costs, only Tunisia, Botswana and Namibia were among the top ten African countries, while Ghana, Uganda and Mozambique received somewhat lower marks. Botswana, Namibia, Tunisia and Ghana were the only frontrunners that received relatively high marks on the quality of their telecommunication infrastructure (ibid.). As for the education and skill level of the workforce, another important factor in attracting efficiency-seeking FDI, it is again only Botswana,[44] Namibia and Tunisia among the frontrunner countries that have educational levels (as measured by school enrolment ratios) that were significantly higher than the African average (table VI.12).

Thus, except for Tunisia (and Botswana judging from its recent FDI in the automobile industry for servicing the South African market), none of the frontrunners owes its recent success to attracting sizeable amounts of efficiency-seeking FDI. In most frontrunner countries, the conditions, in particular as regards infrastructure and the skill level of the workforce, are not yet in place. Considering that it takes time to improve on both of these fronts, it is not surprising that countries like Mozambique and Uganda that have gone through devastating civil wars in their recent history trail other frontrunners as well as other African countries in this respect. However, as these countries pursue policies to reduce their shortcomings in these areas, there are already signs that they too can expect a larger amount of efficiency-seeking FDI in the future.[45]

3. Lessons

The analysis has shown that even within this relatively small group of African countries a host of reasons can be seen to have allowed these countries to attract FDI in recent years: in the case of Equatorial Guinea it was mainly rich reserves in oil and gas accompanied by a reasonably stable political environment. Natural resource reserves also played a role in the case of Botswana, Ghana, Mozambique and Namibia; however, these countries have also received some market-seeking FDI fuelled by the relatively strong growth of their economies in recent years. Privatization has led to considerable FDI into Mozambique, Ghana and also Uganda. Finally, Tunisia has not only attracted market-seeking FDI from investors seeking to explore its own market, but also attracted efficiency-seeking FDI, in particular in the textile and apparel industry.

What are the lessons that can be drawn from this analysis, in particular for those countries in Africa that have so far been less successful in attracting FDI? There is no single determinant that could explain by itself the recent relative success of the frontrunners. The diversity of the success stories analysed above suggests that the stereotype that African countries can be attractive for foreign investors only on the basis of their natural resources

Table VI.12. Africa: selected indicators of the level of education and infrastructure facilities in recent FDI frontrunner countries and for all countries

(Percentage and constant 1987 dollars)

Country/region	School enrolment, primary level 1992-1993 (Per cent)	School enrolment, secondary level 1992-1993 (Per cent)	Government expenditure: real per capita education spending, annual average 1990 to most recent year[a] (dollars)	Telephone services availability (mainlines over 1000 persons), average 1991-1995	Road network: 1000 km road per 1 million persons, annual average 1990 to most recent year[a]
Botswana	115	57	152.7	40	--
Equatorial Guinea	...	...	..	6	...
Ghana	...	...	15.7	4	2.6
Mozambique	60	7	..	5	2.5
Namibia	134	59	..	51	28.7
Tunisia	118	52	77.9	58	...
Uganda	67	11	6.9[b]	2	1.7
Average for all African countries	78	33	...	18	2.3

Source: UNCTAD, based on World Bank, 1997a; World Bank, 1997b.

[a] "Most recent year" refers, in most cases, to 1996.

[b] Average, 1985-1989.

is incorrect. Certainly, rich natural-resource endowments continue to be an important FDI determinant for many African countries, but the experience of most of the frontrunners -- with the exception of Equatorial Guinea -- shows that just relying on natural resources is not enough. In other words, it would take a comprehensive approach that aims at improving investment conditions with respect to all of the determinants mentioned above to increase FDI flows to countries that have been less successful. Although each country has to define its own strategy, some of the lessons that can be drawn from the example of the frontrunner countries apply to all countries regardless of their specific situations.

- A stable and predictable policy and macroeconomic environment is an important factor in attracting FDI. All of the frontrunner countries have made remarkable progress in this respect. A stable and predictable framework regarding FDI also encourages foreign investors and, finally, a high degree of investment protection is a typical characteristic of countries that have been successful in attracting FDI. Thus, countries that wish to follow the example of the more successful countries should provide foreign investors with a clear and reliable set of regulations and a comprehensive scheme for the protection of their invested capital.

- Most of the frontrunner countries have at least made a beginning with privatization programmes. As elaborated above in section VI.A, Africa still trails other regions in this respect. Privatization programmes are therefore a potential source for attracting FDI.

- The fact that the frontrunner group countries had significantly higher GDP growth rates in the past ten years underlines the importance of growth-oriented policies. As market-seeking investment is still probably lower in Africa than in other regions, foreign investors could respond rapidly to the dynamics of economic development in a business-friendly environment.

- As most African countries have a comparatively small market size, regional integration efforts are critical in attracting more market-oriented foreign investors to Africa. The example of other regions shows that regional integration initiatives such as, for example, the MERCOSUR can have a positive impact on FDI inflows, since they not only increase foreign investors' interest in a newly created large market, but also foster the overall credibility of policy reforms. There is evidence of some movement in this direction among frontrunner countries -- in particular in the SADC area, where regional integration efforts to create a free-trade zone among the 15 member countries have attracted market-oriented FDI due to the prospective enlarged market. In the future, such integration arrangements could also lead to flows of FDI wanting to take advantage of intraregional division of labour similar to that in Asia. The revitalization of other regional integration agreements in Africa could contribute to an increased inflow of FDI into an increasing number of countries in the continent. Integration efforts have to focus, apart from the reduction in intraregional tariff and non-tariff barriers, on the improvement of intraregional infrastructure facilities to link the often separated markets on the continent.[46]

- Another lesson that can be drawn, especially from the experience of Tunisia, as well as other (non-frontrunner) countries receiving significant efficiency-seeking investments such as Egypt, Mauritius and Morocco, is that countries that want to attract efficiency-oriented investment should reinforce their efforts to improve the education available to their citizens, particularly at the primary and secondary levels. In addition to a well-educated labour force and a relatively well-developed infrastructure, favourable trade policies have also played an important role in attracting foreign companies into most of the frontrunner countries, in particular, in manufacturing industries and especially in the apparel and textile industries (Sachs and Sievers, 1998, p. 40). In fact, these countries stand out among African countries, the majority of which have pursued restrictive trade policies for a long time, with high tariff barriers on imports as well as exports, representing significant disincentives for export-oriented foreign firms in these industries.

- While natural resources have been among the main determinants for the attraction of FDI to almost all of the frontrunners, some face the problem of sustaining such flows over a longer time as natural resources are limited in the long run. Some frontrunner countries have therefore already started to use revenues deriving from the extraction of these resources to fund the creation of other assets. In the case of Botswana, revenues from the mining industry are strategically invested to build up human capital in the country in order to make the country attractive to other kinds of investment.

- In many of the successful African countries, deregulation was paired with intense investment promotion activities. All successful countries possess an investment promotion agency that also has, in many cases, the facility of a one-stop shop that gives foreign companies quick and non-bureaucratic assistance in all aspects of their investment projects. In investment promotion, African investment promotion agencies have still to adopt world-standard best practices. Such agencies as the Uganda Investment Authority have shown that African agencies can compare -- at least in some aspects -- with the most successful agencies in developing as well as in developed countries and, moreover, that putting effort into improving investment promotion activities can yield increases in FDI inflows provided that determinants in other areas are also improving. As African countries step up their efforts to integrate their markets, they should also join forces in investment promotion. A first step in this direction is currently undertaken by the investment promotion agencies of SADC. The agencies of all SADC countries met in Centurion, South Africa, on 26 June 1998 to form a SADC Committee of Investment Promotion Agencies.

- As to corruption, "African governments that ignore corruption do so at serious peril to their economies, and to the attractiveness of their countries as hosts for FDI" (Sachs and Sievers, 1998, p. 39). While corruption is a complex phenomenon and often difficult to tackle, a simplification of national regulations can make a contribution to reducing the scope of corruption.

Even though Africa as a whole has been less successful than other regions in attracting FDI, the recent performance of the group of frontrunners discussed here shows that being located in Africa per se does not rule out success in attracting foreign firms. What is required is that countries offer a combination of policies, facilities for conducting business and economic factors that foreign investors find appealing. The lessons outlined above are relevant for other countries that seek to increase inward FDI as well as for the frontrunners themselves, if they wish to sustain their recent performance over a longer time.

* * *

In sum, efforts to attract FDI have to include initiatives in a number of areas. Appropriate measures at the overall political and macroeconomic levels have to be undertaken to improve the basic determinants of FDI. Moreover, in Africa, as everywhere else, policies designed to attract foreign investment have to be based on a rigorous analysis of the strengths and weaknesses of a country on the basis of the determinants discussed above.

The fact that there are a number of African countries that have improved their policies but do not fall among the frontrunners analysed in this section not only suggests that one has to allow for some time for the policy changes and their effects to show results in terms of a sizeable increase in absolute FDI inflows (some of the frontrunners are only starting to become major recipients of FDI in Africa) as -- among other things -- investors' perception of the investment condition in a country often take some time to change; it also suggests that the measures mentioned above are not always enough for attracting FDI. In addition to further measures at the domestic level, there is also a need for initiatives on the part of the international community to improve investment conditions in Africa. Although, historically the development process in Africa has been constrained by factors on the supply side, as African countries strengthen their capabilities, the reduction of trade barriers for goods and services produced in Africa could contribute to enhancing FDI both directly and indirectly in many African countries. For instance, Botswana, Cameroon, Cote d'Ivoire, Ghana, Malawi, Mozambique, Nigeria, Tanzania and Zambia all stand a chance of developing a textile and apparel industry capable of competing in the United States market, if they could have quota-free and duty-free status, as is being considered under the planned United States-Africa Growth and Opportunities Act.[47] The same could hold true for other industries and with respect to other developed countries' markets.

Debt relief is another measure that could improve investment conditions in Africa.[48] Since many African countries remain heavily indebted, debt relief could help to reduce the pressure on the foreign exchange regimes in these countries and contribute to the relaxation of exchange restrictions in connection with FDI, thus contributing to an improved regulatory framework for FDI. Additionally, measures by home country governments and business organizations to promote investment by domestic firms in Africa could be enhanced (box VI.3). Technical assistance in the areas of basic education and technical training in the upgrading of infrastructure facilities could also make a contribution.

Box VI.3. The Southern Africa Initiative of German Business

In May 1996, the Southern Africa Initiative of German Business (SAFRI) was launched. Its principal aim, as agreed by three leading German Business Associations -- Africa-Association (Afrika-Verein), Federation of German Industries (BDI), and the Association of German Chambers of Industry and Commerce (DIHT) -- is to strengthen relations between the 14 member states of SADC and the German business community. Among African countries, the SADC region countries play an important role as trade partners and investment locations for German companies: in 1997, about 30 per cent of German trade with Africa was done with the SADC countries; more than 70 per cent of German FDI stock in Africa had been accumulated in the region by the end of 1995, with the Republic of South Africa as the most prominent host country. Economic links have been accompanied by development of strong political ties between the SADC member states and Germany.

/...

(Box VI.3, concluded)

SAFRI's activities include:

- A human resource development initiative for the SADC region: SAFRI organizes business-oriented panels that bring together entrepreneurs from southern Africa and Germany for an exchange of ideas, concepts and visions (the first SAFRI-SADC private business conference will be held in October 1998). SAFRI also considers vocational training schemes to set up SAFRI-sponsored training in the region; these initiatives will be taken in accordance with agreements made with relevant SADC authorities.

- The organization of fairs and conferences as well as trips by company delegations to bring together potential business partners from Germany and SADC: the concept of SAFRI is based upon the assumption that personal contacts between individual entrepreneurs are pivotal for further establishing trade and investment relations. In order to facilitate business-to-business contacts between German and African counterparts, the Africa-Association has established its "Africa Business Platform" - a virtual market-place on the Internet that enables visitors from all over the world to make contact with German companies doing business with and in Africa.

- Active support of the privatization process in the region in order to improve further political and legal parameters for foreign investment and technology transfer.

- SAFRI also welcomes and supports intraregional liberalization efforts, in particular the SADC initiative to create a free-trade zone among its member states by the year 2008, as this could increase the region's attractiveness for market- and resource-seeking investors.

With its emphasis on a good investment climate and an improvement in the human capital formation, SAFRI concentrates on some of the most pivotal factors for attracting FDI into the region. However, these measures are considered long-term investments by SAFRI; essential improvements for the region cannot be expected in the short run. Since its foundation in the summer of 1996, SAFRI has had broad media coverage both in Germany and the SADC states and provides a good example of increasing private sector initiatives to promote interest in Africa as a business location.

Source: UNCTAD, based on information provided by the Africa-Association.

Notes

1 Much of the FDI inflow into Lesotho in recent years has been for the development of the Lesotho Highlands Project; as this nears completion, flows are expected to decline.

2 For an analysis of recent developments in the least developed economies in Africa, see UNCTAD 1998b, forthcoming.

3 A weaker demand and lower price for oil were (correctly) forecast as being among the effects of the Asian crisis and the 30 per cent fall in the price of oil, combined with political uncertainty, meant that the expected return to investment in the oil industry was reduced. Investment had been increasing in the Nigerian manufacturing sector in the late 1980s but the stagnation and then fall in Nigerian GDP per capita since 1993, which have left income per capita below the level of 1978, mean that Nigeria is losing attractiveness as a host country.

4 However, the International Monetary Fund in its balance-of-payment tapes publishes strikingly different figures for FDI inflows into South Africa in 1997. According to the IMF, FDI inflows into South Africa fell for a second consecutive year; the data set for 1997 from the South African Reserve Bank (SARB) used in this chapter represent a revised version of the data as provided in the balance-of-payment tapes by the International Monetary Fund (IMF). Differences in the FDI data for earlier years as reported by the SARB and the IMF derive from differences in the definition of FDI by the two institutions.

5 According to Business Map, a private source of information on FDI into South Africa, FDI unrelated to privatization accounted for inflows of $2.1 billion in 1996 and $1.8 billion in 1997 (Business Map, 1998). These figures do not correspond to the figures by the South African Reserve Bank given in the text because of different definitions of FDI.

6 H. Simonian, and M. Ashurst, in "GM returns to S. Africa with investment in Delta"; *Financial Times*, 11 December 1997, p. 12.

7 However, Malaysian investors, that had become the second most important source of FDI inflows into South Africa in 1996 and 1997, seem to have scaled down their plans for 1998 because of the Asian crisis (Business Map, 1998, p. 3).

8 Malaysian firms have been partners in Zimbabwe's biggest power station and also in forestry (both in 1996).

9 FDI from China is a notable exception, as it spreads over 20 African countries. In most cases, however, Chinese FDI stock is very limited, not exceeding $5 million (Fujita, 1997, p. 14).

10 The decline in the share of services in FDI into Africa in the period 1989 to 1996 is largely matched by an increase in the share of the category "unallocated" that includes holdings and other FDI in non-specified sectors that is not shown in figure VI.5. It should be also emphasized that the analysis of the sectoral distribution of FDI flows to Africa as a whole suffers from the fact that data are scarce and that it has mainly to rely on the information provided by selected major home countries.

11 Of the 38 countries that are regularly surveyed by the United Nations Department of Economic and Social Affairs, 15 achieved a GDP growth rate of 5 per cent or more in 1997 (United Nations, 1998a, p. 20).

12 Hyperinflation in some civil-war-ravaged economies, as well as drought-induced increases in food prices and wages in some countries, are the main factors behind the rise in the inflation rate for 1997 (United Nations, 1998a, p. 20).

13 Tony Hawkins, "Privatization process is taking much longer than expected", *Financial Times*, 22 June 1998, p. 14.

14 As of June 1998, SADC members are Angola, Botswana, Democratic Republic of Congo, Lesotho, Malawi, Mauritius, Mozambique, Namibia, Seychelles, South Africa, Swaziland, the United Republic of Tanzania, Zambia and Zimbabwe.

15 R. Khalaf, "Morocco to seek foreign investors", *Financial Times*, 31 March 1998.

16 Includes South Africa. The survey criteria for the selection of companies changed during the period.

17 Virtually the same indicators were used to identify frontrunners in UNCTAD, 1995b.

18 The methodology used, like any other method to assess performance, has limitations:

- One limitation of the method is that a country that already has a high ratio on a particular indicator might be excluded from the frontrunner group because that might make it more difficult for it to attain an above-average improvement. However, this may also indicate a lack of dynamism. Also, some of the frontrunners already had, in the period 1987-1991, above-developing-country-average values for certain indicators, suggesting that there is no systematic bias against countries that already had a high value for a particular indicator in the earlier period (1987-1991).
- A second factor to be considered is that a country that received virtually no flows in the period 1987-1991, but received rapidly increasing flows in the second period (1992-1996) would have very high values for the growth rates on all of the four flow indicators described in the text, even though absolute inflows may be low. However, as explained, a country would only qualify if it had reached, for at least one indicator, an above-developing-country value. Thus, although there are African countries that received almost no inflows in the period 1987-1991 but had slightly higher inflows in the period 1992-1996, Uganda was the only African country that recovered strongly enough from a situation where FDI inflows had almost ceased to fulfill the frontrunner requirements.

19 These countries are Angola, Egypt, Libyan Arab Jamahiriya, Morocco and Nigeria. Egypt and Nigeria were the only African countries that received above-developing-country average flows during 1992-1996.

20 Furthermore, the interlinkage between trade policies and FDI is ambiguous, as trade liberalization in general does not always have immediate positive impact on FDI. In some cases, for instance, rapid liberalization might lead companies that had undertaken investment to overcome the existing trade barriers to divest. There is some evidence to suggest that a rapid liberalization process in the framework of

adjustment programmes in some sub-Saharan countries may have contributed to divestment by foreign firms (Bennell 1997a, p.135).

21 Some of the tariff rates entered in the table might have changed significantly in recent years, as a consequence of the Uruguay Round negotiations under the General Agreement on Tariffs and Trade (GATT).

22 Botswana has not yet signed the Paris Convention for the Protection of Industrial Property as administered by the World Intellectual Property Organization (WIPO).

23 It is not surprising that most of the frontrunners have concluded considerably fewer such treaties than non-frontrunners (like Egypt and Mauritius) that have a longer history of receiving FDI, as reflected in relatively higher FDI stock indicators. DTTs are often only established between countries once there is a critical mass of foreign investment.

24 For a detailed analysis of the national FDI codes of Mozambique and Namibia see Mutharika (1997); for a brief description of the FDI framework in Botswana see SADC / FISCU, 1998.

25 The frontrunner countries included in the survey reported in the *Africa Competitiveness Report 1998* are Botswana, Ghana, Mozambique, Namibia, Tunisia and Uganda.

26 The list of non-frontrunner countries that received a negative assessment on this point included a much longer list of countries such as Cameroon, Cote d'Ivoire, Ethiopia, Kenya, Malawi, Mauritius, Morocco, Nigeria, South Africa and Zimbabwe. In another survey conducted by the European Round Table of Industrialists (ERT, 1997), the two FDI frontrunner countries covered -- Ghana and Tunisia -- were both evaluated as countries opening up in terms of their investment regulations with a high average speed in the period 1993 to 1996. Furthermore, while Ghana was evaluated to be "quite open" and thus having reached the second highest category on the ERT benchmark, Tunisia was one of the four top-ranked countries with "very open" investment conditions.

27 The same holds true for the share of frontrunner countries in the value of the transaction. The five frontrunner countries for which data are available accounted for $623 million or 27 per cent of the total privatization value of $2.3 billion in sub-Saharan Africa.

28 The large number of privatizations in Mozambique is partially explained by the privatization of many small units and retail outlets (Bennell, 1997b). However, not all frontrunners were active in privatizing in the period until 1998. Botswana, Equatorial Guinea and Namibia all accounted for very few privatization transactions. Some of these countries have only recently started to push privatization forward more decisively.

29 According to Atingi-Ego and Kasekende of the Bank of Uganda: "... FDI inflows have been largely associated with the privatization programme [...]" (Atingi-Ego and Kasekende, 1998, p.22.)

30 Thus, while in Namibia and Botswana it takes only a small fraction of a senior executive's time to negotiate with officials in obtaining licenses, regulations or permits, in Tunisia it takes 10 per cent of the senior manager's time, while in Ghana, more than 20 per cent of the executive's time has to be devoted to these activities.

31 According to the study, the cost of obtaining a commercial registration for an investment of one million dollars in Mozambique can be up to $50,000, while the cost of the same procedure in the state of Maryland, United States would be just $100 (IFC, 1996, p. ii).

32 Tunisia does not have such programmes.

33 No information was available on investment promotion in Equatorial Guinea.

34 The following analysis is based on the findings of the study and therefore refers only to Botswana, Namibia, Tunisia and Uganda.

35 The countries were: Botswana, Mozambique, Namibia, Tunisia and Uganda. The ranking was based on three performance criteria -- the number of projects attracted, total capital investment and the number of jobs created -- while taking into account the incentives offered to companies, the resources of the investment promotion agency, and the overall competitiveness, market size and wealth of the country.

36 The "Best African Investment Promotion Agency Award" event is organized jointly each year by the company Corporate Location in collaboration with Coopers & Lybrand. The assessment is based on a combination of the results of a questionnaire completed by a senior manager within the agency and the findings of a questionnaire completed by several representatives of organizations that advise investors and know how the agencies are perceived by investors (Tillett, 1996, p. 38).

37 Tillett (1996) gives an overview of best practice indicators (annex table A.VI.4).

38 However, Tunisia received significant inflows in the tourism industry, a sector which is to a considerable extent just as location-bound as natural resource extraction.

39 Other surveys confirm the crucial importance of an appropriate regulatory environment, highlighting the ability to repatriate profits, the guaranteeing of management control, and consistency as well as constancy in minerals policies (Oestensson 1997, p.6).

40 Another example of this is South African Breweries setting up new facilities or acquiring existing ones in Mozambique and in Uganda (IDC, 1997, Corporate Location, 1998, p. 22);

41 Tony Hawkins, "High rates choke investment", in *Financial Times*, 22 June 1998, p.14.

42 SACU members are Botswana, Lesotho, Namibia, South Africa and Swaziland.

43 A further factor increasing the transaction costs is poor law enforcement. It should be noted that, apart from the "transaction costs" approach, there are also other theories to explain the poor performance of the manufacturing sector in Africa -- including the "Dutch disease" hyphothesis, according to which the large exports of natural resources push the exchange rates of many African countries upwards, making other products less competitive (Collier, 1997).

44 Botswana has over the years pursued a stringent policy of raising educational levels in its population and workforce by using revenues from the diamond industry to enhance human resource development (Corporate Location, 1998, p.4).

45 FDI in the automobile industry of Botswana, mentioned earlier, to cater for the South African market reflects the potential in that country for efficiency-oriented FDI. Mozambique has attracted $1.7 billion in investment by a consortium composed of South Africa's Billiton, the government-owned Industrial Development Corporation of South Africa, Mitsubishi and the Government of Mozambique as a minor shareholder to build an aluminium smelter near the deep water port of Maputo. The decision was significantly influenced by the plans of the South African and Mozambican Government for the Maputo Development Corridor, including the reconstruction of the transport infrastructure between the Johannesburg/Gauteng area in South Africa and Maputo in Mozambique. Low electricity costs were another key factor (Corporate Location 1998, p. 16).

46 The urgency to make progress in the internal integration of African markets has to be seen also in the context of liberalization efforts vis-à-vis countries outside the continent, in particular developed countries. The latter efforts can only come to full fruition for African countries if intra-African liberalization progresses more quickly than that with external partners. Thus, liberalized trade and investment between African countries and the European Union and the United States are likely to result predominantly in trade integration as opposed to investment integration as long as the markets of the individual African countries are largely separated from each other (Wangwe, 1997, p. 23). In this connection, policy makers need to be aware that regional integration efforts should encourage cross-border FDI within the region, as there is evidence that this substantially increases the positive effects of integration for the participating countries as contrasted with just trade-based integration (Wangwe, 1997, p. 26).

47 United States International Trade Commission 1997 as cited in Sachs and Sievers, 1998, p. 41.

48 For a discussion on the potential role of debt relief in restoring self-sustained economic growth in sub-Saharan Africa, see UNCTAD, 1998a, Part Two, chapter 1, pp. 127-130.

CHAPTER VII

ASIA AND THE PACIFIC

A. Trends

Despite the financial crisis affecting a number of East and South-East Asian economies, foreign direct investment (FDI) in Asia and the Pacific rose by about 8 per cent to an estimated $87 billion in 1997 (annex table B.1), led primarily by increased flows to China (figure VII.1). The growth rate of FDI in 1997 was, however, lower than that of the previous year (17 per cent). The region accounted for 57 per cent of flows into developing countries and over half of their FDI stock. The FDI stock in the region reached $596 billion in 1997, an increase of 17 per cent over 1996 (annex table B.3). However, both the region's FDI inflows as a percentage of gross fixed capital formation in 1994-1996 and its FDI stock as a percentage of gross domestic product (GDP) in 1996 were slightly lower than the corresponding averages for all developing countries (figures VII.2 and VII.3). This is mainly because a number of major host countries in Asia have relatively large domestic economies and/or high ratios of domestic investment to income. Within the region, of course, FDI varies as a proportion of both gross fixed capital formation and GDP.

As in the past, an overwhelming proportion of the region's inward FDI was directed to *East and South-East Asia*. Inflows to that subregion increased by 5 per cent over 1996 to a total of $78 billion, despite the financial crisis in Asia which erupted in July 1997 (UNCTAD, 1998a). This was largely because flows increased to China and, to a lesser extent, to Singapore and Taiwan Province of China by a total of some $5 billion in 1997 (figure VII.1). Even in the five Asian economies most affected by the crisis (Indonesia, the Republic of Korea, Malaysia, the Philippines and Thailand), overall inflows remained at a level similar to that of 1996. There were moderate decreases in flows into Indonesia, Malaysia and the Philippines, a sharp increase in Thailand, and no change in the Republic of Korea (figure VII.1). Furthermore, FDI approvals for these five countries together increased from $29 billion in the first half of 1997 to $32 billion in the second half of 1997 (table VII.1). FDI was thus much less volatile than portfolio capital flows and commercial lending, both of which declined sharply in 1997, no doubt because it generally represents long-term interests in its host economies. (See section B below for further discussion.) In this context, it is worth noting that the share of FDI in total resource flows to East and South-East Asia has increased remarkably in recent years, from 10 per cent in 1990 to 53 per cent in 1997 (World Bank, 1998). Indeed, FDI has become the single most important source of private development financing for the region, and is likely to be particularly important for the economies most affected by the crisis, even if it should decline to some extent in the short-to-medium term.

Within the overall trends in FDI flows into East and South-East Asia, the performance of individual economies has varied:

- As the frontrunner, China (with new record inflows of $45 billion) again accounted for over a half of the flows into Asia and 11 per cent of the world total. The country continued to maintain its position as the second largest FDI recipient in the world and the single largest among developing countries. It was second (after Singapore) among Asian countries in FDI flows relative to gross fixed capital formation in 1994-1996 (figure VII.2). Since China's FDI boom has now lasted for six consecutive years, and since there has been a financial crisis in Asia which could have some spillover effects on China, the question arises as to whether the boom will continue. Indications are that there may well be a decline in FDI flows, as predicted in 1996 (UNCTAD, 1996a), for a number of reasons quite apart from any that might be related to the financial crisis (box VII.1).

- The newly industrializing economies of Asia (Hong Kong, China; Republic of Korea; Singapore; and Taiwan Province of China) achieved a modest combined FDI growth of 6 per cent in 1997, compared to 27 per cent in 1996. Flows into these economies taken together reached a record $17 billion in 1997. With a slight increase to $10 billion in inflows in 1997 -- twice as much as FDI flows to the entire African continent --

Figure VII.1. Asia and the Pacific: FDI flows into the top 20 recipient economies,[a] 1997 and flows to the same economies, 1996

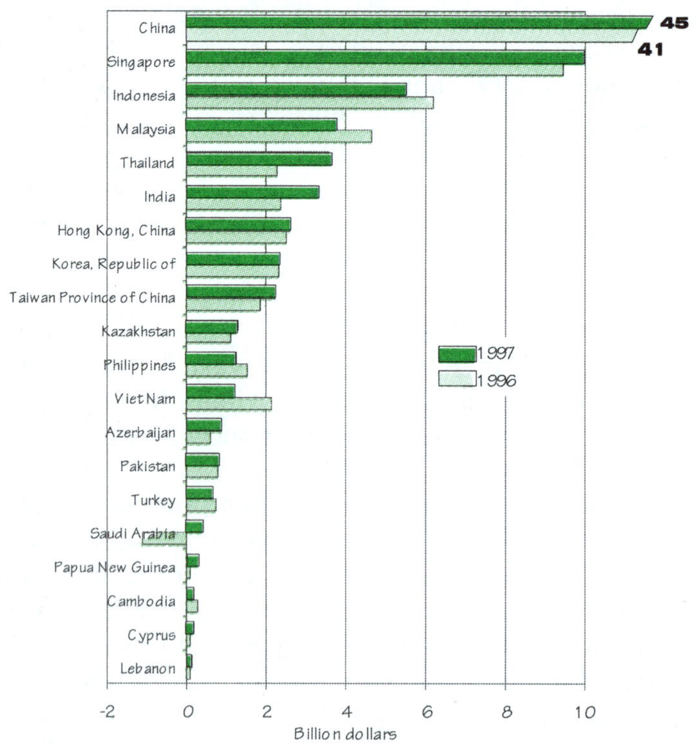

Source: UNCTAD, FDI/TNC database.

[a] Ranked on the basis of the magnitude of FDI inflows in 1997.

Singapore remained the single largest recipient among the four economies and the second largest in the subregion (figure VII.1). Singapore also ranked at the top of the region's countries in the ratio of FDI stock to GDP (figure VII.3), reflecting both the substantial flows it has sustained over time and the relatively small size of its economy. Flows into Hong Kong, China and the Republic of Korea remained at a level similar to that of 1996, while flows into Taiwan Province of China increased.

- Total flows into Indonesia, Malaysia, the Philippines, Thailand and Viet Nam (the "ASEAN 5") remained at a level similar to that in 1996. While flows into the other four declined, those to Thailand increased by over a half, although Thailand was the first Asian country to be stricken by the crisis.

FDI flows to *South Asia* rose to another record level of about $4.4 billion in 1997, as compared with $3.3 billion in 1996, mostly reflecting an increase of about 37 per cent in flows into India. India attracted $3.3 billion in 1997, less than the flows, for example, to Chile, and accounted for about three-quarters of total flows into the sub-region. India's poten-tial for inward FDI remains sub-stantial. Flows into the other economies in South Asia remain low. Those to Pakistan, the second largest reci-pient in South Asia, have remained stag-nant for several years, their growth hampered by structural bottle-necks and a further slowdown in econo-mic growth.

Figure VII.2. Asia and the Pacific: FDI inflows and outflows as a percentage of gross fixed capital formation,[a] top 20 economies, 1994-1996 (annual average)
(Percentage)

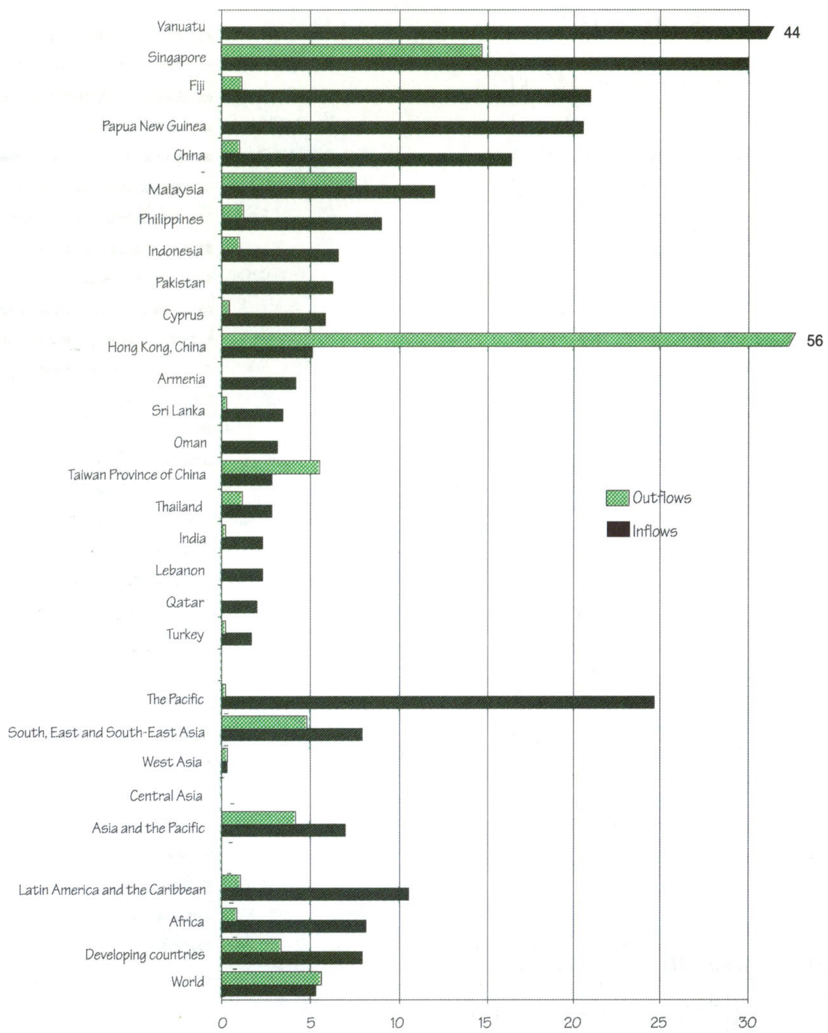

Source: UNCTAD, FDI/TNC database.

[a] Top 20 economies ranked on the basis of the magnitude of FDI inflows as a percentage of gross fixed capital formation in 1994-1996.

FDI flows into the eight *Central Asian* economies increased for a fifth consecutive year, reaching $2.4 billion in 1997. Kazakhstan and Azerbaijan were by far the most important recipients, accounting for nearly four-fifths of the total flows into the subregion. The Republic of Korea was the largest investor in the region (although some divestment by Korean firms took place at the beginning of 1998) followed by the United States, the United Kingdom and China. Most comprised resource-seeking FDI (oil, gas, ferrous and non-ferrous minerals), often attracted by privatization programmes. While FDI was particularly attracted by the openness of the Central Asian economies, it still faces many problems, such as the low transparency of privatization programmes, the unreliable information on investment projects, the uncertainty in legal matters and, in some countries, the inconvertibility of currencies. Nevertheless, FDI prospects for the short and medium term remain bright, particularly in natural resources. For example, in Kazakhstan, investors from China and Indonesia concluded some large deals in early 1997, committing over $4 billion each to oil and natural gas projects.[1]

Flows into *West Asia* increased by a multiple of six, from a level of some $300 million in 1996 to 1.9 billion in 1997, having turned positive (in 1996) after divestments exceeded investments in 1995. Even so, FDI flows into the region fell short of the levels of the early 1990s. Nonetheless, and despite active efforts by countries -- through offset programmes (box VII.2), the promotion of intraregional joint ventures and improvements of the FDI climate (UNCTAD, 1997c) -- investment is lagging in the region. The potential for FDI flows exists in a number of areas, other than oil and gas, such as petrochemicals, agriculture and agro-processing, tourism and infrastructure.

Figure VII.3. Asia and the Pacific: inward and outward FDI stock as a percentage of GDP, top 20 economies, 1996[a]

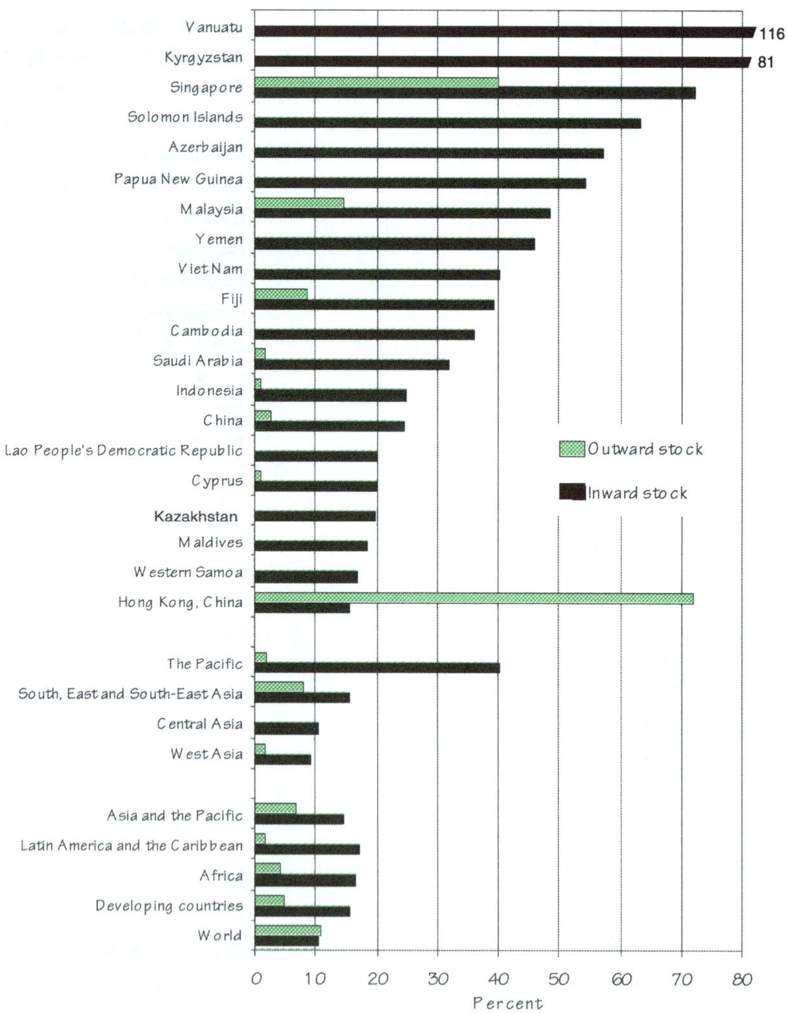

Source: UNCTAD, FDI/TNC database.

[a] Top 20 economies ranked on the basis of the magnitude of inward FDI stock as a percentage of GDP in 1996.

Table VII.1. FDI inflows into the Asian countries most affected by the financial crisis, 1990- first quarter of 1998

(Billions of dollars)

Country	1990	1991	1992	1993	1994	1995	1996	1997	1997 Q1	1997 Q2	1997 Q3	1997 Q4	1998 Q1
(a) Actual FDI (balance-of-payments data)													
Indonesia	1.1	1.5	1.8	2.0	2.1	4.3	6.2	5.4	2.3	1.3	1.4	0.4	0.3
Korea, Republic of	0.8	1.2	0.7	0.6	0.8	1.8	2.3	2.3	0.5	0.8	0.6	0.4	0.4
Malaysia	2.3	4.0	5.2	5.0	4.3	4.1	4.7 [a]	3.8 [a]	..	..	..	..	2.3
Philippines	0.5	0.5	0.2	1.2	1.6	1.5	1.5	1.3	0.6	0.2	0.3	0.2	0.3
Thailand	2.5	2.0	2.1	1.8	1.3	2.0	2.3	3.6	0.6	0.8	1.2	1.0	1.3 [b]
Total for the above countries	7.2	9.2	10.0	10.6	10.2	13.7	16.9	16.4	..	..	..	..	4.6
Memorandum:													
South, East and South-East Asia	20.1	21.2	27.7	47.3	58.3	66.6	77.6	82.4	..	..	..	..	..
China	3.5	4.4	11.2	27.5	33.8	35.8	40.8	45.3	7.8	..	..	10.6	8.6
Share of the five most affected countries in total for South, East and South-East Asia	35.8	43.4	36.2	22.5	17.4	20.6	21.8	19.9	..	..	..	..	..
(b) Approved FDI													
Indonesia[c]	8.8	8.8	10.3	8.1	23.7	39.9	29.9	33.8	—— 16.4 ——		—— 17.4 ——		3.5
Korea, Republic of	0.8	1.4	0.9	1.0	1.3	1.9	3.2	7.0	2.1	2.3	1.0	1.5	0.6
Malaysia[d]	6.5	6.2	7.0	2.4	4.3	3.7	6.8	4.1	0.5	1.4	1.0	1.1	1.0
Philippines	1.0	0.8	0.3	0.5	1.8	1.9	2.8	6.3	1.3	0.7	3.8	0.5	0.2
Thailand	8.0	5.0	10.0	4.3	5.9	16.5	14.0	10.6	2.5	2.1	3.2	2.7	2.3
Total for the above countries	25.1	22.2	28.5	16.3	37	63.9	56.7	61.8	—— 29.3 ——		—— 32.2 ——		7.6

Source: UNCTAD, FDI/TNC database.

[a] Excluding reinvested earnings.
[b] Preliminary data.
[c] Not including FDI in oil and gas, insurance, banking, non-bank financial institutions and leasing.
[d] Manufacturing only.

Box VII.1. Is the current FDI boom in China over?

China has experienced an unprecedented boom in FDI inflows over the past six years, with inflows reaching $45 billion in 1997 (box figure 1). The boom has been fuelled by various factors, including the country's large and continuously growing domestic market, its export-oriented strategy and successful penetration of world markets, the liberalization of its inward-FDI regime, the spillover effects of industrial upgrading in neighbouring economies -- the so-called "flying-geese" pattern (UNCTAD, 1995a, chapter V), as well as the low level of FDI stock relative to the size of the economy until recently. However, the rate of growth of FDI inflows has slowed in recent years, from an average of 165 per cent in 1992-1993 to 17 per cent in 1994-1995; in 1997, it declined further to 11 per cent. This slowdown raises the question of whether the FDI boom in China is nearing its end. The relevance of this question is twofold. First, considering the position of FDI in both gross fixed capital formation and GDP in China (among the highest in the world), a major change in FDI inflows may have wide-ranging consequences for the Chinese economy. Second, developments with respect to FDI in China will have a sizeable impact on FDI trends in Asia and the developing world generally, since China has become the single largest FDI recipient among developing countries and the second largest recipient worldwide (annex table B.1 and box figure 2).

Box figure 1. FDI flows into China, 1991-1997

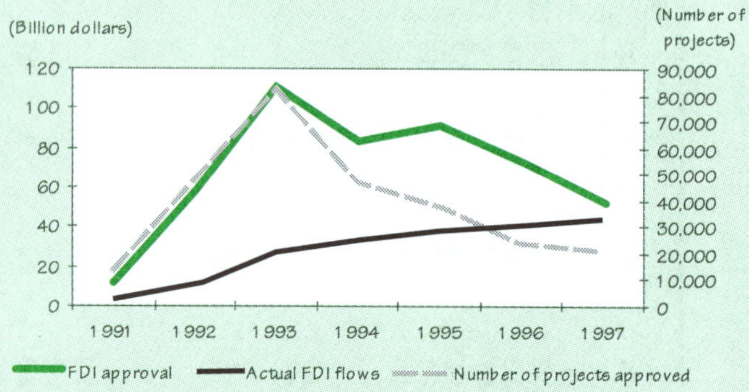

Source: UNCTAD FDI/TNC database.

Box figure 2. Share of China, and selected regions in world FDI inflows, 1997

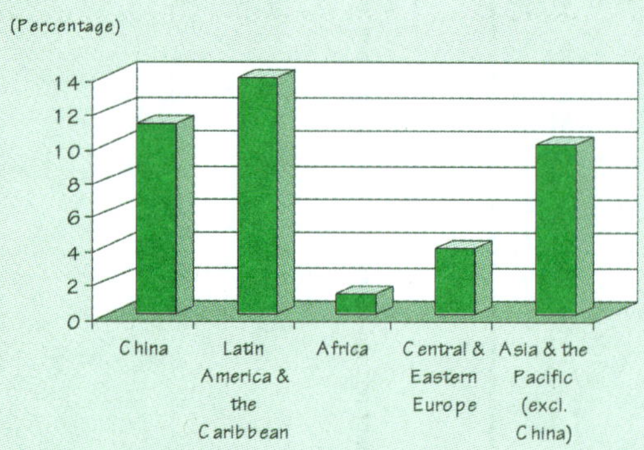

Source: UNCTAD FDI/TNC database.

To the extent that FDI approvals are indicative, they do suggest that actual flows may decline in the coming years, as approvals have been declining for some years, falling from $111 billion in 1993 to $52 billion in 1997 (box figure 1). Experience suggests that increased approvals precede increases in actual FDI. Assuming a lag as in the past between current approvals and future implementation, the decline in approvals by 20 per cent in 1996 and 30 per cent in 1997 may be followed by a decline in actual inflows in the short-to-medium term. Various developments in pull and push factors for inward FDI in China suggest that such a prediction is plausible.

Slowdown of economic growth. FDI tends to be positively correlated with GDP growth. Hence, reduced economic growth in China can be expected to have a negative impact on FDI inflows. Although GDP growth has remained high in China (at 8.8 per cent in 1997), it is below the double-digit growth of earlier years. More importantly, GDP projections point to a further slowdown, to about 7 per cent, in 1998 and 1999 (ADB, 1998). Market-seeking FDI, in particular, would be depressed by weaker demand in China.

Excess capacity. FDI in China's industrial sector will be the first to be affected by worsening demand.[a] It may turn out that the massive -- foreign and domestic -- investment of the recent past has resulted in excess capacity in a number of industries, such as some consumer electrical and electronics products, textiles and clothing, and other light industrial products. The capacity of such industries to

/...

(Box VII.1, continued)

absorb further FDI inflows may thus be limited in the next few years. This is true especially of industries in the coastal area, in which FDI has been concentrated. Competition in the coastal area for sales in the domestic market is becoming more intense and, in addition to foreign enterprises, a few domestic firms are emerging as strong competitors. This suggests that the "gold rush" by investors into certain manufacturing industries in China may be coming to an end. The pressure on profit rates stemming from excess capacity and increased competition could reduce the incentive for the latecomers among TNCs to undertake new FDI. At the same time, established TNCs are likely to postpone sequential FDI unless a reasonable balance between demand and supply is restored.

Declining locational advantages for efficiency-seeking FDI. When China emerged as a major host country for FDI, most investment went into labour-intensive export processing operations. Several factors have played a role in creating a new set of conditions.

- Wage increases, particularly in China's coastal areas where FDI is concentrated, are eroding incentives for TNCs to establish labour-intensive export processing operations.

- Despite special efforts by the Government, TNCs' relocation of investment from China's coastal regions to the interior has not been significant. TNCs have preferred, rather, to move to other low-income countries where transportation costs are lower and infrastructure more advanced than in China's interior provinces.

- For certain labour-intensive products, even though they remain internationally competitive, the potential of exporting from China is constrained by trade barriers in major export markets (import quotas, anti-dumping provisions, et al.). In addition, the demand for labour-intensive products in these markets is likely to decline if expectations of an economic slowdown in the world economy turn out to be correct. The recession in Japan is of particular relevance here.

- China's price competitiveness in international markets has been reduced vis-à-vis that of a number of South-East Asian countries which recently devalued their currencies. This could break the flying-geese pattern of industrialization in Asia, from which labour-intensive industries in China have benefited in the past.

These problems could not only discourage efficiency-seeking FDI in China but also affect the country's impressive export performance. In the short run, export growth is indeed likely to slow down, especially to the South-East Asian countries currently affected by the financial crisis.[b] With regard to total exports, a decline in annual growth from 20 per cent in 1997 to 3 per cent in 1998 and 1999 has been forecast (ADB, 1998).

Reduced outward FDI from Asian neighbours. FDI in China has mainly come from within the Asian region. Hong Kong, China; Taiwan Province of China; Singapore; Japan; the Republic of Korea; Thailand and Malaysia rank among the top investors, accounting for 80 per cent of China's inward FDI stock. The share of these countries in approved FDI in China in 1996-1997 is also high. It is questionable, however, to what extent the approvals in 1996-1997 will be realized, given the current constraints on outward investment facing some of these countries. A significant decline of flows from other Asian economies to China can thus be expected in 1998 (see section B).

To sum up, FDI in China will probably decline in the short run. Although the financial crisis in Asia has not directly affected China, its indirect repercussions are as yet unclear. If they are serious, and if the country's economic growth slows down considerably, various structural weaknesses may come to the surface and erode investors' confidence in the short and medium term. It should be noted, however, that FDI flows are an incremental measure, representing additions to a stock of assets for production; it cannot be expected that they will grow forever at the same rate, even if a host country continues to have a relatively high rate of economic growth. As long as flows fluctuate around a relatively high level, they contribute, other things being equal, to the increase in stocks and play an important role in the host economy (box table 1).

/...

Finally, the *Pacific island economies* experienced a modest gain in FDI flows in 1997 after a sharp decline in 1996. The subregion experienced a negative growth rate of GDP in 1997 (ADB, 1998) and the inflows of $400 million were still below the 1995 level of $600 million. Given the narrow production base characterizing the island economies, their absorptive capacity for FDI is limited.

New trends may be emerging in Asia and the Pacific with respect to the sources, the sectoral distribution and the mode of entry of FDI:

- *Decline of intraregional FDI.* The share of FDI from outside the region is increasing in total FDI in Asia and the Pacific. On the one hand, European TNCs, having largely neglected Asia until recently (European Commission and UNCTAD, 1996), are now taking an active interest in the region. The current financial crisis provides some immediate opportunities for European firms to enter the Asian market or expand existing operations (Section B). Furthermore, governments of the European Union countries and the Asian countries have been actively promoting investment flows between the two continents; important promotion efforts include a comprehensive Investment Promotion Action Plan adopted at the second Asia-Europe summit meeting.[2] On the other hand, the financial crisis in Asia has reduced the capacity of Asian TNCs, particularly those from Malaysia, Thailand and the Republic of Korea,

(Box VII.1, concluded)

Box table 1. The importance of FDI in China, 1991-1997

Item	1991	1992	1993	1994	1995	1996	1997
FDI inflows (billion dollars)	4.4	11.2	27.5	33.8	35.8	40.8	45.3
FDI inflows as a ratio of gross domestic investment (per cent)	3.9	7.4	12.7	17.3	15.1	17.0	14.8
FDI stock as a ratio of GDP (per cent)	5.6	7.1	10.2	17.6	18.8	24.7	..
Exports by foreign affiliates (billion dollars)	12.1	17.4	25.2	34.7	46.9	61.5	75.0
Share of exports by foreign affiliates in total exports (per cent)	17.0	20.4	27.5	28.7	31.3	41.0	41.0
Share of industrial output by foreign affiliates in total industrial output (per cent)	5.0	6.0	9.0	11.0	13.0	..	18.6
Number of employees in foreign affiliates (million)	4.8	6.0	10.0	14.0	16.0	17.0	17.5
Tax contribution as share of total (per cent)	..	4.1	..	..	10.0	..	13.2

Source: UNCTAD, based on information provided by China, Ministry of Foreign Trade and Economic Corporation and UNCTAD, FDI/TNC database.

All these considerations mainly concern the short to medium-run FDI prospects. In the longer run, China can be expected to remain an attractive location for FDI. Lower growth forecasts notwithstanding, China's growth performance is expected to be high by regional and world standards. The liberalization of FDI policies is still under way. Some industries closed to FDI in the past are being opened up gradually; in particular, liberalization is continuing in such service industries as telecommunications, electric power, transportation, banking and insurance, and retail and wholesale trade. Furthermore, a significant potential exists for foreign investors to participate in building infrastructure and restructuring state-owned enterprises. The sources of future FDI inflows will probably shift to a certain extent, reducing the role of firms from neighbouring Asian countries and increasing that of TNCs based in Europe and North America. The latter have traditionally been underrepresented (see section B, figure VII.16) in China as compared with other developing economies and can be expected to respond to available favourable investment opportunities. These factors should also mitigate any slowdown that occurs in FDI in the short to medium term.

Source: UNCTAD.

[a] The growth of industrial production is expected to decline from 12 per cent in 1996 to 7 per cent in 1999 (ADB, 1998).
[b] Exports to these countries accounted for about 15 per cent of China's total exports in 1996-1997.

to invest elsewhere in the region. This was confirmed by a survey of leading TNCs conducted by UNCTAD/ICC in March 1998 (UNCTAD, 1998f).

- *Sectoral distribution.* An increasing share of FDI flows to the region is directed towards the services sector, particularly banking, insurance and telecommunications. In part, this is because the sector is being liberalized, whether through unilateral initiatives or through the framework of international agreements. The restructuring of certain service industries in some of the countries affected by the crisis has also opened up opportunities to foreign investors. The development strategies of some economies -- Hong Kong, China; Singapore; and Taiwan Province of China -- for attracting regional headquarters of TNCs and strengthening them as regional hubs have contributed to this process as well.

- *Mode of entry.* Mergers and acquisitions (M&As) are becoming more important as a mode of entry for FDI in Asia and not only in the economies most affected by the crisis. Majority M&A sales in Asia to foreigners in 1997 more than tripled in value over 1996 (from $4 billion to $13 billion), and cross-border M&A transactions as a percentage of FDI inflows reached 15 per cent (figure VII.4). While this share is

Box VII.2. FDI through offset programmes in West Asia

Offset FDI programmes refer to programmes requiring foreign suppliers (exporters) of large volumes of specific goods and services to invest in the importing country. The first such programme was initiated in 1984 by Saudi Arabia and the United States. Offset programmes have now been expanded to include firms from other countries as well, such as the United Kingdom and France. The number of host countries pursuing such programmes has also grown. The programme as originally conceived required foreign suppliers of arms and aircraft to make an investment in the buyer country amounting to an equivalent of about 30 per cent (exact figures depend on specific projects) of the technology-related products and services provided by them in return for the contract they obtained. The duration for undertaking the investment is about 7-10 years following the supplies of arms and aircraft.

The first offset programme involved Boeing Aerospace and General Electric in Saudi Arabia; under the Peace Shield Offset Programme, these two companies made investments valued at about $600 million in five projects: Advanced Electronics Co. ($160-170 million); Aircraft Accessories & Components Co. ($50-60 million); Al-Salam Aircraft Co. ($115 million); International Systems Engineering ($17 million); Middle East Propulsion Centre ($60 million in phase one and $118 million in phase two) (Japan, Institute of Middle Eastern Economies, 1998). FDI in Saudi Arabia through this programme also came from Hughes (United States), a company that won the contract for Peace Shield II and established Middle East Batteries Co. in return. Similar examples exist for other supplier countries: a United Kingdom firm, British Aerospace, is to invest £1 billion in return for selling aircraft and has already established two out of seven proposed affiliates -- Saudi Development and Training Co. and Aircraft Accessory and Component -- under the Al Yamamah Economic Offset during 1988-1989. Thomson-CSF, a French defence company, also has similar obligatory investment projects (Japan, Institute of Middle Eastern Economies, 1998).

Offset FDI is seen by the governments involved as a means to obtain technology, employment and a boost for the domestic private sector, as suggested by the presence of local partners in many of these investment projects. The affiliates established are not necessarily confined to the arms industry (e.g. Fryma Fabrics). The governments that have offset programmes are, moreover, expanding their scope. For example, the programme in Saudi Arabia has been extended to the non-military area by bringing AT&T, a United States telecommunications firm, into the offset programme in 1994.

Source: UNCTAD, based on information provided by the Japan Institute of Middle Eastern Economies.

almost four times higher than it was the year before, it does not seem very high when the trend in the share over several years in the 1990s is considered: in 1994, for example, the share of M&As in total FDI inflows was 11.5 per cent. Moreover, the value of M&As as a percentage of FDI flows into developing Asia is very low if compared with that in developed countries (figure VII.5). This suggests that the higher the level of development, the stronger the role of M&As as a market-entry vehicle, reflecting industry structure, stronger technology-based competition and the need not only to exploit but to acquire created assets. M&As can, of course, be expected to assume particular importance as firms respond to the restructuring taking place in the economies most affected by the financial crisis (section B).

Figure VII.4. Asia and the Pacific: the relationship between cross-border M&As and FDI flows, 1991-1997

(Billions of dollars and percentage)

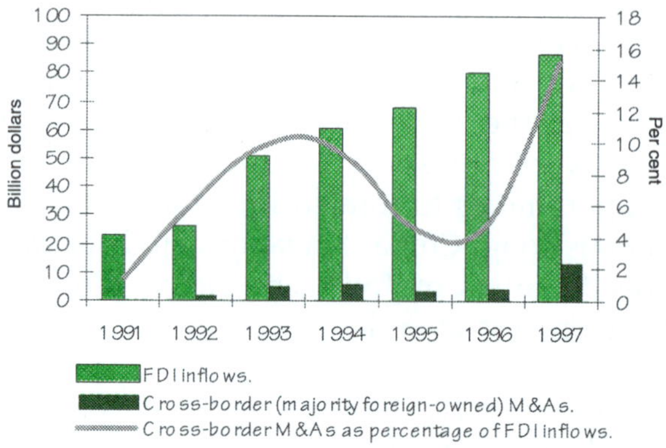

Source: UNCTAD, based on the UNCTAD FDI/TNC database and KPMG Corporate Finance database.

Outward FDI from Asia and the Pacific increased in 1997 by 9 per cent to $51 billion -- an increase of 2 per cent. The main home countries of outward-investing firms in the region were eight East and South-East Asian economies (figure VII.6). Hong Kong, China, was by far the largest outward investor, accounting for over half the total outflows from developing Asia. Indeed, Hong Kong, China has ranked among the top five outward investors in the world since 1993. Outward FDI from West Asia was positive in 1997, from negative outflows in 1996, although it was still lower than its levels in 1994 and 1995. The stock of outward FDI from the region reached $289 billion in 1997, accounting for over four-fifths of the total outward stock from developing countries.

Significant increases occurred in the 1997 outflows from China, Singapore, Taiwan Province of China and, in particular, Indonesia (figure VII.6). Indonesia's increased outflows were largely the result of a few large M&As that took place during the first half of the year, the largest being an investment project in oil and gas in Kazakhstan.[3] The expansion in China's outflows was led mainly by resource-

Figure VII.5. Cross-border M&As as a percentage of FDI inflows, 1996-1997

(Percentage)

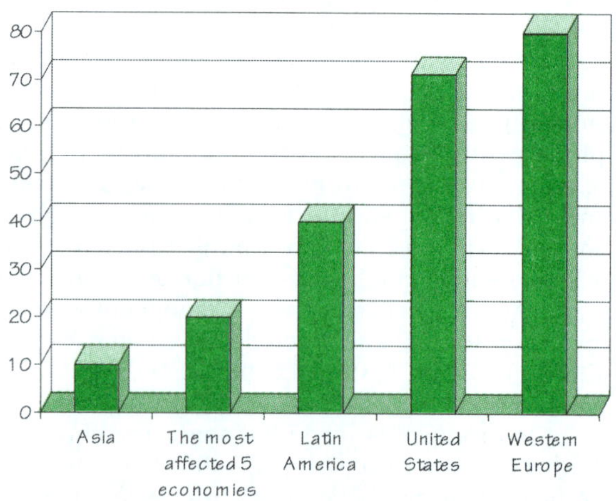

Source: UNCTAD, based on the UNCTAD FDI/TNC database and KPMG Corporate Finance database.

Note: the five most affected economies are Indonesia, Malaysia, Republic of Korea, Philippines and Thailand.

seeking investments, with large investment projects in forest development in New Zealand and oil exploitation in Kazakhstan. Hong Kong, China remained an attractive location for investment by Chinese firms. Investment in the territory was further facilitated by the reversion of Hong Kong, China, to China and the integration of the two economies, so that Chinese firms found it progressively easier to establish a foothold in the territory as a springboard for outward expansion. China also increased its FDI significantly in South Africa, as bilateral relations between the two countries improved. Singapore also remained an active investor in 1997. Notably, firms from Singapore entered into a number of M&As, with a total value of over $2 billion, in the crisis-affected countries of the region in the second half of 1997.

Figure VII.6. Asia and the Pacific: FDI outflows from the top 15 economies[a] in 1997 and flows from the same economies in 1996

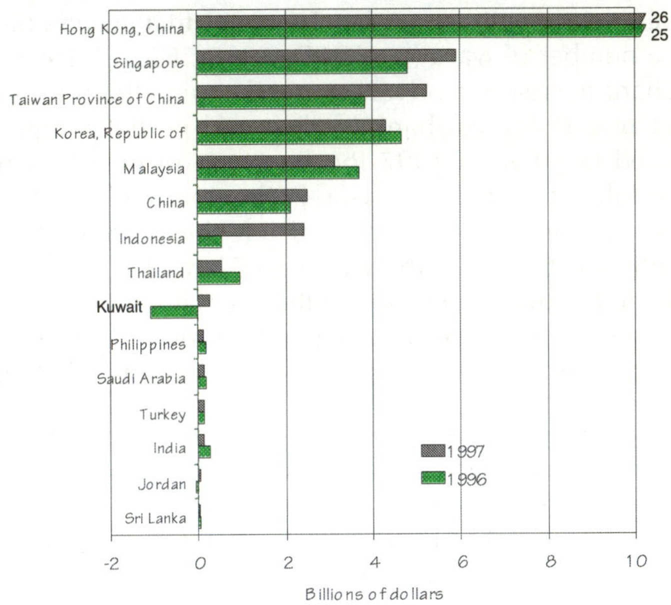

Source: UNCTAD, FDI/TNC database.

[a] Ranked on the basis of the magnitude of FDI outflows in 1997.

The growth of outward FDI on the part of Asian economies was, however, partly offset by a considerable reduction of outflows from Malaysia,Thailand and the Republic of Korea. Transnational corporations from these economies, affected directly by the crisis, slowed their pace of outward FDI because of the financial difficulties and structural problems confronting them. Firms from the Republic of Korea in particular have either scaled down or postponed a large number of their planned investment projects in North America and Europe, with outflows to these regions decreasing by 69 and 37 per cent, respectively (section B).

For the most part, Asia's outward FDI remains within the region, with China continuing to be the single largest recipient of outward FDI from developing Asian economies and especially from Hong Kong, China, absorbing nearly two-thirds of the total outflows in 1997. Asian investors are also among the most important in the lower-income and least developed Asian economies. Greenfield investments remain the preferred mode of entry for most Asian TNCs, although firms from China, Malaysia and Singapore tend increasingly to resort to M&As.

* * *

Looking ahead, the current financial crisis is likely to dampen both FDI flows into and outflows from the region in the short term, the extent of the dampening being determined by the speed with which the impact of the crisis is overcome. The next section analyses this impact in greater detail.

B. The financial crisis in Asia and FDI

In the second half of 1997, turmoil erupted in the financial markets of some countries in East and South-East Asia. The crisis that ensued has affected the economies of the region in a number of ways (UNCTAD, 1998f; ESCAP, 1998). It has involved, among other things, a sharp decrease in private external capital flows to some developing countries in the region. Net private foreign bank lending and portfolio equity investment were estimated to have turned negative in 1997 for the group of countries most affected by the crisis: Indonesia, Republic of Korea, Malaysia, Philippines and Thailand (figure VII.7). However, while large amounts of short-term capital left these countries, FDI inflows remained positive and continued to add to the existing FDI stock. Indeed, FDI inflows in 1997 to the five most affected countries, taken together, remained at a level similar to that of 1996 (figure VII.7) although they slowed considerably during the first quarter of 1998 when compared to the first quarter of 1997, primarily on account of a steep fall in flows to Indonesia (table VII.1).

This is not surprising. FDI flows involve not only financial capital but also technological, managerial and intellectual capital that jointly represents a stock of assets for the production of goods and services. The flows are motivated by the strategic interests of TNCs that invest in host countries in their search for markets, resources, created assets and competitiveness-enhancing efficiencies (chapter IV). They typically involve long-term relationships at the level of production between investors and their foreign affiliates, reflecting the investor's lasting interest in these affiliates and control over them. Since FDI is mainly a real investment in firms, its mobility is limited by such factors as physical assets, networks of suppliers, the local infrastructure, human capital and the institutional environment; FDI stocks are generally not footloose.

Much portfolio investment, on the other hand, is motivated primarily by a search for immediate financial gain and the time horizon for many bank lending decisions is also short term. This short-term orientation may make these investment flows quite volatile at times (box I.1; UNCTAD, 1997a, chapter III) and may contribute to the emergence of bubbles (UNCTAD, 1997a). Unlike FDI, portfolio investment is fully mobile at low cost. Because of their volatility, portfolio investments can cause drastic disruptions in private capital flows during crises which may then spill over into the real sector since such investments are a significant source of productive resources, especially for developing countries.

The behaviour of these two types of investment flows to the Asian economies most affected by the crisis is reminiscent of their behaviour during the crisis that struck Mexico in 1994-1995: total portfolio investment to Mexico fell by nearly 40 per cent, from $12 billion in 1994 to $7.5 billion, with portfolio equity investment falling by almost 90 per cent, from $4.5 billion to $0.5 billion.[4] FDI flows, in contrast, which had more than doubled in 1994, fell by only 13 per cent in 1995.

Figure VII.7. FDI flows, foreign portfolio equity flows and foreign bank lending to the Asian countries most affected by the financial crisis,[a] 1994-1997

(Billions of dollars)

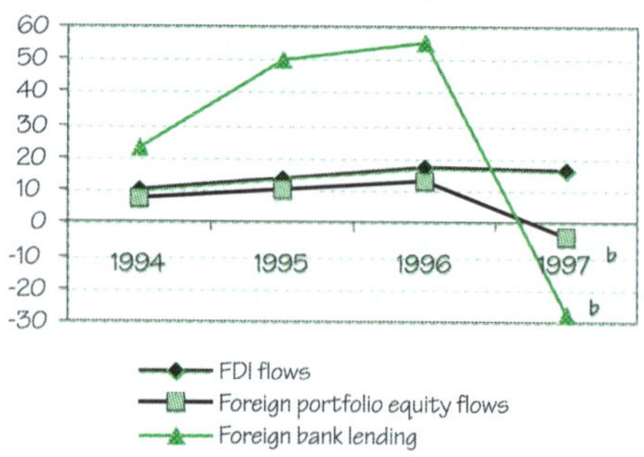

Source: UNCTAD, FDI/TNC database and Institute of International Finance, 1998.

[a] Indonesia, Republic of Korea, Malaysia, Philippines and Thailand.

[b] Estimates.

Even though FDI is more stable than portfolio investment, it is not insensitive to crises and especially to changes in the determinants of investment induced by a crisis (chapter IV). The eruption of the financial crisis in East and South-East Asia has in fact changed a number of major FDI determinants, at least in the short and medium term. This raises the question of what the effects of the crisis are likely to be on FDI flows to and from Asia and, in particular, to and from the most seriously affected economies.

This is a relevant question because FDI plays an important role in the growth and development of Asian economies, including those most affected by the crisis. Among other things, inward FDI provides a useful supplement to domestic investment, with the ratio of inward FDI flows to gross fixed capital formation ranging from about 5 per cent in Thailand to 12 per cent in Malaysia (figure VII.2 and annex table B.5). It also accounts for a considerable share of exports in some industries (UNCTAD, 1995a, chapter IV). Maintaining and increasing the level of FDI flows to and within the region could therefore assist in the process of economic recovery in the region.

This section considers, first, the implications of the crisis for inward FDI into the five most affected economies in the region in the short and medium term on account of a number of changes resulting from the crisis. It then proceeds to discuss the implications of the crisis for *outward* FDI from the countries of the region and inward FDI to developing economies *not* directly affected by the crisis. In conclusion, it considers the possible overall impact of the crisis on FDI flows to Asian host countries in the short and medium term and the long-term FDI prospects of developing Asia.

1. Implications for FDI into the most affected economies

The most important locational determinants of FDI are the economic factors determining the prospects for TNCs to engage profitably in production activities (chapter IV). If these factors are favourable, there is an inducement for TNCs to invest in a country, provided that the country's policy framework allows them to do so. The extent and nature of any FDI will depend upon the precise combination of the economic opportunities available, the friendliness of the policy framework, and the ease of doing business in a country.

The Asian countries most affected by the crisis have ranked high among developing host countries in the attractiveness of their economies to foreign investors. In particular, they have built up fundamental strengths that make for long-term growth, such as high domestic savings rates and skilled and flexible human resources, thereby creating opportunities for FDI that is competitiveness-enhancing for TNCs. They have also substantially liberalized their FDI policies and taken steps to facilitate business. All of these factors can be expected to remain favourable. Nevertheless, in the short and medium term, the financial crisis and its economic consequences will affect FDI flows to these countries, because they are likely to influence some of the determinants of FDI -- some in a manner conducive to attracting more FDI and others in a manner less favourable.

(a) Effects on FDI entry and expansion

One reason why inflows of FDI to the crisis-affected countries could be expected to *increase* in the short and medium term is the decrease in the costs, for all firms, of establishing and expanding production facilities in these countries. The decrease is the result of exchange-

Table VII.2. Currency depreciation, fall in share prices and interest rate changes in the most affected economies, July 1997 - February 1998
(Percentage)

Country	Depreciation of the currency vis-à-vis the dollar (Per cent)	Change in the share price index (Per cent)	Change in interest rates (Basis points)[a]
Indonesia	231.0	-81.7	2 398
Korea, Republic of	83.0	-63.1	965
Malaysia	55.4	-58.4	373
Philippines	51.4	-49.2	-
Thailand	87.1	-48.4	-25

Source: Ortiz, 1998.

[a] 100 basis points are equivalent to 1 per cent.

rate depreciations, lower property prices and more company assets offered for sale, given the heavy indebtedness of domestic firms and their reduced access to liquidity. Companies wishing to establish a presence in the region or seeking to increase the scale of their existing operations may see in the crisis an opportunity for doing so, especially if they react quickly, before recovery starts and the prices of assets and other productive resources rise again. There is some evidence that this may be taking place: in Thailand, for example, according to preliminary data, there were large increases in actual FDI flows into a number of industries (annex table A.VII.1) during the second half of 1997 and the first quarter of 1998.

The currency devaluations that have occurred in the affected countries (table VII.2), as well as the lowered property prices, have reduced the foreign currency costs of acquiring fixed assets such as land, buildings and capital goods manufactured locally. In addition, falling valuations of many Asian firms in the aftermath of the financial crisis have reduced the costs of acquiring firms. For example, as the crisis unfolded, stock market prices -- a rough measure of the price of acquisitions -- plunged (table VII.2). As a result, foreign firms require much smaller resources in home country currencies to establish new production capacities or add to existing ones.[5] Indeed, for firms already planning to invest or expand their investments in Asia, the current situation presents a unique opportunity to do so at lower than anticipated costs. In Thailand, for example, FDI flows into financial services tripled in 1997 in comparison with 1996 and flows in the first quarter of 1998 alone are 30 per cent higher than total flows in 1997 (annex table A.VII.1).

Moreover, the re-structuring of firms faced with large debt repayments and rising interest rates (table VII.2) and their urgent need for funds, combined with lower stock prices and a more liberal policy towards M&As, provide opportunities for TNCs to undertake direct investments in the region through M&As involving host country firms, including firms that might otherwise go bankrupt. Indeed, a number of large M&As have already taken place in the five most affected countries since the turmoil began (annex table A.VII.2), led by firms from the United States and Singapore during the second half of 1997 (figure VII.8). However, so far, no clear trend towards an increase in the total value of cross-border M&As in the five crisis-stricken countries taken together is discernible;[6] among individual host countries, substantial increases were evident only in the case of the Republic of Korea (figure VII.9). Overall, the value of M&As as a percentage of FDI flows into the five most affected countries was relatively low as compared to that for Latin America, but higher than that for Asia as a whole (figure VII.5).

Naturally, there are growing concerns over the loss of national control over enterprises, especially as there has been a noticeable increase in the value of M&As in which foreign firms acquired majority shares (figure VII.4). Although M&As are generally regarded as less desirable than greenfield investments, much depends on the specific circumstances and on the available alternatives, which may include bankruptcy (box VII.3). Still, concerns are understandable, particularly when M&As seem like "fire sales" (Krugman, 1998). In any case, foreign control of large portions of any industry -- or even small portions of key industries -- is often a sensitive issue in developed as well as developing countries. Hostile takeovers, in particular, are therefore viewed cautiously in a number of countries. Sensitivities in this respect must be appreciated, as otherwise the prospects for a long-term partnership between foreign investors and host countries through FDI could be affected adversely.

Figure VII.8. Cross border M&A purchases in the five Asian countries most affected by the financial crisis,[a] by selected home economy, 1997-1998 (first half)
(Millions of dollars)

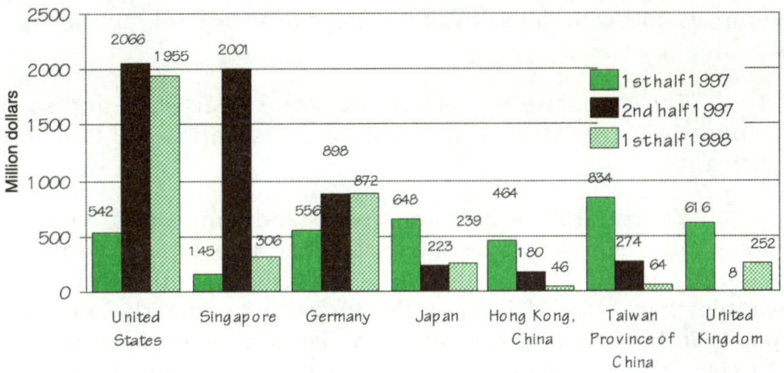

Source: data provided by KPMG Corporate Finance.

[a] Indonesia, Republic of Korea, Malaysia, Philippines and Thailand. Data for the first half of 1998 are preliminary.

(b) Effects on TNC operations

i. Export-oriented FDI

Currency devaluations can increase the attractiveness of the affected Asian economies to foreign investors by lowering the costs of production. As wages and other operating costs decrease in terms of foreign currency values, efficiency-seeking mobile foreign investors might find it advantageous to invest in the affected economies, even though inflation might eventually eliminate the advantage.[7] Such advantages are particularly relevant for export-oriented foreign affiliates, since they improve their international competitiveness vis-à-vis firms located in other countries that have not devalued.[8] In Thailand, for example, FDI in such export-oriented industries as electrical

Figure VII.9. Cross border M&A sales in the five Asian countries most affected by the financial crisis,[a] by host country, 1997-1998
(Millions of dollars)

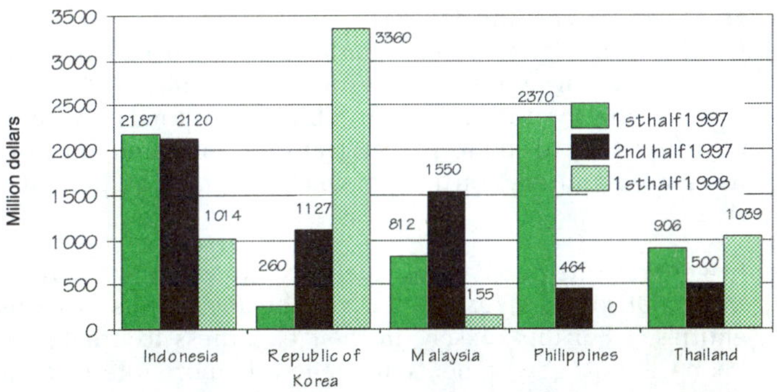

Source: data provided by KPMG Corporate Finance.

[a] Indonesia, Republic of Korea, Malaysia, Philippines and Thailand. Data for the first half of 1998 are preliminary.

Box VII. 3. M&As and greenfield investment: a comparison

Cross-border M&As have been on the rise for some time, accounting for about half the global FDI inflows in 1997. Although they are concentrated in the United States and Western Europe, international M&As are also a phenomenon increasingly associated with the privatization of state enterprises and with the sales of bankrupt or near-bankrupt business units in various regions, including Asia.

The corporate motivations for M&A deals vary and so do the effects of cross-border M&As for countries. The private and public costs and benefits of cross-border M&As can also diverge significantly.

Viewed from a host country's standpoint, cross-border M&As are one form of FDI inflows, along with greenfield investments. These two types of inward FDI are often compared in their desirability for host countries. It is argued that, other things being equal, greenfield FDI is more desirable than M&A FDI, since the former immediately and directly adds to the existing industrial capacity in host countries, whereas the latter merely transfers ownership of local assets from domestic to foreign interests. This may be true as far as the immediate impact is concerned, and greenfield FDI is normally preferred by host countries for this reason. In addition to this short-term capital stock effect, however, there are a host of possible long-term effects that also need to be taken into account in evaluating the relative merits of these two kinds of FDI.

- **Capital formation.**
  Greenfield FDI is, by definition, investment in new productive facilities. Hence, assuming that no viable domestic investment will take place in the absence of such FDI, it immediately adds to the stock of capital in the host country. Furthermore, it is necessarily accompanied by the transfer of foreign TNCs' intangible assets such as technology and managerial skills, which are internalized/ embodied in their greenfield projects, assets that enable foreign TNCs to stay competitive relative to host country firms in the latter's own backyard. Greenfield projects are thus likely to result in new capital formation, both physical and human.

  In contrast, M&As may not lead to capital formation in the short run. The immediate effect is merely an asset transfer from a host country owner to a foreign TNC. But the acquirer may carry out modernization and capacity expansion (perhaps as a condition of the deal, as is usually the case with privatized state properties in developing countries and Central and Eastern Europe) or induce other related investments (perhaps other related FDI undertaken by suppliers). New incremental or supplementary capital formation may then eventually occur in the form of both *sequential* and *associated* FDI which is larger than the original purchase (UNCTAD, 1995a). Furthermore, if the acquired firm would otherwise have gone bankrupt, thereby decreasing the capital stock involved, the M&A may have been instrumental in maintaining or revitalizing a host country's capital formation. There is, of course, the danger that the acquisition may have been undertaken for the sole purpose of eliminating competition by eventually closing down the acquired firm (UNCTAD, 1997a).

- **Employment and the tax base.**
  Just as with capital accumulation, greenfield FDI immediately creates new jobs (assuming again the absence of credible domestic investment). M&As would have no such positive employment effect in the short run. In fact, job reduction may ensue if an acquisition involves a troubled high-cost firm that needs to be restructured and slimmed down. In the long run, however, if a TNC turns an acquired firm into a successful unit as part of its corporate network, employment may rise.

  In general, the tax base is likely to expand more favourably under greenfield FDI than through M&As for the very reason that new business units are created by the former as additional taxable entities. For this reason, in their eagerness to create employment opportunities and expand the tax base, host governments are generally more interested in attracting greenfield FDI than in seeing existing local firms sold off to foreign TNCs. It is thus no surprise that special incentives are often given to greenfield FDI.

/...

(Box VII.3, continued)

Nonetheless, it is conceivable that an acquired firm will end up contributing as much or more to the local tax base, depending on whether it might have gone bankrupt in the absence of the acquisition or on the effectiveness with which it handles new infusions of capital and technology under foreign ownership.

- **Structural diversification.**
  From a host country's point of view, FDI is desirable in part because it may bring new assets (e.g. industrial knowledge) in new fields, thereby contributing to industrial diversification in the local economy. Since M&As mostly involve transfers of existing productive assets, they are not likely to help a host economy diversify into new industrial activities, unless the acquired firm itself later diversifies. If the acquired units become integrated with the foreign TNCs' corporate systems, however, they may have an opportunity to move into new fields. Besides, there is no guarantee that greenfield FDI necessarily opens up new industrial sectors, although the chances of structural diversification are probably greater in greenfield FDI than in M&As.

- **Competition.**
  Market competition is desirable because it stimulates and improves efficiency, resulting in lower prices for consumers. Greenfield FDI can enhance local competition if its superior assets/market power are harnessed in such a way as to prevent predatory practices and to attract competitors. In contrast, while M&As will not generate new competition in the short run, they can maintain the level of competition that prevailed before, if the acquired firms might have gone out of business in the absence of a deal. In addition, if a new owner revitalizes a moribund local firm, local competition will be revitalized as well. On the other hand, if the acquiring firm were part of a small number of firms at the global level, the takeover might reduce global competition as well as competition in the host country.

- **Political and cultural considerations.**
  Since M&As involve the transfer of ownership of a local productive activity and assets, a national security issue arises when local assets (e.g. technology) have military applications and can thus damage national security if they fall into foreign hands. Greenfield FDI does not directly pose this problem but some greenfield ventures may be aimed at monitoring local technological progress. Similar considerations apply with respect to national sentiment and culture. For example, some countries may consider the broadcasting or film-making industry a cultural industry critical to the preservation of national traditions. It all depends upon the nature of the industry involved, the market power of the new entrant, and the characteristics of the host countries themselves.

- **Liquidity (new capital injection).**
  FDI is often welcomed because it brings liquidity, whether in the form of foreign exchange at the national level or in the form of needed funds at the company level. Liquidity is usually a priority for any country that experiences a balance-of-payments crisis and is in dire need of foreign exchange. In terms of national liquidity considerations, greenfield FDI and M&As are equally desirable alternatives.

  In developed countries with flexible exchange rates, however, this "foreign reserves" rationale hardly exists. Only a company-level need for liquidity may arise. For example, founders may want to sell because they wish to retire or some young start-up ventures may reach a point where they need additional capital. Here, obviously, greenfield FDI is not an alternative to M&As from the point of view of the individual enterprise.

  In some developing countries, on the other hand, the sales of local businesses to foreign firms can become important, precisely because both the governments and the local firms are desperately in need of liquidity. Partial M&A deals may also occur to secure a minimum level of liquidity.

- **Supplementary resources.**
  Both M&As and greenfield FDI can bring in some critical supplementary resources such as new managerial, production and marketing techniques that are lacking in host countries. The new owners of local firms may apply new techniques to make their acquired businesses profitable. M&As are also often motivated by the desire to capture synergies by combining sets of corporate assets between the deal-making parties; the intra-corporate supplementing of local assets with

/...

appliances and electronics has risen considerably (annex table A.VII.1). A specific example is Seagate, which has expanded its operations in Malaysia to serve the European market (box VII.4). Something very similar had happened in Mexico after the Peso crisis, when FDI in export-oriented manufacturing and assembly of electrical and electronic equipment more than doubled in 1995 over the previous year (annex table A.VII.3).[9]

In making or expanding FDI in export-oriented production, or switching the output of production from the domestic to the international market, TNCs can draw on their international production systems which can serve as channels to reach markets and access inputs. In these corporate systems, intermediate goods and tradable services produced by an affiliate in one country are exported to the parent firm, or to affiliates of the same parent firm in other countries. Indeed, about one-third of world trade consists of such "intra-firm" trade. Being part of a TNC system therefore gives affiliates "privileged" access to the TNC system, a market in itself, and to markets located elsewhere (UNCTAD, 1996a). This in turn offers a strong motivation for foreign affiliates to take advantage of the lower costs of production following devaluation.

(Box VII.3, concluded)

foreign assets is a possibility unique to cross-border M&As. The Daimler-Chrysler merger and the VW-Rolls Royce merger are examples. Synergy-creating M&As certainly add to both the host and home countries' stock of resources and may bring both public and private benefits.

Similarly, greenfield FDI is likely to transplant supplementary resources at the national level, since the ownership-specific advantages they internalize are supposed to be superior to their local counterparts if such FDI is to succeed. Hence, the upshot is an augmentation of the host country's resource base. A prime example of such greenfield FDI is NUMMI (New United Motor Manufacturing Incorporated), a joint venture between GM and Toyota, in the United States, which has served as a learning conduit for GM in flexible manufacturing.

In contrast, an M&A may not involve any transfer of new resources from the acquiring foreign firm. It may even cause a reverse transfer, particularly if the new owner's intention is to siphon off knowledge from the acquired firm to the new owners, as is the case with some asset-seeking FDI. In such a case, an M&A results in the draining of resources (e.g. technology) from host countries.

* * *

So which is better from a host country's point of view? "It all depends" is the appropriate answer. Depending upon specific circumstances and the policy priorities of host countries, one or the other may be preferable. At the individual firm level, M&As can enable local firms directly to become parts of transnational corporate systems with a number of competitiveness-enhancing advantages. This source of gain is important, especially when dealing with distressed, non-performing local businesses. They require immediate and direct transfusions of new capital and supplementary resources at the firm level.

In fact, when it comes to distressed local business units, whether privately or publicly owned, the requirement is simply a buyer, whether foreign or domestic. These units need to be sold off, if not entirely then at least partially, for they have to be acquired by or merged into other firms if they are to avoid their ever-accumulating losses or debts and eventual demise. They need transfusions of both new capital and new managerial resources to survive and prosper. In many cases, these existing businesses cannot be purchased and upgraded by domestic firms, simply because they may themselves be short of capital and deficient in technological resources. In these cases, foreign firms may be the only possible suitors.

Source: Ozawa, 1998.

Many corporate systems of integrated international production already exist in Asia, led by Japanese TNCs, and closely followed by United States TNCs (UNCTAD, 1996a). Increasingly, these also include small and medium-sized firms which, in the case of Japan, account for more than a half of the country's outward FDI in numbers of projects (UNCTAD, 1998g, pp. 31-32), although their share of FDI in dollar value is much lower (UNCTAD, 1993b). To the extent that data for Japanese and United States foreign affiliates in the most affected countries are indicative, TNCs have already had relatively high export propensities in most instances, ranging (for United States majority-owned affiliates) from 14 per cent in the Republic of Korea to 57 per cent in Malaysia and Thailand in 1995 (table VII.3). Foreign affiliates in industries such as electrical machinery have had even higher export propensities in some countries, reaching 69 per cent and 82 per cent in the case of United States affiliates in Thailand and the Philippines. Export propensities of United States majority-owned foreign affiliates in manufacturing as a whole have been considerably higher for the five most affected countries as a group (42 per cent in 1995) than for Latin America (26 per cent in 1995).[10]

Box VII.4. TNCs, restructuring and the Asian crisis: Seagate Technology, Inc.

Seagate Technology, Inc. is a leading provider of technology and of products for storing, accessing, and managing information, with nearly $7 billion in revenues for its 1997-1998 fiscal year. Based in the United States, the company has the vast majority of its production facilities located in Asia, which account for over four-fifths of its output. It has also been the engine driving the exports of electronic products from Malaysia and Thailand; as the single largest exporter in Thailand, its exports accounted for 4 per cent of the country's GDP during the past few years (TDRI, 1998).

Seagate was affected by the Asian financial crisis both in production and sales, and experienced currency losses because of the devaluations of the Thai baht and the Malaysian ringgit. However, the negative effects of the crisis on its Asian operations are not as obvious as the effects of other economic factors. The company reported a loss for the fiscal year 1997/1998, largely on account of the slump in global computer prices and the consequent cost of restructuring.[a] Its sales revenues in Asia for the first quarter of 1998 remained at a level similar to that in the previous quarter, while its revenues in Europe fell. Overall, the Asia-Pacific region contributes about 15-17 per cent of the company's worldwide sales revenues, with sales in the ASEAN region constituting a major portion.

Faced with worldwide excess capacity, weak demand, technological advances that have intensified competition, the emergence of newcomers and intense pricing pressures in the disk- drive industry, Seagate restructured its global operations in late 1997, aiming at enhancing its competitive position through improvements in productivity and reduction of costs. The restructuring included the closure of certain manufacturing facilities, the consolidation of its five disk-drive product design centres in the United States into three, the consolidation of its domestic media operations, and the downsizing of its worldwide sales and administrative functions.[b]

As part of the restructuring, Seagate announced in December 1997 that it would close a plant in Clomnel, Ireland, which had been opened only in 1995, laying off 1,400 employees and paying back a $15.8 million grant to the Irish authorities. It also postponed the expansion of its production facilities for a read-write head plant in Springtown in Ireland. As a result of the devaluation of Asian currencies, the competitiveness of the Clomnel plant was weakened. Production costs in Ireland became almost three times those in the affected countries in Asia.[c] The company therefore decided to use the surplus capacity at its plants in Asia to service European markets, which had previously been supplied by the Clomnel plant.[d]

Source: UNCTAD, based on information obtained from various sources.

[a] Seagate, *Annual Report*, 1998.
[b] Seagate, press release, June 1998.
[c] *The Irish Times*, 13 December 1998.
[d] *Sunday Times*, 14 December 1997.

Being part of TNC networks also makes it easier for firms to switch from domestic sales to exports, as could be seen during the Mexican crisis of December 1994-1995. In the case of the Mexican automobile industry, a number of foreign affiliates reacted to the slump in domestic demand by switching -- sometimes within a few months -- a part of their production to foreign markets: exports increased both in absolute terms and as a percentage of total production, from 58 per cent in 1994 to 86 per cent in 1995 (annex table A.VII.4). Naturally, access to the large North American market in the context of NAFTA and buoyant demand conditions also helped, as did the fact that foreign automobile affiliates in Mexico were already producing at internationally competitive quality standards.

There are signs that some Asian TNCs are also switching some of their sales from domestic to export markets. Toyota, for example, expects to increase its exports of motor vehicles, both absolutely and relatively to total production, as well as substantially to increase exports of parts and components (box VII.5). Survey data for Thailand also indicate plans for increased exports by some foreign affiliates (box VII.6). The most immediate implications of the currency realignment has been that some TNCs are shifting orders from factories from other countries in the region to their affiliates in the most affected countries. For example, Honda is shifting some production activities from Japan to its facilities in Thailand (box VII.7).

The impact of the current crisis could therefore be mitigated somewhat for a number of the most affected Asian countries because international integration at the level of production allows TNCs (and firms linked to them) to compensate for declining domestic sales through increased exports spurred by devaluation. Whether and to what extent this potential is realized depends, of course, on the strategies of firms. Moreover, the extent of the cost advantages enjoyed by export-oriented firms varies among industries and firms and is determined in part by their import-dependence. This further underlines the importance of integrating foreign affiliates into their host economies: such integration not only contributes to the building up of local capacities; but the more foreign affiliates can draw on backward linkages with local enterprises, the less import-dependent they are.

Table VII.3. Export propensity[a] of Japanese and United States affiliates in the Asian countries most affected by the financial crisis, 1995

(Percentage)

Sector/ industry	Japanese affiliates in Indonesia, Malaysia, Philippines, and Thailand[c] combined	United States affiliates[b]					
		Indonesia	Republic of Korea	Malaysia	Philippines	Thailand	All 5 countries
Primary	76.0	79.0 [d]	14.0	..	..	..	..
Manufacturing	39.9	8.0	4.0	57.0	40.0	57.0	42.0
Chemicals	18.5	2.0	19.0	14.0	2.0	6.0	4.0
Electrical machinery	70.7	46.0	..	51.0	82.0	69.0	51.0
Transport equipment	8.1	..	1.0	..	..	..	..
Services	25.3	1.0	6.0	1.0	..	..	2.0
All industries	35.9	65.0	10.0	40.0	27.0	25.0	34.9

Source: UNCTAD, based on Japan, Ministry of International Trade and Industry,1998a, and United States, Department of Commerce, 1998.

[a] Exports as a percentage of total sales.
[b] Majority-owned foreign affiliates only.
[c] Data for the Republic of Korea are not available.
[d] Petroleum only.

Box VII.5. Toyota's response to the Asian crisis: changes in production and exports from Thailand, 1997-1998

Toyota Motor Corporation, one of the first TNCs to establish operations in the automotive industry of Thailand, increased production capacity in Thailand in the 1990s, principally to serve the domestic market in that country but also to export to other countries inside and outside the region. Toyota's facilities in Thailand include two plants for the assembly of vehicles, mostly pick-up trucks, and plants for the production of components, including diesel engines, engine blocks and camshafts. The changes in production levels and the shares of output for the domestic and export markets during 1997-1998 illustrate how a TNC can respond to rapidly changing economic conditions, including a significant reduction in demand in the local economy and a dramatic depreciation of currency.

On 5 November 1997, Toyota halted production in two of its Thai plants because of declining demand. In mid-November, production was partly resumed. Within a few weeks, however, Toyota announced that it was planning to increase production, especially for export. During the following few weeks it made small changes in the production processes -- for instance, it increased inventory of certain parts used in vehicles for export and undertook some additional maintenance of its facilities. On 7 January 1998, it resumed near-normal production schedules at both of its assembly plants in Thailand, each producing two of Toyota's passenger or commercial vehicle models.

The company then began to expand the volume of exports of assembled vehicles and parts to some countries (Indonesia, Laos, Malaysia, New Zealand, Pakistan and Portugal) to which it had already been exporting prior to the crisis. In addition, it began exporting diesel engines to Japan from Thailand for the first time. The expansion of exports is evident in the box table below, which compares projections for 1997 with 1996 levels of exports and production. Even though the total production of assembled vehicles is expected to decline in 1998 because of the fall in demand within Thailand, the number of vehicles for export is expected to increase from 1,600 in 1997 to 4,800 in 1998, and the value of exports of components was expected to increase from about $50 million in 1997 to about $96 million in 1998. Further substantial increases in exports of both vehicles and components are expected by the end of 1998.

Car sales continued to decline as expected in Thailand during the first four months of 1998. Total vehicle sales in April 1998 dropped to 11,000 units, as compared with 15,200 units in December 1997. Altogether, Thailand's car market is reported to have shrunk by more than 70 per cent since September 1997. The continued slump has forced Toyota to revise its production, marketing, and employment plans once again.

The new plan calls for a temporary halt in the production of the new 1.8 litre Corolla launched in January 1998 because sales (less than 400 units per month) do not justify the investment. It also involves reducing the number of employees through an early retirement scheme for factory workers. Some workers have been sent to Japan, and jobs previously done by outside subcontractors, such as initial quality surveys, will now be done in-house. Toyota has also taken advantage of the redundant capacity resulting from the crisis to provide a six-month training term at the Japanese headquarters to 50 production-team employees of its Thai affiliate, in order to improve further the quality and competitiveness of its production in Thailand. Toyota is also postponing indefinitely a model change for its pick-up trucks, which was originally planned for the third quarter of 1998.

To help its parts suppliers survive, Toyota Motor Thailand has accepted price increases ranging from 6 per cent to 20 per cent and is providing preshipment payments. Partly for this reason, the parent company had to inject an additional capital of 4,000 million baht into Toyota Motor Thailand, increasing the latter's registered capital to 4.5 billion baht in June 1998. The capital increase also allows Toyota Leasing to provide financing support for car buyers, while dealers have received a credit extension from Toyota Motor Thailand.

Toyota Motor Corporation is helping Toyota Motor Thailand to develop export markets, which is crucial if the local factories are to achieve their minimum production volume of 100,000 units a year. (Toyota Motor Thailand is expected to sell only 60,000-70,000 units in 1998 including exports.) Because

/...

(Box VII.5, concluded)

of its global production system that includes parts production and vehicle assembly facilities in many countries, Toyota Motor Corporation is able to shift towards a larger share of exports in its production in Thailand in quick response to the crisis. At the same time, Toyota Motor Corporation has used its financial strength to help solve the immediate liquidity problems of Toyota Motor Thailand, which is in turn expected to revise its production, marketing and employment plans so that it becomes leaner and can maintain its competitive edge.

Box table. Production and exports by Toyota Motor Thailand in 1997 and forecasts for 1998

Item	1997	1998 (forecast)	Change (1997-1998)
Assembled vehicles (units)			
Total production	97 000	60 000	-37 000 units
Total exports	1 600	4 800	+3 200 units
Total exports as percentage of production	1.6	8.0	
Automotive parts and components			
Exports (million dollars)			
Diesel engines	47	89	+$42 million
Engine blocks and camshafts	3	7	+$4 million

Source: Toyota Motor Corporation, press release of 8 December 1997, and additional information provided to UNCTAD.

Box VII.6. Implications of the financial crisis for foreign affiliates' operations: survey results for Thailand

An annual survey covering foreign affiliates in all industries in Thailand was conducted by the Thai Board of Investment[a] in early 1998 to provide insights, among other things, into how the crisis has affected foreign affiliates, how firms are responding and how they view future prospects:

- In 1997, 43 per cent of all respondents enjoyed an increase in revenues, while 34 per cent experienced reduced revenues (box table). There is considerable variation among industries: more firms in mining, metal and ceramics, metal products, machinery and transport equipment faced reduced revenues than in agricultural products, light industry and chemicals, and paper and plastics.

Box table. Performance of foreign affiliates in Thailand, 1997, by industry: survey results

Sector/industry	Total number of firms responding	Revenue increased	Revenue reduced	Remain unchanged
			(Per cent)[a]	
Agriculture and agricultural products	9	78	11	11
Mining metal and ceramics	15	33	47	20
Light industry	19	53	32	15
Metal productions machinery and transport equipment	55	35	40	25
Electronic products and electrical appliances	59	37	34	29
Chemical paper and plastic	46	52	26	22
Services and infrastructure	19	42	37	21
Total	222	43	34	23

Source: Thailand, Board of Investment.

[a] Percentage of respondents indicating a particular response.

/...

(Box VII.6, continued)

- Exports of many companies have been increasing in value since 1997. The trend towards increased exports appears to be gaining momentum in 1998. Over 60 per cent of the respondent companies indicated that exports in dollar value were expected to increase (box figure 1).

- Most companies alleviated their crisis-related problems by reducing production costs such as transportation, packaging and stock. Seeking new export markets presented another important solution. Many firms suffering from the decline in the domestic market have resorted to overseas markets. Among other measures, nearly half the respondents reported turning to the use of domestic raw materials in place of imported inputs. Some laid off employees. 47 per cent of firms in mining, metal and ceramics reduced the number of their employees; electronic products and appliances were at the other end of the spectrum, with only 5.1 per cent of the respondents reporting such an action.

Box figure 1. Foreign affiliates in Thailand: changes in export value in terms of dollars survey results

(Percentage)[a]

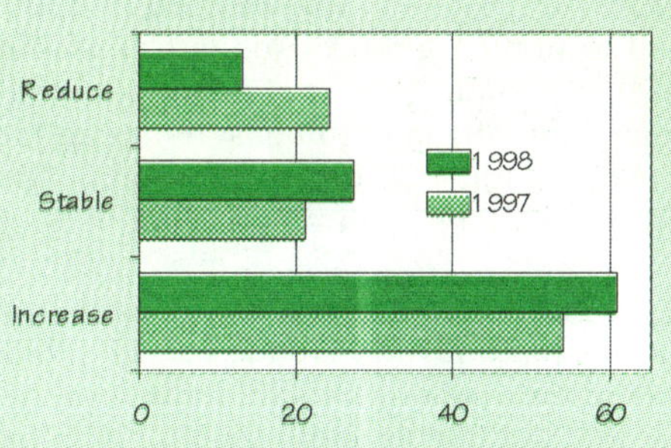

Source: Thailand, Board of Investment.

[a] Percentage of respondents indicating reduced, stable, or increased exports in 1997 and expected changes in 1998.

- The measures to be taken in the future to deal with the economic crisis are more or less the same as those taken over the past months. The most important one is cost reduction. More firms will resort to currency hedging to protect themselves from baht fluctuation.

- In the light of the economic recession that has set in following the crisis, more than half the responding companies do not plan to expand their investments in 1998. However, 38 per cent still have plans to invest more in Thailand as labour costs and investment incentives remain attractive. The industries with the most ambitious investment-expansion plans are electronics and electrical appliances. Moreover, the percentage of firms planning to shift production to other countries is quite small, with only 1 per cent of respondents indicating such plans (box figure 2).

Box figure 2. Investment plans of TNCs in Thailand

(Percentage)

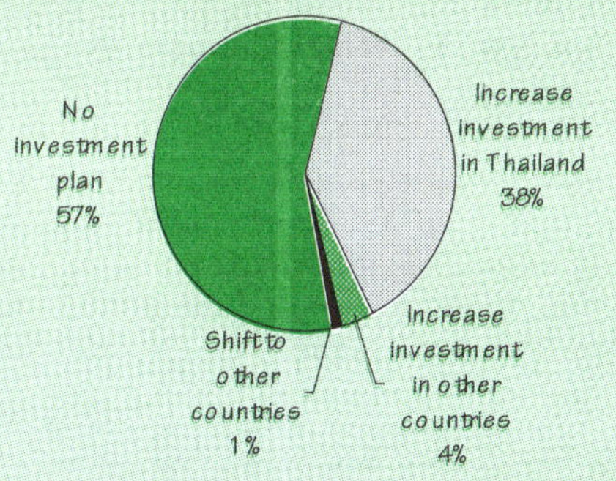

- Finally, although Thai exports have gained greater price competitiveness thanks to a weaker baht, the fluctuation in the value of the baht has been a major concern among foreign investors (slightly over a half of the respondents). Other problems include the decline in domestic demand and the financial liquidity crunch.

Source: Thailand, Board of Investment.

[a] Questionnaires were sent to 592 foreign affiliates operating in Thailand, of which 236 firms (40 per cent) responded. The majority (58 per cent) of the respondents were Japanese companies, followed by Taiwanese and United States' investors. Two-thirds of the respondent companies had been operating in Thailand for more than five years. Most of them are medium- and large-scale firms, with 29 per cent of them having more than Bt 1 billion in asset value. Two-thirds of respondent companies exported more than 20 per cent of their production. The industrial breakdown of the respondents was: agriculture and agricultural products — 4 per cent; mining, metals and ceramics — 7 per cent; light industry — 9 per cent; metal products, machinery and transport equipment — 24 per cent; electronic products and electrical appliances — 26 per cent; chemicals, paper and plastics — 21 per cent; and service and infrastructure — 9 per cent.

Box VII.7. TNCs' response to the Asian crisis: the case of Honda in Thailand

In the wake of the financial crisis, some leading Japanese automobile makers and their parts producers have been injecting capital into their affiliates located in the most affected countries. This has not only helped the affiliates to deal with their financial problems, but also boosted their parent firms' equity share in their affiliates at a cheaper price than might have been possible in normal times. The crisis has also acted as a catalyst in this restructuring of global production by automobile TNCs, as illustrated by Honda's relocation programme.

Honda's parent company has decided to inject three billion baht into its Thai holding company, of which Bt 2.16 billion will be used to double the capital base of its Thai affiliates. The remainder will be used to purchase those Honda Car Manufacturing (Thailand) shares not fully subscribed by Honda. In addition, Honda Motors of Japan plans to inject 600 million baht into its cash-strapped parts supply subsidiaries in Thailand to boost their capital during the liquidity crunch.[a] Showa Corp., an automobile parts manufacturer affiliated to Honda Motor Co., plans to raise its stake in a joint shock-absorber venture in Thailand from 49 per cent to 53 per cent by doubling the capital of the affiliate.

Furthermore, the cheaper baht has accelerated Honda's restructuring programme to relocate production to Thailand. Honda has 27 subsidiaries in Thailand, most of which are parts manufacturers. The relocation plan envisages the use of existing facilities without new investments. Honda's production facilities in Japan are to cease producing some parts and to transfer the responsibility to its Thai affiliates. The programme is expected to benefit more than 20 parts producers in Thailand in which Honda has a stake. The plan starts with parts production and then proceeds to car and motorcycle manufacturing.[b] Honda is also working on a plan to boost automotive parts exports from Thailand. It has been able to increase exports back to Japan and to outside the region.

The relocation of parts production, boosting exports and injecting capital into its affiliates are a few of the measures Honda has adopted in response to the financial crisis in Thailand. Other measures include increasing local content in its Thai automobile production, negotiating for a price reduction of completely-knocked-down imported units from its Japanese parent, and cutting expenditures.

Source: UNCTAD.

[a] *The Nation*, 24 March 1998.
[b] *The Nation*, 24 March 1998.

Box VII. 8. TNCs' response to the crisis: the electrical and electronics industry in Malaysia

The electrical and electronics industry in Malaysia is dominated by TNCs. It is also the country's single largest foreign exchange earner, accounting for two-thirds of total manufactured exports in 1997 (Malaysia, Bank Negara, 1998). There are currently over 100 sizeable electrical and electronics foreign affiliates in Malaysia. The industry grew by 14 per cent in 1997 (Malaysia, Bank Negara, 1998), stimulated mainly by global demand for semiconductors, particularly from the United States, Europe and the Asia-Pacific countries (excluding Japan).

A survey of foreign affiliates in the industry was carried out by UNCTAD between April and May 1998, with a view to obtaining an understanding of the impact of the crisis on FDI and TNC activities in this key industry.[a] The results of the survey are as follows:

Financing and financial transactions

- A majority of the foreign affiliates surveyed depend on offshore sources of financing. Only one-sixth are self-financing from sales and profits. Local banks are used mainly for day-to-day local transactions.
- Most of the respondents service their debt in dollars, although some Japanese and Asian firms use the ringgit.

/...

Survey data suggest also that in Malaysia (box VII.8) and Thailand (box VII.6) industries that are more export-oriented have been less affected by the crisis than other industries.

There are, however, important preconditions that need to be fulfilled if increased export competitiveness is to be effectively exploited, be it by export-oriented foreign affiliates or by domestic firms: the principal export markets in other parts of the world need to remain open to exports from the affected Asian countries and, equally important, demand in these markets needs to remain strong enough to absorb additional imports. This is particularly important since demand in the Asian regional market as a whole, which has been absorbing increasing shares of exports from within the region, has been adversely affected by the crisis and by the current economic slowdown in Japan.

(Box VII.8, concluded)

- The dollar is the currency required to pay for principal inputs. Hence the devaluation has affected the cost of production. Since most foreign affiliates export more than a half of their output, however, the impact of sourcing through dollar-bought imports has not been critical.
- Profit repatriations are normally made in ringgit, through dividend payments from the Malaysian affiliate to a parent company. However, one-fifth of the affiliates do not repatriate profits to their parent firm.

Plans for investment or expansion

- None of the foreign affiliates surveyed intended to close down or relocate elsewhere. Some consumer electronic firms (28 per cent) have adopted a wait-and-see attitude towards the crisis, partly due to the fact that some of their products target domestic and/or regional markets. Half of the respondents see some opportunities to expand Malaysian operations in the wake of the crisis.

Coping with the crisis

- Almost all of the respondents see cost reduction as a priority arising from the crisis. In addition, improvements in efficiency and marketing are seen as necessary for coping with the crisis.

Expectations of future performance

- Despite the crisis, the firms surveyed have positive expectations regarding various production parameters. More than 60 per cent expressed the view that production, sales and exports will increase in the next three years. Others felt they would remain at the present level. None of the respondents suggested that they would decline significantly.

To sum up, there is some negative impact on the operations of foreign affiliates in the electrical and electronics industry of Malaysia resulting from the economic turmoil, but the impact does not appear to be significant. The surveyed companies still have confidence in Malaysia as a destination for FDI and are optimistic about the next three years. Some of them see the current crisis as an opportunity for expansion. In the meantime, because FDI in the electrical and electronic industry is mostly export-oriented, the ups and downs of the global electrical and electronic industry represent more of a challenge than the domestic or subregional economic upheavals such as the one now affecting Malaysia.

Source: UNCTAD survey.

[a] Responses were obtained from 20 major TNCs with manufacturing facilities in the electrical and electronic industry in Malaysia; some of the TNCs have more than one plant. The total value of output from these affiliates (about $5.7 billion) comprised a large proportion of the industry in 1997. Most of the TNCs surveyed utilize Malaysia as a base for component manufacturing, assembly and testing.

ii. Domestic-market-oriented FDI

The downturn in domestic demand in Asia (annex table A.VII.5) obviously has some adverse consequences for foreign affiliates producing for sale in local and regional markets. Reduced demand and slower growth can be expected to lead to some cancelling, scaling down or postponement of FDI in the most affected countries and perhaps elsewhere in the region.

The impact on domestically-oriented foreign affiliates varies among sectors and industries. Foreign affiliates in the services sector are particularly susceptible to local demand conditions because of the non-tradability of most services. According to a survey conducted by UNCTAD and ICC (box VII.9), expectations of reduced investment in the East and South-East Asian region in the short and medium term were reported most frequently for services: 18 per cent as compared to 12 per cent overall (box VII.10). FDI declined in real estate in Thailand (annex table A.VII.1) and is expected to fall significantly in construction and civil engineering in the Republic of Korea (box VII.11). Nevertheless, in certain service industries, FDI could increase. These include banking, insurance and other financial services, and telecommunication, where the combination of the recent liberalization and the availability of assets for acquisition would suggest an increase in FDI inflows. This is precisely what has happened in Thailand where FDI in financial services tripled in 1997 and in the first quarter of 1998 alone stood nearly a third higher than the total for 1997 (annex table A.VII.1). In the Republic of Korea, the largest increases in FDI are expected to take place in consulting services (box VII.11).

Box VII.9. The UNCTAD/ICC global survey

The UNCTAD Secretariat and the International Chamber of Commerce (ICC) jointly conducted a survey of large TNCs in February-March 1998 (UNCTAD and ICC, 1998; UNCTAD, 1998f). The aim was to ascertain the companies' intentions with respect to FDI in the short-to-medium term in East and South-East Asia in the light of the financial crisis and their opinions regarding the long-term prospects for the region as an investment destination. The survey covered 500 companies. These included the world's 100 largest TNCs (not including banking and finance companies) in foreign assets, drawn from the list of such corporations prepared for UNCTAD's *World Investment Report 1997*; 200 companies that were potential candidates for inclusion in that list; the world's 50 largest TNCs (not including banking and finance companies) headquartered in developing countries, drawn from the list of such corporations published in UNCTAD's *World Investment Report 1997*; 50 companies that were potential candidates for inclusion in that list; and 100 additional firms with significant operations in Asia. A total of 198 firms responded to the survey, for a response rate of 40 per cent. The composition of the sample in terms of countries/regions in which the respondents are located ("home regions") and in terms of economic sectors is contained in the following two box figures:

Box figure. Breakdown of responses to the questionnaire by home region

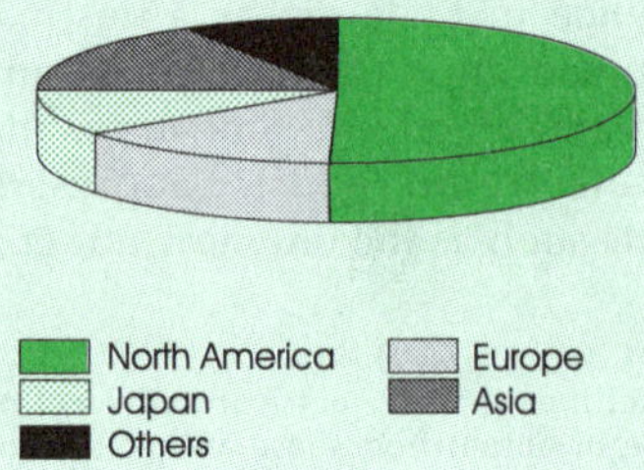

Box figure. Breakdown of responses to the questionnaire by main sector

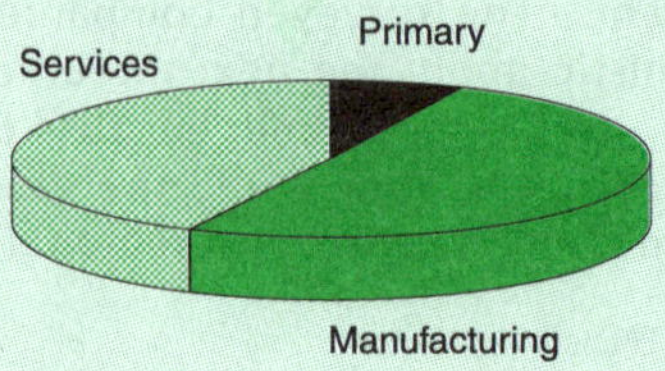

Source: UNCTAD.

Among manufacturing industries, foreign affiliates in light industries which produce non-luxury consumer goods are less likely to be affected than affiliates producing durable goods and luxury items. Affiliates producing goods and services that depend mainly on domestic sources of raw materials and intermediate inputs would also be less affected than those relying on imports from countries whose exchange rates have changed little. The automotive industry, in which TNCs figure prominently, is a good example of the impact of the crisis and the range of responses by firms. Demand for passenger cars in the most affected economies has declined dramatically (figure VII.10), where considerable capacity

Box VII.10. The UNCTAD/ICC global survey: implications for FDI in Asia in the short and medium term

The findings of the UNCTAD/ICC survey (box VII.9) show that more than one-quarter of the responding firms expect to increase their FDI in East and South-East Asia as a whole in the short-to-medium term (box figure 1). North American and Japanese firms are close to this average, while firms from Europe are distinctly above it and those from developing Asia distinctly below it (box figure 2). In the case of European firms, this may well reflect the fact that, after having largely neglected Asia until recently (European Commission and UNCTAD, 1996), they are now taking an active interest in this region. In the case of the developing Asia TNCs, the low proportion may reflect the impaired capacity of some TNCs to undertake outward FDI (most of which has traditionally gone to other developing countries). However, they remain committed to the region; 69 per cent expect to maintain their investment at the pre-crisis level. Predictably, firms in manufacturing from all regions have the highest proportion of responses indicating expected expansion of their FDI in Asia, with over one-third of them providing this response, as compared to one-fifth of service firms and less than one-tenth of primary sector firms (box figure 3).

Box figure 1. Short and medium-term prospects: overall response of companies worldwide

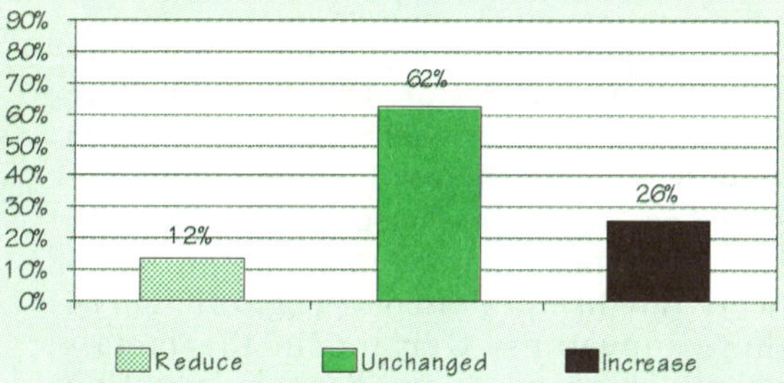

Box figure 2. Short and medium-term prospects: company intentions by home region of parent company

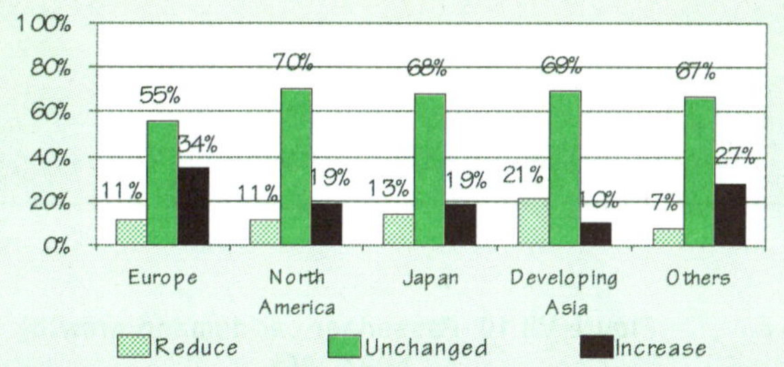

Box figure 3. Short and medium-term prospects: company intentions by sector

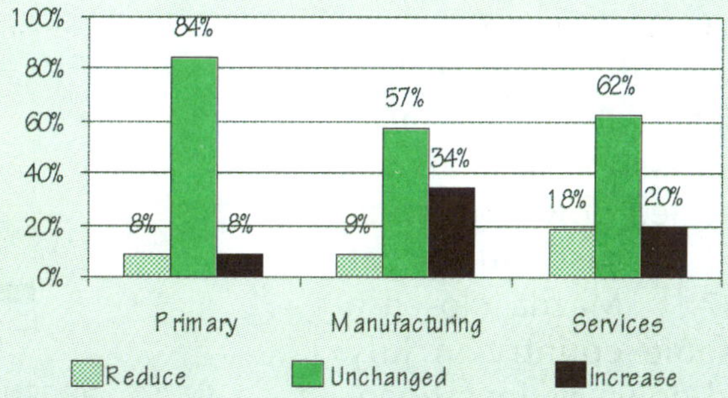

Source: UNCTAD/ICC global survey, March 1998

Box VII.11. Prospects for inward FDI in various industries in the Republic of Korea

The financial crisis is expected to influence the prospects for FDI in the Republic of Korea differently in different industries. According to a survey of foreign affiliates in the Republic of Korea, conducted jointly by UNCTAD and the Federation of Korean Industries (FKI), the consulting industry appears to be the brightest spot for FDI in the light of the financial crisis (box figure) -- presumably because the need for professional advice increases as the full-scale restructuring of domestic corporations begins and firms engage actively in M&As.

Other areas expected to attract more FDI are the semiconductor and communication equipment industries, and the electrical and electronics industries. Domestic demand for these products is increasing rapidly and because national technologies in the industry are relatively advanced. Furthermore, these industries are export-oriented, and their products are internationally competitive. Investment in trading services is also expected to increase as the import and export regulations have been substantially liberalized and will be further streamlined in the future.

However, the surveyed firms were pessimistic about the prospects for FDI in shipping, finance and insurance, industries in which FDI grew rapidly prior to the crisis. The predicted contraction of the economy in general, and a rapid fall in consumer spending in particular, are likely to discourage growth of FDI in these industries. Demand in the metals industry, which produces basic production materials and intermediate goods, may also drop precipitously due to decreased domestic investment and demand and lower levels of production. Finally, FDI in the construction and civil engineering industries is expected to fall substantially, given the serious stagnation in the real estate market.

Source: UNCTAD/FKI survey, April 1998.

Box figure. Prospects for inward FDI in the Republic of Korea in the light of crisis, 1997: survey results

(Points)

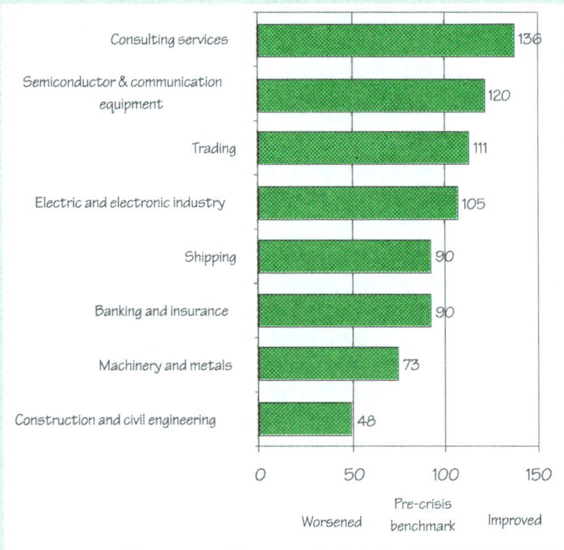

Source: UNCTAD/FKI survey, April 1998.

had been built up, and a number of automotive TNCs have scaled down, postponed or even cancelled investment projects in some of these countries. One-third of the 18 respondents from that industry to the UNCTAD/ICC survey indicated that they planned to postpone some of their investment projects and another one-sixth indicated a scaling down. Volvo scaled down output at its affiliate inThailand by suspending car production in late 1997;[11] Mazda closed a joint venture in the same country in July 1998;[12] and GM scaled down its investment plans for a plant in Rayong, Thailand, from

Figure VII.10. Passenger car demand growth, 1997-1998

(Percentage)

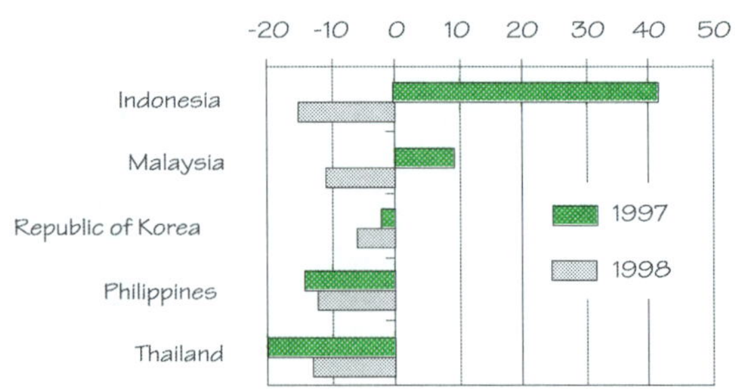

Source: Standard and Poor's DRI, as cited in *Financial Times*, 25 November 1997.

$750 million to $450 million (a reduction in planned capacity from 100,000 units to 40,000 units) and postponed its implementation (TDRI, 1998). At the same time, the same companies sometimes increased, or sought to increase, their investment in the most affected countries. For example, GM acquired an additional 40 per cent in General Motors Buana, Indonesia. In January 1998,[13] Honda increased its share in Honda Thailand, thus injecting funds to help its financially distressed affiliate as well as increasing its level of control over it (box VII.7); and GM and Ford were competing with each other and with domestic firms to acquire Kia, an automobile producer in the Republic of Korea.[14] At the aggregate level, this is reflected, for example, in the fact that FDI flows into the automobile industry in Thailand remained relatively strong during the second half of 1997 and the first quarter of 1998 (annex table A.VII.1). TNCs also reacted by reallocating production from elsewhere to affiliates in the most seriously affected countries (box VII.7), switching production into exports (boxes VII.5, VII.6) and/or increasing local content (boxes VII.7 and VII.12).

These examples illustrate both the risks and opportunities that the crisis entails for firms, in the automobile industry as well as in other industries. They show how TNCs can turn adverse effects to their advantage by strategic positioning, among other things by the acquisition of assets. They also show that foreign affiliates are often in a better position than domestic firms to weather difficulties, an example of the protective influence that

Box VII.12. The Asian crisis and its implications for TNCs: the case of Motorola

Despite the deterioration of economic conditions in some Asian markets and its negative impact on sales and profits, Motorola is holding to its investment plans in Asia. In Malaysia, Motorola plans to invest RM50 million in the Multimedia Super Corridor, the Malaysian silicon valley to develop, among other products, smart cards based on the open systems architecture.[a] The investment is to be spread over two years. In addition, Motorola Malaysia is investing RM3.3 million in the first phase of its wastewater recycling project which would be using the latest "membrane technology". The project, in which the company plan to recycle up to 40 per cent of current water usage from its plants, is expected to involve a total investment of RM5 million. The company also has an R&D centre in Malaysia. Motorola Malaysia expects to recruit 200 engineers by the year 2000, and 80 to 90 per cent of its 12,000-strong workforce in its five manufacturing facilities in Malaysia are expected to be Malaysian nationals. Motorola is also planning to relocate its ASEAN regional headquarters to Malaysia.[b]

As one of its measures to reduce costs, Motorola Malaysia expects its annual purchases from its local component suppliers to increase, reaching a total value of RM1 billion in the year 2000, compared to RM785 million in 1997. The company sources from more than 100 local suppliers: various types of components including semiconductor lead frames, flexible circuit boards, liquid crystal device, precision tooling, engineering plastic parts and packaging. It also has another 500 local partners which supply and service the company's daily factory maintenance, repairs and operational requirements for each of its five manufacturing facilities in Malaysia. Motorola intends actively to develop local suppliers and to provide overall support to them in technology, management and training.[c]

In the Republic of Korea, Motorola acquired in May 1998 a stake in Pantech, Seoul, a Korean electronics firm, becoming its second largest shareholder with 20 per cent equity. Exports are expected to account for more than 80 per cent of the company's annual sales by 1999, an increase from about 60 per cent expected for 1998. Pantech and Motorola plan to work together to develop Code Division Multiple Access (CDMA) digital cellular telephones. Motorola plans to invest $300 million in the Republic of Korea to expand its operations and set up new partnerships.[d]

Source: UNCTAD, based upon information obtained from the media and Motorola.

a *SUNS: South-North Development Monitor*, 24 January 1998.
b ibid.
c *New Straits Times*, 11 June 1998.
d *New Straits Times*, 15 May 1998.

transnational corporate systems can spread over their affiliates. For countries, all of this helps to alleviate the immediate impact of the crisis.

(c) Regulatory changes affecting FDI

The shortage of capital, not only for investment but also for financing production operations and trade, combined with a recognition of the role that FDI can play in restoring growth and development, is leading to an even more flexible attitude towards FDI in the region. As a result, some countries have in recent months further liberalized their FDI regimes (annex table A.VII.6). In addition to unilateral measures and measures implemented in pursuit of multilateral commitments (such as, for example, those made under the General Agreement on Trade in Services), liberalization measures have also been taken in the context of the adjustment programmes linked to the package of financial support from the International Monetary Fund. Recent moves by the five most affected countries include opening industries like banking and other financial services to FDI and relaxing rules with respect to ownership, mode of entry and financing.

Governments in the countries most affected by the crisis have also intensified their efforts to attract FDI both individually and collectively. For example, the Republic of Korea has introduced an automatic approval system (table VII.4), and Thailand has established a unit to assist foreign companies to bring expatriates to work in promoted projects. At the regional level, ASEAN members are implementing their Plan of Action on Cooperation and Promotion of Investment and, in July 1998, the heads of the ASEAN investment promotion agencies announced that the framework agreement to establish the ASEAN Investment Area would be submitted to Ministers for adoption late in 1998 (chapter III). At the interregional level, at the second Asia-Europe Meeting (ASEM) in London in April 1998, leaders "urged full and rapid implementation by all ASEM partners of the Trade Facilitation Action Plan and the Investment Promotion Action Plan ....".[15] The Asia-Europe Investment Promotion Action Plan is focused on a number of activities under two broad headings: investment promotion and investment policies and regulations. The proposed activities to promote investment between and within the two regions include a virtual exchange network to disseminate information to investors, a round table with business leaders and a business-to-business exchange programme, as well as high-level dialogue on key investment issues.[16]

Taken together, these liberalization moves and promotion efforts make the policy determinants of FDI in the most affected countries more favourable for foreign investors. There is a danger,

Table VII.4. Republic of Korea: major elements of the FDI promotion programme

According to an announcement on 30 March 1998, the following programme will be implemented in order to encourage FDI in the country: [a]

Provisions of one-stop service

- Streamline laws and regulations on FDI.
- Introduce an automatic approval system.
- Korean Trade and Investment Promotion Agency (KOTRA) will be given full responsibility for the Republic of Korea's relationship with foreign investors.

Offering incentives

- Extend the tax concession period from the current 8 years to 10 years.
- Expand the range of tax exemptions to include high-tech, and value-added service industries.
- Provide local government with greater autonomy when dealing with certain tax exemptions.

Source: Republic of Korea, Ministry of Finance and Economy, 1998.

[a] For changes in the regulatory regime, see annex table A.VII.7.

however, that countries eager to attract FDI may provide foreign investors incentives that they would not grant under normal circumstances. This could lead to market distortions and intensify incentives competition in the region (UNCTAD, 1996d), especially since the crisis-affected economies have similar industries and demand structures.

2. Implications for outward FDI

Outward FDI by TNCs headquartered in developing Asia has increased substantially in recent years, with the greatest proportion of such flows going to other countries in the region. For the major Asian developing home economies taken together, the stock of FDI located in other developing Asian economies was at least one-half of their total outward FDI (figure VII.11). The financial crisis is likely to reduce both the capacities and the incentives of a number of Asian TNCs to undertake FDI, both intraregionally and elsewhere.

The region's TNCs have been financially weakened by the crisis for a number of reasons:

- *Valuation losses.* The book value of the assets of a number of firms has fallen due to the drastic currency devaluations and the sharp fall of stock prices (see table VII.2). This applies both to parent firms and their affiliates in affected countries within the region. The impact is much more pronounced for Asian TNCs than for investors from other regions, since a much higher proportion of Asian TNCs' assets are located in other Asian countries. Judging from changes in the ranking of Asian companies on the 1997 *Financial Times* "Global 500 list" of the largest companies in the world, several large TNCs from developing Asian economies have experienced considerable losses of the value of their assets.[17] Of the 25 companies that have fallen the most in their ranking on the 1997 list, as compared to the 1996 list, seven were based in developing Asia (and 14 in Japan). In 1996, four newcomers on the 500 list were from the most affected economies;[18] in 1997, there were none and, moreover, an additional six firms from that group of countries departed from the list in 1997. With the worsening of the situation at the end of 1997 and the beginning of 1998, valuation losses may have increased, further impairing their FDI potential, as well as current FDI stocks in some cases.

- *Debt burden.* Asian TNCs that are mainly Asia-oriented face another possible source of loss if they have relied on borrowed funds denominated in dollars. Such borrowing appeared reasonable as long as various Asian currencies were pegged to the dollar. Higher interest rates in some Asian host countries encouraged dollar-denominated borrowing. Like domestic borrowers, Asian parent firms and their foreign affiliates were caught by surprise when the dollar pegs of some Asian currencies proved unsustainable.[19] Substantial

Figure VII.11. Developing Asia's [a] outward FDI stock, by destination, 1995/1996[b]

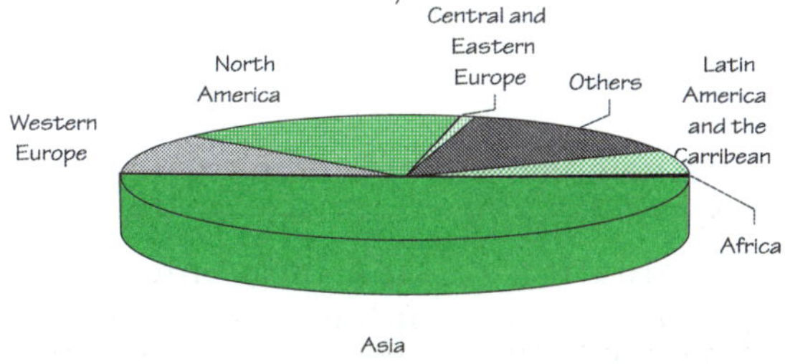

Source: UNCTAD, FDI/TNC database.

[a] China, India, Malaysia, Republic of Korea, Taiwan Province of China, Thailand, Singapore. Data for Hong Kong, China were not available by destination; the greater proportion of its outward FDI is in China.

[b] For India, stock data for 1992 have been included.

borrowing in foreign currencies has therefore aggravated the debt-servicing burden of TNCs with high debt-equity ratios. The largest Korean conglomerates, for example, had debt-equity ratios (annex table A.VII.7) that were high by international standards (UNCTAD, forthcoming d). In the case of banks, a rise in non-performing debt as well as more demanding prudential regulations may further restrict the room for manoeuvre. The problems arising from devaluation in servicing dollar-denominated debt tend to be more pronounced for foreign affiliates oriented to local markets, since they do not earn foreign currency.[20] The effect is again to impair the ability of the affected firms to finance outward FDI.

- *Reduced profitability.* To the extent that parent firms and affiliates are located in countries that have experienced a decline in demand, their ability to self-finance their operations or to expand further, through reinvestment or in other ways, may also have decreased. Consumption has indeed declined in a number of Asian economies, reflecting in many cases a decline in growth rates or the onset of a recession (annex table A.VII.5). The result has been a steep decline in profits in 1997, averaging 18 per cent for the 15 companies from developing Asia included in the 1998 *Fortune 500* list, compared to an increase of 25 per cent in the profits of European firms at the other end of the spectrum with respect to profits (figure VII.12).

The impact of these factors is further compounded by high interest rates (and in some cases, a general credit crunch) at home, the increased cost of foreign operations due to depreciation of domestic currency, and the difficulty of raising funds abroad due to lowered credit ratings (table VII.2). As a result, the financial capacities of a number of Asian TNCs have been weakened, including their capacity to undertake outward FDI. A shortage of cash has induced a number of Asian firms to divest assets abroad, especially in Asia, Europe and the United States, to raise funds (annex table A.VII.8).[21] At the same time, the crisis has changed some of the parameters that induced some Asian firms to invest abroad in the past, at least as far as other parts of Asia are concerned:

- To the extent that growth and demand in other Asian countries has declined (annex table A.VII.5), TNCs from Asian developing countries seeking national or regional markets have less of an incentive to invest or reinvest in those countries. On the other hand, market-seeking TNCs could switch to countries unaffected by the crisis, if their financial capabilities and ownership advantages this permitted.

- The calculations of efficiency-seeking TNCs depend very much on the devaluation-related movement of production costs at home as against in other Asian countries. In particular, TNCs headquartered in home countries whose currencies have been significantly devalued (table VII.2) may find that devaluations have so far

Figure VII.12. Profits growth of world's largest 500 firms, by home region, 1996 and 1997
(Percentage)

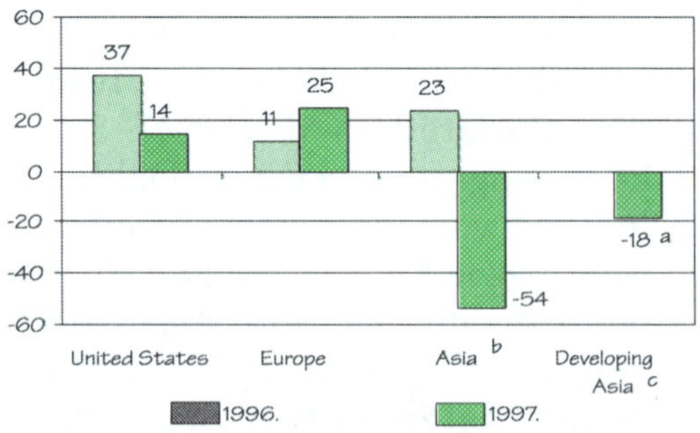

Source: based on *Fortune*, 3 August 1998.

a Includes data for 12 firms from the Republic of Korea, 2 from Taiwan Province of China and 1 from Malaysia.
b Includes developing Asia and Japan.
c Profit data for 1996 for developing Asia are not available.

reduced the cost differentials between producing at home and producing abroad that it is no longer worthwhile for them to move labour-intensive production abroad in order to be competitive in world markets.

In either case, the incentive for Asian TNCs to invest abroad and to invest in Asia in particular is weakened, at least in the short-to-medium term.

In addition to the factors affecting the capacities and incentives of Asian TNCs to invest abroad, policy measures adopted by governments to deal with the crisis could also discourage some outward FDI. Some of these measures may not be targeted at outward FDI but, to the extent that they aim at minimizing outflows of capital in general, they could also affect FDI. Other measures are specifically FDI-related. For example, the Government of Malaysia had encouraged its firms to invest abroad before the crisis (UNCTAD, 1995a). After the crisis reached that country, the Government began to discourage outward (or "reverse") investment by Malaysian firms, so as to maintain liquidity. The Government declared that "reverse" investment, which amounted to 7 billion Malaysian ringgit during the first half of 1997, "will have to be deferred even if these investments are to be financed through foreign borrowing. However, investments which have significant linkages with domestic economy and earn foreign exchange will be continued".[22]

All in all, FDI outflows from developing Asia in general, and from the five most affected countries in particular, can be expected to remain at low levels in the short and perhaps the medium term, as Asian TNCs' capacities to sustain existing operations and initiate new FDI projects are weakened. The year 1997 witnessed a decline of outward FDI from four of the five most affected countries (annex table A.VII.9), including a substantial decrease in cross-border M&As over the second half of 1997 (figure VII.13). First quarter data for the Republic of Korea and Malaysia suggest that this decline will continue.[23] Furthermore, according to a survey conducted by UNCTAD and the Federation of Korean Industries (FKI) in March 1998,[24] some two-thirds of the 46 large TNC respondents based in the Republic of Korea indicated that they had either cancelled, scaled down or postponed their investment plans (figure VII.14). This was the case for both manufacturing and non-manufacturing firms (figure VII.14). It was also the case for investment intentions for 1998-1999, suggesting that Korean firms expect to invest less in virtually every one of their major investment destinations (figure VII.15) and that reductions in FDI are likely to be particularly large in the four other crisis-stricken economies. Outside Asia, the expected declines in FDI from the Republic of Korea are considerably less pronounced. A survey conducted by the Export and Import Bank of the Republic of Korea in March 1998 corroborates these findings: 108 of 140 Korean TNCs responding had cancelled or postponed their FDI plans[25] and the bank estimated that total outward FDI by Korean TNCs could fall by 60 per cent in 1998.

Figure VII.13. Cross border M&A purchases by firms headquartered in the countries most affected by the crisis, 1997-1998
(Billions of dollars)

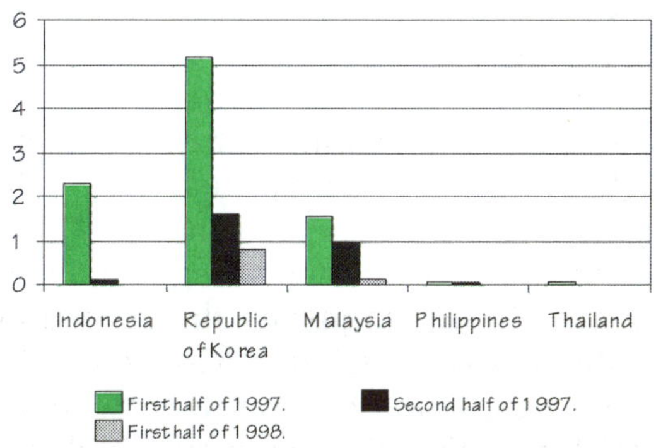

Source: UNCTAD, based on KPMG Corporate Finance.

The picture looks different when the less affected major home economies of Asia (China, Hong Kong, China, Singapore and Taiwan Province of China) are considered: their performance regarding outward FDI improved slightly in 1997 over 1996 (see section A), indicating that the combination of financial capabilities and economic incentives has remained favourable for them so far. This is also reflected in the fact that total M&A purchases outside Asia by firms from major outward-investing economies among the less affected Asian economies increased in 1997 over 1996 (annex table A.VII.10). Whether this will continue in 1998 is uncertain, even though there were a number of M&As by firms from other major developing countries in Asia in the five most affected economies during the first half of 1998 (annex table A.VII.10). When it comes to the longer term, it can be expected that outward FDI from the region (including the crisis-affected economies) will resume its upward trend. This reflects the belief of the corporate executives responding to the survey that most of the fundamental determinants of Asian outward FDI can be expected to reassert themselves once the present difficulties have been overcome. One determinant is marketing and management know-how. Another is accumulated technological capacity, especially in medium-technology industries. This includes the capacity to adapt technology to the needs of developing economies as well as advantages deriving from R&D activities, especially in the newly industrializing economies. Furthermore, the painful lessons of the crisis and the restructuring in its light could strengthen the competitiveness of Asian TNCs. Over the long term, they can be expected to resume their position as leading developing-country

Figure VII.14. TNCs headquartered in the Republic of Korea: effects on outward FDI, survey responses[a]

(Percentage)

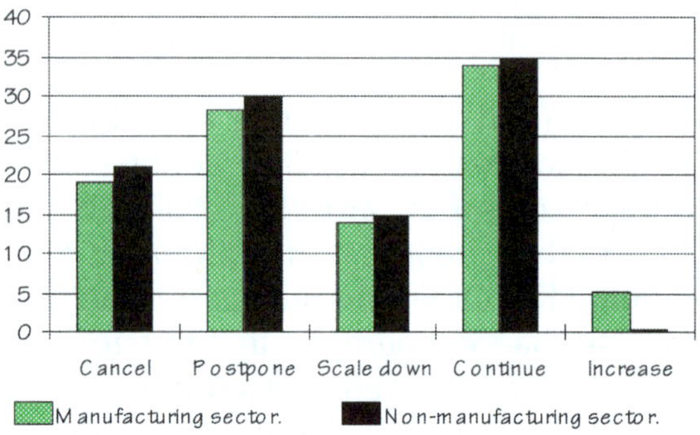

Source: UNCTAD/FKI survey, 1998.

[a] Percentage of respondents indicating each of the responses shown.

Figure VII.15. TNCs headquartered in the Republic of Korea: changes in investment intentions for 1998-1999 in the light of the crisis

(Points)

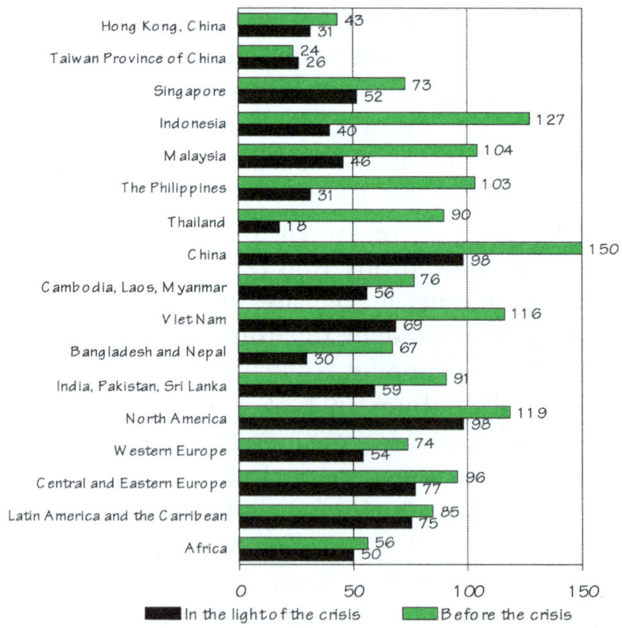

Degrees of priority: 0 - 50 points: low.
50-100 points: medium.
100-150 points: strong.

Source: UNCTAD/FKI survey, 1998.

investors, although they may well be more cautious and more focused in their internationalization in the future.

3. Implications for FDI flows into other countries

The implications of the financial crisis for inward FDI are not confined to the five most seriously affected countries. Other countries, especially in developing Asia, may also be affected. Three factors are particularly relevant here:

- The reduced capacity of TNCs in the region to invest abroad, be it for market-seeking or efficiency-seeking reasons.
- The possibility of reduced growth in the non-affected countries in the region, making them less attractive as destinations for market-seeking FDI.
- The reduced export competitiveness of the less affected countries, brought about by the devaluations in the most affected countries, which makes them less attractive for efficiency-seeking FDI.

Developing countries in the region in which any or all of these factors come into play are likely to experience a fall in FDI. In particular, FDI flows into countries that receive significant amounts of investment from within the region -- especially from the most affected countries -- could fall. These are mainly the countries of East and South-East Asia, including China, Viet Nam, the Asian least developed countries (Bangladesh, Cambodia, Lao People's Democratic Republic, Myanmar) and Central Asia (figures VII.16 to VII.19). The same considerations could also influence FDI flows from developed countries to the less affected Asian developing countries; in particular, Japanese FDI may be affected (box VII.13).

Figure VII.16. FDI in China, by region/country of investment, cumulative flows, 1979-1997

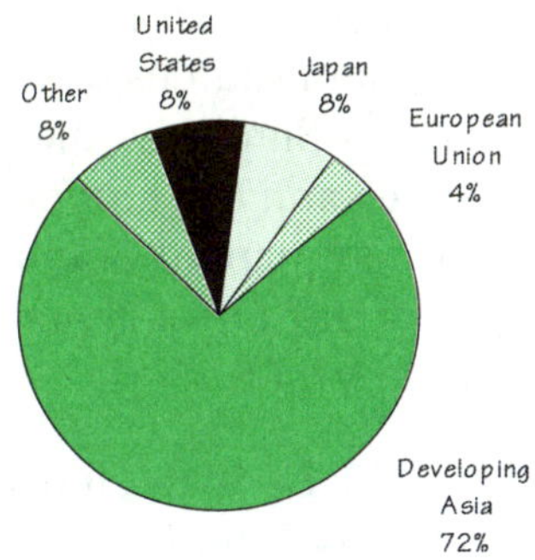

Source: UNCTAD, FDI/TNC database.

Figure VII.17. FDI in Viet Nam, by region/country of investment, cumulative flows, 1993-1996

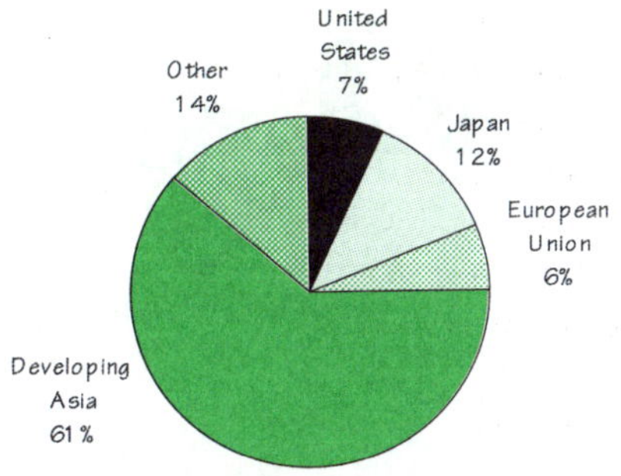

Source: UNCTAD, FDI/TNC database.

Note: data are for approved investment flows. Data for developing Asia include data for Hong Kong, China, Republic of Korea, Malaysia, Singapore and Taiwan Province of China.

To the extent that FDI flows into other developing countries in Asia do decline, there could be broader implications, since interactive TNC-assisted restructuring has been one of the dynamic forces that has assisted Asian development, in the framework of the "flying-geese" pattern (UNCTAD, 1995a). In the first instance, this process took place between Japan (and the United States) on the one hand and the newly industrializing Asian countries on the other hand (UNCTAD, 1995a). At a second stage, a number of other Asian countries joined in, also receiving outward FDI from the newly industrializing economies. For the major developing host economies, FDI originating in other developing Asian economies was at least 40 per cent higher than the share of Europe, Japan or the United States taken singly (European Commission and UNCTAD, 1996). The current crisis could therefore lead to a slowing down or interruption of the process.

Furthermore, countries in the region less closely linked, including through intraregional FDI, to the most affected countries may well gain in relative attractiveness, provided that at least some of their basic FDI determinants are in good shape. Indeed, the UNCTAD/ICC survey suggested that FDI to South Asia, where FDI from other developing Asian economies has been relatively low (figure VII.20),[26] could well increase (table VII.5). Countries further away -- in Africa, Latin America and the Caribbean, and Central and Eastern Europe -- are unlikely to be touched by the developments in Asia as far as FDI is concerned, although, if there is a global recession -- and there are some signs of deflationary tendencies, such as recession in Japan and slowing down of growth in the United States -- they could be. Despite some increases in FDI from developing Asian economies, particularly from the Republic of Korea, the main sources of FDI to those regions are still Europe and the United States (figures VII.21-23).[27] Similarly, the share of the Asian developing countries in FDI in Japan, the United States and the European Union amounted to between 1.1 per cent (European Union) to 6.3 per cent (Japan) of total inflows, and between 0.5 per cent (European Union) and 4.6 per cent (Japan) of total stock in the first half of the 1990s (table VII.6).

It might be expected that, in the light of the crisis, some TNCs may find sites in other regions more attractive relative to those in Asia for new investment projects in the short-to-medium term, if not in the longer term. Survey results suggest that some firms are indeed looking at expansion in Latin America and also in Central and Eastern Europe and Africa in the short-to-medium term (table VII.5). However, this finding should not be interpreted as necessarily indicating an FDI switch to these regions in response to the crisis. The ability of investors to substitute actual or potential FDI in one host region (or country) with FDI in another depends largely on the type of FDI as well as on the sector or industry concerned. The following points among others are relevant:

- Natural-resource-seeking FDI is largely location-specific and substitution is limited.

Figure VII.18. FDI in Asian LDCs, by region/country of investment, cumulative flows, 1992-1995

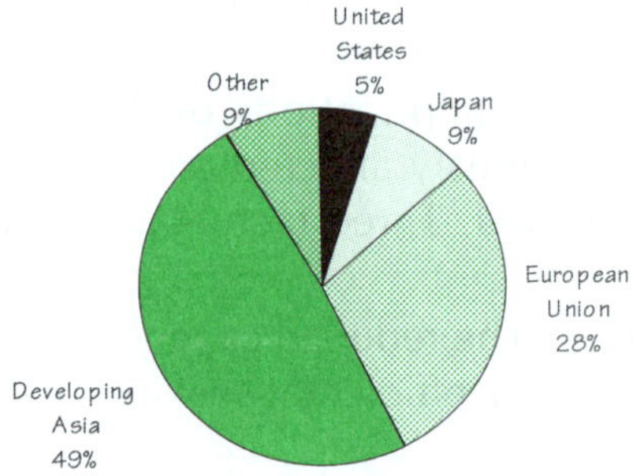

Source: UNCTAD, FDI/TNC database.

Note: data are for approved investment. Data for developing Asia include data for China, Hong Kong, China, Indonesia, Republic of Korea, Malaysia, Singapore, Taiwan Province of China and Thailand.

Figure VII.19. FDI in Central Asia, by region/country of investment, cumulative flows, 1993-1996

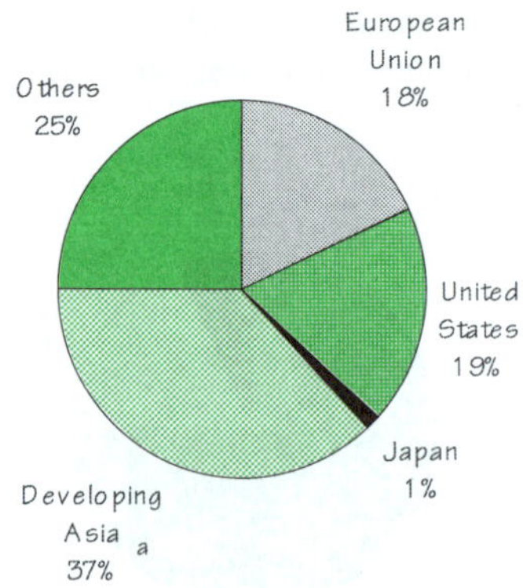

Source: UNCTAD, FDI/TNC database.

Note: data are for approved investment. Data for developing Asia include data for China, Hong Kong, China, Indonesia, Republic of Korea, Malaysia, Philippines, Singapore, Taiwan Province of China and Thailand.

Box VII.13. Impact of the Asian financial crisis on Japanese FDI

Japan has a particularly important role in FDI flows into Asia, and many of the considerations discussed in relation to Asian developing-country TNCs are also relevant to Japanese TNCs.

The crisis has meant considerable difficulties for Japanese TNCs. Like other Asian TNCs, their stock has lost value because of devaluations by affected countries, and they too have dollar-denominated debt to service. Asia, including the most affected countries, is an important host region for Japanese TNCs (European Commission and UNCTAD, 1996), and Japan is in turn important for Asia. Japanese TNCs held almost one-third of the inward FDI stock of the Republic of Korea in 1996, and about one-quarter of it in the ASEAN 4 (Indonesia, Malaysia, the Philippines and Thailand) in the mid-1990s. In comparison, the European Union held around 15 per cent and the United States 13 per cent of the inward stock of the ASEAN 4.[a]

When it comes to the adverse effects of depressed demand on the profitability of foreign affiliates focusing on local markets, it is relevant to note that local market-oriented FDI is fairly important for Japanese affiliates in Asia. It accounted for 60 per cent of the total sales of these affiliates in South, East and South-East Asia in 1995 (box figure 1) and exports to the countries of the region accounted for another 15 per cent.[b] The future prospects of local market-oriented FDI in Asia from Japan depend critically on how fast East and South-East Asia overcomes the crisis. The critical industries for Japanese foreign affiliates are chemicals, transport equipment, and iron and steel, in which the proportion of local sales is particularly high (Japan, MITI, 1998a, table 2-21-6). In the transport industry, for example, three-quarters of the Japanese affiliates incurred losses in 1997.[c]

Box figure I. Japan: destination of sales of Japanese affiliates abroad in manufacturing, 1995

(Billions of dollars and percentage)

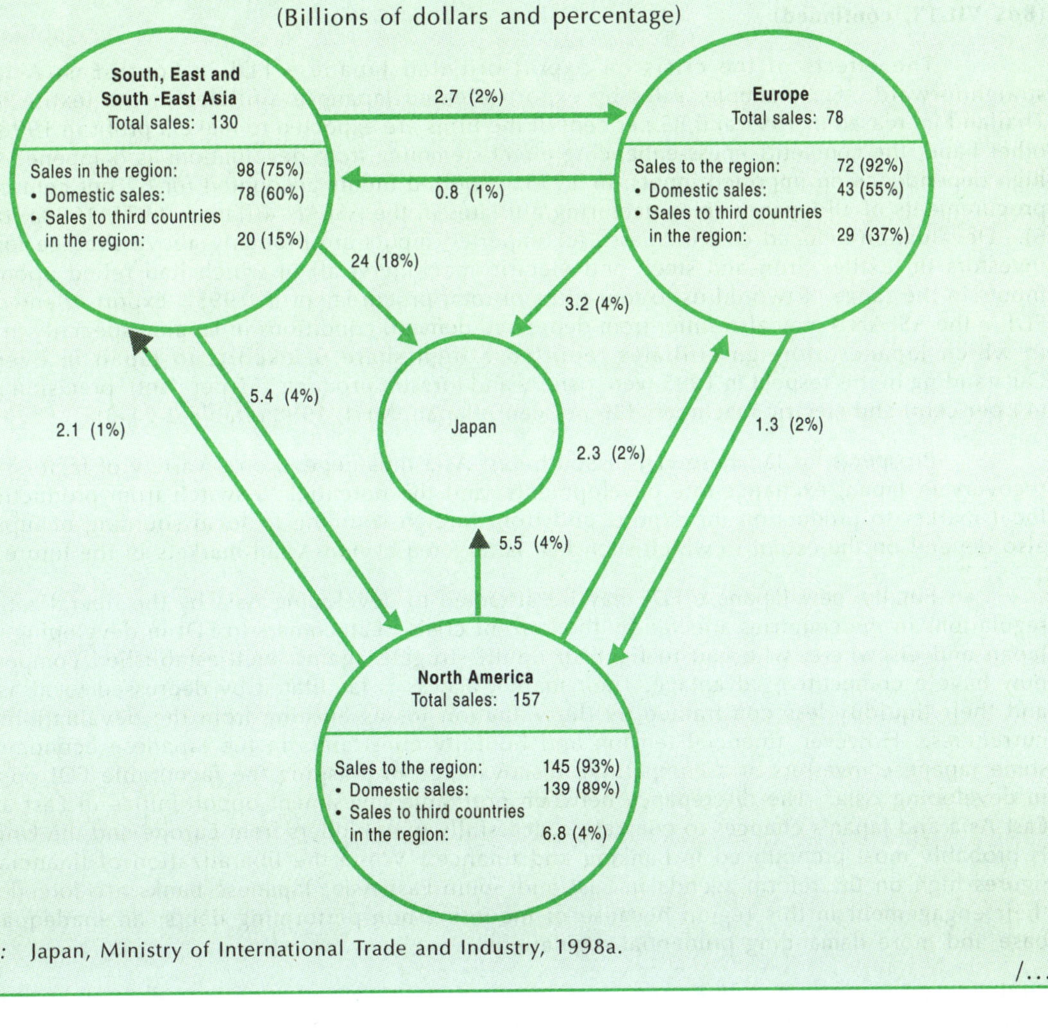

Source: Japan, Ministry of International Trade and Industry, 1998a.

/...

- Asset-seeking FDI, as discussed above, may be attracted by the new opportunities in Asia.

- Efficiency-seeking FDI may also be attracted by falling costs in Asia.

- Market-seeking FDI depends mainly on the size and income growth of host countries. The contraction of markets in the affected countries in Asia is thus likely to reduce some market-seeking FDI in the short-to-medium term, but this does not necessarily mean a switch to other regions. That would depend on how attractive other regions are, either relatively or absolutely. Furthermore, FDI is not a zero-sum game and it need not be assumed that FDI for other regions must involve some withdrawal from Asia.

Thus the extent of a shift of FDI from the crisis-affected countries to other regions is likely to be limited. Indeed, an overwhelming majority (90 per cent) of the UNCTAD/ICC survey respondents who indicated that they expect to increase their investments in Latin America and the Caribbean and in Central and Eastern Europe did *not* intend to reduce their investments in East and South-East Asia in the short-to-medium term. Furthermore, nearly 50 per cent of them also indicated that they expect to *increase* their investments in

(Box VII.13, continued)

The effects of the crisis on export-oriented Japanese FDI in South-East Asia are less straightforward. For example, sales by export-oriented Japanese affiliates in the textile industry in Thailand increased in 1997 and 85 per cent of the firms are expected to make a profit in 1998.[d] On the other hand, the competitiveness-enhancing effect stemming from devaluations is dampened by a fairly high dependence on imported inputs: in 1995, imported inputs accounted for 62 per cent of the total procurements of all Japanese manufacturing affiliates in the ASEAN 4 (Japan, MITI, 1998a, table 2-22-6). Devaluation-induced cost increases for imported inputs are probably above average for Japanese investors in textiles, iron and steel, and electric machinery, all of which had relied upon imported inputs in the range of two-thirds to four-fifths of total procurement in 1995. Export-oriented Japanese FDI in the ASEAN 4 may also suffer from depressed demand conditions in Japan, especially in industries in which Japanese foreign affiliates reported a high share of exports to Japan in overall sales. Outstanding in this respect in 1995 were fishery and forestry products (65 per cent), precision machinery (44 per cent) and electric machinery (36 per cent) (Japan, MITI, 1998a, table 2-21-6).

Prospects for Japanese FDI in South-East Asia thus depend on a variety of factors: economic recovery in Japan, exchange-rate developments, and the potential to switch from production for the local market to production for exports and from foreign sourcing to local sourcing of inputs. They also depend on the extent to which such FDI is targeted at non-Asian markets in the future.

Finally, new Japanese FDI may be attracted to developing Asia by the liberalization of FDI regulations in the countries affected by the current crisis. Latecomers to FDI in developing Asia, from Japan and elsewhere, who had to fight an uphill struggle against well-established competitors may now have a competitive advantage. Their market access is facilitated by depressed local asset prices and their liquidity less constrained by the valuation losses ensuing from the devaluations of Asian currencies. However, financial tension and liquidity constraints in the Japanese economy may put some Japanese investors at a competitive disadvantage in grasping the favourable FDI opportunities in developing Asia. The discrepancy between profitable investment opportunities in East and South-East Asia and Japan's chances to compete successfully with bidders from Europe and the United States is probably most pronounced in banking and finance. While the liberalization of financial services figures high on the reform agenda in East and South-East Asia, Japanese banks are forced to reduce their engagement in this region because of mounting non-performing debts, an inadequate capital base and more demanding prudential regulations.

/...

East and South-East Asia. In other words, firms see profitable investment opportunities across the spectrum of developing countries and do not necessarily see these countries as alternatives to one another. This is also confirmed by survey responses of foreign affiliates in Thailand, only 1 per cent of which indicated an intention to shift investments to other countries (box VII.6).

Table VII.5. Short- and medium-term investment intentions of the world's leading TNCs in the light of the Asian crisis, by host region

(Percentage)[a]

Item	East and South-East Asia	South Asia	Latin America and the Caribbean	Central and Eastern Europe	Africa
Increase	23	18	37	27	11
No change	55	61	47	52	62
Reduce	11	5	2	2	3
No answer	10	16	14	18	24

Source: UNCTAD/ICC global survey, 1998.

[a] Percentage of respondents indicating a particular response.

(Box VII.13, concluded)

All in all, however, Japanese TNCs seem to be responsive to the changing environment in South-East Asia and some of them could turn the recent events to their advantage. This view is supported by the increasing exports of Japanese affiliates in developing Asia. Examples abound. Sharp, Matsushita, Hino Motors, as well as automobile parts and component firms, all plan to increase exports from their affiliates in Asia.[e] Furthermore, in the UNCTAD/ICC survey, two-thirds of Japanese TNCs stated that their investment plans in the region remained unchanged, and almost one-fifth of them even intended to increase their investments despite the crisis. Another survey undertaken in mid-1998 indicates that between 44 per cent (Indonesia) and 75 per cent (Philippines) of Japanese TNCs in the countries affected by the crisis expected to maintain or increase their FDI in the next one-to-three years. Declines are expected to be most pronounced in Indonesia (56 per cent) and Thailand (53 per cent) (box figure 2).[f]

Box figure 2. Investment plans of Japanese TNCs in the next 1-3 years in the most affected Asian countries, compared to the FDI level in 1997, 1998

(Percentage)

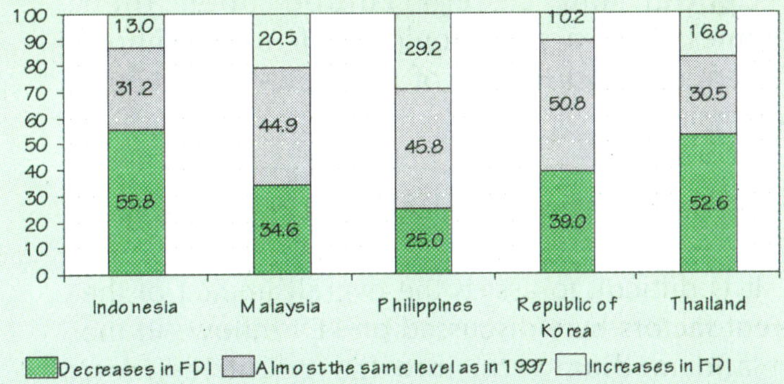

Source: Tejima, 1998.

Source: UNCTAD.

[a] Based on UNCTAD, FDI/TNC database.

[b] These shares, taken together, were somewhat lower, however, than the corresponding shares for Japanese affiliates in Europe and North America. Similarly, United States affiliates in South, East and South-East Asia have lower shares of domestic sales (53 per cent in 1994) than in Europe (65 per cent) (United States, Department of Commerce, 1997c).

[c] *Nihon Keizai Shimbum*, 16 December 1997, p. 11.

[d] ibid.

[e] *Nihon Keizai Shimbum*, 20 April 1998 and 5 May 1998.

[f] This survey was conducted by the Research Institute for International Investment and Development, Export-Import Bank of Japan, in the mid-1998; see Tejima, forthcoming.

Figure VII.20. FDI in South Asia by region/country of investment, cumulative flows, 1993-1996

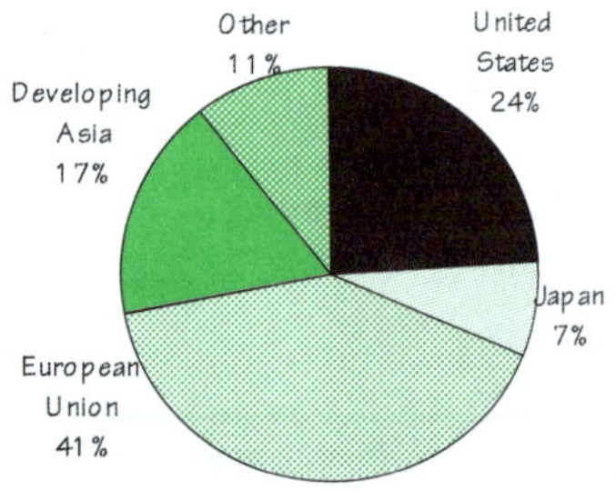

Source: UNCTAD, FDI/TNC database.

Note: data are for approved investment. Data for developing Asia include data for China, Hong Kong, China, Indonesia, Republic of Korea, Malaysia, Singapore, Taiwan Province of China and Thailand.

Indeed, FDI flows to Latin America and the Caribbean and to Central and Eastern Europe already showed a substantial upward trend before the Asian crisis (chapters VIII and IX). Central and Eastern Europe, in any event, is a region which offers much potential for further increases. As regards Africa, the characteristics of the host countries in that region and in Asia are so different from those of Asian host countries that there is little direct competition between the two regions (chapter VI).

Finally, it needs to be recognized that, with or without a crisis, Asia's share in the total FDI going to all developing countries would decline in any case, as other regions improved their FDI appeal. In other words, the relative FDI position Asia attained during the past decade is being readjusted as Latin America and the Caribbean emerge from their "lost decade" and Central and Eastern Europe open their economies. Thus a shift would occur even without any interregional diversion of FDI flows on account of the crisis.

4. Conclusions

It is difficult to assess the overall impact of the different factors here discussed on FDI inflows in the short and medium term into the countries most affected by the crisis (table VII.7). The extent to which the financial crisis spills over into the real sector and the way it is handled will determine how it affects the size and nature of TNCs' operations in the region. There is a growing consensus that economic growth will slow in 1998 and perhaps also in 1999, but there is far less agreement over how much it will fall and how quickly the affected economies will recover

Figure VII.21. FDI in Latin America and the Caribbean, by source region/country of investment, cumulated flows, 1993-1996

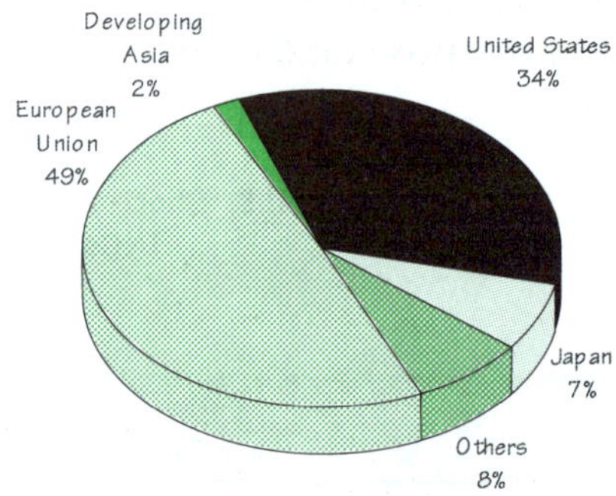

Source: UNCTAD, FDI/TNC database and national sources.

Figure VII.22. FDI in Africa, by source region/country of investment, cumulated flows, 1993-1996

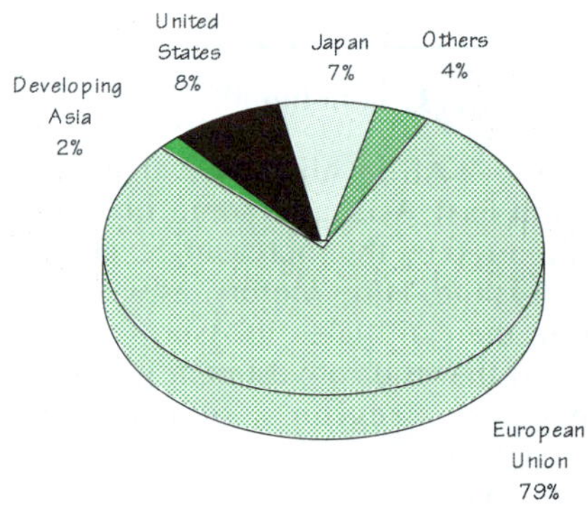

Source: UNCTAD, FDI/TNC database and national sources.

Figure VII.23. Central and Eastern Europe, by source region/country of investment, cumulated flows, 1993-1996

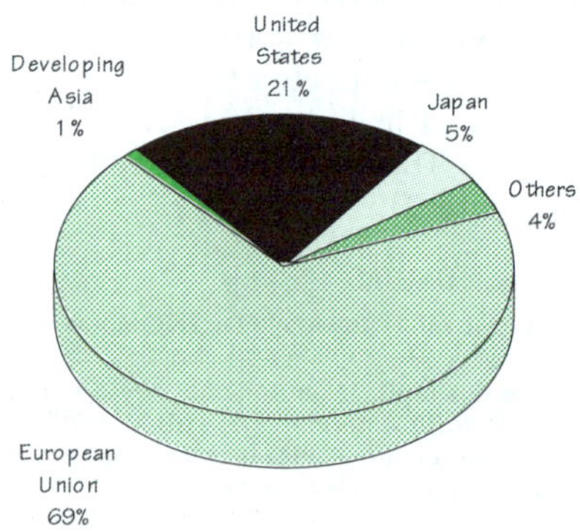

Source: UNCTAD, FDI/TNC database and national sources.

(International Monetary Fund, 1997b; UNCTAD, 1998a). Much will depend upon how quickly the efforts to stabilize the financial markets and external financing positions of the crisis-affected economies are broadly successful.

Table VII.6. The share of Asian developing countries in FDI in Japan, the United States and the European Union, 1990s
(Percentage)

	Flows		Stock	
Economy	1983-1990	1990-1995	1985	1995
European Union	0.9	1.1 [a]	0.1	0.5 [b]
United States	0.7	2.4 [c]	0.6	1.3 [d]
Japan [e]	3.3 [f]	6.3	4.0 [f]	4.6 [g]

Source: UNCTAD, 1997d.

[a] 1990-1993.
[b] 1993.
[c] 1990-1994.
[d] 1994.
[e] On approval/notification basis.
[f] Only Hong Kong, China.
[g] 1990 stock from Hong Kong, China plus 1991-1995 flows from South, East and South-East Asia.

When it comes to FDI determinants proper, many of them remain attractive. First, regulatory frameworks, which were already quite open and hospitable to FDI prior to the crisis, have become even more so. Second, business facilitation has been strengthened and promotional efforts have been accelerated. Further policy measures and promotional efforts could be considered, especially to deal with the short- and medium-term effects (box VII.14). Third, as regards the economic determinants of investment, the size of host country markets is bound to contract in countries affected by the crisis and thus discourage some market-oriented investments in the short term. FDI, like domestic investment, is pro-cyclical, declining during recessions and rising as recovery gathers speed, although FDI stock does not fall as a rule and foreign affiliate output and employment show less cyclical variation than FDI flows (Ramstetter, 1998). The crisis also creates opportunities for FDI, specifically for efficiency-seeking and asset-seeking FDI in the form of devaluation-driven cost advantages and cheaper and more easily available assets.

The combination of these factors should allow for cautious optimism about FDI flows in the short- to medium-term to the region as a whole, including the five most affected countries. There will, of course, be variations among countries depending on the speed and thoroughness with which they master the crisis and restore macroeconomic stability. If flows are maintained or increased, that would contribute to counteracting, even if modestly, the expected fall in income and employment and would help in the process of recovery.

The extent to which the three sets of FDI determinants mentioned above translate into actual FDI inflows depends upon the longer-term views TNCs take of the future of the region. If they take a negative view, they will be reluctant to invest, especially as far as market-seeking FDI is concerned, and cautious in acquiring assets in the region. They might even consider divesting. If they take a positive view, they would position themselves in the region strategically, by strengthening their portfolio of locational assets to service markets, access resources and improve efficiency. In brief, they would see the crisis as an opportunity for competitiveness-enhancing FDI. The rationale for taking the second view would be that the economic fundamentals of the region remain sound and attractive for FDI. These include high domestic savings rates, skilled and flexible human resources, substantial infrastructure capacity and access to regional markets.

The same determinants are crucial for the long-term prospects for FDI flows to Asian countries. This includes flows from Asian TNCs, even from the most affected countries, since the competitive strengths of firms headquartered in the region remain unchanged and they can be expected to resume their outward FDI once financial strength is restored. Expectations of a continued growth of FDI flows to Asia in the long run are supported by the findings of the UNCTAD/ICC Survey (box VII.9). The great majority (over four-fifths) of the respondents reported that their confidence in the region as an investment destination had remained unchanged (figure VII.24). The pattern of the findings in this regard is similar across firms in different sectors (figure VII.25) and from different home regions (figure VII.26). Similar findings emerge from surveys of foreign affiliates in Thailand (box VII.6), the Republic of Korea[28] and Malaysia's electrical and electronics industries (box VII.8). In each case, the majority of the respondents expressed their confidence in the long-term prospects of those economies as profitable destinations for FDI. Even if these positive expectations may have become more cautious since the surveys were conducted in the first half of 1998, they reflect the fact that Asia remains an attractive region despite the crisis.

Table VII.7. Summary of effects of the crisis and possible implications for FDI in the short and medium term in and from countries affected by the crisis

Host-country variable affected	Changes related to/ resulting from the crisis	Implications for inward FDI	Implications for outward FDI
Exchange rate	Large depreciation of currencies leading to: - Lower home-currency costs of establishing or expanding affiliates for TNCs from countries with stable exchange rates. - Lower costs and prices, in terms of currencies of home and third countries with stable exchange rates.	Encourages all kinds of FDI with locally-sourced assets/inputs for establishment/expansion (+) Encourages export-oriented FDI and efficiency-seeking FDI (+)	Discourages outward FDI due to: - Higher costs in home country currency to finance new investments (-) - Higher costs in home country currency to support existing foreign operations (-)
GDP (market size)	Reduced rate of GDP growth, leading to reduction of or slower expansion of demand/market size	Discourages domestic or regional market oriented FDI (-)	Could discourage some intra-regional outward FDI (-)
Asset prices	Drastic decline of asset prices. Depreciation of foreign currency value of assets in existing affiliates.	Lower costs for entry, encouraging greenfield, and (especially) cross-border M&As (+) Reduces financial capacities of some foreign affiliates, with adverse effects on reinvestment (-)	
Supply of capital/finance	Lower supply due to: - tightened monetary policy; - interest-rate increases; - heavy debt burden; - lower supply of foreign capital by banks and portfolio investors.	Creates opportunities for FDI generally, especially by larger firms, due to exit of some domestic or other firms adversely affected by capital/ liquidity constraints (+) Reduces availability of and increases costs for foreign firms to raise funds in host-country markets, affecting FDI by some (especially smaller) firms adversely (-) Increases opportunities for FDI through M&As by foreign firms (+)	Discourages outward FDI due to difficulties in financing new investments and difficulties in financing existing operations (-)
FDI policy changes	Further liberalization of inward FDI policy; some controls on capital flows	Creates opportunities for new FDI (+)	Discourages outward FDI (-)

Source: UNCTAD.

Note: '+' and '-' signs indicate possible increase or decrease in FDI.

As regards the implications of the crisis for Asian countries not directly caught up in the crisis, a number of them -- China, Vietnam, the Asian LDCs and the countries of Central Asia -- that have depended heavily on outward investments from some of the crisis-stricken countries, as well as competed with them for export-oriented FDI, are likely to receive lower FDI inflows in the short-to-medium term. Effects on FDI to South Asian countries as well as to Asian newly industrializing economies are likely to be modest. Indeed, they might become

Box VII.14. Policy measures

Since continued FDI flows could make a useful contribution to restoring economic growth and maintaining export levels in Asian countries affected by the crisis, policy measures to encourage them deserve attention. Some specific measures that might be considered in this context include the following:

- Governments of the affected countries could make an extra effort - perhaps helped by regional and international institutions - to provide information about greenfield and joint venture investment opportunities, especially in activities they consider as priority areas. Special attention might be given to industries whose prospects remain (or have become) particularly attractive, such as those in which costs are denominated in local currencies while revenues are obtained in hard currencies. Attractive opportunities could also be highlighted in component or other supplier sectors that are often less visible to foreign investors than final-goods manufactures.

- Countries might pay greater attention to providing assistance to dynamic and innovative small- and medium-sized enterprises which are also transnationalizing and the role of which as potential partners in international networks and technology alliances would thus be enhanced. These enterprises are even more likely than large TNCs to generate early beneficial effects, such as improvements in the trade balance, the use of local subcontracting, joint venture operations and the transfer of appropriate technologies (UNCTAD, 1993a). They often face obstacles related to their size and governments need to address these if they wish to attract small- and medium-term enterprises (UNCTAD, 1998g) as investors.

- Where appropriate, Asian TNCs could consider adopting international accounting standards as soon as possible.

- Within the framework of regional integration arrangements and other fora for international cooperation -- such as the ASEAN Investment Area -- Asian countries could formulate joint measures to encourage FDI and its contributions to the economies of member countries.

- Home countries whose tax policies allow the use of optional reserves and grant tax deductions for the depreciated value of their firms' foreign affiliates could consider recognizing the present circumstances in Asian countries as meeting the criteria for such reserves and deductions.

- Home country political-risk-insurance programmes for investors could consider expanding their coverage of foreign affiliates to sudden, steep and debilitating devaluations of foreign currencies.

- Countries that are hosts to foreign affiliates of Asia-based TNCs in financial distress could consider temporary measures of assistance to help sustain existing affiliates, where this is warranted. This would be akin to investment incentives for new inward FDI projects, but adapted to the special present circumstances in the post-investment stage. Care would need to be taken in formulating these measures to avoid introducing undue discrimination against other investors.

Naturally, such efforts would have to be embedded in more general policies aimed at restoring macroeconomic stability and economic performance, as well as strengthening institutional capacities to advance the process of development. While specific efforts aimed at maintaining and increasing FDI flows can make a contribution to the process of overcoming the impact of the crisis, much more will depend on the quality of those more general policies.

more attractive to foreign investors looking for new locations for investment in the light of reduced scope for expanding FDI in the most affected countries.

Finally, the extraregional impact of the crisis will probably be modest, although the possibility of adverse indirect effects cannot be ruled out if a global economic slowdown were to occur. The changing parameters for outward FDI by Asian TNCs are unlikely to affect other regions substantially, since Asian firms have not yet made significant inroads as investors in countries outside the region. The likelihood of diversion of non-Asian investors from Asia and, especially from the most affected Asian countries to other regions are also quite limited. In any event, FDI flows to Africa, Latin America and the Caribbean, and Central and Eastern Europe had already showed an upward trend independently of the Asian crisis, because of favourable economic performance and other changes conducive to FDI. This suggests that, while there may be no diversion of FDI to those regions because of the crisis, Asian countries face increasing competition for FDI.

Figure VII.24. Long-term prospects: overall response of companies worldwide

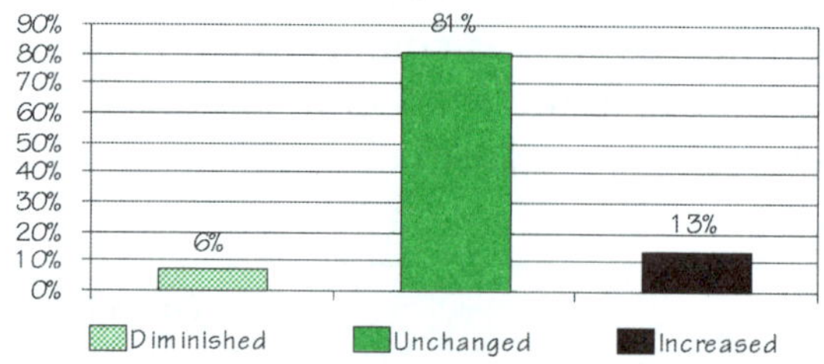

Source: UNCTAD/ICC global survey, March 1998.

Figure VII.25. Long-term prospects: company intentions by sector

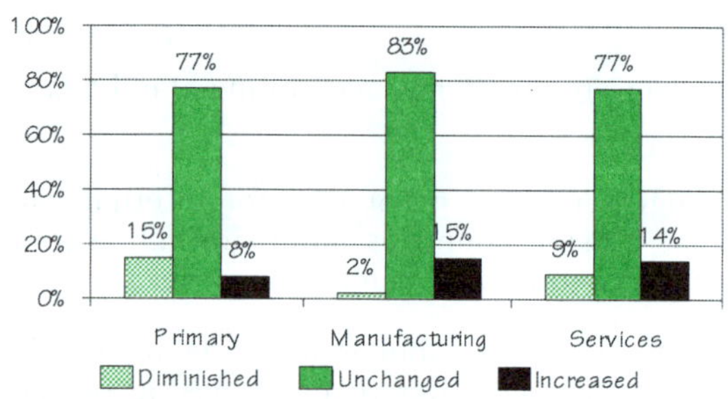

Source: UNCTAD/ICC global survey, March 1998.

Figure VII.26. Long-term prospects: company intentions by home region of parent company

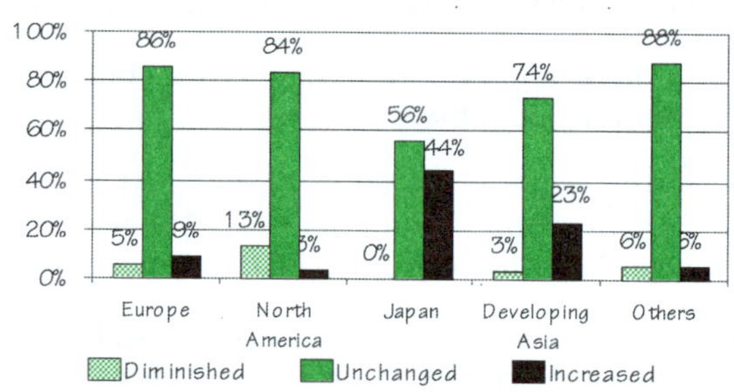

Source: UNCTAD/ICC global survey, March 1998.

Notes

1 "Kazakstan sells 60% of largest oil firm", *International Herald Tribune*, 13 May 1997, p. 15; and "China buys oil firm in Kazakstan: $4 billion deal aims to bolster supplies", *International Herald Tribune,* 6 June 1997, p. 17.

2 Chairperson's statement at the Second Asia-Europe Meeting, London, 3-4 April 1998 (Internet: http://asema.flo.goVII.uk/asema/texts/closing/chairmans.statement/).

3 The deal was made during the first half of 1997 between the SETDCO Group, based in Indonesia, and Mangistaumunaigaz in Kazakhstan.

4 Based on UNCTAD's FDI/TNC database and data provided by the World Bank.

5 Levels of FDI flows into the most affected countries which are similar to past levels in dollar terms would therefore signal increased interest by TNCs in Asia.

6 The value of M&A sales in the five most affected countries to cross-border purchasers was $6.5 billion in the first half of 1997, $5.8 billion in the second half of 1997 and $5.5 billion in the first half of 1998. (Data provided by KPMG Corporate Finance).

7 Inflation in South-East Asia is estimated to be 13 per cent in 1998, compared with 6 per cent in 1997 (ADB, 1998, p. 10).

8 However, the extent of the improvement will depend on how far export-oriented foreign affiliates rely upon imported inputs.

9 Based on data obtained from SECOFI, Mexico City, Mexico.

10 Based on data from United States, Department of Commerce, 1997a, tables III.F.2, III.F.7 and III.F.8.

11 "Fall out from Asian Turmoil starts to affect multinationals", *Financial Times,* 14 January 1998.

12 "Mazda closes Thai plant", *Financial Times,* 27 July 1998.

13 "Big three auto makers go shopping for deals in Asia", *International Herald Tribune*, 21 January 1998.

14 "GM decides not to bid for Kia, leaving race to Ford", *International Herald Tribune*, 22-23 August 1998.

15 "ASEM 2 Statement: The Financial and Economic Situation in Asia", Asia-Europe Summit Meeting, London, 3 April 1998.

16 "The Asia-Europe Investment Promotion Action Plan", in European Commission and ASEM, *Terms of Reference for the ASEM Investment Experts Group*, Economic Ministers' Meeting, Makuhari, Japan, 27-28 September 1997, mimeo..

17 *"Financial Times Global 500", Financial Times,* 1997 (n.d.).

18 *"Financial Times Global 500", Financial Times,* 1998 (n.d.).

19 It is only since the outbreak of the financial crisis that Asian TNCs appear to have adopted strategies to avoid currency risk.

20 Foreign affiliates of developed and other country firms in the crisis-stricken countries that have also borrowed heavily face less of a problem since their home country currencies have maintained their value vis-à-vis the dollar.

21 As discussed in chapter V (box V.I), divestment is a normal occurrence, a part of changing corporate strategies. It is therefore not always easy to determine the reason for a particular divestment. In the specific circumstances mentioned, a firm may judge it preferable to sell foreign assets than to sell domestic ones, especially at unfavourable exchange rates. It is also difficult to ascertain to what extent some of these are distress sales. For example, Hyundai Electronics Industries Co. of the Republic of Korea is reported to have sold its affiliate Symbios (acquired from AT&T Corp. for $300 million in 1994) in the United States to Adaptec Inc., a Silicon valley company, at a price of $775 million, a price considered low by analysts. ("Asian firms beat retreat from U.S.", *Financial Times,* 4 March 1998.)

22 Ibrahim (1997). This proposal was recently reiterated by the National Economic Advisory Council of Malaysia, which proposed, as a part of its plan to strengthen the ringgit, "to reduce or suspend reverse investment temporarily with the assurance that overseas investment would be allowed when conditions improve". ("Measures to strengthen ringgit", 1998 Star Publications (M) Bhd (No. 10894-D). (Retrieved on 28 July 1998 from http://the star.com.my/archives/neac).

23 According to preliminary data obtained from the Bank of Korea, outward FDI from the Republic of Korea during the first quarter of 1998 decreased by 51 per cent as compared to outward FDI over the same

period in 1997. As for Malaysia, outward FDI declined from RM1.9 billion in the first quarter of 1997 to RM1.1 billion in the first quarter of 1998 (Malaysia, Bank Negara, 1988; figures subject to revision).

24 The survey on the implications of the financial crisis for outward FDI was conducted by the UNCTAD secretariat and the Federation of Korean Industries in March 1998 and covered the 100 largest TNCs headquartered in the Republic of Korea. A total of 46 firms responded to the survey questionnaires, some of which were followed up with interviews.

25 Cited in *SUNS: South-North Development Monitor*, No. 4193, 16 April 1998.

26 Intraregional FDI in South Asia, particularly from the Republic of Korea, gained momentum during the mid-1990s. For example, in 1996, the pace of investment from the Republic of Korea in India started outstripping that of India's traditionally important trade and investment partners. Firms from the Republic of Korea had planned to invest $4 billion in India between 1997 and 1999 (UNCTAD, 1997d). That growth momentum may have suffered because of the financial crisis.

27 However, the Republic of Korea accounts for 11 per cent of the FDI stock in Romania and 6 per cent of that in Poland.

28 Based on the results of the UNCTAD/FKI survey, 1998.

CHAPTER VIII

LATIN AMERICA AND THE CARIBBEAN

A. Trends

Inward foreign direct investment (FDI) in Latin America and the Caribbean was comparatively low between the early 1970s and the early 1990s, and even declined during a part of the "lost decade" of the 1980s. This was largely a consequence of poor economic performance, mainly resulting from the debt crisis in the region. From 1991 onwards, however, this trend was reversed, as Latin America began to receive substantial and growing FDI inflows. Even Mexico's 1994-1995 peso crisis did not discourage foreign *direct* investors. Indeed, during 1995-1997, FDI flows into the region grew more than twice as fast as flows to all other developing countries as a whole.

In 1997 Latin America and the Caribbean attracted a record $56 billion in FDI inflows.[1] This represented an increase of 28 per cent over 1996. FDI flows to the region accounted for 38 per cent of total flows into all developing countries in 1997 and the increase in inflows accounted for two-thirds of the overall increase in flows into all developing countries. Thirty countries received more FDI inflows in 1997 than in 1996 (annex table B.1), including thirteen of the top twenty recipients (figure VIII.1). Among the larger recipients, the countries that experienced the largest percentage increases were Venezuela, Mexico and Brazil and, among the smaller ones, Aruba, Saint Vincent and the Grenadines, Saint Lucia and Suriname (figure VIII.2).

In terms of their role in host economies, FDI inflows reached 11 per cent of gross fixed capital formation in the region during 1994-1996, with ratios for the largest countries ranging from around 7 per cent to over 40 per cent (annex table B.5 and figure VIII.3). This compares to ratios of 8 per cent for South, East and South-East Asia, and 5 per cent for the world as a whole. FDI stock as a percentage of gross domestic product was even higher for Latin America and the Caribbean as a whole, reaching 17 per cent in 1996. This compares with 16 per cent for South, East and South-East Asia and 11 per cent for the world as a whole. Ratios for the largest economies of the region ranged from around 8 per cent to 29 per cent, and ratios for some smaller Caribbean nations exceeded 100 per cent (annex table B.6 and figure VIII.4).

Figure VIII.1. Latin America and the Caribbean: FDI flows into the top 20 recipient economies in 1997 and flows to the same economies in 1996[a]

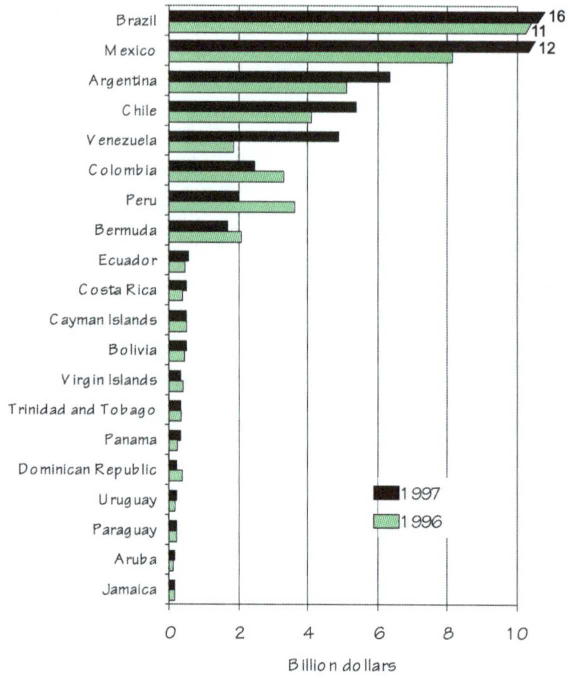

Source: UNCTAD FDI/TNC database.

In absolute terms, the larger economies of the region were, not surprisingly, by far the largest recipients of inward FDI flows in 1997 (figure VIII.1), with Argentina, Brazil and Mexico accounting for 62 per cent of total flows to the region. Venezuela, Peru, Colombia and Chile accounted for a further 26 per cent. Among the remaining countries, the absolute level of FDI flows received was low, although significant relative to their size in most cases, as measured in relation to either gross fixed capital formation or GDP (figures VIII.3 and VIII.4). Indeed, inward FDI flows relative to gross fixed capital formation were much higher for many smaller countries than for the larger ones (figure VIII.3).

Within this context of overall growth, significant shifts in attractiveness occurred among the larger recipient countries. The rising star was Brazil. During the first half of the 1990s, Brazil had fallen behind the rest of the region, receiving FDI inflows well below what might have been expected given the size of its economy and its total FDI stock, which continued to be the largest in the region even during these years. In 1996, Brazil regained its position as the region's champion by overtaking Mexico, which had held this position for the preceding six years (box VIII.1). Brazil consolidated its position in 1997, attracting more than $16 billion in FDI and increasing its lead over Mexico, the second largest recipient.

Flows of FDI into Central America not including Mexico amounted to $1.2 billion in 1997, up from $900 million in 1996. Flows into Caribbean countries, excluding offshore financial centres, increased from an annual average of $800 million in the 1990-1993 period to $1.2 billion during 1994-1997. The largest recipient among the financial centres was Bermuda, accounting for over half the flows into the entire subregion in 1990-1997 (figure VIII.5). Among Central American countries, Costa Rica was particularly successful in attracting FDI into more sophisticated activities. In 1997, INTEL, a major United States chip maker, started work on a $500 million regional production and testing system and other high-tech companies are following suit.

The United States remains the largest investor in Latin America and the Caribbean, with outward FDI of $24 billion in 1997 and cumulative flows of $121 billion during 1990-1997. Flows from Europe, which have been growing steadily since 1994, came primarily from Germany, France, Spain and the United Kingdom. Investment flows from Japan were comparatively low but have been growing recently. FDI inflows from developing Asian economies, mainly from the Republic of Korea and Taiwan Province of China, increased considerably, mostly in apparel to supply the United States market. Intraregional investment has also grown noticeably (UNCTAD, 1997a; Garay and Vera, 1998).

Key destination industries for United States FDI in the region are automobiles, electronics and other manufacturing, mainly in Mexico, and apparel in the Caribbean Basin. European FDI is concentrated most strongly in services and manufacturing in the larger MERCOSUR countries: Argentina and Brazil. (MERCOSUR also includes Paraguay and

Figure VIII.2. Latin America and the Caribbean: growth of FDI, top 20 economies, 1996-1997

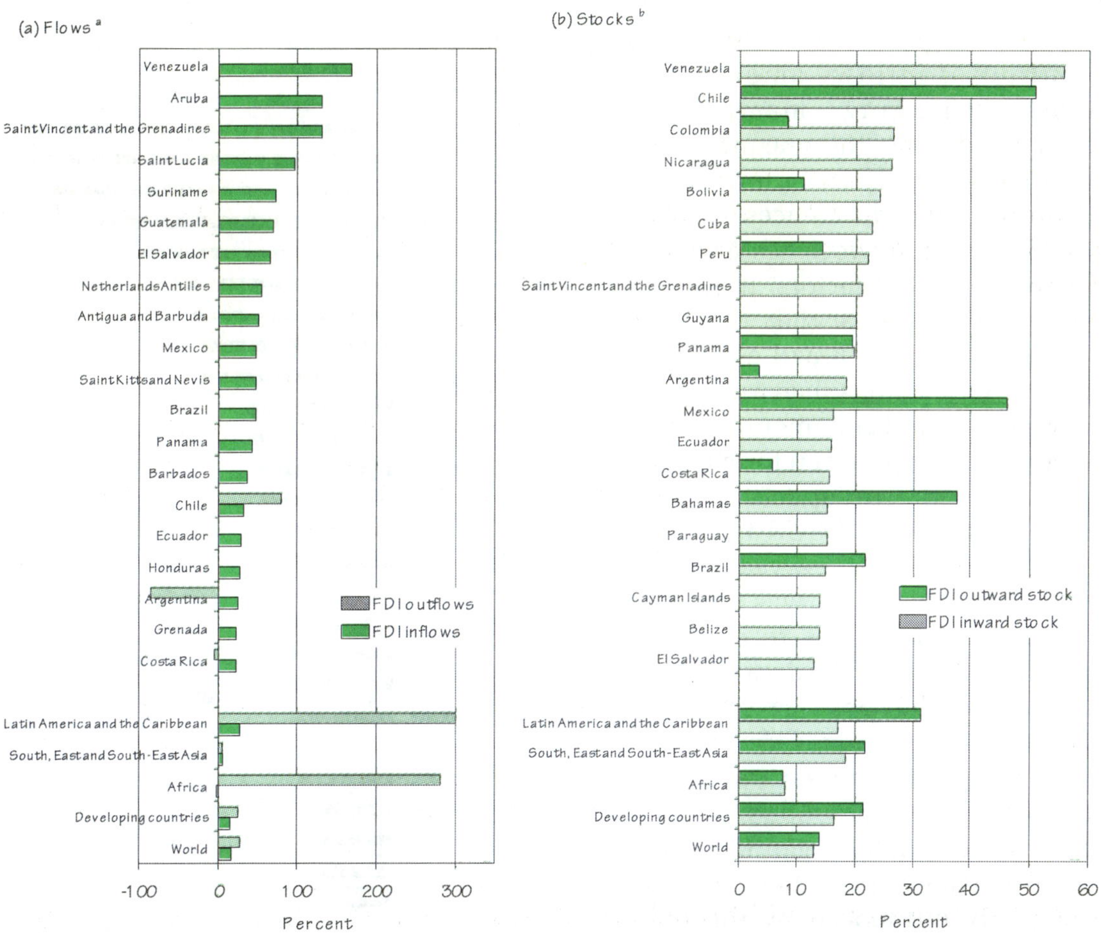

Source: UNCTAD, FDI/TNC database.

[a] Ranked on the basis of the magnitude of FDI inflows growth rates.
[b] Ranked on the basis of the magnitude of FDI inward stock growth rates.

Uruguay, with Bolivia and Chile as associated members.) In terms of size, 33 of the largest 100 companies in the region (ranked by sales) are foreign affiliates (América Economía, 1997/1998). The largest foreign firms in the region are mostly affiliates of United States and European firms in manufacturing industries, mainly in automobiles, and in oil extraction (table VIII.1)

Several factors help to explain both the restored attractiveness for FDI of the region as a whole and the changes in the distribution of FDI flows among the region's economies. These include macroeconomic stabilization, trade liberalization, wide-ranging privatization programmes, deregulation of policies regarding private investment (both domestic and foreign) and advances in regional integration (CEPAL, 1998a, p. 4). Macroeconomic fundamentals, in particular, have improved considerably in recent years (CEPAL, 1997). The average annual rate of GDP growth rose from 1 per cent in the 1980s to 3.5 per cent in the 1990s, with per capita growth rates rising from -1.0 per cent to 1.8 per cent in the current decade. The average rate of inflation dropped from 200 per cent in 1990 to 11 per cent in 1997, and the export index of the region (1990=100) has more than doubled since 1990, surpassing the 200 mark in 1997.

With regard to the distribution of inflows among countries, changing macro-economic conditions, the unequal timing of reforms (particularly privatizations) and differences in regional integration processes all seem to be important factors. It is indeed no coincidence that the relative importance of Brazil as a recipient of inflows has increased as macroeconomic fundamentals have improved, the pace of reforms increased and the prospects of integration in the MERCOSUR area consolidated in the past few years. Mexico, on the other hand, was the main recipient of inflows to the region in the first half of the decade, when, before the peso crisis, macroeconomic conditions seemed most promising and integration through NAFTA was consolidating. The pace of flows into Argentina, on the other hand, appears to have been strongly influenced by the timing of the privatization process and integration in MERCOSUR, with inflows growing faster since 1993.

Figure VIII.3. Latin America and the Caribbean: FDI flows as a percentage of gross fixed capital formation, top 20 economies, 1994-1996 (annual average)[a]

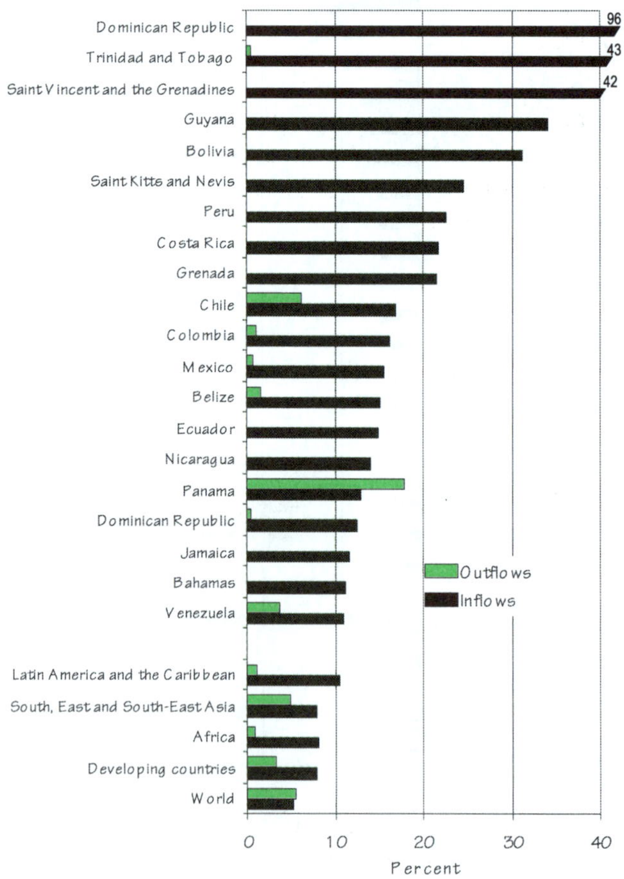

Source: UNCTAD, FDI/TNC database.

[a] Ranked on the basis of the magnitude of FDI inflows as a percentage of gross fixed capital formation.

Independently of the factors that help to explain changes in the regional composition of FDI inflows in the past few years, transnational corporations (TNCs) have shown great flexibility in adapting to shifting opportunities in the region. As a result, concerns about the sustainability of FDI flows into Latin America have proved unfounded (Nunnenkamp, 1997b). The principal concern was that privatization-related acquisitions of state assets by foreign investors, particularly during the 1990-1993 period, would have only a one-off effect on inflows. Instead, during 1994-1996 major new investments were made in new assets or in the modernization of privatized companies and of existing foreign affiliates (figure VIII.6), often in the form of new greenfield investments. This trend appears to be most pronounced in manufacturing, in which certain industries have attracted substantial FDI, in an increasing number of cases through mergers and acquisitions (M&As). Indeed, as privatization-related opportunities in some countries have declined, M&As have gained increasing prominence. In 1997, M&As by foreign firms in the region represented 13 per cent of the world total, surpassing the corresponding value for Asia (see annex table B.7).

Corporate investment strategies in Latin America and the Caribbean have been driven by a variety of different strategic motives on the part of TNCs, including the pursuits of efficiency, markets and resources (table VIII.2). The pursuit of strategic assets, on the other hand, has not played a major role thus far. The motivations behind individual investment projects vary according to the recipient country, the home country and the economic sector in which the investment is made:

- In MERCOSUR the main driving force of FDI appears to be market expansion. In the context of increasing global competition among TNCs, firms from Europe, the United States and Asia, particularly in the automobile and chemical industries, have invested strongly in the MERCOSUR area to defend and increase their shares in these markets, which are expanding rapidly on account of economic

Figure VIII.4. Latin America and the Caribbean: FDI stock as a percentage of gross domestic product, top 20 economies, 1996[a]

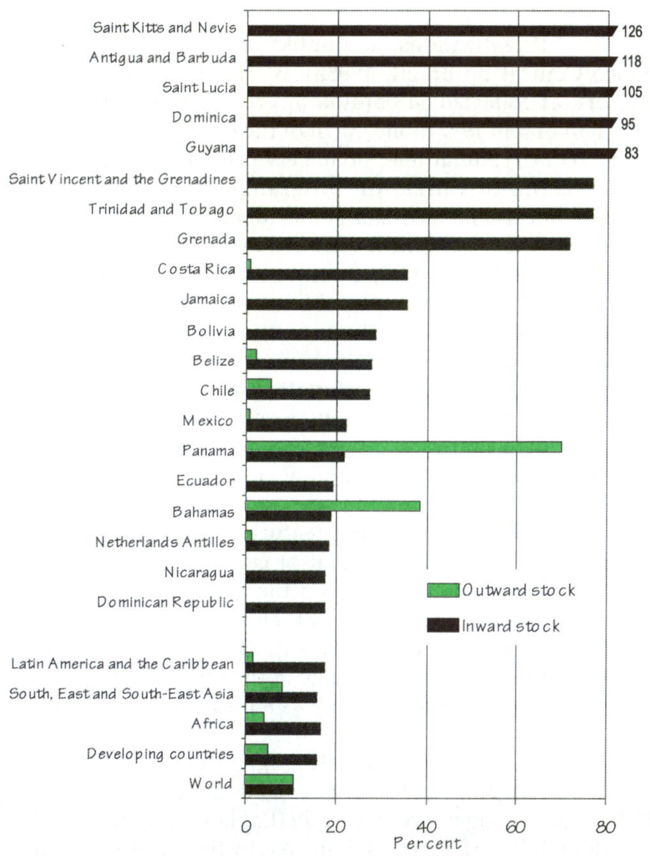

Source: UNCTAD, FDI/TNC database.

[a] Ranked on the basis of the magnitude of FDI inward stock as a percentage of gross domestic product.

Box VIII.1. Brazil: the new champion

FDI flows into Brazil increased from $1.3 billion in 1993 to $16.3 billion in 1997. This was mostly the result of macroeconomic stabilization (especially the successful implementation of the Plan Real), the attractiveness of a large market, the opening up of the economy and the privatization programme.

Recent FDI flows have gone to a variety of industries, through different mechanisms. Among these are: the growth of greenfield FDI and cross-border M&A; aimed strategically at acquiring or improving shares in the growing markets of Brazil and MERCOSUR; the participation of foreign investors in the widespread privatization of state-owned firms; the growth of FDI aimed at penetrating Brazil's domestic and regional market (MERCOSUR) in protected industries like automobiles; and the rationalization, reorganization and restructuring of established foreign affiliates.

Some 600 M&As took place between January 1992 and 1997. In these operations, 61 per cent of the buyers were foreign firms (mainly from North America) and 59 per cent of the transactions involved firms in the manufacturing sector. The most targeted industries were food and beverages (14 per cent), metallurgy (13 per cent), electrical machinery (12 per cent) and pharmaceuticals (8 per cent). Within the service sector, which accounted for one-third of all M&As in this period, finance and insurance, telecommunications and information services were the prime recipients. This surge in M&As is partly the result of the fact that domestic industries, particularly in the case of paper, automobile components and steel, have had outdated capital stock and limited access to international financial services and have therefore been unprepared to compete on a global basis. Thus, a number of these firms have been sold to TNCs or have formed alliances with TNCs looking for cost-efficient ways of accessing the expanding and profitable local market (FIPE, 1998).

Privatizations, accounted for almost 27 per cent of FDI flows over the past two years (Brazil, Banco Central do Brazil, 1998a). Between January 1991 and April 1998, the Brazilian federal and state authorities collected $43 billion in privatization revenues excluding the transfer of entreprise debts, more than half of it in 1997 alone. Most of the revenues came from the sale of enterprises in the electronics industry (42 per cent), cellular telephone networks (19 per cent), steel (13 per cent) and mining (8 per cent). The first phase of the privatization programme, involving the transfer of aircraft, mining, steel, chemicals, petrochemicals and fertilizer plants to private hands, was completed with a minority participation by foreign investors. Thus, until now only around 30 per cent of the privatized assets have been acquired by foreign investors (BNDES, 1998). In state-level sales, mainly in electronics and telecommunications (cellular telephones), the involvement of foreign firms has been somewhat higher (38 per cent and 40 per cent, respectively).

Most of the foreign investors participating in privatizations originate in the United States, followed by Spain (16 per cent of the revenues), Chile (8 per cent), Sweden (5 per cent) and France (4 per cent). Bell South (United States) has been the most prominent, having paid, in association with local investors, $3 billion for the right of operation of cellular telephones in two of the ten zones of Brazil.

Another interesting feature of Brazil's recent FDI flows is its sectoral pattern, which has been significantly different from that of earlier years. Indeed, during 1990-1993, only a small part of FDI was directed into manufacturing and that was aimed principally at the rationalization of existing enterprises (Bielchowsky and Stumpo, 1996). However, from 1991 onwards, as growth accelerated and the economy stabilized, there was an increase in FDI in the manufacturing sector aimed at serving local and regional markets. The most salient change in the sectoral composition of FDI, however, is the increase in the share of services in total inflows, mainly as a result of privatizations in that sector.

On the other hand, although foreign affiliates already established in Brazil account for the bulk of recent investment, there is also a considerable number of newcomers, particularly in the automobile industry. Indeed, according to a recent study (Laplane and Sarti, 1997), FDI by newcomers has been mostly concentrated in automobiles (51 per cent), followed by the electronics industry (19 per cent), chemicals and pharmaceuticals (9 per cent) and food and beverages (6 per cent). Most FDI has been used to establish new production facilities (58 per cent), followed by the modernization of existing facilities (23 per cent).

/...

Table VIII.1. Latin America: the 20 biggest foreign affiliates, by sales, 1996

Rank	TNC	Home country	Industry	Host country	Sales (Millions of dollars)
1	Volkswagen	Germany	Automotive	Brazil	7 000
2	Chrysler	United States	Automotive	Mexico	6 455
3	General Motors	United States	Automotive	Mexico	6 346
4	General Motors	United States	Automotive	Brazil	5 433
5	FIAT	Italy	Automotive	Brazil	4 743
6	Shell	United Kingdom/Netherlands	Petroleum	Brazil	4717
7	Carrefour	France	Commerce	Brazil	4 510
8	Ford	United States	Automotive	Mexico	3 879
9	Ford	United States	Automotive	Brazil	3 830
10	Nestlé	Switzerland	Food products	Brazil	3 592
11	Telefónica	Spain	Telecommunications	Argentina	2 751
12	Gessy Lever	United Kingdom/Netherlands	Chemical products	Brazil	2 749
13	Texaco	United States	Petroleum	Brazil	2 639
14	Pepsi	United States	Food products	Mexico	2 600
15	Exxon	United States	Petroleum	Brazil	2 470
16	Mercedes Benz	Germany	Automotive	Brazil	2 131
17	IBM	United States	Machinery and equipment	Brazil	1 950
18	Telecom	France	Telecommunications	Argentina	1 930
19	Shell	United Kingdom/Netherlands	Petroleum	Argentina	1 866
20	Nissan	Japan	Automotive	Mexico	1 800

Source: ECLAC, Unit on Investment and Corporate Strategies.

(Box VIII.1, concluded)

Perspectives in the automobile industry continue to be promising as, with sales of more than 2 million units per year, Brazil's industry has become a favourite destination for the world's leading automobile companies:

* Daimler-Benz (Germany) moved its assembly operation of 2,000 trucks and buses from Argentina to Brazil. The company now has two assembly plants in Brazil, together producing 40,000 units per year, and expects to invest $1 billion by the year 2000.
* Ford (United States) plans to invest $1 billion in the year 2000 to produce two new models . This would increase its Brazilian investment to $3.5 billion (Bustos, 1998).
* Fiat (Italy) announced plans to invest $1 billion by the year 2000 to produce a new model (Palio) to be exported from its plant in Betim to other developing countries.
* By the same year, Volkswagen (Germany) plans to build another factory in Parana to export vehicles to its affiliates in Mexico.
* General Motors (United States) has announced its intention to invest $3.6 billion.

It is not only flows into the automobile industry that are expected to grow. Given the evolution of the economy and advances in the process of reforms (particularly privatization), the prospects for future inflows continue to be bright across most industries. As to the external environment, the impact of the Asian crisis on FDI flows into Brazil has been limited. This is mostly explained by the fact that FDI represents a long-term commitment to Brazil's economy and is associated to an important extent with the dynamics of the privatization process. Indeed, preliminary figures indicate that, in the first four months of 1998, FDI inflows have exceeded $4.2 billion (Brazil, Banco Central do Brasil, 1998b), an amount equivalent to twice the total inflows in 1994.

Source: UNCTAD.

growth and advances in the process of regional integration. To some extent, this has also been the case in such services as banking, telecommunications, power generation, and distribution and commercial activities. Partly because of strong historic links with the subregion and because of their focus on local markets, European TNCs have shown particular preference for the MERCOSUR region (IDB-IRELA, 1998).

Figure VIII.5. The Caribbean: FDI inflows by major host economies, 1990-1997

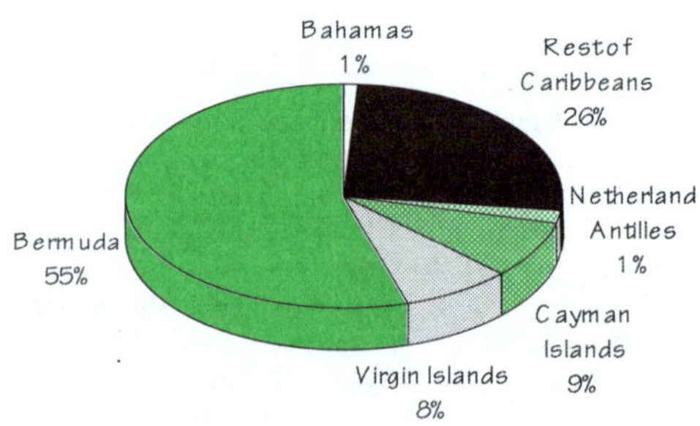

Source: UNCTAD, FDI/TNC database.

- In Mexico and the Caribbean Basin, manufacturing FDI has mostly been efficiency-seeking and motivated by efforts to improve exports, overwhelmingly to the United States market, taking advantage of relatively low labour costs, geographic proximity to the United States, and the opportunities opened by NAFTA and the Caribbean Basin Initiative. The lead in this respect has been taken by United States TNCs attempting to obtain a competitive edge in their home market vis-à-vis other firms. On a much smaller scale, Asian and European TNCs have also followed this trend.

- In the services and primary sectors, both market-seeking and resource-seeking appear to be the major motivations of TNCs from all regions, which have taken advantage of liberalization and deregulation processes ocurring across most Latin American economies. In these sectors, which had been off-limits to foreign capital in previous decades, wide-ranging privatization programmes have provided opportunities for expansion. This is the case, for example, in energy, financial services, mining and petroleum.

Apart from the region's attractivess because of its markets, labour and natural resources, government policy has played a crucial role in generating the conditions under which the current boom in FDI has occured. In this respect, the case of Brazil is again illustrative. As discussed, the recovery of FDI inflows coincided with comprehensive macroeconomic stabilization and structural adjustment measures (Nunnenkamp, 1997b), among which the Plan Real of 1993-1994 was a decisive step. With its fiscal consolidation programme of November 1997, the Government of Brazil has further underscored its determination to sustain macroeconomic stability. As to future FDI flows, much will depend on the pace of Brazil's privatization programme now under way; the

Figure VIII.6. Latin America and the Caribbean: FDI inflows by mode of entry, in selected countries of Latin America,[a] 1990-1996

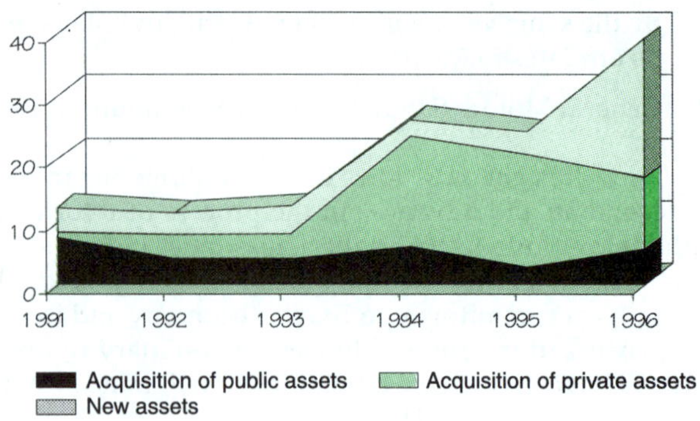

Source: UNCTAD, FDI/TNC database.

[a] Includes Argentina, Bolivia, Brazil, Chile, Colombia, Ecuador, Mexico, Paraguay, Peru, Uruguay, Venezuela.

privatization of Telebras at the end of July 1998 for $19 billion (of which 63.6 per cent came from foreign investors) may well be indicative in this respect. Similar experiences can be found in most Latin American countries, in which the acceleration of institutional reforms and the stabilization of the economy, as well as the implementation of specific policies to attract FDI, have very much coincided with or preceded the growth of inflows.

Regional integration policies have also provided a stimulus to FDI in Latin America. The large subregional integration schemes, MERCOSUR and NAFTA, have generated new opportunities for foreign investors by enlarging and enhancing access to markets and applying the rules-of-origin principle on a regional basis. This facilitates the establishment of regional production systems, as witnessed by the automobile industry. Investment in the automobile industries of Mexico, Brazil and Argentina has indeed been substantial, amounting to $12 billion during 1990-1995; further projects worth $23 billion have been announced for 1996-2000 (Voduzeck and Calderon, 1998). Still, the effect of regional integration on overall FDI in Latin America, and on the distribution of FDI within the region, is far from clear, as it is almost impossible to isolate the effects of regional integration from the effects of such domestic-policy reforms as macroeconomic stabilization, privatization and opening to world markets. The effects also vary among integration schemes:

- FDI flows driven by regional integration are most likely to have occurred in the case of Mexico's integration with the economies of the United States and Canada in the framework of NAFTA. An example is the integration of Mexican plants into the corporate production systems of United States automobile TNCs. Something similar appears to be taking place in textile and apparel production.
- In the case of MERCOSUR, both Brazil and Argentina have attracted much higher FDI inflows since the constitution of that market in 1995, as, on a smaller scale, has Uruguay which aspires to be the administrative centre of the subregion.

Table VIII.2. Latin America and the Caribbean: FDI in terms of types of corporate strategies, 1997

Sector	Corporate strategy			
	Efficiency-seeking	Resource/asset-seeking: Natural resources	Resource/asset-seeking: Assets	Market-seeking (national or regional)
Primary		Petroleum and gas: Venezuela, Argentina, Colombia Minerals: Chile, Argentina, Peru		
Manufacturing	Automotive: Mexico Electronics: Mexico, Caribbean Basin Apparel: Caribbean Basin and Mexico			Automotive: (MERCOSUR) Chemicals: Brazil Food products: Argentina, Brazil Cement: Colombia, Dominican Republic, Venezuela
Services				Financial: Mexico, Chile, Argentina, Venezuela, Colombia Telecommunications: Argentina, Chile, Brazil, Peru Electric energy: Colombia, Brazil, Argentina, Central America Gas distribution: Argentina, Chile, Colombia

Source: ECLAC, Unit on Investment and Corporate Strategies.

- Regional integration may not (yet) have greatly improved the FDI prospects of smaller countries in the region. A recent analysis of the distribution of German FDI within MERCOSUR, the Andean Group and the Central American Common Market showed that integration-induced FDI, if there was any, was still primarily directed to the traditionally preferred host countries (Nunnenkamp, 1998).[2] With few exceptions, these countries consisted of the largest and most advanced members of regional integration schemes.

One interesting new FDI feature in Latin America and the Caribbean is the fast growth of *outward* flows, even though systematic statistical information remains scarce (figure VIII.2). Outward FDI flows from the region reached $9 billion in 1997, a rise of almost $7 billion over 1996. In some cases, this represented the response of firms to the opportunities offered by the privatization of companies in their sectors in other countries of the region; in others they appear to have responded to the incentive provided by subregional integration schemes. Some examples are:

* Outward FDI by Chilean electricity companies in the electricity generation industry of Argentina, Brazil, Colombia and Peru; in the the financial industry in Argentina, Colombia, Venezuela and Peru; and in the commercial sector in Argentina and Peru.

* Outward FDI by Mexican companies in cement in the United States, Europe and various Latin American countries (including the Dominican Republic, Venezuela, Colombia and Guatemala); in the glass industry in the United States; in food and drink in Venezuela, Argentina and Nicaragua; and in financial services in Argentina.

* Within MERCOSUR, outward FDI by Argentinian companies in the agriculture/food industry of Brazil; Brazilian outward FDI in the automobile and autoparts industries and the financial industry in Argentina; and Uruguayan outward FDI in the commercial sector of Argentina.

This trend towards increased outward FDI can be expected to continue, especially if regional growth and integration efforts maintain their momentum in the future, and should generate a platform for the growth and development of regional TNCs.

* * *

The prospects for FDI remain positive in the region. The financial crisis in Asia does not seem to have affected FDI flows into Latin America and the Caribbean so far and may not do so in the future either. One reason for this is that the bulk of FDI in the region is still oriented towards local or regional markets. Export-oriented FDI may, in principle, be more affected as devaluations in East and South-East Asia have improved that region's relative locational attractiveness. But FDI diversion is likely to remain modest as the exports of East and South-East Asia and Latin America to major markets (the United States and Western Europe) are more or less complementary.[3] Still, 37 per cent of the firms that replied to the UNCTAD/ICC survey on the effect of the Asian financial crisis on FDI to and from Asia indicated that they would expect to expand their engagement in Latin America and the

Caribbean,[4] although some reduction in FDI from crisis-affected developing Asian economies is likely in the short and medium term, given the financial constraints Asian TNCs currently face. On the other hand, export-oriented FDI in manufacturing in the region is mostly directed to the United States market and based in Mexico or the Caribbean Basin. It is not likely that devaluations in Asia will seriously affect the competitiveness of these operations, given the relatively low transaction costs associated with them on account of geographic proximity and the institutional framework within which they take place (NAFTA; Caribbean Basin Initiative; HTS 9802 tariff item).[5]

In the immediate future, the main forces driving FDI into the region should remain strong. Although they have become less important for the region as a whole, privatizations (especially in Brazil) will remain an important factor. Investment in the modernization of previously privatized firms and of foreign affiliates in the services sector should also continue, as TNCs compete for fast-growing local markets. Some manufacturing industries are also likely to draw in new FDI as TNCs consolidate their regional production systems, especially in the automobile industry. Efficiency-seeking FDI should continue to grow as United States TNCs continue to take up the opportunities provided by Mexico, Central America and the Caribbean as export platforms, particularly to serve their home market. European and Asian TNCs may also become active in this respect, as they follow the lead of United States TNCs. Finally, TNCs in home countries that have not paid much attention to the region thus far -- including, eventually, Japan -- may increasingly turn to it, if the region's strong economic performance continues.

B. FDI, exports and the balance of payments

Prior to recent trade policy reforms and the increasingly outward orientation of countries in Latin America and the Caribbean, TNCs used FDI largely to overcome import barriers. This applied especially to FDI in such capital-and-skill-intensive manufacturing industries as chemicals and transport equipment in which the region lacked comparative advantage.[6] Thus, foreign firms established local production facilities in order to serve local markets and, as import protection supported high rates of return, the efficiency and international competitiveness of these facilities was not a major concern.

The policy environment for FDI has, however, changed substantially in the region over the past few years. After the difficult decade of the 1980s, most countries stabilized their economies and implemented --or began to implement-- large-scale structural reform programmes. They have privatized a large number of state-owned firms and opened their economies to international competition. While the timing, intensity and scope of these reforms have differed across countries, they appear to have acquired "full and generalized force in the late 1980s and early 1990s" (Edwards, 1995, p. 8).

Since FDI has boomed in this new environment, it seems pertinent to ask whether its nature has also changed. What factors have motivated TNCs to return with such force to the region in the 1990s? Have recent FDI flows into the region increasingly sought resources and efficiency rather than markets? The answers to these questions have implications for a wide range of development dimensions. Given the region's long history of problems with its *external balance*, however, this section concentrates on this particular dimension. More specifically, since the region no longer enjoys the high rates of return guaranteed by protectionism, has recent FDI become more export-oriented as might be expected? And, whatever the answer to this question, what are the possible implications of recent and current FDI flows for the balance-of-payments position of the region?

1. The export orientation of FDI

When the model of import-substitution industrialization predominated in much of Latin America and the Caribbean until the 1980s, the export performance of the region was poor. In the 1990s, the countries of Latin America and the Caribbean have certainly improved in this respect.[7] Overall, exports have soared from $15 billion in 1970 to $288 billion in 1997 (IMF, 1997a; IDB, 1998). The export propensity of foreign affiliates was low until the 1990s. Indeed, through the 1980s, exports by majority-owned manufacturing affiliates of United States firms in Latin America and the Caribbean, for example, never went much over 20 per cent of total sales, while they never fell below 60 per cent in the Asian economies (table VIII.3).

The partial evidence available in this area appears to show that modest changes are occuring. The export propensity of United States manufacturing affiliates in Latin America as a whole increased to 26 per cent in 1995 (table VIII.3) and the contribution of *all* foreign affiliates to the manufactured exports of Brazil reached 48 per cent in 1996 (SOBEET, 1997). More generally the 33 largest foreign affiliates among the 100 largest companies in the region generated 37 per cent of the total exports of these companies in 1996 (América Economía, 1997/1998).

Even if structural policy conditions seem appropiate for integration into the world economy, several factors can affect the export propensity of foreign affiliates. Among these are exchange-rate management, the sectoral composition of FDI and the existence of specific policies to attract export-oriented FDI, particularly in the manufacturing sector. In recent years, all of these elements have combined in different forms across different subregions of Latin America and the Caribbean to determine quite different patterns of FDI.

Even though trade liberalization and other structural reforms may be aimed at integration into the world economy, good macroeconomic management is an important condition of their success. In particular, FDI is not likely to become more world-market-oriented if exchange-rate policies work against the international competitiveness of local production. This, of course, applies equally to domestic companies. In Latin America, this point is specially relevant as the

Table VIII.3. Latin America and the Caribbean: export propensities of United States majority-owned foreign affiliates in manufacturing,[a] 1983-1995
(Percentage)

Region/economy	1983	1986	1990	1995
Latin America and the Caribbean	15	20	21	26
Argentina	12	16 [b]	26 [b]	19
Brazil	16	17	14	15
Chile	20	0	40	28
Colombia	4	4 [b]	5	12
Costa Rica	0	0	35	46
Dominican Republic	0	0	49	88
Ecuador	12	2	21 [b]	20
Jamaica	1	46	4	49 [b]
Mexico	20	34	29	40
Peru	3	1	7	8 [b]
Venezuela	1	2	9	11
South, East and South-East Asia and the Pacific	60	63	63	51
Asian newly industrializing economies	70	64	65	63 [c]

Source: United States, Department of Commerce, various years.

[a] Exports as per cent of total sales.
[b] Total sales minus local sales as per cent of total sales.
[c] 1994.

exchange rate has frequently been used as a nominal anchor in macroeconomic stabilization programmes. This has been done to break inflationary expectations but has typically led to the real appreciation of national currencies (Nazmi, 1997), impairing the export performance of both domestic companies and foreign affiliates.

The sectoral composition of FDI is also relevant in its potential effect on exports. In general, investments in the primary sector are mostly export-oriented. FDI in the secondary sector has a more mixed character, depending on the size of the local market, relative comparative advantages and the policy environment. Companies operating in the tertiary sector are very strongly, if not exclusively, focused on local markets, although FDI in this sector can have indirect effects on the export performance of other sectors of the economy. These sectoral distinctions are important as they allow some indirect evidence to be obtained on current trends in the export orientation of FDI in the region.

FDI in the primary sector tends to generate a stream of foreign-exchange revenues, as local sales are typically of marginal importance. FDI in this sector constituted 12 per cent of FDI inflows in 1990-1996 for a group of countries accounting for two-thirds of inflows in 1996 (table VIII.4). Examples of natural-resource-seeking FDI are mining in Argentina, Chile and Peru, as well as petroleum and gas in Colombia and Venezuela. The region's share of FDI in this sector has basically remained constant throughout the 1990s,[8] although with considerable variation among countries. Resource-seeking FDI accounted for almost half the flows to Chile and Colombia during 1990-1996, while its share was exceptionally low in Brazil, dropping to less than 1 per cent in 1996.

FDI in service industries provides a sharp contrast to FDI in natural resources, as most services are not tradable across borders and thus generate only marginal export revenues. In Brazil, FDI in services accounted for about two-thirds of total inflows during 1990-1996, the highest share among the countries for which data are available, except for Peru (table VIII.4). For seven Latin American countries taken together, the share of FDI in services doubled in total inflows from 31 per cent in 1990 to 61 per cent in 1993, but declined thereafter to 47 per cent in 1996. In the 1990-1996 period as a whole, however, FDI in services constituted more than a half of the total.[9] Privatization programmes in various Latin American and Caribbean countries were the major policy determinant underlying the shift of FDI into services, including infrastructure, energy and telecommunications.

Although recent investment in services in the region is in non-tradable industries, technological change is allowing some services, especially business-related services like data processing and accounting, to become tradable (Sauvant, 1990; UNCTAD, 1994b). Advances in micro-electronics have offered some developing countries opportunities to generate foreign currency receipts by supplying such services to clients all over the world. While Latin America and the Caribbean have lagged behind Asian countries (notably India) in this respect, FDI in these service industries may offer some limited opportunities for catching up. Other service industries in which FDI can contribute directly to exports include tourism, air transport and distribution networks. In Argentina, for example, investment in the generation, transport and distribution of electricity and gas is thought to offer good prospects of exports to neighbouring countries, especially Brazil and Chile. In Costa Rica, opportunities for investment have been identified in call centres to support the electronics industry, which could then be developed to support other potentially exportable services such as telemarketing. Nonetheless, most FDI in the tertiary sector in Latin America and the Caribbean still goes into non-tradable services. In 1996, none of the foreign affiliates in the service sector belonging to the top 100 companies in the region reported any exports (América Economía, 1997/1998).

Table VIII.4. FDI inflows in selected Latin American countries, by sector, 1990-1996

(Millions of dollars)

Country	1990	1991	1992	1993	1994	1995	1996
Argentina	1 836	2 439	4 014	2 514	3 116	4 783	5 090
Primary	..	..	1 015	234	452	454	1 014
Manufacturing	..	..	438	677	1 601	1 779	1 538
Services	..	..	2 561	1 603	1 063	2 550	2 538
Brazil [a b]	2 857	1 437	1 395	7 054	9 520	4 860	10 409
Primary	4	100	53	-88	252	..	96
Manufacturing	1 340	427	-585	1 730	1 654	..	1 843
Services	1 377	831	1 884	5 241	8 041	..	4 749
Chile[c]	1 320	982	999	1 730	2 531	3 028	4 801
Primary	837	471	588	923	1 849	1 818	1 052
Manufacturing	104	271	145	495	362	378	951
Services	379	240	266	312	320	832	2 798
Colombia	501	457	729	959	1 667	2 317	3 322
Primary	324	314	521	585	904	859	1 172
Manufacturing	160	131	89	217	398	614	675
Services	17	12	119	157	366	844	1 475
Mexico [b d]	2 400	6 012	7 397	4 535	11 503	8 430	6 122
Primary	157	80	120	213	104	142	94
Manufacturing	1 199	3 088	4 013	1 281	6 153	3 902	3 498
Services	1 019	2 710	3 079	3 092	5 232	4 380	2 530
Peru[e]	45	33	176	129	2 808	1 094	618
Primary	2	9	129	-	310	173	91
Manufacturing	17	15	10	54	52	147	331
Services	26	9	37	75	2 445	774	197
Venezuela	..	224	1 950	375	701	333	395
Primary	..	19	28	14	40	40	25
Manufacturing	..	187	400	280	347	127	235
Services	..	18	1 522	81	314	167	135
Latin America[f]	8 958	11 583	16 659	17 295	31 846	24 845	30 757
Primary	1 325	992	2 454	1 880	3 911	3 487	3 543
Manufacturing	2 819	4 120	4 509	4 733	10 568	6 946	9 071
Services	2 817	3 820	9 468	10 561	17 781	9 546	14 422

Source: UNCTAD, based on data provided by ECLAC, Unit on Investment and Corporate Strategies.

[a] Refers to gross incomes, not including capital repatriation to the country of origin or the FDI income under intra-firm loan form. Figures for the period 1990-1995 correspond to stock variation, whereas those for 1996 correspond to flow distribution.

[b] Includes unspecified FDI.

[c] Refers only to FDI operations developed under L-D 600, including related loans. Does not include FDI incomes under Article 14 of the "Summary of International Exchange Guidelines of the Central Bank".

[d] Including imports of capital goods by in-bond processors, starting from 1994 but not including re-invested earnings or intra-firm loans.

[e] Not including intra-firm loans. Corresponding to a stock variation.

[f] Only countries included in this table.

Note: figures presented in this table are not necessarily based on balance-of-payments data. So they do not correspond to FDI cited elsewhere in the *World Investment Report 1998*.

Investments in the tertiary sector can, however, still have important indirect export-enhancing effects, although they are almost impossible to measure. While FDI in non-tradable service industries typically depends heavily on imports of capital goods, it can be important for modernizing FDI stocks and improving export capabilities in manufacturing industries. Indeed, infrastructure and service bottlenecks have been among the biggest burdens on the international competitiveness of local production in Latin America.[10] Some of the recent service inflows may thus make a useful contribution to eventual exports in other sectors.

On the whole, however, a large proportion of primary and tertiary operations have their relative export capacity pre-defined by markets and technologies. Given their large scale of production and the location of their main markets, companies in the primary sector generally have very little choice but to export large proportions of their production. Given the non-tradable character of their products, on the other hand, most companies operating in the service sector must generally gear their production to local markets. Thus, if there have been any major changes in the export orientation of FDI in the region, they should mostly be found in the *manufacturing* sector, as TNCs operating in this sector have a much clearer choice between producing for exports and producing for local markets.

During the 1980-1994 period, the share of manufactures in overall exports from Latin America increased from 15 per cent to almost 50 per cent (UNCTAD, 1997e). This increase, however, has not necessarily allowed the countries in the region to keep up with their main competitors in this sector from other regions. The region's share in OECD imports of manufactures (mainly apparel, automobiles, electrical machinery and electronic equipment) rose from 1.8 per cent in 1980 to 3.1 per cent in 1995, a rather modest increase in comparison with developing Asia, which doubled its share to 15.3 per cent in 1995 (Mortimore et al., 1997).

With respect to the operations of TNCs, trade liberalization in the region seems to have provided greater opportunities to integrate foreign manufacturing affiliates into the regional or global networks of their parent companies. This applies particularly to United States TNCs, for which the significance of intra-firm trade is a relevant indicator. The share of intra-firm trade involving foreign manufacturing affiliates majority-owned by United States TNCs increased from 17 per cent in 1989 (UNCTAD, 1995a, figure II.4) to 22 per cent in 1995 in the total trade between the United States and Latin America and the Caribbean (United States, Department of Commerce, 1997a). The export propensity of the foreign manufacturing affiliates among the largest 100 companies in the region increased even more, from 18 per cent in 1994 to 34 per cent in 1996, compared to 10 and 22 per cent for domestic firms (table VIII. 5). Thus, as a whole, FDI in manufacturing industry does seem to have played a role in improving the region's export performance.

Table VIII.5. Latin America and the Caribbean: export propensity of the top 100 companies in Latin America in selected countries,[a] by sector of activity and company status, 1994 and 1996

Region/Country	1994		1996	
	Domestic firms	Foreign affiliates	Domestic firms	Foreign affiliates
Latin America				
(all sectors)	15,9	15,1	31,0	26,2
Manufacturing	9,5	17,7	21,5	33,7
Brazil (all sectors)	4,7	5,2	6,1	4,3
Manufacturing	8,8	5,9	22,4	5,3
Mexico (all sectors)	17,2	48,6	29,3	71,4
Manufacturing	10,3	48,6	20,6	71,4

Source : América Economía, 1997/1998.

[a] Export propensity is defined as the ratio of exports to sales multiplied by 100.

What this means is that, in some manufacturing industries, foreign investors' adjustment to the new policy environment in Latin America and the Caribbean has resulted in a progressive integration of parts of the region into regionalised or globalized production based on comparative advantage. However, both export achievements and the role FDI has played in them vary considerably. The integration of manufacturing affiliates in the region into global production networks is an uneven phenomenon. Company strategies in this respect have differed in accordance with the countries (or subregions) in which they invest and with respect to their country of origin. The strongest movement towards integration of manufacturing affiliates into global production networks has taken place in Mexico and the Caribbean Basin, pushed forward by TNCs from the United States. Manufacturing companies investing in South America, particularly in MERCOSUR countries, on the other hand, still seem to be very much oriented to serving local or subregional markets, operating more or less independently of their parent companies or sister affiliates in other regions (IDB-IRELA, 1998).

Mexico ranked second behind China in gaining OECD import-market shares of manufacturers during 1980-1995 (1.4 percentage points).[11] It accounted for 40 per cent of exports from Latin America and the Caribbean and was the largest recipient of FDI in the region during the first half of the 1990s.[12] 60 per cent of the inflows were concentrated in manufacturing, precisely in those industries reporting increasing shares in Mexico's exports: automobiles and their parts, electrical machinery and electronic equipment, and apparel.[13] European TNCs accounted for around 20 per cent of FDI flows into the region during 1994-1997 and Japanese firms for less than 4 per cent. The lion's share -- almost 60 per cent -- originated from the United States.

In the case of United States TNCs, Mexico alone accounted for more than 60 per cent of intra-firm trade of United States manufacturing affiliates in the region in 1995. Brazil ranked second with a much lower share of 10 per cent. Within Mexico, the share of intra-firm trade of United States foreign affiliates in total Mexican trade with the United States increased from 24 per cent in 1989 to 29 per cent in 1995, while in Brazil the corresponding figures were 21 and 23 per cent, respectively (United States, Department of Commerce, 1997a).[14]

The evidence regarding the Caribbean Basin seems relatively clear. United States TNCs have increasingly established assembly sites in the area, making use of low wages, tax-free operations in export processing zones and special access to the United States market, particularly in order to meet the competition from Asian suppliers in the United States (Mortimore, 1995). This is especially the case with apparel, footwear and simple electronic equipment (e.g. alarms), where FDI has been the principal factor behind the rise of exports emanating from export processing zones in the Caribbean Basin (box VIII.2). European and Asian companies have lagged far behind in this respect. In consequence, the North American import shares of manufactures from the Caribbean Basin have increased considerably. FDI in export processing zones was the driving force behind the 150 per cent increase during 1990-1997 in the share of United States textile and clothing imports coming from the Caribbean Basin and Mexico (Mortimore, 1997b). The privileged market access of these trading partners is reflected in the fact that, of the 19 per cent of all textile and clothing imports that came by way of the production-sharing mechanism of the United States tariff schedule, the Caribbean Basin and Mexico together provided over 90 per cent (United States, Department of Commerce, various years).

The export performance of Brazil and Argentina (box VIII.3), on the other hand, has remained relatively poor in manufactures, although these countries ranked next to Mexico in attracting FDI inflows during 1990-1996. Their share in OECD imports of manufactures declined from 0.44 and 0.11 per cent, respectively, in 1980, to 0.43 and 0.06 per cent in 1995 (OECD, various issues). Moreover, while intra-MERCOSUR trade relations expanded, Brazil's and Argentina's combined share in world exports remained more or less constant, fluctuating around 1.3 per cent in 1990-1996 (IMF, 1997a).

Box VIII.2. FDI in the Caribbean Basin and the NAFTA challenge

FDI in the Caribbean Basin has many distinct sectoral destinations -- tourist resorts, petroleum and mining operations, infrastructure and services -- but much of it goes into the establishment of assembly operations, usually in export processing zones. The final products of these zones (primarily apparel, footwear and electronics) are aimed at the United States market. A combination of special access to the United States market in the form of production sharing (the HTS 9802 tariff regulation and the Caribbean Basin Initiative), coupled with tax-free operations in export processing zones, allows United States firms to take maximum advantage of the relatively low wages in the Caribbean Basin. This permits them to improve their ability to compete with rising imports (particularly from Asia) in the United States market. The sharp rise in FDI flows into the Caribbean Basin since the mid-1980s, following the steep devaluations of national currencies associated with the debt crisis, is closely linked to the expansion of assembly operations.

FDI in these operations has positive as well as negative aspects. On the one hand, the expansion of export processing zones based on FDI represented a solution to the crisis in the external sector of Caribbean Basin countries, where natural resource exports were collapsing while foreign debt charges mounted. For countries such as the Dominican Republic and Costa Rica, the production of apparel, footwear and electronics activities in export processing zones became the primary link to their principal export market, the United States. Their import-market shares for manufactures in that market increased considerably, as did their net receipts of foreign exchange. On the other hand, the sharp competition among Caribbean Basin countries to attract such FDI meant that tax incentives thought to be temporary became permanent and fiscal benefits for the host countries were much smaller than expected (Mortimore and Peres, 1998). Moreover, the nature of the special-access and low-wage mechanism for these exports, especially in the case of apparel, did not strengthen local industrialization processes (Mortimore, 1997b).

The implementation of the North American Free Trade Agreement (NAFTA) beginning in 1994 represented a major challenge to assembly operations in the Caribbean Basin, especially those in the apparel industry, because Mexico benefited from several advantages not available to the Caribbean Basin Initiative countries: the equivalent of a six-point tariff advantage, no quotas on many items, and local inputs counted as having "North American" content. Mexican advantages, measured in local production costs, also improved as a result of the devaluation of the Mexican currency in 1995. Relatively higher-wage Caribbean Basin countries, such as Costa Rica and the Dominican Republic, saw their import market shares decline or the growth of their shares in the United States market slow down.

Those affected reacted in different ways. Costa Rica, for example, attempted to move its export processing zone activities into technologically more sophisticated areas which required more educated (and better remunerated) workers. It succeeded in 1997 in attracting a large new investment in the order of $500 million from the United States computer firm INTEL for a chip-making and testing facility, and other computer TNCs may be following suit. The Dominican Republic took a different stance. It attempted to extend export-processing-zone advantages to national apparel companies, even though these were not physically located in such zones, to facilitate a more integrated industry.

These last two examples suggest that FDI in the Caribbean Basin, in part sparked by challenges such as Mexico's NAFTA advantage, might be evolving towards activities that respond better to local developmental needs.

Source: UNCTAD.

Box VIII.3. Trade by foreign affiliates in Argentina

During the 1993-1996 period, exports by the largest 1,000 exporters of the country (accounting for 92 per cent of exports) increased by 80 per cent, while exports by foreign firms in this group grew by 105 per cent. In the same period, exports to MERCOSUR by foreign firms grew almost 50 per cent faster than those by domestic firms (Chudnovsky and López, 1998). Thus, the share of foreign firms in the external sales of the leading 1,000 exporters increased from 34 per cent in 1993 to 38 per cent in 1996. In the case of exports to MERCOSUR, the share increased from 42 per cent to 50 per cent. Foreign firms have obviously been quicker than local firms in taking advantage of the opportunities created by subregional integration.

On the other hand, foreign firms also had a higher share than domestic firms in the total imports of the 1,000 leading exporters in 1996, accounting for 58 per cent of these imports. Although foreign firms registered a positive trade balance in 1996, the principal reason was that they are the leading exporters of commodities. Though significant, exports in the automobile industry and other manufacturing industries, with the exception of food processing, were far lower than imports into them.

The greater share of foreign affiliates in imports than in exports in these estimates is in line with the information collected in firm surveys. During 1990-1994, imports increased from $264 to $2,102 million, much faster than exports, which increased from $796 to $1,978 million. Imports of final goods increased the most, though intermediate products also grew rapidly. Whereas all surveyed firms increased imports, increases in exports were mostly registered by foreign affiliates producing agricultural commodities and by affiliates in the automobile industry. The remaining firms had low export coefficients. Intra-firm trade by surveyed firms accounted for 83 per cent of exports and for 92 per cent of imports in 1994. This trade increased the most within MERCOSUR (Chudnovsky and López, 1998), partly reflecting the progressive integration of Argentinian plants into regional production systems.

The sharp increase in imports during this period was mostly due to trade liberalization and greater economic activity. Affiliates complemented local production with imports from parent companies or sister affiliates. Imported final goods, which generally require more advanced technologies in their manufacturing, were aimed at more wealthy consumers or meant to replace local goods, the production of which was discontinued. The increase in imported inputs was partly a consequence of a reduction in the domestic content of automobiles, which was explicitly allowed by the regulatory framework. Greenfield investments and investments in the modernization of existing stocks, on the other hand, led to growing imports of capital goods.

In the automobile industry, the allocation of one model to an Argentine plant to export to regional or world markets has been a key factor in allowing scale economies and contributing to the feasibility of exports. In fact, exports of vehicles have grown significantly, particularly to the Brazilian market, increasing from 1,126 units in 1990 to 208,217 in 1997. However, with the exception of traditional resource-seeking investment geared to the world market (i.e. in agricultural commodities) and efficiency-seeking investment in automobile and autoparts production (which lead in both imports and exports), imports of final or intermediate goods are generally far more important than exports for the remaining foreign firms.

This situation may change in the future. Once ongoing investments are made and efficiency gains are consolidated, foreign firms may be in a better position to increase their exports, especially if a more favourable macro environment for export growth emerges. Larger export coefficients by foreign affiliates in Argentina and their greater integration into the production systems of their parent firms does not, however, depend only on local conditions. Much of it will depend on the global and regional strategies of the TNCs to which the affiliates belong. Finally, though no study of the balance-of-payments effects of FDI in Argentina is yet available, the growing trend observed in dividend payments to parent companies may soon become a policy issue.

Source: Chudnovsky and López, 1997; and 1998.

Although these figures suggest that United States manufacturing affiliates in Latin America and the Caribbean are shifting from a stand-alone and domestic-market-orientation strategy towards globally integrated production systems, they also reflect regional differences. Export propensities of United States affiliates were similar in Brazil and Mexico in the early 1980s (table VIII.3). In the case of Brazil, however, the export propensity had declined by 1995, while in the case of Mexico it had doubled. This is also true more generally of the export propensities of the largest foreign manufacturing affiliates in these two countries. The export propensity of foreign manufacturing affiliates belonging to the 100 largest companies in the region that are located in Mexico increased from 49 per cent in 1994 to 71 per cent in 1996; in Brazil, on the other hand, it decreased slightly from an already low 6 per cent to 5 per cent (table VIII.5).

There are several factors which combine to explain this difference. One is clearly Mexico's membership in NAFTA and its geographical proximity to the North American market, which have helped domestic and foreign firms located in Mexico to penetrate the North American market. Other factors include the effect of the *maquiladora* (assembly) programme in Mexico,[15] the different strategies followed by TNCs from different home countries, the size of the potential internal and subregional markets of these countries, and issues related to exchange-rate management.

TNCs from different home countries have manifested different sectoral and geographic orientations in their investment in the region. Thus, 55 per cent of accumulated net flows from Western Europe to the region (again excluding offshore financial centres) during 1990-1996 went to Argentina and Brazil, while only 13 per cent went to Mexico. On the other hand, during the same period, only 43 per cent of net FDI flows from the United States to the region (again excluding offshore financial centres) went to Argentina and Brazil, while 33 per cent had Mexico as their country of destination (IDB-IRELA, 1998). Even though causal relationships are not clear, recent research into the motivations of the investment behaviour of TNCs from different regions suggests that European TNCs, particularly from Germany, France and Spain, have a marked orientation towards the provision of local markets. This partly responds to the peculiarities of their historical links with the region and to the better opportunities for re-localization they find in other areas, such as Central and Eastern Europe and North Africa (IDB-IRELA, 1998, especially chapters V and VII).

Another factor that may help in explaining these differences is the exchange-rate regime of the host countries. Indeed, the export propensity of foreign affiliates did not increase, or even declined, when exchange-rate-based stabilization programmes induced a real appreciation in Argentina, Brazil and Mexico and thus reduced the international competitiveness of local production. Although these trends also respond to longer-term factors, the recent developments of the automobile exports of Brazil and Mexico underscore the importance of this factor. Mexico's exports of passenger cars, as a percentage of total production, jumped from 58 per cent in 1994 to 86 per cent in 1995, before declining slightly to 80 per cent in 1996 (annex table A.VII.5). In part, this is the result of the sudden decline of domestic demand and of the devaluation of the Mexican peso. The devaluation restored international competitiveness at a time when the Mexican foreign affiliates in the automobile industry had become more deeply integrated into the corporate networks of their parent firms, which involved an upgrading of quality and facilitated the switch to exports. At the same time, the export share of Brazil's production of passenger cars declined from 22 per cent in 1994 to 15 per cent in 1996 (Germany, VDA, various issues); during this period, the Brazilian currency appreciated by about 25 per cent in real terms.

All this suggests that the export potential of FDI depends in part on host countries themselves. Corporate strategies adapt themselves to country-specific policy environments. The automobile industry again provides an illustration. Foreign automobile manufacturers have planned to make heavy investments in Argentina, Brazil and Mexico over the next few years (section A). Although many of the same corporations are involved in these three countries, the strategies they pursue are different in different countries. In the first two, TNCs take advantage of the large domestic markets and the potential of a division of labour within MERCOSUR.[16] Some TNCs (mainly FIAT, Ford, General Motors and Volkswagen) are investing to defend their market shares in Argentina and Brazil, particularly for economy-class cars; others (like BMW, Chrysler and some Asian firms) are seeking new market niches. In Mexico, on the other hand, TNCs use the country as a production base for supplying developed country markets, notably in North America. Chrysler, Ford, General Motors, Nissan and Volkswagen are modernizing, extending and diversifying their productive capacities in Mexico and adapting them to international standards for export purposes. As a consequence, Mexico has good prospects of improving its global performance in the automobile industry.

The potential contribution of FDI to the developmental prospects of host countries, however, is much broader than its contribution to foreign exchange earnings. Specifically, FDI can make a contribution to economic restructuring in host countries, as the example of Asia has shown (UNCTAD, 1995a). The evidence available in this respect for Latin America and the Caribbean is, however, mixed and suggests that the magnitude and character of these effects vary across sectors and countries.

Through the introduction and dissemination of new technological and organizational capabilities, FDI can promote some limited restructuring in the primary sector. The generation of forward linkages, moreover, may facilitate industrialization in products with high natural resource contents, helping to upgrade the position of the country in the vertical production chain. Apart from making the sector more dynamic, this can lead to the export of goods based on natural resources with higher domestic value added and can promote efficient import substitution in other sectors. The role of FDI in the development of the agro-industry in Chile provides an example of the former and the prospects for development of the petrochemical industry in Argentina (box VIII.4) may constitute an example of the latter. Notwithstanding these examples, however, most primary production by TNCs in the region still concentrates on the extraction and export of natural resources with little domestic value added and little effect on domestic restructuring.

When it comes to FDI in services, the effects on economic restructuring are mostly indirect. By helping to ease bottlenecks in areas such as communication and transport, FDI may help to expand the productive capabilities of other sectors of the economy. These effects are very difficult to measure but the operation of TNCs in this sector in the 1990s, given its quantitative importance, is likely to have had a productivity-enhancing impact in recent years. More broadly, FDI in this sector can help economies in intersectoral restructuring, helping them move towards becoming service economies.

The most important restructuring effects, however, are likely to take place in relation to FDI in the manufacturing sector. Here the evidence for the region is uneven. In assembly operations that take advantage of relatively low wages, where a large proportion of recent FDI in manufacturing has been concentrated, internal linkages are typically weak and the effect on economic restructuring low, if any. This is the case with an important proportion of manufacturing FDI in Mexico and the Caribbean Basin, which has had little effect on economic restructuring. There is also some evidence, however, of TNC operations that have aided economic restructuring and advanced development. An example is the Mexican automobile industry, where the modernization of management methods and the introduction of new technology have very much improved the competitive position of the industry in recent years (Mortimore, 1995).

Government policies have an important role to play in attracting FDI into activities with a greater potential effect on development. Policies that improve skills and human resources, that promote industrial upgrading, that support the deepening of the supplier base and that foster the formation of industrial clusters can work towards the strengthening of internal linkages, the incorporation of a larger and more sophisticated domestic component in manufactured goods and, at the same time, help to attract FDI in more dynamic manufacturing activities.

2. Balance-of-payments concerns

The export performance of foreign affiliates is often of particular interest in the context of the balance of payments.[17] As noted earlier, when import-substitution strategies prevailed in the region, foreign affiliates had relatively low export propensities and, even though they were often obliged to meet local content requirements, their reliance on imports tended to be higher than that of domestic companies (UNCTAD, 1995a, p. 218).

This became increasingly obvious towards the end of the import-substitution period, especially in manufacturing. At the early stage of FDI projects, machinery and equipment has to be imported in order to set up local production facilities. At a later stage, there are profit remittances as well as royalties and licence fees to be paid to parent companies. All of these affect a host country's balance-of-payments situation. Under conditions of import substitution, these direct effects of FDI are not compensated for by indirect effects. Import protection reduced competition and hindered the development of efficient local suppliers. Backward linkages of FDI -- which could have created indirect growth effects -- tended to be weak, even though local content requirements induced foreign investors to assist local suppliers in getting access to technical information and licences (Londero et al., 1998).

The balance-of-payments effects of FDI continue to be widely debated after various countries in the region have opened up to world markets in order to integrate their economies more closely into the international division of labor. This is an issue that has received special attention in Brazil. Indeed, the fact that the recent FDI boom in Latin America has been accompanied by large and rising current-account deficits has revived concerns over the negative balance-of-payments impact of FDI. In Brazil, for instance, the current-account deficit increased from $1.2 billion in 1994 to $33 billion in 1997 (IDB, 1998), in parallel with FDI inflows rising from $3 to $17 billion.

The coincidence of booming FDI and high current-account deficits can be analysed from different angles. First of all, the development effects of FDI go far beyond its direct balance-of-payments implications. In addition to foreign capital, FDI typically supplies access to technology, to managerial and organizational skills, and to foreign markets. More broadly, it can also contribute to economic restructuring and thus contribute to growth and development (United Nations, Department of Economic and Social Development, 1992a; UNCTAD, 1995a). These points apart, one might also ask how far moderate current-account deficits are a cause for alarm. In the case of Latin America and the Caribbean, they may be no more what is to be expected, since the process of opening up to world markets involves considerable restructuring related to production and trade. Trade policy reforms tend to have the immediate consequence of rising imports whereas their effect on exports may be delayed.

During the first stage, FDI inflows can generate higher imports not only of capital but also of consumer goods because TNCs may begin by establishing sales affiliates and distribution networks. Thus, the first-round effects of trade liberalization on the balance of payments may be negative, even though it may be inducing more export-oriented FDI. However, even export-oriented projects usually require imports of capital goods and intermediates, unless local enterprises can provide them. If they can, the negative balance-of-payments impact is softened -- a reminder of the importance of strengthening the domestic enterprise sector. Countries such as Brazil, which have been latecomers to trade liberalization, may still be in this early phase. In the longer run, however, successful economic restructuring may induce higher export growth, while import growth should normalize once the adjustment of foreign and domestic investors to the new policy environment is completed.

The new environment can also bring about efficient import substitution. In Argentina, for instance, it has been estimated that two large FDI projects in the petrochemical industry -- each with an investment outlay of more than one billion dollars -- will substitute for imports worth about $500 million, which was about 10 per cent of Argentina's trade deficit in 1997 (box VIII.4). Not that there is no reason for concern. The sustainability of current-account deficits cannot be taken for granted during the difficult transition period. If foreign investors consider the deficits unsustainable, this judgment may prove to be a self-fulfilling prophecy and trade-policy reforms may even have to be reversed.

As for its significance as a source of financing, the share of FDI in the total external capital inflows of Latin America and the Caribbean has increased and has come to represent the largest source of net external capital inflows in the 1990s, although this share has varied by country. During 1990-1997, the share of FDI in total net capital inflows averaged 45 per cent for Latin America and the Caribbean as a whole, with Argentina registering 55 per cent and Brazil 30 per cent (IDB, 1998). This might create concerns over the potential effect of FDI inflows on current account deficits, since they may induce an appreciation of the host country's currency. It would appear, however, that the exchange-rate regime itself contributes more significantly to balance-of-payments problems than do capital inflows. This is especially true in countries that have implemented exchange-rate-based stabilization programmes: fixed or quasi-fixed exchange-rate regimes can work against a favourable FDI balance-of-payments impact.

The increasing outward orientation of Latin American and Caribbean countries in the aftermath of trade policy reforms could, under the right conditions, eventually lead to FDI having a more favourable balance-of-payments impact. The policy conditions required for this are, among others, exchange-rate policies that do not work against the international competitiveness of local production and policies that promote the generation of domestic backward linkages, to reduce the import content of foreign affiliates. The import propensity of foreign affiliates may rise temporarily while TNCs are adjusting to the new more open trade framework, having a negative effect on the balance of payments. In the longer run, however, import propensities should not increase and may even decline if governments encourage the strengthening of local supply capacities. Stronger backward linkages of foreign affiliates would also imply that the indirect trade and development effects of FDI would turn more positive: FDI could not only induce capital formation by domestic suppliers, but also improve their capacity to export on their own.

Other FDI-related balance-of-payments items are likely to change only modestly. On the one hand, payments of royalties and licence fees may increase if a more global orientation creates an incentive to use more advanced foreign technologies. On the other hand, the relative amount of direct investment income transferred to the home countries of foreign investors (notably profit remittances) may decline, if the competition-reducing effect of earlier import-substitution policies had resulted in high profit rates for foreign affiliates.[18]

Box VIII.4. Argentina: two cases of investment in the petrochemical industry

The petrochemical industry is fundamental to the Argentinian economy due to its strong linkage with other economic activities. During the 1990s, in the context of a strong FDI boom, an important number of the leading TNCs in the industry expanded facilities in Argentina. Two projects are particularly worth mentioning since, given their scale, they will have considerable direct and indirect effects on production, trade and capital formation. In both of these cases, the projects are implemented by TNCs in association with important local groups.

The first of these is the Mega project. This is an undertaking to develop a rich natural reserve of natural gas located at Loma de la Lata, Province of Neuquen. A plant will be established to separate liquid components from the gas which will be transported (by a poliduct, the construction of which is also part of the project) to the city of Bahia Blanca, where fractioning and storage facilities are being built. The project involves a production plan of 562,000 tons of ethane, 610,000 tons of LPG and 223,000 tons of naturale gasoline per year. The ethane production will be used to supply Petroquimica Bahia Blanca (a firm privatized in 1995 and now controlled by foreign investors), while the LPG and gasoline will be exported.

Foreign investors from the United States and Brazil will supply 62 per cent of the $430 million of capital for this project, which is expected to start production by the year 2000. In terms of its potential effect on the balance of payments, the project is expected to allow for the substitution of imports worth around $320 million and to generate exports worth around $225 million.

The second of these large investments in the petrochemical industry is the Profertil project. It seeks to establish the largest fertilizer plant in the world. Based on natural gas processing, this project involves the construction of a plant in Bahia Blanca with a production capacity of 1.1 million tons per year of urea and 625,000 tons of ammonia. Production will be geared to the domestic market and is expected to generate high levels of import substitution and contribute to increased productivity in the farming sector.

Foreign investors from Canada will supply 33 per cent of the $600 million of capital for this project, which is expected to start production by the year 2000. In terms of its potential effect on the balance of payments, the project is expected to allow for the substitution of imports worth around $175 million and to generate exports worth around $70 million.

Source: Argentina, Center for Production Research, Investment Database, Industry, Commerce and Mining Secretariat, based on data provided by the firms.

An empirical assessment of these possibilities suffers from considerable data constraints. Frequently, the relevant balance-of-payments items cannot be divided into TNC-related and non-TNC-related transactions. Most importantly, systematic data on the imports of foreign affiliates operating in Latin America and the Caribbean are not available. As noted earlier, the import propensity of foreign affiliates seems generally to have exceeded that of indigenously owned firms. This propensity is also illustrated by the relatively high intra-firm exports shipped by United States and Japanese parent companies to all their affiliates abroad, which typically exceeded intra-firm imports shipped by the affiliates to their parent companies (UNCTAD, 1995a, table IV.1).

However, this kind of information does not provide insights into whether the new policy environment in Latin America and the Caribbean has had negative FDI-related balance-of-payments effects due to an increasing import propensity and whether such effects have been particularly pronounced in countries like Mexico, which have been relatively successful in increasing exports to developed countries. Since United States manufacturing TNCs have been at the forefront in this development, it may be instructive to compare the intra-firm shipments from United States parent companies to their affiliates in Latin America with the converse shipments (table VIII.6). If greater openness towards world markets involves negative balance-of-payments effects in trade, the exports-to-imports ratio of the United States parent companies should rise over time and be particularly high in countries that are more world-market-oriented.

For Latin America and the Caribbean as a whole, the exports of United States parent companies to their foreign affiliates are only slightly higher than the imports of parent companies from their affiliates. The exports-to-imports ratio has in fact remained relatively stable during 1989-1995, although the ratio varies significantly across host countries. Thus, in Argentina and Brazil, the ratio has indeed increased considerably during this period (from a level below one in the case of Brazil). This is probably related to two important factors mentioned above: exchange-rate-based stabilization programmes and corporate restructuring of foreign affiliates, the latter ensuing from trade liberalization and resulting in a temporary boom in exports of capital goods of United States parent companies to their affiliates in Argentina and Brazil.

Table VIII.6. Latin America and the Caribbean: exports of goods of United States parent companies to affiliates in Latin America, relative to imports of goods of parent companies from affiliates, 1989 and 1995

(Ratio)

Region/economy	1989	1995
Latin America	1.07	1.05
Argentina	1.68	11.94
Brazil	0.57 [a]	1.45
Chile	1.35	1.07
Colombia	0.55 [a]	..
Costa Rica	1.82 [a]	..
Dominican Republic	0.77	0.39
Mexico	1.06	0.94
Peru	1.17	0.77
Venezuela	18.54	4.17 [b]
Developing Asia	0.53	0.73
All developed and developing countries	1.05	1.14

Source: United States, Department of Commerce, Survey of Current Business, October 1997 and August 1992

[a] 1990.
[b] 1994.

By contrast, the exports of United States parent companies to their affiliates in most other Latin American host countries have declined relative to the imports of United States parent companies from their affiliates. In the case of the Dominican Republic, for example, the exports-to-imports ratio of parent companies to affiliates reached an exceptionally low level in 1995. This is most probably related to the expansion and consolidation of export processing zone activities in the country, for which the dependence on capital goods provided by United States parent companies is now relatively low. For Mexico, the exports-to-imports ratio is likely to have declined further after 1995, in the wake of the longer-term effects of the devaluation of the Mexican peso and the consolidation of heavy investments made by United States TNCs in the first part of the decade.

Similarly, the partial evidence on payments of direct investment income as well as royalties and licence fees does not point to the high costs of a stronger export orientation on the part of foreign affiliates in Latin America. Payments of direct investment income increased by a factor of 2.7 between 1985-1990 and 1994-1996 (table VIII.7). Relative to FDI inflows, however, payments of direct investment income decreased for Latin America as a whole. It should be noted though that because of the time-lag affecting direct investment payments with respect to inflows, this ratio could be underestimating the long-term effect in a context of growing inflows.

Among Latin American countries, Peru and Argentina experienced the steepest increase in payments of direct investment income, but payments still accounted for a small percentage of inflows in 1994-1996. Brazil experienced a rather modest increase in payments of direct investment income but a declining payments-to-inflows ratio. This ratio, however, was still twice as high in Brazil as in Mexico, despite the stronger global orientation of the latter. Again, caution is required in interpretation. The differences across countries could reflect the different points in the maturity cycle that investments in different countries may occupy. Given the high inflows Mexico received in the first half of the 1990s, low foreign direct investment payments could simply reflect the fact that the new stocks have not yet consolidated.

Payments of royalties and licence fees were rather low in comparison with payments of direct investment income, even when payments unrelated to TNC operations are included

Table VIII.7. Latin America and the Caribbean: payments of direct investment income[a] by Latin American host countries, 1985-1996

(Millions of dollars and percentage)

Country	Millions of dollars[b]			Percentage of FDI inflows[b]			Percentage of FDI stocks		
	1985-1990	1991-1993	1994-1996	1985-1990	1991-1993	1994-1996	1985	1990	1996
Latin America and the Caribbean	3 889	5 742	10 408	47.9	34.7	30.2	3.4	4.4	3.7
Argentina	94	502	992	3.9	17.8	5.1	0.9	4.6	3.3
Brazil	1 503	1 072	2 425[c]	136.2	72.2	60.6[c]	4.4	4.4	2.6[d]
Chile	262	752	1 128	50	111.1	44.5	6.8	3.3	7.3
Colombia	665	892	1 301	121.2	124.7	53.5	14.9	25.9	11.1
Costa Rica	16	20	18[c]	15.5	9.2	5.0[c]	0.7	1.2	0.7[d]
Dominican Republic	165	180	118.8	45	15.7	7.2			
Mexico	628	1 163	2 756	24	25.8	29.4	2.1	3.8	4.3
Peru	9	94	187	28.3	35.3	6.4	2.8	0.6	2.6
Venezuela	164	436	461	114.8	44.9	38.4	6.8	5.8	5

Source: IMF, various years.

[a] Excluding reinvested earnings, i.e. "other direct investment income" as defined in the source.
[b] Annual average.
[c] 1994-1995.
[d] 1995.

(table VIII.8). Opposing trends prevailed in different Latin American host countries. For example, payments of royalties and licence fees declined in Argentina, where payments accounted for an exceptionally high percentage of inward FDI stocks in 1985 and 1990. By contrast, payments of royalties and licence fees increased in both Brazil and Mexico, notwithstanding the different TNC strategies in these two countries. In Brazil, payments accounted for almost 10 per cent of FDI inflows in 1994-1995, significantly above the corresponding ratio for Mexico (5.4 per cent), whereas the payments-to-FDI-stocks ratio was the same for the two countries.

3. Conclusion

With differences in emphasis across subregions, foreign investors have begun to respond to the new policy environment and to assist, to some extent, the integration of Latin America and the Caribbean into regionalized or globalized production systems, particularly in manufacturing. Trade reforms and greater openness to world markets may cause a temporary deterioration in the trade balance. In the longer run, however, and with appropriate governmental policies, the positive effect of trade reforms on the export propensity of foreign affiliates could reverse, together with a competitive real exchange rate, the negative balance-of-payments effect resulting from the high import propensity of foreign affiliates, particularly in the first stages of their investment. This is still an open question and promoting FDI with a long-term positive balance-of-payments effect therefore constitutes one of the great challenges facing the region. On the other hand, there is no conclusive evidence that a closer integration of Latin America into the world economy has led to a negative balance-of-payments impact of FDI, resulting from higher payments of direct investment income as well as royalties and licence fees.

Governments can improve the developmental contribution of FDI and its impact on the balance of payments in several ways. On the macroeconomic front, the existence of a competitive real exchange rate is important to provide both foreign and domestic investors

Table VIII.8. Latin America and the Caribbean: payments of royalties and licence fees by Latin American host countries, 1985-1996

(Millions of dollars and percentage)

Country	Millions of dollars[a]			Percentage of FDI inflows[a]			Percentage of FDI stocks		
	1985-1990	1991-1993	1994-1996	1985-1990	1991-1993	1994-1996	1985	1990	1996
Latin America and the Caribbean	861	1073	1566[b]	10.6	6.5	5.1[b]	1	0.9	0.6[c]
Argentina	370	266	206	15.2	9.4	1.1	6.4	4.7	0.7
Brazil	46	76	384[b]	4.2	5.1	9.6[b]	0.1	0.1	0.5
Chile	32	39	49	6.1	5.8	1.9	1	0.4	0.3
Colombia	10	18	37	1.8	2.6	1.5	0.3	0.4	0.4
Costa Rica	9	9	11[b]	8.8	3.9	3.2[b]	1	0.6	0.4[c]
Dominican Republic	...	...	7	...	...	1.7	...	...	0.5
Mexico	228	462	504	8.7	10.2	5.4	0.8	1.2	0.5
Peru	4	16	50	14.4	6	1.7	0.3	0.4	0.7

Source: IMF, various years.

[a] Annual average
[b] 1994-1995
[c] 1995

with stronger export incentives and to reduce their import propensities. On the microeconomic front, policies encouraging industrial upgrading by fostering backward linkages, improving the physical and human resource infrastructure, supporting the formation of industrial clusters and facilitating international partnering between enterprises can all enhance the developmental effect. Finally, host countries should not neglect the potential indirect trade and development effects of FDI, even though they cannot be easily quantified. FDI in business-related services and infrastructure may enhance the international competitiveness of manufacturing industries and thus contribute to improving existing FDI stocks.

Notes

1 For a comprehensive analysis of FDI trends in Latin America and the Caribbean, see CEPAL, 1998b.

2 It needs to be kept in mind, however, that German TNCs have been among the slowest in their reaction to new opportunities in the region (IDB-IRELA, 1998).

3 Complementarity in exports to the European Union, for example, is revealed by the fact that four-fifths of European Union imports from developing Asia consisted of manufactured goods in 1995, whereas four-fifths of European Union imports from Latin America consisted of non-manufactured goods (OECD, 1997).

4 An overwhelming majority of these respondents also indicated that they do not intend to reduce their investments in Asia, suggesting that increased FDI in Latin America and the Caribbean does not represent a switch from Asian host countries (see chapter VII for further discussion).

5 The HTS 9802 tariff regulation allows United-States-based companies that assemble goods abroad which include components produced in the United States to pay tariffs only on the value added abroad when the assembled goods return to the United States market. Thus, the re-imported components are tariff-exempt.

6 For a discussion of revealed comparative advantage in these industries see, for example, Nunnenkamp, 1998.

7 For details, see CEPAL, 1998a, and Mortimore et al., 1997.

8 Latin America in fact received the highest amount of mining FDI in the world in 1996. *The Economist*, 6 December 1997, p. 17.

9 Worldwide, some 50 to 60 per cent of FDI flows are in the services sector, reflecting a trend for services to become the single largest economic sector in most countries.

10 See, for example, WEF, 1997; for a detailed discussion, see Nunnenkamp, 1997 and UNCTAD, forthcoming b.

11 See Mortimore et al., 1997.

12 Mexico's inward FDI stock more than doubled from $33 billion in 1990 to $72 billion in 1996 (UNCTAD, 1997a, p. 315).

13 FDI inflows in the last two industries were related to assembly activities (*maquiladora*). For a more detailed analysis of Mexico's integration into globalized production, see Calderon, et al., 1996; Mortimore, 1995; 1997a; and UNCTC, 1992.

14 These figures tend to underrate the significance of intra-firm trade, as they do not cover trade relations among United States foreign affiliates in different Latin American host countries, but only their trade with United States parent companies. This qualification may be important for Brazil in particular, as United States foreign affiliates are likely to contribute considerably to intra-Mercosur trade (e.g. in the automobile industry).

15 This programme of the Government of Mexico aims to simplify requirements and provides incentives for the operation of export-oriented economic units. Among these is the exemption from tariffs of their imports of components.

16 Special rules for the automobile industry in MERCOSUR require a certain degree of compensating exports within members' trade flows. Local content requirements are defined on the MERCOSUR level. For details, see Mortimore, 1997a.

17 For a more detailed discussion of the balance-of-payments effects of FDI, see UNCTAD, 1997a, ch. II.

18 Note, however, that changes in profit remittances may also be attributable to changes in tax policies, as the accounting practices of TNCs adapt to them.

CHAPTER IX

CENTRAL AND EASTERN EUROPE

A. Trends

The basic FDI trend in Central and Eastern Europe resumed its upward growth in 1997 after a decline in 1996. The trend was uneven, with twelve countries showing growth and five showing declines, with neither group homogenous in terms of progress in transition. With the exception of the Russian Federation, most of the FDI growth occurred in the secondary and tertiary sectors. The Russian Federation emerged as the leader in attracting FDI for the first time, mainly on account of the interest of investors in its natural resources and its infrastructure potential in basic telecommunications. The relation between FDI growth and GDP growth continued to be weak, with causal links apparently extending both ways in different circumstances. Finally, outward FDI from Central and Eastern Europe showed significant growth, with the Russian Federation again taking the lead, but outward FDI stocks remained very low in comparison with inward stocks.

Following a decline in 1996 that proved to be temporary, FDI flows into Central and Eastern Europe[1] bounced back in 1997, reaching $19 billion (FDI trends of the transition economies of Central Asia are discussed in chapter VII). While high, this new record level was only slightly higher than inflows to Brazil in 1997. FDI inflows increased in 12 countries of the region. The Russian Federation, Romania, Poland and Bulgaria experienced the largest increases of FDI in absolute terms, as compared with flows in 1996 and, in comparison, FDI inflows decreased in five countries (figure IX.1). The Czech Republic witnessed a decline in inflows for the second year since the 1995 peak, although the rate of decrease was lower than in the previous year.[2]

The Russian Federation, Poland and Hungary were the largest recipients of FDI in the region (figure IX.1). Together with the Czech Republic, these countries accounted for 79 per cent in 1996 and 77 per cent in 1997 of total inflows. However, the relative weight of the individual members of this group changed. In particular, the Russian Federation increased its share from 18 per cent to 33 per cent, driven mainly by large projects in infrastructure and natural resources.[3] The share of the next four largest recipients (Romania, Ukraine, Bulgaria and Latvia) increased from 10 per cent to 15 per cent. By the end of 1997, Poland had become the region's leader in terms of inward FDI stock, followed by Hungary and the Russian Federation (annex table B.3). But if only the equity component of inward FDI is taken into account (and reinvested earnings and intra-company loans are excluded), Poland is third, behind Hungary and the Russian Federation. In terms of FDI stock, the growth of inward FDI in 1997 was exceptionally high in Belarus, Lithuania, Bulgaria, Romania and the Russian Federation, though typically from fairly low levels.

Figure IX.1. Central and Eastern Europe: FDI flows into the recipient economies 1997 and flows to the same economies, 1996[a]

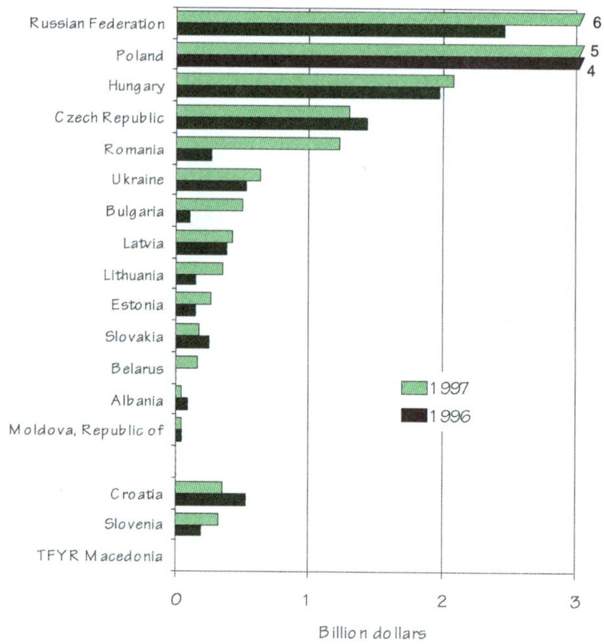

Source: UNCTAD, FDI/TNC database.

[a] Ranked on the basis of the magnitude of FDI inflows in 1997.

Judging from data on home country shares in FDI in individual host countries, the United States was in 1997 the biggest single source of inward FDI stock in Central and Eastern Europe, followed by Germany and the Netherlands. Taken together, however, the countries of Western Europe accounted for the bulk of inward FDI stock. The share of Japan, as well as developing Asian countries, is low, except for the share of developing Asia in Romania and Poland. In three (Russian Federation, Poland and Ukraine) of the seven most important recipient countries,[4] United States TNCs were the most important sources of FDI, and they were only slightly behind German firms in Hungary (table IX.1). Germany is the most important source of FDI for the Czech Republic and Hungary, and the second most important source for Poland and Slovenia. In Slovenia, neighbouring Austria is the foremost source of inward FDI, while FDI in Romania comes mostly from France and the Republic of Korea.

Except in the Russian Federation, the primary sector accounts for a low share of inward FDI (table IX.2). On average, secondary and tertiary activities are of equal importance in the region's inward FDI. The tertiary sector accounts for a leading share of inward FDI in Hungary, the Czech Republic, Slovenia and the Russian Federation. Manufacturing dominates FDI in Poland, Romania and Ukraine. Within that sector, the food industry, machinery and equipment and the chemical industry are the most notable recipients. In services, the financial industry, commercial activities and transport and communications attracted most of the inward FDI.

Table IX.1. Central and Eastern Europe: geographical distribution of inward FDI stock in selected countries, 1997

(Percentage)

Home country	Czech Republic	Hungary	Poland	Romania	Russian Federation	Slovenia[a]	Ukraine
United States	13	20	23	7	29	1	19
Germany	28	22	12	9	12	14	10
Netherlands	14	13	7	9	4	2	10
United Kingdom	3	4	7	4	17	5	8
France	8	8	9	13	2	7	1
Switzerland	11	3	3	..	15	4	10
Austria	7	10	4	3	2	34	2
Italy	1	6	9	6	3	7	2
Korea, Republic of	..	1	6	11	..	..	..
Belgium	..	4	1	..	..	..	..
Japan	..	2	..	..	..	..	..
Others	15	9	18	39	17	25	37
Total	**100**	**100**	**100**	**100**	**100**	**100**	**100**

Source: UNCTAD estimates, based on national reports and Helmstedt, 1998. These estimates are based on national statistical surveys and are not necessarily comparable with FDI data based on balance-of-payments figures.

[a] End 1996.

When it comes to individual economies -- and using various indicators -- FDI plays a role that can be quite considerable as, for example, in Hungary (table IX.3). As a percentage of gross fixed-capital formation, inflows (in 1994-1996) were highest in the Republic of Moldova, followed by Hungary and Estonia (figure IX.2), with ratios comparable to those of newly industrializing economies in Asia, such as Singapore. On the same basis, FDI inflows were of minor importance in the Russian Federation. Moreover, FDI relative to gross fixed-capital formation was slightly lower in Central and Eastern Europe than in all developing countries taken as a group.

The discrepancy in the relative importance of FDI between Central and Eastern Europe and developing countries as a group is much more pronounced with regard to the ratio of inward FDI stock to GDP in 1996; 8 per cent versus 16 per cent (figure IX.3). (As a percentage of GDP, the inward stock (1996) was the highest in Hungary, Estonia and Latvia). This is not surprising, considering that Central and Eastern Europe was a latecomer in drawing on FDI for capital or other resources. Before 1989, government policy had made FDI virtually impossible, except in the case of Hungary and former Yugoslavia and, to a lesser degree, Poland. Moreover, at that time, only five of the 19 states currently constituting the region had existed as independent entities.

Various factors have to be taken into account in order to explain the uneven distribution of FDI among countries within Central and Eastern Europe. First of all, the countries in the region differ significantly in terms of the stage of transformation to market-based economies. The Czech Republic, Estonia, Hungary, Poland and Slovenia have been the frontrunners in the transition to a market-based economic system.[5] For example, the European Bank for Reconstruction and Development (EBRD) assigned an average transition indicator of more than 3 to all of these countries (EBRD, 1997).[6] It can reasonably be expected that this group is more attractive to foreign investors than those countries which are still facing considerable transitional uncertainty. Indeed, during 1993-1997, the pattern of FDI inflows to the region was clearly dominated by the first wave of reformers (which also includes countries that

Table IX.2. Central and Eastern Europe: sectoral and industrial distribution of inward FDI stock in selected countries, 1997

(Percentage)

Sector/industry	Czech Republic	Hungary	Poland[a]	Romania	Russian Federation	Slovenia[a]	Ukraine
Primary sector	..	**2**	**2**	**6**	**16**	..	**2**
Agriculture, hunting, forestry & fishing	..	1	0	2	..	..	2
Mining, quarrying & petroleum	..	1	2	4	16 [b]	..	..
Secondary sector	**38**	**39**	**61**	**53**	**23**	**30**	**50**
Food, beverages & tobacco	16 [c]	9	21	14	9	2	20
Textiles, leather & clothing	..	2	3 [d]	4 [d]	..	..	2 [d]
Wood, paper, publishing & printing	..	3	5	2	4	7	3
Chemicals, chemical products & coke &, petroleum products	8	8	5	5	3	6	7
Non-metallic mineral products (cement & building materials)	..	3	6	6	..	2	7
Basic metals & metal products	..	2	1	1	3	..	3
Machinery & equipment	..	12 [e]	17 [e]	14	4 [f]	5	9
Electrical machinery & apparatus	1	..	..	3	..	..	..
Automotive	13	..	..	3	..	..	..
Unspecified secondary	..	0	3	..	..	7	..
Tertiary sector	**45**	**59**	**38**	**35**	**51**	**55**	**40**
Electricity & water distribution	4	14	..	..	..	14	..
Construction	1	4	5	1	..	..	..
Wholesale trade & distributive trade	9	12	6	16	11	11	19
Hotels & restaurants (tourism)	..	2	..	4	5	..	..
Transport, storage & telecommunications	18	8	5	4	2	..	5
Finance (& banking & insurance)	9	9	21	5	32	17	9
Real estate, rental activities & business services	3	8	..	4	..	13 [g]	2
Public administration, health & social services	..	2	0	1	1	..	5
Unspecified	**17**	-	-	**6**	**10**	**15**	**8**

Source: UNCTAD, based on national reports and Helmstedt, 1998. These estimates are based on national statistical surveys and are not necessarily comparable with FDI data based on balance-of-payments figures.

a End 1996.
b Fuel industry.
c Includes "consumer goods".
d Includes other light industries.
e Includes electrical machinery & automotive industries.
f Includes basic metals & metal products.
g Includes trade in vehicles and gases.

Table IX.3. Central and Eastern Europe: relative importance of foreign-owned companies in manufacturing, 1996

(Percentage)

Country	Equity capital	Employment	Investment	Sales	Export sales
Czech Republic	21.5 [a]	13.1	33.5	22.6	..
Hungary	67.4 [b]	36.1	82.5	61.4	77.5
Slovakia	16.9	11.7	24.3	21.6	..
Slovenia	15.6	10.1	20.3	19.6	25.8

Source: Hunya, 1998, p. 6.

a Own capital.
b Nominal capital in cash.

had gone far in privatization open to foreigners) (figure IX.4).[7] A comparison of the rankings of Central and Eastern European countries in terms of the average transition indicator and inward FDI stock also confirms the relationship: the rank correlation coefficient between FDI stock and the transition indicator for the region's 17 countries was 0.91 and that between FDI flows and the transition indicator was 0.85 in 1997.[8]

Even so, FDI inflows also increased in countries less advanced in the process of economic transformation. In the case of the Russian Federation, for instance, FDI is largely motivated by the opportunity for exploiting that country's vast natural resources. In this sector, economic policies and economic prospects of host countries have traditionally been less important as determinants of FDI. Indeed, the competitiveness index provided in the 1998 *Global Competitiveness Report* was the lowest for Ukraine and second lowest for the Russian Federation among the 53 countries under consideration in 1998 (WEF, 1998b).[9] In cases such as Belarus and the Republic of Moldova, high FDI growth on the basis of very low starting levels may stem from just a few FDI projects, undertaken by foreign investors who want to benefit from first-mover advantages.

Investment related to privatization has been a dominant form of inflows for a number of countries (figure IX.5). For example, privatization-related inflows accounted for virtually all FDI until 1995 in both the Czech Republic and the Republic of Moldova until 1995, although the latter was ranked much lower by the EBRD in terms of progress in respect to the transition. Likewise, privatization-related inflows accounted for the bulk of FDI in Croatia until 1995, followed by a slight decline in 1996 and 1997. In Bulgaria, the share of privatization-related FDI increased to about 70 per cent. Hungary is the only country believed to have nearly exhausted its potential for privatization-related FDI (Hunya, 1998, p. 7).[10] Accordingly, the share of this type of FDI decreased from 68 per cent in 1995 to 13 per cent in 1997, with other FDI flows compensating for the levelling of privatization-related flows. In Hungary, during 1995-1997, non-privatization-related inflows alone averaged $1.5 billion per year; this compares with total average annual inflows of $1.7 billion during 1992-1994 (figure IX.5).

Three factors may together explain most of the unevenness of the link between FDI inflows and GDP growth in Central and Eastern Europe. The most general factor is uncertainty about the future pace of economic transition. The specific factors are the "lumpiness" of FDI associated with privatization and the

Figure IX.2. Central and Eastern Europe: FDI flows as a percentage of gross fixed capital formation, 1994-1996 (annual average)[a]

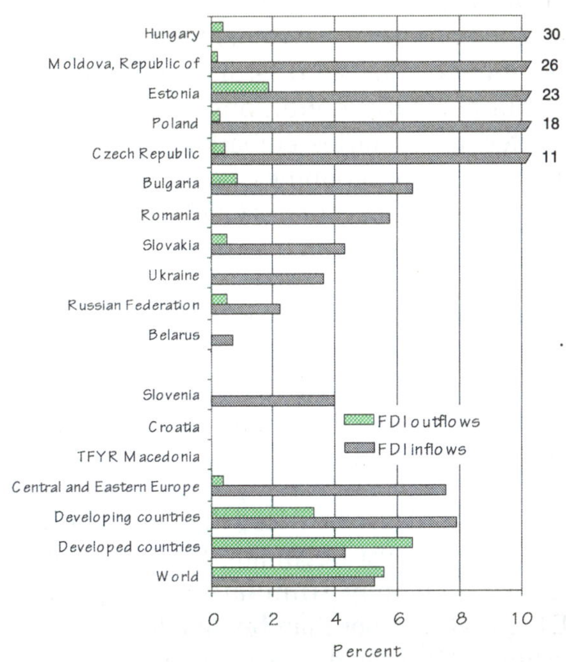

Source: UNCTAD, FDI/TNC database.

[a] Ranked on the basis of the magnitude of FDI inflows as a percentage of gross fixed capital formation.

relative indifference of natural-resource investors to broader economic conditions. High GDP growth between 1995-1997 tended to go hand in hand with increasing FDI in some countries, notably in Poland and Croatia (table IX.4); in some other countries, FDI increased although GDP growth was relatively low (e.g. Hungary, Latvia, Romania and Belarus) or even negative (Russian Federation, Republic of Moldova, Bulgaria, and Ukraine). In 1997, FDI inflows increased dramatically in Romania and Bulgaria, against the backdrop of declining GDP. Most strikingly, perhaps, high GDP growth in Slovakia attracted little FDI in 1995-1997. In this case, one reason was host country policy: the country practically excluded foreign investors from participating in the privatization of state-owned enterprises.

Figure IX.3. Central and Eastern Europe: FDI stock as a percentage of gross domestic product, 1996[a]

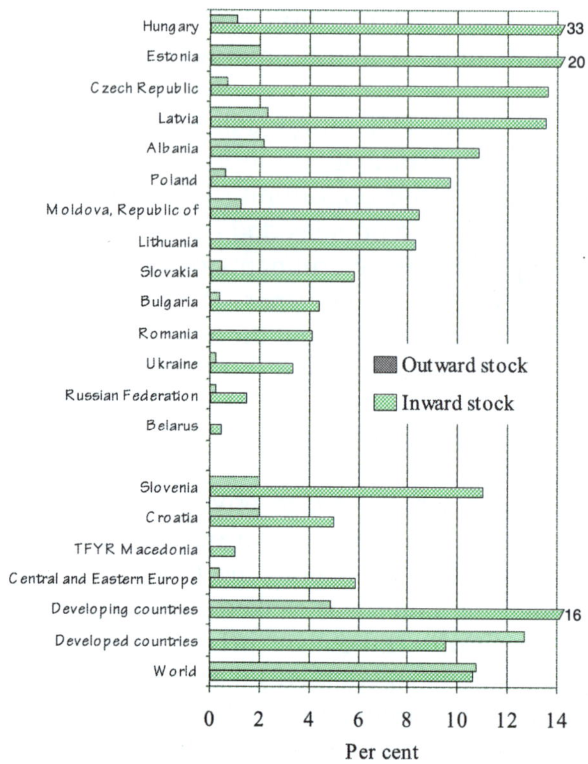

Source: UNCTAD, FDI/TNC database.

[a] Ranked on the basis of the magnitude of FDI stock as a percentage of gross domestic product.

At an early stage of foreign investment, the low starting levels may also partly explain the weak relationship of FDI growth with GDP growth. The decisions of foreign investors tend to be less influenced by short-term changes in GDP under early conditions of economic transition. Foreign investors may be strongly attracted to countries embarking on far-reaching and consistent reforms, especially when privatization programmes facilitate entry, even though the required structural change is likely to result in declining GDP in the short run. Countries in which structural reforms are delayed may thus have a more favourable GDP growth performance for some time. Nonetheless, FDI inflows will remain static or will decline if foreign investors consider long-term GDP growth to be unsustainable.

Figure IX.4. Central and Eastern Europe: stock of inward FDI, by country/group of countries, 1993-1997
(Billions of dollars)

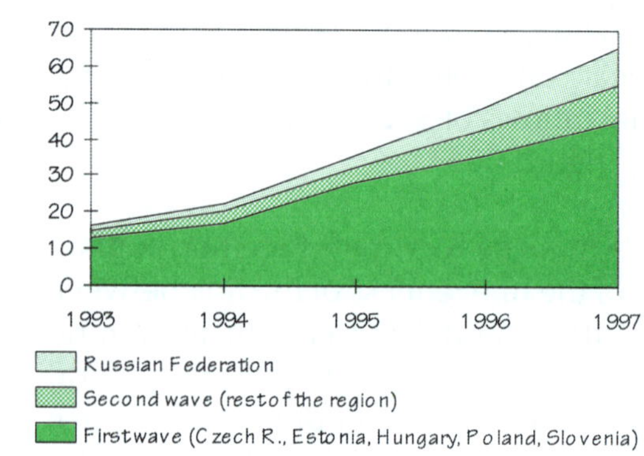

Source: UNCTAD, FDI/TNC database.

It should also be noted that, especially in economies just beginning the transition process, FDI may stimulate subsequent GDP growth, rather than being attracted by existing GDP growth. A good example is privatization-related FDI, which results in the restructuring and upgrading of inefficient state-owned enterprises. It is not surprising, therefore, that FDI boomed in Hungary in 1995, while GDP growth picked up only in 1997. Likewise, in the Russian Federation, FDI inflows increased steadily from 1994, while GDP did not recover until 1997.[11]

Figure IX.5. Central and Eastern Europe: privatization-related FDI flows as percentage of total FDI inflows, 1993-1997

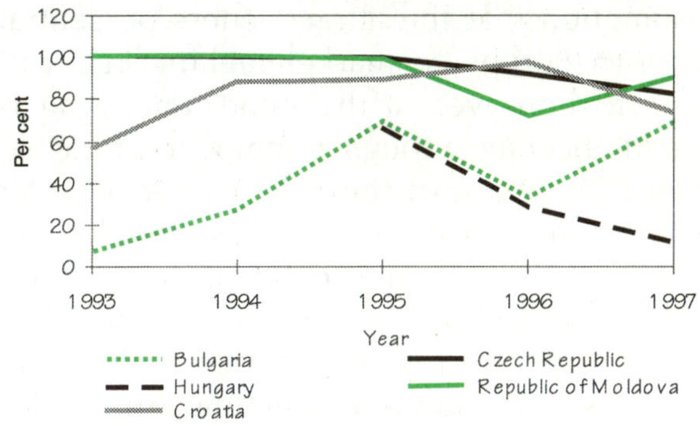

Source: UNCTAD, FDI/TNC database.

Note: the definition of "privatization-related FDI flows" varies. In the case of Hungary, for instance, only the revenues of the privatization agency are included, and capital increases are excluded. The Czech Republic includes all non-greenfield investments. The data are, therefore, not strictly comparable.

Recent developments in FDI patterns have some implications for the future of FDI in Central and Eastern Europe. First, countries that are relatively attractive to FDI -- whether because of the pace of transition or of economic growth, opportunities in privatization, or for other reasons -- will have a better chance to overcome economic recession. Second, new competitors for FDI among the latecomers in transition may attract additional inflows to the region, without impairing FDI prospects for the currently most attractive countries. For instance, the potential of privatization-related FDI is still untapped or not exhausted in several countries in Central and Eastern Europe; this type of FDI can thus be expected to play a leading role in these countries in the near future. Finally, countries in the region that are likely to become members of the European Union may become more attractive to foreign investors as their economic systems and regulatory frameworks become more similar to those of the Union, and as the dynamic effects of the association agreements begin to manifest themselves.

An UNCTAD survey of the region's investment-promotion agencies conducted in 1998 (to be discussed below; see box IX.3) sheds some further light on this issue. Just two of 15 respondent countries considered intraregional FDI diversion to be a significant problem. Ten respondents expressed the view that the FDI attractiveness of other countries in the region would not affect their own level of FDI, while three respondents had seen a positive bandwagon effect of other countries' attractiveness on flows into their own country. According to the same survey, the Asian financial crisis is expected to have only minor effects on FDI in Central and Eastern Europe: eight out of 13 respondents argued that the impact would be neutral or balanced; three respondents expected more

Table IX.4. Central and Eastern Europe: average annual rates of growth of inward FDI and gross domestic product, 1995-1997

(Percentage)

Country	Growth of FDI inflows	GDP growth
Poland	43.1	6.7
Slovakia	-8.0	6.5
Croatia	135.5	6.4
Estonia	14.3	5.4
Czech Republic	47.9	3.6
Lithuania	124.8	3.4
Albania	4.6	3.3
Slovenia	38.6	3.0
Latvia	35.2	3.0
Hungary	79.4	2.4
Romania	115.9	1.7
Belarus	136.5	0.8
Macedonia, TFYR	-28.2	0.3
Russian Federation	129.1	-2.9
Moldova, Republic of	139.3	-2.9
Bulgaria	120.7	-5.4
Ukraine	60.9	-8.5

Source: UNCTAD, based on UNCTAD FDI/TNC database and national sources.

FDI inflows as a result of the Asian crisis, while two respondents considered the impact to be negative. This evaluation appears to be based on the assumption that the attractiveness of Central and Eastern Europe to market-seeking FDI will continue to improve. At the same time, Asia is expected to become a tougher competitor for cost-sensitive FDI. As has been seen earlier (chapter VII), this response pattern coincides entirely with the views expressed by transnational corporations (TNCs) in the survey carried out by UNCTAD/ ICC in March 1998 as regards the effect of the Asian crisis on FDI. Romania and Poland, the major recipients of FDI in Central and Eastern Europe from the Republic of Korea, which accounted, in 1997, for 11 per cent and 6 per cent respectively of their inward stock (table IX.2), may nevertheless see some negative effects on their inward FDI due to the financial constraints on Korean enterprises.

Figure IX.6. Central and Eastern Europe: FDI flows from the economies in 1997 and flows from the same economies in 1996 [a]

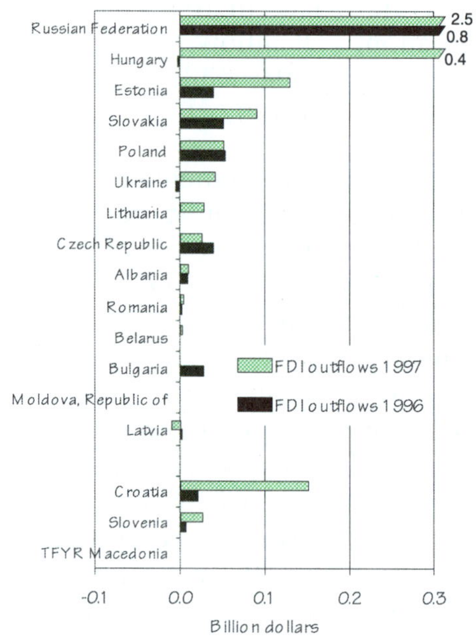

Source: UNCTAD, FDI/TNC database.

[a] Ranked on the basis of the magnitude of FDI outflows in 1997.

Investment outflows from Central and Eastern Europe increased more than three times in 1997, to an estimated $3.4 billion, though from a very low level (figure IX.6). Outflows still represented a mere 18 per cent of the region's FDI inflows. The Russian Federation continued to account for the bulk of the outflows ($2 billion), followed by Hungary, Croatia and Estonia. The outflows of other countries of the region are still very low (box IX.1). The reasons for the low level of reported outward FDI are related to incomplete reporting as well as to features of the real economy. The statistics of some countries probably capture only a small part of FDI outflows and outward stocks. This is the result of inadequate statistical methods and of the reluctance of domestic firms to report their outward FDI. Furthermore, it is difficult to account for foreign assets acquired before the transition (box IX.2). But the low level of outward FDI may also be a consequence of the relative lack of ownership advantages among enterprises in the midst of economic transformation. Yet the cases of Hungary and Estonia suggest that, when transition is sufficiently advanced, firm-specific ownership advantages do tend to develop. This improves the chances of investing abroad, especially in order to overcome the profit constraints of small domestic markets and to maintain corporate competitiveness. The case of the Russian Federation seems to be different: a part of FDI outflows appear to be motivated by the desire of investors to diversify assets as a safeguard against domestic instability. Thus, in 1997, only 0.1 per cent of the Russian Federation's outward FDI was directed to other countries in the Commonwealth of Independent States, where Russian enterprises might have been expected to be in the best position to use their ownership advantages.

In the longer run, outward FDI is likely to gain in importance as countries, especially in Central Europe, begin to lose comparative advantage based on low wages, particularly in industries such as textiles, footwear and other labour-intensive industries. Indeed, firms from some more advanced transition economies like Hungary have already begun to invest abroad -- in a Central and Eastern European version of the Asian flying-geese phenomenon -- in labour-intensive industries.[12]

Box IX.1. Outward FDI in Slovenia

In 1996, the outward FDI stock of Slovenia was only $366 million (Slovenia, Bank of Slovenia, 1998, p. 65). When independence came in 1991, with the consequent transition to a full market economy, one might have expected Slovenian firms to change ahead with outward FDI -- after all, they had made moderate investment abroad since the 1960s (Svetlicic, 1997, p. 291). On the contrary, faced with some serious challenges -- the loss of former Yugoslav markets, uncertainties related to privatization, legal barriers[a] and a sceptical public opinion (ibid.) -- they discontinued outward FDI, some going so far as to divest. Outward FDI resumed in 1995 but most recent changes in the outward investment stock[b] have been more a matter of accounting in claims and liabilities between parent firms and affiliates than of an increase in equity holdings.

The outward FDI data, however, do not reveal the underlying restructuring taking place in this area. A recent survey of major Slovenian enterprises (Kra□ovec, 1996)[c] revealed that the motives for outward FDI have changed radically, resulting in considerable structural changes. The new motive is the search for new markets and it has brought new firms into the FDI arena. Establishing and strengthening market shares[d] and accessing cheaper labour abroad[e] are the main purposes of these investments, and they are being made in Central and Eastern European countries in general and Croatia in particular. As much as 83 per cent of leading Slovenian firms see this region as the most important destination for potential outward FDI until the year 2000. Almost half of them (49 per cent) plan to start or increase investment abroad by the year 2000, with the establishment of joint ventures (60 per cent), the establishment of majority-owned affiliates (41 per cent), increasing investment in existing affiliates (35 per cent) and takeovers of foreign firms (22 per cent) all mentioned as major avenues for investment.[f]

With advances in privatization, Slovenian firms are now better positioned to take advantage of opportunities for international production, as evidenced by the survey of major Slovenian companies cited earlier. Similarly, improving the access of Slovenian firms to Western European markets may compensate for the loss of the former Yugoslav markets, contributing to an improved financial position. Slovenia has also been quite successful in attracting *inward* FDI, and the presence of foreign TNCs is expected not only to have a positive demonstration effect on local firms but also to facilitate their integration with international production networks. Finally, public opinion has come to recognize the benefits of outward FDI for the economy.

Source: UNCTAD, based on Svetlicic and Rojec, 1998.

[a] In the early 1990s, outward investment was authorized only if it was financed from the investing firm's profits. Firms were not allowed to draw on loans to finance investment abroad.

[b] $ 281million in 1994, $ 404 million in 1995 and $ 366 million in 1996 (Slovenia, Bank of Slovenia, 1998, p. 65). Data on outward FDI are also changing as a result of modifications in the statistical reporting system. A major revision was undertaken in 1997, implying retroactive corrections for 1993-1996 as well.

[c] The survey, undertaken in 1996, was based on interviews with 120 managers of leading Slovenian firms. These firms account for more than half of Slovenia's exports.

[d] As much as 81 per cent of the leading Slovenian enterprises consider maintaining and strengthening market shares a major motive for outward FDI (Kra□ovec, 1996, p. 6).

[e] Wages in Slovenia are substantially higher than in any other Central and Eastern European country.

[f] Firms are planning many forms simultaneously; so shares do not add up to 100 per cent.

B. Is Central and Eastern Europe attracting enough foreign direct investment?

1. The relative position of the region

The trends discussed in the preceding section raise the question of whether Central and Eastern Europe has indeed attracted as much FDI as one would expect for a region at its level of development, especially given the early expectations that FDI would be "crucial in the transition" process (IMF, World Bank, OECD and EBRD, 1991, p. 75). In fact, the region's share in world inward FDI stock is low, much lower than the region's share in world GDP, world population, or world imports (table IX.5), although the region has begun

Box IX.2. How high is the outward FDI stock of the Russian Federation?

While the low level of outward FDI flows from Central and Eastern Europe may be viewed as a natural consequence of the lack of ownership advantages possessed by enterprises in transition, there are also indications that, at least in some countries, the imperfections of statistics lead to an overestimation of difference between inflows and outflows. For various reasons (a lack of interest in reporting outflows, differences in formal reporting requirements, difficulties in accounting for assets accumulated abroad before transition, etc.), the statistics of some countries are believed to capture only a small part of FDI outflows and outward stocks.

Counting on cumulative FDI outflows since 1992, the accumulated FDI outflows of the Russian Federation amounted to about $3.7 billion at the end of 1997,[a] on the basis of balance-of-payments data. However, a recent study has suggested that a figure of $20 to $30 billion might be more realistic for Russian FDI outward stock (Bulatov, 1998). There are other estimates suggesting even higher FDI outward stock figures. In 1995, two independent studies suggested that the stock of Russian investment abroad -- direct, portfolio and other -- was of the order of $130 billion at the beginning of 1995 (Rybkin, 1995; Gorshenin, 1995). In 1996, another study concluded that the volume of Russian investment abroad was more than $300 billion, of which direct and portfolio investments each represented $30 to $40 billion, while the 'other' category accounted for roughly $230 billion (Khaldin and Andrianov, 1996).

Why do such big differences exist between balance-of-payments data and other estimates? There may be various reasons:

- The balance-of-payments data do not capture fully the value of assets accumulated by the Soviet Union abroad. The bulk of these assets was inherited by the Russian Federation. The book value of Soviet companies abroad was considered to be $2 billion at the beginning of the 1990s (Sokolov, 1991) and the market value $10 billion (Gorshenin, 1995). Indeed, the market value of outward FDI may have increased over time, as compared with its original book value. Given decline of the ruble against the dollar in the 1990s, the market value may now be significantly higher when expressed in rubles.

- The balance-of-payments data do not account either for the assets that the Russian Federation inherited in other former Soviet Republics. These investments had in fact been registered as domestic investment by the Union of Soviet Socialist Republics and became foreign assets once these republics gained independence.

- Some part of Russian assets abroad may be financed through outflows registered under other flows (such as portfolio flows, trade finance or service payments), increasing the whole outward FDI stock substantially (Bulatov, 1998).

- Finally, some of the outward flows may go completely unregistered. The above-mentioned studies suggest that the registration of FDI and other outflows is far less advanced than the reporting of FDI inflows.

These considerations suggest that the measurement of outward stock based on cumulative outflows needs to be supplemented, particularly for countries that have recently become independent. (Besides the Russian Federation, Croatia, which holds assets in Slovenia, may be another country in a similar situation; see Kopec, 1997, p. 145.) There may also be a need for a periodic re-evaluation of assets held abroad when outward FDI stocks are calculated. Finally, there may be some policy implications, for example, in countries where some of the outflows are believed to go unregistered because of capital flight.

Source: UNCTAD.

[a] For an estimate of earlier FDI outflows see United Nations, Department of Economic and Social Development, 1992b.

Table IX.5. Central and Eastern Europe: share in world inward FDI stock and flows, compared with shares in population, GDP and imports

(Percentage)

Item	World population (1996)	World GDP (1996)	World trade (imports) (1996)	World inward FDI stock (1996)	World FDI inflows	
					1996	1997
Central and Eastern Europe's share	6.1	2.4	2.3	1.5	3.6	4.0

Source: UNCTAD/TNC database.

Table IX.6. Selected indicators of the importance of inward FDI, by region, 1996

Region	FDI inward stock over GDP, 1996 (Per cent)	FDI inward stock per capita, 1996 (Dollars)	FDI inflows over gross fixed capital formation, 1994-1996 (Per cent)
World	11	528	5
Developed countries	9	2 425	4
Developing countries	16	194	8
Africa	17	86	8
Latin America and the Caribbean	17	660	11
Developing Europe	8	347	14
Asia and the Pacific	15	150	7
West Asia	9	259	0.5
Central Asia	11	71	..
South, East and South-East Asia	16	143	8
Pacific	40	618	25
Central and Eastern Europe[a]	6	151	8
Selected group of countries for comparison[b]	26	848	15

Source: UNCTAD, FDI/TNC database.

[a] Including Croatia, Slovenia and TFYR Macedonia.

[b] Includes 18 countries with a gross domestic product per capita in the range of $2,000-$5,000. The countries are listed in table IX.7.

to catch up, as witness its much higher shares in the world's FDI inflows in both 1996 and 1997 than its shares of the world's FDI stock, imports or GDP in those same years.

Not surprisingly, the ratio of FDI stock to GDP for Central and Eastern Europe falls behind not only the world average, but also the average for developed countries and the averages for all developing regions, although the gap differs according to region (table IX.6). With FDI stock per capita, Central and Eastern Europe is also still considerably behind the world average, even further behind the average for all developed countries, and behind the average for the developing countries taken as a whole; but it is ahead of Central Asia and, more strikingly, South, East and South-East Asia, reflecting its higher relative GDP. With the ratio of FDI inflows to gross fixed capital formation (1994-1996 average), matters improve even further: there the Central and Eastern Europe average is above both the world average and the average of developed countries, and about the same as (table IX.6) or just slightly below (figure IX.2) the average for developing countries, reflecting the region's greater similarity with developing countries in this respect.

When Central and Eastern Europe's average ratios of FDI relative to various economic variables are contrasted with those of a comparable group of countries at roughly similar levels of economic development (countries with GDP per capita in the range of $2,000-

$5,000, excluding OPEC members), it is seen that the latter group of countries has higher averages in all of the measures indicated in table IX.6. As might be expected from the previous discussion, however, the difference is least noticeable with respect to gross fixed capital formation. (If Central and Eastern Europe had had the same FDI/GDP ratio in 1996 as the reference group, its inward FDI stock would have been $216 billion instead of the actual figure of $50 billion).[13]

Naturally, the picture differs from country to country (table IX.7). Hungary's ratio of FDI stock to GDP, for example, is three times the world average, over twice the developing country average, and 15 per cent higher than that of the reference group. However, Hungary

Table IX.7. Central and Eastern Europe: selected indicators of the importance of inward FDI, by country

Country	FDI inward stock over GDP, 1996 (Per cent)	FDI inward stock per capita, 1996 (Dollars)	FDI inflows over gross fixed capital formation, 1994-1996 (Per cent)
Central and Eastern Europe average[a]	6 [b]	151 [b]	8[b]
Hungary	34	1 490	30
Estonia	19	551	23
Latvia	17	335	..
Albania	11	84	..
Czech Republic	11	537	11
Poland	11	339	18
Moldova, Republic of	9	34	36
Slovakia	5	161	4
Bulgaria	4	51	5
Lithuania	4	80	..
Romania	4	55	6
Croatia	4	185	..
Slovenia	4	366	5
Ukraine	3	26	4
Russian Federation	1	45	2
TFYR Macedonia	1	20	..
Belarus	-	6	1
Reference group[c]			
Trinidad and Tobago	77	2 996	46
Grenada	71	2 016	22
Malaysia	49	2 014	12
Fiji	39	925	21
Costa Rica	36	915	22
Botswana	33	942	31
Chile	27	1 356	17
Mexico	22	783	15
Panama	22	646	13
Tunisia	22	470	7
Belize	15	762	15
Peru	15	374	23
Thailand	12	328	3
Colombia	11	261	16
Mauritius	7	252	2
Turkey	3	92	2
Syrian Arab Republic	2	74	1
Lebanon	2	61	2
Average, reference group	26	848	15

Source: UNCTAD, FDI/TNC database.

[a] Including Croatia, Slovenia and TFYR Macedonia.

[b] Unweighted averages (ratios for the region or group taken as a whole).

[c] This group, selected for comparison, includes countries with GDP per capita ranging from $2,000 to $5,000 per annum.

is the only country with a ratio of FDI stock to GDP and FDI stock per capita exceeding the corresponding average ratios for the reference group, although there are five other countries in Central and Eastern Europe (Albania, Czech Republic, Estonia, Latvia, Poland) in which the ratio of FDI stock to GDP is equal to or exceeds the world average. In eight of the twelve Central and Eastern European countries for which data are available, FDI inflows as a ratio of gross fixed capital formation are equal to or above the average for the world; but only in four countries (Estonia, Hungary, Republic of Moldova and Poland) is this ratio higher than that for the reference group. Indeed, some major Central and Eastern European economies such as the Russian Federation, Ukraine and Slovakia perform below world, developing-country and developed-country averages, as well as below the averages for the reference group in all of the measures.

To a large extent, the gap between the inward FDI of the region and the level that would be expected judging from the region's economic significance, size and other characteristics (as reflected in its GDP, gross fixed capital formation and population) is explained by the fact that, as mentioned in section A, the overwhelming majority of Central and Eastern European countries opened up to inward FDI relatively recently and have thus accumulated FDI stocks over a relatively short period. Nevertheless, it remains surprising that the share of FDI in gross fixed capital formation in GDP is not higher in the region, since one might expect that foreign investors would take advantage of the newly opened opportunities, as they have done in China, and would be particularly interested in the locational advantages of these countries. That they have not done so probably reflects the influence of various factors: legal and regulatory problems, a deeper and longer than expected transition-related recession, a prolonged privatization process, and the lack of local experience in business facilitation. The countries of Central and Eastern Europe are conscious of a number of these obstacles as shown by the results of the UNCTAD mail questionnaire survey (box IX.3) of investment-promotion agencies.

Box IX.3. UNCTAD's survey of investment-promotion agencies in Central and Eastern Europe

To gather first-hand insights into issues related to FDI flows into Central and Eastern Europe, the UNCTAD secretariat conducted, in early 1998, a mail questionnaire survey covering the 17 investment-promotion agencies of this region. They were asked to give an evaluation of their country's ability to attract and absorb FDI during 1993-1997, and to do the same for 1998-2002. (The year 1993 was chosen as a starting date for analysis because it was by 1 January 1993 that the current state structure of the region took shape.) They were also asked to identify major factors that determined their countries' FDI attractiveness in 1993-1997, and to pinpoint the factors that, in their opinion, would most improve during 1998-2002. Finally, they were invited to specify three industries that they considered most successful and three they thought least successful in attracting FDI, both in 1993-1997 and in 1998-2002.

Between January and April 1998, responses were received from 15 countries --- Albania, Belarus, Bulgaria, Croatia, Czech Republic, Estonia, the Former Yugoslav Republic of Macedonia, Hungary, Lithuania, Poland, Republic of Moldova, Romania, Slovakia, Slovenia, and Ukraine.[a] Even though the Russian Federation did not respond, the survey results can be considered representative of the region not only because of the response rate (88 per cent), but also because the countries of the respondents account for 99 per cent of the region's population and GDP if the Russian Federation is excluded. The differentiation between the Russian Federation and the rest of the region is based on the fact that the former shows more similarities with other large, natural-resource-rich economies of the world than with the other countries of its own region, which are characterized by smaller territories, populations and resource endowments, and by greater reliance on created investment opportunities.

Source: UNCTAD.

[a] The response received from Hungary was based on the consensus view of 16 locally established banks and six other institutions.

The empirical comparisons and explanations discussed above suggest that there is considerable room for an increase in FDI flows into Central and Eastern European countries. As the enabling framework evolves-- of which some elements already exist but others, such as well-functioning competitive markets and policy coherence, need strengthening -- and as various economic determinants as well as business facilitation efforts improve, more FDI is likely to be attracted to countries in the region.

2. Strengths and weaknesses

The investment-promotion agencies of the region certainly think that the FDI potential of their countries is far from exhausted and that their economies could productively attract more investment. Indeed, the respondents to the UNCTAD survey of investment-promotion agencies felt that only about a half of the region's capacity to attract and absorb FDI was utilized during 1993-1997.[14] (The views of representatives of investment-promotion agencies are important since they are perhaps the best judges of the economic strengths and weaknesses of their countries.) Most respondents also considered that their countries' success in attracting FDI was below that of South, East and South-East Asia, but comparable to that of Latin America and the Caribbean, and higher than that of Africa (table IX.8).

While the region's potential for attracting FDI was perceived as being largely untapped, the general view of the respondents was that it would improve markedly between 1998 and 2002. The overwhelming majority of the respondents, especially from the laggard countries, gave a substantially higher rating for their expected degree of success in attracting FDI during 1998-2002 than they did for their (actual) degree of success during 1993-1997: the average mark given by the respondents to their expected success in attracting FDI in the future was close to 7 (on a scale of 0-10) as compared with about 4 for the period 1993-1997. Only the response for Hungary indicated that the expected level of FDI in the future was anticipated to remain at the 1993-1997 level. All others foresaw some advancements in their FDI performance, sometimes significant improvements .

At the industry level, judging from the survey responses, there is considerable variation in both 1993-1997 and 1998-2002 (table IX.9). According to the responses, the secondary and tertiary sectors on balance have performed quite well, while the primary sector has been disappointing. Food, chemicals (including pharmaceuticals), cement and building materials, and automotives were success cases most often cited. Chemicals and automotives are relatively skill- and technology-intensive, and major contributors to the modernization of Central and Eastern European economies. The success of the building materials industry is linked to both the availability of competitively priced raw materials

Table IX.8. Central and Eastern Europe: inward FDI performance, compared by respondents with other regions, 1993-1997

Item	Average mark[a]
Respondent countries' inflows compared with the average of:	
Central and Eastern Europe	4.2
Africa	7.5
Latin America	3.7
South, East and South-East Asia	2.1
Respondent countries' inward stock compared with the average of:	
Central and Eastern Europe	4.0
Africa	7.5
Latin America	4.0
South, East and South-East Asia	2.3

Source: UNCTAD survey.

[a] Average of the marks assigned by the respondents on a scale of 0 to 10, with 0 signifying the lowest degree of success, 5 meaning the same degree of success and 10 meaning the highest degree of success compared with the other regions in the utilization of FDI absorptive capacity.

(including those required for exports) and the needs of economic reconstruction, while that of the food industry is related to the basic need to improve the quality and safety of food products and the attractiveness of newly opening local markets. These success cases stand in sharp contrast with the experience of electrical machinery and apparatus, and of machinery and equipment generally, which were marked by a number of respondents as not having attracted enough FDI.

Of the past successes in attracting FDI, the food industry and, to a lower degree, chemicals are expected to continue to perform well in the near future (1998-2000). Not so for the cement, building materials and automotive industries, because in these industries first mover advantages had already been reaped during 1993-1997. The electrical machinery and apparatus industry, as well as machinery and equipment, are expected to continue to lag behind in the near future. Textiles and basic metals and metal products are also believed by the respondents to have little additional FDI potential during 1998-2002.

Table IX.9. Central and Eastern Europe: survey responses with respect to degree of success in terms of attracting and absorbing FDI, by industry, 1998

(Number of responses)

	1993-1997		1998-2002	
Sector and industry	Mentioned as best performing industry	Mentioned as less performing industry	Mentioned as best performing industry	Mentioned as less performing industry
Primary sector				
Agriculture, hunting, forestry and fishing	-	8	3	5
Mining and quarrying	-	3	1	3
Secondary sector	31	19	23	16
Food, beverages & tobacco	7	2	6	1
Textiles, leather & clothing	1	1	1	3
Wood and paper	1	2	2	1
Publishing and printing	1	-	1	-
Chemicals and chemical products (including pharmaceutic	5	1	3	-
Rubber and plastic products	-	-	-	1
Non-metallic mineral products (cement and building materi	4	-	-	1
Basic metals and metal products	2	1	-	3
Machinery and equipment	2	3	2	2
Electrical machinery and apparatus	-	4	1	2
Precision instruments	2	1	2	-
Motor vehicles and other transport equipment (automotiv	3	-	1	-
Unspecified secondary	3	4	4	2
Tertiary sector	20	15	24	6
Electricity and water distribution	-	2	3	2
Construction	1	-	-	-
Wholesale trade and distributive trade	5	-	-	2
Hotels and restaurants (tourism)	-	4	5	-
Transport and storage	1	3	2	1
Post and telecommunications	3	2	2	1
Finance (including banking and insurance)	5	1	5	-
Real estate	1	-	1	-
Rental activities	1	-	1	-
Business services (including engineering and information	3	2	5	-
Health and social services	-	1	-	-

Source: UNCTAD survey.

Note: the table tabulates the responses according to UNCTAD's standard classification of industries. It should be noted that standardization has resulted in a certain amount of double counting, as some of the answers are reflected under more than one industry.

According to the evaluation of the respondents, most industries successful in attracting FDI have been in the secondary sector during 1993-1997. For 1998-2002, however, services were viewed as having more potential to attract FDI than manufacturing, being cited almost as often as manufacturing industries. It is even more striking that services rarely appeared on the list of industries less attractive in the future: they were mentioned in this category less than a third as often as manufacturing industries.

Some of the services that have performed well, or are expected to do so, in attracting FDI could make significant contributions to the transition to market economies. These include wholesale and distributive trade, telecommunications and finance (including banking and insurance). Business services (including engineering and information services) are also important for the transition process, and have been identified by a larger number of respondents as having considerable potential for FDI. Prospects for tourism are also expected to improve significantly: the responses indicate that this industry's potential has been largely untapped in the past, but its FDI performance could improve markedly in the near future. A common feature of all services industries mentioned as past or potential successes in terms of FDI performance is that they rely critically on well-trained labour, an asset that Central and Eastern European countries either already possess or expect to acquire in the future.

Key to any improved utilization of the region's FDI potential is, of course, the nature of the various factors determining the location decisions of TNCs. The UNCTAD survey throws some light on what the investment-promotion agencies consider to be their countries' strengths and weaknesses in this respect (table IX.10):

Economic factors

- Local markets have apparently not yet attained the size and growth rate that would help raise substantial market-seeking FDI. Only a few respondents saw the size of their local markets as a major factor enhancing their FDI attractiveness during 1993-1997.

Table IX.10. Central and Eastern Europe: factors enhancing or constraining inward FDI, 1993-1997

(Number of responses)

Factor	Enhancing factor[a]	Constraining factor[b]
Economic factors		
Labour cost	13	-
Labour skills	12	1
Integration prospects	7	1
Market size	2	8
Market growth	2	3
Natural resources	1	5
Management skills	1	1
Physical infrastructure	1	4
Financial infrastructure	1	3
Access to Russian market	-	1
Niche industries	-	1
Policy factors		
Macro-economic stability	9	1
Currency convertibility	5	-
Favourable privatization strategies	4	3
Readiness of local firms	3	2
Economic reconstruction possibilities	3	3
Progress of privatization	2	2
BITs	1	2
Legal stability	-	5
Enterprise restructuring	-	3
Business facilitation		
Subjective proximity to investors	11	-
Information	3	5
Political environment	3	2
Country image	1	8
Financial incentives	1	8
Market incentives	1	3
Enterprise registration	1	4

Source: UNCTAD survey.

[a] Number of respondents who identified a particular item as an enhancing factor.

[b] Number of respondents who identified a particular factor as an obstacle.

Note: the questionnaire asked the respondents to list the factors (not exceeding six in each case) that, in their view, had most enhanced, or represented the biggest obstacles to realizing their FDI potential.

Consistent with this is the perception of low purchasing power and low or negative growth as disincentives for FDI.

- Low labour costs, combined with the availability of skilled labour, are seen by the majority of respondents as major factors contributing positively to the region's ability to attract FDI.
- The availability of natural resources is not seen as a major factor helping to attract FDI, but the absence of such resources is seen by some as a constraint. (It should be recalled that the responses do not cover the Russian Federation, the principal resource-abundant country of the region.)
- The state of the physical and financial infrastructure was seen as a limiting factor by nearly a third of the respondents.

Taken together, the survey responses suggest that the region's capacity to attract market- and natural-resource-seeking FDI has been limited by small markets, low growth, and inadequate resource endowments. However, the respondents considered that the opportunities for efficiency-seeking investment have been better used, given the availability of low-cost, high-skill labour.

Policy-related factors

- According to the majority of the respondents, macroeconomic stability and currency convertibility contribute positively to the ability of the region to attract and absorb FDI.
- Surprisingly, privatization strategies were assessed very differently by the respondents. While progress in privatization and favourable privatization strategies were seen as factors enhancing FDI flows into advanced countries, the slowness of privatization and the reluctance to accept foreign investors in privatization strategies were still regarded as major handicaps hindering FDI flows into other countries.
- Legal uncertainties are major impediments to attracting FDI: they were mentioned as problems by more respondents than any other single policy-related factor.

Factors related to business facilitation

- The overwhelming majority of the respondents identified geographical and psychological proximity as the single most important factor enhancing their countries' attractiveness as FDI locations during 1993-1997.
- Image problems and a perceived lack of financial incentives were cited as the most important business-facilitation factors hindering the realization of the FDI potential. Only one response judged that no special improvement in this category was needed.
- Only three respondents of 15 expressed satisfaction with the current availability of information on investment opportunities, while five considered it inadequate.

As observed earlier, the respondents overall were optimistic when it came to the ability of the region to attract higher FDI flows. In keeping with that optimism, various locational determinants are expected to change over the period 1998-2002 (table IX.11):

- A number of economic determinants are expected to improve. These include, in particular, the region's physical and financial infrastructure. Prospects for economic integration with investor countries are also expected to improve. This suggests that the possibility of wider regional markets would improve prospects for market-seeking and possibly efficiency-seeking investment.

- As regards policy factors, the stabilization of the legal environment is the single most important factor expected to boost FDI flows in the future. Other factors expected to contribute in this respect include further advancement in enterprise restructuring, improvements in macroeconomic stability, major advances in privatization, and a more welcoming attitude towards FDI on the part of local firms.

- Most respondents forecast improved country images, reflecting improvements in the economic and regulatory determinants, coupled with better information about investment opportunities. Many also envisage better incentives and are moving in this direction (box IX.4).[15]

If the countries in Central and Eastern Europe succeed in improving the various conditions that determine the locational decisions of TNCs, they can expect to attract more FDI. If that were the case, a scenario under which FDI would become more important in more countries -- and in the region as a whole -- seems most likely. In such a scenario, the inward FDI stock in the region by the year 2000 may well exceed the figure of $ 100 billion that was predicted in 1993 (Dunning, 1993b).

Table IX.11. Central and Eastern Europe: factors expected to enhance inward FDI, 1998-2002

Factor	Number of responses[a]
Economic factors	
R&D potential	11
Physical infrastructure	9
Integration prospects	5
Financial infrastructure	4
Market size	2
Niche industries	2
Labour skills	2
Access to Russian market	1
Management skills	1
Labour cost	1
Policy factors	
Legal stability	9
Enterprise restructuring	5
Macro-economic stability	4
Progress of privatization	4
Readiness of local firms	3
BITs	2
Favourable privatization strategies	1
Economic reconstruction possibilities	1
Business facilitation	
Country image	8
Information	6
Financial incentives	6
Political environment	3
Tax system	1
Enterprise registration	1

Source: UNCTAD survey.

[a] Refers to the number of respondents who identified a particular item as a factor improving the country's attractive or absorptive potential with respect to FDI.

Note: the questionnaire asked the respondents to list the factors (not exceeding six in each case) that in their view would most improve their countries' FDI potential.

Box IX.4. Investment incentives in the Czech Republic

Until 1998, the Czech Republic offered only a handful of one-off agreements to attract potential investors. Most of the benefits of these agreements were to be offered by the local authorities and not by the central government.

Mainly as a reaction to two consecutive years (1996 and 1997) of declining FDI inflows, and prompted by the belief that the Czech Republic could absorb much more FDI, the Government of the Czech Republic announced a comprehensive six-point investment package on 29 April 1998, to boost investment. In line with the Czech Republic's OECD obligations for equal treatment of domestic and foreign investors, the package applies, in principle, to both categories of investors, although foreign firms are widely believed to be in a better position to apply for it, given the minimum investment requirements. It covers corporate taxation, waivers of customs duty and value-added taxes on imported equipment, the possibility of special customs zones for major investors, job-training grants, special job-creation benefits for firms locating in underdeveloped regions, and the provision of low cost land (box table).

All incentives apply only to firms investing more than $ 25 million in a manufacturing operation falling under the OECD classification of "high-technology products and industries". The investment must be made through a newly registered company, whether greenfield or joint venture, and satisfy authorities that the production process is environmentally friendly. Investors must apply for these incentives through CzechInvest, although each ministry or government body concerned issues a separate contract directly to the applicant firm to cover the incentive granted under its responsibility.

Box table. The investment incentives scheme of the Czech Republic, April 1998

Area	Description of incentives	Conditions and limits
Corporate taxation	1. Deferred payment of corporate tax over five years; remission of tax liabilities if requirements are met; and provision of a tax bonus equal to the remitted amount which shall be deductible from future tax obligations.	For 1: independent accounting; machinery bought must not previously have been subject to depreciation in the Czech Republic; losses carried forward must be offset from first year profit.
	2. Accelerated tax depreciation (will be offered from January 1999).	For 2: none.
Customs-free zone	Location of the new production in an existing customs-free zone; or creation of a new customs-free zone for the new production.	At least 40 per cent of the total project value invested into machinery; machinery brought must not have been subject to depreciation in any country; significant long-term benefits.
Customs and value-added tax	Remission of customs duty on high-technology machinery, deferred value-added tax on high-technology machinery for 90 days in view of refunding by the revenue office after registration in the Czech Republic.	At least 40 per cent of total project value invested into machinery; machinery brought must not have been subject to depreciation in any country.
Job creation benefits	Interest-free loan for jobs for Czech citizens, to be converted into a subsidy if requirements are met.	Only for investment in underdeveloped regions; direct employment for a given number of people for two years; use of financial resources in conformity with a given objective.
Training benefits	Interest-free loan for training and re-training of Czech citizens, up to 50 per cent of training costs, to be converted into a subsidy if requirements met.	Employment for a given number of people in a relevant region for a given period; up to the total limit in a designed budget.

Source: CzechInvest (1998).

Notes

1 For the purpose of this analysis, this region is defined to include the following countries: Albania, Belarus, Bosnia and Herzegovina, Bulgaria, Croatia, Czech Republic, Estonia, Former Yugoslav Republic of Macedonia, Hungary, Latvia, Lithuania, Poland, Republic of Moldova, Romania, Russian Federation, Slovakia, Slovenia, Ukraine, Yugoslavia. (The data for Croatia, Former Yugoslav Republic of Macedonia and Slovenia can be found in the annex under the heading "Developing Europe".) There are no official FDI data available for Bosnia and Herzegovina and for Yugoslavia. The inward FDI stock of Yugoslavia was unofficially estimated at $1.1 billion in 1997, mostly due to investment in telecommunications (Scepanovic, 1998, p. 40). For 1990, the inward FDI stock of Serbia (accounting for 94 per cent of Yugoslavia's population) was unofficially estimated to be $ 371 million ("Foreign investment in Serbia - a three decade long tradition", http://ww.yugoslavia.com/Economy/invest.htm).

2 The cost-competitiveness of export-oriented production in the Czech Republic had deteriorated and, in May 1997, the fixed-exchange-rate regime proved to be unsustainable. Austerity measures to reduce the massive current account deficit led to lower GDP growth, which amounted to 2 per cent per annum between the fourth quarter of 1996 and the fourth quarter of 1997. (*The Economist*, 9 May 1998, p. 120.)

3 This increase also reflects some "round-tripping" as indicated by a fast parallel rise of inflows and outflows and a growing discrepancy between home and host country statistics. ('Round-tripping' refers to the transfer of funding abroad in order to bring some or all of the investment back as FDI and claim the tax and other benefits to foreign investors.) In 1995-1997, inflows grew at 129 per cent per annum, while outflows grew even faster -- at 191 per cent per year. That a part of the fast growing inflows may be financed from outflows is further suggested by the fact that, since 1995, the reports of the OECD source countries show only half of the volume of FDI inflows reported in the balance of payments of the Russian Federation (Meyer and Pind, 1998, p.21). Much of the round-tripping FDI is not covered by source country statistical surveys either because the transactions undertaken are too small to be registered or are transferred through third countries, typically outside the OECD area (Sheets, 1996).

4 The Czech Republic, Hungary, Poland, Romania, the Russian Federation, Slovenia and Ukraine together account for almost 90 per cent of the region's inward FDI stock.

5 For a detailed analysis of FDI in Estonia, including a comparison with other Central and Eastern European countries, see Varblane (1998).

6 The transition indicator produced by the EBRD is based on the following criteria: Large-scale privatization of enterprises; small-scale privatization of enterprises; governance and restructuring of enterprises; price liberalization; trade and foreign exchange system; competition policy; banking reform and interest rate liberalization; and securities markets and non-bank financial institutions; the maximum value that the indicator can reach is 4 (EBRD, 1997, p. 14). While the bulk of the components constituting the transition index are not related to FDI, the factor of enterprise restructuring may indirectly reflect conditions for FDI.

7 Economic transition and inward FDI are intricately linked in Central and Eastern Europe, particularly at the enterprise level. During the process of their transformation to market-oriented entities, Central and Eastern European firms require an injection of high amounts of capital and managerial skills. It is distinctively specific to the formerly state-owned firms of the region that the costs of post-acquisition restructuring exceed the costs of the acquisition itself (Meyer, 1998, p. 242). This leads to "brownfield investments", involving the "acquisition of a firm in the region for market share reasons, but entirely new production facilities are then developed within the firm" (Estrin, Hughes and Todd, 1997, p. 23). Only companies with very good capital endowment and managerial know-how -- mostly TNCs -- are capable of overcoming this constraint. In return, the acquired firms offer skilled labour and easy access to local distribution networks.

8 A similar exercise carried out in 1996 and covering 17 Central and Eastern European and five Central Asian countries obtained a rank correlation coefficient between cumulative FDI inflows during 1989-1996 and the average transition indicator of 0.88, and a coefficient between 1996 FDI inflows and the average indicator of 0.86 (Lankes and Stern, 1998). Meyer and Pind (1998, pp. 16-17) also found a close relationship between progress in transition and per capita and per GDP FDI in Central and Eastern Europe and Central Asia.

9 In 1997, the Russian Federation was the last and Ukraine the last but one on the *Global Competitiveness Report* list. Of the other Central and Eastern European countries, Poland was 49th in 1998 (up from 50th in 1997), Slovakia 48th (down from 35th), Hungary 43rd (up from 46th), and Czech Republic 35th (down from 32nd). In the ranking by the *World Competitiveness Yearbook 1998*, of the 46 countries analysed, the Russian Federation ranks last both in 1997 and 1998. In 1998, Poland is 45th (down from 43rd), the Czech Republic 38th (down from 35th), and Hungary 28th (up from 36th) (IMD, 1998).

10 Virtually all of the potential privatization was considered to have been accomplished in Hungary by the end of 1997: *"By and large it is ready ... 85 to 90 per cent of the task has been accomplished. What is left is only minor work, tidying up, checking up and settlement..."* (Mihalyi, 1998, p. 461).

11 A study by Baldwin, Francois and Portes (1997) found a significant positive impact of inward FDI on GDP growth in the Czech Republic, Estonia, Hungary, Poland and Slovenia. Recent empirical surveys of the Czech Republic (Charap and Zemplinerova, 1994), Slovenia (Rojec, 1998) and Hungary (Hunya, 1996) also suggest that, largely by outperforming local companies, foreign affiliates do, indeed, contribute to the transition.

12 See UNCTAD, 1997a, pp. 98-99, for a discussion on Hungary's nascent outward investors.

13 However, 53 per cent of the 1996 global inward FDI stock had been accumulated before 1990 when the Central and Eastern European countries had joined the rest of the world in actively seeking FDI. If this 53 per cent is discounted from these $216 billion, the FDI stock in Central and Eastern Europe still could have been $100 billion - twice the actual figure.

14 On a scale of 0 to 10 -- with "0" signifying no or practically no utilization of a country's FDI potential and "10" full utilization of such potential -- the majority of respondents gave a mark of 5 or less in answer to the question as regards the success with which their country's absorptive capacity had been utilized during 1993-1997. Only two countries (Hungary and Poland) obtained higher marks (7 and 8, respectively). Unweighted average marks for a country in the region stood at 3.8. (The weighted average, using inward FDI stock, is 5.7.)

15 Respondents envisage more incentives even though the value of incentives in significantly influencing locational decisions is questionable (UNCTAD, 1996d).

References

African Development Bank (1998). *African Development Report 1998* (Oxford: Oxford University Press).

América Economía (1997/1998). "Las 500 mayores empresas de América Latina", *Annual Edition 1995/1996* (América Economía).

Asian Development Bank (ADB) (1998). *Asian Development Outlook 1998* (New York: Oxford University Press).

Atingi-Ego, M. and Kasekende, L. (1998). "Uganda's growth experience and prospects", in World Economic Forum, *Africa Competitiveness Report 1998* (Geneva: World Economic Forum), pp. 62-71.

Austria, National Bank (1993). *Berichte und Studien der Oesterreichischen Nationalbank*, Heft 3 (Vienna: Austrian National Bank).

Bach, Christopher (1998). "U.S. international transactions: fourth quarter and year 1997", *Survey of Current Business*, 78, 4 (April), pp. 51-78.

Bachtler, John and Keith Clement (1990). *The Impact of the Single European Market on Foreign Direct Investment in the United Kingdom* (London: HMSO).

Baldwin, Richard, Joseph Francois and Richard Portes (1997). "The costs and benefits of Eastern enlargement: the impact on the EU and Central Europe", *Economic Policy: A European Forum*, 24, pp. 125-170.

Barry, Frank and John Bradley (1997). "FDI and trade: the Irish host-country experience", *The Economic Journal*, 107, 445 (November), pp. 1798-1811.

Basant, R., P. Chandra and L. K. Mytelka (1998). "Strategic partnering in telecom software: Northern Telecom's technology network in India" (Geneva: UNCTAD), mimeo..

Bellak, Christian and John Cantwell (1996). "Foreign direct investment: how much is it worth? Comments on S. J. Gray and A.M. Rugman", *Transnational Corporations*, 5, 1 (April), pp. 85-97.

Bennell, Paul (1997a). "Foreign direct investment in Africa: rhetoric and reality", *SAIS Review* (Summer/Fall), pp. 127-139.

________ (1997b). "Privatization in Sub-Saharan Africa: progress and prospects during the 1990s", *World Development*, 25, 11, pp. 1785-1803.

Bielchowsky, Ricardo and G. Stumpo (1996). "Empresas transnacionales manufactureras en cuatro estilos de restructuración en América Latina: los casos de Argentina, Brasil, Chile y México despues de la sustitución de importaciones" in Jorge Katz, ed., *Estabilización Macroeconómica, Reforma Estructural y Comportamiento Industrial: Estructura y Fincionamiento del Sector Manufacturero Latinoamericano en los Años 90* (Buenos Aires: CEPAL/IDRC/Alianza Editorial).

Blomström, Magnus and Ari Kokko (1997). "Regional integration and foreign direct investment", National Bureau of Economic Research, Working Paper No. 6019 (Cambridge, Massachusetts: National Bureau of Economic Research), mimeo..

Bora, Bijit (forthcoming). "Potential for investment liberalization between AFTA and CER", in Robertson, David and Chia Siew Yue, eds. *AFTA-CER Linkage: The Way Forward* (Singapore: Institute for South East Asia Studies).

Brazil, Banco Central do Brasil (1998a). *Censo de Capitais Estrangeiros no Brasil: Ano-Base 1995* (Brasilia: Banco Central do Brasil).

________ (1998b). *Informantes Economicas: Balança de Pagamentos - 1er Trimestre de 1998* (Brasilia: Banco Central do Brasil).

Brazil, Banco Nacional de Desenvolvimento Económico e Social (BNDES) (1998). *Privatização: Resultados* (Brasilia: Banco Nacional de Desenvolvimiento Economico e Social).

Brewer, Thomas L. and Stephen Young (1998). *The Multilateral Investment System and Multinational Enterprises* (Oxford: Oxford University Press).

Bridge, J. (1998). "Supply-chain-dynamics: a case study of the automotive sector". Paper presented at the International Workshop on Global Production and Local Jobs: New Perspectives on Enterprise Networks, Employment and Local Development Policy, Geneva, ILO, 9-10 March, mimeo..

Bulatov, Alexander S. (1998). "Russian direct investment abroad: main motivations in the post-Soviet period", *Transnational Corporations*, 7, 1 (February), forthcoming.

Burgenmeier, Beat and Jean-Louis Mucchielli (1991). *Multinationals and Europe 1992: Strategies for the Future* (London: Routledge).

Business Map (1998). *SA Insider South African Investment Report 1998* (Johannesburg: Business Map).

Bustos, Sergio (1998). "Prosperar Brasil?", *Latin Trade*, 6, 6 (June).

Calderon, Alvaro, M. Mortimore, W. Peres (1996). "Mexico: foreign investment as a source of international competitiveness", in J. Dunning and R. Narula, eds., *Foreign Direct Investment and Governments: Catalysts for Economic Restructuring* (London: Routledge).

Canada, Minister of Supply and Services (1985). "Foreign Investment Review Act: Final Annual Report, 1984-1985". Presented to the Governor General of Canada by the Minister of Regional Industrial Expansion (Ottawa), mimeo..

Canada, Statistics Canada (1980). *Annual Report of the Ministry of Supply and Services under the Corporations and Labour Unions Returns Act, Part 1: Corporations, 1978* (Ottawa: Ministry of Supply and Services).

Cantwell, J. and R. Harding (1997). "The internationalization of German companies' R&D", Discussion paper in International Investment and Management, No. 233 (Reading: University of Reading), mimeo..

Charap, Joshua and Alena Zemplinerova (1994). "Foreign direct investment in the privatization and restructuring of the Czech economy", *Development and International Cooperation*, 10, 18, pp. 27-44.

Chudnovsky, D. and A. López (1997). "Market or policy driven? The foreign direct investment boom in Argentina", *Oxford Development Studies*, 25, 2.

________ and A. López (1998). "La inversión extranjera directa en la Argentina en los años 1990: tendencias, determinantes y modalidades", in Argentina, Ministerio de Relaciones Exteriores, Comercio Internacional y Culto, *Argentina de Cara al Mundo III*, (Buenos Aires: Ministry of Foreign Affaires).

Clarke, Tony (1998). "Towards a citizens MAI". Paper prepared by the Polaris Institute, Canada, mimeo..

Collier, Paul (1997). "Globalisation: what should be the African response?" (Oxford: Centre for the Study of African Economies), mimeo..

Cornford, Andrew and Jim Brandon (forthcoming). "The WTO agreement on financial services: problems of financial globalization in practice", in UNCTAD, *International Monetary and Financial Issues, vol. X* (New York and Geneva: UNCTAD), forthcoming.

Corporate Location (1994). "Botswana: an objective study of investment conditions" (Milton Keynes: Century House Information).

________ (1997). *Corporate Location Magazine*, November/December 1996 (London: Corporate Location).

________ (1998). "The foreign investor's gazetteer: Africa" (London: Corporate Location).

Coughlin, Cletus C., Joseph V. Terza, and Vachira Arromdae (1991). "State characteristics and the location of foreign direct investment within the United States", *The Review of Economics and Statistics*, LXXIII, 4 (November), pp. 675-683.

Council of Canadians (CoC) (1998). "The Multilateral Agreement on Investment (MAI). Towards a Citizens MAI: an alternative approach to developing a global investment treaty based on citizens' rights and democratic control". Working Instruments (Canada: Polaris Institute), mimeo..

Consumer International (CI) (1996). "Briefing on the OECD Multilateral Agreement on Investment (London: CI), mimeo..

Consumer Unity and Trust Society (CUTS) (1996). "Globalising liberalisation without regulations! Briefing on the OECD Multilateral Agreement on Investment" (Delhi: CUTS), mimeo..

________ (1998). "Multilateral frameworks for investment: what and where next?". Briefing kit (Jaipur: CUTS).

CzechInvest (1998). "A list of investment incentives for investors in the Czech Republic" (http://www.czechinvest.cz/news/press-releases/latest-pr.html#incentive package), 29 April.

Deutsche Bundesbank (1988). "Patent and licence transactions with foreign countries and other exchanges of technological know-how through service transactions in 1986 and 1987", *Monthly Report of the Deutsche Bundesbank*, 40, 5 (May).

________ (1998). "Technology services in the balance of payments". Special Statistical Publication 12.

________ (various issues). *Kapitalverflechtung mit dem Ausland* (Frankfurt/Main: Deutsche Bundesbank).

Dun and Bradstreet (1997). *Who Owns Whom: Worldwide Corporate Structure* (London: Dun and Bradstreet), 3rd quarter (CD-ROM based publication).

Dunning, John H. (1993a). *Multinational Enterprises and the Global Economy* (Wokingham: Addison-Wesley).

________ (1993b). "The prospects for foreign direct investment in Eastern Europe", in Patrick Artisien, Matija Rojec and Marjan Svetlicic, eds., *Foreign Direct Investment in Central and Eastern Europe* (London: Macmillan), pp. 16-33.

________ (1996). "The geographical sources of the competitiveness of firms: some results of a new survey", *Transnational Corporations*, 5, 3 (December), pp. 1-30.

________ (1997). "The European internal market programme and inbound foreign direct investment", *Journal of Common Market Studies*, 35, 1 (March), pp. 1-30.

________ (1998a). *American Investment in British Manufacturing Industry*, Revised and updated edition (London and New York: Routledge).

________ (1998b). "The changing geography of foreign direct investment", in Nagesh Kumar, ed., *Globalization, Foreign Direct Investment, and Technology Transfer: Impact and Prospects for Developing Countries* (London and New York: Routledge and UNU Press), forthcoming.

________ (1998c). "Location and the multinational enterprise: a neglected factor?", *Journal of International Business Studies*, 29, 1, pp. 45-66.

Eden, Lorraine and Maureen Appel Molot (1993). "Insiders and outsiders: defining 'who is us' in the North American automobile industry", *Transnational Corporations*, 2, 3 (December), pp. 31-64.

Edwards, Sebastian (1995). *Crisis and Reform in Latin America: From Despair to Hope* (Oxford: Oxford University Press).

El Hedi Lahouel, Mohamed (1998). "Morocco and Tunisia: offsetting the decline of aid", in UNDP, *Perspectives on International Financial Liberalisation*, Office of Development Studies Discussion Paper Series No. 15 (New York: UNDP), pp.12-19.

Engering, Frans (1996). "The Multilateral Investment Agreement",*Transnational Corporations*, 5, 3 (December), pp. 147-162.

Estrin, Saul, Kirsty Hughes and Sara Todd (1997). *Foreign Direct Investment in Central and Eastern Europe: Multinationals in the Transition* (London: Pinter and The Royal Institute of International Affairs).

European Bank for Reconstruction and Development (EBRD) (1997). *Transition Report 1997* (London: EBRD).

European Commission and UNCTAD (1996). *Investing in Asia's Dynamism: European Union Direct Investment in Asia* (Luxembourg: Office for Official Publications of the European Communities).

European Parliament (1998). "Resolution containing parliament's recommendations to the Commission on negotiations in the framework of the OECD on a multilateral agreement on investment (MAI) and Explanatory Statement" (document A4-0073/98), European Parliament's Committee on External Economic Relations, Brussels.

European Round Table of Industrialists (ERT) (1997). "Investment in the developing world: new openings and challenges for European industry" (Brussels: European Round Table of Industrialists), mimeo..

EUROSTAT (1997). *European Union Direct Investment: Yearbook 1996* (Luxembourg: Office for Official Publications of the European Communities).

________ (1998a). "EU FDI positions at the end of 1995" (Luxembourg: Eurostat), mimeo..

________ (1998b). *European Union Direct Investment: Yearbook 1997* (Luxembourg: Office for Official Publications of the European Communities).

Fors, Gunnar and Mario Zejan (1996). "Overseas R&D in foreign centers of excellence", Working Paper 458 (Stockholm: The Research Institute of Industrial Economics), mimeo..

Free Trade Area of the Americas (FTAA) (1998). "Working programme for the FTAA negotiating groups" (Washington, D.C.: FTAA) (June), mimeo..

Friends of the Earth - International (FoE-I) (1998). "Updated Joint NGOs Statement on the Multilateral Agreement on Investment (MAI) to the Organisation for Economic Cooperation and Development", Internet communication on MAI ad-hoc list server of 10 February 1998 (up to date information available form Mvalli_at_aol.com).

Fujita, Masataka (1989). "TNBs in developing countries", *The CTC Reporter*, 27 (Spring), pp. 44-49.

________ (1997). "Asian foreign direct investment in Africa". Paper prepared for the UNCTAD first subregional workshop on Asia-Africa trade and investment diversification and networking, Harare, Zimbabwe, 25-28 November (Geneva: UNCTAD), mimeo..

________ (1998). *The Transnational Activities of Small and Medium-sized Enterprises* (Boston, Dordrecht and London: Kluwer Academic Publishers).

Garay, Luis Jorge and Arturo Vera (1998). "Nature and evolution of intra-regional foreign direct investment in Latin America", in IDB-IRELA, *Foreign Direct Investment in Latin America: Perspectives of the Main Investors* (Madrid:IDB-IRELA), pp. 197-215.

Germany, Verband der Automobilindustrie (VDA) (various issues). "Tatsachen und Zahlen aus der Kraftverkehrswirtschaft" (Frankfurt: VDA), mimeo..

Goldberg, Linda S. and Charles D. Kolstad (1994). "Foreign direct investment, exchange rate variability and demand uncertainty", NBER Working Paper 4815 (Cambridge, Massachusetts: National Bureau of Economic Research), mimeo..

Goldberg, H. Lynn (1983). "Conventions for the elimination of international double taxation: toward a developing country model", *Law and Policy in International Business*, 15, 3, pp. 833-909.

Gorshenin, Vladimir (1995). "Zarubezhnoye dostoyanie Rossii", *Ekonomika i Zhizn*, 19, p. 38.

Graham, E. M. (1998). "NGOs and multilateral rules on investment" (Washington D.C.: Institute for International Economics), mimeo..

Gray, Sidney J. and Alan M. Rugman (1994), "Does the United States have a deficit with Japan in foreign direct investment?", *Transnational Corporations*, 3, 2 (August), pp. 127-137.

Guisinger, Stephen, and Associates (1985). *Investment Incentives and Performance Requirements* (New York: Praeger).

________ (1989). "Total protection: a new measure of the impact of government intervention on investment profitability", *Journal of International Business Studies*, 20, pp. 280-295.

________ (1992). "Rhetoric and reality in international business: a note on the effectiveness of incentives", *Transnational Corporations*, 1, 2 (August), pp. 111-123.

Head, Keith C., John C. Ries and Deborah L. Swenson (1994). "The attraction of foreign manufacturing investment: investment promotion and agglomeration economics", NBER Working Paper 4878 (Cambridge: National Bureau of Economic Research), mimeo..

Helmstedt, Katharina (1998). "Ausländische Direktinvestitionen in den Oststaaten" (Vienna: Ministry of Economy), mimeo..

Hufbauer, Clyde Gary and Jeffrey J. Schott (1993). *NAFTA: An Assessment* (Washington, D.C.: Institute of International Economics).

Hunya, Gabor (1996). "Foreign direct investment in Hungary: a key element of economic modernization" (Vienna: Vienna Institute for Comparative Economic Studies), mimeo..

__________ (1998). "Recent developments of FDI and privatization", *The Vienna Institute Monthly Report*, 5, pp. 1-7.

Ibrahim, Anwar (1997). "Press statement by Yab Dato' Seri Anwar Ibrahim, Deputy Prime Minister, Ministry of Finance, Malaysia, on strategic measures to strengthen economic and financial stability" (5 December), mimeo..

Ietto-Gillies, G. (forthcoming). "Different conceptual frameworks in the assessment of the degree of internationalization: empirical analysis of various indices for the top 100 TNCs", *Transnational Corporations*, 7, 1 (forthcoming).

Industrial Development Agency of Ireland (IDA) (1998). "Foreign investment" (http://www.ida.ie/fi.html and http://www.ida.ie/fio.html), 31 July.

Industrial Development Corporation (IDC) (1997). "Profile of Mozambique for the potential investor", IDC Research paper series, November (Johannesburg: Industrial Development Corporation of South Africa), mimeo..

Institute of International Finance, Inc. (1998). *Capital Flows to Emerging Market Economies* (Washington, D.C.: The Institute of International Finance, Inc.), 20 April.

Instituto de Pesquisas Económicas (FIPE) da Universidade de Sao Paulo (1998). "O Brasil e globalização: oportunidades e desafios", *Revista da Indústria*, 3, 74, (12 January).

InterAmerican Development Bank (IDB) (1998). "IDB Basic socioeconomic data" (from IDB website).

________ and Institute for European Latin American Relations (IDB-IRELA) (1998), *Foreign Direct Investment in Latin America: Perspectives of the Main Investors* (Madrid: IDB-IRELA).

International Bureau of Fiscal Documentation (IBFD) (1998). *Annual Report 1997-1998* (Amsterdam: IBFD Publications BV).

International Finance Corporation (IFC) (1996). "Mozambique: administrative barriers to investment. The red tape analysis" (Washington D.C.: World Bank), mimeo..

International Institute for Management Development (IMD) (1998). *World Competitiveness Yearbook 1998* (Lausanne: IMD).

International Monetary Fund (IMF) (1993). *Balance of Payments Manual, 5th edition* (Washington, D.C.: IMF).

________ (1997a). *International Financial Statistics Yearbook 1997* (Washington, D.C.: IMF).

________ (1997b). *World Economic Outlook* (Washington, D.C.: IMF).

________ (1998a). *International Financial Statistics, February 1998* (Washington, D.C.: IMF).

________ (1998b). *World Economic Outlook* (Washington, D.C.: IMF).

________ (various issues). *Balance of Payments Statistics Yearbook* (Washington, D.C.: IMF).

________, World Bank, OECD and EBRD (1991). *A Study of the Soviet Economy* (Paris: OECD).

Invest in France Mission, Arthur Andersen and United Nations (1998). *International Investment: Towards the Year 2002* (Paris and Geneva: United Nations).

Japan, Bank of Japan (1987). *Balance of Payments Monthly: April* (Tokyo: Bank of Japan).

________ (1997). *Balance of Payments Monthly: April* (Tokyo: Bank of Japan).

Japan, Export-Import Bank (1998). "EXIM Japan FY1997 survey: the outlook of Japanese foreign direct investment", *Journal of Research Institute for International Investment and Development*, 24, 1 (January), pp. 4-84.

Japan, Institute of Middle Eastern Economies (1998). "Special report on the Saudi economic offset program", prepared by the Economic Bureau (Saudi Arabia), mimeo..

Japan, Ministry of International Trade and Industry (MITI) (1989). *Dai 3-kai Kaigai Jigyo Katsudo Kihon Chosa: Kaigai Toshi Tokei Soran* (Tokyo: Keibun Shuppan).

________ (1998a). *Dai 26-kai Wagakuni Kigyo no Kaigai Jigyo Kaisudo* (Tokyo: Ministry of Finance Printing Bureau).

________ (1998b). *Dai 30-kai Giashikei Kigyo no Doko* (Tokyo: Ministry of Finance Printing Bureau).

Jegathesan, J. (1998). "Investment environment in developing countries in the context of foreign direct investments" (Kuala Lumpur: Malaysian Industrial Development Authority), mimeo..

JETRO (1991). *The 11th Survey of European Operations of Japanese Companies in the Manufacturing Sector* (Tokyo: JETRO).

________ (1996). *The 12th Survey of European Operations of Japanese Companies in the Manufacturing Sector* (Tokyo: JETRO).

Johanson, Jan and Finn Wiedersheim-Paul (1993). "The internationalization of the firm - four Swedish cases", in Peter F. Buckley and Pervez N. Ghauri, eds., *The Internationalization of the Firm* (London: Academic Press), pp. 16-31.

Kaufmann, D. (1998). "Challenging some myths about corruption", in World Economic Forum, *Africa Competitiveness Report 1998* (Geneva: World Economic Forum), p. 28.

Khaldin, Mikhail A., and Vladimir D. Andrianov (1996). "Kapital Rossii: poteriat ili preumnozhit?", *Ekonomika Series*, 1 (Moscow: Centre for Complex Social Research and Marketing).

Kopec, Urszula (1997). "Foreign direct investment in countries of Central and Eastern Europe", in Barbara Durka, ed., *Foreign Investments in Poland* (Warsaw: Foreign Trade Research Institute), pp. 142-163.

Korn, M. (1997). "The Multilateral Agreement on Investment (MAI): policy implications for developing countries" (Kuala Lumpur: Third World Network), mimeo..

Krasovec, T. (1996). "Internationalizacija slovenska gospodarstva: zdruzenje manager" (Ljubljana), mimeo..

Kravis, Irving B. and Robert E. Lipsey (1982). "The location of overseas production and production for export by U.S. multinational firms", *Journal of International Economics*, 12, 3/4 (May), pp. 201-223.

Krugman, Paul (1998). "Fire sale FDI" (http://web.mit.edu/krugman/www/FIRESALE.htm.)

Kudrle, Robert T. (1995). "Canada's foreign investment review agency and United States direct investment in Canada", *Transnational Corporations*, 4, 2 (August), pp. 58-91.

Kurylko, D. (1996). "Makers aim for vertical disintegration", *Automotive News Europe*, 24 June 1996, p. 14.

Lall, Sanjaya and G. Wignaraja (1998). *Mauritius: Dynamising Export Competitiveness*, Commonwealth Secretariat economic paper series No.32 (London: Commonwealth Secretariat).

Lang, Jeffrey (1997). "Testimony before the Subcommittee on Africa and on International Economic Policy and Trade of the House Committee on International Relations", 21 May (Washington, D.C.: United States Government Printing Office), mimeo..

Lankes, Hans-Peter and N. Stern (1998). "Capital flows to Eastern Europe and the former Soviet Union", EBRD Working Paper No. 27 (London: EBRD), mimeo..

Laplane, Mariano and Fernando Sarti (1997). "Investimento directo estrangeiro e a retomada do crescimento sustentado nos anos 90", *Economia e Sociedade*, 8 (June).

Lateef, A. (1997). "Linking up with the global economy: A case study of the Bangalore software industry", Discussion paper DP/96/1997 (Geneva: International Institute of Labour Studies, ILO), mimeo..

Lindert, P. and T. Pugel (1996). *International Economics* (Homewood: Irwin Publishers).

Lipsey, Robert E. (1990). "American firms face Europe: 1992", NBER Working Paper 1612 (Cambridge, Massachusetts: National Bureau of Economic Research), mimeo..

________, Magnus Blomström and Eric Ramstetter (1998). "Internationalized production in world output," in Robert E. Baldwin, Robert E. Lipsey and J. David Richardson, eds.

Geography and Ownership as Bases for Economic Accounting, Studies in Income and Wealth, 59 (Chicago: University of Chicago Press), forthcoming.

Lloyd, Peter J. (1996). "The changing nature of regional trade agreements", in Bijit Bora and Christopher Findlay, eds., *Regional Integration and the Asia Pacific* (Melbourne: Oxford University Press), pp. 25-48.

Londero, Elio, Simón Teitel et al. (1998). *Resources, Industrialization and Exports in Latin America. The Primary Input Content of Sustained Exports of Manufactures from Argentina, Colombia and Venezuela* (London-New York: Macmillan Press/St. Martin's Press).

Malaysia, Bank Negara (1998). *Monthly Statistical Bulletin* (http://www.bnm.gov.my).

Mataloni, Raymond J., Jr. (1997). "U.S. multinational companies: operations in 1995", *Survey of Current Business*, 78, 10 (October), pp. 44-68.

________ and M. Fahim-Nader (1996) "Operations of U.S. multinational companies: preliminary results from the 1994 benchmark survey", *Survey of Current Business* (December), pp. 11-37.

Mauro, Paolo (1995). "Corruption and growth", *Quarterly Journal of Economics*, CX, 3 (August), pp. 681-712.

Meyer, Klaus E. (1998). *Direct Investment in Economies in Transition* (Cheltenham and Northampton: Edward Elgar).

________ and Christina Pind (1998). "Ten years of foreign direct investment in the former Soviet Union: a survey with special focus on Kazakhstan" (Copenhagen: Copenhagen Business School), mimeo..

Mihalyi, Peter (1998). *A magyar privatizacio kronikaja* [Chronicle of Hungarian Privatization] (Budapest: Közgazdasagi és Jogi Könyvkiado).

Mortimore, Michael (1995). *Transforming Sitting Ducks into Flying Geese: The Mexican Automobile Industry* (Santiago: ECLAC).

________ (1997a). "The automobile industry in NAFTA (Mexico), MERCOSUR (Brazil and Argentina) and ASEAN (Thailand)". Paper prepared for the UNCTAD research project on Industrial Restructuring and International Competition (Geneva: UNCTAD), mimeo..

________ (1997b). "When does apparel become a peril? On the nature of industrialization in the Caribbean Basin". Paper presented to "Global Production, Regional Responses and Local Jobs: Challenges and Opportunities in the North American Apparel Industry" held at Bucke University, Durham, 7-8 November 1997, mimeo..

________ and Wilson Peres (1998). "Competition policy for foreign direct investment in the Caribbean Basin: Costa Rica, Dominican Republic and Jamaica", *Serie Desarrollo Productivo*, 49 (LG/G.1991) (Santiago: ECLAC).

________, J. L. Bonifaz and J. L. Duarte de Oliveira (1997). *La Competitividad Internacional: un CANálisis de las Experiencias de Asia en Desarrollo y América Latina* (Santiago: ECLAC).

Motta, Massimo and George Norman (1996). "Does economic integration cause foreign direct investment?", *International Economic Review*, 37, 4 (November), pp. 757-783.

Muchlinski, Peter (1995). *Multilateral Enterprises and the Law* (Cambridge: Blackwell Publishers).

Mutharika, Peter (1997). "Creating an attractive investment climate in the Common Market for Eastern and Southern Africa (COMESA) region", *ICSID Review*, 12, 2 (Washington, D.C.: International Centre for Settlement of Investment Disputes), pp. 237-286.

Mytelka, Lynn K. (1987). "Knowledge-intensive production and the changing internationalization strategies of multinational firms", in James A. Caporaso, ed., *A Changing International Division of Labour* (London: Francis Pinter Publishers), pp. 44-70.

________ (1991). "Technological change and the global relocation of production in textiles and clothing", *Studies in Political Economy*, 36 (Autumn), pp. 109-143.

________ (1994). "Regional cooperation and the new logic of international competition", in Lynn K. Mytelka, ed., *South-South Co-operation in a Global Perspective* (Paris: OECD), pp. 21-54.

________ and Michel Delapierre (1997). "Industrial dynamics, knowledge-based networked oligopolies and the emergence of new modes of competition". Paper prepared for the Druid workshop on Industrial Dynamics and New Modes of Competition, Skagen, Denmark, 1-3 June, mimeo..

________ (forthcoming). "Locational tournaments for FDI: inward investment into Europe in a global world", in Neil Hood and Stephen Young, eds., The Globalization of Multinational Enterprise Activity and Economic Development (London: Macmillan).

Naciones Unidas, Comisión Económica Para América Latina y El Caribe (CEPAL) (1997). *Notas sobre la economia y el desarollo* (Santiago: CEPAL).

________ (1998a). *Panorama de la inserción internacional de América Latina y el Caribe, 1997: notas sobre la economía y el desarollo* (Santiago: CEPAL).

________ (1998b). *Informe Sobre la Inversion Extranjera en America Latina y Caribe, 1997* (Santiago: CEPAL).

Nazmi, N. (1997), "Exchange rate-based stabilization in Latin America", *World Development*, 25, 4, pp. 519-535.

Nunnenkamp, Peter (1997a). "Aufhol- und Abkopplungsprozesse im europäischen Binnenmarkt", *Die Weltwirtschaft*, 2, pp. 190-203.

________ (1997b). "Foreign direct investment in Latin America in the era of globalized production", *Transnational Corporations*, 6, 1 (April), pp. 51-81.

________ (1998). "German direct investment in Latin America: triking peculiarities, unfounded fears, and neglected issues" (Kiel: Kiel Institute of World Economics), mimeo..

Oestensson, O. (1997). "Global mining taxation in relation to foreign direct investment flows to developing countries". Paper presented at the ESCAP workshop on mining taxation, Bangkok, 6-7 November, mimeo..

Organization of American States (OAS) (1996). "Inter-American Convention against Corruption" (Washington D.C.: OAS), mimeo. (http://www.oas.org/EN/PROG/JURIDICO/corr-eng.htm).

Organisation for Economic Co-operation and Development (OECD) (1996). *OECD Benchmark Definition of Foreign Direct Investment, third Edition* (Paris: OECD).

________ (1997a). "Convention on Combating Bribery of Foreign Officials in International Business Transactions and Related Instruments" (Paris: OECD), document DAFFE. IME/BR(97)20.

________ (1997b). *Model Double Taxation Convention on Income and on Capital* (Paris: OECD).

________ (1998a). "Ministerial statement on the Multilateral Agreement on Investment (MAI)", *OECD News Release*, doc. SG/COM/NEWS/(98)50, 28 April (Paris: OECD).

________ (1998b). *Harmful Tax Competition: An Emerging Global Issue* (Paris: OECD).

________ (various issues). *Foreign Trade by Commodities* (Paris: OECD).

Ortiz Martinez, Guillermo (1998). "What lessons does the Mexican crisis hold for the recovery in Asia", *Finance and Development* (June), pp. 6-9.

Ozawa, Terutomo (1998). "M&As and greenfield investments in host countries", paper prepared for UNCTAD, mimeo..

Oxfam (1998). "Briefing on the OECD Multilateral Agreement on Investment" (Oxford, Oxfam), mimeo..

Phelps, N. A., J. Lovering and K. Morgan (1998). "Tying the firm to the region or tying the region to the firm? Early observations on the case of LG in South Wales", *European Union and Regional Studies*, 5, 2, pp. 119-137.

Pires, Manuel (1989). *International Juridical Double Taxation of Income* (Deventer, Boston: Kluwer).

Plasschaert, Sylvain (1994). "Introduction: transfer pricing and taxation", in Sylvain Plasschaert, ed.,*Transnational Corporations: Transfer Pricing and Taxation*, United Nations Library on Transnational Corporations, 14 (London and New York: Routledge on behalf of the United Nations), p. 1-21.

Pomfret, Richard (1996). "Sub-regional economic zones", in Bijit Bora and Christopher Findlay, eds., *Regional Integration and the Asia Pacific* (Melbourne: Oxford University Press), pp. 207-222.

Price Waterhouse (1989). "Doing business in the Republic of Ireland" (New York: Price Waterhouse), mimeo..

Project Link (1998). "World outlook: countries and regions" (New York, Philadelphia and Toyota: United Nations, University of Pennsylvania and University of Toronto), 1 May.

Public Citizen (1998). "The Multilateral Agreement on Investment (MAI) will impose the same rules on the US that the IMF is now imposing on Asia" (Washington, D.C.: Public Citizen), mimeo..

Ramstetter, Eric D. (1995a). "Sectoral flows of foreign direct investment in Malaysia," in Economic and Social Commission for Asia and the Pacific, *Sectoral Flows of Foreign Direct Investment in Asia and the Pacific,* Studies in Trade and Investment 5, ST/ESCAP/ 1501 (New York: United Nations), pp. 115-148.

________ (1995b). "Sectoral flows of foreign direct investment in Thailand" in Economic and Social Commission for Asia and the Pacific, *Sectoral Flows of Foreign Direct Investment in Asia and the Pacific,* Studies in Trade and Investment 5, ST/ESCAP/1501 (New York: United Nations), pp. 149-182.

________ (1996). "Estimating economic activities by Japanese transnational corporations: how to make sense of the data?", *Transnational Corporations,* 5, 2 (August), pp. 107-143.

________ (1998). "Turmoil in asset markets and the prospects for foreign transnational corporations in Southeast Asia" in Mitsuru Toida and Daisuke Hiratsuka, eds., *Ajia Kogyoken no Keizai Tenbo (Projections for Asian Industrializing Region)* (Tokyo: Institute of Developing Economies), pp. 114-122.

Republic of Korea, Ministry of Finance and Economy (1998). *Investing in Korea's Future: New Opportunities in a New System* (Seoul: Ministry of Finance and Economy).

Reuber, G. L., H. Crookell, M. Emmerson and G. Gallais-Hamonno (1973). *Private Foreign Investment in Development* (Oxford: Claredon Press).

Robson, Peter, ed. (1993). *Transnational Corporations and Regional Economic Integration,* United Nations Library on Transnational Corporations, vol. 9 (London: Routledge on behalf of the United Nations).

Rojec, Matija (1998). *Restructuring with Foreign Direct Investment: The Case of Slovenia* (Ljubljana: Institute of Macroeconomic Analysis and Development).

Ruane, Frances and Holger Görg (1997). "The impact of foreign direct investment on sectoral adjustment in the Irish economy", *National Institute Economic Review,* 160 (April) (London: National Institute of Economic and Social Research), pp. 76-86.

Ruigrok, W. and R. van Tulder (1995). *The Logic of International Restructuring* (London and New York: Routledge).

Rybkin, Ivan (1995). "Tri dokhodnya chasti biudzheta", *Ekonomika I Zhizn,* 14, p. 1.

Sachs, Jeffrey and Sara Sievers (1998). "FDI in Africa", in World Economic Forum, *Africa Competitiveness Report 1998* (Geneva: World Economic Forum), pp. 36-44.

SADC Finance and Investment Sector Co-ordinating Unit (FISCU) (1998). "1998 Southern Africa economic summit Windhoek, Namibia, 17-19 May 1998". Prepared by the SADC Finance and Investment Sector Co-ordinating Unit (Pretoria: SADC Finance and Investment Sector Co-ordinating Unit), mimeo..

Sauvant, Karl (1990). "The tradability of services", in UNCTC and the World Bank, *The Uruguay Round: Services in the World Economy* (Washington and New York: The World Bank), pp. 114-122.

Scepanovic, Nina (1998). "Legal basis of foreign investments in FRY", *Review of International Affairs*, XLIX, 1066 (15 March), pp. 40-44.

Sheets, Nathan (1996). "Capital flight from the countries in transition: some empirical evidence", *Journal of Policy Reform*, 1, pp. 259-270.

Slovenia, Bank of Slovenia (1998). *Monthly Bulletin* (June/July).

Sociedade Brasileira de Estudos de Empresas Transnacionais e da Globalizacao Economica (SOBEET) (1997). *Carta da Sobeet* (Sao Paulo: SOBEET).

Sokolov, Sergey (1991). "Sovetskiy kapital za rubezhom", *Ekonomika i Zhizn*, 41, supplement, p. 7.

Stewart, T. A. (1997). *Intellectual Capital* (London: Nicholas Bradley).

Svetlicic, Marjan (1997). "Outward foreign direct investment by Central European economies and restructuring", in Klaus Macharzina, Michael-Jörg Oesterle and Joachim Wolf, eds., *Global Business in the Information Age*, Proceedings of the 23rd Annual EIBA Conference, Stuttgart, 14-16 December 1997 (Brussels: European International Business Academy), pp. 281-312.

________ and Matija Rojec (1998). "Restructuring role of foreign direct investment by Central European firms: the case of Slovenia". Paper presented at the Conference on Globalization, the International Firm and Emerging Economies, Izmir, Turkey, 27-31 May, mimeo..

Tejima, Shigeki (1998). "The effects of the Asian crisis on Japan's manufacturing FDI", paper prepared for UNCTAD, mimeo..

Thailand Development Research Institute (TDRI) (1998). "Effects of recent financial and macroeconomic developments on inward and outward FDI in Thailand". Background paper prepared for UNCTAD (Bangkok: TDRI), mimeo..

Tillett, Chris (1996). "Foreign investment: targeting and promotional strategies", Commonwealth Secretariat Occasional Paper 2 (London: Commonwealth Secretariat), mimeo..

Toyo Keizai (1998). *Kaigai Shinshutsu Kigyo Soran 1998* (Tokyo: Toyo Keizai Shimposha).

United Nations (1980). *United Nations Model Double Taxation Convention between Developed and Developed Countries* (New York: United Nations), United Nations publication, Sales No. E.80.XVI.3.

________ (1997). "Manual for the negotiation of bilateral tax treaties between developed and developing countries: Ad Hoc Group of Experts on International Cooperation in Tax Matters", eighth meeting, Geneva, 15-19 December (ST/SG/AC.8/1997/L.12, 13 October), mimeo..

________ (1998a). *Africa Recovery*, 11, 3 (February) (New York: United Nations Office for Communications and Public Relations).

________ (1998b). *World Economic and Social Survey* (New York: United Nations), United Nations publication, forthcoming.

United Nations Conference on Trade and Development (UNCTAD) (1993a). *World Investment Report 1993: Transnational Corporations and Integrated International Production* (New York: United Nations), United Nations publication, Sales No. E.93.II.A.14.

________ (1993b). *Small and Medium-sized Transnational Corporations: Role, Impact and Policy Implications* (New York and Geneva: United Nations), United Nations publication, Sales No. E.93.II.A.5.

________ (1994a). *World Investment Report 1994: Transnational Corporations, Employment and the Workplace* (Geneva: United Nations), United Nations publication, Sales No.E.94.II.A.14.

________ (1994b). *The Tradability of Banking Services: Impact and Implications* (Geneva: United Nations), United Nations publication, Sales No. E.94.II.A.12.

________ (1995a). *World Investment Report 1995: Transnational Corporations and Competitiveness* (New York and Geneva: United Nations), United Nations publication, Sales No. E.95.II.A.9.

________ (1995b).*Foreign Direct Investment in Africa* (New York and Geneva: United Nations), United Nations publication, Sales No. E.95.II.A.6.

________ (1996a). *World Investment Report 1996: Investment, Trade and International Policy Arrangements* (New York and Geneva: United Nations), United Nations publication, Sales No. E.96.II.A.14.

________ (1996b). *International Investment Instruments: A Compendium, vol. I, II and III* (Geneva: UNCTAD) United Nations publication, Sales Nos. E.96.II.A.9, 10, 11.

________ (1996c). "A Partnership for Growth and Development" (Geneva: UNCTAD), United Nations document, No. TD/378.

________ (1996d). *Incentives and Foreign Direct Investment* (Geneva and New York: United Nations), United Nations publication, Sales No. E.96.II.A.6.

________ (1997a). *World Investment Report 1997: Transnational Corporations, Market Structure and Competition Policy* (Geneva and New York: United Nations), United Nations publication, Sales No. E.97.II.D.10.

________ (1997b). *Survey of Best Practices in Investment Promotion* (Geneva: United Nations), United Nations publication, Sales No.E.97.II.D.11.

________ (1997c). *World Investment Directory: Volume VI. West Asia* (Geneva: United Nations), United Nations publication, Sales No. E.97.II.A.2.

________ (1997d). *Sharing Asia's Dynamism: Asian Direct Investment in the European Union* (New York and Geneva: United Nations), United Nations publication, Sales No. E.97.II.D.1.

________ (1997e). *Handbook of International Trade and Development Statistics* (New York and Geneva: United Nations), United Nations publication, Sales No. E/F.97.II.D.7.

________ (1997f). "Foreign direct investment in LDCs: prospects and constraints". Report prepared by the UNCTAD secretariat for the pilot seminar on the mobilization of the private sector in order to encourage foreign investment flows towards least developed countries (LDCs), "Investment opportunities in pre-emerging markets", Geneva, 23-25 June (Geneva: United Nations), United Nations document, No. UNCTAD/GDS/GFSB/2.

________ (1997g). *World Investment Directory 1996, Volume V, Africa*(Geneva: United Nations), United Nations publication, Sales No. E.97.II.A. 1.

________ (1997h). "WAIPA Directory 1997" (Geneva: United Nations), mimeo..

________ (1998a). *Trade and Development Report 1998* (Geneva: United Nations), United Nations publication, forthcoming.

________ (1998b). *Least Developed Countries Report 1988* (Geneva: United Nations), United Nations publication, forthcoming.

________ (1998c). "The growth of domestic capital markets, particularly in developing countries and its relationship with foreign portfolio investment" (Geneva: UNCTAD), United Nations document, No. TD/B/CM.2/EM.4/2, 19 March.

________ (1998d). "Foreign portfolio investment implications for the growth of emerging capital markets" (Geneva: UNCTAD), United Nations document, No. UNCTAD/GDS/GFSB/4, 22 May.

________ (1998e). *Issues Note*, No. 1 (Geneva: UNCTAD), 31 March, mimeo..

________ (1998f). "The financial crisis in Asia and foreign direct investment", Background Note (Geneva: UNCTAD), 18 March, mimeo..

________ (1998g).*Handbook on Foreign Direct Investment by Small and Medium-sized Enterprises: Lessons from Asia* (New York and Geneva: United Nations), United Nations publication, Sales No. E.98.II.D.4.

________ (forthcoming, a). "UNCTAD's relations with Civil Society" (Geneva: United Nations), mimeo..

________ (forthcoming, b). *FDI Determinants and TNC Strategies: The Case of Brazil* (Geneva: United Nations), United Nations publication, forthcoming.

________ (forthcoming, c). *Bilateral Investment Treaties in the Mid-1990s* (Geneva: United Nations), United Nations publication, forthcoming.

________ (forthcoming, d). *The Role of Accounting in the East Asian Financial Crisis: Lessons Learned* (Geneva: United Nations), United Nations publication, forthcoming.

________ and the International Chamber of Commerce (ICC) (1998). "Leading multinationals vote their confidence in Asia: the Asian crisis and prospects for foreign direct investment", Press Release, 18 March, mimeo..

United Nations Centre on Transnational Corporations (UNCTC) (1978-1994). *National Legislation and Regulations Relating to Transnational Corporations*, vols. I-XX (New York and Geneva, United Nations).

________ (1992). *Foreign Direct Investment and Industrial Restructuring in Mexico* (New York: United Nations), United Nations publication, Sales No. E.92.II.A.9.

________ (1993). *From the Common Market to EC92: Regional Economic Integration in the European Community and Transnational Corporations*(New York: United Nations), United Nations publication, Sales No. E.93.II.A.2.

United Nations, Department of Economic and Social Development (1992a). *World Investment Report 1992: Transnational Corporations as Engines of Growth* (New York: United Nations), United Nations publication, Sales No. E92.II.A.19.

________ (1992b). *World Investment Directory. Volume II: Central and Eastern Europe* (New York: United Nations), United Nations publication, Sales No. E.93.II.A.1.

________ (1993). *Transnational Corporations from Developing Countries: Impact on their Home Countries* (New York: United Nations), United Nations publication, Sales No. E.93.II.A.8.

United Nations, Economic Commission for Latin America and the Caribbean (ECLAC) (1998). *La Inversión Extranjera en América Latina y el Caribe: Informe 1997* (Santiago de Chile: ECLAC).

United Nations, Economic and Social Commisson for Asia and the Pacific (ESCAP) (1998). *Economic Survey of Asia and the Pacific* (New York: United Nations), United Nations publication, Sales No. E.98.II.F.59.

United States, Department of Commerce (1985). *U.S. Direct Investment Abroad, 1982 Benchmark Survey Data* (Washington, D.C.: United States Government Printing Office).

________ (1992). "U.S. international sales and purchases of services: U.S. cross-border transactions in 1991 and sales by affiliates in 1990", *Survey of Current Business*, 72, 9 (September), pp. 82-115.

________ (1993a). *Foreign Direct Investment in the United States: Operations of U.S. Affiliates of Foreign Companies, Revised 1990 Estimates* (Washington, D.C.: United States Department of Commerce).

________ (1993b). *U.S. Direct Investment Abroad: Operations of U.S. Parent Companies and their Foreign Affiliates, Revised 1990 Estimates* (Washington, D.C.: United States Government Printing Office).

________ (1997a). *U.S. Direct Investment Abroad: Operations of U.S. Parent Companies and their Foreign Affiliates, Preliminary 1995 Estimates* (Washington, D.C.: United States Government Printing Office).

________ (1997b). *Foreign Direct Investment in the United States: Operations of U.S. Affiliates of Foreign Companies, Preliminary 1995 Estimates* (Washington, D.C.: United States Government Printing Office).

________ (1997c). "US direct investment abroad: details for historical-cost position and related capital and investment flows, 1996", *Survey of Current Business*, 77, 9 (September).

________ (1997d). "U.S. international sales and purchases of services: U.S. cross-border transactions in 1996 and sales by affiliates in 1995", *Survey of Current Business*, 77, 10 (October), pp. 95-138.

________ (1998). *U.S. Direct Investment Abroad: 1994 Benchmark Survey, Final Results* (Washington, D.C.: United States Government Printing Office).

________ (various issues). *Survey of Current Business* (Washington, D.C.: United States Government Printing Office).

Vallanchain, B. and M. A. Satterthwaite (1992). "Sectoral growth at the metropolitan level: an evaluation of economic development incentives", *Journal of Economics*, 31, pp. 25-58.

Varblane, Urmas (1998). "Foreign direct investment in Estonia as a factor of integration to the world economy" (Tartu: University of Tartu), mimeo..

Voduzeck, Ziga and Alvaro Calderon (1998). "Foreign direct investment in Latin America: an overview", in IDB-IRELA, *Foreign Direct Investment in Latin America: Perspectives of the Main Investors* (Madrid: IDB-IRELA), pp. 25-60.

Wangwe, Samuel (1997). "Conditions under which African manufacturing industries in sub-Saharan Africa have been able to break into export markets". Paper prepared for the UNCTAD Workshop on Conditions under which African manufacturing industries in sub-Saharan Africa have been able to break into export markets: lessons from East Asia, Mauritius, 4-5 December, mimeo..

Wei, Shang-Jin (1997a). "How taxing is corruption on international investors?", National Bureau of Economic Research, Working Paper No. 6030 (Cambridge, Massachusetts: National Bureau of Economic Research), mimeo..

________ (1997b). "Why is corruption so much more taxing than tax?", National Bureau of Economic Research, Working Paper No. 6255 (Cambridge, Massachusetts: National Bureau of Economic Research), mimeo..

Wells, Louis T. (1993). "Promoting foreign investment: opportunities and pitfalls for host countries", in Organisation for Economic Co-operation and Development, *Promoting Foreign Direct Investment in Developing Countries* (Paris: OECD), pp. 45-46.

________ and Alvin G. Wint (1990). "Marketing a country: promotion as a tool for attracting foreign investment", FIAS Occasional Paper 1 (Washington, D.C.: Foreign Investment Advisory Services), mimeo..

________ and Alvin G. Wint (1991). "Facilitating foreign investment: government institutions to screen, monitor and service investment from abroad", FIAS Occasional Paper 2 (Washington, D.C.: FIAS), mimeo..

Western Governors' Association (WGA) (1997). "Multilateral Agreement on Investment: potential effects on state and local government" (Washington, D.C.: WGA), April, mimeo..

Wint, Alvin G. (1993). "Promoting transnational investment: organizing to service approved investors", *Transnational Corporations*, 2, 1 (February), pp. 71-90.

Witherell, William H. (1995). "The OECD Multilateral Agreement on Investment", *Transnational Corporations*, 4, 2 (August), pp. 1-14.

World Bank (1997a). *World Development Report 1997* (Oxford: Oxford University Press).

________ (1997b). *African Development Indicators* (Washington D.C.: The World Bank).

________ (1997c). *World Development Indicators* (Washington D.C.: The World Bank).

________ (1998). *Global Development Finance* (Washington, D.C.: The World Bank).

World Council of Churches (WCC) (1998). "The MAI: a threat to social rights, the environment and democracy?" (Washington, D.C.: WCC), mimeo..

World Development Movement (WDM) (1997). "Pulling up the drawbridge: the OECD Multilateral Agreement on Investment" (London: WDM), mimeo..

World Economic Forum (WEF) (1997). *The Global Competitiveness Report 1997* (Geneva: World Economic Forum).

________ (1998a). *Africa Competitiveness Report 1998* (Geneva: World Economic Forum).

________ (1998b). *The Global Competitiveness Report 1998* (Geneva: World Economic Forum).

World Export Processing Zones Association (WEPZA) (1997). *WEPZA International Directory of Export Processing Zones and Free Trade Zones* (Flagstaff, Arizona: The Flagstaff Institute).

World Trade Organization (WTO) (1997a). "Fourth Protocol to the General Agreement on Trade in Services" (Geneva: WTO), document S/L/20, 30 April 1996.

________ (1997b). "Fifth Protocol to the General Agreement on Trade in Services" (Geneva: WTO), document S/L/45, 3 December 1997.

________ (1997c). "Working Group on the Relationship between Trade and Investment: Report (1997) to the General Council" (Geneva: WTO), document WT/WGTI/1, 25 November 1997.

WWF - International (World Wide Fund for Nature) (1996). "OECD Briefing on the Multilateral Agreement on Investment" (Geneva:WWF), mimeo..

________ (1997). "Is the MAI sustainable?". WWF Discussion Paper (Geneva: WWF), mimeo..

________ (1998a). "Enhancing the environmental review of the Multilateral Agreement on Investment" (Geneva: WWF), mimeo..

________ (1998b). "The OECD Multilateral Agreement on Investment: ripe for reform or ready for rejection?" (Geneva: WWF), mimeo..

WWF - UK (forthcoming). "Defending the legacy of Rio: the civil society campaign against the MAI), mimeo..

Yamazawa, Ippei (1997). "Recent developments of APEC: issues and prospects of the Osaka Agenda", in Takatoshi Ito and Anne O. Krueger, eds, *Regionalism Versus Multilateral Trade Arrangements*, NBER East Asia Seminar on Economics, 6 (Chicago and London: University of Chicago Press), pp. 203-222.

Young, Stephen and Neil Hood (1994). "Designing developmental after-care programmes for foreign direct investors in the European Union", *Transnational Corporations*, 3, 2 (August), pp. 45-72.

Zeile, William J. (1997). "U.S. intrafirm trade in goods", *Survey of Current Business*, 78, 2 (February), pp. 23-38.

ANNEXES

Annex A. Additional text tables

Annex table A.I.1. Cross-border M&A deals over $1 billion announced in 1997

Deal value (Billion dollars)	Acquiring company	Home economy	Industry of acquiring company	Acquired company	Host economy	Industry of acquired company
18.4	Zurich Versicherungs GmbH	Switzerland	Insurance	BAT Industries PLC-Financial	United Kingdom	Insurance
10.2	Roche Holding AG	Switzerland	Drugs	Corange Ltd.	Bermuda	Drugs
10.0	Allianz AG Holding Berlin	Germany	Insurance	AGF	France	Insurance
8.0	ICI PLC	United Kingdom	Chemicals and allied products	Quest International,3 Others	Netherlands	Chemicals and allied products
6.2	Assicurazioni Generali SpA	Italy	Insurance	Aachener und Muenchener	Germany	Commercial banks, bank holding companies
5.3	Tyco International Ltd	United States	Machinery	ADT Ltd.	Bermuda	Business services
5.3	Merrill Lynch & Co. Inc.	United States	Investment & commodity firms, dealers, exchanges	Mercury Asset Management Group	United Kingdom	Investment & commodity firms, dealers, exchanges
4.8	Rhone-Poulenc SA(France)	France	Chemicals and allied products	Rhone-Poulenc Rorer Inc.	United States	Drugs
4.5	ING Groep NV	Netherlands	Insurance	Banque Bruxelles Lambert SA	Belgium	Commercial banks, bank holding companies
4.3	Nordbanken(Venantius/Sweden)	Sweden	Commercial banks, bank holding companies	Merita Oy	Finland	Commercial banks, bank holding companies
3.8	Investor Group	United States	Investment & commodity firms, dealers, exchanges	Victoria-Loy Yang A Power	Australia	Electric, gas, and water distribution
3.2	Ameritech Corp.	United States	Telecommunications	TeleDanmark A/S(Denmark)	Denmark	Telecommunications
3.0	Lafarge SA	France	Stone, clay, glass, and concrete products	Redland PLC	United Kingdom	Rubber and miscellaneous plastic products
3.0	EI du Pont de Nemours and Co.	United States	Chemicals and allied products	Imperial Chem Ind-White Pigment	United Kingdom	Chemicals and allied products
3.0	Metro AG (Metro International	Germany	Wholesale trade-nondurable goods	SHV Makro NV(Metro AG)	Netherlands	Wholesale trade-durable goods
2.8	Metro AG (Metro International	Germany	Wholesale trade-nondurable goods	Makro Holdings(SHV Holdings)	Netherlands	Wholesale trade-durable goods
2.7	Coca-Cola Amatil Ltd	Australia	Food and kindred products	Coca-Cola Bottlers Philippines	Philippines	Food and kindred products
2.6	Metro Group	Germany	Real estate; mortgage bankers and brokers	Makro Holdings-European	United Kingdom	Retail trade-food stores
2.6	ING Groep NV	Netherlands	Insurance	Equitable of Iowa Cos	United States	Insurance
2.4	LVMH Moet-Hennessy L Vuitton	France	Soaps, cosmetics, and personal-care products	Grand Metropolitan PLC	United Kingdom	Food and kindred products
2.2	Federal-Mogul Corp.	United States	Transportation equipment	T&N PLC	United Kingdom	Transportation equipment
2.1	Verenigd Bezit VNU	Netherlands	Printing, publishing, and allied services	ITT World Directories Inc.	United States	Printing, publishing, and allied services
2.0	GPU Inc.	United States	Electric, gas, and water distribution	PowerNet Victoria(GPU Inc.)	Australia	Electric, gas, and water distribution
2.0	Hellenic Bottling Co. SA	Greece	Food and kindred products	Molino Beverages Holding SA	Luxembourg	Food and kindred products
1.9	QAF Ltd(Qualif/KMP/Salim Grp)	Singapore	Wholesale trade-nondurable goods	Indofood Sukses Makmur PT	Indonesia	Food and kindred products
1.9	Mustcom Ltd.	Cyprus	Investment & commodity firms, dealers, exchanges	Svyazinvest(Russia)	Russian Federation	Investment & commodity firms, dealers, exchanges
1.7	Richemont(Rembrandt Group Ltd.)	Switzerland	Tobacco products	Vendome Luxury Group PLC	United Kingdom	Miscellaneous manufacturing
1.7	BAT Industries PLC	United Kingdom	Tobacco products	Cigarrera La Moderna SA	Mexico	Tobacco products
1.7	Seagram Co. Ltd.	Canada	Food and kindred products	USA Network	United States	Radio and television broadcasting stations
1.7	Newcourt Credit Group Inc.	Canada	Real estate; mortgage bankers and brokers	AT&T Capital Corp.	United States	Credit institutions
1.7	Zurich Versicherungs GmbH	Switzerland	Insurance	Scudder Stevens & Clark Inc.	United States	Investment & commodity firms, dealers, exchanges
1.7	Incentive AB	Sweden	Measuring, medical, photo equipment; clocks	Vivra Inc.	United States	Health services
1.6	Energy Group PLC	United Kingdom	Electric, gas, and water distribution	Peabody Holding Co(Hanson PLC)	United States	Mining
1.6	Xerox Corp.	United States	Computer and office equipment	Rank Xerox(Xerox,Rank Organis)	United Kingdom	Machinery
1.5	Siemens AG	Germany	Electronic and electrical equipment	Westinghouse-Conven Power Gen	United States	Machinery
1.5	China Everbright Holdings	China	Electronic and electrical equipment	HK Telecomm(Cable & Wireless)	Hong Kong, China	Telecommunications
1.5	SITA(Suez Lyonnaise des Eaux)	France	Sanitary services	Browning-Ferris-Non Amer Asts	Germany	Sanitary services

/...

Annex table A.I.1. Cross-border M&A deals over $1 billion announced in 1997 (continued)

Deal value (Billion dollars)	Acquiring company	Home economy	Industry of acquiring company	Acquired company	Host economy	Industry of acquired company
1.4	AES Corp.	United States	Electric, gas, and water distribution	Cie Centro Oeste	Brazil	Electric, gas, and water distribution
1.4	Daewoo Corp.	Republic of Korea	Construction firms	Kaztelekom(Kazakhstan)	Kazakhstan	Telecommunications
1.4	News Corp. Ltd.	Australia	Printing, publishing, and allied services	Heritage Media Corp.	United States	Radio and television broadcasting stations
1.3	Caterpillar Inc.	United States	Machinery	Perkins Engines Group Ltd.	United Kingdom	Machinery
1.3	Sappi Ltd.	South Africa	Paper and allied products	KNP Leykam(KNP BT)	Luxembourg	Paper and allied products
1.3	Amvescap PLC	United Kingdom	Investment & commodity firms, dealers, exchanges	Chancellor LGT Asset Mgmt	United States	Investment & commodity firms, dealers, exchanges
1.3	Investor Group	United States	Investment & commodity firms, dealers, exchanges	Telkom South Africa(SA)	South Africa	Telecommunications
1.2	National Australia Bank Ltd.	Australia	Commercial banks, bank holding companies	HomeSide Inc.	United States	Real estate; mortgage bankers and brokers
1.2	CEA-Industrie SA	France	Electric, Gas, and Water Distribution	SGS-Thomson Microelectronics	Italy	Electronic and electrical equipment
1.2	Investor Group	Spain	Investment & commodity firms, dealers, exchanges	Codensa	Colombia	Electric, gas, and water distribution
1.2	Doughty Hanson	United Kingdom	Investment & commodity firms, dealers, exchanges	Geberit International SA	Switzerland	Metal and metal products
1.2	Investor Group	Italy	Investment & commodity firms, dealers, exchanges	Retevision(Kingdom of Spain)	Spain	Radio and television broadcasting stations
1.2	Wal-Mart Stores Inc.	United States	Retail trade-general merchandise and apparel	CIFRA SA de CV	Mexico	Retail trade-general merchandise and apparel
1.2	Pioneer Natural Resources Co.	United States	Oil and gas; petroleum refining	Chauvco Resources Ltd.	Canada	Oil and gas; petroleum refining
1.1	Investor Group	United Kingdom	Investment & commodity firms, dealers, exchanges	Elis Group	France	Personal services
1.1	Panamerican Beverages Inc.	Mexico	Food and kindred products	Coca-Cola Hitt de Venezuela	Venezuela	Food and kindred products
1.1	Roche Holding AG	Switzerland	Drugs	Tastemaker	United States	Chemicals and allied products
1.1	Amersham International PLC	United Kingdom	Chemicals and allied products	Nycomed ASA	Norway	Drugs
1.1	Southern Electric Brazil	United States	Investment & commodity firms, dealers, exchanges	Cemig(Minas Gerais)	Brazil	Electric, gas, and water distribution
1.0	PartnerRe Holdings Ltd.	Bermuda	Insurance	Societe Anonyme Francaise de	France	Insurance
1.0	Tesco PLC	United Kingdom	Retail trade-general merchandise and apparel	Associated British Foods-Irish	Ireland	Retail trade-food stores

Source: UNCTAD, based on data provided by Securities Data Company, Inc. (New York).

Annex table A.II.1. Country breakdown of the world's top 100 TNCs, by transnationality index, foreign assets, foreign sales and foreign employment, 1990

(Percentage)

Country	Average TNI[a]	Foreign assets	Foreign sales	Foreign employment	Number of entries
European Union	56.7	45.5	41.2	54.5	48
France	50.9	10.4	9.0	12.0	14
United Kingdom[b]	68.5	16.8	12.4	19.2	12
Germany	44.4	8.9	10.6	11.0	9
Sweden	71.7	2.7	2.7	4.5	5
Italy	38.7	3.5	3.3	2.4	4
Netherlandsb	68.5	8.9	6.5	10.9	4
Belgium	60.4	1.0	1.0	1.0	2
North America	41.2	32.5	30.5	28.7	30
United States	38.5	31.5	29.9	27.9	28
Canada	79.2	1.0	0.6	0.8	2
Japan	35.5	12.0	21.1	5.0	12
Remaining countries[c]	71.0	10.0	7.2	11.8	11
Total of all 100 listed TNCs	51.1	100	100	100	100[a]

Source: UNCTAD/Erasmus University database.

[a] Expressed in percentage points.

[b] Due to dual nationality, Royal Dutch Shell and Unilever are counted as an entry for both the United Kingdom and the Netherlands. In the aggregate for the European Union they are only counted once.

[c] Remaining countries are Australia, New Zealand, Norway and Switzerland.

Annex table A.II.2. Country breakdown of the world's top 100 TNCs, by transnationality index, foreign assets, foreign sales and foreign employment, 1996

(Percentage)

Country	Average TNI[a]	Foreign assets	Foreign sales	Foreign employment	Number of entries
European Union	64.8	41.0	40.1	51.2	41
France	59.7	9.2	7.6	10.2	11
United Kingdom[b]	71.2	11.4	11.7	13.6	10
Germany	56.9	10.9	11.3	13.4	9
Sweden	78.9	3.5	4.0	6.4	4
Italy	46.7	3.4	2.1	2.3	3
Netherlands[b]	77.9	7.8	7.7	10.5	4
Belgium	81.9	0.8	1.1	0.6	2
North America	47.8	35.0	29.7	29.5	32
United States	43.2	32.2	27.6	26.5	28
Canada	79.9	2.8	2.1	3.0	4
Japan	36.2	15.8	23.1	10.3	18
Remaining countries[c]	71.3	8.2	7.1	9.0	10
Total of all 100 listed TNCs	54.8	100	100	100	101 [a]

Source: UNCTAD/Erasmus University database.

[a] Expressed in percentage points.

[b] Due to dual nationality, Royal Dutch Shell and Unilever are counted as an entry for both the United Kingdom and the Netherlands. In the aggregate for the European Union they are only counted once. RTZ CRA is counted as an entry for both the United Kingdom and Australia.

[c] Remaining countries are Australia, Republic of Korea, Norway, Switzerland and Venezuela.

Annex table A.II.3. Averages in transnationality index, assets, sales and employment of the top 5 TNCs in each industry,[a] 1990 and 1996

(Percentage points, and in per cent of top 100 total)

Industry	Transnationality index	Assets Foreign	Assets Total	Sales Foreign	Sales Total	Employment Foreign	Employment Total
Petroleum							
1990	57.7	15.1	10.6	15.8	11.9	5.5	4.2
1996	61.9	9.8	7.1	12.2	9.4	3.6	3.1
Automotive							
1990	34.7	11.9	15.3	10.4	11.8	9.7	14.2
1996	39.1	12.5	17.1	11.2	13.1	9.0	13.5
Electronics/electrical equipment							
1990	36.1	6.4	7.4	4.7	6.3	6.5	9.6
1996	36.4	4.4	7.0	5.8	6.9	7.7	11.3
Pharmaceuticals							
1990	47.1	1.5	1.3	1.6	1.4	2.4	2.3
1996	47.8	2.7	2.9	2.7	2.4	3.5	3.1
Chemicals							
1990	51.6	5.3	4.2	5.9	4.5	4.8	5.4
1996	60.8	6.0	3.8	4.7	3.9	4.8	4.5
Trading							
1990	28.3	5.0	9.1	14.7	22.2	0.4	0.6
1996	32.1	4.9	7.4	10.3	15.4	0.3	0.4

Source: UNCTAD/Erasmus University database.

[a] Only industries that have at least five entries and in which the same five top TNCs featured in the lists of the top 100 TNCs of 1990 and 1996.

Annex table A.II.4. Number of banking entities from selected developing and transition economies[a] in selected OECD host countries, 1996

Host country	Number of foreign banking entities	Number of home economies represented	Foreign banking entities per home economy
United States	171	34	5.0
United Kingdom	153	46	3.3
France	46	25	1.8
Germany	36	19	1.9
Japan	35	11	3.2
Luxembourg	16	8	2.0
Netherlands	14	8	1.8
Switzerland	12	8	1.5
Belgium	9	6	1.5
Australia	9	5	1.8
Austria	7	7	1.0
Spain	7	5	1.4
Italy	5	5	1.0
Greece	3	3	1.0
Other[b]	1	1	1.0

Source: Cornford and Brandon, forthcoming.

[a] Algeria, Argentina, Bangladesh, Brazil, Bulgaria, Chile, China, Colombia, Croatia, Cuba, Cyprus, Czech Republic, Democratic People's Republic of Korea, Dominican Republic, Ecuador, Egypt, El Salvador, FYR Macedonia, Ghana, Hong Kong, China, Hungary, India, Indonesia, Iran (Islamic Republic of), Jamaica, Jordan, Kenya, Kuwait, Lebanon, Malaysia, Malta, Mexico, Morocco, Montenegro, Nigeria, Pakistan, Panama, Peru, Phillippines, Poland, Qatar, Republic of Korea, Romania, Russian Federation, Saudia Arabia, Senegal, Singapore, Slovenia, South Africa, Sri Lanka, Taiwan Province of China,Thailand, Tunisia, Turkey, Ukraine, United Arab Emirates, Uruguay, Venezuela, Yugoslavia and Zambia.

[b] Within this category, Portugal has one branch from Brazil; and Denmark, Finland, Ireland and Sweden have no entities at all.

Annex table A.II.5. The ten selected developing and transition economies[a] with most banking entities in selected OECD[b] host countries, 1996

Home economy	Number of foreign banking entities	Number of host countries represented	Foreign banking entities per host country
Korea, Republic of	76	9	8.4
Brazil	42	10	4.2
Taiwan Province of China	31	8	3.9
Turkey	25	8	3.1
Singapore	22	4	5.5
Iran, Islamic Republic of	21	6	3.5
India	20	6	3.3
Indonesia	19	6	3.2
Pakistan	17	8	2.1
Hong Kong, China	17	5	3.4

Source: Cornford and Brandon, forthcoming.

[a] The offshore banking centres Bahrain and Bermuda are excluded.

[b] Australia, Austria, Belgium, France, Germany, Greece, Italy, Japan, Luxembourg, Netherlands, Spain, United Kingdom and United States.

Annex table A.II.6. Number of banking entities from selected OECD countries[a] in selected developing and transition economies, 1996

Host economy	Number of foreign banking entities	Number of home countries represented	Foreign banking entities per home country
Asia			
Hong Kong, China	108	14	7.7
Singapore	87	17	5.1
Republic of Korea	41	7	5.9
Taiwan Province of China	31	8	3.9
China	31	10	3.1
Thailand	26	8	3.3
India	22	8	2.8
Philippines	9	6	1.5
Malaysia	9	6	1.5
Indonesia	7	5	1.4
Vietnam	7	4	1.8
Brunei	3	2	1.5
Latin America and the Caribbean			
Brazil	18	9	2.0
Argentina	14	9	1.6
Chile	12	5	2.4
Mexico	9	5	1.8
Panama	9	5	1.8
Peru	9	5	1.8
Uruguay	9	5	1.8
Venezuela	9	5	1.8
Colombia	4	3	1.3
Ecuador	3	2	1.5
Central and Eastern Europe			
Czech Republic	43	11	3.9
Russian Federation	34	14	2.4
Poland	16	6	2.7
Romania	14	8	1.8
Croatia	11	3	3.7
Slovakia	10	5	2.0
Bulgaria	7	5	1.4
Albania	4	2	2.0
Estonia	4	3	1.3
Slovenia	4	2	2.0
Latvia	3	2	1.5
Hungary	1	6	0.2

Source: Cornford and Brandon, forthcoming.

[a] Australia, Austria, Belgium, Canada,Denmark, Finland, France, Germany, Greece, Ireland, Italy, Luxembourg, Japan, Netherlands, Norway, Portugal, Spain, Sweden, Switzerland, United Kingdom and United States.

Annex table A.II.7. The ten OECD countries with most banking entities in selected developing and transition economies,[a] 1996

Home country	Number of foreign banking entities	Number of host economies represented	Foreign banking entities per host economy
Japan	116	15	7.7
United States	113	28	4.0
France	76	25	3.0
Germany	66	20	3.3
Netherlands	53	27	2.0
United Kingdom	42	17	2.5
Austria	33	11	3.0
Italy	23	9	2.6
Spain	21	14	1.5
Switzerland	13	7	1.9

Source: Cornford and Brandon, forthcoming.

[a] For the list of countries, see footnote a in annex table A.II.4.

Annex table A.II.8. The world's top 100 TNCs: measures of transnationality, 1996

(Percentage)

	Approach I				Approach II	
Corporation[a]	Foreign assets as a percentage of total assets	Foreign sales as a percentage of total sales	Foreign employment as a percentage of total employment	Transnationality index[b]	No. of Countries	Network-spread index[c]
General Electric Company	30	27	35	31	34	19
Shell, Royal Dutch	66	55	78	67	109	61
Ford Motor Company	31	45	38	38	46	26
Exxon Corporation	58	87	73	73	34	19
General Motors Corporation	25	32	34	30	59	33
IBM	51	61	51	54	50	28
Toyota Motor Corporation	35	47	23	35	34	19
Volkswagen Group	55	64	47	55	23	13
Mitsubishi Corporation	41	39	43	41	36	20
Mobil Corporation	68	66	53	62	42	24
Nestlé SA	91	98	97	95	94	53
Asea Brown Boveri (ABB)	96	97	95	96	84	47
Elf Aquitaine SA	62	59	49	57	..[d]	..[d]
Bayer AG	91	82	66	80	70	39
Hoechst Aktiengesellschaft	79	54	63	66	93	52
Nissan Motor Co., Ltd.	46	54	-50	50	13	7
Fiat Spa	38	39	38	38	43	24
Unilever	85	86	90	87	92	52
Daimler-Benz AG	40	63	23	42	38	21
Philips Electronics N.V.	77	95	82	85	72	40
Roche Holding AG	83	98	80	87	54	30
Siemens AG	43	61	46	50	79	44
Alcatel Alsthom Cie	49	78	62	63	43	24
Sony Corporation	51	72	58	60	47	26
Total SA	76	76	76	76	88	49
Novartis (former Ciba Geigy)	49	98	78	75	69	39
British Petroleum Company	65	56	70	64	70	39
Philip Morris Companies, Inc.	37	44	61	48	45	25
ENI Group	33	33	33	33	44	25
Renault SA	45	54	31	43	29	16
B.A.T. Industries	30	81	91	67	79	44
Du Pont (E.I.) de Nemours	48	48	35	44	49	28
Rhone-Poulenc SA	67	79	56	67	51	29
Seagram Company Ltd.	98	97	97	97	35	20
BASF AG	63	73	41	59	68	38
Honda Motor Co., Ltd.	53	62	54	57	22	12
BMW AG	59	73	45	59	22	12
Mitsui & Co., Ltd.	28	43	35	35	47	26
Nissho Iwai Corporation	35	32	30	32	53	30
Itochu Corporation	23	26	26	25	36	20
Hewlett-Packard Company	55	56	40	50	45	25
Ferruzzi/Montedison	69	76	59	68	29	16
Daewoo Corporation	46	39	79	55	42	24
News Corporation	60	87	65	71	48	27
Chevron Corporation	41	35	30	35	21	12
Dow Chemical Company	58	56	52	56	48	27
Robert Bosch GmbH	62	62	62	62	25	14
Marubeni Corporation	21	39	30	30	45	25
Cable And Wireless PLC	84	72	79	78	56	32
Thomson Corporation	97	94	93	95	19	11
Texaco Incorporated	47	48	39	45	61	34
Michelin	85	85	85	85	24	14
Matsushita Electric Industries	18	38	28	28	39	22
Xerox Corporation	45	51	48	48	58	33
Ericsson	71	93	53	73	57	32

/...

Annex table A.II.8. The world's top 100 TNCs: measures of transnationality, 1996 (continued)

(Percentage)

	Approach I					Approach II
Corporation[a]	Foreign assets as a percentage of total assets	Foreign sales as a percentage of total sales	Foreign employment as a percentage of total employment	Transnationality index[b]	No. of Countries	Network-spread index[c]
Holderbank Glarus	92	86	91	90	35	20
BCE Inc.	38	65	38	47	..d	..d
Saint-Gobain SA	53	65	67	62	32	18
Broken Hill Comp. (BHP)	41	37	34	37	32	18
Hitachi, Ltd.	14	29	17	20	39	22
Sumitomo Corporation	26	28	31	28	13	7
Electrolux AB	86	92	88	89	49	28
At&T Corp.	19	17	18	18	17	10
Procter & Gamble Company	39	49	44	44	67	38
International Paper Company	37	30	36	34	42	24
Amoco Corporation	32	22	22	26	17	10
Volvo AB	50	89	37	58	33	19
Mcdonald's Corporation	55	57	65	59	7	4
Grand Metropolitan PLC	54	90	84	76	60	34
Glaxo Wellcome PLC	66	92	75	78	66	37
BTR PLC	66	75	71	71	59	33
Johnson & Johnson	46	50	53	50	57	32
Petroleos de Venezuela	20	94	22	45	..[d]	..[d]
Fujitsu Limited	23	30	32	28	58	33
Hanson PLC	58	94	63	72	26	15
Motorola, Inc.	36	60	46	47	30	17
Generale des Eaux	19	31	26	25	32	18
Nippon Steel Corporation	23	23	23	23	12	7
Akzo Nobel N.V.	71	74	75	73	51	29
Chrysler Corporation	15	13	21	16	26	15
Canon Electronics Inc.	37	68	51	52	26	15
Coca-Cola Company	68	68	67	67	22	12
Solvay SA	92	96	89	92	42	24
Mitsubishi Motors Corp.	31	29	25	28	14	8
Northern Telecom Limited	72	89	81	81	..[d]	..[d]
Petrofina SA	67	80	68	72	33	19
Bridgestone Corporation	51	56	54	54	27	15
Pepsico, Inc.	32	29	30	30	23	13
Danone Groupe SA	40	56	69	55	35	20
Crown Cork & Seal Company	60	60	60	60	40	23
Toshiba Corporation	16	32	24	24	27	15
Kvaerner ASA	82	77	86	82	48	27
Atlantic Richfield Company	29	18	23	23	26	15
RTZ CRA	46	50	61	53	58	33
Mannesmann AG	47	36	35	39	44	25
Pharmacia & Upjohn, Inc.	65	68	66	66	..[d]	..[d]
GTE Corporation	19	13	16	16	22	12
American Home Products	34	41	47	41	20	11
Eridania Beghin-Say SA	75	79	76	76	..[d]	..[d]
Société au Bon Marché	31	64	48	48	..[d]	..[d]

Source: Ietto-Gilles, forthcoming, based on UNCTAD/Erasmus University database and on Dun and Bradstreet, 1997. All data involving the number of countries in which TNCs operate are based on the location of foreign affiliates.

a Ranked by foreign assets, based on data for 1996.

b The index of transnationality is calculated as the average of the ratios: foreign assets to total assets, foreign sales to total sales and foreign employment to total employment.

c The number of countries in which a company has foreign affiliates is denoted as "N". An index in percentage terms (and thus comparable to the transnationality index) is derived by taking N as a percentage of N*, the number of foreign countries in which, potentially, the company could have located affiliates. N* is chosen to be the number of countries in the world that have inward FDI. In practice, N* is estimated as the number of countries that are in receipt of inward stock of FDI minus 1 (to exclude the home country of the TNC); on the basis of the data in the *WIR 97*, N* is equal to 178. The index N/N* is the network spread index.

d Complete data were not available.

Annex table A.II.9. Measures of transnationality: rank correlations between variables/indices, 1996

Variable	Total assets	Total sales	Total employment	Foreign assets	Foreign sales	Foreign employment	Approach 1: Indices Assets index	Sales index	Employment index	Transnationality index	Approach II Network-spread index
Total assets	1.00	0.89	0.39	0.67	0.66	0.12	-0.56[a]	-0.46	-0.52	-0.54[a]	0.06[b]
Total sales	1.00	0.35	0.63	0.80	0.11	-0.46	-0.44[a]	-0.49	-0.49[a]	0.08[b]	
Total employment	1.00	0.35	0.32	0.83	-0.14	-0.06	-0.11[a]	-0.10[a]	0.14[b]		
Foreign assets	1.00	0.79	0.36	0.18	0.13	0.09	0.15	0.38[b]			
Foreign sales	1.00	0.30	-0.01	0.13	-0.03	0.04	0.35[b]				
Foreign employment	1.00	0.24	0.30	0.39	0.33	0.36[b]					
Assets index	1.00	0.79	0.83	0.93	0.33[b]						
Sales index	1.00	0.79	0.92	0.36[b]							
Employment index	1.00	0.93	0.44[b]								
Transnationality index	1.00	0.40[b]									
Network spread	1.00[b]										

Source: Ietto-Gilles, forthcoming, based on UNCTAD/Erasmus University database and Dun and Bradstreet, 1997.

[a] These coefficients are affected by the way the indices were constructed.

[b] Coefficient calculated for a sample of 93 companies. In all other cases, a sample of 100 companies was used.

Annex table A.II.10. Measures of transnationality: averages of transnationality and network-spread indices, by industry, and respective rankings for the largest TNCs worldwide, 1996

Industry	Transnationality index (average) (Per cent)	Transnationality index (average) Rank	No. of countries[a]	Network-spread index (average) Rank	Network-spread index (average) (Per cent)
Construction	80.7	1	31	11	17.1
Food and beverages[b]	67.2	2	54	1	30.3
Media, Printing and paper	66.6	3	36	6	20.4
Chemical/pharmaceutical	65.4	4	52	2	29.5
Electronics/electrical equipment	52.8	5	49	4	27.7
Oil, petroleum and mining	52.1	6	50	3	27.8
Telecommunications	47.9	7	32	8	17.8
Automotive	43.8	8	32	8	17.8
Metals	43.3	9	36	7	19.9
Diversified	39.2	10	40	5	22.6
Trading and services	35.0	11	31	10	17.3

Source: Ietto-Gilles, forthcoming, based on UNCTAD/Erasmus University database and Dun and Bradstreet, 1997.

[a] All data involving the number of countries in which TNCs operate are based on the location of foreign affiliates.

[b] Includes tobacco firms.

Annex table A.II.11. Measures of transnationality: averages of the transnationality and network-spread indices, by country and respective rankings, 1996

Country	Transnationality index[a] (Per cent)	Transnationality index[a] Rank	No. of countries[b]	Network-spread index[a] Rank	Network-spread index[a] (Per cent)
Switzerland	88.7	1	67	3	37.8
Belgium	82.0	2	38	11	21.1
Netherlands	81.7	3	72	1	40.3
Norway	81.7	3	48	6	27.0
Canada	79.9	4	27	14	15.2
Sweden	78.9	5	56	4	31.3
United Kingdom	71.2	7	68	2	37.9
France	59.7	8	42	9	23.5
Germany	57.0	9	51	5	28.8
Korea, Republic of	54.5	10	42	8	23.6
Australia	53.4	11	46	7	25.8
Italy	46.7	12	39	10	21.7
Venezuela	44.9	13	..[c]	..[c]	..[c]
United States	43.2	14	37	12	21.0
Japan	36.3	15	33	13	18.4

Source: Ietto-Gilles, forthcoming, based on UNCTAD/Erasmus University database and Dun and Bradstreet, 1997.

[a] The number calculated represents the average for each country.

[b] All data involving the number of countries in which TNCs operate are based on the location of foreign affiliates.

[c] Data not available.

Annex table A.II.12. Country breakdown of the top 50 TNCs from developing countries by transnationality index, foreign assets, foreign sales and foreign employment for 1993 and 1996

(Per cent of total and number of entries)

	1993					1996				
	Number of entries	Average TNI	Foreign assets	Foreign sales	Foreign employment	Number of entries	Average TNI	Foreign assets	Foreign sales	Foreign employment
South, East and South-East Asia	33	20.0	70.6	83.4	8.9	31	31.8	65.7	64.5	79.0
China	-	-	-	-	-	4	30.0	8.2	8.7	0.7
Hong Kong, China	7	26.4	22.0	22.2	42.2	11	50.7	20.4	18.9	50.3
India	1	6.4	0.4	0.5	-	1	7.7	0.8	0.0	0.2
Korea, Republic of	9	16.7	24.8	47.9	30.3	6	45.6	24.4	22.4	18.4
Malaysia	4	20.0	4.7	4.3	4.9	3	34.4	3.2	7.0	1.8
Philippines	2	6.9	1.4	0.5	1.3	1	16.1	0.9	0.2	0.7
Singapore	3	41.0	5.3	2.1	3.9	3	38.1	3.7	4.0	3.1
Taiwan Province of China	7	19.6	12.3	6.0	6.7	2	32.1	4.2	3.2	3.8
Latin America	17	14.0	29.9	16.6	1.1	15	28.9	28.9	31.4	13.3
Argentina	-	-	-	-	-	1	19.5	2.6	0.6	0.4
Brazil	10	17.4	12.0	9.9	0.9	5	13.1	6.2	3.0	0.2
Chile	2	12.1	1.0	0.7	0.6	3	29.0	3.6	0.8	1.4
Colombia	-	-	-	-	-	1	17.9	0.5	0.3	0.5
Mexico	5	12.5	16.9	6.0	9.1	4	48.7	7.5	3.5	8.4
Venezuela	-	-	-	-	-	1	44.9	8.6	23.1	2.3
Africa/South Africa	-	-	-	-	-	4	40.2	5.4	4.2	7.7
Total of all listed TNCs	50	19	100	100	100	50	35	100	100	100

Source: UNCTAD database.

Annex table A.IV.1. WAIPA members, as of July 1998

Economy	Agency
Albania	Albanian Center for Foreign Investment Promotion
Algeria	Agence de Promotion de Soutien et de Suivi des Investissements (APSI)
Angola	Instituto do Investimento Estrangeiro (IIE)
Anguilla	Ministry of Finance, Planning and Economic Development
Antigua and Barbuda	Ministry of Trade, Industry and Commerce
Armenia	Armenian Development Agency
Aruba	Department of Economic Affairs, Commerce and Industry
Austria	Austrian Business Agency
Bahrain	Bahrain Promotions and Marketing Board
Bangladesh	Board of Investment (BOI)
Belarus	Belarussian Foreign Investment Promotion Agency
Belgium	Flanders' Foreign Investment Office
	Office for Foreign Investors (Wallonia)
Bolivia	Ministry of Foreign Trade and Investment
Bulgaria	Foreign Investment Agency
Cameroon	Investment Code Management Unit (ICMU)
Cape Verde	Center for Investment, Export and Tourism Promotion (PROMEX)
Chile	Comité de Inversiones Extranjeras
China	Ministry of Foreign Trade and Economic Cooperation (MOFTEC)
Colombia	Invest in Colombia Corporation (COINVERTIR)
Congo, Democratic Republic of	Fonds de Promotion de l'Industrie (FPI)
Costa Rica	Costa Rican Investment and Trade Development Board (CINDE)
Côte d'Ivoire	Centre de Promotion des Investissements en Côte d' Ivoire (CEPICI)
Croatia	Croatian Investment Promotion Agency (CIPA)
Cuba	Centro de Promoción de Inversiones
Cyprus	Central Bank of Cyprus
Czech Republic	Czech Agency for Foreign Investment (CZECHINVEST)
Dominica, Commonwealth of	National Development Corporation
Dominican Republic	Dominican Republic Investment Promotion Office (OPI-RD)
Egypt	General Authority for Investment (GAFI)
Estonia	Estonian Investment Agency
Ethiopia	Ethiopian Investment Authority (EIA)
Fiji	Fiji Trade and Investment Board
Finland	Invest in Finland Bureau
Gambia, The	National Investment Promotion Authority (NIPA)
Ghana	Ghana Investment Promotion Centre (GIPC)
Greece	Hellenic Center for Investment S.A. (ELKE S.A.)
Guatemala	Fundación para el Desarollo de Guatemala (FUNDESA)
Guyana	Guyana Office for Investment (GO-INVEST)
Haiti	Ministry of Commerce and Industry
Hungary	Hungarian Investment and Trade Development Agency (ITDH)
Iceland	Invest in Iceland Bureau
India (Rajasthan)	Bureau of Industrial Promotion
Indonesia	Investment Coordination Board, Ministry of Investment
Iran, Islamic Republic of	Organization for Investment, Economic and Technical Assistance of Iran
Ireland	Industrial Development Agency of Ireland (IDA Ireland)
Israel	Investment Promotion Center, Ministry of Industry and Trade
Italy	Institute for Industrial Promotion
Jamaica	Jamaica Promotions Corporation (JAMPRO)
Jordan	Investment Promotion Corporation
Kazakhstan	State Committee of the Republic of Kazakhstan on Investment
Kenya	Investment Promotion Centre (IPC)
Kiribati, Republic of	Foreign Investment Commission
Kyrgyz Republic	Kyrgyz Project Promotion Agency (KPPA)
Latvia	Latvian Development Agency
Lesotho	Lesotho Investment Promotion Centre (LIPC)
Lithuania	Lithuanian Investment Agency
Malaysia	Malaysian Industrial Development Authority (MIDA)
Maldives	Foreign Investment Services Bureau (FISB)
Mali	Centre National de Promotion des Investissements (CNPI)

/...

Annex table A.IV.1. WAIPA members, as of July 1998 (continued)

Economy	Agency
Malta	Malta Development Corporation
Moldova, Republic of	National Agency for Attracting Investment
Mongolia	Board of Foreign Investment
Morocco	Ministère des Finances et des Investissements Extérieurs
Namibia	Namibia Investment Centre
Nepal	Industrial Promotion Division, Ministry of Industry
Nicaragua	Centro de Exportaciones e Inversiones (CEI)
Nigeria	Nigerian Investment Promotion Commission (NIPC)
Pakistan	Board of Investment
Papua New Guinea	Investment Promotion Authority (IPA)
Paraguay	PROPARAGUAY
Peru	PROMPERU
Philippines	Board of Investments (BOI)
Poland	Polish Agency for Foreign Investment (PAIZ)
Romania	Romanian Development Agency
Russia	Foreign Investment Promotion Center of Russia (FIPC)
Senegal	Guichet Unique
Seychelles	Seychelles International Business Authority (SIBA)
Sierra Leone	Ministry of Trade, Industry and State Enterprises
Slovak Republic	Slovak National Agency for Foreign Investment and Development
Solomon Islands	Foreign Investment Division, Ministry of Commerce, Industries and Employment
Sri Lanka	Board of Investment of Sri Lanka
St. Lucia	St. Lucia National Development Corporation
Sudan	General Administration for Investment Promotion
Tajikistan	Aid Coordination Unit
Tanzania, United Republic of (Zanzibar)	Zanzibar Investment Promotion Agency (ZIPA)
Thailand	Office of the Board of Investment
Trinidad and Tobago	Tourism and Industrial Development Company of Trinidad and Tobago Ltd.
Tunisia	Foreign Investment Promotion Agency (FIPA Tunisia)
Uganda	Uganda Investment Authority (UIA)
Ukraine	Ukrainian Foreign Investments Promotion Agency
Uzbekistan	Foreign Investment Agency
Vanuatu	Department of Trade, Industry and Investment
Western Samoa	Department of Trade, Commerce and Industry
Yemen, Republic of	General Investment Authority
Yugoslavia	Foreign Investment Bureau, Yugoslav Chamber of Commerce and Industry
Zambia	Zambia Investment Centre
Zimbabwe	Zimbabwe Investment Centre

Source: UNCTAD.

Annex table A.V.1. Survey results on reasons for divestment by Japanese TNCs, by selected region, 1995

(Percentage)

Reason	Number of Japanese foreign affiliates that cited the reason as a major factor, as percentage of all Japanese affiliates surveyed				
	World	United States	European Union	Latin America and the Caribbean	South, East and South-East Asia
Deterioration of sales and profits due to:					
Wrong forecast of demand for products	14.2	19.8	18	8.3	9
Intensified competition with local firms	4.9	7.4	6.6	-	1.5
Intensified competition with Japanese affiliates in the same host country	2.6	4.9	3.3	-	1.5
Intensified competition with non-Japanese affiliates in the same host country	4.5	3.7	8.2	-	6
Other reasons	16.8	14.8	16.4	20.8	16.4
Deterioration of profits due to increases in wages	2.2	-	-	-	7.5
Deterioration of profits due to increased prices of raw materials and parts	-	-	-	-	-
Difficulties of labour procurement	0.7	1.2	-	-	1.5
Difficulties of obtaining raw materials and parts	0.7	1.2	1.6	-	-
Human resources constraints on the Japanese side, such as death or retirement of Japanese managers	1.5	2.5	-	4.2	-
Conflict with local partners	1.9	1.2	1.6	-	4.5
Requirement for localization	1.5	-	1.6	-	3
Restrictions on remittance of profits and royalty to Japan	0.4	-	-	-	1.5
Changes in tax system	1.1	-	-	-	3
Changes in foreign exchange policy in host country such as appreciation of local currency	1.1	-	1.6	4.2	-
Others	45.9	43.2	41	62.5	44.8
Total	100	100	100	100	100
Memorandum:					
Number of affiliates surveyed	268	81	61	24	67

Source: Japan, Ministry of International Trade and Industry, 1998a, pp. 433-445.

Annex table A.V.2. Share of FDI in Austria, by source country, corrected for the ultimate source of capital, 1983-1991

(Percentage share)

Year	Item	Switzerland / Liechtenstein	Germany	United States	Other foreign countries	Austria[a]
1983	Reported	23	24	10	20	23
	Corrected	13	28	11	24	24
1985	Reported	24	23	10	19	24
	Corrected	13	27	11	23	25
1987	Reported	23	23	6	21	27
	Corrected	16	24	7	26	27
1989	Reported	21	24	6	22	27
	Corrected	14	26	6	26	28
1991	Reported	19	25	5	25	26
	Corrected	13	27	5	28	26

Source: UNCTAD, based on Austria, National Bank, 1993, p. 6.

[a] Domestic investment in Austria by foreign firms located in Austria (nominal capital).

Note: the table may be understood as follows: in 1991, according to data on Swiss FDI in Austria, only 13 per cent of FDI in Austria was made by Swiss TNCs per se, although 19 per cent of FDI in Austria is reported as originating in Switzerland. The difference of 6 per cent presumably constitutes investment in Austria by foreign affiliates of non-Swiss TNCs in Switzerland. Of this 6 per cent, 2 percentage points are traceable to Germany, and 3 to other foreign countries. Similar, and larger, discrepancies between reported and corrected FDI from Switzerland in Austria for other years can be attributed to higher FDI by the other countries shown in the table.

Annex table A.V.3. Foreign assets in the United States owned by firms based in countries other than FDI-originating countries, 1995

(Millions of dollars and percentage)

Economy	Foreign assets of FDI-originating countries (A)	Foreign assets of ultimate beneficiary countries (B)	Foreign assets of non FDI-originating countries (C=A-B)	Foreign assets of non FDI-originating countries (C) as percentage of foreign assets of FDI-originating countries (A)
Developed countries				
Canada	270 520	267 378	3 142	1.2
France	221 502	232 662	-11 160	-5.0
Germany	207 366	210 408	-3 042	-1.5
Italy	9 366	22 718	-13 352	-142.6
Japan	516 626	519 577	-2 951	-0.6
Netherlands	220 305	154 877	65 428	29.7
Sweden	41 128	42 067	- 939	-2.3
Switzerland	225 179	229 335	-4 156	-1.8
United Kingdom	344 121	381 241	-37 120	-10.8
Developing economies				
Bermuda	15 415	8 660	6 755	43.8
Brazil	1 101	8 661	-7 560	-686.6
China	1 024	1 029	- 5	-0.5
Hong Kong, China	3 031	7 719	-4 688	-154.7
Republic of Korea	13 605	13 689	- 84	-0.6
Malaysia	1 197	1 645	- 448	-37.4
Mexico	7 749	9 593	-1 844	-23.8
Netherlands Antilles	10 976	3 211	7 765	70.7
Saudi Arabia	7 528	10 700	-3 172	-42.1
Singapore	3 252	3 402	- 150	-4.6
Taiwan Province of China	4 532	10 217	-5 685	-125.4
United Kingdom Islands, Caribbean	20 750	3 328	17 422	84.0
Venezuela	3 997	12 011	-8 014	-200.5

Source: UNCTAD, based on United States, Department of Commerce, 1997a, table A.7.

Annex table A.VI.1. African countries:[a] selected FDI stock indicators, 1987 and 1996

	FDI inward stock			FDI inward stock as a percentage of GDP			FDI inward stock per capita	
	1987	1996		1987	1996		1987	1996
Country	(Million dollars)		Country	(Per cent)		Country	(Dollars)	
Nigeria	5 222.0	16 578.1	Equatorial Guinea	9.6	386.7	Seychelles	1 805.2	4 507.4
Egypt	7 864.7	14 733.9	Liberia	11.2	97.8	Equatorial Guinea	38.1	1 499.7
Tunisia	1 977.9	4 255.0	Seychelles	48.5	71.4	Namibia	1 576.8	944.4
Morocco	501.1	3 301.0	Namibia	113.5	48.0	Botswana	505.3	942.0
Namibia	1 960.0	1 492.2	Nigeria	19.3	39.9	Gabon	983.5	750.2
Botswana	583.1	1 442.2	Congo	23.7	36.9	Tunisia	260.4	469.8
			Swaziland	40.5	35.5	Swaziland	349.9	463.0
			Chad	27.2	33.9	Liberia	53.8	438.7
			Botswana	37.8	32.8	Congo	266.9	278.5
			Zambia	10.8	29.4	Mauritius	60.1	252.2
			Egypt	12.2	24.4	Egypt	150.3	229.5
			Gambia, The	8.3	24.2	Nigeria	59.3	144.1
			Lesotho	8.6	22.9	Morocco	22.0	119.8
			Tunisia	20.5	21.8	Zambia	30.4	102.6
			Gabon	30.4	20.0			
			Togo	18.0	19.8			
			Malawi	13.9	19.4			
			Rwanda	7.7	18.5			
			Niger	10.6	17.2			
			Mozambique	1.8	15.4			
			Ghana	5.8	15.3			
Memorandum:								
Average for developing countries including South Africa	1 832.1	6 097.7		8.7	15.5		69.3	195.3
Average for Africa including South Africa	807.0	1 432.0		9.6	14.9		71.0	97.8

Source: UNCTAD, FDI/TNC database.

[a] Ranked according to 1996 values of the indicators. Countries shown are those with values of at least one indicator exceeding the African average.

Annex table A.VI.2. FDI framework of African countries: Membership in international agreements concerning FDI, by 1 January 1998

Country	Convention establishing the Multilateral Investment Guarantee Agency	Convention on the Settlement of Investment Disputes between States and Nationals of other States	Convention on the Recognition and Enforcement of Foreign Arbitral Awards	World Intellectual Property Organisation (WIPO)
	Year of accession	Year of accession	Year of accession	Year of accession
Algeria	1996	1996	1989	1966
Benin	1994	1966	1974	1967
Botswana	1990	1970	1971	-
Burkina Faso	1988	1966	1987	1963
Burundi	-	1969	-	1977
Cameroon	1988	1967	1988	1964
Cape Verde	1993	-	-	-
Central African Rep	-	1966	1962	1963
Chad	-	1966	-	1963
Comoros	-	1978	-	-
Congo, Republic of	1991	1966	-	1963
Congo, Dem.Rep.of	1989	1970	-	1975
Cote d'Ivoire	1988	1966	1991	1963
Djibouti	-	-	1983	-
Egypt,Arab Rep.of	1988	1972	1959	1951
Equatorial Guinea	1994	-	-	1997
Eritrea	1996	-	-	-
Ethiopia	1991	-	-	-
Gabon	-	1966	-	1964
Gambia, The	1992	1975	-	1992
Ghana	1988	1966	1968	1976
Guinea	1995	1968	1991	1982
Guinea-Bissau	-	-	-	1988
Kenya	1988	1967	1989	1965
Lesotho	1988	1969	1989	1989
Liberia	-	1970	-	1994
Libya	1993	-	-	1976
Madagascar	1988	1966	1962	1963
Malawi	1988	1966	-	1964
Mali	1992	1978	1994	1983
Mauritania	1992	1966	1997	1985
Mauritius	1990	1969	1996	1976
Morocco	1992	1967	1959	1917
Mozambique	1994	1995	-	-
Namibia	1990	-	-	-
Niger	-	1966	1964	1964
Nigeria	1990	1966	1970	1963
Rwanda	-	1979	-	1984
Sao Tome & Principe	-	-	-	-
Senegal	1988	1967	1994	1963
Seychelles	1992	1978	-	-
Sierra Leone	1996	1966	-	1977
Somalia	-	1968	-	-
South Africa	1994	-	1976	1947
Sudan	1990	1973	-	1984
Swaziland	1990	1971	-	1991
Tanzania	1992	1992	1964	-
Togo	1988	1967	-	1967
Tunisia	1988	1966	1967	1884
Uganda	1990	1966	1992	1965
Zambia	1988	1970	-	1965
Zimbabwe	1992	1994	1994	1980
Total	40	42	26	40

Source: UNCTAD, FDI/TNC database.

Annex table A.VI.3. Africa: The investor-friendliness of the business environment as ranked according to selected indicators, 1997

Country	Government regulations [a]	State interference[b]	Share of management time spent on dealing with bureaucratic issues (per cent)[c]
Botswana	4.9	5.9	4
Burkina Faso	4.0	5.9	0
Cameroon	2.6	4.2	15
Côte d'Ivoire	3.4	5.0	12
Egypt	3.3	5.2	11
Ethiopia	3.5	4.4	11
Ghana	4.0	5.9	21
Kenya	3.3	5.1	13
Malawi	4.2	5.3	10
Mauritius	4.1	5.6	13
Morocco	4.5	4.7	12
Mozambique	2.4	4.2	21
Namibia	4.6	5.5	3
Nigeria	2.2	4.4	12
South Africa	3.5	4.8	7
United Republic of Tanzania	3.5	5.2	15
Tunisia	4.7	5.2	10
Uganda	4.5	5.8	11
Zambia	3.8	5.8	22
Zimbabwe	2.2	4.0	4
Average, FDI frontrunner countries	4.2	5.4	17
Average, other countries	3.4	5.0	10

Source: UNCTAD, based on World Economic Forum, 1998a.

Note*:* investors in the countries were asked to give ratings between 1 and 7 (1: strongly disagree and 7: strongly agree) for statements a and b and to assign a percentage in the case of c:

[a] Government regulations do not impose a heavy burden on business competitiveness.

[b] Excepting the state controlled sector, state interference in private business is minimal.

[c] What percentage of senior management's time is spent with officials negotiating or obtaining licences, regulations, permits or tax assessments?

Annex table A.VI.4. Best practice indicators for inward investment promotion for selected investment promotion agencies in the mid-1990s

Indicator	Agencies										
	Belgium	France	India	Ireland	Malaysia	Netherlands	Oregon	Singapore	Uganda	Wales	Zambia
Proactive (P) or reactive (R) policy	P	P	R	P	P	P	P	P	P	P	R
Long-term (3 years plus) or short-term (1 year) strategy	Short	Long	Short	Long	Long	Long	Long	Long	Short	Long	Long
Set targets?	√ (5)	No	No	√ (5)	√ (20)	√ (4)	√(..)	√ (6)	√ (8)	√ (6)	√ (10)
Number of monitoring criteria	3	8	3	8	3	5	8	6	2	5	1
Range of services											
Image building	√	√		√	√	√		√	√	√	
Promote to investors	√	√	√	√	√	√	√	√	√	√	
Promote to brokers				√	√	√	√	√		√	
Involved in "product improvement"[a]		√		√	√	√	√	√		√	
Handle enquiries and project	√ (post)	√ (post)	√ (post)	√	√	√	√	√	√	√	√ (post)
Facilitation services			√	√			√	√		√	√
"Aftercare" (post investment support) services				√	√	√	√	√		√	
Other bodies involved in investment attraction (beyond national government)	Provinces	Regions, Utilities	States	Private sector	States, private sector	Provinces, private sector	Local authorities, private sector	..	..	Local authorities, private sector	..

Source: UNCTAD, based on Tillett, 1996, p. 9.

[a] Investment promotion agency is involved in decision-making processes as regards issues that affect the attractiveness of the country as an investment location.

Annex table A.VII.1. Thailand: FDI inflows,[a] by industry, 1995-first quarter 1998

(Millions of dollars)

Industry	1995	1996	1997[b]	1996 Q1	1996 Q2	1996 Q3	1996 Q4	1997 Q1	1997 Q2	1997 Q3	1997 Q4[b]	1998 Q1[b]
Manufacturing	566.4	759.3	1228.1	447.6	96.3	85.3	131.5	231.4	183.3	449.0	644.4	534.4
Food & sugar	39.0	45.1	129.7	15.8	6.4	13.8	9.1	90.8	9.1	25.9	32.5	14.0
Textiles	37.8	49.2	38.8	34.3	13.8	-4.5	5.8	5.9	-0.1	3.5	38.3	-15.2
Metal & non-metallic	92.4	112.5	177.6	33.6	10.5	23.4	45.0	48.1	54.7	45.7	69.3	119.1
Electrical appliances	233.2	291.5	501.9	164.5	41.7	-6.4	91.9	119.2	161.3	182.7	152.8	36.0
Machinery & transport equipment	144.3	108.8	339.7	62.6	31.0	21.2	-5.7	-13.4	51.5	279.0	101.3	135.2
Chemicals	93.6	182.2	157.8	41.1	48.3	33.1	59.6	-4.6	36.7	16.9	145.3	64.3
Petroleum products	-161.3	-249.9	-262.1	15.9	-83.7	-83.4	-98.2	-55.9	-153.6	-128.5	16.2	125.4
Construction materials	25.1	4.0	-7.5	-3.6	5.0	-0.3	2.8	3.9	-0.2	-8.6	-4.4	0.0
Others	62.2	215.9	158.0	83.4	23.3	88.4	21.2	37.3	23.9	32.4	100.2	55.7
Financial institutions	25.8	71.9	212.8	3.9	24.8	44.8	-1.4	8.9	7.6	69.7	175.5	316.6
Trade	445.9	522.3	1021.7	141.6	128.8	108.0	143.9	196.0	244.1	446.0	368.4	237.0
Construction	36.4	69.5	222.1	-3.9	19.4	30.1	23.9	21.1	48.2	27.0	176.6	79.9
Mining & quarrying	56.9	19.3	27.2	26.7	4.7	6.6	-18.5	6.9	6.6	-6.9	26.8	13.9
Agriculture	9.3	2.0	1.5	-0.3	-0.4	-0.4	3.1	-0.5	0.5	0.1	1.8	0.3
Services	87.7	125.1	232.8	-13.7	41.9	4.8	91.5	33.3	114.3	23.0	115.5	77.7
Real estate	852.6	703.0	399.6	141.1	182.5	187.4	192.0	147.9	153.1	158.8	29.8	5.8
Others	-79.1	-25.4	67.5	32.7	-47.5	-14.3	3.7	-6.2	11.8	18.3	59.3	67.3
Total	2001.9	2247.0	3413.3	775.7	450.4	452.4	569.7	638.9	769.4	1185.0	1598.2	1332.9
Exchange rate[c]	(24.9)	(25.3)	(31.4)	(25.2)	(25.3)	(25.3)	(25.5)	(25.9)	(25.9)	(33.0)	(40.7)	(47.1)

Source: UNCTAD, based on data provided by the Bank of Thailand.

[a] Equity Investment plus loans from related companies.

[b] Preliminary.

[c] Baht per dollar. There may be a problem with conversion because of the volatility of the exchange rate during the second half of 1997 and the first half of 1998.

Annex table A.VII.2. Asia: the largest 30 cross-border M&As in the five most affected economies, July 1997-June 1998

Date of M&A	Acquired company	Industry	Acquiring company	Acquiring economy	Deal type	Value (Million dollars)
Indonesia						
15 July 1997	*Indofood Sukses Makmur Pt*	Food, drink and tobacco manufacturing	*QAF Ltd.*	Singapore	FA	1920
22 Sept. 1997	*Branta Mulia (20%)*	Production of man-made fibres	*El Du Pont De* Nemours & Co.	United States	MI	65
6 Jan. 1998	*Puncakjaya Power (PJP) PT*	Business services	*US Investor Group*	United States	FA	360
6 Jan. 1998	*Asia Pulp & Paper Co's certain* Power Production Assets	Production and distribution of electricity, gas and other forms of energy	*Singapore Power Ltd.*	Singapore	FA	175
31 Jan. 1998	*Power Plant Project*	Production and distribution of electricity, gas and other forms of energy	*Westcoast Energy Inc.*	Canada	MI	360
Korea, Republic of						
30 Sept. 1997	*LG Chemical Ltd.*	Chemical industry	*Huels AG (acq. 50%)*	Germany	JV	390
10 Nov. 1997	*Doosan Group's Drinks Bottling* Plants	Food, drink and tobacco manufacturing industries	*The Coca-Cola Co.*	United States	FA	441
27 Nov. 1997	*Ssangyong Paper Co. Ltd.*	Manufacture of paper and paper products; printing and publishing	*Procter & Gamble*	United States	FA	169
31 Dec. 1997	*Hanwha Chemical Corp.*	Chemical industry	*BASF AG*	Germany	FA	60
18 Mar. 1998	*Daesang Group's Lysine Business*	Chemical industry	*BASF AG*	Germany	FA	600
31 Mar. 1998	*Tungsten Co.*	Metal industry	*Iscar Ltd.*	Israel	FA	150
13 Apr. 1998	*Halla Pulp & Paper Co's Daebul* Newsprint Mill	Manufacture of paper and paper products; printing and publishing	*Bowater Inc.*	United States	FA	175
20 Apr. 1998	*Dongsuh Securities Co*	Business services	*Horizon Holdings Ltd.*	United States	FA	250
7 May 1998	*Samsung Heavy Industries Co Ltd.'s* Construction Equipment Arm	Mechanical engineering	*Volvo AB*	Sweden	FA	572
27 May 1998	*Korea Exchange Bank (30%)*	Banking and finance	*Commerzbank AG*	Germany	MI	250
28 May 1998	*Hanwha Energy Co's* Power Generation Business	Production and distribution of electricity, gas and other forms of energy	*AES Corp.*	United States	FA	874
Malaysia						
31 Aug. 1997	*Petronas Petroliam Nasional BHD*	Oil processing	*BASF AG (acq. 60%)*	Germany	JV	420
14 Oct. 1997	*Kedah Wafer Plant/Jv Khazanah* National BHD	Electrical and electronic engineering	*Amtel (acq. 60%)*	United States	JV	490
16 Oct. 1997	*Khazanah Nasional BHD + Bank* Industri BHD + BI Walden International	Electrical and electronic engineering	*VISI Technologies Inc.*	United States	JV	600
16 Oct. 1997	*Khazanah Nasional BHD + Bank* Industri BHD + VSLI Technology	Electrical and electronic engineering	*BI Walden International*	United States	JV	..

/...

Annex table A.VII.2. Asia: the largest 30 cross-border M&As in the five most affected economies, July 1997-June 1998 (continued)

Date of M&A	Acquired company	Industry	Acquiring company	Acquiring economy	Deal type	Value (Million dollars)
Philippines						
31Aug. 1997	*Filinvest Group (16%)*	Banking and finance	*Metro Pacific Corp.*	Hong Kong(China)	MI	179
19 Oct. 1997	*Manila Electric Co. (10%)*	Production and distribution of electricity, gas and other forms of energy	*Union Electrica-* Fenosa SA	Spain	MI	168
Thailand						
31 Oct. 1997	*Bangkok Investment PLc*	Banking and finance	*AIG American* International Group Inc.	United States	FA	262
3 Mar. 1998	*Asia Credit PLC*	Banking and finance	*Societe Generale SA*	France	FA	72
18 Mar. 1998	*BOA Bank of Asia Ltd.*	Banking and finance	*Abn Amro Holding NV*	Netherlands	FA	184
18 May 1998	*Lotus*	Retail distribution	*Tesco PLC*	United Kingdom	FA	181
31 Mar. 1998	*Thai Danu Bank Ltd.*	Banking and finance	*DBS Bank*	Singapore	FA	132
31 Mar. 1998	*The Cogeneration PLC (33%)*	Extraction of oil and natural gas	*Sithe Energies Group*	United States	MI	100
24 Apr. 1998	*Thainox Steel Co. Ltd.*	Metal manufacturing	*Usinor-Sacilor SA*	France	FA	60
28 Apr. 1998	*Bangkok Bank of Commerce Ltd.* (2%)	Banking and finance	*The Sakura Bank Ltd.*	Japan	MI	73
30 Apr. 1998	*The Siam Commercial Bank Ltd.* (Increase Stake from 7% to 13%)	Banking and finance	*The Sanwa Bank Ltd.*	Japan	MI	100

Source: UNCTAD, based on data provided by KPMG Corporate Finance.

Key: FA - full acquisition; JV - joint venture; MI - minority acquisition.

Annex table A.VII.3. FDI flows into Mexico: the 10 largest recipient industries,[a] 1994-1997

(Thousands of dollars)

Industry	1994	1995	1996	1997
Automobiles	914 214	895 985	590 560	679 954
Tobacco	123	337	..	2 134 157
Services of credit, banking and auxiliary credit institutions	673 174	715 949	296 991	376 454
Trade of non-food products (wholesale)	854 300	557 241	345 708	124 931
Basic iron and steel industries	1 336 835	117 112	311 956	93 975
Communications	545 359	708 537	401 362	175 940
Beverage industries	853 954	258 015	90 560	605 400
Trade of food products in supermarkets, etc. (retail)	114	18 515	94 088	1 661 646
Manufacturing and/or assembly of electric machinery, equipment	259 490	676 857	399 159	412 422
Manufacturing and/or assembly of electronic equipment (radios, televisions, communications, etc.)	240 181	550 001	243 560	232 251
Total	10 209 579	7 720 411	6 597 735	7 980 086
Growth rate				
Automobiles	..	- 2.0	- 34.1	15.1
Tobacco	..	174.1	..	..
Services of credit, banking and auxiliary credit institutions	..	6.4	- 58.5	26.8
Trade of non-food products (wholesale)	..	- 34.8	- 38.0	- 63.9
Basic iron and steel industries	..	- 91.2	166.4	- 69.9
Communications	..	29.9	- 43.4	- 56.2
Beverage industries	..	- 69.8	- 64.9	568.5
Trade of food products in supermarkets, etc. (retail)	..	16 184.2	408.2	1 666.0
Manufacturing and/or assembly of electric machinery, equipment	..	160.8	- 41.0	3.3
Manufacturing and/or assembly of electronic equipment (radios, televisions, communications, etc.)	..	129.0	- 55.7	- 4.6
Total	..	- 24.4	- 14.5	21.0

Source: UNCTAD, based on data from SECOFI, Mexico.

[a] Does not include reinvestments of profits and accounts/flows between firms.

Annex table A.VII.4. Mexico: automobile production[a] and exports by selected TNCs, 1993-1997

(Thousands of units and percentage)

Producer	Market	1993	1994	1995	1996	1997[b]
Ford	Total	169.6	189.7	211.3	170.5	159.6
	Exports	117.2	162.8	200.6	154.5	142.3
	Export share[c]	69.1	85.8	94.9	90.6	89.2
GM	Total	141.3	111.1	140.7	142.7	146.3
	Exports	90.7	70.5	124.5	101.1	86.0
	Export share[c]	64.2	63.4	88.5	70.8	58.8
Chrysler	Total	159.4	163.8	80.4	144.5	122.6
	Exports	101.7	117.5	64.6	124.9	90.1
	Export share[c]	63.8	71.7	80.3	86.4	73.5
VW	Total	229.2	243.0	183.7	227.5	237.2
	Exports	77.5	97.7	156.2	176.7	175.7
	Export share[c]	33.8	40.2	85.0	77.7	74.1
Nissan	Total	120.5	147.0	79.1	117.7	120.8
	Exports	37.4	48.6	52.9	78.7	63.3
	Export share[c]	31.0	33.1	66.9	66.9	52.4
All[d]	Total	823.2	855.3	699.3	795.0	790.9
	Exports	424.5	497.1	598.8	635.9	557.4
	Export share[c]	51.6	58.1	85.6	80.0	70.5

Source: UNCTAD, data provided by the Unit on Investment and Corporate Strategies, ECLAC, United Nations, February 1998.

a Sales of passenger vehicles.
b Through November 1997. Data are for production, not sales.
c Share of exports in total sales/production (percentage).
d Includes also production by others, such as BMW, Honda and Mercedes-Benz.

Annex table A.VII.5. Forecasts of changes in domestic demand and GDP/GNP in the economies most affected by the Asian crisis, 1997-2001[a]

(Percentage)

Item	1997	1998	1999	2000	2001
Indonesia[b]					
Private consumption	1.7	-3.0	-1.3	1.5	3.7
Public consumption	5.0	4.0	5.0	5.0	5.0
Fixed investment	9.5	-23.0	10.3	13.9	12.0
GDP	4.8	-5.1	1.7	3.6	4.8
Korea, Republic of [c]					
Private consumption	4.1	-4.0	3.0	3.8	4.3
Public consumption	5.3	-	2.0	2.0	2.0
Fixed investment	-4.7	-28.9	7.2	7.9	11.5
GNP	5.3	-1.5	3.4	5.3	6.0
Malaysia[d]					
Private consumption	3.8	1.7	2.1	3.3	3.7
Public consumption	1.5	1.5	2.5	2.4	1.5
Fixed investment	12.1	7.3	8.8	9.4	9.4
GNP	5.1	2.6	4.8	5.4	5.5
Philippines[e]					
Private consumption	5.0	3.1	3.6	3.7	4.0
Public consumption	3.6	2.0	3.0	3.0	3.0
Fixed investment	12.1	7.3	8.8	9.4	9.4
GNP	5.1	2.6	4.8	5.4	5.5
Thailand[f]					
Private consumption	-1.3	-3.1	2.2	4.9	6.3
Public consumption	-2.5	-8	-1	4	5
Fixed investment	-9.8	-20.6	-2.7	6.2	7.1
GNP	0.6	-2.1	2	5.4	5.8
Memorandum					
GDP					
Newly industrializing Asian economies[g]	6.0	2.2	4.3	..	..
China and Mongolia	8.8	7.2	6.8	..	..
South-East Asia[h]	3.9	-0.4	2.4	..	..
South Asia	4.8	6.4	6.7	..	..
Developing Asia, total	6.1	4.0	5.1	..	..

Source: Project Link, 1998. GDP data under the memorandum item are from ADB, 1998.

a Forecasts prepared by the LINK forecasting exercise at the end of April 1998. It is expected that changes since that time would require downward revisions in the forecasts for 1998, including a decline in output reflecting the recessions in Indonesia, the Republic of Korea, Malaysia and Thailand (United Nations, 1998b, forthcoming). UNCTAD's forecasts of percentage GDP growth in 1998 for the five countries shown above are: Indonesia: -12.0; Republic of Korea: -6.0; Malaysia: -2.5; Philippines: 1.0; and Thailand: -8.0 (UNCTAD, 1998a).

b Billions of rupiahs. 1975 prices.

c Billions of won. 1980 prices.

d Billions of ringgit. 1975 prices.

e Billions of Philippine pesos. 1972 prices.

f Billions of baht. 1975 prices.

g Including Hong Kong, China, Republic of Korea, Singapore and Taiwan Province of China.

h Excluding Singapore.

Annex table A.VII.6. Changes in the regulatory framework regarding FDI in the five most seriously affected countries, June 1997 - June 1998

Indonesia:

- Eliminated the 49 per cent limit on foreign share holdings in firms other than financial firms in September 1997.
- Allowed 100 per cent foreign ownership of non-bank financial firms, including insurance companies.
- Guaranteed existing foreign ownership in financial institutions.
- Under the new "reformation policy on investment " announced by the Office of the Ministry of Investment/ Investment Coordinating Branch on 29 May 1998, opened retail and wholesale trading and palm oil sectors to foreign investment. (Import-export trading had been opened earlier for foreign investment.) For the time being, foreign investment in retail and wholesale trading should be in the form of joint ventures with Indonesian nationals/companies.
- Under the above-mentioned "reformation policy" package, simplified various procedures applying to foreign investors.
- Presidential Decree Number 96/1998 revised the list of industries and activities fully or partially closed to foreign investment. The new list is valid for three years but subject to annual review, if necessary. All other industries and activities are open to FDI.

Korea, Republic of:

- Hostile takeovers of Korean companies were fully liberalized in May 1998.
- With the exception of those companies determined as having national security concerns, the requirement of government approval for takeovers of Korean companies with assets of 2 trillion won or more was abolished in April 1998.
- Allowed the establishment of subsidiaries of foreign banks and foreign securities firms in March 1998.
- Restrictions on the use of long-term loans with maturities of over five years, brought into the country by foreign manufacturers were abolished.
- The ceiling on individual and aggregate foreign ownership of listed Korean shares were abolished in May 1998.
- Korea's major FDI Promotion Programme established the Foreign Investment Promotion Act, which fully permits M&As, opens all types of businesses to foreign investors in principle, allows foreign participation in equity transactions in large public enterprises and key industries, provides for a one-stop service and introduces an automatic approval system, liberalizes the real estate market and offers tax and other incentives for foreign investors.
- The number of industries restricted to FDI will be diminished from 42 to 31; of these remaining industries, 13 are closed and 18 partially restricted. There are 1,148 industries in the Republic of Korea.

Malaysia:

- Relaxed the limits on foreign equity holdings. The limit now is 30 per cent foreign equity, except for export-oriented industries, high-technology industries and multimedia companies with MSC status. Foreign equity holding in the local licences basic telecommunications companies has been raised from a previous maximum of 30 per cent to a new maximum of 49 per cent. Malaysia is prepared to consider applications to raise the foreign equity holdings up to a maximum of 61 per cent, provided that the companies concerned shall reduce their foreign equity holdings to a maximum of 49 per cent within 5 years.
- Guaranteed up to 51 per cent foreign equity participation in existing insurance companies by current holders. Malaysia's revised offers following the WTO negotiation concluded in December 1997 in respect of foreign equity participation in the insurance sector are as follows:
    - New foreign entrants into the local insurance industry will be restricted to an equity stake of 30 per cent. However, foreigners with an existing presence in the local industry will be allowed a maximum of 51 per cent foreign equity participation under the following circumstances:

/...

Annex table A.VII.6. Changes in the regulatory framework regarding FDI in the five most seriously affected countries, June 1997 - June 1998 (continued)

- a foreign direct insurer operating in Malaysia as a branch, and which locally incorporates its operation in compliance with the Insurance Act, 1996, can retain up to 51 per cent of the equity of the locally-incorporated entity;
- an existing foreign owner of a locally-incorporated insurer which has yet to restructure can retain up to 51 per cent of the equity of the restructured company, provided aggregate foreign shareholding does not exceed 51 per cent; and
- the present foreign shareholders which were the original owners of locally-incorporated insurance companies that have restructured in line with requirements under the National Development Policy, can increase their shareholdings to 51 per cent provided aggregate foreign shareholdings do not exceed 51 per cent.

These restrictions do not apply to foreign professional reinsurers that are allowed to operate as branches in Malaysia, or in the case of locally-incorporated joint venture reinsurance companies, the foreign partner may retain up to an aggregate of 49 per cent of the equity in the joint venture company.

- Fully/majority foreign-owned fund-management companies will be allowed.

- Relaxed bumiputera policy. Relaxation of regulations on the release of a 30 per cent share of listed firms owned by bumiputera to non-bumiputera. Approval on a case by case basis of acquisitions of bumiputera firms by non-bumiputera.

- The Minister of International Trade and Industry relaxed the country's equity policy for the manufacturing sector as follows [from 31 July 1998]:

  - With the exception of activities in a specific exclusion list,[a] all new projects in manufacturing, including for expansion and diversification will be exempted from both equity and export conditions. This means that project owners can hold 100 per cent equity and will not need to meet any export requirements.
  - This policy will apply to all applications received from 31 July 1998 to 31 December 2000, as well as applications already received, but for which decisions are pending.
  - All projects approved under the new policy will not be required to restructure their equity after the period.
  - The Government will review this policy after 31 December 2000.

Philippines:

Amendments were made to The Investment House Act (October 1997) and the Financing Company Act (February 1998). Key changes which affect foreign investment are:

- Allowable foreign equity participation has been increased to 60 per cent for both investment houses and finance and leasing companies, subject to reciprocity rights.

- Paid up capital for investment houses is now 300 million pesos.

- Paid up capital for finance and leasing companies is now:

  - at least 10 million pesos for those located in Metro Manila and other first class cities;
  - 5 million pesos for those situated in other classes of cities; and
  - 2.5 million pesos in municipalities.

/...

Annex table A.VII.6. Changes in the regulatory framework regarding FDI in the five most seriously affected countries, June 1997 - June 1998 (concluded)

Thailand:

- Foreign equity holdings were limited to no more than 49 per cent except for export-oriented projects with at least 80 per cent export share located in Zone 3, where 100 per cent foreign ownership was allowed. The Board of Investment relaxed this regulation in 1997 for companies with financial difficulties so that they could have foreign ownership of more than 51 per cent on the condition that Thai shareholders of that company agree and confirm their acceptance in writing of the change in ownership to the Board of Investment.
- The Minister of Finance, upon the recommendation of the Bank of Thailand, may release the 25 per cent limit for foreign interests in locally-incorporated banks and finance and credit companies for 10 years. The absolute amount of foreign equity holdings up to 100 per cent will be protected if acquired during this period.
- Existing shareholding structures of foreign bank branches are guaranteed.
- Announced that majority foreign ownership of existing promoted firms in certain industrial zones would be permitted if agreed by existing Thai shareholders.
- The 30 per cent export requirement for exemption of import duties used in the manufactures of exports has been eliminated.

Source: UNCTAD, based on information from national sources.

[a] Paper packaging; plastic packaging (bottles, films, sheets and bags); plastic injection moulding components; metal stamping, metal fabrication and electroplating; wire harness; printing, and steel service centre.

Annex table A.VII.7. Debt to equity ratio of leading TNCs from the Republic of Korea

(Percentage)

Group	Number of affiliates	Debt to equity ratio
Hanwha	31	1 215
Kumho	32	944
Hanjin	25	908
Doosan	23	590
Hyundai	62	579
Daelim	21	514
LG	52	506
Daewoo	37	472
SK	45	468
Hyosung	21	465
Hansol	19	400
Ssangyong	22	400
Samsung	61	371
Dong Ah	22	360
Lotte	28	216

Source: *Far Eastern Economic Review*, 30 April 1998, p. 12.

Annex table A.VII.8. Examples of sales of foreign assets by TNCs headquartered in the countries most affected by the Asian crisis, late 1997-1998

Affiliate divested and host country	Industry	Parent firm	Home country	Buyer	Value (Million dollars)
United Commercial Bank of California (United States) [a]	Banking	First Pacific Co. of Salim Group	Indonesia	UCBH Holdings Inc. (bank's holding company) (United States)	170
Six hotel and office properties in Dallas (United States) [b]	Property	Sinar Mas	Indonesia	Pacific Reality Trust and Angelo Gordon & Co. (United States based partnership).	265
SR Gent (United Kingdom) [c]	Textiles (garments)	Prospero Investment	Indonesia	3i, venture capital group (United Kingdom)	(GB£40 million)
50% stake in Shanghai Ek Chor Motorcycle (China) [d]	Motorcycle manufacture	Charoen Pokphand	Thailand	Shanghai Automotive Co. (China)	12.8
212.3 million shares in Coca-Cola Beverages (United Kingdom) [e]	Beverages	San Miguel Corp.	Philippines	112.3 million shares to Crescent Holding of the Olayan Group, and 100 million to public auction.	554.1
Sandestin Resorts Inc., (Canada) [f]	Property	Sime Darby Berhad	Malaysia	Intrawest Corp., a resort operator (Canada)	131.5
36.8% stake in Gourmet Direct Investment Ltd (New Zealand) [g]	Investment bank	Mega First Corp.	Malaysia	..	(NZ$350,000)
London Hotel (United Kingdom) [h]	Property	Johor Hotels International of Johor Corp.	Malaysia	..	(RM35.36 million)
40% stake in Kazakhtelecom (Kazakhstan) [i]	Telecommunications	Daewoo Corp.	Korea, Republic of	Kazhommerts Securities (Investment bank in Kazakhstan)	..
50% stake in power plant project (India) [j]	Engineering	Daewoo Corp.	Korea, Republic of	Asea Brown Boveri (Sweden)	650
A controlling stake in Bank of Athens (Greece) [k]	Banking	Hanwha Group	Korea, Republic of	EFG Eurobank, Greece (part of the Latsis shipping and oil refining group (United Kingdom)	(GB£20 million)
Riverside Cement Co. (United States) [l]	Building materials	Ssangyong Cement Industrial Co. of Ssangyong Group	Korea, Republic of	Texas Industries Inc. (United States)	120
2 Marriott Residence Inn hotels (United States) [m]	Property	Ssangyong Engineering & Construction Co. of Ssangyong Group	Korea, Republic of	Sunstone Hotel Investor, United States. (Investment trust co.)	30.5
Symbios Inc. (United States) [n]	Semiconductors	Hyundai Electronics Industries Co. of Hyundai Group	Korea, Republic of	Adaptec Inc. (United States)	775

Source:

- a *Thomson's International Banking Regulator*, 11 May 1998.
- b *Dallas Business Journal*, 1 May 1998.
- c *The Daily Telegraph*, 31 May 1998.
- d *Asian Wall Street Journal*, 4 May 1998.
- e *South China Morning Post*, 14 July 1998.
- f *Business Times*, 27 May 1998.
- g *Business Times*, 13 July 1998.
- h *New Straits Times*, 1 July 1998.
- i *Financial Times*, 25 March 1998.
- j *Korea Economic Daily*, 28 April 1998.
- k *Financial Times*, 18 June 1998.
- l *Korea Herald*, 13 January 1998.
- m *Korea Herald*, 13 January 1998.
- n *Financial Times*, 4 March 1998.

Annex table A.VII.9. FDI from the top 10 outward investors from South, East and South-East Asia, 1994-1997

(Billions of dollars and percentage)

Economy	1994	1995	1996	1997	Percentage change 1996-1997
Five most affected economies					
Indonesia	0.6	0.6	0.5	2.4[a]	369
Korea, Republic of	2.5	3.5	4.7	4.3	-9
Malaysia	1.8	2.6	3.7	3.1	-16
Philippines	0.3	0.4	0.2	0.1	-50
Thailand	0.5	0.9	0.9	0.5	-46
Total	5.7	8.0	10.0	10.4	4
Others					
China	2.0	2.0	2.1	2.5	18
Hong Kong, China[b]	21.4	25.0	26.4	26.0	-
India	0.1	0.1	0.2	0.1	-50
Singapore	3.7	4.0	4.8	5.9	23
Taiwan Province of China	2.6	3.0	3.8	5.2	35
Memorandum:					
Total for South, East and South-East Asia	35.6	41.8	47.4	50.2	6
Share of the five most affected countries in total for South, East and South-East Asia	16.1	18.4	21.1	20.7	-2

Source: UNCTAD, FDI/TNC database.

[a] A large proportion of outflows took place during the first half of the year.

[b] Estimated on the basis of data on inflows to China, ASEAN members, the European Union and the United States.

Annex table A.VII.10. Largest purchases in the 5 most affected countries by TNCs based in Hong Kong, China, Singapore and Taiwan Province of China, first half, 1998

Deal date and economy of acquiring company	Acquiring company	Acquired company	Industry	Deal type	Value (Million dollars)
Hong Kong, China					
17 February 1998	Dairy Farm International Holdings	The Hero Group (31 %)	Retail distribution	MI	36
23 February 1998	Regent Pacific Group	DAE YU Securities (21.5 %)	Business services	MI	10
Singapore					
6 January 1998	Singapore Power Ltd.	Asia Pulp & Paper Co., certain power production assets	Production and distribution of electricity, gas and other forms of energy	FA	175
31 March 1998	DBS Bank	Thai Danu Bank Ltd.	Banking and finance	FA	131
Taiwan Province of China					
31 March 1998	YUANTA Group	Nava Finance & Securities Plc. (10 %)	Banking and finance	MI	25
31 March 1998	CDC China Development Corp.	BFIT Bangkok First Investment & Trust	Business services	FA	17
28 April 1998	TUNTEX Distinct	Bangkok Bank of Commerce Ltd.	Banking and finance	MI	8
28 April 1998	President Enterprises Corp.	Bangkok Bank of Commerce Ltd.	Banking and finance	MI	8
28 April 1998	China Development Corp.	Bangkok Bank of Commerce Ltd.	Banking and finance	MI	8

Source: UNCTAD, based on KPMG Corporate Finance.

Key: FA - full acquisition; MI - minority acquisition.

Annex B. Statistical annex

DEFINITIONS AND SOURCES

A. General definitions

1. *Transnational corporation*

Transnational corporations are incorporated or unincorporated enterprises comprising parent enterprises and their foreign affiliates. A *parent enterprise* is defined as an enterprise that controls assets of other entities in countries other than its home country, usually by owning a certain equity capital stake. An equity capital stake of 10 per cent or more of the ordinary shares or voting power for an incorporated enterprise, or its equivalent for an unincorporated enterprise, is normally considered as a threshold for the control of assets.[1] A *foreign affiliate* is an incorporated or unincorporated enterprise in which an investor, who is resident in another economy, owns a stake that permits a lasting interest in the management of that enterprise (an equity stake of 10 per cent for an incorporated enterprise or its equivalent for an unincorporated enterprise). In the *World Investment Report*, subsidiary enterprises, associate enterprises and branches are all referred to as *foreign affiliates* or *affiliates.*

- *Subsidiary:* an incorporated enterprise in the host country in which another entity directly owns more than a half of the shareholders voting power and has the right to appoint or remove a majority of the members of the administrative, management or supervisory body.

- *Associate:* an incorporated enterprise in the host country in which an investor owns a total of at least 10 per cent, but not more than a half, of the shareholders' voting power.

- *Branch:* a wholly or jointly owned unincorporated enterprise in the host country which is one of the following: (i) a permanent establishment or office of the foreign investor; (ii) an unincorporated partnership or joint venture between the foreign direct investor and one or more third parties; (iii) land, structures (except structures owned by government entities), and /or immovable equipment and objects directly owned by a foreign resident; (iv) mobile equipment (such as ships, aircraft, gas or oil-drilling rigs) operating within a country other than that of the foreign investor for at least one year.

2. *Foreign direct investment*

Foreign direct investment (FDI) is defined as an investment involving a long-term relationship and reflecting a lasting interest and control of a resident entity in one economy (foreign direct investor or parent enterprise) in an enterprise resident in an economy other than that of the foreign direct investor (FDI enterprise or affiliate enterprise or foreign affiliate).[2] Foreign direct investment implies that the investor exerts a significant degree of influence on the management of the enterprise resident in the other economy. Such investment involves both the initial transaction between the two entities and all subsequent transactions between them and among foreign affiliates, both incorporated and unincorporated. Foreign direct investment may be undertaken by individuals as well as business entities.

Foreign-direct-investment inflows and *outflows* comprise capital provided (either directly or through other related enterprises) by a foreign direct investor to a FDI enterprise, or capital received from a FDI enterprise by a foreign direct investor. There are three components in FDI: equity capital, reinvested earnings and intra-company loans.

- *Equity capital* is the foreign direct investor's purchase of shares of an enterprise in a country other than its own.

- *Reinvested earnings* comprise the direct investor's share (in proportion to direct equity participation) of earnings not distributed as dividends by affiliates or earnings not remitted to the direct investor. Such retained profits by affiliates are reinvested.

- *Intra-company loans* or *intra-company debt transactions* refer to short- or long-term borrowing and lending of funds between direct investors (parent enterprises) and affiliate enterprises.

Foreign-direct-investment stock is the value of the share of their capital and reserves (including retained profits) attributable to the parent enterprise, plus the net indebtedness of affiliates to the parent enterprise.[3] Foreign-direct-investment flow and stock data used in the *World Investment Report* are not always defined as above, because these definitions are often not applicable to disaggregated FDI data. For example, in analysing geographical and industrial trends and patterns of FDI, data based on approvals of FDI may also be used because they allow a disaggregation at the country or industry level. Such cases are denoted accordingly.

3. *Non-equity forms of investment*

Foreign direct investors may also obtain an effective voice in the management of another business entity through means other than acquiring an equity stake. These are non-equity forms of FDI, and they include, *inter alia*, subcontracting, management contracts, turnkey arrangements, franchising, licensing and product sharing. Data on transnational corporate activity through these forms are usually not separately identified in balance-of-payments statistics. These statistics, however, usually present data on royalties and licensing fees, defined as "receipts and payments of residents and nonresidents for: (i) the authorized use of intangible non-produced, non-financial assets and proprietary rights such as trade-marks, copyrights, patents, processes, techniques, designs, manufacturing rights, franchises, etc., and (ii) the use, through licensing agreements, of produced originals or prototypes, such as manuscripts, films, etc."[4]

B. Availability and limitations of foreign-direct-investment data presented in the World Investment Report

Data on FDI flows in annex tables B.1 and B.2, as well as some tables in the text, are on a net basis (capital transactions' credits less debits between direct investors and their foreign affiliates). Net decreases in assets or net increases in liabilities are recorded as credits (recorded with a positive sign in the balance of payments), while net increases in assets or net decreases in liabilities are recorded as debits (recorded with a negative sign in the balance of payments). In the annex tables, as well as in the tables in the text, the negative signs are deleted for practical use. Hence, FDI flows with a negative sign in the *World Investment Report* indicate that at least one of the three components of FDI (equity capital, reinvested earnings or intra-company loans) is negative and not offset by positive amounts of the remaining components. These are instnces of reverse investment or disinvestment.

Not all countries record every component of FDI flows. Tables 1 and 2 summarize the availability of each component of FDI during 1980-1996, the period covered in the *World Investment Report* for, respectively, FDI inward flows and FDI outward flows. Comparison of data among countries should therefore be made bearing these limitations in mind.

1. *Inflows*

The most reliable and comprehensive data on FDI flows that are readily available from international sources and follow the above definition are reported by the International Monetary Fund (IMF). For the purpose of assembling balance-of-payments statistics for its member countries, IMF collects and publishes data annually on FDI inflows and outflows in the *Balance of Payments Statistics Yearbook*. The same data are also available in IMF's *International Financial Statistics* for certain countries. Therefore, data from IMF used in the *World Investment Report* were obtained directly from IMF's computer tapes containing balance-of-payments statistics and international financial statistics. In those cases in which economies do not report to IMF (e.g., Taiwan Province of China), or their reporting does not cover the entire 1980-1997 period that is used in the *World Investment Report*, data from UNCTAD FDI/TNC database, which contains published or unpublished national official FDI data obtained from central banks, statistical offices or national authorities, were used. These data were also supplemented with data of the Organisation for Economic Co-operation and Development, *Geographical Distribution of Financial Flows to Developing Countries* (retrieved by OECD from a computer tape). Data reported by OECD are based on FDI outflows to developing countries from the member countries of the Development Assistance Committee of OECD.[5] Inflows of FDI to developing countries reported by OECD are therefore underestimated. Those countries and territories for which OECD data, or estimates based on OECD data, were used for the 1980-1994 period, or part of that period, are listed below.

1980-1994	Bermuda, Cayman Islands, Democratic Republic of Congo, Cuba, Ethiopia and United States Virgin Islands.
1980-1993	Afghanistan, Hong Kong, United Arab Emirates and Western Samoa.
1980-1991	Nepal and United Republic of Tanzania.
1980-1990	Iraq and Uganda.
1980-1989	Islamic Republic of Iran, Kuwait, Lebanon and Syrian Arab Republic.
1980-1988	Madagascar and Myanmar.
1980-1986	Viet Nam.
1980-1985	Guinea, India and Mozambique.
1980-1984	Angola, Burundi, Maldives and Yugoslavia (former).
1981-1988	Equitorial Guinea.
1982-1994	Benin, Gibraltar, Macau and Sudan.

1983-1992	Qatar.
1983-1991	Djibouti.
1983-1986 and 1990	Gambia.
1983-1985 and 1989-1991	Uruguay.
1984-1994	Guinea-Bissau and Malawi.
1985-1994	New Caledonia.
1985-1989	Namibia.
1986-1991	Guyana and Somalia.
1987-1994	Democratic People's Republic of Korea.
1987-1991	Nicaragua.
1988-1993	Liberia.
1989-1994	Congo.
1990-1994	Burkina Faso.
1992-1993	Togo.

As of 1 July 1998, data on FDI inflows for 1997 were available for Albania, Argentina, Armenia, Azerbaijan, Bangladesh, Belarus, Belgium and Luxembourg, Bolivia, Brazil, Bulgaria, China, Colombia, Croatia, Czech Republic, Denmark, Estonia, Finland, Georgia, Germany, Hungary, India, Indonesia, Israel, Italy, Japan, Kazakhstan, Republic of Korea, Kyrgyzstan, Latvia, Lithuania, TFYR Macedonia, Malaysia, Mexico, Republic of Moldova, New Zealand, Norway, Paraguay, Peru, Philippines, Poland, Romania, Russian Federation, Slovakia, Slovenia, South Africa, Sweden, Taiwan Province of China, Thailand, Tajikistan, Ukraine, United States and Uraguay, and (from UNCTAD FDI/TNC database) and Aruba, Australia, Austria, Canada, Chile, Ecuador, Netherlands, Portugal, Spain, United Kingdom and Venezuela (from IMF's balance-of-payments and international-financial-statistics tapes).

For many of other countries FDI inflows for 1997 are estimated. For France FDI inflows for 1997 are estimated by annualizing the data for the first three quarters; for Bahamas, Ireland and Turkey, the first two quarters; and for Nicaragua and Turkmenistan, the first quarter (data from IMF's balance-of-payments and international-financial-statistics tapes).

Table 1. List of economies for which at least one component of FDI inflows is not available [a]

Equity investment	*Reinvested earnings*	*Intra-company loans*
Developed countries:		
Denmark [b], Canada, Iceland [c], Ireland, Israel, Italy, Spain, Sweden, Switzerland [b], United Kingdom [d]	Austria [e], Belgium and Luxembourg, Canada [b], Denmark, France [e], Greece [f], Iceland, Ireland[g], Italy, Japan, Norway, Spain, Sweden [h], Switzerland [b]	Austria, Denmark [i], Greece [j], Iceland [k], Italy, Spain [g], Switzerland[d]
Developing economies:		
Africa:		
Angola [f], Benin, Burkina Faso, Burundi [l], Cape Verde [m], Chad [d], Comoros [m], Djibouti [n], Egypt, Equitorial Guinea [o], Gambia [m], Guinea [c], Lesotho [c], Libyan Arab	Algeria, Angola [f], Benin [e], Burundi, Cape Verde, Central African Republic [h], Chad [r], Comoros [m], Djibouti [r], Egypt, Equitorial Guinea, Gambia [m], Ghana [s],	Algeria, Angola [l], Benin [e], Burundi, Cape Verde, Chad [c], Comoros, Djibouti, Equitorial Guinea, The Gambia [e], Ghana [e], Guinea [o], Kenya[m], Lesotho [s], Madagascar,

/...

(Table 1, concluded)

Equity investment	*Reinvested earnings*	*Intra-company loans*
Africa (continued):		
Jamahiriya, Madagascar [o], Mali, Mauritius, Morocco [f], Mozambique[c], Namibia [g], Niger [p], Nigeria, Seychelles [o], Sierra Leone[q], Somalia, Uganda [n], United Republic of Tanzania [r], Zambia [o]	Guinea[c], Libyan Arab Jamahiriya [t], Lesotho, Madagascar, Malawi, Mali [o], Mauritania, Mauritius [u], Mozambique, Namibia [g], Nigeria, Somalia, Sudan, Tunisia, Uganda [n], United Republic of Tanzania, Zimbabwe [s]	Malawi, Mauritania, Mozambique, Namibia [g], Somalia [p], Sudan, Uganda [f], United Republic of Tanzania, Zimbabwe [c]
Latin America and the Caribbean:		
Antigua and Barbuda [c], Aruba, Bolivia [q], Colombia,Guyana, Jamaica [m], Nicaragua [r], Peru [l], Saint Kitts and Nevis [c], Saint Lucia [c], Saint Vincent and the Grenadines [c]	Antigua and Barbuda [c], Argentina[w], Aruba, Bahamas, Chile [m], Dominica[c], Dominican Republic [n], Grenada [c], Guyana [p], Haiti, Paraguay [g], Nicaragua [r], Saint Kitts and Nevis [c], Saint Lucia [u], Saint Vincent and the Grenadies [c], Suriname, Uruguay [c], Venezuela	Argentina, Aruba [g], Bolivia [m], Barbados [h], Chile, Dominica [c], Dominican Republic [n], Ecuador, Guatemala [u], Grenada [c], Haiti, Honduras [m], Nicaragua, Paraguay[u], Peru [s], Uraguay [c], Venezuela [x]
Developing Europe:		
Croatia, Slovenia [r], TFYR Macedonia [x]	Croatia, Slovenia, TFYR Macedonia	Croatia [n], Slovenia, TFYR Macedonia [x]
West Asia:		
Bahrain, Cyprus, Islamic Republic of Iran [x], Jordan [m], Saudi Arabia, Syrian Arab Republic [c]	Bahrain, Islamic Republic of Iran, Jordan, Saudi Arabia, Syrian Arab Republic, Turkey [y],Yemen	Islamic Republic of Iran, Oman, Syrian Arab Republic, Turkey, Yemen [f]
Central Asia:		
Armenia [x]	Armenia	Armenia
South, East and South-East Asia:		
Cambodia [r], Indonesia [b], Lao People's Democratic Republic, Malaysia, Maldives, Mongolia [r], Myanmar [o]	Bangladesh, Cambodia [n], China, Indonesia, Republic of Korea [o], Lao People's Democratic Republic, Malaysia, Maldives [c], Mongolia, Myanmar, Pakistan [n], Singapore, Sri Lanka [c], Thailand	Bangladesh [c], Cambodia, China, Republic of Korea, Lao People's Democratic Republic [u], Maldives, Mongolia, Myanmar, Pakistan [n], Singapore, Sri Lanka
The Pacific:		
Kiribati [b], Papua New Guinea [f], Tonga [m], Vanuatu	Kiribati [l], Solomon Islands, Tonga	Kiribati, Solomon Islands [m], Tonga[c]
Central and Eastern Europe:		
Albania [r], Bulgaria [g], Czech Republic [n], Hungary [f], Latvia [r], Lithuania [n], Republic of Moldova [y], Romania [f], Russian Federation, Slovakia [x], Ukraine	Albania, Bulgaria, Czech Republic, Hungary, Latvia, Lithuania [y], Republic of Moldova, Poland [g], Romania, Russian Federation, Slovakia, Ukraine	Albania, Bulgaria, Czech Republic, Hungary, Latvia, Lithuania [y], Republic of Moldova [y], Poland [x], Romania, Russian Federation, Slovakia [y], Ukraine

Source: UNCTAD, based on International Monetary Fund, balance-of-payments tape, retrieved in May 1998.

a Countries not available at least one year are all reported in the table.
b Started reporting since 1983.
c Started reporting since 1986.
d Started reporting since 1984.
e Stopped reporting since 1981.
f Started reporting since 1991.
g Started reporting since 1990.
h Started reporting since 1982.
i Stopped reporting since 1982.
j Stopped reporting since 1990.
k Stopped reporting since 1989.
l Started reporting since 1985.
m Started reporting since 1987.
n Started reporting since 1993
o Started reporting since 1989.
p Stopped reporting since 1985.
q Stopped reporting since 1987.
r Started reporting since 1992.
s Stopped reporting since 1984.
t Stopped reporting since 1983.
u Started reporting since 1988.
v Stopped reporting since 1986.
w Stopped reporting since 1991.
x Started reporting since 1994.
y Started reporting since 1995.

For those countries for which FDI data were not available througout the period (up to 1997), data have been estimated by UNCTAD. Those economies for which estimation was made are listed below:

1997: Antigua and Barbuda, Bahrain, Barbados, Belize, Bosnia and Herzegovina, Botswana, Cambodia, Dominica, Dominican Republic, Equitorial Guinea, Fiji, Gambia, Ghana, Guinea, Greece, Grenada, Guatemala, Haiti, Honduras, Iceland, Islamic Republic of Iran, Jordan, Kenya, Lao People's Democratic Republic, Madagascar,, Maldives, Malta, Mauritius, Morocco, Nigeria, Oman, Panama, Papua New Guinea, Rwanda, Saint Lucia, Saint Vincent and the Grenadines, Seychelles, Singapore, Sri Lanka, Syrian Arab Republic, Swaziland, Switzerland, Tunisia, Uganda, United Republic of Tanzania, Uzbekistan, Viet Nam and Zimbabwe.

1996-1997: Cameroon, Cape Verde, Comoros, Costa Rica, Côte d'Ivoire, Cyprus, Djibouti, El Salvador, Gabon, Guyana, Jamaica, Mauritania, Mongolia, Mozambique, Myanmar, Netherlands Antilles, Niger, Pakistan, Senegal, Sierra Leone, Suriname, Trinidad and Tobago, Vanuatu and Yemen

1995-1997: Angola, Bermuda, Brunei Darussalam, Burkina Faso, Cayman Islands, Central African Republic, Chad, Congo, Democratic Republic of Congo, Cuba, Ethiopia, Gibraltar, Guinea-Bissau, Hong Kong, China, Kiribati, Democratic People's Republic of Korea, Lesotho, Malawi, Mali, Macau, New Caledonia, Saint Kitts and Nevis, Tonga, Virgin Islands.

1994-1997: Burundi, Liberia, Sudan, Togo, United Arab Emirates and Western Samoa.

1993-1997: Afghanistan, Qatar and Solomon Islands.

1992-1997: Algeria, Benin, Nepal, Somalia and Zambia.
1991-1997: Iraq, Libyan Arab Jamahiriya.
1990-1997: Kuwait and Lebanon.

For Viet Nam, data from 1988 to 1997 are estimated by applying an average implementation ratio of about 20 per cent (the ratio of realized FDI to approved FDI), to the approved data. The data for India are converted to those on a calandar year basis from those reported on the basis of fiscal year.

2. *Outflows*

As of 1 July 1998, FDI outflows for 1997 were available for Belgium and Luxembourg, Brazil, Bulgaria, Croatia, Czech Republic, Estonia, Finland, Germany, Hungary, Israel, Italy, Japan, Republic of Korea, Latvia, Lithuania, TFYR Macedonia, Republic of Moldova, Namibia, New Zealand, Norway, Philippines, Poland, Romania, Russian Federation, Slovakia, Slovenia, South Africa, Taiwan Province of China, Ukraine and the United States (from UNCTAD, FDI/TNC database) and for Australia, Austria Argentina, Canada, Chile, Kazakhstan, Netherlands, Portugal, Spain, Venezuela and United Kingdom (from the IMF's balance-of-payments tape).

For France FDI outflows in 1997 is estimated by annualizing the first three quarters, for Denmark, Ireland and Turkey on the basis of the first two quarters and for Sweden on the basis of the first quarter.

Table 2. List of economies for which at least one component of FDI outflows is not available [a]

Equity investment	*Reinvested earnings*	*Intra-company loans*
Developed countries:		
Denmark [b], Canada, Iceland [c], Ireland, Israel, Sweden, Switzerland [d], United Kingdom [d]	Austria, Belgium and Luxembourg, Canada [b], Denmark, France [e], Iceland, Ireland [f], Italy, Japan, Norway,Portugal [g], Spain, Switzerland [b]	Austria [h], Denmark [e], Iceland [i], Ireland, Italy, Spain [f], Switzerland [d]
Developing economies:		
Africa:		
Benin, Burkina Faso [e], Cape Verde[g], Chad [d], Comoros [f], Djibouti[j], Egypt [f], Equitorial Guinea[k], Kenya [k], Lesotho, Mauritania [c], Mauritius, Morocco [l], Namibia [f], Niger [m], Seychelles, Zimbabwe [n]	Algeria, Angola, Benin, Botswana[o], Burkina Faso Burundi, Cape Verde, Cameroon [k], Central African Republic, Chad, Comoros [f], Djibouti [p], Egypt, Equitorial Guinea, Gabon, Libyan Arab Jamahiriya, Lesotho, Mauritania, Mauritius [q], Morocco, Namibia [f], Niger [c], Nigeria, Senegal [r], Tunisia, Zimbabwe	Algeria, Angola, Burkina Faso Burundi, Cameroon [k], Cape Verde, Central African Republic, Chad, Comoros, Djibouti, Equitorial Guinea, Gabon, Kenya [s], Libyan Arab Jamahiriya, Mauritania, Mauritius [n], Morocco , Namibia [f], Zimbabwe
Latin America and the Caribbean:		
Barbados [o], Bolivia [t], Belize l, Chile[d], Colombia, Trinidad and Tobago [b], Venezuela [o]	Argentina, Belizer, Bolivia [m], Brazil, Chile,, Haiti, Trinidad and Tobago, Uraguay, Venezuela [g]	Argentina, Bolivia, Barbados [o], Belize, Chile, Colombia, Costa Rica [l], Haiti [f], Haiti, Trinidad and Tobago, Uraguay, Venezuela
Developing Europe:		
Malta [b]	Malta [u]	Malta [u]
West Asia:		
Cyprus, Jordan, Turkey, Yemen [l]	Cyprus, Jordan, Kuwait, Turkey, Yemen	Cyprus [g], Kuwait, Turkey, Yemen [h]
South, East and South-East Asia:		
Indonesia [v], Pakistan [d], Philippines [j], Sri Lanka	China, Indonesia,Pakistan, Philippines, Singapore, Sri Lanka, Thailand	China, Indonesia, Pakistan, Philippines, Singapore, Sri Lanka, Thailand
The Pacific:		
Fiji [d], Papua New Guinea,	Fiji [n], Papua New Guine,	Kiribati
Central and Eastern Europe:		
Bulgaria [w], Czech Republic [j], Estonia, Hungary [j], Latvia [p], Lithuania [w], Republic of Moldova, Romania [f], Slovakia [u]	Bulgaria, Czech Republic, Estonia, Hungary, Latvia, Lithuania, Republic of Moldova, Poland [l], Romania, Slovakia	Bulgaria, Czech Republic, Estonia, Hungary, Latvia [p], Lithuania, Republic of Moldova [w], Poland [l], Romania, Slovakia [w]

Source: UNCTAD, based on International Monetary Fund, balance-of-payments tape, retrieved in May 1998.

[a] Countries not available at least one year are all reported in the table.
[b] Started reporting since 1983.
[c] Started reporting since 1986.
[d] Started reporting since 1984.
[e] Stopped reporting since 1982.
[f] Started reporting since 1990.
[g] Started reporting since 1985.
[h] Stopped reporting since 1981.
[i] Stopped reporting since 1986.
[j] Started reporting since 1993.
[k] Started reporting since 1989.
[l] Started reporting since 1991.
[m] Stopped reporting since 1983.
[n] Stopped reporting since 1988.
[o] Started reporting since 1982.
[p] Started reporting since 1992.
[q] Reported 1989 only.
[r] Reported 1982 only.
[s] Started reporting since 1989.
[t] Stopped reporting since 1987.
[u] Started reporting since 1994.
[v] Reported 1993 only.
[w] Started reporting since 1995.

In the case of countries for which FDI outflows were unavailable from national authorities, inflows to large recipient economies were used as a proxy. Thus, for Greece - up to 1996, India - up to 1995, Indonesia - up to 1992, Mexico - up to 1996 and the Philippines - up to 1992, inflows to the European Union and the United States were used as a proxy. In the case of Hong Kong - up to 1996, inflows to China, the European Union and the United States are used as a proxy. For Argentina (1984-1991), Bahamas (1981-1998), Bahrain (1981-1996), Bermuda (1981-1997), Bosnia and Herzegovenia (1992-1996), Central African Republic (1995), Chad (1995), Gabon, (1995-1996), Iraq (1992-1996), Ireland (1984-1989), Lebanon (1982-1997), Liberia (up to 1996), Netherlands Antilles (up to 1989), Nigeria (1982-1995), Oman (1988-1996), Panama (1981-1997), Saudi Arabia (1981-1997), Trinidad and Tobago (1993-1995), United Arab Emirates (1981-1997) and Uruguay (1989-1996) inflows into the United States were used as a proxy of their outflows. For Iran, Islamic Republic (1992-1996) inflows to the European Union were used as a proxy of their outflows.

The United States data on FDI outflows and outward stocks were adjusted for the financial sector of the Netherlands Antilles. This is because considerable intra-company loans between United States parent enterprises and their financial affiliates in the Netherlands Antilles are in many respects more akin to portfolio investment than to FDI.

For Albania, Bahrain, Bangladesh, Bolivia, Botswana, Bosnia and Herzegovina, Burundi, Cameroon, Central African Republic, Chad, China, Colombia, Costa Rica, Cyprus, Dominican Republic, Egypt, Fiji, Gabon, Greece, Hong Kong, China, Iceland, India, Indonesia, Iraq, Islamic Republic of Iran, Jordan, Kenya, Liberia, Malaysia, Malta, Mauritius, Morocco, Netherlands Antilles, Nigeria, Oman, Pakistan, Peru, Senegal, Seychelles, Sri Lanka, Swaziland, Switzerland, Thailand, Trinidad and Tobago, Tunisia and Uraguay 1997 are based on UNCTAD's own estimates.

3. *Stocks*

Various tables in the *World Investment Report* present data on FDI stocks at book value or historical cost, reflecting prices at the time when the investment was made. For a large number of countries (as indicated in annex tables B.3 and B.4), FDI stocks are estimated by cumulating FDI flows over a period of time. For a number of countries (indicated in annex tables B.3 and B.4), estimates of FDI stocks are obtained by adding flows to a FDI stock estimate that has been obtained for a particular year from national sources or the International Monetary Fund data series on assets and liabilites of direct investment. Almost all estimates of FDI stocks for 1997 are obtained by adding FDI flows for 1997 to the stock figures of 1996. For further detail, refer to notes to annex tables B.3 and B.4.

*****

All data, unless otherwise indicated, are expressed in United States dollars. Data reported in national currencies or Special Drawing Rights are converted to United States dollars by using the period's average exchange rate for flow data and the end-of-the-period exchange rate for stock data.

All FDI data and estimates in the *World Investment Report* are continuously revised. Because of the on-going revision, FDI data reported in the *World Investment Report* may differ from those reported in earlier *Reports* or other publications of UNCTAD. In particular, recent FDI data are being revised in many countries according to the fifth edition of the IMF's balance-of-payments manual. Data taken from the IMF are based on the balance-of-payments and international financial statistics tapes, retrieved in June 1998.

C. Definitions and sources of the data in annex tables B.5-11

Annex tables B.5 and B.6

These two annex tables show the ratio of inward and outward FDI flows to gross fixed capital formation (annex table B.5) and inward and outward FDI stock to GDP (annex table B.6), respectively. All of these data are in current prices. The data on both gross fixed capital formation and GDP were obtained from the IMF's international-financial-statistics tape, retrieved on 1 June 1998. For some economies such as Taiwan Province of China, the data are supplemented from national sources. Data on FDI are from annex tables B.1-B.4.

Annex tables B.7, B.8 and B.9

Data on cross-border M&As are obtained from the KPMG. This consulting firm collects information through a variety of secondary sources including newspapers and other periodicals, and a quarterly meeting of the 42-member KPMG Corporate Finance Network. All data in the text refer to only cross-border M&A transactions which result in the equity holding of more than 50 per cent (unless otherwise indicated). Data on minority investments are not included in the discussion on the assumption that portfolio investments account for the bulk of minority-held investments. However, in annex tables B.7, B.8 and B.9, all M&As (including minority-held investments) are also presented for information. Cross-border M&As are recorded in both directions of transactions; i.e., when a cross-border M&A takes place, it registers as both a sale in the country of the target firm, and as a purchase in the home country of the acquiring firm. Data showing cross-border M&A activities on an industrial basis refer to only sales figures (annex table B.9). Thus, if a food company acquires a chemical company, this transaction is recorded in the chemical industry.

Notes

1 In some countries such as Germany and the United Kingdom, the stake of 20 per cent or more is a threshold.

2 This general definition of FDI is based on OECD, *Detailed Benchmark Definition of Foreign Direct Investment*, second edition (Paris, OECD, 1992) and International Monetary Fund, *Balance of Payments Manual*, fifth edition (Washington, D.C., IMF, 1993).

3 There are, however, some exceptions. For example, in the case of Germany, loans granted by affiliate enterprises to their parent enterprises are not deducted from the stock.

4 International Monetary Fund, op. cit., p. 40.

5 Includes Austria, Belgium, Canada, Denmark, Finland, France, Germany, Italy, Japan, Netherlands, Norway, Spain, Sweden, United Kingdom and United States.

Annex table B.1. FDI inflows, by host region and economy, 1986-1997

(Millions of dollars)

Host region/economy	1986-1991 (Annual average)	1992	1993	1994	1995	1996	1997 [a]
World	**159 331**	**175 841**	**217 559**	**242 999**	**331 189**	**337 550**	**400 486**
Developed countries	**129 583**	**120 294**	**138 887**	**141 503**	**211 465**	**195 393**	**233 115**
Western Europe	**66 470**	**85 837**	**83 877**	**78 417**	**122 779**	**99 954**	**114 857**
European Union	**63 186**	**83 794**	**80 935**	**71 580**	**116 792**	**92 398**	**108 172**
Austria	439	947	977	1 312	639	3 826	1 700
Belgium and Luxembourg	5 454	11 286	10 750	8 514	10 565	14 125	12 550
Denmark	754	1 017	1 713	5 006	4 139	773	2 570
Finland	361	407	866	1 577	1 063	1 109	1 543
France	9 254	21 840	20 754	15 799	23 733	21 972	18 280
Germany	2 942	2 640	1 911	1 790	13 448	-2 721	- 195
Greece	826	1 144	977	981	1 053	1 058	1 500
Ireland	368	1 442	1 121	838	1 447	2 456	4 152
Italy	3 630	3 951	4 383	2 163	4 878	3 377	3 523
Netherlands	6 362	7 836	8 561	7 517	11 498	7 760	8 725
Portugal	1 403	1 873	1 534	1 270	685	708	1 713
Spain	8 325	13 276	8 144	9 359	6 201	6 454	5 556
Sweden	2 257	- 5	3 705	6 269	14 939	5 492	9 659
United Kingdom	20 812	16 140	15 540	9 185	22 504	26 009	36 897
Other Western Europe	**3 284**	**2 042**	**2 942**	**6 837**	**5 987**	**7 555**	**6 685**
Gibraltar	34	89	40	- 1	1	1	1
Iceland	14	- 11	-	- 2	- 9	82	3
Norway	601	716	2 003	2 736	2 392	3 960	3 181
Switzerland	2 635	1 249	899	4 104	3 603	3 512	3 500
North America	**54 674**	**23 662**	**48 302**	**53 571**	**69 596**	**82 851**	**98 994**
Canada	5 586	4 777	4 768	8 476	10 824	6 398	8 246
United States	49 088	18 885	43 534	45 095	58 772	76 453	90 748
Other developed countries	**8 439**	**10 796**	**6 708**	**9 515**	**19 090**	**12 588**	**19 263**
Australia	6 236	5 458	3 724	4 968	13 402	5 473	9 584
Israel	197	539	580	626	1 974	2 442	3 407
Japan	556	2 756	210	888	41	228	3 224
New Zealand	1 478	2 085	2 213	2 694	2 691	3 686	1 343
South Africa	- 27	- 42	- 19	338	981	760	1 705
Developing countries	**29 090**	**51 108**	**72 528**	**95 582**	**105 511**	**129 813**	**148 944**
Africa	**2 869**	**3 171**	**3 647**	**5 693**	**5 136**	**4 828**	**4 710**
North Africa	**1 196**	**1 582**	**1 579**	**2 364**	**1 262**	**1 313**	**1 811**
Algeria	8	10	13	15	5	13	7
Egypt	932	459	493	1 256	598	636	834
Libyan Arab Jamahiriya	45	165	120	110	105	100	110
Morocco	132	423	492	551	290	311	500
Sudan	- 4	-	-	-	-	-	-
Tunisia	83	526	462	432	264	253	360
Other Africa	**1 673**	**1 589**	**2 068**	**3 329**	**3 874**	**3 515**	**2 899**
Angola	169	288	302	170	250	290	350
Benin	3	1	-	-	1	1	3
Botswana	59	- 2	- 287	326	380	272	100
Burkina Faso	2	-0.3	13	4	2	3	1

/...

Annex table B.1. FDI inflows, by host region and economy, 1986-1997 (continued)

(Millions of dollars)

Host region/economy	1986-1991 (Annual average)	1992	1993	1994	1995	1996	1997 [a]
Burundi	1	1	1	1	2	-	1
Cameroon	- 16	29	5	- 9	7	35	45
Cape Verde	1	- 1	3	2	10	12	13
Central African Republic	2	- 11	- 10	4	2	5	6
Chad	12	2	15	27	13	18	15
Comoros	3	- 2	-	-	1	2	2
Congo	15	4	149	3	8	9	9
Congo, Democratic Republic of	- 10	- 1	7	- 2	-	-	1
Côte d'Ivoire	49	- 231	88	27	19	21	50
Djibouti	-	2	1	1	3	4	5
Equatorial Guinea	10	6	22	17	127	376	40
Ethiopia	1	-	-	3	8	5	15
Gabon	53	127	- 114	- 100	- 113	65	- 100
Gambia, The	4	6	11	10	8	11	13
Ghana	11	23	125	233	107	120	200
Guinea	18	20	3	-	1	24	1
Guinea-Bissau	1	6	- 2	-	-	-	2
Kenya	35	6	2	4	33	13	40
Lesotho	11	3	15	19	23	28	29
Liberia	200	- 11	30	14	21	17	15
Madagascar	12	21	15	6	10	10	17
Malawi	15	2	10	9	13	17	2
Mali	-	- 8	- 20	45	17	23	15
Mauritania	3	8	16	2	7	5	3
Mauritius	24	15	15	20	19	37	38
Mozambique	8	25	32	35	45	29	35
Namibia	26	118	55	98	118	152	131
Niger	16	56	- 34	- 11	7	-	1
Nigeria	728	897	1 345	1 959	2 201	1 391	1 000
Rwanda	14	2	6	- 1	2	2	1
Senegal	13	21	- 1	67	32	45	30
Seychelles	20	9	19	30	40	30	49
Sierra Leone	- 10	- 6	- 8	- 3	- 2	-	4
Somalia	- 2	-	-	-	1	1	1
Swaziland	53	83	70	56	26	14	75
Togo	10	- 2	1	2	-	1	1
Uganda	-	3	55	88	121	121	250
United Republic of Tanzania	-	12	20	50	120	150	250
Zambia	100	45	52	56	67	58	70
Zimbabwe	10	20	38	68	118	98	70
Latin America and the Caribbean	**9 460**	**17 611**	**17 247**	**28 687**	**31 929**	**43 755**	**56 138**
South America	**4 252**	**8 885**	**7 554**	**13 673**	**18 068**	**30 432**	**38 993**
Argentina	1 168	4 045	2 555	3 116	4 783	5 090	6 327
Bolivia	40	122	124	130	374	474	500
Brazil	1 258	2 061	1 291	2 149	5 043	11 112	16 330
Chile	763	699	808	1 772	1 667	4 092	5 417
Colombia	455	729	959	1 667	2 317	3 322	2 447
Ecuador	134	178	469	531	470	447	577
Guyana	3	147	70	107	74	81	90
Paraguay	31	137	111	180	184	225	200
Peru	29	136	670	3 084	2 035	3 581	2 000
Suriname	- 120	- 54	- 47	- 30	- 21	7	12
Uruguay	41	58	173	155	157	169	200
Venezuela	451	629	372	813	985	1 833	4 893

/...

Annex table B.1. FDI inflows, by host region and economy, 1986-1997 (continued)

(Millions of dollars)

Host region/economy	1986-1991 (Annual average)	1992	1993	1994	1995	1996	1997 [a]
Other Latin America and the Caribbean	**5 208**	**8 726**	**9 693**	**15 014**	**13 861**	**13 323**	**17 145**
Antigua and Barbuda	42	20	15	25	32	19	28
Aruba	53	- 37	- 18	- 73	- 6	85	196
Bahamas	7	-	27	23	107	87	89
Barbados	9	14	9	13	12	13	18
Belize	12	16	9	15	21	22	23
Bermuda	1 381	3 231	2 707	1 079	1 350	2 100	1 700
Cayman Islands	44	27	447	447	470	510	500
Costa Rica	118	226	247	298	396	410	500
Cuba	2	7	3	14	9	12	13
Dominica	13	21	13	22	54	18	20
Dominican Republic	105	180	225	360	404	394	250
El Salvador	17	15	16	23	38	25	41
Grenada	12	23	20	19	20	18	22
Guatemala	127	94	143	65	75	77	130
Haiti	5	- 2	- 3	-	7	4	3
Honduras	44	48	27	35	50	63	80
Jamaica	61	142	78	117	167	175	180
Mexico	3 081	4 393	4 389	10 973	9 526	8 169	12 101
Netherlands Antilles	31	40	11	22	10	11	17
Nicaragua	-	15	39	40	70	85	92
Panama	- 115	139	156	354	179	238	340
Saint Kitts and Nevis	25	13	14	15	20	17	25
Saint Lucia	29	41	34	32	30	23	45
Saint Vincent and the Grenadines	8	15	31	47	31	18	42
Trinidad and Tobago	85	178	379	516	299	320	340
Virgin Islands	15	- 131	675	532	490	410	350
Developing Europe	**88**	**214**	**264**	**405**	**467**	**1 029**	**796**
Bosnia and Herzegovina	..	..	..	..	..	..	1
Croatia	..	..	95	102	98	533	348
Malta	43	40	56	152	184	300	110
Slovenia	12	111	113	128	176	186	321
TFYR Macedonia	..	..	..	24	9	11	16
Yugoslavia (former)	33	64	..	..	..	..	..
Asia	**16 468**	**29 651**	**51 218**	**60 679**	**67 386**	**80 011**	**86 923**
West Asia	**1 329**	**1 827**	**3 447**	**1 518**	**- 746**	**303**	**1 886**
Bahrain	54	- 9	- 5	- 31	- 27	47	15
Cyprus	73	107	83	75	119	100	175
Iran, Islamic Republic of	- 120	- 170	- 50	2	17	26	50
Iraq	3	- 1	1	..	..	..	..
Jordan	18	41	- 34	3	13	16	70
Kuwait	- 1	35	13	16	15	20	45
Lebanon	4	4	6	7	35	80	150
Oman	109	104	142	77	46	67	90
Qatar	3	40	29	37	35	35	55
Saudi Arabia	531	- 79	1 369	350	-1 877	-1 129	400
Syrian Arab Republic	67	67	176	251	100	89	80
Turkey	459	844	636	608	885	722	606
United Arab Emirates	49	130	183	113	110	130	100
Yemen	80	714	897	11	- 218	100	50
Central Asia	**4**	**142**	**424**	**896**	**1 561**	**2 084**	**2 627**
Armenia	4	2	1	2	8	18	43

/...

Annex table B.1. FDI inflows, by host region and economy, 1986-1997 (continued)

(Millions of dollars)

Host region/economy	1986-1991 (Annual average)	1992	1993	1994	1995	1996	1997 [a]
Azerbaijan	..	..	..	22	275	601	872
Georgia	..	..	..	8	6	103	100
Kazakhstan	..	100	150	185	941	1 137	1 320
Kyrgyzstan	..	..	228	519	96	47	83
Tajikistan	..	..	..	10	15	16	4
Turkmenistan	..	..	..	100	100	108	121
Uzbekistan	..	40	45	50	120	55	85
South, East and South-East Asia	**15 135**	**27 683**	**47 348**	**58 265**	**66 571**	**77 624**	**82 411**
Afghanistan	-	-	-	-	-	-	-
Bangladesh	6	18	10	8	2	14	145
Brunei Darussalam	-	4	14	6	7	9	5
Cambodia	..	33	54	69	151	294	200
China	3 105	11 156	27 515	33 787	35 849	40 800	45 300
Hong Kong, China	1 711	2 051	1 667	2 000	2 100	2 500	2 600
India	177	233	574	973	1 964	2 382	3 264
Indonesia	746	1 777	2 004	2 109	4 348	6 194	5 350
Korea, Democratic People's Republic of	95	42	6	7	3	4	2
Korea, Republic of	863	727	588	809	1 776	2 325	2 341
Lao People's Democratic Republic	3	8	30	59	95	160	90
Macau	1	2	3	-	2	2	2
Malaysia	1 605	5 183	5 006	4 342	4 132	4 672	3 754
Maldives	5	7	7	9	7	8	10
Mongolia	..	2	8	7	10	5	7
Myanmar	68	171	149	91	115	100	80
Nepal	2	1	4	6	5	19	20
Pakistan	188	335	347	419	719	770	800
Philippines	501	228	1 238	1 591	1 459	1 520	1 253
Singapore	3 592	2 204	4 686	8 368	8 210	9 440	10 000
Sri Lanka	41	123	195	166	56	120	140
Taiwan Province of China	1 034	879	917	1 375	1 559	1 864	2 248
Thailand	1 325	2 114	1 804	1 322	2 002	2 268	3 600
Viet Nam	68	385	523	742	2 000	2 156	1 200
The Pacific	**205**	**460**	**152**	**118**	**593**	**190**	**378**
Fiji	25	104	91	68	70	10	12
Kiribati	-	-	- 1	-	-	1	1
New Caledonia	7	17	20	10	17	13	10
Papua New Guinea	150	294	- 2	- 5	455	111	300
Solomon Islands	9	14	13	11	18	21	22
Tonga	-	1	2	1	1	2	2
Vanuatu	12	26	26	30	31	28	30
Western Samoa	2	4	2	3	2	4	1
Central and Eastern Europe	**658**	**4 439**	**6 143**	**5 914**	**14 214**	**12 344**	**18 428**
Albania	..	20	58	53	70	90	48
Belarus	..	7	10	15	7	18	163
Bulgaria	10	42	40	105	90	109	497
Czech Republic	99	1 003	568	862	2 559	1 428	1 301
Czechoslovakia (former)	..	..	..	..	..	..	..
Estonia	..	82	162	215	202	150	262
Hungary	430	1 471	2 339	1 146	4 453	1 982	2 085
Latvia	..	29	45	215	180	382	418
Lithuania	..	10	30	31	73	152	355
Moldova, Republic of	..	17	14	12	64	45	43

/...

Annex table B.1. FDI inflows, by host region and economy, 1986-1997 (concluded)

(Millions of dollars)

Host region/economy	1986-1991 (Annual average)	1992	1993	1994	1995	1996	1997 [a]
Poland	84	678	1 715	1 875	3 659	4 498	5 000
Romania	7	80	94	342	420	265	1 224
Rusian Federation	..	700	700	640	1 976	2 452	6 241
Slovakia	29	100	168	245	195	251	170
Ukraine	..	200	200	159	267	521	623
Memorandum:							
Least developed countries [b]							
Total	781	1 463	1 747	844	1 096	1 965	1 813
Africa	590	470	558	548	880	1 214	1 162
Latin America and the Caribbean	5	- 2	- 3	-	7	4	3
Asia	164	951	1 151	252	157	694	595
West Asia	80	714	897	11	- 218	100	50
South, East and South-East Asia	84	238	254	241	375	594	545
The Pacific	23	45	40	44	51	54	54
Oil-exporting countries [c]							
Total	8 786	15 019	17 214	23 820	21 786	24 106	30 890
Africa	2 017	2 505	2 775	3 837	3 325	2 792	2 615
North Africa	1 067	1 160	1 088	1 813	972	1 002	1 311
Other Africa	949	1 345	1 688	2 024	2 353	1 790	1 304
Latin America and the Caribbean	3 790	5 500	5 733	12 963	11 655	11 243	18 411
South America	625	929	965	1 474	1 829	2 754	5 970
Other Latin America and the Caribbean	3 165	4 571	4 768	11 489	9 825	8 489	12 441
Asia	2 979	7 014	8 706	7 020	6 806	10 071	9 864
West Asia	629	50	1 682	563	-1 681	- 804	755
South, East and South-East Asia	2 351	6 964	7 024	6 457	8 487	10 875	9 109
All developing countries minus China	**25 985**	**39 952**	**45 013**	**61 795**	**69 662**	**89 013**	**103 644**

Source: UNCTAD, FDI/TNC database.

a Estimates. For details, see "definitions and sources" in annex B.

b Least developed countries include: Afghanistan, Angola, Bangladesh, Benin, Burkina Faso, Burundi, Cambodia, Cape Verde, Central African Republic, Chad, Comoros, Democratic Republic of Congo, Djibouti, Equatorial Guinea, Ethiopia, The Gambia, Guinea, Guinea-Bissau, Haiti, Kiribati, Lao People's Democratic Republic, Lesotho, Liberia, Madagascar, Malawi, Maldives, Mali, Mauritania, Mozambique, Myanmar, Nepal, Niger, Rwanda, Western Samoa, Sierra Leone, Solomon Islands, Somalia, Sudan, Togo, Uganda, United Republic of Tanzania, Vanuatu, Yemen and Zambia. Not included are Bhutan, Eritrea, Sao Tome and Principe and Tuvalu due to unavailability of data.

c Oil-exporting countries include: Algeria, Angola, Bahrain, Brunei Darussalam, Cameroon, Congo, Ecuador, Egypt, Gabon, Indonesia, Islamic Republic of Iran, Iraq, Kuwait, Libyan Arab Jamahiriya, Malaysia, Mexico, Nigeria, Oman, Qatar, Saudi Arabia, Trinidad and Tobago, Tunisia, United Arab Emirates and Venezuela.

Annex table B.2. FDI outflows, by home region and economy, 1986-1997

(Millions of dollars)

Home region/economy	1986-1991 (Annual average)	1992	1993	1994	1995	1996	1997 [a]
World	**180 510**	**200 800**	**240 900**	**284 261**	**352 514**	**333 629**	**423 666**
Developed countries	**169 155**	**179 984**	**205 810**	**241 481**	**306 465**	**283 476**	**359 236**
Western Europe	**100 367**	**115 629**	**107 063**	**133 579**	**174 287**	**168 459**	**195 600**
European Union	**93 652**	**109 157**	**97 410**	**120 595**	**159 234**	**150 927**	**179 801**
Austria	800	1 872	1 465	1 203	1 046	1 391	1 437
Belgium and Luxembourg	4 560	11 407	4 904	1 371	11 794	8 370	6 706
Denmark	1 232	2 236	1 373	4 162	2 969	2 510	3 240
Finland	1 674	- 753	1 409	4 297	1 497	3 595	4 407
France	17 894	31 269	20 605	24 438	15 824	30 362	24 565
Germany	15 928	19 670	15 260	17 180	38 838	29 519	34 340
Greece	2	42	- 16	- 90	66	- 18	5
Ireland	357	215	220	438	820	727	806
Italy	4 289	6 502	9 271	5 638	6 925	6 185	10 194
Netherlands	10 627	14 409	12 069	17 355	19 626	23 094	20 370
Portugal	130	687	147	287	688	765	1 642
Spain	1 966	2 192	2 652	3 831	3 650	5 208	10 042
Sweden	8 067	419	1 471	6 685	11 399	5 112	3 896
United Kingdom	26 127	18 990	26 580	33 800	44 091	34 107	58 150
Other Western Europe	**6 715**	**6 472**	**9 653**	**12 984**	**15 053**	**17 532**	**15 799**
Gibraltar	..	..	..	..	..	..	..
Iceland	7	4	12	25	24	66	10
Norway	1 344	411	877	2 166	2 859	5 867	3 789
Switzerland	5 365	6 057	8 764	10 793	12 170	11 599	12 000
North America	**31 278**	**42 525**	**80 716**	**82 379**	**103 247**	**83 348**	**127 511**
Canada	5 530	3 547	5 879	9 127	11 173	8 515	12 974
United States [b]	25 748	38 978	74 837	73 252	92 074	74 833	114 537
Other developed countries	**37 509**	**21 830**	**18 030**	**25 523**	**28 931**	**31 668**	**36 125**
Australia	3 238	2 235	1 768	4 537	3 759	6 184	6 355
Israel	138	651	763	735	646	743	670
Japan	33 095	17 390	13 830	18 090	22 508	23 428	25 993
New Zealand	930	792	1 387	2 019	1 747	1 256	759
South Africa	109	762	282	143	271	57	2 349
Developing countries	**11 331**	**20 714**	**34 929**	**42 512**	**45 642**	**49 161**	**61 138**
Africa	**1 032**	**528**	**812**	**659**	**591**	**297**	**1 130**
North Africa	**94**	**41**	**23**	**73**	**100**	**33**	**48**
Algeria	13	..	..	..	..	..	..
Egypt	22	4	-	43	93	5	20
Libyan Arab Jamahiriya	53	..	..	..	..	..	..
Morocco	4	32	23	24	12	27	25
Sudan	..	..	..	..	..	..	..
Tunisia	2	5	..	6	- 5	1	3
Other Africa	**938**	**487**	**789**	**586**	**491**	**265**	**1 082**
Angola	-	..	2	- 2	..	..	..
Benin	..	..	..	..	..	..	..
Botswana	3	10	10	14	45	117	10
Burkina Faso	..	..	..	..	..	..	..

/...

Annex table B.2. FDI outflows, by home region and economy, 1986-1997 (continued)

(Millions of dollars)

Home region/economy	1986-1991 (Annual average)	1992	1993	1994	1995	1996	1997 [a]
Burundi	-	..	-	-	1	-	-
Cameroon	20	33	22	-	1	8	8
Cape Verde	-	..	..	1	..	..	..
Central African Republic	3	6	5	7	6	6	5
Chad	8	14	11	1	12	8	10
Comoros	-	..	..	..	..	..	..
Congo	..	..	..	..	..	..	..
Congo, Democratic Republic of	..	..	..	..	..	..	..
Côte d'Ivoire	..	..	..	..	..	..	..
Djibouti	..	..	..	..	..	..	..
Equatorial Guinea	..	..	..	..	..	..	..
Ethiopia	..	..	1	- 1	..	..	..
Gabon	13	26	3	1	- 1	- 1	15
Gambia, The	..	..	..	..	..	..	..
Ghana	..	..	..	..	..	..	..
Guinea	..	..	..	..	..	1	..
Guinea-Bissau	..	..	..	..	..	..	..
Kenya	7	..	..	..	..	- 1	5
Lesotho	-	..	..	..	..	..	..
Liberia	61	50	57	85	- 45	- 392	200
Madagascar	..	..	..	..	..	..	..
Malawi	..	..	..	..	..	..	..
Mali	..	..	..	..	..	..	..
Mauritania	-	..	..	..	..	..	..
Mauritius	2	43	33	1	4	3	3
Mozambique	..	..	..	..	..	..	..
Namibia	1	- 2	9	- 6	1	1	1
Niger	8	41	6	- 2	7	..	..
Nigeria	784	176	593	386	385	455	800
Rwanda	..	..	..	..	..	..	..
Senegal	- 2	51	-	17	- 3	5	4
Seychelles	3	1	1	13	16	13	15
Sierra Leone	..	..	..	..	..	..	..
Somalia	..	..	..	..	..	..	..
Swaziland	12	33	29	63	50	- 18	5
Togo	..	..	..	..	..	..	..
Uganda	..	..	..	..	..	..	..
United Republic of Tanzania	..	..	..	..	..	..	..
Zambia	..	..	..	..	..	..	..
Zimbabwe	15	4	7	8	13	60	..
Latin America and the Caribbean	**1 305**	**1 378**	**2 827**	**5 194**	**2 346**	**2 270**	**9 097**
South America	**739**	**686**	**2 711**	**2 913**	**3 017**	**1 530**	**4 220**
Argentina	18	- 7	..	125	155	205	28
Bolivia	1	2	2	2	2	2	2
Brazil	443	137	1 094	1 037	1 559	- 77	1 569
Chile	27	378	434	926	696	1 079	1 949
Colombia	29	50	240	152	284	68	100
Ecuador	..	..	..	..	..	..	..
Guyana	..	- 2	2	..	..	..	..
Paraguay	..	..	..	..	..	..	..
Peru	..	- 1	21	..	48	10	20
Suriname	..	..	..	..	..	..	..
Uruguay	3	- 27	32	- 6	- 26	5	5
Venezuela	218	156	886	677	299	238	547

/...

Annex table B.2. FDI outflows, by home region and economy, 1986-1997 (continued)

(Millions of dollars)

Home region/economy	1986-1991 (Annual average)	1992	1993	1994	1995	1996	1997 [a]
Other Latin America and the Caribbean	**566**	**692**	**117**	**2 280**	**- 672**	**740**	**4 877**
Antigua and Barbuda	..	..	..	..	..	..	..
Aruba	..	..	..	..	..	-	..
Bahamas	1	-	-	-	-	-	444
Barbados	2	1	3	1	3	4	..
Belize	-	2	2	2	2	2	..
Bermuda	92	- 378	- 16	378	- 555	174	2 293
Cayman Islands	..	..	..	..	..	..	..
Costa Rica	4	4	2	5	6	4	4
Cuba	..	..	..	..	..	..	..
Dominica	..	..	..	..	..	..	..
Dominican Republic	..	- 1	11	12	15	14	13
El Salvador	..	..	..	..	..	..	..
Grenada	..	..	..	..	..	..	..
Guatemala	..	..	..	..	..	..	..
Haiti	- 4	..	..	..	..	..	..
Honduras	..	..	..	..	..	..	..
Jamaica	..	..	..	..	..	..	..
Mexico	146	655	609	2 006	- 482	- 319	1 037
Netherlands Antilles	2	2	- 2	1	-	-	1
Nicaragua	..	..	..	..	..	..	..
Panama	321	407	- 494	- 130	336	858	1 082
Saint Kitts and Nevis	..	..	..	..	..	..	..
Saint Lucia	..	..	..	..	..	..	..
Saint Vincent and the Grenadines	..	..	..	..	..	..	..
Trinidad and Tobago	1	..	3	5	3	3	3
Virgin Islands	..	..	..	..	..	..	..
Developing Europe	**9**	**- 4**	**22**	**7**	**67**	**92**	**247**
Bosnia and Herzegovina	..	- 2	1	4	..	..	5
Croatia	..	..	19	7	6	20	150
Malta	..	..	1	- 1	56	63	65
Slovenia	9	- 2	1	- 3	6	8	26
TFYR Macedonia	..	..	..	..	..	1	1
Yugoslavia (former)	..	..	..	..	..	..	..
Asia	**8 975**	**18 786**	**31 240**	**36 653**	**42 641**	**46 491**	**50 663**
West Asia	**660**	**1 308**	**821**	**1 091**	**825**	**- 871**	**505**
Bahrain	1	..	..	- 20	..	- 19	1
Cyprus	4	15	12	6	7	8	5
Iran, Islamic Republic of	..	18	50	6	3	0	3
Iraq	..	..	..	..	..	..	..
Jordan	1	- 3	- 53	- 23	- 27	- 43	10
Kuwait	425	1 211	848	1 031	717	-1 095	254
Lebanon	6	- 3	- 2	- 2	- 2	- 2	- 3
Oman	- 1	- 2	- 3	5	1	1	4
Qatar	..	..	..	..	..	..	..
Saudi Arabia	217	5	- 53	81	13	180	125
Syrian Arab Republic	..	..	..	..	..	..	..
Turkey	3	65	14	49	113	110	116
United Arab Emirates	5	3	7	- 42	1	- 11	- 10
Yemen	-	..	..	..	..	..	..
Central Asia	**..**	**..**	**..**	**..**	**-**	**-**	**1**
Armenia	..	..	..	..	..	..	..

/...

Annex table B.2. FDI outflows, by home region and economy, 1986-1997 (continued)

(Millions of dollars)

Home region/economy	1986-1991 (Annual average)	1992	1993	1994	1995	1996	1997 [a]
Azerbaijan	..	..	..	..	..	..	..
Georgia	..	..	..	..	..	..	..
Kazakhstan	..	..	..	..	-	-	1
Kyrgyzstan	..	..	..	..	..	..	..
Tajikistan	..	..	..	..	..	..	..
Turkmenistan	..	..	..	..	..	..	..
Uzbekistan	..	..	..	..	..	..	..
South, East and South-East Asia	**8 315**	**17 478**	**30 419**	**35 562**	**41 816**	**47 362**	**50 157**
Afghanistan	..	..	..	..	..	..	..
Bangladesh	-	-	-	-	-	-	-
Brunei Darussalam	..	..	..	..	..	..	..
Cambodia	..	..	..	..	..	..	..
China	745	4 000	4 400	2 000	2 000	2 114	2 500
Hong Kong, China	2 373	8 254	17 713	21 437	25 000	26 356	26 000
India	3	24	41	83	117	239	100
Indonesia	7	52	356	609	603	512	2 400
Korea, Democratic People's Republic of	..	..	..	..	..	..	..
Korea, Republic of	923	1 208	1 340	2 461	3 552	4 670	4 287
Lao People's Democratic Republic	..	..	..	..	..	..	..
Macau	..	..	..	..	..	..	..
Malaysia	311	514	1 325	1 817	2 575	3 700	3 100
Maldives	..	..	..	..	..	..	..
Mongolia	..	..	..	..	..	..	..
Myanmar	..	..	..	..	..	..	..
Nepal	..	..	..	..	..	..	..
Pakistan	12	- 12	- 2	1	6	3	3
Philippines	- 1	5	374	302	98	182	136
Singapore	658	1 317	2 021	3 746	3 988	4 805	5 900
Sri Lanka	2	2	7	8	7	8	8
Taiwan Province of China	3 191	1 967	2 611	2 604	2 983	3 843	5 222
Thailand	92	147	233	493	886	931	500
Viet Nam	..	..	..	..	..	..	..
The Pacific	**11**	**26**	**29**	**-**	**- 3**	**10**	**2**
Fiji	13	26	29	-	- 3	10	2
Kiribati	..	..	..	..	..	..	..
New Caledonia	..	..	..	..	..	..	..
Papua New Guinea	- 2	..	..	..	..	..	..
Solomon Islands	..	..	..	..	..	..	..
Tonga	..	-	-	..	..	..	..
Vanuatu	..	..	..	..	..	..	..
Western Samoa	..	..	..	..	..	..	..
Central and Eastern Europe	**25**	**102**	**161**	**268**	**408**	**993**	**3 292**
Albania	..	20	7	9	12	10	10
Belarus	..	..	..	..	..	..	3
Bulgaria	..	..	..	..	8	29	1
Czech Republic	..	21	101	120	37	41	25
Czechoslovakia (former)	6	..	..	..	..	..	..
Estonia	..	2	6	2	3	40	130
Hungary	5	28	11	49	43	- 3	431
Latvia	..	2	- 5	- 65	- 65	3	- 8
Lithuania	..	..	..	..	1	-	27
Moldova, Republic of	..	..	..	..	-	-	-
Poland	11	13	18	29	42	53	50

/...

Annex table B.2. FDI outflows, by home region and economy, 1986-1997 (concluded)

(Millions of dollars)

Home region/economy	1986-1991 (Annual average)	1992	1993	1994	1995	1996	1997 [a]
Romania	4	7	7	1	3	2	4
Rusian Federation	..	..	..	101	306	771	2 489
Slovakia	..	9	15	14	8	52	90
Ukraine	..	..	..	8	10	- 5	41
Memorandum:							
Least developed countries [c]							
Total	78	111	82	89	- 19	- 377	215
Africa	81	110	82	89	- 19	- 377	215
Latin America and the Caribbean	- 4	..	..	..	..	..	..
Asia	-	-	-	-	-	-	-
West Asia	-	..	..	..	..	..	..
South, East and South-East Asia	-	-	-	-	-	-	-
The Pacific	..	..	..	-	..	..	..
Oil-exporting countries [d]							
Total	2 238	2 858	4 650	6 612	4 207	3 659	8 312
Africa	907	244	620	434	473	467	846
North Africa	90	9	-	49	88	6	23
Other Africa	817	235	620	385	385	461	823
Latin America and the Caribbean	366	813	1 500	2 691	- 178	- 76	1 589
South America	219	158	888	679	301	240	549
Other Latin America and the Caribbean	147	655	612	2 011	- 479	- 316	1 040
Asia	965	1 801	2 530	3 487	3 913	3 268	5 877
West Asia	647	1 235	849	1 061	735	- 944	377
South, East and South-East Asia	319	566	1 681	2 426	3 178	4 212	5 500
All developing countries minus China	**10 586**	**16 714**	**30 529**	**40 512**	**43 642**	**47 047**	**58 638**

Source: UNCTAD, FDI/TNC database.

a Estimates. For details, see "definitions and sources" in annex B.

b Excluding FDI in the financial sector of the Netherlands Antilles. For details, see definitions and sources.

c Least developed countries include: Afghanistan, Angola, Bangladesh, Benin, Burkina Faso, Burundi, Cambodia, Cape Verde, Central African Republic, Chad, Comoros, Democratic Republic of Congo, Djibouti, Equatorial Guinea, Ethiopia, The Gambia, Guinea, Guinea-Bissau, Haiti, Kiribati, Lao People's Democratic Republic, Lesotho, Liberia, Madagascar, Malawi, Maldives, Mali, Mauritania, Mozambique, Myanmar, Nepal, Niger, Rwanda, Western Samoa, Sierra Leone, Solomon Islands, Somalia, Sudan, Togo, Uganda, United Republic of Tanzania, Vanuatu, Yemen and Zambia. Not included are Bhutan, Eritrea, Sao Tome and Principe and Tuvalu due to unavailability of data.

d Oil-exporting countries include: Algeria, Angola, Bahrain, Brunei Darussalam, Cameroon, Congo, Ecuador, Egypt, Gabon, Indonesia, Islamic Republic of Iran, Iraq, Kuwait, Libyan Arab Jamahiriya, Malaysia, Mexico, Nigeria, Oman, Qatar, Saudi Arabia, Trinidad and Tobago, Tunisia, United Arab Emirates and Venezuela.

Annex table B.3. FDI inward stock, by host region and economy, 1980, 1985, 1990, 1995, 1996 and 1997

(Millions of dollars)

Host region/economy	1980	1985	1990	1995	1996	1997 [a]
World	**479 985**	**756 663**	**1 736 326**	**2 732 649**	**3 065 299**	**3 455 509**
Developed countries	**371 917**	**546 808**	**1 377 609**	**1 929 336**	**2 122 668**	**2 349 442**
Western Europe	**198 710**	**254 026**	**766 221**	**1 068 630**	**1 162 892**	**1 276 449**
European Union	**183 664**	**236 457**	**719 782**	**991 423**	**1 088 770**	**1 195 643**
Austria	3 163	6 122	10 765	18 636	19 886	21 586 [b]
Belgium and Luxembourg	7 306	18 447	58 388	116 446 [c]	130 572 [c]	143 121 [c]
Denmark	4 193	3 613	9 192	22 620 [d]	23 393 [d]	25 963 [d]
Finland	540	1 339	5 132	8 465	8 797	9 040
France	22 617	33 629	86 845	143 670	155 872	174 152 [b]
Germany	36 630	36 926	111 232	140 647	137 926 [e]	137 731 [e]
Greece	4 524	8 309	14 016 [f]	19 306 [f]	20 364 [f]	21 864 [f]
Ireland	3 749	4 649	5 501 [g]	11 706 [g]	14 162 [g]	18 314 [g]
Italy	8 892	18 976	57 985	63 456	74 991	78 514 [b]
Netherlands	19 167	25 071	73 991	111 460 [c]	119 220 [c]	127 945 [c]
Portugal	1 102	1 339	5 132	6 171 [h]	6 879 [h]	8 592 [h]
Spain	5 141	8 939	65 234	98 580	105 034 [e]	110 590 [e]
Sweden	3 626	5 071	12 461	30 489	34 202	43 861 [b]
United Kingdom	63 014	64 028	203 907	199 772	237 472	274 369 [b]
Other Western Europe	**15 046**	**17 570**	**46 438**	**77 207**	**74 122**	**80 807**
Gibraltar	..	32 [i]	197 [i]	363 [i]	364 [i]	365 [i]
Iceland	.. [j]	71 [k]	147	129	197	200 [b]
Norway	6 572 [l]	7 408 [k]	12 402	19 652	20 520	23 701 [b]
Switzerland	8 506	10 058	33 693	57 063	53 041	56 541 [b]
North America	**137 209**	**249 272**	**507 965**	**683 319**	**758 912**	**857 906**
Canada	54 163	64 657	113 054	122 469	128 867 [e]	137 113 e
United States	83 046	184 615	394 911	560 850	630 045	720 793 b
Other developed countries	**35 998**	**43 510**	**103 424**	**177 386**	**200 864**	**215 086**
Australia	13 173	25 049	74 348	96 811	116 679	126 263 [b]
Israel [m]	727	1 132	1 963	6 031	8 473	11 880
Japan	3 270	4 740	9 850	33 531	29 940	33 164 [b]
New Zealand	2 363	2 043	8 065	26 182	33 234	29 536
South Africa	16 465	10 546	9 198	14 832	12 538	14 243 [b]
Developing countries	**108 068**	**209 856**	**357 815**	**768 364**	**896 023**	**1 043 666**
Africa	**13 367**	**23 082**	**37 497**	**56 253**	**60 480**	**65 177**
North Africa	**4 546**	**9 273**	**15 472**	**22 467**	**23 680**	**25 381**
Algeria [m]	1 320	1 281	1 315	1 370	1 383	1 390
Egypt [n]	2 256	5 700	11 039	14 098	14 734	15 568
Libyan Arab Jamahiriya	..	..	..	..	..	..
Morocco [m]	189	441	918	2 990	3 301	3 801
Sudan	..	29 [i]	7 [i]	7 [i]	7 [i]	7 i
Tunisia [m]	781	1 822	2 193	4 002	4 255	4 615
Other Africa	**8 821**	**13 809**	**22 025**	**33 786**	**36 800**	**39 796**
Angola [m]	61	675	1 024	2 699	2 989	3 339
Benin [m]	32	34	36	52	53	56

/...

Annex table B.3. FDI inward stock, by host region and economy, 1980, 1985, 1990, 1995, 1996 and 1997 (continued)

(Millions of dollars)

Host region/economy	1980	1985	1990	1995	1996	1997 [a]
Botswana	150 [o]	399 [p]	761 [p]	1 170 [p]	1 442 [p]	1 542 [p]
Burkina Faso [m]	18	25	38	58	61	62
Burundi [m]	7	23	29	34	34	35
Cameroon [m]	330	1 125	1 044	1 062	1 097	1 142
Cape Verde	..	..	2 [q]	18 [q]	30 [q]	43 [q]
Central African Republic [m]	50	77	96	76	81	87
Chad [m]	123	186	255	317	335	350
Comoros	..	..	15 [r]	17 [r]	19 [r]	21 [r]
Congo [s]	309	479	563	733	742	751
Congo, Democratic Republic of [p]	440	351	277	293	293	294
Côte d'Ivoire [m]	530	699	975	895	916	966
Djibouti [t]	3	3	6	14	18	23
Equatorial Guinea	..	5 [u]	25 [u]	239 [u]	615 [u]	655 [u]
Ethiopia [m]	110	114	120	133	138	153
Gabon [m]	511	833	1 208	954	1 019	919
Gambia, The [m]	21	21	36	81	92	105
Ghana [m]	229	272	316	823	943	1 143
Guinea [t]	2	2	70	132	156	157
Guinea-Bissau [n]	-	4	8	14	15	17
Kenya [m]	344	434	626	689	702	742
Lesotho [v]	5	24	84	150	178	207
Liberia	..	104 [i]	1 297 [i]	1 360 [i]	1 377 [i]	1 392 [i]
Madagascar [m]	36	47	103	168	179	196
Malawi [m]	100	143	215	267	284	286
Mali [s]	13	35	29	67	90	105
Mauritania [m]	.. [j]	33	51	86	91	94
Mauritius [m]	20	37	163	248	285	323
Mozambique [m]	15	17	42	202	231	266
Namibia	1 935 [w]	1 951 [w]	2 047	1 727	1 492	1 721
Niger [m]	188	203	284	317	318	318
Nigeria [m]	2 406	4 418	8 073	15 187	16 578	17 578
Rwanda [m]	54	133	213	226	229	230
Senegal [m]	150	191	277	389	434	464
Seychelles [x]	37	87	187	304	334	383
Sierra Leone [m]	77	66	.. [j]	.. [j]	.. [j]	.. [j]
Somalia [s]	29	4	.. [j]	.. [j]	.. [j]	.. [j]
Swaziland	243 y	104	336	507	407	482 [b]
Togo [m]	176	210	264	271	272	273
Uganda [m]	9	7	4	272	393	643
United Republic of Tanzania [m]	47	91	89	294	444	694
Zambia [m]	25	121	684	938	996	1 066
Zimbabwe [z]	-	21	63	321	420	490
Latin America and the Caribbean	**47 713**	**76 788**	**123 964**	**278 393**	**320 563**	**375 414**
South America	**29 243**	**42 068**	**65 988**	**166 230**	**195 488**	**233 810**
Argentina	5 344	6 563	7 442	25 698	30 414	36 070
Bolivia	420	592	708	1 554	2 063	2 563 [b]
Brazil	17 480	25 665	37 143	98 839	109 951 [e]	126 281 [e]
Chile	886	2 321	10 067	15 547	19 639 [e]	25 056 [e]
Colombia	1 061	2 231	3 500	6 818	9 305	11 752 [b]
Ecuador	719	982	1 370	3 178 [d]	3 625 [d]	4 202 [d]
Guyana [m]	.. [j]	.. [j]	.. [j]	366	447	537
Paraguay [m]	218	298	401	1 095	1 321	1 521
Peru	898	1 152	1 293	5 477	9 058 [e]	11 058 [e]
Suriname [m]	.. [j]	.. [j]	.. [j]	.. [j]	.. [j]	.. [j]
Uruguay [z]	700	766	980	1 554	1 723	1 923
Venezuela	1 604	1 548	3 865	6 975	8 808 [e]	13 701 [e]

/...

Annex table B.3. FDI inward stock, by host region and economy, 1980, 1985, 1990, 1995, 1996 and 1997 (continued)

(Millions of dollars)

Host region/economy	1980	1985	1990	1995	1996	1997 [a]
Other Latin America and the Caribbean	**18 470**	**34 720**	**57 976**	**112 163**	**125 076**	**141 604**
Antigua and Barbuda [z]	23	94	292	437	456	484
Aruba	..	..	131 [aa]	182 [aa]	266 [aa]	196 [aa]
Bahamas [t]	298	294	336	493	580	668
Barbados [m]	102	123	169	225	238	256
Belize [m]	12	10	72	146	168	191
Bermuda [m]	5 132	8 052	13 849	24 705	26 805	28 505
Cayman Islands [m]	223	1 479	1 749	3 132	2 642	4 142
Costa Rica	672	957	1 447	2 791 [d]	3 201 [d]	3 701 [d]
Cuba [v]	-	1	3	45	57	70
Dominica	..	6 [i]	66 [i]	192 [i]	210 [i]	230 [i]
Dominican Republic	239	265	572	1 885 [d]	2 279 [d]	2 529 [d]
El Salvador	154	181	212	293	318 [e]	359 [e]
Grenada [m]	1	13	70	168	186	208
Guatemala [m]	701	1 050	1 723	2 190	2 267	2 397
Haiti [m]	79	112	141	141	146	149
Honduras [m]	93	172	383	594	657	737
Jamaica [m]	501	458	690	1 327	1 502	1 682
Mexico [m]	8 105	18 802	32 523	66 566	74 735	86 836
Netherlands Antilles [ab]	568	55	206	321	332	349
Nicaragua [m]	109	109	105	270	355	447
Panama	387	533	623 [f]	1 492 [f]	1 729 [f]	2 069 [f]
Saint Kitts and Nevis [v]	1	32	160	243	260	285
Saint Lucia [z]	94	197	315	510	533	578
Saint Vincent and the Grenadines [ac]	1	9	48	181	199	241
Trinidad and Tobago	976	1 719	2 093	3 634 d	3 954 [d]	4 294 [d]
Virgin Islands	..	..	..	..	..	..
Developing Europe	**297**	**465**	**1 507**	**3 320**	**4 334**	**5 128**
Bosnia and Herzegovina	..	..	..	..	..	..
Croatia	..	..	..	455 [ad]	988 [ad]	1 336 [ad]
Malta [m]	156	286	465	974	1 274	1 384
Slovenia	..	..	784 [ae]	1 857	2 028	2 349
TFYR Macedonia	..	..	..	33 [af]	44 [af]	60 [af]
Yugoslavia (former) [m]	141	179	257 ..	..	..	..
Asia	**45 524**	**108 350**	**192 720**	**426 694**	**506 751**	**593 674**
West Asia	**13 221**	**43 103**	**48 172**	**56 124**	**56 427**	**58 313**
Bahrain	..	306 [ag]	638 [a]	559 [ag]	606 [ag]	621 [ag]
Cyprus [m]	460	789	1 146	1 613	1 713	1 888
Iran, Islamic Republic of [m]	1 106	925	184	5	31	81
Iraq	..	..	..	..	..	..
Jordan [ab]	155	493	615	627	642	712
Kuwait t	30	33	26	106	126	171
Lebanon [s]	20	34	53	107	187	337
Oman [ah]	476	1 195	1 716	2 220	2 288	2 378
Qatar [t]	83	77	55	239	274	329
Saudi Arabia [m]	10 306	38 217	41 241	41 164	40 035	40 435
Syrian Arab Republic	..	37 [ai]	374 [ai]	1 030 [ai]	1 119 [ai]	1 199 [ai]
Turkey	107	360	1 320	5 103 [d]	5 825 [d]	6 431 [d]
United Arab Emirates [m]	409	482	751	1 312	1 442	1 542
Yemen [s]	68	155	53	2 039	2 139	2 189
Central Asia	**..**	**..**	**6**	**3 047**	**5 132**	**7 759**
Armenia	..	..	6 [aj]	37 [aj]	55 [aj]	98 [aj]
Azerbaijan	..	..	..	297 [af]	898 [af]	1 770 [af]

/...

Annex table B.3. FDI inward stock, by host region and economy, 1980, 1985, 1990, 1995, 1996 and 1997 (continued)

(Millions of dollars)

Host region/economy	1980	1985	1990	1995	1996	1997 [a]
Georgia	..	..	..	14 [af]	117 [af]	217 [af]
Kazakhstan	..	..	..	1 376 [ak]	2 513 [ak]	3 833 [ak]
Kyrgyzstan	..	..	..	843 [ad]	890 [ad]	973 [ad]
Tajikistan	..	..	..	25 [af]	41 [af]	45 [af]
Turkmenistan	..	..	..	200 [af]	308 [af]	429 [af]
Uzbekistan	..	..	..	255 [ak]	310 [ak]	395 [ak]
South, East and South-East Asia	**32 302**	**65 247**	**144 543**	**367 523**	**445 192**	**527 602**
Afghanistan [m]	11	12	12	12	12	12
Bangladesh	63	112	158 [al]	212 [al]	226 [al]	370 [al]
Brunei Darussalam [m]	19	33	30	62	71	76
Cambodia	..	..	..	198 [a]	849	1 049 [b]
China	57	4 305	18 568 [f]	131 241 [f]	172 041 [f]	217 341 [f]
Hong Kong, China	1 729	3 520	13 413 [m]	21 769 [f]	24 269 [f]	26 869 [f]
India	1 177	1 075	1 667 [al]	5 566 [al]	7 948 [al]	11 212 [al]
Indonesia	10 274	24 971	38 883	50 603 [d]	56 797 [d]	62 147 [d]
Korea, Democratic People's Republic of	..	..	572 [r]	630 [r]	634 [r]	636 [r]
Korea, Republic of	1 140	1 806	5 727	10 478	12 491	14 832 [b]
Lao People's Democratic Republic [m]	2	2	14	213	373	463
Macau [ab]	2	10	11	20	22	24
Malaysia	6 078	8 510	14 117 [al]	36 778 [al]	41 450 [al]	45 203 [al]
Maldives [t]	5	3	25	61	68	78
Mongolia	..	..	..	26 [ak]	31 [ak]	38 [ak]
Myanmar [ab]	5	5	173	937	1 037	1 117
Nepal [ah]	1	2	12	29	49	69
Pakistan	688	1 079	1 887	4 570 [c]	5 340 [c]	6 140 [c]
Philippines	1 225	1 302	2 098 [f]	7 158 [f]	8 678 [f]	9 931 [f]
Singapore	6 203	13 016	28 565	58 622 [c]	68 062 [c]	78 062 [c]
Sri Lanka	231	517	681 [al]	1 269 [al]	1 389 [al]	1 529 [al]
Taiwan Province of China	2 405	2 930	9 735 [al]	15 736 [al]	17 600 [al]	19 848 [al]
Thailand	981	1 999	7 980 [f]	17 236 [f]	19 504 [f]	23 104 [f]
Viet Nam [m]	7	38	216	4 096	6 252	7 452
The Pacific	**1 167**	**1 171**	**2 127**	**3 705**	**3 894**	**4 272**
Fiji	358	393	390 [f]	727 [f]	737 [f]	749 [f]
Kiribati	..	- [ai]	1 [ai]	2 [ai]	3 [ai]	4 [ai]
New Caledonia	..	- [ai]	40 [ai]	107 [ai]	120 [ai]	130 [ai]
Papua New Guinea	748	683	1 508 [f]	2 453 [f]	2 564 [f]	2 864 [f]
Solomon Islands [n]	28	32	69	140	161	183
Tonga	..	- [an]	1 [an]	6 [an]	8 [an]	10 [an]
Vanuatu [t]	33	62	110	249	277	307
Western Samoa [ah]	1	1	8	22	26	27
Central and Eastern Europe	**..**	**..**	**901**	**34 949**	**46 608**	**62 401**
Albania	..	..	..	201 [ak]	291 [ak]	339 [ak]
Belarus	..	..	..	39 [ak]	57 [ak]	220 [ak]
Bulgaria	..	..	4 [aa]	337 [aa]	446 [aa]	943 [aa]
Czech Republic	..	..	59 [ae]	5 923	7 061	6 763
Czechoslovakia (former)	..	..	..	..	..	..
Estonia	..	..	..	736 ao	886	1 148
Hungary	..	..	648 a	11 919	14 690	15 882
Latvia	..	..	..	511	679	901
Lithuania	..	..	..	495	647	1 041
Moldova, Republic of	..	..	..	92	137	180
Poland	..	..	109	7 843	11 463	16 463 [b]
Romania	..	..	..	978 [aq]	1 243 [aq]	2 467 [aq]

/...

Annex table B.3. FDI inward stock, by host region and economy, 1980, 1985, 1990, 1995, 1996 and 1997 (concluded)

(Millions of dollars)

Host region/economy	1980	1985	1990	1995	1996	1997 [a]
Russian Federation	..	..	..	4 016 [ak]	6 468 [ak]	12 709 [ak]
Slovakia	..	..	81 [ar]	950	1 109	1 293
Ukraine	..	..	..	910	1 431	2 054
Memorandum:						
Least developed countries [as]						
Total	1 921	3 287	6 169	13 039	15 362	17 175
Africa	1 626	2 789	5 394	8 784	9 998	11 160
Latin America and the Caribbean	79	112	141	141	146	149
Asia	155	292	446	3 701	4 752	5 347
West Asia	68	155	53	2 039	2 139	2 189
South, East and South-East Asia	88	137	394	1 662	2 613	3 158
The Pacific	61	95	188	412	466	520
Oil-exporting countries [at]						
Total	54 919	132 121	193 332	313 554	343 295	380 546
Africa	7 974	16 332	26 460	40 106	42 797	45 302
North Africa	4 357	8 803	14 547	19 470	20 372	21 573
Other Africa	3 617	7 529	11 913	20 636	22 426	23 730
Latin America and the Caribbean	18 163	41 041	69 231	140 400	157 378	182 260
South America	2 743	3 121	5 943	11 707	14 496	20 466
Other Latin America and the Caribbean	9 081	20 521	34 616	70 200	78 689	91 130
Asia	28 782	74 748	97 641	133 049	143 120	152 983
West Asia	12 411	41 235	44 611	45 606	44 802	45 557
South, East and South-East Asia	16 370	33 513	53 030	87 443	98 318	107 426
All developing countries minus China	**108 011**	**205 551**	**339 247**	**637 123**	**723 981**	**826 325**

Source: UNCTAD, FDI/TNC database.

a Estimates. For details, see "definition and sources" in annex B.
b Estimated by adding flows to the stock of 1996.
c Estimated by adding flows to the stock of 1994.
d Estimated by adding flows to the stock of 1990.
e Estimated by adding flows to the stock of 1995.
f Estimated by adding flows to the stock of 1989.
g Estimated by adding flows to the stock of 1986.
h Estimated by adding flows to the stock of 1993.
i Estimated by accumulating flows since 1982.
j Negative accumulation of flows. However, this value is included in the regional and global total.
k Stock data prior to 1988 are estimated by subtracting flows.
l Stock data prior to 1987 are estimated by subtracting flows.
m Estimated by accumulating flows since 1970.
n Estimated by accumulating flows since 1975.
o Estimated by UNCTAD.
p Estimated by adding flows to the stock of 1980.
q Estimated by accumulating flows since 1986.
r Estimated by accumulating flows since 1987.
s Estimated by accumulating flows since 1971.
t Estimated by accumulating flows since 1973.
u Estimated by accumulating flows since 1981.
v Estimated by accumulating flows since 1980.
w Stock data prior to 1990 are estimated by subtracting flows.
x Estimated by accumulating flows since 1976.
y Stock data prior to 1981 are estimated by subtracting flows.
z Estimated by accumulating flows since 1977.
aa Estimated by accumulating flows since 1990.
ab Estimated by accumulating flows since 1972.
ac Estimated by accumulating flows since 1978.
ad Estimated by accumulating flows since 1993.
ae Stock data prior to 1993 are estimated by subtracting flows.
af Estimated by accumulating flows since 1994.
ag Estimated by accumulating flows since 1983.

[ah] Estimated by accumulating flows since 1974.
[ai] Estimated by accumulating flows since 1985.
[aj] Estimated by accumulating flows since 1988.
[ak] Estimated by accumulating flows since 1992.
[al] Estimated by adding flows to the stock of 1988.
[am] Stock data prior to 1995 are estimated by subtracting flows.
[an] Estimated by accumulating flows since 1984.
[ao] Stock data prior to 1997 are estimated by subtracting flows.
[ap] Stock data prior to 1991 are estimated by subtracting flows.
[aq] Estimated by accumulating flows since 1991.
[ar] Stock data prior to 1992 are estimated by subtracting flows.
[as] Least developed countries include: Afghanistan, Angola, Bangladesh, Benin, Burkina Faso, Burundi, Cambodia, Cape Verde, Central African Republic, Chad, Comoros, Democratic Republic of Gongo, Djibouti, Equatorial Guinea, Ethiopia, The Gambia, Guinea, Guinea-Bissau, Haiti, Kiribati, Lao People's Democratic Republic, Lesotho, Malawi, Maldives, Mali, Mauritania, Mozambique, Myanmar, Nepal, Niger, Rwanda, Western Samoa, Sierra Leone, Solomon Islands, Somalia, Sudan, Togo, Uganda, United Republic of Tanzania, Vanuatu, Yemen and Zambia. Not included are Bhutan, Eritrea, Sao Tome and Principe and Tuvalu due to unavailability of data.
[at] Oil-exporting countries include: Algeria, Angola, Bahrain, Brunei Darussalam, Cameroon, Congo, Ecuador, Egypt, Gabon, Indonesia, Islamic Republic of Iran, Iraq, Kuwait, Libyan Arab Jamahiriya, Malaysia, Mexico, Nigeria, Oman, Qatar, Saudi Arabia, Trinidad and Tobago, Tunisia, United Arab Emirates and Venezuela.

Annex B.4. FDI outward stock, by home region and economy, 1980, 1985, 1990, 1995, 1996 and 1997
(Millions of dollars)

Home region/economy	1980	1985	1990	1995	1996	1997 [a]
World	**524 636**	**688 908**	**1 704 544**	**2 793 542**	**3 115 870**	**3 541 384**
Developed countries	**509 235**	**659 367**	**1 629 834**	**2 557 415**	**2 830 918**	**3 192 496**
Western Europe	**236 346**	**305 727**	**865 772**	**1 426 353**	**1 584 793**	**1 786 035**
European Union	**212 926**	**279 709**	**789 079**	**1 260 644**	**1 411 422**	**1 596 865**
Austria	530	1 908	4 656	12 887	13 542	14 979 [b]
Belgium and Luxembourg	6 037	9 551	40 636	81 335 [c]	89 705 [c]	96 411 [c]
Denmark	2 065	1 801	7 342	19 934 [d]	22 444 [d]	25 684 [d]
Finland	743	1 829	11 227	15 177	17 666	20 332
France	23 604	31 459	110 126	184 380	202 234	226 799 [b]
Germany	43 127	58 690	151 581	262 169	291 688 [e]	326 028 [e]
Greece	..	..	851 [f]	863 [f]	845	850
Ireland	..	202 [g]	2 150 [g]	4 038 [g]	4 765 [g]	5 571 [g]
Italy	7 319	14 514	56 105	97 043	107 497	125 074
Netherlands	42 116	44 772	108 976	169 697 [c]	192 791 [c]	213 161 [c]
Portugal [h]	116	186	503	2 775	3 540	5 182
Spain	1 226	2 076	16 128	33 540	38 748 [e]	48 790 [e]
Sweden	5 611	12 408	49 491	71 941	70 878	74 774 [b]
United Kingdom	80 434	100 313	229 307	304 865	355 079	413 229 [b]
Other Western Europe	**23 419**	**26 018**	**76 693**	**165 708**	**173 372**	**189 171**
Gibraltar	..	..	..	..	..	..
Iceland	58 [i]	59 [i]	75	182	244	254 [b]
Norway	1 870 [j]	4 609 [j]	10 888	22 514	28 381 [e]	32 170 [e]
Switzerland	21 491	21 350	65 731	143 013	144 747	156 747 [b]
North America	**243 961**	**294 177**	**520 026**	**832 207**	**917 701**	**1 045 212**
Canada	23 783	43 143	84 807	117 576	124 741	137 715 [b]
United States	220 178	251 034	435 219	714 631	792 960	907 497 [b]
Other developed countries	**28 928**	**59 463**	**244 035**	**298 856**	**328 424**	**361 249**
Australia	2 260	6 653	30 536	39 107	46 038	52 393 [b]
Israel [k]	28	510	912	4 130	4 873	5 543
Japan	19 610	43 970	201 440	238 452	258 612	284 605 [b]
New Zealand	1 308	1 826	3 320	7 675	9 352	6 811
South Africa	5 722	6 504	7 827 [l]	9 492 [l]	9 549 [l]	11 898 [l]
Developing countries	**15 397**	**29 516**	**74 428**	**233 914**	**281 612**	**342 202**
Africa	**529**	**6 353**	**11 629**	**14 838**	**15 094**	**16 225**
North Africa	**300**	**450**	**876**	**1 251**	**1 284**	**1 332**
Algeria [m]	99	157	185	235	235	235
Egypt [m]	39	91	163	365	370	390
Libyan Arab Jamahiriya [h]	162	206	526	526	526	526
Morocco	..	..	..	114 [n]	141 [n]	166 [n]
Sudan	..	..	..	..	..	..
Tunisia	..	.. [o, p]	2 [o]	11 [o]	12 [o]	15 [o]
Other Africa	**229**	**5 903**	**10 753**	**13 587**	**13 811**	**14 893**
Angola	..	..	- [q]	- [q]	- [q]	- [q]
Benin [r]	-	2	2	2	2	2

/...

Annex B.4. FDI outward stock, by home region and economy, 1980, 1985, 1990, 1995, 1996 and 1997 (continued)

(Millions of dollars)

Home region/economy	1980	1985	1990	1995	1996	1997 [a]
Botswana [s]	3	3	10	97	214	224
Burkina Faso [t]	3	3	3	3	3	3
Burundi	..	..	- [u]	- [u]	1 [u]	1 [u]
Cameroon [v]	23	53	150	227	235	243
Cape Verde	..	..	1 [u]	2 [u]	2 [u]	2 [u]
Central African Republic [w]	3	4	21	49	55	60
Chad [x]	-	1	36	84	92	102
Comoros	..	..	1 [q]	1 [q]	1 [q]	1 [q]
Congo	..	..	..	..	..	..
Congo, Democratic Republic of	..	..	..	..	..	..
Côte d'Ivoire	..	..	..	..	..	..
Djibouti	..	..	..	..	..	..
Equatorial Guinea	..	..	- [u]	- [u]	- [u]	- [u]
Ethiopia	..	..	..	..	..	..
Gabon [t]	77	102	163	205	204	219
Gambia, The	..	..	..	..	..	..
Ghana	..	..	..	..	..	..
Guinea	..	..	..	..	..	..
Guinea-Bissau	..	..	..	..	..	..
Kenya [w]	18	60	99	99	99	104
Lesotho	..	..	- [y]	- [y]	- [y]	[y]
Liberia [z]	48	361	453	768 [c]	376 [c]	576 [c]
Madagascar	..	..	..	..	..	..
Malawi	..	..	..	..	..	..
Mali [w]	22	22	22	22	22	22
Mauritania	..	..	3 [aa]	3 [aa]	3 [aa]	3 [aa]
Mauritius	..	..	1 [y]	93 [y]	96 [y]	99 [y]
Mozambique	..	..	..	..	..	..
Namibia	..	..	80	15	13	16
Niger [t]	2	8	54	109	109	109
Nigeria [r]	5	5 193	9 508	11 438	11 893	12 693
Rwanda	..	..	..	..	..	..
Senegal [t]	-	37	43	90	94	98
Seychelles [s]	14	44	61	93	106	121
Sierra Leone	..	..	..	..	..	..
Somalia	..	..	..	..	..	..
Swaziland	9	9	40	155	100	105 [b]
Togo [ab]	2	2	2	2	2	2
Uganda	..	..	..	..	..	..
United Republic of Tanzania	..	..	..	..	..	..
Zambia	..	..	..	..	..	..
Zimbabwe	..	..	..	28 [ac]	88 [ac]	88 [ac]
Latin America and the Caribbean	**2 942**	**7 240**	**12 686**	**25 307**	**27 339**	**35 889**
South America	**960**	**2 280**	**4 727**	**15 432**	**16 724**	**20 397**
Argentina [z]	70	280	420	675 [ad]	880 [ad]	908 [ad]
Bolivia	-	-	6	16	18	20 [b]
Brazil	652	1 361	2 397	7 238 [d]	7 161 [d]	8 730 [d]
Chile	42	102	178	2 769 [ae]	3 848 [ae]	5 797 [ae]
Colombia	137	301	402	1 152 [d]	1 220 [d]	1 320 [d]
Ecuador	..	..	..	..	..	..
Guyana	..	..	..	2 [ac]	2 [ac]	2 [ac]
Paraguay [s]	30	30	30	30	30	30
Peru	3	38	63	131 [d]	141 [d]	161 [d]
Suriname	..	..	..	..	..	..
Uruguay [z]	3	2	9	.. [c, p]	- 4 [c]	1 [c]
Venezuela	23	165	1 221	3 427	3 427 [e]	3 427 [e]

/...

Annex B.4. FDI outward stock, by home region and economy, 1980, 1985, 1990, 1995, 1996 and 1997 (continued)

(Millions of dollars)

Home region/economy	1980	1985	1990	1995	1996	1997 [a]
Other Latin America and the Caribbean	**1 982**	**4 960**	**7 959**	**9 876**	**10 615**	**15 492**
Antigua and Barbuda	..	..	..	..	..	..
Aruba	..	..	..	..	..	..
Bahamas [z]	285	154	1 535	1 184 [ad]	1 184 [ad]	1 628 [ad]
Barbados [k]	5	12	22	31	35	35
Belize	..	..	..	10 [n]	12 [n]	12 [n]
Bermuda [z]	724	2 002	1 550	1 265 [ad]	1 439 [ad]	3 732 [ad]
Cayman Islands	..	..	..	..	..	..
Costa Rica [x]	6	26	43	66	70	74
Cuba	..	..	..	..	..	..
Dominica	..	..	..	..	..	..
Dominican Republic	..	..	..	38 [ac]	51 [ac]	64 [ac]
El Salvador	..	..	..	..	..	..
Grenada	..	..	..	..	..	..
Guatemala	..	..	..	..	..	..
Haiti	..	..	..	..	..	..
Honduras	..	..	..	..	..	..
Jamaica [ab]	5	5	5	5	5	5
Mexico [z]	136	533	575	2 564 [ad]	2 245 [ad]	3 282 [ad]
Netherlands Antilles [ab]	10	12	23	26	25	26
Nicaragua	..	..	..	..	..	..
Panama [z]	811	2 204	4 188	4 660 [ad]	5 518 [ad]	6 600 [ad]
Saint Kitts and Nevis	..	..	..	..	..	..
Saint Lucia	..	..	..	..	..	..
Saint Vincent and the Grenadines	..	..	..	..	..	..
Trinidad and Tobago	..	12 [af]	17 [af]	28 [af]	31 [af]	34 [af]
Virgin Islands	..	..	..	..	..	..
Developing Europe	..	..	**258**	**891**	**937**	**1 182**
Bosnia and Herzegovina	..	..	..	- [ag]	0 [ag]	5 [ag]
Croatia	..	..	..	432 [ah]	453	603 [b]
Malta	..	..	..	55 [ac]	118 [ac]	183 [ac]
Slovenia	..	..	258 [y]	404 [y]	366 [y]	391 [y]
TFYR Macedonia	..	..	..	..	..	..
Yugoslavia (former)	..	..	..	..	..	..
Asia	**11 906**	**15 878**	**49 754**	**192 717**	**238 072**	**288 733**
West Asia	**1 202**	**1 865**	**6 008**	**9 705**	**8 834**	**9 339**
Bahrain [z]	..	10	46 [ai]	.. [ai, p]	- 20 [ai, p]	- 19 [ai,p]
Cyprus	..	- [aj]	9 [aj]	63 [aj]	71 [aj]	76 [aj]
Iran, Islamic Republic	..	..	..	77 [ak]	77 [ak]	80 [ak]
Iraq	..	..	..	..	..	..
Jordan [q]	23	26	16	.. [p]	.. [p]	.. [p]
Kuwait [w]	944	1 306	4 039	7 660	6 565	6 819
Lebanon [z]	1	40	.. [p]	.. [ad, p]	.. [ad,p]	.. [ad,p]
Oman [z]	1	40	7	5 [ad]	6 [ad]	10 [ad]
Qatar	..	..	..	..	..	..
Saudi Arabia [z]	228	420	1 811	1 685 [ad]	1 865 [ad]	1 990 [ad]
Syrian Arab Republic	..	..	..	..	..	..
Turkey	..	..	.. [al, p]	261 [al]	371 [al]	487 [al]
United Arab Emirates [z]	5	19	99	66 [ad]	55 [ad]	45 [ad]
Yemen	..	4 [am]	5 [am]	5 [am]	5 [am]	5 [am]
Central Asia	..	..	..	..	..	..
Armenia	..	..	..	..	..	..

/...

Annex B.4. FDI outward stock, by home region and economy, 1980, 1985, 1990, 1995, 1996 and 1997 (continued)

(Millions of dollars)

Home region/economy	1980	1985	1990	1995	1996	1997 [a]
Azerbaijan	..	..	..	..	..	..
Georgia	..	..	..	..	..	..
Kazakhstan	..	..	..	..	..	..
Kyrgyzstan	..	..	..	..	..	..
Tajikistan	..	..	..	..	..	..
Turkmenistan	..	..	..	..	..	..
Uzbekistan	..	..	..	..	..	..
South, East and South-East Asia	**10 704**	**14 013**	**43 745**	**183 013**	**229 238**	**279 395**
Afghanistan	..	..	..	..	..	..
Bangladesh	..	..	- [q]	2 [q]	2 [q]	2 [q]
Brunei Darussalam	..	..	..	..	..	..
Cambodia	..	..	..	..	..	..
China	..	131	2 489 [an]	15 802 [an]	17 916 [an]	20 416 [an]
Hong Kong, China [ao]	148	2 345	13 242	85 156	111 512	137 512
India [z]	4	19	30	282 [ad]	521 [ad]	621 [ad]
Indonesia [z]	..	49	25	1 295 [ad]	1 807 [ad]	4 207 [ad]
Korea, Democratic People's Republic of	..	..	..	..	..	..
Korea, Republic of	142	526	2 301	10 224	13 757	18 044 [b]
Lao People's Democratic Republic	..	..	..	..	..	..
Macau	..	..	..	..	..	..
Malaysia	414	749	2 283 [l]	8 903 [l]	12 603 [l]	15 703 [l]
Maldives	..	..	..	..	..	..
Mongolia	..	..	..	..	..	..
Myanmar	..	..	..	..	..	..
Nepal	..	..	..	..	..	..
Pakistan	40	126	244	272 [c]	275 [c]	278 [c]
Philippines	171	171	155 [l]	909 [l]	1 091 [l]	1 227 [l]
Singapore	9 675 [i]	9 675 [i]	9 675	32 695	37 500 [e]	43 400 [e]
Sri Lanka	..	1 [aj]	8 [aj]	37 [aj]	44 [aj]	52 [aj]
Taiwan Province of China	97	204	12 894 [l]	25 113 [l]	28 956 [l]	34 178 [l]
Thailand	13	16	398 [an]	2 324 [an]	3 255 [an]	3 755 [an]
Viet Nam	..	..	..	..	..	..
The Pacific	**21**	**45**	**102**	**160**	**170**	**172**
Fiji [ab]	10	23	95	153	163	165
Kiribati	..	..	..	- [ap]	- [ap]	- [ap]
New Caledonia	..	..	..	..	..	..
Papua New Guinea	10	22	7 [an]	7 [an]	7 [an]	7 [an]
Solomon Islands	..	..	..	..	..	..
Tonga	..	..	..	- [n]	- [n]	- [n]
Vanuatu	..	..	..	..	..	..
Western Samoa	..	..	..	..	..	..
Central and Eastern Europe	**4**	**25**	**282**	**2 213**	**3 340**	**6 686**
Albania	..	..	..	48 [ak]	58 [ak]	68 [ak]
Belarus	..	..	..	..	..	..
Bulgaria	..	..	..	8 [ag]	37 [ag]	37 [ag]
Czech Republic	..	..	..	346	386	384
Czechoslovakia (former)	..	..	..	..	..	..
Estonia	..	..	..	46 [f]	86	215
Hungary	..	..	169	489	493	990
Latvia	..	..	..	124	116	123
Lithuania	..	..	..	2	3	26
Moldova, Republic of	..	..	..	18	19	20
Poland	4	25	95	539	735	785 [b]

/...

Annex B.4. FDI outward stock, by home region and economy, 1980, 1985, 1990, 1995, 1996 and 1997 (concluded)
(Millions of dollars)

Home region/economy	1980	1985	1990	1995	1996	1997 [a]
Romania	..	..	18 [u]	41 [u]	43 [u]	47 [u]
Russian Federation	..	..	..	407 [ap]	1 178 [ap]	3 667 [ap]
Slovakia	..	..	..	48	95	190
Ukraine	..	..	..	97	92	134
Memorandum:						
Least developed countries [ar]						
Total	80	408	604	1 052	675	890
Africa	80	404	599	1 046	668	883
Latin America and the Caribbean	..	..	..	..	..	..
Asia	..	4	5	6	6	7
West Asia	..	4	5	5	5	5
Asia	..	4	5	6	6	7
The Pacific	..	..	..	..	..	..
Oil-exporting countries [as]						
Total	2 269	9 480	20 191	37 882	40 985	49 788
Africa	405	5 798	10 697	13 009	13 476	14 322
North Africa	300	450	876	1 137	1 143	1 166
Other Africa	105	5 348	9 821	11 872	12 333	13 156
Latin America and the Caribbean	272	1 089	1 184	5 183	4 551	6 631
South America	24	166	1 227	3 443	3 445	3 447
Other Latin America and the Caribbean	136	545	592	2 592	2 276	3 316
Asia	1 592	2 593	8 310	19 690	22 958	28 835
West Asia	1 178	1 795	6 002	9 492	8 548	8 925
South, East and South-East Asia	414	798	2 308	10 198	14 410	19 910
All developing countries minus China	**15 397**	**29 385**	**71 939**	**218 112**	**263 697**	**321 786**

Source: UNCTAD, FDI/TNC database.

c Estimates. For details, see "definitions and sources" in annex B.
b Estimated by adding flows to the stock of 1996.
c Estimated by adding flows to the stock of 1994.
d Estimated by adding flows to the stock of 1990.
e Estimated by adding flows to the stock of 1995.
f Stock data prior to 1997 are estimated by subtracting flows.
g Estimated by accumulating flows since 1984.
h Estimated by accumulating flows since 1972.
i Stock data prior to 1988 are estimated by subtracting flows.
j Stock data prior to 1990 are estimated by subtracting flows.
k Estimated by accumulating flows since 1970.
l Estimated by adding flows to the stock of 1988.
m Estimated by accumulating flows since 1977.
n Estimated by accumulating flows since 1991.
o Estimated by accumulating flows since 1981.
p Negative accumulation of flows. However, this value is included in the regional and global total.
q Estimated by accumulating flows since 1990.
r Estimated by accumulating flows since 1979.
s Estimated by accumulating flows since 1976.
t Estimated by accumulating flows since 1974.
u Estimated by accumulating flows since 1989.
v Estimated by accumulating flows since 1973.
w Estimated by accumulating flows since 1975.
x Estimated by accumulating flows since 1978.
y Estimated by accumulating flows since 1988.
z Estimated by using the inward stock of the United States as a proxy.
aa Estimated by accumulating flows since 1986.
ab Estimated by accumulating flows since 1980.
ac Estimated by accumulating flows since 1993.
ad Estimated by adding flows to the stock of 1993.
ae Estimated by adding flows to the stock of 1992.
af Estimated by accumulating flows since 1983.

[ag] Estimated by accumulating flows since 1995.
[ah] Stock data prior to 1996 are estimated by subtracting flows.
[ai] Stock data prior to 1986 are estimated by subtracting flows.
[aj] Estimated by accumulating flows since 1985.
[ak] Estimated by accumulating flows since 1992.
[al] Estimated by accumulating flows since 1987.
[am] Estimated by accumulating flows since 1982.
[an] Estimated by adding flows to the stock of 1989.
[ao] Estimated by using the inward stock of the United States and China as a proxy and accumulating flows since 1994.
[ap] Estimated by accumulating flows since 1994.
[aq] Stock data prior to 1995 are estimated by subtracting flows.
[ar] Least developed countries include: Afghanistan, Angola, Bangladesh, Benin, Burkina Faso, Burundi, Cambodia, Cape Verde, Central African Republic, Chad, Comoros, Democratic Repunlic of Congo, Djibouti, Equatorial Guinea, Ethiopia, The Gambia, Guinea, Guinea-Bissau, Haiti, Kiribati, Lao People's Democratic Republic, Lesotho, Liberia, Malawi, Maldives, Mali, Mauritania, Mozambique, Myanmar, Nepal, Niger, Rwanda, Western Samoa, Sierra Leone, Solomon Islands, Somalia, Sudan, Togo, Uganda, United Republic of Tanzania, Vanuatu, Yemen and Zambia. Not included are Bhutan, Eritrea, Sao Tome and Principe and Tuvalu due to unavailability of data.
[as] Oil-exporting countries include: Algeria, Angola, Bahrain, Brunei Darussalam, Cameroon, Congo, Ecuador, Egypt, Gabon, Indonesia, Islamic Republic of Iran, Iraq, Kuwait, Libyan Arab Jamahiriya, Malaysia, Mexico, Nigeria, Oman, Qatar, Saudi Arabia, Trinidad and Tobago, Tunisia, United Arab Emirates and Ve1nezuela.

Annex table B.5. Inward and outward FDI flows as a percentage of gross fixed capital formation, by region and economy, 1986-1996

(Percentage)

Region/economy	1986-1991 (Annual average)	1992	1993	1994	1995	1996
Total						
inward	***3.6***	***3.3***	***4.4***	***4.5***	***5.6***	***5.6***
outward	***4.1***	***3.7***	***4.9***	***5.3***	***5.9***	***5.5***
Developed countries						
inward	***3.5***	***2.6***	***3.0***	***2.8***	***3.9***	***3.6***
outward	***4.5***	***3.8***	***4.5***	***4.9***	***5.6***	***5.2***
Western Europe						
inward	***5.6***	***5.3***	***6.1***	***5.4***	***7.2***	***5.9***
outward	***8.4***	***7.1***	***7.8***	***9.2***	***10.3***	***10.0***
European Union						
inward	***5.7***	***5.5***	***6.2***	***5.2***	***7.3***	***5.8***
outward	***8.4***	***7.1***	***7.5***	***8.8***	***10.0***	***9.4***
Austria						
inward	*1.4*	*2.0*	*2.2*	*2.7*	*1.1*	*6.6*
outward	*2.5*	*4.0*	*3.3*	*2.4*	*1.8*	*2.4*
Belgium and Luxembourg						
inward	*17.5*	*25.2*	*26.1*	*19.4*	*20.4*	*28.3*
outward	*14.6*	*25.5*	*11.9*	*3.1*	*22.8*	*16.8*
Denmark						
inward	*3.8*	*4.6*	*8.4*	*23.6*	*15.3*	*2.7*
outward	*6.2*	*10.1*	*6.8*	*19.7*	*10.9*	*8.7*
Finland						
inward	*1.4*	*2.1*	*6.9*	*11.1*	*5.6*	*5.8*
outward	*6.3*	*-3.8*	*11.3*	*30.3*	*7.9*	*18.8*
France						
inward	*4.5*	*8.2*	*9.0*	*6.6*	*8.6*	*8.2*
outward	*8.7*	*11.8*	*8.9*	*10.2*	*5.7*	*11.3*
Germany						
inward	*1.1*	*0.6*	*0.5*	*0.4*	*2.6*	*-0.6*
outward	*6.1*	*4.3*	*3.7*	*3.8*	*7.4*	*6.0*
Greece						
inward	*5.9*	*5.5*	*5.2*	*5.3*	*4.8*	*4.4*
outward	-	*0.2*	*-0.1*	*-0.5*	*0.3*	-
Ireland						
inward	*5.9*	*17.0*	*15.3*	*10.1*	*14.2*	*20.4*
outward	*5.7*	*2.5*	*3.0*	*5.3*	*8.1*	*6.0*
Iltaly						
inward	*2.0*	*1.7*	*2.6*	*1.3*	*2.6*	*1.6*
outward	*2.4*	*2.8*	*5.6*	*3.3*	*3.7*	*3.0*
Netherlands						
inward	*12.8*	*12.2*	*14.2*	*11.7*	*14.8*	*9.9*
outward	*21.4*	*22.4*	*20.1*	*26.9*	*25.3*	*29.6*
Portugal						
inward	*9.9*	*8.3*	*7.9*	*6.1*	*2.7*	*2.7*
outward	*0.9*	*3.0*	*0.8*	*1.4*	*2.8*	*2.9*
Spain						
inward	*9.6*	*10.5*	*8.6*	*9.8*	*5.4*	*5.5*
outward	*2.3*	*1.7*	*2.8*	*4.0*	*3.2*	*4.4*
Sweden						
inward	*5.9*	-	*14.0*	*23.1*	*44.3*	*14.8*
outward	*21.0*	*1.0*	*5.6*	*24.7*	*33.8*	*13.7*
United Kingdom						
inward	*13.6*	*9.8*	*11.0*	*6.0*	*13.1*	*14.6*
outward	*17.1*	*11.6*	*18.8*	*22.0*	*25.7*	*19.1*

/...

Annex table B.5. Inward and outward FDI flows as a percentage of gross fixed capital formation, by region and economy, 1986-1996 (continued)

(Percentage)

Region/economy	1986-1991 (Annual average)	1992	1993	1994	1995	1996
Other Western Europe						
inward	***4.3***	***2.5***	***3.9***	***8.1***	***6.2***	***8.2***
outward	***8.9***	***7.9***	***12.8***	***15.5***	***15.5***	***19.0***
Gibraltar						
inward	..	..	..	..	..	..
outward	..	..	..	..	..	..
Iceland						
inward	*1.3*	*-0.9*	*-*	*-0.2*	*-0.9*	*6.4*
outward	*0.6*	*0.3*	*1.3*	*2.6*	*2.4*	*5.2*
Norway						
inward	*2.4*	*2.8*	*8.4*	*10.8*	*7.9*	*12.3*
outward	*5.4*	*1.6*	*3.7*	*8.5*	*9.4*	*18.2*
Switzerland						
inward	*5.3*	*2.2*	*1.8*	*7.1*	*5.5*	*6.0*
outward	*10.8*	*10.8*	*17.2*	*18.8*	*18.5*	*19.8*
North America						
inward	***6.3***	***2.7***	***5.1***	***5.1***	***6.3***	***6.9***
outward	***3.6***	***4.8***	***8.5***	***7.8***	***9.3***	***7.0***
Canada						
inward	*5.3*	*4.5*	*4.8*	*8.4*	*11.0*	*6.2*
outward	*5.3*	*3.3*	*5.9*	*9.0*	*11.4*	*8.2*
United States						
inward	*6.5*	*2.4*	*5.1*	*4.7*	*5.8*	*7.0*
outward	*3.4*	*5.0*	*8.8*	*7.7*	*9.1*	*6.9*
Other developed countries						
inward	***0.9***	***0.9***	***0.5***	***0.7***	***1.2***	***0.8***
outward	***4.1***	***1.8***	***1.3***	***1.7***	***1.8***	***2.1***
Australia						
inward	*10.7*	*9.3*	*6.5*	*7.2*	*18.8*	*7.0*
outward	*5.6*	*3.8*	*3.1*	*6.6*	*5.3*	*7.9*
Israel						
inward	*1.0*	*1.5*	*1.7*	*1.6*	*4.3*	*4.9*
outward	*0.7*	*1.9*	*2.2*	*1.9*	*1.4*	*1.5*
Japan						
inward	*-*	*0.2*	*-*	*0.1*	*-*	*-*
outward	*4.0*	*1.5*	*1.1*	*1.3*	*1.5*	*1.7*
New Zealand						
inward	*19.2*	*31.6*	*27.7*	*25.8*	*21.4*	*26.7*
outward	*12.1*	*12.0*	*17.4*	*19.3*	*13.9*	*9.1*
South Africa						
inward	*-0.2*	*-0.2*	*-0.1*	*1.7*	*4.3*	*3.5*
outward	*0.6*	*3.8*	*1.6*	*0.7*	*1.2*	*0.3*
Developing countries						
inward	***3.4***	***4.2***	***6.1***	***7.6***	***7.4***	***8.7***
outward	***1.3***	***1.7***	***3.0***	***3.4***	***3.2***	***3.3***
Africa						
inward	***3.9***	***5.2***	***6.1***	***9.5***	***7.9***	***7.3***
outward	***1.4***	***0.9***	***1.4***	***1.1***	***0.9***	***0.4***
North Africa						
inward	***2.5***	***4.4***	***4.4***	***6.6***	***3.2***	***3.3***
outward	***0.2***	***0.1***	***0.1***	***0.2***	***0.3***	***0.1***

/...

Annex table B.5. Inward and outward FDI flows as a percentage of gross fixed capital formation, by region and economy, 1986-1996 (continued)

(Percentage)

Region/economy	1986-1991 (Annual average)	1992	1993	1994	1995	1996
Algeria						
inward	-	-	0.1	0.1	-	0.1
outward	-	..	..	..	..	..
Egypt						
inward	4.8	5.3	5.4	12.0	5.3	5.1
outward	0.1	-	-	0.4	0.8	-
Libyan Arab Jamahiriya						
inward	1.1	4.7	4.8	5.4	3.9	4.2
outward	1.4	..	..	..	..	..
Morocco						
inward	2.7	6.6	8.1	8.8	3.9	4.2
outward	-	0.5	0.4	0.4	0.2	0.4
Sudan						
inward	-	-	-	-	-	-
outward	..	..	..	..	..	..
Tunisia						
inward	3.4	12.5	11.2	10.2	6.1	5.6
outward	-	0.1	-	0.1	-0.1	-
Other Africa						
inward	**6.7**	**6.4**	**8.8**	**14.1**	**14.8**	**13.2**
outward	**3.8**	**2.0**	**3.4**	**2.5**	**1.9**	**1.0**
Angola						
inward	28.4	67.4	85.3	65.4	72.0	90.4
outward	-	..	0.6	-0.8	..	..
Benin						
inward	1.1	0.3	0.1	0.2	0.3	0.3
outward	..	..	..	..	..	..
Botswana						
inward	7.6	-0.1	-29.1	32.0	34.5	25.7
outward	0.3	0.8	1.0	1.3	4.1	11.0
Burkina Faso						
inward	0.3	-	2.1	0.6	0.4	0.4
outward	..	..	..	..	..	..
Burundi						
inward	0.7	0.3	0.3	0.7	1.7	0.5
outward	-	..	-	0.1	0.5	0.3
Cameroon						
inward	-0.5	2.5	0.5	-0.8	0.7	3.2
outward	0.7	2.9	2.0	-	-	0.7
Cape Verde						
inward	0.6	-	3.6	3.5	10.5	14.7
outward	0.2	..	..	1.4	..	..
Central African Republic						
inward	1.5	-6.8	-9.4	3.4	1.9	4.7
outward	2.2	3.7	5.0	6.8	5.6	5.8
Chad						
inward	11.0	1.8	13.5	24.0	11.5	16.0
outward	6.8	12.4	9.7	0.5	10.6	7.0
Comoros						
inward	6.2	-3.2	0.4	0.4	1.8	4.0
outward	0.4	..	..	..	..	..
Congo						
inward	3.7	0.9	40.2	0.8	2.2	2.4
outward	..	..	..	..	..	..

/...

Annex table B.5. Inward and outward FDI flows as a percentage of gross fixed capital formation, by region and economy, 1986-1996 (continued)

(Percentage)

Region/economy	1986-1991 (Annual average)	1992	1993	1994	1995	1996
Congo, Democratic Republic of						
inward	-0.9	-0.2	2.9	-0.8	-	-
outward	..	..	..	..	..	..
Côte d'Ivoire						
inward	5.1	-29.1	10.7	3.3	1.5	1.6
outward	..	..	..	..	..	..
Djibouti						
inward	0.3	2.7	1.9	2.6	4.5	6.7
outward	..	..	..	..	..	..
Equatorial Guinea						
inward	29.7	16.0	54.0	46.8	330.5	972.3
outward	0.2	..	..	..	..	..
Ethiopia						
inward	0.1	-	-	0.4	0.9	0.4
outward	..	..	0.1	-0.1	..	..
Gabon						
inward	4.9	10.5	-9.6	-8.4	-9.6	5.5
outward	1.2	2.1	0.2	-	-	-
Gambia, The						
inward	9.8	8.8	27.5	26.6	15.8	25.6
outward	..	..	..	..	..	..
Ghana						
inward	1.6	2.5	14.0	30.2	13.8	15.6
outward	..	..	..	..	..	..
Guinea						
inward	4.2	4.0	0.5	-	0.2	4.6
outward	..	..	..	..	..	0.1
Guinea-Bissau						
inward	1.8	10.0	-4.1	..	0.5	0.3
outward	..	..	..	..	..	..
Kenya						
inward	2.2	0.5	0.2	0.3	1.7	0.7
outward	0.4	..	..	..	..	-
Lesotho						
inward	3.9	0.5	2.6	3.3	4.0	4.9
outward	..	..	..	..	..	..
Liberia						
inward	186.8	-17.1	58.0	36.2	40.7	35.7
outward	57.2	78.6	108.5	219.6	-87.2	-823.2
Madagascar						
inward	3.5	6.2	4.0	1.8	2.8	2.2
outward	..	..	..	..	..	..
Malawi						
inward	6.3	0.8	4.9	6.3	6.9	5.6
outward	..	..	..	..	..	..
Mali						
inward	-	-1.4	-4.2	10.4	3.0	3.5
outward	..	..	..	..	..	..
Mauritania						
inward	1.7	2.8	6.7	0.9	2.9	2.1
outward	0.2	..	..	..	..	..
Mauritius						
inward	4.2	1.7	1.6	1.9	1.9	3.3
outward	0.4	4.9	3.6	0.1	0.4	0.2
Mozambique						
inward	1.1	3.2	3.5	3.5	4.9	3.2
outward	..	..	..	..	..	..

/...

Annex table B.5. Inward and outward FDI flows as a percentage of gross fixed capital formation, by region and economy, 1986-1996 (continued)

(Percentage)

Region/economy	1986-1991 (Annual average)	1992	1993	1994	1995	1996
Namibia						
inward	8.1	20.2	9.4	15.1	16.3	22.5
outward	0.4	-0.3	1.5	-0.9	0.1	0.2
Niger						
inward	5.2	16.6	-10.1	-6.9	4.2	0.2
outward	2.6	12.0	1.7	-1.1	4.1	..
Nigeria						
inward	23.2	26.3	36.5	50.5	56.7	35.9
outward	25.0	5.2	16.1	10.0	9.9	11.7
Rwanda						
inward	4.6	0.9	1.7	-0.3	1.2	1.1
outward	..	..	..	..	..	..
Senegal						
inward	2.1	2.6	-0.1	12.6	4.2	5.4
outward	-0.3	6.3	-	3.3	-0.4	0.6
Seychelles						
inward	29.6	9.9	14.8	23.5	32.1	23.7
outward	4.6	1.3	0.9	10.2	12.5	10.4
Sierra Leone						
inward	-16.0	-10.4	-15.6	-6.3	-4.2	0.4
outward	..	..	..	..	..	..
Somalia						
inward	-0.6	0.2	0.2	0.1	0.4	0.4
outward	..	..	..	..	..	..
Swaziland						
inward	39.0	33.8	27.7	16.9	6.1	3.7
outward	8.5	13.6	11.5	18.9	11.9	-4.8
Togo						
inward	3.9	-0.5	0.9	1.4	0.2	0.3
outward	..	..	..	..	..	..
Uganda						
inward	-	0.6	10.1	11.7	11.9	12.5
outward	..	..	..	..	..	..
United Republic of Tanzania						
inward	-	1.0	1.9	4.5	11.6	14.0
outward	..	..	..	..	..	..
Zambia						
inward	32.8	12.9	13.8	18.1	20.4	15.5
outward	..	..	..	..	..	..
Zimbabwe						
inward	0.7	1.3	2.5	4.5	6.4	5.3
outward	1.2	0.3	0.4	0.5	0.7	3.3
Latin America and the Caribbean						
inward	**5.3**	**7.6**	**6.4**	**8.9**	**9.8**	**12.8**
outward	**0.7**	**0.6**	**1.1**	**1.6**	**0.7**	**0.7**
South America						
inward	**3.2**	**5.8**	**4.2**	**6.1**	**6.9**	**11.4**
outward	**0.6**	**0.4**	**1.5**	**1.3**	**1.1**	**0.6**
Argentina						
inward	5.6	10.6	5.4	5.5	9.5	9.7
outward	-	-	..	0.2	0.3	0.4
Bolivia						
inward	6.7	13.3	12.9	14.7	35.9	39.8
outward	0.2	0.2	0.2	0.2	0.2	0.2

/...

Annex table B.5. Inward and outward FDI flows as a percentage of gross fixed capital formation, by region and economy, 1986-1996 (continued)

(Percentage)

Region/economy	1986-1991 (Annual average)	1992	1993	1994	1995	1996
Brazil						
inward	1.6	2.9	1.5	1.9	3.5	7.5
outward	0.6	0.2	1.3	0.9	1.1	-0.1
Chile						
inward	14.1	7.4	7.3	15.0	10.7	23.8
outward	0.5	4.0	3.9	7.8	4.5	6.3
Colombia						
inward	6.8	10.6	10.0	11.9	14.6	22.2
outward	0.4	0.7	2.5	1.1	1.8	0.5
Ecuador						
inward	6.2	7.2	16.5	17.0	14.1	13.7
outward	..	..	..	..	..	..
Guyana						
inward	2.1	73.0	28.6	41.7	29.1	31.6
outward	..	-1.0	0.8	..	..	..
Paraguay						
inward	2.5	9.7	7.3	10.2	8.9	10.4
outward	..	..	..	..	..	..
Peru						
inward	0.4	2.1	9.7	29.3	14.7	25.7
outward	..	-	0.3	..	0.3	0.1
Suriname						
inward	-38.3	-8.3	-3.4	-2.2	-1.6	0.5
outward	..	..	..	..	..	..
Uruguay						
inward	4.6	3.9	9.0	7.4	7.6	7.6
outward	0.3	-1.8	1.7	-0.3	-1.3	0.2
Venezuela						
inward	4.5	4.9	3.2	7.9	7.9	17.6
outward	2.2	1.2	7.6	6.6	2.4	2.3
Other Latin America and the Caribbean						
inward	**11.3**	**10.9**	**11.0**	**15.7**	**22.2**	**18.0**
outward	**1.2**	**0.9**	**0.1**	**2.4**	**-1.1**	**1.0**
Antigua and Barbuda						
inward	..	..	..	..	..	..
outward	..	..	..	..	..	..
Aruba						
inward	..	..	..	..	..	..
outward	..	..	..	..	..	..
Bahamas						
inward	1.2	-	5.1	3.8	15.3	14.2
outward	0.2	-	-	-	-	-
Barbados						
inward	3.2	9.6	4.5	5.6	5.0	5.7
outward	0.7	0.5	1.2	0.5	1.4	1.5
Belize						
inward	14.6	11.6	5.8	12.8	15.5	16.9
outward	0.4	1.5	1.3	1.7	1.5	1.5
Bermuda						
inward	..	..	..	..	..	..
outward	..	..	..	..	..	..
Cayman Islands						
inward	..	..	..	..	..	..
outward	..	..	..	..	..	..

/...

Annex table B.5. Inward and outward FDI flows as a percentage of gross fixed capital formation, by region and economy, 1986-1996 (continued)

(Percentage)

Region/economy	1986-1991 (Annual average)	1992	1993	1994	1995	1996
Costa Rica						
inward	*11.7*	*16.2*	*14.1*	*18.0*	*22.7*	*24.7*
outward	*0.4*	*0.3*	*0.1*	*0.3*	*0.3*	*0.3*
Cuba						
inward	..	..	..	..	..	..
outward	..	..	..	..	..	..
Dominica						
inward	*24.6*	*46.3*	*34.7*	*80.5*	*147.3*	*52.8*
outward	..	..	..	..	..	..
Dominican Republic						
inward	*6.9*	*9.2*	*10.2*	*15.5*	*12.4*	*10.7*
outward	..	-	*0.5*	*0.5*	*0.4*	*0.4*
El Salvador						
inward	*2.4*	*1.5*	*1.3*	*1.6*	*2.1*	*1.5*
outward	..	..	..	..	..	..
Grenada						
inward	*19.0*	*32.5*	*27.6*	*21.8*	*22.5*	*20.3*
outward	..	..	..	..	..	..
Guatemala						
inward	*12.6*	*5.8*	*7.8*	*3.5*	*3.5*	*3.7*
outward	..	..	..	..	..	..
Haiti						
inward	*1.4*	*-0.9*	*-1.4*	..	*3.8*	*2.3*
outward	*-1.1*	..	..	..	..	..
Honduras						
inward	*6.7*	*6.2*	*2.6*	*3.6*	*5.2*	*6.4*
outward	..	..	..	..	..	..
Jamaica						
inward	*6.9*	*13.7*	*5.8*	*8.9*	*12.7*	*13.3*
outward	..	..	..	..	..	..
Mexico						
inward	*8.3*	*6.4*	*5.9*	*13.5*	*20.6*	*14.2*
outward	*0.4*	*1.0*	*0.8*	*2.5*	*-1.0*	*-0.6*
Netherlands Antilles						
inward	..	..	..	..	..	..
outward	..	..	..	..	..	..
Nicaragua						
inward	*-0.1*	*4.2*	*9.5*	*8.6*	*15.2*	*18.4*
outward	..	..	..	..	..	..
Panama						
inward	*-16.8*	*11.3*	*9.3*	*19.4*	*8.7*	*11.5*
outward	*46.8*	*33.1*	*-29.4*	*-7.1*	*16.3*	*41.4*
Saint Kitts and Nevis						
inward	*40.0*	*17.6*	*19.3*	*21.6*	*28.2*	*23.9*
outward	..	..	..	..	..	..
Saint Lucia						
inward	..	..	..	..	..	..
outward	..	..	..	..	..	..
Saint Vincent and the Grenadines						
inward	*16.6*	*26.1*	*47.8*	*65.8*	*38.4*	*22.9*
outward	..	..	..	..	..	..
Trinidad and Tobago						
inward	*11.0*	*24.0*	*61.5*	*74.7*	*31.0*	*33.2*
outward	*0.1*	..	*0.5*	*0.7*	*0.3*	*0.3*
Virgin Islands						
inward	..	..	..	..	..	..
outward	..	..	..	..	..	..

/...

Annex table B.5. Inward and outward FDI flows as a percentage of gross fixed capital formation, by region and economy, 1986-1996 (continued)

(Percentage)

Region/economy	1986-1991 (Annual average)	1992	1993	1994	1995	1996
Developing Europe						
inward	***0.4***	***28.4***	***8.5***	***11.1***	***9.3***	***19.9***
outward	**-**	***-0.5***	***0.7***	***0.2***	***1.3***	***1.8***
Bosnia and Herzegovina						
inward	..	..	..	..	..	..
outward	..	..	..	..	..	..
Croatia						
inward	..	..	..	..	..	..
outward	..	..	..	..	..	..
Malta						
inward	*7.8*	*5.2*	*7.8*	*19.0*	*18.0*	*31.8*
outward	..	..	*0.1*	*-0.1*	*5.5*	*6.7*
Slovenia						
inward	..	..	*4.7*	*4.5*	*4.4*	*4.4*
outward	..	..	-	*-0.1*	*0.1*	*0.2*
TFYR Macedonia						
inward	..	..	..	..	..	..
outward	..	..	..	..	..	..
Yugoslavia (former)						
inward	*0.2*	..	..	..	..	..
outward	..	..	..	..	..	..
Asia						
inward	***2.8***	***3.2***	***6.0***	***7.0***	***6.6***	***7.4***
outward	***1.5***	***2.0***	***3.7***	***4.2***	***4.2***	***4.3***
West Asia						
inward	***0.8***	***0.6***	***2.8***	***1.2***	***-0.6***	***0.2***
outward	***0.4***	***0.4***	***0.7***	***0.9***	***0.6***	***-0.6***
Bahrain						
inward	*5.5*	*-0.6*	*-0.4*	*-2.0*	*-1.9*	*3.3*
outward	*0.1*	..	..	*-1.3*	..	*-1.3*
Cyprus						
inward	*6.6*	*6.1*	*5.6*	*4.9*	*7.0*	*5.8*
outward	*0.3*	*0.8*	*0.8*	*0.4*	*0.4*	*0.5*
Iran, Islamic Republic of						
inward	*-0.1*	-	*-0.3*	-	*0.1*	*0.1*
outward	..	-	*0.3*	-	-	..
Iraq						
inward	-	..	..	..	..	..
outward	..	..	..	..	..	..
Jordan						
inward	*1.6*	*2.6*	*-1.8*	*0.1*	*0.6*	*0.6*
outward	-	*-0.2*	*-2.8*	*-1.2*	*-1.3*	*-1.8*
Kuwait						
inward	-	*1.0*	*0.3*	*0.4*	*0.4*	*0.5*
outward	*12.8*	*35.1*	*20.6*	*25.7*	*19.7*	*-29.7*
Lebanon						
inward	*1.0*	*0.4*	*0.3*	*0.4*	*1.9*	*4.4*
outward	*1.6*	*-0.3*	*-0.1*	*-0.1*	*-0.1*	*-0.1*
Oman						
inward	*7.0*	*5.1*	*6.5*	*3.8*	*2.2*	*3.2*
outward	-	-	*-0.1*	*0.2*	-	-
Qatar						
inward	*0.3*	*2.8*	*2.2*	*2.0*	*1.9*	*2.1*
outward	..	..	..	..	..	..

/...

Annex table B.5. Inward and outward FDI flows as a percentage of gross fixed capital formation, by region and economy, 1986-1996 (continued)

(Percentage)

Region/economy	1986-1991 (Annual average)	1992	1993	1994	1995	1996
Saudi Arabia						
inward	*2.9*	*-0.3*	*5.2*	*1.6*	*-8.2*	*-4.9*
outward	*1.2*	-	*-0.2*	*0.4*	*0.1*	*0.8*
Syrian Arab Republic						
inward	*1.5*	*0.9*	*1.8*	*1.9*	*0.7*	*0.6*
outward	..	..	..	..	..	..
Turkey						
inward	*1.8*	*2.3*	*1.4*	*1.4*	*2.0*	*1.6*
outward	-	*0.2*	-	*0.1*	*0.3*	*0.2*
United Arab Emirates						
inward	*0.8*	*1.6*	*1.8*	*1.1*	*1.0*	*1.2*
outward	*0.1*	-	*0.1*	-	-	-
Yemen						
inward	*8.6*	*32.8*	*35.9*	*0.4*	*-8.7*	*4.0*
outward	..	..	..	..	..	..
Central Asia						
inward	..	..	..	..	..	..
outward	..	..	..	..	..	..
Armenia						
inward	..	..	*1.3*	*1.4*	*3.4*	*6.0*
outward	..	..	..	..	..	..
Azerbaijan						
inward	..	..	..	..	..	..
outward	..	..	..	..	..	..
Georgia						
inward	..	..	..	..	..	..
outward	..	..	..	..	..	..
Kazakhstan						
inward	..	..	..	..	..	..
outward	..	..	..	..	..	..
Kyrgyzstan						
inward	..	..	..	..	..	..
outward	..	..	..	..	..	..
Tajikistan						
inward	..	..	..	..	..	..
outward	..	..	..	..	..	..
Turkmenistan						
inward	..	..	..	..	..	..
outward	..	..	..	..	..	..
Uzbekistan						
inward	..	..	..	..	..	..
outward	..	..	..	..	..	..
South, East and South-East Asia						
inward	***3.6***	***4.5***	***6.5***	***7.9***	***7.5***	***8.3***
outward	***2.0***	***2.9***	***4.2***	***4.8***	***4.7***	***5.0***
Afghanistan						
inward	..	..	..	..	..	..
outward	..	..	..	..	..	..
Bangladesh						
inward	*0.3*	*0.6*	*0.3*	*0.2*	-	*0.3*
outward	-	-	-	-	-	-
Brunei Darussalam						
inward	..	..	..	..	..	..
outward	..	..	..	..	..	..

/...

Annex table B.5. Inward and outward FDI flows as a percentage of gross fixed capital formation, by region and economy, 1986-1996 (continued)

(Percentage)

Region/economy	1986-1991 (Annual average)	1992	1993	1994	1995	1996
Cambodia						
inward	..	..	..	..	..	..
outward	..	..	..	..	..	..
China						
inward	2.9	7.4	12.2	17.3	15.0	17.0
outward	0.7	2.7	2.0	1.0	0.8	0.9
Hong Kong, China						
inward	10.7	7.4	5.3	5.1	4.9	5.2
outward	14.9	29.9	55.9	55.0	58.6	54.6
India						
inward	0.3	0.4	1.0	1.4	2.4	2.9
outward	-	-	-	0.1	0.1	0.3
Indonesia						
inward	2.3	3.9	4.3	3.8	6.7	8.5
outward	-	0.1	0.8	1.1	0.9	0.7
Korea, Democratic People's Republic of						
inward	..	..	..	..	..	..
outward	..	..	..	..	..	..
Korea, Republic of						
inward	1.3	0.6	0.5	0.6	1.1	1.3
outward	1.4	1.1	1.1	1.8	2.1	2.6
Lao People's Democratic Republic						
inward	..	..	..	..	..	..
outward	..	..	..	..	..	..
Macau						
inward	..	..	..	..	..	..
outward	..	..	..	..	..	..
Malaysia						
inward	14.7	26.0	20.3	14.9	11.0	11.1
outward	2.9	2.6	5.4	6.2	6.9	8.8
Maldives						
inward	..	..	..	..	..	..
outward	..	..	..	..	..	..
Mongolia						
inward	..	..	..	..	..	..
outward	..	..	..	..	..	..
Myanmar						
inward	3.0	3.3	2.4	1.0	0.8	0.5
outward	..	..	..	..	..	..
Nepal						
inward	0.3	145.9	0.5	0.6	0.5	2.1
outward	..	..	..	..	..	..
Pakistan						
inward	2.6	3.7	3.8	4.6	7.1	7.1
outward	0.2	-0.1	-	-	-	-
Philippines						
inward	6.6	2.1	9.6	10.5	8.9	7.8
outward	-	-	2.9	2.0	0.6	0.9
Singapore						
inward	37.6	12.4	23.0	35.0	28.9	27.5
outward	6.9	7.4	9.9	15.7	14.0	14.0
Sri Lanka						
inward	2.5	5.4	7.5	5.3	1.7	3.6
outward	0.1	-	0.3	0.3	0.2	0.2
Taiwan Province of China						
inward	3.6	1.8	1.8	2.5	2.7	3.2
outward	11.1	4.0	5.0	4.7	5.2	6.6

/...

Annex table B.5. Inward and outward FDI flows as a percentage of gross fixed capital formation, by region and economy, 1986-1996 (continued)

(Percentage)

Region/economy	1986-1991 (Annual average)	1992	1993	1994	1995	1996
Thailand						
inward	*5.5*	*4.8*	*3.6*	*2.3*	*2.9*	*3.0*
outward	*0.4*	*0.3*	*0.5*	*0.9*	*1.3*	*1.2*
Viet Nam						
inward	..	..	..	..	..	..
outward	..	..	..	..	..	..
The Pacific						
inward	***20.2***	***38.2***	***12.6***	***9.9***	***47.9***	***15.6***
outward	***1.0***	***2.1***	***2.4***	***-0.0***	***-0.2***	***0.8***
Fiji						
inward	*13.7*	*50.1*	*38.0*	*30.6*	*27.3*	*4.3*
outward	*7.2*	*12.5*	*12.0*	*-0.1*	*-1.1*	*4.3*
Kiribati						
inward	..	..	..	..	..	..
outward	..	..	..	..	..	..
New Caledonia						
inward	..	..	..	..	..	..
outward	..	..	..	..	..	..
Papua New Guinea						
inward	*19.5*	*31.0*	*-0.2*	*-0.5*	*49.8*	*12.2*
outward	*-0.3*	..	..	..	..	..
Solomon Islands						
inward	*41.5*	..	..	..	..	..
outward	..	..	..	..	..	..
Tonga						
inward	..	..	..	..	..	..
outward	..	..	..	..	..	..
Vanuatu						
inward	*30.2*	*53.1*	*51.9*	*52.4*	*42.8*	*38.6*
outward	..	..	..	..	..	..
Western Samoa						
inward	..	..	..	..	..	..
outward	..	..	..	..	..	..
Central and Eastern Europe						
inward	***0.1***	***1.1***	***7.4***	***4.7***	***10.2***	***7.5***
outward	**-**	**-**	***0.2***	***0.2***	***0.3***	***0.4***
Albania						
inward	..	..	..	..	..	..
outward	..	..	..	..	..	..
Belarus						
inward	..	*0.4*	*1.9*	*3.1*	*0.3*	*0.7*
outward	..	..	..	..	..	..
Bulgaria						
inward	-	*3.0*	*2.9*	*7.9*	*4.5*	*8.0*
outward	..	..	..	..	*0.4*	*2.1*
Czech Republic						
inward	..	..	*6.8*	*8.0*	*17.5*	*7.7*
outward	..	..	*1.2*	*1.1*	*0.3*	*0.2*
Czechoslovakia (former)						
inward	-	..	..	..	..	..
outward	*0.1*	..	..	..	..	..
Estonia						
inward	..	..	*40.6*	*35.6*	*22.3*	*16.6*
outward	..	..	*1.6*	*0.4*	*0.3*	*4.4*

/...

Annex table B.5. Inward and outward FDI flows as a percentage of gross fixed capital formation, by region and economy, 1986-1996 (continued)

(Percentage)

Region/economy	1986-1991 (Annual average)	1992	1993	1994	1995	1996
Hungary						
inward	6.8	20.1	32.5	13.9	52.8	23.5
outward	-	0.4	0.2	0.6	0.5	-
Latvia						
inward	..	..	..	..	..	..
outward	..	..	..	..	..	..
Lithuania						
inward	..	..	..	..	..	..
outward	..	..	..	..	..	..
Moldova, Republic of						
inward	..	23.2	18.3	8.8	38.6	27.1
outward	..	..	..	..	..	..
Poland						
inward	0.6	4.8	12.6	12.5	18.1	22.2
outward	-	0.1	0.1	0.2	0.2	0.3
Romania						
inward	0.1	2.1	2.0	5.8	7.1	4.5
outward	-	0.2	0.1	-	-	-
Russian Federation						
inward	..	0.2	2.0	0.9	2.8	2.7
outward	..	..	..	0.1	0.4	0.4
Slovakia						
inward	..	..	4.3	6.0	3.8	3.6
outward	..	..	0.4	0.3	0.2	0.7
Ukraine						
inward	..	9.3	2.5	1.8	3.1	5.7
outward	..	..	..	-	0.1	-0.1
Memorandum:						
Least developed countries [a]						
Total						
inward	1.3	1.9	2.0	1.3	1.3	2.2
outward	0.1	0.1	0.1	0.1	-	-
Africa						
inward	5.1	4.2	5.4	5.6	8.2	10.9
outward	0.7	1.0	0.8	0.9	-0.2	-3.4
Latin America and the Caribbean						
inward	1.4	-0.9	-1.4	..	3.8	2.3
outward	-1.1	..	..	..	..	..
Asia						
inward	0.3	1.5	1.5	0.5	0.2	0.9
outward	..	..	..	..	..	..
West Asia						
inward	8.6	32.8	35.9	0.4	-8.7	4.0
outward	..	..	..	..	..	..
South, East and South-East Asia						
inwrad	0.2	0.4	0.3	0.5	0.5	0.8
outward	..	..	..	..	..	..
The Pacific						
inward	37.2	89.5	80.4	77.7	70.8	74.1
outward	..	..	..	-	..	..

/...

Annex table B.5. Inward and outward FDI flows as a percentage of gross fixed capital formation, by region and economy, 1986-1996 (concluded)

(Percentage)

Region/economy	1986-1991 (Annual average)	1992	1993	1994	1995	1996
Oil-exporting countries [b]						
Total						
inward	3.3	3.3	6.6	8.7	8.0	8.2
outward	0.8	0.6	1.8	2.4	1.6	1.2
Africa						
inward	4.0	7.1	7.8	10.8	8.9	7.3
outward	1.8	0.7	1.8	1.2	1.3	1.2
North Africa						
inward	2.5	4.0	3.8	6.3	3.2	3.2
outward	0.2	-	..	0.2	0.3	-
Other Africa						
inward	11.6	20.1	25.3	29.9	34.3	26.2
outward	9.9	3.5	9.3	5.7	5.6	6.7
Latin America and the Caribbean						
inward	7.5	6.4	6.3	13.4	18.2	15.3
outward	0.7	1.0	1.7	2.8	-0.3	-0.1
South America						
inward	4.9	5.8	6.3	10.3	10.9	18.5
outward	1.7	1.0	5.8	4.7	1.8	1.6
Other Latin America and the Caribbean						
inward	8.3	6.6	6.3	14.0	20.8	14.5
outward	0.4	0.9	0.8	2.4	-1.0	-0.5
Asia						
inward	1.8	2.1	6.6	4.9	4.0	5.5
outward	0.6	0.5	1.9	2.4	2.3	1.8
West Asia						
inward	0.5	-	2.7	1.0	-2.5	-1.2
outward	0.5	0.5	1.4	1.8	1.1	-1.4
South, East and South-East Asia						
inwrad	5.5	10.6	9.9	7.7	8.3	9.5
outward	0.7	0.9	2.4	2.9	3.1	3.7
All developing countries minus China						
inward	3.5	3.7	4.7	5.9	5.9	7.1
outward	1.4	1.6	3.2	3.8	3.7	3.8

Source: UNCTAD, FDI/TNC database.

a Least developed countries include: Afghanistan, Angola, Bangladesh, Benin, Burkina Faso, Burundi, Cambodia, Cape Verde, Central African Republic, Chad, Comoros, Democratic Repunlic of Congo, Djibouti, Equatorial Guinea, Ethiopia, The Gambia, Guinea, Guinea-Bissau, Haiti, Kiribati, Lao People's Democratic Republic, Lesotho, Liberia, Malawi, Maldives, Mali, Mauritania, Mozambique, Myanmar, Nepal, Niger, Rwanda, Western Samoa, Sierra Leone, Solomon Islands, Somalia, Sudan, Togo, Uganda, United Republic of Tanzania, Vanuatu, Yemen and Zambia. Not included are Bhutan, Eritrea, Sao Tome and Principe and Tuvalu due to unavailability of data.

b Oil-exporting countries include: Algeria, Angola, Bahrain, Brunei Darussalam, Cameroon, Congo, Ecuador, Egypt, Gabon, Indonesia, Islamic Republic of Iran, Iraq, Kuwait, Libyan Arab Jamahiriya, Malaysia, Mexico, Nigeria, Oman, Qatar, Saudi Arabia, Trinidad and Tobago, Tunisia, United Arab Emirates and Venezuela.

Annex table B.6. Inward and outward FDI stock as a percentage of gross domestic product, by region and economy, 1980, 1985, 1990 and 1996

(Percentage)

Region/economy	1980	1985	1990	1996
Total				
inward	***4.6***	***6.5***	***8.0***	***10.6***
outward	***5.0***	***5.9***	***7.8***	***10.8***
Developed countries				
inward	***3.8***	***4.9***	***6.6***	***7.6***
outward	***5.2***	***5.9***	***7.8***	***10.1***
Western Europe				
inward	***5.6***	***8.7***	***11.0***	***13.1***
outward	***6.7***	***10.5***	***12.5***	***17.9***
European Union				
inward	***5.4***	***8.6***	***10.9***	***13.0***
outward	***6.3***	***10.2***	***12.0***	***16.8***
Austria				
inward	*4.1*	*9.4*	*6.8*	*8.5*
outward	*0.7*	*2.9*	*2.9*	*5.8*
Belgium and Luxembourg				
inward	*6.0*	*22.1*	*28.5*	*45.8*
outward	*4.9*	*11.5*	*19.8*	*31.4*
Denmark				
inward	*6.3*	*6.2*	*7.1*	*13.4*
outward	*3.1*	*3.1*	*5.7*	*12.9*
Finland				
inward	*1.1*	*2.5*	*3.8*	*7.1*
outward	*1.4*	*3.4*	*8.3*	*14.3*
France				
inward	*3.4*	*6.4*	*7.3*	*10.1*
outward	*3.6*	*6.0*	*9.2*	*13.1*
Germany				
inward	*4.5*	*6.0*	*7.4*	*5.9*
outward	*5.3*	*9.5*	*10.1*	*12.4*
Greece				
inward	*11.3*	*24.9*	*16.9*	*16.6*
outward	..	..	*1.0*	*0.7*
Ireland				
inward	*19.5*	*24.5*	*12.2*	*21.0*
outward	..	*1.1*	*4.8*	*7.1*
Italy				
inward	*2.0*	*4.5*	*5.3*	*7.4*
outward	*1.6*	*3.4*	*5.1*	*10.6*
Netherlands				
inward	*11.3*	*19.6*	*26.1*	*30.4*
outward	*24.9*	*35.0*	*38.4*	*49.1*
Portugal				
inward	*4.4*	*6.5*	*7.6*	*6.4*
outward	*0.5*	*0.9*	*0.7*	*3.3*
Spain				
inward	*2.4*	*5.4*	*13.3*	*18.1*
outward	*0.6*	*1.3*	*3.3*	*6.7*
Sweden				
inward	*2.9*	*5.0*	*5.4*	*13.7*
outward	*4.5*	*12.3*	*21.5*	*28.3*
United Kingdom				
inward	*11.7*	*14.0*	*20.8*	*20.5*
outward	*14.9*	*21.9*	*23.4*	*30.7*

/...

Annex table B.6. Inward and outward FDI stock as a percentage of gross domestic product, by region and economy, 1980, 1985, 1990 and 1996 (continued)

(Percentage)

Region/economy	1980	1985	1990	1996
Other Western Europe				
inward	***9.3***	***11.4***	***13.3***	***16.1***
outward	***14.4***	***16.9***	***21.9***	***37.7***
Gibraltar				
inward	..	..	..	..
outward	..	..	..	..
Iceland				
inward	..	*2.4*	*2.4*	*2.7*
outward	*1.8*	*2.0*	*1.2*	*3.3*
Norway				
inward	*11.4*	*12.7*	*10.7*	*13.0*
outward	*3.2*	*7.9*	*9.4*	*18.0*
Switzerland				
inward	*8.4*	*10.8*	*14.8*	*18.0*
outward	*21.1*	*23.0*	*28.8*	*49.2*
North America				
inward	***4.6***	***5.7***	***8.0***	***9.2***
outward	***8.2***	***6.7***	***8.2***	***11.2***
Canada				
inward	*20.4*	*18.5*	*19.7*	*22.0*
outward	*9.0*	*12.3*	*14.8*	*21.3*
United States				
inward	*3.1*	*4.6*	*6.9*	*8.3*
outward	*8.1*	*6.2*	*7.6*	*10.4*
Other developed countries				
inward	***2.7***	***2.7***	***3.0***	***3.8***
outward	***2.2***	***3.7***	***7.0***	***6.2***
Australia				
inward	*8.7*	*15.6*	*25.2*	*29.7*
outward	*1.5*	*4.1*	*10.3*	*11.7*
Israel				
inward	*1.5*	*2.1*	*1.6*	*3.9*
outward	*0.1*	*0.9*	*0.8*	*2.3*
Japan				
inward	*0.3*	*0.4*	*0.3*	*0.7*
outward	*1.9*	*3.3*	*6.8*	*5.6*
New Zealand				
inward	*10.5*	*9.0*	*18.7*	*51.8*
outward	*5.8*	*8.1*	*7.7*	*14.6*
South Africa				
inward	*21.3*	*19.1*	*8.6*	*9.9*
outward	*7.4*	*11.8*	*7.3*	*7.6*
Developing countries				
inward	***4.3***	***8.2***	***8.5***	***15.6***
outward	***0.6***	***1.2***	***1.8***	***4.9***
Africa				
inward	***3.7***	***6.9***	***10.0***	***16.6***
outward	***0.1***	***1.9***	***3.1***	***4.1***
North Africa				
inward	***3.3***	***5.9***	***7.2***	***12.1***
outward	***0.2***	***0.3***	***0.4***	***0.7***

/...

Annex table B.6. Inward and outward FDI stock as a percentage of gross domestic product, by region and economy, 1980, 1985, 1990 and 1996 (continued)

(Percentage)

Region/economy	1980	1985	1990	1996
Algeria				
inward	*3.1*	*2.2*	*2.1*	*3.4*
outward	*0.2*	*0.3*	*0.3*	*0.6*
Egypt				
inward	*9.6*	*12.0*	*23.0*	*24.4*
outward	*0.2*	*0.2*	*0.3*	*0.6*
Libyan Arab Jamahiriya				
inward	..	..	..	..
outward	*0.5*	*0.8*	*1.3*	*1.9*
Morocco				
inward	*1.0*	*3.4*	*3.6*	*9.0*
outward	..	..	..	*0.4*
Sudan				
inward	..	*0.4*	-	*0.1*
outward	..	..	..	..
Tunisia				
inward	*9.0*	*22.0*	*17.8*	*21.8*
outward	..	-	-	*0.1*
Other Africa				
inward	***4.0***	***7.8***	***13.5***	***21.8***
outward	***0.1***	***3.3***	***6.6***	***8.2***
Angola				
inward	*1.7*	*11.1*	*13.2*	*59.8*
outward	..	..	-	-
Benin				
inward	*2.7*	*3.1*	*2.0*	*2.3*
outward	-	*0.2*	*0.1*	*0.1*
Botswana				
inward	*15.5*	*35.1*	*21.7*	*32.8*
outward	*0.3*	*0.2*	*0.3*	*4.9*
Burkina Faso				
inward	*1.4*	*2.4*	*1.5*	*2.1*
outward	*0.2*	*0.3*	*0.1*	*0.1*
Burundi				
inward	*0.7*	*2.0*	*2.5*	*3.3*
outward	..	..	-	*0.1*
Cameroon				
inward	*4.4*	*13.8*	*8.5*	*13.3*
outward	*0.3*	*0.6*	*1.2*	*2.8*
Cape Verde				
inward	..	..	*0.9*	*9.0*
outward	..	..	*0.4*	*0.6*
Central African Republic				
inward	*6.2*	*11.0*	*6.6*	*7.3*
outward	*0.3*	*0.6*	*1.4*	*5.0*
Chad				
inward	*13.0*	*27.9*	*20.9*	*33.9*
outward	*0.1*	*0.2*	*2.9*	*9.3*
Comoros				
inward	..	..	*6.2*	*9.2*
outward	..	..	*0.5*	*0.5*
Congo				
inward	*18.1*	*22.1*	*20.1*	*36.9*
outward	..	..	..	..

/...

Annex table B.6. Inward and outward FDI stock as a percentage of gross domestic product, by region and economy, 1980, 1985, 1990 and 1996 (continued)

(Percentage)

Region/economy	1980	1985	1990	1996
Congo, Democratic Republic				
inward	7.1	11.8	9.9	14.6
outward	..	..	..	..
Côte d'Ivoire				
inward	5.2	10.0	9.9	8.6
outward	..	..	..	..
Djibouti				
inward	0.9	0.9	1.4	3.9
outward	..	..	..	..
Equatorial Guinea				
inward	..	6.3	17.4	386.7
outward	..	..	0.2	0.2
Ethiopia				
inward	2.7	2.4	1.5	2.3
outward	..	..	..	..
Gabon				
inward	11.9	22.7	22.3	20.0
outward	1.8	2.8	3.0	4.0
Gambia, The				
inward	8.7	9.4	11.1	24.2
outward	..	..	..	..
Ghana				
inward	1.5	4.3	5.1	15.3
outward	..	..	..	..
Guinea				
inward	0.1	0.1	2.5	4.4
outward	..	..	..	..
Guinea-Bissau				
inward	-	0.8	3.4	6.0
outward	..	..	..	..
Kenya				
inward	4.8	7.1	7.3	7.7
outward	0.2	1.0	1.2	1.1
Lesotho				
inward	1.2	9.8	13.4	22.9
outward	..	..	-	-
Liberia				
inward	..	9.7	105.2	97.8
outward	5.2	33.8	36.7	26.7
Madagascar				
inward	1.1	1.7	3.3	4.4
outward	..	..	..	..
Malawi				
inward	8.1	12.6	11.6	19.4
outward	..	..	..	..
Mali				
inward	0.9	2.8	1.2	3.6
outward	1.5	1.8	0.9	0.9
Mauritania				
inward	..	4.8	4.9	9.0
outward	..	..	0.2	0.2
Mauritius				
inward	1.8	3.5	6.4	6.6
outward	..	..	0.1	2.2
Mozambique				
inward	0.6	0.7	2.9	15.4
outward	..	..	..	..

/...

Annex table B.6. Inward and outward FDI stock as a percentage of gross domestic product, by region and economy, 1980, 1985, 1990 and 1996 (continued)

(Percentage)

Region/economy	1980	1985	1990	1996
Namibia				
inward	*101.5*	*152.3*	*90.2*	*48.0*
outward	..	..	*3.5*	*0.4*
Niger				
inward	*7.4*	*14.1*	*11.7*	*17.2*
outward	*0.1*	*0.6*	*2.2*	*5.9*
Nigeria				
inward	*2.6*	*5.5*	*24.9*	*39.9*
outward	-	*6.4*	*29.3*	*28.6*
Rwanda				
inward	*4.6*	*7.8*	*9.1*	*18.5*
outward	..	..	..	..
Senegal				
inward	*5.1*	*7.6*	*4.9*	*8.4*
outward	-	*1.5*	*0.8*	*1.8*
Seychelles				
inward	*24.9*	*51.7*	*50.6*	*71.4*
outward	*9.4*	*25.9*	*16.6*	*22.8*
Sierra Leone				
inward	*7.0*	*5.0*	..	..
outward	..	..	..	..
Somalia				
inward	*1.1*	*0.2*	*-0.6*	*-0.5*
outward	..	..	..	..
Swaziland				
inward	*44.8*	*31.1*	*39.1*	*35.5*
outward	*1.7*	*2.7*	*4.7*	*8.7*
Togo				
inward	*15.6*	*27.9*	*16.1*	*19.8*
outward	*0.2*	*0.3*	*0.1*	*0.1*
Uganda				
inward	-	*0.2*	*0.1*	*6.2*
outward	..	..	..	..
United Republic of Tanzania				
inward	*0.9*	*1.4*	*2.1*	*6.8*
outward	..	..	..	..
Zambia				
inward	*0.6*	*5.4*	*18.3*	*29.4*
outward	..	..	..	..
Zimbabwe				
inward	-	*0.5*	*0.9*	*7.7*
outward	..	..	..	..
Latin America and the Caribbean				
inward	***6.4***	***10.8***	***11.5***	***17.4***
outward	***0.4***	***1.0***	***1.2***	***1.5***
South America				
inward	***5.8***	***8.9***	***8.6***	***13.8***
outward	***0.2***	***0.5***	***0.6***	***1.2***
Argentina				
inward	*6.9*	*7.4*	*5.3*	*10.2*
outward	*0.1*	*0.3*	*0.3*	*0.3*
Bolivia				
inward	*13.7*	*14.7*	*14.6*	*28.6*
outward	-	-	*0.1*	*0.3*

/...

Annex table B.6. Inward and outward FDI stock as a percentage of gross domestic product, by region and economy, 1980, 1985, 1990 and 1996 (continued)

(Percentage)

Region/economy	1980	1985	1990	1996
Brazil				
inward	*6.9*	*11.3*	*8.5*	*14.2*
outward	*0.3*	*0.6*	*0.5*	*0.9*
Chile				
inward	*3.2*	*14.1*	*33.1*	*27.3*
outward	*0.2*	*0.6*	*0.6*	*5.4*
Colombia				
inward	*3.2*	*6.4*	*8.7*	*10.8*
outward	*0.4*	*0.9*	*1.0*	*1.4*
Ecuador				
inward	*6.1*	*6.2*	*12.8*	*19.0*
outward	..	..	..	..
Guyana				
inward	..	..	..	*82.8*
outward	..	..	..	*0.4*
Paraguay				
inward	*4.9*	*6.5*	*7.6*	*13.8*
outward	*0.7*	*0.7*	*0.6*	*0.3*
Peru				
inward	*4.3*	*6.7*	*3.8*	*14.9*
outward	-	*0.2*	*0.2*	*0.2*
Suriname				
inward	..	..	..	..
outward	..	..	..	..
Uruguay				
inward	*6.9*	*16.2*	*11.7*	*9.1*
outward	-	-	*0.1*	-
Venezuela				
inward	*2.7*	*2.6*	*8.0*	*13.1*
outward	-	*0.3*	*2.5*	*5.1*
Other Latin America and the Caribbean				
inward	***7.7***	***14.5***	***18.4***	***29.7***
outward	***0.8***	***2.1***	***2.5***	***2.5***
Antigua and Barbuda				
inward	*24.6*	*54.2*	*87.3*	*117.8*
outward	..	..	..	..
Aruba				
inward	..	..	..	..
outward	..	..	..	..
Bahamas				
inward	*25.5*	*12.7*	*10.7*	*18.6*
outward	*24.4*	*6.6*	*49.0*	*38.1*
Barbados				
inward	*11.8*	*10.3*	*9.9*	*12.7*
outward	*0.6*	*1.0*	*1.3*	*1.9*
Belize				
inward	*6.4*	*5.0*	*17.7*	*27.7*
outward	..	..	..	*2.0*
Bermuda				
inward	..	..	..	..
outward	..	..	..	..
Cayman Islands				
inward	..	..	..	..
outward	..	..	..	..

/...

Annex table B.6. Inward and outward FDI stock as a percentage of gross domestic product, by region and economy, 1980, 1985, 1990 and 1996 (continued)

(Percentage)

Region/economy	1980	1985	1990	1996
Costa Rica				
inward	*13.9*	*24.4*	*25.3*	*35.5*
outward	*0.1*	*0.7*	*0.8*	*0.8*
Cuba				
inward	..	..	..	..
outward	..	..	..	..
Dominica				
inward	..	*5.7*	*40.0*	*94.8*
outward	..	..	..	..
Dominican Republic				
inward	*3.6*	*5.2*	*8.1*	*17.3*
outward	..	..	..	*0.4*
El Salvador				
inward	*4.3*	*3.2*	*4.0*	*3.0*
outward	..	..	..	..
Grenada				
inward	*1.7*	*11.0*	*31.7*	*71.3*
outward	..	..	..	..
Guatemala				
inward	*8.9*	*9.4*	*22.5*	*14.4*
outward	..	..	..	..
Haiti				
inward	*5.7*	*5.6*	*5.6*	*5.0*
outward	..	..	..	..
Honduras				
inward	*3.6*	*4.7*	*12.6*	*16.4*
outward	..	..	..	..
Jamaica				
inward	*18.7*	*22.7*	*16.2*	*35.4*
outward	*0.2*	*0.2*	*0.1*	*0.1*
Mexico				
inward	*4.2*	*10.2*	*13.2*	*22.3*
outward	*0.1*	*0.3*	*0.2*	*0.7*
Netherlands Antilles				
inward	*57.6*	*4.6*	*13.2*	*18.4*
outward	*1.0*	*1.0*	*1.5*	*1.4*
Nicaragua				
inward	*5.1*	*4.1*	*0.9*	*17.4*
outward	..	..	..	..
Panama				
inward	*10.8*	*10.8*	*11.7*	*21.9*
outward	*22.6*	*44.5*	*78.8*	*69.8*
Saint Kitts and Nevis				
inward	*2.1*	*40.5*	*105.4*	*125.6*
outward	..	..	..	..
Saint Lucia				
inward	*95.4*	*105.5*	*79.0*	*104.6*
outward	..	..	..	..
Saint Vincent and the Grenadines				
inward	*2.0*	*7.5*	*24.9*	*76.7*
outward	..	..	..	..
Trinidad and Tobago				
inward	*15.7*	*23.3*	*41.3*	*76.5*
outward	..	*0.2*	*0.3*	*0.6*
Virgin Islands				
inward	..	..	..	..
outward	..	..	..	..

/...

Annex table B.6. Inward and outward FDI stock as a percentage of gross domestic product, by region and economy, 1980, 1985, 1990 and 1996 (continued)

(Percentage)

Region/economy	1980	1985	1990	1996
Developing Europe				
inward	***0.3***	***1.1***	***3.5***	***8.1***
outward	..	..	***0.6***	***1.8***
Bosnia and Herzegovina				
inward	..	..	..	..
outward	..	..	..	..
Croatia				
inward	..	..	..	*5.0*
outward	..	..	..	*2.3*
Malta				
inward	*13.8*	*28.2*	*20.1*	*39.3*
outward	..	..	..	*3.6*
Slovenia				
inward	..	..	..	*10.8*
outward	..	..	..	*1.9*
TFYR Macedonia				
inward	..	..	..	*1.1*
outward	..	..	..	..
Yugoslavia (former)				
inward	*0.2*	*0.4*	*1.0*	..
outward	..	..	..	..
Asia				
inward	***3.5***	***7.4***	***7.1***	***14.6***
outward	***0.9***	***1.1***	***1.8***	***6.9***
West Asia				
inward	***2.9***	***9.1***	***5.0***	***9.4***
outward	***0.3***	***0.4***	***0.6***	***1.5***
Bahrain				
inward	..	*8.4*	*15.9*	*12.0*
outward	..	*0.3*	*1.1*	*-0.4*
Cyprus				
inward	*21.4*	*32.6*	*20.6*	*20.1*
outward	..	..	*0.2*	*0.8*
Iran, Islamic Republic of				
inward	*1.2*	*0.5*	-	-
outward	..	..	..	-
Iraq				
inward	..	..	..	..
outward	..	..	..	..
Jordan				
inward	*4.0*	*9.6*	*15.3*	*8.8*
outward	*0.6*	*0.5*	*0.4*	*-1.7*
Kuwait				
inward	*0.1*	*0.2*	*0.1*	*0.4*
outward	*3.3*	*6.1*	*21.9*	*21.2*
Lebanon				
inward	*0.5*	*2.2*	*1.9*	*2.0*
outward	-	*2.6*	*-0.6*	*-0.4*
Oman				
inward	*8.0*	*12.0*	*16.3*	*15.0*
outward	-	*0.4*	*0.1*	-
Qatar				
inward	*1.1*	*1.2*	*0.7*	*3.6*
outward	..	..	..	..

/...

Annex table B.6. Inward and outward FDI stock as a percentage of gross domestic product, by region and economy, 1980, 1985, 1990 and 1996 (continued)

(Percentage)

Region/economy	1980	1985	1990	1996
Saudi Arabia				
inward	*6.6*	*44.1*	*39.4*	*32.0*
outward	*0.1*	*0.5*	*1.7*	*1.5*
Syrian Arab Republic				
inward	..	*0.2*	*1.6*	*2.3*
outward	..	..	..	..
Turkey				
inward	*0.2*	*0.7*	*0.9*	*3.4*
outward	..	..	..	*0.2*
United Arab Emirates				
inward	*1.4*	*1.8*	*2.2*	*3.2*
outward	-	*0.1*	*0.3*	*0.1*
Yemen				
inward	*2.4*	*3.7*	*0.8*	*46.0*
outward	..	*0.1*	*0.1*	*0.1*
Central Asia				
inward	..	..	..	***10.5***
outward	..	..	..	..
Armenia				
inward	..	..	*0.1*	*2.1*
outward	..	..	..	..
Azerbaijan				
inward	..	..	..	*57.3*
outward	..	..	..	..
Georgia				
inward	..	..	..	*5.4*
outward	..	..	..	..
Kazakhstan				
inward	..	..	..	*19.8*
outward	..	..	..	..
Kyrgyzstan				
inward	..	..	..	*80.7*
outward	..	..	..	..
Tajikistan				
inward	..	..	..	*2.0*
outward	..	..	..	..
Turkmenistan				
inward	..	..	..	*5.7*
outward	..	..	..	..
Uzbekistan				
inward	..	..	..	*1.5*
outward	..	..	..	..
South, East and South-East Asia				
inward	***3.8***	***6.6***	***8.8***	***15.8***
outward	***1.3***	***1.4***	***2.7***	***8.1***
Afghanistan				
inward	*0.3*	*0.3*	*0.1*	*0.1*
outward	..	..	..	..
Bangladesh				
inward	*0.4*	*0.7*	*0.7*	*0.7*
outward	..	..	-	-
Brunei Darussalam				
inward	*0.4*	*0.9*	*0.8*	*1.8*
outward	..	..	..	..

/...

Annex table B.6. Inward and outward FDI stock as a percentage of gross domestic product, by region and economy, 1980, 1985, 1990 and 1996 (continued)

(Percentage)

Region/economy	1980	1985	1990	1996
Cambodia				
inward	..	..	..	36.3
outward	..	..	..	..
China				
inward	-	1.5	4.8	24.7
outward	..	-	0.6	2.6
Hong Kong, China				
inward	6.3	10.5	17.9	15.7
outward	0.5	7.0	17.7	71.9
India				
inward	0.7	0.5	0.5	2.6
outward	-	-	-	-
Indonesia				
inward	14.2	28.6	36.6	25.0
outward	..	0.1	-	0.8
Korea, Democratic People's Republic of				
inward	..	..	2.6	3.0
outward	..	..	..	..
Korea, Republic of				
inward	1.8	1.9	2.3	2.6
outward	0.2	0.6	0.9	2.8
Lao People's Democratic Republic				
inward	..	0.1	1.6	20.1
outward	..	..	..	..
Macau				
inward	..	..	..	..
outward	..	..	..	..
Malaysia				
inward	24.8	27.2	33.0	48.6
outward	1.7	2.4	5.3	14.8
Maldives				
inward	11.4	3.8	20.3	18.6
outward	..	..	..	..
Mongolia				
inward	..	..	..	3.2
outward	..	..	..	..
Myanmar				
inward	0.1	0.1	0.7	0.9
outward	..	..	..	..
Nepal				
inward	0.1	0.1	0.3	1.1
outward	..	..	..	..
Pakistan				
inward	2.4	3.3	4.8	8.9
outward	0.1	0.4	0.6	0.5
Philippines				
inward	3.8	4.2	4.7	10.4
outward	0.5	0.6	0.4	1.3
Singapore				
inward	52.9	73.6	76.3	72.4
outward	82.6	54.7	25.8	39.9
Sri Lanka				
inward	5.7	8.6	8.5	10.8
outward	..	..	0.1	0.3
Taiwan, Province of China				
inward	5.8	4.7	6.1	7.3
outward	0.2	0.3	8.1	12.0

/...

Annex table B.6. Inward and outward FDI stock as a percentage of gross domestic product, by region and economy, 1980, 1985, 1990 and 1996 (continued)

(Percentage)

Region/economy	1980	1985	1990	1996
Thailand				
inward	*3.0*	*5.1*	*9.3*	*11.6*
outward	-	-	*0.5*	*1.9*
Viet Nam				
inward	..	*0.2*	*3.3*	*40.2*
outward	..	..	..	..
The Pacific				
inward	***26.4***	***31.2***	***28.6***	***40.3***
outward	***0.5***	***1.2***	***1.4***	***1.8***
Fiji				
inward	*29.8*	*34.4*	*28.2*	*39.4*
outward	*0.8*	*2.0*	*6.9*	*8.7*
Kiribati				
inward	..	..	*4.0*	*8.1*
outward	..	..	..	*0.1*
New Caledonia				
inward	..	..	*1.8*	*5.4*
outward	..	..	..	..
Papua New Guinea				
inward	*27.1*	*31.1*	*46.8*	*54.3*
outward	*0.4*	*1.0*	*0.2*	*0.1*
Solomon Islands				
inward	*19.2*	*19.9*	*32.8*	*63.5*
outward	..	..	..	..
Tonga				
inward	..	*0.2*	*0.7*	*5.0*
outward	..	..	..	-
Vanuatu				
inward	*29.0*	*60.0*	*71.8*	*116.2*
outward	..	..	..	..
Western Samoa				
inward	*0.4*	*0.8*	*5.4*	*16.8*
outward	..	..	..	..
Central and Eastern Europe				
inward	..	..	***0.1***	***5.9***
outward	..	..	..	***0.4***
Albania				
inward	..	..	..	*10.8*
outward	..	..	..	*2.2*
Belarus				
inward	..	..	..	*0.5*
outward	..	..	..	..
Bulgaria				
inward	..	..	-	*4.5*
outward	..	..	..	*0.4*
Czech Republic				
inward	..	..	..	*13.6*
outward	..	..	..	*0.7*
Czechoslovakia (former)				
inward	..	..	..	..
outward	..	..	..	..
Estonia				
inward	..	..	..	*20.4*
outward	..	..	..	*2.0*

/...

Annex table B.6. Inward and outward FDI stock as a percentage of gross domestic product, by region and economy, 1980, 1985, 1990 and 1996 (continued)

(Percentage)

Region/economy	1980	1985	1990	1996
Hungary				
inward	..	..	2.0	33.2
outward	..	..	0.5	1.1
Latvia				
inward	..	..	..	13.5
outward	..	..	..	2.3
Lithuania				
inward	..	..	..	8.3
outward	..	..	..	0.0
Moldova, Republic of				
inward	..	..	..	8.4
outward	..	..	..	1.2
Poland				
inward	..	..	0.2	9.7
outward	..	-	0.2	0.6
Romania				
inward	..	..	..	4.1
outward	..	..	-	0.1
Russian Federation				
inward	..	..	..	1.5
outward	..	..	..	0.2
Slovakia				
inward	..	..	..	5.8
outward	..	..	..	0.5
Ukraine				
inward	..	..	..	3.3
outward	..	..	..	0.2
Memorandum:				
Least developed countries [a]				
Total				
inward	1.8	3.4	3.9	6.1
outward	0.1	0.4	0.4	0.3
Africa				
inward	2.1	4.7	6.2	13.9
outward	0.1	0.7	0.7	0.9
Latin America and the Caribbean				
inward	5.7	5.6	5.6	5.0
outward	..	..	..	..
Asia				
inward	0.5	0.8	0.7	2.7
outward	..	-	-	-
West Asia				
inward	2.4	3.7	0.8	46.0
outward	..	0.1	0.1	0.1
South, East and South-East Asia				
inward	0.3	0.4	0.7	1.5
outward	..	-	-	-
The Pacific				
inward	15.4	27.0	34.7	68.7
outward	..	..	..	-

/...

Annex table B.6. Inward and outward FDI stock as a percentage of gross domestic product, by region and economy, 1980, 1985, 1990 and 1996 (concluded)

(Percentage)

Region/economy	1980	1985	1990	1996
Oil-exporting countries [b]				
Total				
inward	*5.0*	*11.7*	*11.7*	*22.1*
outward	*0.2*	*0.8*	*1.2*	*2.6*
Africa				
inward	*3.6*	*6.8*	*11.8*	*20.3*
outward	*0.2*	*2.4*	*4.8*	*6.4*
North Africa				
inward	*4.0*	*6.4*	*8.9*	*13.7*
outward	*0.3*	*0.3*	*0.5*	*0.8*
Other Africa				
inward	*3.3*	*7.5*	*19.6*	*36.2*
outward	*0.1*	*5.3*	*16.2*	*19.9*
Latin America and the Caribbean				
inward	*4.5*	*10.7*	*13.7*	*23.1*
outward	*0.1*	*0.3*	*0.2*	*0.7*
South America				
inward	*3.7*	*3.9*	*9.3*	*15.5*
outward	-	*0.2*	*1.9*	*3.7*
Other Latin America and the Caribbean				
inward	*4.5*	*10.7*	*13.7*	*23.1*
outward	*0.1*	*0.3*	*0.2*	*0.7*
Asia				
inward	*6.0*	*14.7*	*10.6*	*21.5*
outward	*0.3*	*0.5*	*0.9*	*3.5*
West Asia				
inward	*3.3*	*10.7*	*5.8*	*12.9*
outward	*0.3*	*0.5*	*0.8*	*2.5*
South, East and South-East Asia				
inwrad	*16.1*	*27.5*	*34.8*	*31.0*
outward	*0.4*	*0.7*	*1.5*	*4.5*
All developing countries minus China				
inward	***4.9***	***9.1***	***8.9***	***14.4***
outward	***0.7***	***1.3***	***1.9***	***5.2***

Source: UNCTAD, FDI/TNC database.

a Least developed countries include: Afghanistan, Angola, Bangladesh, Benin, Burkina Faso, Burundi, Cambodia, Cape Verde, Central African Republic, Chad, Comoros, Democratic Repunlic of Congo, Djibouti, Equatorial Guinea, Ethiopia, The Gambia, Guinea, Guinea-Bissau, Haiti, Kiribati, Lao People's Democratic Republic, Lesotho, Liberia, Malawi, Maldives, Mali, Mauritania, Mozambique, Myanmar, Nepal, Niger, Rwanda, Western Samoa, Sierra Leone, Solomon Islands, Somalia, Sudan, Togo, Uganda, United Republic of Tanzania, Vanuatu, Yemen and Zambia. Not included are Bhutan, Eritrea, Sao Tome and Principe and Tuvalu due to unavailability of data.

b Oil-exporting countries include: Algeria, Angola, Bahrain, Brunei Darussalam, Cameroon, Congo, Ecuador, Egypt, Gabon, Indonesia, Islamic Republic of Iran, Iraq, Kuwait, Libyan Arab Jamahiriya, Malaysia, Mexico, Nigeria, Oman, Qatar, Saudi Arabia, Trinidad and Tobago, Tunisia, United Arab Emirates and Venezuela.

Annex table B.7. Cross-border M&A sales, by region/economy of seller, 1990-1997

(Millions of dollars)

Region/economy	1990		1991		1992		1993		1994		1995		1996		1997	
	Majority	Total	Majority	Total	Majority	Total	Majority	Total	Majority	Total	Majority	Total	Majority	Total	Majority	Total
World	**115 637**	**159 959**	**49 062**	**85 279**	**73 769**	**121 894**	**66 812**	**162 344**	**109 549**	**196 367**	**140 813**	**237 184**	**162 686**	**274 611**	**236 216**	**341 653**
Developed economies	**107 128**	**132 762**	**46 544**	**71 439**	**61 611**	**83 712**	**54 956**	**97 832**	**96 669**	**129 123**	**127 880**	**168 420**	**142 292**	**186 411**	**190 983**	**233 768**
Western Europe	**48 395**	**65 688**	**25 266**	**39 753**	**44 379**	**59 248**	**28 531**	**52 420**	**41 290**	**60 932**	**53 787**	**76 295**	**60 221**	**81 822**	**112 116**	**138 313**
European Union	**43 294**	**60 320**	**24 523**	**38 678**	**42 637**	**56 906**	**27 911**	**51 740**	**38 885**	**58 368**	**52 594**	**74 812**	**56 195**	**76 772**	**108 038**	**133 621**
Austria	15	204	317	355	34	549	223	242	249	728	595	1 287	909	949	169	1 316
Belgium and Luxembourg	722	1 095	1 189	1 882	270	1 246	375	3 823	898	2 154	1 616	5 313	1 800	2 068	6 528	7 251
Denmark	439	719	94	130	245	258	599	732	1 860	1 860	260	260	257	417	535	4 452
Finland	129	129	489	526	160	179	436	551	35	203	256	340	1 090	1 151	352	410
France	4 494	6 268	2 618	4 965	6 678	8 772	3 756	5 042	8 859	12 491	10 208	12 751	5 673	11 414	12 582	14 518
Germany	5 995	7 920	2 666	4 992	5 269	7 651	1 541	5 930	5 987	9 871	5 336	6 212	5 408	6 550	16 663	19 262
Greece	100	120	40	40	739	739	-	34	-	96	153	555	47	49	309	464
Ireland	460	537	144	264	230	230	1 431	1 588	73	275	522	1 154	260	587	1 489	1 600
Italy	3 727	4 731	1 227	1 971	3 146	4 635	2 802	3 212	3 259	5 311	2 480	3 441	2 871	5 206	4 499	9 173
Netherlands	1 416	2 029	1 331	2 462	5 129	5 994	4 253	10 813	1 242	2 346	2 381	2 542	2 970	3 647	8 536	8 837
Portugal	279	3 581	99	232	519	833	196	414	243	856	408	551	683	748	4	912
Spain	3 970	6 241	3 362	6 371	3 575	4 390	1 028	2 775	2 854	5 153	1 340	1 996	823	1 786	2 130	6 213
Sweden	1 102	1 509	1 026	1 499	1 566	2 684	3 388	3 771	2 331	2 468	1 600	2 074	1 558	2 630	3 116	3 803
United Kingdom	20 216	25 005	8 987	12 057	15 078	18 747	7 100	12 029	10 901	14 460	25 439	36 337	31 502	39 226	51 126	55 411
Unspecified	232	232	933	933	-	-	783	783	94	94	-	-	344	344	-	-
Other Western Europe	**5 101**	**5 368**	**744**	**1 075**	**1 742**	**2 341**	**620**	**680**	**2 404**	**2 564**	**1 193**	**1 483**	**4 026**	**5 050**	**4 078**	**4 692**
Gibraltar	-	-	-	9	-	-	-	-	-	-	-	-	-	-	-	-
Iceland	-	1	-	-	-	-	-	-	-	-	-	-	3	3	-	18
Monaco	-	75	-	-	-	-	-	-	10	11	-	-	-	-	2	2
Norway	984	1 049	65	358	1 622	1 931	144	182	422	422	349	458	480	493	963	1 407
Switzerland	4 117	4 243	679	707	120	411	454	475	1 973	2 131	844	1 025	3 375	4 386	2 946	3 098
Unspecified	-	-	-	-	-	-	22	22	-	-	-	-	167	167	167	167
North America	**53 215**	**60 042**	**19 604**	**26 092**	**14 023**	**19 183**	**23 103**	**40 277**	**52 165**	**62 866**	**60 625**	**74 019**	**70 465**	**81 358**	**66 517**	**77 167**
Canada	5 417	5 746	1 753	2 277	3 561	5 246	3 311	5 550	5 609	6 494	9 680	11 115	9 512	10 437	8 351	12 016
United States	47 798	54 297	17 851	23 815	10 463	13 938	19 792	34 727	46 556	56 372	50 944	62 903	60 953	70 921	58 166	65 151
Other developed economies	**5 517**	**7 033**	**1 673**	**5 595**	**3 209**	**5 281**	**3 322**	**5 135**	**3 216**	**5 325**	**13 468**	**18 106**	**11 605**	**23 231**	**12 350**	**18 288**
Australia	2 137	3 499	1 003	2 921	1 016	2 098	2 026	3 182	1 462	2 628	10 304	12 349	3 935	10 043	10 013	12 693
Israel	-	27	-	-	40	257	9	101	60	85	381	1 321	1 376	1 711	149	1 108
Japan	24	102	84	1 399	309	775	81	279	1 302	1 690	681	1 573	2 163	4 780	342	1 053
New Zealand	3 357	3 388	577	1 265	1 844	2 141	1 183	1 459	322	696	1 404	1 821	1 527	3 519	923	983
South Africa	-	17	9	9	1	10	23	115	70	226	279	622	2 604	3 179	923	2 452
Unspecified	-	-	1	1	-	-	-	-	-	-	420	420	-	-	-	-
Developing economies	**7 785**	**18 177**	**1 425**	**10 659**	**8 460**	**32 174**	**9 648**	**48 670**	**9 297**	**60 983**	**9 166**	**52 746**	**18 443**	**83 396**	**41 029**	**95 620**
Africa	**244**	**254**	**73**	**129**	**290**	**422**	**701**	**1 446**	**447**	**2 014**	**75**	**2 475**	**543**	**2 784**	**1 813**	**2 117**
North Africa	**-**	**-**	**-**	**56**	**221**	**298**	**185**	**239**	**398**	**1 926**	**18**	**1 937**	**154**	**1 926**	**1 106**	**1 253**
Algeria	-	-	-	-	-	66	-	23	-	1 300	-	1 750	-	254	-	-
Egypt	-	-	-	56	125	133	180	211	9	124	18	162	84	1 288	78	89
Morocco	-	-	-	-	-	2	5	5	390	502	-	25	70	84	1 009	1 144
Sudan	-	-	-	-	8	8	-	-	-	-	-	-	-	300	-	-

/...

Annex table B.7. Cross-border M&A sales, by region/economy of seller, 1990-1997 (continued)

(Millions of dollars)

Region/economy	1990		1991		1992		1993		1994		1995		1996		1997	
	Majority	Total	Majority	Total	Majority	Total	Majority	Total	Majority	Total	Majority	Total	Majority	Total	Majority	Total
Tunisia	-	-	-	-	88	88	-	-	-	-	-	-	-	-	19	19
Other Africa	**244**	**254**	**73**	**74**	**69**	**125**	**516**	**1 207**	**49**	**88**	**58**	**537**	**389**	**858**	**707**	**864**
Angola	-	10	-	-	-	-	-	-	-	9	-	-	-	-	-	5
Bostwana	-	-	-	-	8	8	-	-	5	5	-	-	-	-	-	-
Central African Republic	-	-	-	-	-	-	4	4	-	-	-	-	-	-	-	-
Congo	-	-	-	-	-	-	-	-	-	-	-	-	14	14	-	-
Côte d'Ivoire	-	-	-	-	21	21	-	-	-	-	1	1	2	2	193	193
Gabon	-	-	-	-	-	-	-	-	-	-	-	139	-	-	0	-
Ghana	-	-	-	-	-	4	-	-	-	30	-	-	-	47	124	124
Guinea	-	-	-	-	-	-	-	-	-	-	-	39	-	-	3	3
Kenya	-	-	73	73	8	8	-	-	-	-	-	-	-	25	-	25
Lesotho	-	-	-	-	-	-	-	-	5	5	-	-	-	-	-	-
Madagascar	-	-	-	-	-	-	-	-	-	-	-	-	58	58	-	-
Mali	-	-	-	-	-	-	-	160	-	-	-	-	53	53	-	
Mozambique	-	-	-	-	-	-	-	1	20	20	14	14	2	2	-	-
Namibia	-	-	-	-	-	-	-	-	5	5	-	-	-	4	-	
Nigeria	-	-	-	-	-	4	-	285	-	-	-	95	-	252	-	
Senegal	-	-	-	-	-	3	-	-	-	-	-	-	-	137	-	109
Sierra Leone	-	-	-	-	-	-	34	34	8	8	-	-	-	-	-	
Swaziland	-	-	-	-	-	-	-	-	5	5	-	136	-	-	-	-
Uganda	-	-	-	-	8	53	-	-	-	-	-	-	-	-	-	11
United Republic of Tanzania	-	-	-	-	-	-	-	-	2	2	-	56	13	13	-	-
Zaire	-	-	-	-	8	8	-	-	-	-	-	-	247	247	-	-
Zambia	-	-	-	-	8	8	1	34	-	-	-	15	-	-	-	7
Zimbabwe	-	-	-	-	8	8	1	212	-	-	43	43	1	4	16	16
Unspecified	244	244	-	-	-	-	477	477	-	-	-	-	-	-	371	371
Latin America and the Caribbean	**6 838**	**8 426**	**953**	**3 898**	**6 146**	**10 372**	**3 806**	**13 659**	**3 126**	**14 831**	**6 034**	**11 374**	**11 162**	**22 257**	**25 579**	**43 809**
South America	**5 774**	**6 156**	**646**	**2 850**	**4 648**	**8 238**	**3 225**	**8 419**	**2 452**	**10 648**	**4 877**	**7 894**	**9 998**	**18 359**	**17 541**	**31 280**
Argentina	5 267	5 541	110	280	3 917	4 843	1 097	2 050	699	2 177	1 505	2 346	2 399	3 907	2 612	5 900
Bolovia	7	7	-	-	-	14	-	6	-	2 551	704	802	-	571	104	104
Brazil	57	57	67	68	392	470	1 084	1 226	8	1 351	1 458	2 557	3 112	4 675	10 381	12 568
Chile	397	467	131	283	10	2 295	81	275	817	1 377	183	1 036	1 116	2 135	1 263	2 253
Colombia	7	22	22	22	-	-	1	1	23	85	50	152	1 672	1 672	1 411	3 110
Ecuador	-	-	-	-	-	-	-	-	80	80	22	60	-	-	28	28
Guyana	17	-	-	-	-	45	-	-	-	-	-	-	-	-	-	-
Peru	-	-	-	-	324	324	584	903	445	2 628	668	688	1 042	1 225	544	582
Uraguay	18	18	-	-	-	-	5	5	55	55	20	20	14	14	1	1
Venezuela	6	45	192	2 197	-	247	16	3 953	325	344	120	234	635	4 161	1 197	6 734
Unspecified	-	-	125	-	5	-	358	-	-	-	147	-	7	-	-	-
Other Latin America and the Caribbean	**1 063**	**2 270**	**307**	**1 048**	**1 499**	**2 133**	**581**	**5 240**	**674**	**4 183**	**1 157**	**3 480**	**1 164**	**3 898**	**8 038**	**12 530**
Aruba	23	23														

/...

Annex table B.7. Cross-border M&A sales, by region/economy of seller, 1990-1997 (continued)

(Millions of dollars)

Region/economy	1990		1991		1992		1993		1994		1995		1996		1997	
	Majority	Total	Majority	Total	Majority	Total	Majority	Total	Majority	Total	Majority	Total	Majority	Total	Majority	Total
Bahamas	14	14	-	-	915	915	135	214	-	80	-	-	70	70	35	35
Barbados	-	-	-	-	-	-	4	4	-	-	-	8	64	64	153	153
Belize	-	-	-	-	-	-	-	-	-	-	-	-	-	-	-	-
Bermuda	546	554	10	10	55	180	-	139	47	52	241	1 028	-	447	1 068	1 368
Cayman Islands	-	-	-	-	-	-	-	-	-	-	10	10	-	100	46	46
Costa Rica	-	-	-	-	-	-	-	-	16	16	75	93	22	68	1	1
Cuba	-	-	-	-	-	-	-	20	-	1 100	10	15	40	43	3	1 297
Dominican Republic	-	-	-	-	-	-	-	-	-	6	-	-	47	62	-	-
El Salvador	-	-	-	-	-	-	-	-	-	-	40	40	-	-	24	24
Grenada	-	-	-	-	-	-	-	-	-	-	-	-	-	-	-	-
Guatemala	-	-	-	-	-	-	-	-	-	-	2	2	26	26	-	-
Guyana	-	17	-	100	-	-	-	-	-	-	-	-	-	-	-	23
Honduras	122	122														
Jamaica	-	-	-	-	-	-	63	63	22	196	-	-	6	12	-	1
Martinique	-	4	-	-	-	-	-	-	-	-	-	-	-	-	-	-
Mexico	503	1 681	297	813	529	797	183	3 947	295	2 326	503	1 435	791	2 847	5 821	8 034
Netherlands Antilles	-	-	-	-	-	-	-	-	216	216	-	-	-	-	-	-
Nicaragua	-	-	-	-	-	-	1	1	6	6	-	-	18	18	122	122
Panama	-	-	-	-	-	-	-	-	71	71	259	260	-	-	3	655
Saint Kitts and Nevis	-	-	-	-	-	-	-	-	-	-	-	-	78	78	-	-
Trinidad and Tobago	-	-	-	-	-	238	175	475	-	112	-	125	-	-	205	205
Virgin Islands	-	-	-	-	-	-	-	-	-	-	17	17	2	57	412	421
Unspecified	-	-	-	125	-	5	20	378	1	1	-	447	-	7	-	-
Developing Europe	**22**	**108**	**50**	**158**	**127**	**127**	**1**	**1**	**9**	**69**	**89**	**227**	**-**	**-**	**191**	**1 144**
Croatia	-	-	-	-	-	-	-	-	-	60	55	187	-	-	57	91
Slovenia	-	-	-	-	127	127	1	1	9	9	34	34	-	-	120	120
Former Yugoslavia	22	108	50	158	-	-	-	-	-	-	-	6	-	-	14	934
Asia	**681**	**9 386**	**321**	**6 437**	**1 879**	**21 235**	**5 136**	**33 542**	**5 657**	**44 011**	**2 958**	**38 610**	**3 921**	**55 538**	**13 374**	**48 377**
West Asia	**31**	**208**	**18**	**198**	**184**	**4 251**	**29**	**1 289**	**-**	**1 395**	**273**	**2 400**	**31**	**5 528**	**54**	**4 870**
Bahrain	-	309														
Cyprus	-	-	-	-	-	-	-	-	-	-	-	-	31	1 431	-	-
Iran, Islamic Republic	-	-	-	-	-	520	-	5	-	-	-	-	-	180	-	1
Jordan	-	-	-	-	-	216	-	-	-	-	-	-	-	152	-	-
Kuwait	-	-	-	51	-	-	-	-	-	1 100	-	-	-	42	-	-
Lebanon	-	-	-	-	5	5	-	-	-	-	-	-	-	-	-	-
Oman	-	-	-	-	-	3 019	-	15	-	-	-	1	-	1 875	-	92
Qatar	-	-	-	-	-	1	-	300	-	281	-	-	-	-	-	368
Saudi Arabia	-	-	-	100	24	24	-	8	-	-	8	34	-	1 100	-	75
Syria	-	11														
Turkey	31	208	18	47	93	402	29	961	-	13	265	265	-	542	15	1 028
United Arab Emirates	-	-	-	-	-	1	-	-	-	-	-	-	-	207	39	437
Yemen	-	-	-	-	-	-	-	-	-	-	-	2 100	-	-	-	2 549

/...

Annex table B.7. Cross-border M&A sales, by region/economy of seller, 1990-1997 (continued)

(Millions of dollars)

Region/economy	1990		1991		1992		1993		1994		1995		1996		1997	
	Majority	Total	Majority	Total	Majority	Total	Majority	Total	Majority	Total	Majority	Total	Majority	Total	Majority	Total
Unspecified	-	-	-	-	63	63	-	-	-	-	-	-	-	-	-	-
Central Asia	-	-	-	**40**	-	**45**	**510**	**1 547**	**300**	**685**	**450**	**859**	**512**	**7 051**	**3 556**	**5 865**
Armenia	143	143														
Azerbaijan	-	-	-	-	-	30	-	713	-	300	-	-	-	5 330	..	245
Kazakhstan	-	-	-	40	-	-	510	510	100	185	450	859	512	1 551	3 163	5 033
Tajikistan	150	150														
Turkmenistan	-	-	-	-	-	-	-	70	-	-	-	-	-	50	..	..
Uzbekistan	-	-	-	-	-	15	-	254	200	200	-	-	-	120	100	294
South, East and South-East Asia	**650**	**9 178**	**304**	**6 198**	**1 695**	**16 939**	**4 598**	**30 707**	**5 357**	**41 932**	**2 234**	**35 352**	**3 378**	**42 959**	**9 764**	**37 643**
Bangladesh	-	-	-	-	-	-	-	-	-	-	-	17	-	-	-	15
Brunei Darussalam	-	1	-	-	-	-	-	-	-	-	-	-	-	-	-	667
Cambodia	-	-	-	-	-	-	-	-	-	30	25	667	-	63	-	-
China	-	1 938	16	2 988	94	5 197	639	13 458	976	20 126	636	11 993	602	15 533	960	11 011
Hong Kong, China	191	1 856	90	371	1 252	3 225	2 882	7 372	891	1 769	458	880	637	2 886	2 031	6 160
India	-	5	52	213	13	262	105	1 854	327	2 880	148	3 311	45	3 768	194	2 855
Indonesia	-	792	13	275	42	2 287	286	1 421	199	6 507	126	4 125	118	2 654	2 328	4 312
Korea, Democratic People's Republic	-	223	-	712	31	-	34	-	-	-	102	-	122	-	-	-
Korea, Republic of	-	-	14	-	-	122	-	59	-	827	-	270	-	716	724	1 387
Lao People's Democratic Republic	-	-	-	-	-	-	10	10	-	-	-	-	-	2	-	-
Macau	-	6	-	-	-	-	-	-	-	38	-	-	-	-	-	-
Malaysia	72	842	57	1 004	14	1 197	139	541	215	393	16	821	40	4 497	198	2 361
Mongolia	-	-	-	-	-	-	-	-	-	1	-	5	-	-	3	3
Myanmar	-	64	-	5	-	-	10	15	10	104	-	632	-	134	-	6
Nepal	-	-	-	-	-	-	-	-	-	-	-	12	-	-	-	-
Pakistan	-	22	-	-	-	8	5	5	1 730	2 146	-	15	151	2 501	39	243
Philippines	-	2 576	55	123	89	576	30	679	577	1 824	177	2 966	956	2 708	2 059	2 835
Singapore	386	633	4	127	149	450	403	2 071	306	1 145	323	597	659	1 692	95	1 208
Sri Lanka	-	-	-	-	-	1	12	24	59	61	43	2 873	19	19	35	267
Taiwan Province of China	1	93	4	145	-	822	22	165	32	581	-	860	21	2 410	724	1 108
Thailand	-	116	-	152	-	2 556	20	330	36	605	171	2 963	5	2 063	317	1 405
Viet Nam	-	10	-	49	11	227	-	2 329	-	2 894	10	1 975	5	1 300	57	901
Unspecified	-	-	-	33	-	7	-	374	-	-	-	371	-	13	-	900
The Pacific	-	**3**	**28**	**37**	**18**	**18**	**4**	**22**	**58**	**58**	**10**	**60**	**2 817**	**2 817**	**72**	**173**
Borneo	-	-	-	10	-	-	-	-	-	-	-	-	-	-	..	..
Fiji	-	3	-	-	-	-	-	-	-	-	-	-	-	-	72	72
Papua New Guinea	-	-	28	28	18	18	2	20	58	58	10	60	117	117	..	45
Solomon Islands	-	-	-	-	-	-	2	2	-	-	-	-	-	-	..	..
Vanuatu	56															
Unspecified	-	-	-	-	-	-	-	-	-	-	-	-	2 700	2 700	..	..

/...

Annex table B.7. Cross-border M&A sales, by region/economy of seller, 1990-1997 (concluded)

(Millions of dollars)

Region/economy	1990		1991		1992		1993		1994		1995		1996		1997	
	Majority	Total	Majority	Total	Majority	Total	Majority	Total	Majority	Total	Majority	Total	Majority	Total	Majority	Total
Central and Eastern Europe	**60**	**8 355**	**949**	**3 038**	**3 692**	**6 008**	**1 850**	**15 843**	**2 045**	**4 904**	**3 459**	**16 018**	**1 579**	**4 147**	**4 069**	**9 883**
Albania	-	-	-	-	-	-	-	-	-	70	-	-	-	27	-	-
Belarus	-	-	-	-	-	-	-	7	-	-	-	-	-	10	-	-
Bulgaria	-	-	-	2	-	25	18	38	194	272	18	18	203	203	168	174
Czech Republic	-	-	387	-	-	-	21	160	740	1 009	112	2 330	61	157	492	781
Czechoslovakia (former)	-	5 159	-	969	750	1 222	-	-	-	-	-	-	-	-	-	-
Estonia	-	-	-	-	-	42	-	10	9	9	41	41	-	13	10	10
Hungary	60	560	147	534	369	902	299	1 509	54	247	1 578	1 770	448	607	1 016	1 162
Latvia	-	-	-	-	2	2	25	25	2	162	-	25	-	10	-	75
Lithuania	-	-	-	-	-	2	56	56	-	2	-	2	-	-	7	7
Macedonia, Republic of	-	-	-	-	-	-	-	-	-	-	-	-	2	2	-	18
Moldova, Republic of	-	-	-	-	-	-	-	-	-	-	-	10	-	-	-	-
Poland	-	522	398	748	2 545	3 017	728	1 112	851	1 167	1 518	2 037	788	1 167	513	2 108
Romania	-	1	14	51	-	53	650	720	21	209	24	86	18	117	414	421
Russian Federation	-	-	-	1	-	272	50	12 155	174	1 698	140	9 480	-	1 686	1 449	4 077
Slovakia	-	-	-	-	-	-	3	27	-	39	3	62	59	59	-	-
Former Soviet Union	-	2 114	3	733	26	452	-	-	-	-	-	-	-	-	-	-
Ukraine	-	-	-	-	-	18	-	23	-	20	25	157	-	88	-	150
Unspecified CEE	900															
Dual nationality	665	665	3	3	-	-	-	-	-	-	-	-	1	1	135	1 626
Multinational[a]	-	-	140	140	-	-	-	-	-	-	-	-	248	545	-	737
Unknown country	-	-	-	-	-	-	358	-	1 344	1 357	308	-	124	656	-	19

Source: UNCTAD, based on data provided by KPMG Corporate Finance.

[a] Involving sellers in more than two economies.

Note: "Majority" refers to business combinations in which the foreign investor acquires more than 50 per cent of the voting securities of the resulting business.

Annex table B.8. Cross-border M&A purchases, by region/economy of purchaser, 1990-1997

(Millions of dollars)

Region/economy	1990		1991		1992		1993		1994		1995		1996		1997	
	Majority	Total	Majority	Total	Majority	Total	Majority	Total	Majority	Total	Majority	Total	Majority	Total	Majority	Total
World	**115 637**	**159 959**	**49 062**	**85 279**	**73 769**	**121 894**	**66 812**	**162 344**	**109 356**	**196 367**	**140 813**	**237 184**	**162 686**	**275 156**	**236 216**	**341 653**
Developed economies	**111 195**	**152 201**	**47 351**	**79 900**	**58 824**	**99 168**	**59 292**	**134 895**	**100 223**	**163 010**	**132 344**	**212 084**	**152 224**	**239 139**	**217 251**	**299 173**
Western Europe	**71 132**	**97 436**	**34 071**	**53 820**	**35 089**	**55 197**	**36 584**	**77 047**	**65 368**	**92 644**	**70 235**	**108 130**	**81 688**	**129 846**	**127 148**	**168 316**
European Union	**65 232**	**90 967**	**31 577**	**50 537**	**30 960**	**50 017**	**35 531**	**74 770**	**51 879**	**75 333**	**64 161**	**98 725**	**72 339**	**114 316**	**89 677**	**127 787**
Austria	163	509	128	198	167	197	17	94	-	44	238	448	2	51	208	798
Belgium and Luxembourg	1 067	1 425	1 061	1 572	1 387	1 794	1 899	2 626	1 754	1 929	4 297	8 720	725	1 430	2 493	4 564
Denmark	541	642	354	1 090	797	1 064	429	613	221	706	376	1 263	3 405	3 846	1 238	1 319
Finland	1 131	1 460	349	700	19	287	348	572	476	496	1 133	1 419	305	402	1 584	1 956
France	16 842	22 312	11 174	15 904	8 858	14 204	6 818	10 684	6 140	11 497	8 079	13 318	7 921	11 514	12 495	21 620
Germany	7 038	15 975	4 680	7 501	4 106	6 508	3 264	6 731	8 523	13 191	15 536	22 616	12 111	27 380	10 191	16 047
Greece	-	-	-	5	7	7	661	679	67	68	-	-	2	12	143	545
Ireland	774	861	484	602	427	527	576	591	2 311	2 431	1 189	1 695	3 682	3 869	3 318	3 709
Italy	3 673	5 601	2 119	4 799	6 034	7 642	571	5 902	1 184	2 378	2 983	3 805	1 236	3 046	939	4 041
Netherlands	2 287	4 166	3 754	6 672	1 397	6 038	4 696	12 004	2 484	4 584	5 970	9 620	16 113	19 987	18 224	20 748
Portugal	-	1	165	165	309	309	11	162	218	242	227	247	180	222	442	442
Spain	2 178	2 608	354	690	676	1 159	247	1 392	455	2 346	1 298	1 944	3 283	6 273	7 055	13 162
Sweden	9 434	9 842	840	2 310	691	1 091	1 703	3 385	1 033	2 067	3 020	6 619	959	1 455	4 677	6 219
United Kingdom	20 103	25 566	5 901	8 087	6 085	9 183	14 258	29 146	27 013	33 355	19 816	26 958	22 415	34 822	26 672	32 615
Unspecified	-	-	215	240	1	9	33	189	-	-	-	53	-	9	-	-
Other Western Europe	**5 901**	**6 470**	**2 494**	**3 283**	**4 130**	**5 180**	**1 053**	**2 277**	**13 489**	**17 311**	**6 074**	**9 404**	**9 349**	**15 531**	**37 471**	**40 530**
Liechtenstein	-	15	53	53	-	-	-	1	-	14	2	82	317	317	-	-
Norway	1 234	1 473	85	228	320	1 140	214	377	482	1 026	1 431	3 535	3 044	4 937	748	1 793
Switzerland	4 667	4 981	2 356	3 002	3 810	4 040	839	1 900	13 007	16 271	4 641	5 788	5 988	10 277	36 723	38 737
North America	**19 971**	**26 234**	**8 446**	**15 690**	**16 065**	**26 361**	**19 763**	**44 655**	**28 921**	**52 042**	**52 223**	**80 386**	**60 967**	**87 496**	**77 356**	**106 149**
Canada	3 956	4 544	1 349	2 498	1 680	3 562	4 465	6 849	4 185	8 570	12 652	14 806	18 757	22 150	21 301	24 707
United States	16 015	21 691	7 096	13 192	14 385	22 798	15 298	37 806	24 736	43 472	39 571	65 580	42 210	65 346	56 055	81 442
Other developed economie	**20 092**	**28 531**	**4 835**	**10 390**	**7 670**	**17 610**	**2 946**	**13 194**	**5 934**	**18 324**	**9 887**	**23 568**	**9 569**	**21 797**	**12 747**	**24 708**
Australia	1 842	2 084	819	1 039	1 595	2 733	1 171	2 966	1 400	3 856	4 870	5 569	4 290	5 437	6 691	9 914
Israel	32	41	4	24	35	35	357	357	127	141	85	102	376	1 236	171	682
Japan	17 342	25 133	3 675	8 959	4 188	12 525	437	7 194	1 143	10 467	4 113	16 963	4 096	12 573	4 123	11 710
New Zealand	664	974	128	141	429	603	329	808	-	78	440	481	232	1 060	223	375
South Africa	211	298	208	226	1 423	1 713	652	1 870	3 264	3 783	378	453	575	1 491	1 538	2 027
Unspecified	-	-	1	1	-	-	-	-	-	-	-	-	-	-	-	-
Developing economies	**4 442**	**7 548**	**1 605**	**5 199**	**14 546**	**22 319**	**7 378**	**26 858**	**9 183**	**32 365**	**8 463**	**24 464**	**10 264**	**32 827**	**18 414**	**40 853**
Africa	**140**	**140**	**104**	**156**	-	**306**	**41**	**56**	**74**	**74**	-	**78**	**708**	**708**	-	**110**
North Africa	**140**	**140**	-	**52**	-	**306**	**41**	**56**	**49**	**49**	-	-	**645**	**645**	-	**60**
Egypt	-	-	-	51	-	-	-	-	-	-	-	-	-	-	-	60
Libyan Arab Jamahiriya	-	140	-	1	-	306	5	5	-	-	-	-	-	-	-	-
Morocco	140	-	-	-	-	-	36	51	-	-	-	-	-	-	-	-
Other Africa	-	-	**104**	**104**	-	-	-	-	**25**	**25**	-	**78**	**63**	**63**	-	**50**
Cameroon	-	-	-	-	-	-	-	-	25	25	-	-	-	-	-	-
Central African Republic	-	-	-	-	-	-	-	-	-	-	-	-	63	63	-	
Gabon	-	-	-	104	-	-	-	-	-	-	-	-	-	-	-	-
Gambia, The	-	-	104	-	-	-	-	-	-	-	-	78	-	-	-	-
Ghana	-	-	-	-	-	-	-	-	-	-	-	-	519	519	-	
Mauritius	50															

/...

Annex table B.8. Cross-border M&A purchases, by region/economy of purchaser, 1990-1997 (continued)

(Millions of dollars)

Region/economy	1990 Majority	1990 Total	1991 Majority	1991 Total	1992 Majority	1992 Total	1993 Majority	1993 Total	1994 Majority	1994 Total	1995 Majority	1995 Total	1996 Majority	1996 Total	1997 Majority	1997 Total
Latin America and the Caribbean	**3**	**383**	**129**	**728**	**4 542**	**5 092**	**2 222**	**3 380**	**2 495**	**8 538**	**2 113**	**2 794**	**4 200**	**5 204**	**4 293**	**7 221**
South America	-	-	**17**	**187**	**184**	**533**	**1 105**	**1 345**	**582**	**5 001**	**1 720**	**2 111**	**2 849**	**3 126**	**1 717**	**4 022**
Argentina	-	-	-	-	-	-	57	57	42	96	837	902	404	414	333	1 103
Bolovia	-	-	-	-	-	-	-	-	-	1 200	-	-	-	-	-	-
Brazil	-	-	17	17	2	30	433	447	105	3 032	167	275	14	14	-	120
Chile	-	-	-	170	182	435	609	609	16	249	658	763	2 172	2 210	1 201	2 615
Colombia	-	-	-	-	-	-	-	-	-	-	53	83	-	100	83	83
Peru	-	-	-	-	-	-	-	-	-	-	5	5	-	-	-	-
Surinam	-	-	-	-	-	-	-	4	-	-	-	-	-	-	-	-
Uruguay	-	-	-	-	-	-	-	-	-	4	-	8	-	-	-	-
Venezuela	-	-	-	-	-	68	5	229	420	420	-	75	259	388	100	100
Other Latin America and the Caribbean	**3**	**383**	**112**	**541**	**4 358**	**4 559**	**1 117**	**2 035**	**1 913**	**3 538**	**393**	**683**	**1 351**	**2 078**	**2 576**	**3 199**
Bahamas	3	5	-	-	-	-	-	-	-	-	-	31	1	701	40	40
Barbados	-	-	-	-	-	-	-	-	-	8	-	-	-	-	-	-
Belize	-	-	-	-	-	-	-	-	14	14	-	18	-	-	-	-
Bermuda	-	-	107	107	1 500	1 500	697	922	6	182	299	414	424	434	1 131	1 136
Cayman Islands	-	-	-	-	-	-	31	52	-	140	-	-	-	-	2	33
Dominican Republic	-	-	-	-	-	-	-	-	100	100	-	-	-	-	-	-
Grenada	-	-	-	-	-	-	-	-	-	4	-	-	-	-	-	-
Mexico	-	-	-	79	2 828	2 999	357	587	1 784	3 063	94	169	717	733	290	743
Netherlands Antilles	-	6	-	-	-	30	32	474	-	14	-	-	-	-	12	12
Panama	-	373	5	355	30	30	-	-	-	-	-	-	14	14	1 100	1 200
Saint Kitts and Nevis	-	-	-	-	-	-	-	-	-	2	-	-	-	-	-	-
Trinidad and Tobago	-	-	-	-	-	-	-	-	-	3	-	-	-	-	-	-
Virgin Islands	-	-	-	-	-	-	-	-	9	9	-	51	195	195	-	35
Developing Europe	-	-	-	-	-	-	**5**	**5**	-	-	-	-	-	-	-	-
Malta	-	-	-	-	-	-	5	5	-	-	-	-	-	-	-	-
Asia	**4 299**	**7 024**	**1 372**	**4 315**	**10 003**	**16 921**	**5 110**	**23 417**	**6 614**	**23 753**	**6 350**	**21 591**	**5 356**	**26 915**	**14 120**	**33 522**
West Asia	**2 122**	**2 230**	**563**	**1 832**	**509**	**853**	**942**	**2 814**	**1 897**	**3 781**	**825**	**2 114**	**1 096**	**4 729**	**1 922**	**5 742**
Bahrain	1 500	1 500	-	-	403	403	746	746	585	585	-	1	347	347	879	879
Cyprus	-	-	34	34	-	13	-	10	-	1	-	-	-	-	-	1 880
Iran, Islamic Republic	-	-	-	-	-	-	-	-	-	659	-	-	-	2 750	-	-
Kuwait	300	350	500	549	-	-	-	-	-	-	500	515	162	162	-	4
Lebanon	-	-	-	-	-	-	20	20	-	-	-	-	-	-	-	-
Oman	-	-	-	-	-	-	-	-	-	-	-	-	-	105	-	-
Saudi Arabia	311	311	-	1 190	32	32	177	1 321	1 258	2 056	325	1 535	175	585	1 004	2 314
Turkey	8	18	29	58	75	181	-	719	-	-	-	7	262	622	-	250
United Arab Emirates	3	51	-	-	-	225	-	-	54	479	-	56	151	158	39	416
Central Asia	-	-	-	-	-	-	-	**715**	-	-	-	**6**	-	**285**	**0**	**0**
Azerbaijan	-	-	-	-	-	-	-	700	-	-	-	-	-	-	-	-
Kazakhstan	-	-	-	-	-	-	-	6	-	-	-	-	-	285	-	-
Kyrgyzstan	-	-	-	-	-	-	-	-	-	-	-	3	-	-	-	-
Uzbekistan	-	-	-	-	-	-	-	9	-	-	-	3	-	-	-	-

/...

Annex table B.8. Cross-border M&A purchases, by region/economy of purchaser, 1990-1997 (concluded)

(Millions of dollars)

Region/economy	1990 Majority	1990 Total	1991 Majority	1991 Total	1992 Majority	1992 Total	1993 Majority	1993 Total	1994 Majority	1994 Total	1995 Majority	1995 Total	1996 Majority	1996 Total	1997 Majority	1997 Total
South, East and South-East Asia	**2 176**	**4 794**	**809**	**2 484**	**9 494**	**16 068**	**4 168**	**19 887**	**4 717**	**19 972**	**5 525**	**19 471**	**4 260**	**21 901**	**12 198**	**27 779**
Bangladesh	-	-	-	-	-	-	-	-	-	-	-	12	-	-	-	-
Brunei Darussalam	-	-	-	4	-	-	202	202	-	1	60	82	58	182	-	-
Cambodia	-	-	-	-	-	-	-	-	-	8	-	-	-	-	-	-
China	-	1 336	-	103	786	1 688	1 083	5 450	183	1 636	53	200	332	1 416	950	4 641
Hong Kong, China	756	1 132	427	852	7 885	9 559	2 023	8 388	719	3 414	1 255	3 921	1 062	3 642	2 451	5 635
India	-	-	270	270	-	422	-	-	16	619	159	201	-	-	3	8
Indonesia	-	187	58	58	32	106	173	247	390	519	141	615	504	614	2 321	2 416
Korea, Democratic People's Republic	-	-	-	-	-	-	-	-	-	-	-	-	-	-	-	-
Korea, Republic of	76	475	14	375	156	779	47	847	606	3 555	2 095	6 012	186	3 158	917	6 744
Laos	-	40														
Macau	-	-	-	-	-	-	-	-	-	10	-	-	-	-	-	-
Malaysia	139	160	-	235	74	143	301	1 220	1 737	7 021	391	1 253	1 128	5 413	1 349	2 490
Myanmar	-	-	-	-	-	-	-	-	-	-	-	-	-	1	-	-
Nepal	-	-	-	-	-	-	-	-	-	-	-	-	-	3	-	-
Pakistan	-	-	-	-	-	107	-	-	-	-	-	-	1	1	-	-
Philippines	-	-	12	18	44	51	-	-	-	433	-	11	-	2	30	66
Singapore	144	243	29	417	203	554	230	2 117	820	1 811	977	2 765	290	4 006	3 955	4 841
Sri Lanka	-	-	-	-	-	-	-	-	-	-	-	-	-	-	-	-
Taiwan Province of China	1 062	1 259	-	137	234	1 001	-	882	169	760	211	821	687	2 116	222	884
Thailand	-	-	-	15	80	1 638	110	533	77	181	182	3 577	12	1 346	-	15
Viet Nam	-	-	-	-	-	20	-	-	-	4	-	2	-	-	-	-
Central and Eastern Europe	**-**	**-**	**-**	**53**	**207**	**207**	**31**	**297**	**-**	**916**	**5**	**551**	**30**	**1 579**	**552**	**1 627**
Czech Republic	-	-	-	-	-	-	-	-	-	-	-	-	-	700	39	969
Estonia	-	-	-	-	-	-	-	512	512							
Hungary	-	-	-	-	-	-	-	-	-	-	-	66	-	43	1	3
Latvia	-	-	-	-	-	-	18	18	-	-	-	-	-	-	-	-
Romania	-	-	-	-	-	-	-	266	-	916	-	435	-	836	-	-
Russian Federation	-	-	-	53	-	-	-	14	-	-	5	-	30	-	-	144
Slovakia	-	-	-	-	-	-	14	-	-	-	-	-	-	-	-	-
Former Soviet Union	-	-	-	-	207	207	-	-	-	-	-	-	-	-	-	-
Ukraine	-	-	-	-	-	-	-	-	-	-	-	50	-	-	-	-
Dual nationality	-	210	105	105	-	-	-	-	-	-	-	-	90	90	-	-
Multinational[a]	-	-	-	-	-	-	-	-	-	-	-	-	-	-	-	-
Unknown	-	-	-	22	192	200	110	294	-	76	1	85	86	1 521	-	-

Source: UNCTAD, based on data provided by KPMG Corporate Finance.

[a] Involving purchasers from more than two economies.

Note: Majority refers to business combinations in which the investor acquires at least 50 per cent of the voting securities of the resulting business.

Annex table B.9. Cross-border M&As, by sector and industry, 1991-1997

(Millions of dollars)

Sector/industry	1991		1992		1993		1994		1995		1996		1997	
	Majority	Total	Majority	Total	Majority	Total	Majority	Total	Majority	Total	Majority	Total	Majority	Total
All industries	**49 062**	**85 279**	**73 769**	**121 894**	**66 812**	**162 344**	**109 356**	**196 367**	**140 813**	**237 184**	**162 686**	**274 611**	**236 216**	**341 653**
Primary sector	**1 628**	**2 994**	**803**	**3 246**	**1 568**	**24 308**	**3 762**	**9 588**	**3 477**	**22 215**	**6 577**	**23 408**	**13 673**	**23 812**
Agriculture, forestry and fishing	47	302	67	266	213	294	1 906	1 920	410	796	396	471	789	989
Agriculture and horticulture	-	1	56	56	83	109	1 742	1 756	372	522	283	358	393	534
Forestry	47	301	11	166	130	185	164	164	-	8	113	113	300	356
Fishing	-	-	-	44	-	-	-	-	38	266	-	-	96	99
Mining and Petroleum	1 581	2 692	736	2 981	1 355	24 014	1 856	7 668	3 067	21 419	6 181	22 937	12 884	22 823
Extraction of mineral oil and natural gas	1 169	2 267	582	2 763	1 239	23 763	1 760	7 525	2 339	20 413	5 317	22 064	12 649	22 425
Extraction of minerals not elsewhere specified	412	425	154	218	116	251	96	143	728	1 006	864	873	235	398
Secondary sector	**29 813**	**47 011**	**43 766**	**64 026**	**36 739**	**63 758**	**66 667**	**109 164**	**68 465**	**105 664**	**59 515**	**96 128**	**87 755**	**117 786**
Food, beverages and tobacco	3 626	5 157	12 358	13 561	6 552	9 548	11 376	16 092	13 865	16 363	6 505	10 151	15 636	17 954
Textile, leather and clothing	1 817	2 091	510	612	901	1 410	983	1 748	570	1 141	326	486	1 570	1 632
Textile industry	577	717	179	193	573	674	289	944	315	589	74	156	903	930
Manufacture of leather and leather good	128	128	3	3	187	205	164	165	4	84	146	166	226	226
Footwear and clothing industries	1 112	1 246	328	416	141	531	530	639	251	468	106	164	441	476
Timber and wooden furniture industries	43	248	461	477	54	449	715	1 215	366	434	537	666	277	312
Manufacture of paper and paper products; printing and publishing	2 981	6 227	2 366	4 185	1 893	3 480	7 610	10 861	7 548	8 603	8 100	11 272	7 358	7 911
Coke, petroleum products and nuclear fuel	1 044	5 880	912	4 187	1 888	5 048	2 381	9 191	217	1 212	754	5 015	1 118	2 280
Mineral oil processing	1 044	4 898	747	3 872	70	1 862	1 744	8 554	21	1 013	687	4 783	1 057	1 930
Coal extraction and manufacture of solid	-	982	165	315	1 818	3 186	637	637	196	199	67	232	60	350
Chemicals and chemical products	5 942	7 873	5 288	7 893	11 619	21 240	18 282	23 631	17 655	26 388	16 795	21 182	16 767	22 838
Chemical industry	5 934	7 561	5 284	7 789	11 616	21 038	18 159	23 464	17 563	26 157	16 795	20 422	16 767	22 766
Production of man-made fibres	8	312	4	104	3	202	123	167	92	231	-	760	-	72
Processing of rubber and plastics	1 306	1 403	655	888	595	816	2 203	3 226	2 470	3 059	2 303	2 915	1 157	1 328
Manufacture of non-metallic products	967	1 453	5 613	6 393	912	2 251	2 224	9 235	2 925	5 706	2 582	3 555	5 127	5 642
Basic metals and metal products	2 635	3 275	2 783	7 195	3 910	6 928	5 681	10 711	10 101	14 328	4 568	8 773	5 924	14 492
Extraction and preparation of metallifer	124	418	509	3 016	2 816	3 586	3 217	3 889	744	2 194	2 751	4 068	2 477	4 869
Metal manufacturing	1 125	1 437	1 805	3 308	758	2 887	2 007	6 081	3 698	6 132	670	3 518	2 765	7 943
Manufacture of metal goods not elsewhere specified														
Machinery and equipment	1 114	1 422	1 578	2 514	2 623	2 934	4 028	4 602	2 998	5 520	2 955	5 848	4 499	5 078
Mechanical engineering	1 114	1 422	1 566	2 502	2 623	2 934	4 028	4 602	2 998	5 508	2 955	5 848	4 499	5 078
Coke ovens	-	-	12	12	-	-	-	-	-	12	-	-	-	-
Office machinery and data processing equipment	851	1 001	156	635	538	805	623	826	1 425	2 328	940	1 613	2 075	2 652
Electrical and electronic engineering	4 970	7 302	7 153	9 872	3 979	6 110	5 782	9 407	4 929	11 595	6 137	10 186	8 016	11 486
Instrument engineering	734	1 074	449	506	324	347	1 619	1 749	1 322	1 472	1 707	1 859	12 518	12 605
Motor vehicles and other transport equipment	1778	2790	3135	4879	785	2610	2994	6972	2349	7810	5732	13058	3 673	9 515
Manufacture of motor vehicles and parts	527	1 050	2 459	3 771	258	1 512	2 291	4 238	2 016	6 506	3 952	10 998	2 568	7 806
Manufacture of other transport equipment	1 251	1 740	676	1 108	527	1 098	703	2 734	333	1 304	1 780	2 060	1 105	1 709
Other manufacturing industries	49	64	810	840	221	232	882	911	90	139	109	215	2 041	2 061
Tertiary sector	**17 620**	**35 273**	**29 199**	**54 486**	**28 504**	**74 279**	**38 927**	**77 615**	**68 871**	**109 305**	**96 564**	**155 075**	**134 788**	**200 055**
Electricity and water distribution	-	350	3 727	8 848	2 487	10 320	2 342	10 541	13 108	17 490	14 211	25 419	15 307	32 337
Production and distribution of electricity, gas and other forms of energy	-	212	3 726	8 823	2 452	9 482	2 342	10 506	11 760	16 039	13 904	24 203	15 296	32 103

/...

Annex table B.9. Cross-border M&As, by sector and industry, 1991-1997 (concluded)

(Millions of dollars)

Sector/industry	1991		1992		1993		1994		1995		1996		1997	
	Majority	Total	Majority	Total	Majority	Total	Majority	Total	Majority	Total	Majority	Total	Majority	Total
Water supply industry	-	138	1	25	35	838	-	35	1 348	1 451	307	1 216	11	234
Construction	186	503	259	4 720	155	1 122	511	2 854	662	2 084	1 713	7 189	1 319	4 881
Wholesale distribution (except dealing in scrap and waste materials)	1 395	1 675	1 791	1 895	1 587	2 260	4 433	5 335	4 469	4 996	6 324	6 563	5 955	9 023
Retail distribution	1 334	1 729	2 389	2 666	2 809	3 052	3 422	4 036	1 195	1 948	6 972	8 638	10 206	12 138
Hotels and catering	617	1 223	1 195	2 910	1 923	2 999	2 519	3 811	4 515	5 228	3 463	4 401	4 670	5 954
Transport and storage	1 481	2 332	972	4 317	1 426	4 146	2 194	7 888	1 185	4 571	3 265	10 540	4 984	6 732
Railways	-	-	-	-	-	716	25	45	-	-	-	700	-	-
Sea transport	56	242	74	222	715	739	288	289	281	511	43	693	2 554	2 920
Air transport	243	435	2	1 748	78	406	178	416	8	346	494	1 937	0	200
Other inland transport	123	142	101	101	12	24	227	3 994	269	719	1 916	4 664	495	571
Supporting services to transport	174	298	113	1 113	41	1 563	180	1 323	334	961	199	1 150	318	1 017
Miscellaneous transport services and storage not elsewhere specified	885	1 215	682	1 133	580	698	1 296	1 821	293	2 034	613	1 396	1 618	2 025
Postal services and telecommunications	338	3 400	210	2 572	194	17 062	386	8 958	2 497	17 921	3 475	15 529	3 426	20 154
Banking and finance	2 965	6 073	11 435	13 432	5 651	10 134	5 032	6 961	14 478	16 805	14 296	21 303	28 136	33 676
Insurance, except for compulsory social	4 863	10 024	810	3 525	4 412	5 851	8 589	9 958	2 308	3 025	12 339	13 128	23 752	24 730
Owning and dealing in real estate	526	1 005	1 908	3 166	2 224	8 181	2 350	4 596	3 250	6 438	9 035	11 579	6 927	9 646
Renting of movables	481	566	194	296	1 611	1 621	825	834	181	190	1 130	1 141	2 111	2 199
Business services	1 973	3 353	1 337	1 914	1 677	2 454	3 927	4 895	11 268	13 185	12 131	14 914	15 888	18 339
Business services	1 973	3 349	1 231	1 802	1 677	2 415	3 905	4 673	10 867	12 627	11 433	14 112	15 017	17 433
Research and development	-	4	106	112	-	39	22	222	401	558	698	802	871	906
Public Administration	344	401	539	664	304	1 177	253	306	233	242	392	396	1 040	1 149
Sanitary services	311	368	119	189	290	1 162	253	283	14	23	222	222	950	1 059
Education	33	33	420	475	14	15	-	13	-	-	170	174	78	78
Public administration, national defence and compulsory social security	-	-	-	-	-	-	-	10	219	219	-	-	12	12
Medical and other health services: veterinary services	92	92	14	16	173	173	60	261	884	1 188	1 092	5 083	2 605	2 605
Other services	980	2300	1960	3069	1817	3279	1371	5167	8273	13560	6221	8586	8 462	16 490
Recreational services and other cultural services	797	2 106	1 803	2 889	1 708	3 163	1 020	4 724	7 577	12 766	5 808	8 104	5 981	13 483
Personal services	146	157	16	29	99	99	326	349	684	686	122	171	464	468
Commission agents	-	-	-	-	-	-	-	-	-	12	263	264	43	43
Repair of consumer goods and vehicles	10	10	-	-	-	7	8	9	7	7	3	8	54	69
Dealing in scrap and waste materials	27	27	91	101	10	10	17	82	5	89	25	29	1 920	2 370
Other services provided to the general public	-	-	50	50	-	-	-	3	-	-	-	10	-	56

Source: UNCTAD, based on data provided by KPMG Corporate Finance.

Note: "Majority" refers to business combinations in which the foreign investor acquires more than 50 per cent of the voting securities of the resulting business.

Selected UNCTAD publications on transnational corporations and foreign direct investment

A. Individual studies

Bilateral Investment Treaties in the mid-1990s. 314 p. (forthcoming).

Handbook on Foreign Direct Investment by Small and Medium-Sized Enterprises: Lessons from Asia. 200 p. Sales No. E.98.II.D.4. $ 48.

Handbook on Foreign Direct Investment by Small and Medium-Sized Enterprises: Lessons from Asia. Executive Summary and Report on the Kunming Conference. 74 p. Free-of-charge.

International Investment Towards the Year 2002. 166 p. Sales No. GV.E.98.0.15. $29. (Joint publication with Invest in France Mission and Arthur Andersen, in collaboration with DATAR.)

World Investment Report 1997: Transnational Corporations, Market Structure and Competition Policy. 420 p. Sales No. E.96.II.D.10. $45.

World Investment Report 1997: Transnational Corporations, Market Structure and Competition Policy. An Overview. 70 p. Free-of-charge.

International Investment: Towards the Year 2001. 81 p. Sales No. GV.E.97.0.5. $35. (Joint publication with Invest in France Mission and Arthur Andersen, in collaboration with DATAR.)

World Investment Directory. Volume VI: West Asia 1996. 192 p. Sales No. E.97.II.A.2. $35.

World Investment Directory. Volume V: Africa 1996. 508 p. Sales No. E.97.II.A.1. $75.

Sharing Asia's Dynamism: Asian Direct Investment in the European Union. 162 p. Sales No. E.97.II.D.1. $26.

Transnational Corporations and World Development. 656 pp. ISBN 0-415-08560-8 (hardback), 0-415-08561-6 (paperback). £65 (hardback), £20.99 (paperback).

Companies without Borders: Transnational Corporations in the 1990s. 224 pp. ISBN 0-415-12526-X. £47.50.

The New Globalism and Developing Countries. 336 pp. ISBN 92-808-0944-X. $25.

Investing in Asia's Dynamism: European Union Direct Investment in Asia. 124 p. ISBN 92-827-7675-1. ECU 14. (Joint publication with the European Commission.)

World Investment Report 1996: Investment, Trade and International Policy Arrangements. 332 p. Sales No. E.96.II.A.14. $45.

World Investment Report 1996: Investment, Trade and International Policy Arrangements. An Overview. 51 p. Free-of-charge.

International Investment Instruments: A Compendium. Sales No. E.96.IIA.12 (the set). $125.

World Investment Report 1995: Transnational Corporations and Competitiveness. 491 p. Sales No. E.95.II.A.9. $45.

World Investment Report 1995: Transnational Corporations and Competitiveness. An Overview. 51 p. Free-of-charge.

Small and Medium-sized Transnational Corporations: Executive Summary and Report on the Osaka Conference. p. 60. UNCTAD/DTCI/6. Free-of-charge.

World Investment Report 1994: Transnational Corporations, Employment and the Workplace. 482 p. Sales No. E.94.II.A.14. $45.

World Investment Report 1994: Transnational Corporations, Employment and the Workplace. An Executive Summary. 34 p. Free-of-charge.

World Investment Directory. Volume IV: Latin America and the Caribbean. 478 p. Sales No. E.94.II.A.10. $65.

Liberalizing International Transactions in Services: A Handbook. 182 p. Sales No. E.94.II.A.11. $45. (Joint publication with the World Bank.)

Accounting, Valuation and Privatization. 190 p. Sales No. E.94.II.A.3. $25.

Environmental Management in Transnational Corporations: Report on the Benchmark Corporate Environment Suvey. 278 p. Sales No. E.94.II.A.2. $29.95.

Management Consulting: A Survey of the Industry and Its Largest Firms. 100 p. Sales No. E.93.II.A.17. $25.

Transnational Corporations: A Selective Bibliography, 1991-1992. 736 p. Sales No. E.93.II.A.16. $75. (English/French.)

Small and Medium-sized Transnational Corporations: Role, Impact and Policy Implications. 242 p. Sales No. E.93.II.A.15. $35.

World Investment Report 1993: Transnational Corporations and Integrated International Production. 290 p. Sales No. E.93.II.A.14. $45.

World Investment Report 1993: Transnational Corporations and Integrated International Production. An Executive Summary. 31 p. ST/CTC/159. Free-of-charge.

Foreign Investment and Trade Linkages in Developing Countries. 108 p. Sales No. E.93.II.A.12. $18.

World Investment Directory 1992. Volume III: Developed Countries. 532 p. Sales No. E.93.II.A.9. $75.

Transnational Corporations from Developing Countries: Impact on Their Home Countries. 116 p. Sales No. E.93.II.A.8. $15.

Debt-Equity Swaps and Development. 150 p. Sales No. E.93.II.A.7. $35.

From the Common Market to EC 92: Regional Economic Integration in the European Community and Transnational Corporations. 134 p. Sales No. E.93.II.A.2. $25.

World Investment Directory 1992. Volume II: Central and Eastern Europe. 432 p. Sales No. E.93.II.A.1. $65. (Joint publication with ECE.) $65.

World Investment Report 1992: Transnational Corporations as Engines of Growth: An Executive Summary. 30 p. Sales No. E.92.II.A.24. Free-of-charge.

World Investment Report 1992: Transnational Corporations as Engines of Growth. 356 p. Sales No. E.92.II.A.19. $45.

World Investment Directory 1992. Volume I: Asia and the Pacific. 356 p. Sales No. E.92.II.A.11. $65.

World Investment Report 1991: The Triad in Foreign Direct Investment. 108 p. Sales No. E.91.II.A.12. (out of print).

B. Serial publications

Current Studies, Series A

No. 30. *Incentives and Foreign Direct Investment.* 98 p. Sales No. E.96.II.A.6. $30. (English/French.)

No. 29. *Foreign Direct Investment, Trade, Aid and Migration.* 100 p. Sales No. E.96.II.A.8. $25.

No. 28. *Foreign Direct Investment in Africa*. 119 p. Sales No. E.95.II.A.6. $25

No. 27. *The Tradability of Banking Services: Impact and Implications*. 195 p. Sales No. E.94.II.A.12. $50.

No. 26. *Explaining and Forecasting Regional Flows of Foreign Direct Investment*. 58 p. Sales No. E.94.II.A.5. $25.

No. 25. *International Tradability in Insurance Services*. 54 p. Sales No. E.93.II.A.11. $20.

No. 24. *Intellectual Property Rights and Foreign Direct Investment*. 108 p. Sales No. E.93.II.A.10. $20.

No. 23. *The Transnationalization of Service Industries: An Empirical Analysis of the Determinants of Foreign Direct Investment by Transnational Service Corporations*. 62 p. Sales No. E.93.II.A.3. $15.00.

No. 22. *Transnational Banks and the External Indebtedness of Developing Countries: Impact of Regulatory Changes*. 48 p. Sales No. E.92.II.A.10. $12.

No. 20. *Foreign Direct Investment, Debt and Home Country Policies*. 50 p. Sales No. E.90.II.A.16. $12.

No. 19. *New Issues in the Uruguay Round of Multilateral Trade Negotiations*. 52 p. Sales No. E.90.II.A.15. $12.50.

No. 18. *Foreign Direct Investment and Industrial Restructuring in Mexico*. 114 p. Sales No. E.92.II.A.9. $12.

UNCTAD Issues Paper Series on a Possible Multilateral Framework on Investment

No. 1. *Transnational Corporations, Foreign Direct Investment and Development*. 30 p. DITE/PMFI/SERIES/1 (forthcoming).

The United Nations Library on Transnational Corporations. (Published by Routledge on behalf of the United Nations.)

Set A (Boxed set of 4 volumes. ISBN 0-415-08554-3. £350):

Volume One: *The Theory of Transnational Corporations*. 464 p.

Volume Two: *Transnational Corporations: A Historical Perspective*. 464 p.

Volume Three: *Transnational Corporations and Economic Development*. 448 p.

Volume Four: *Transnational Corporations and Business Strategy*. 416 p.

Set B (Boxed set of 4 volumes. ISBN 0-415-08555-1. £350):

Volume Five: *International Financial Management*. 400 p.

Volume Six: *Organization of Transnational Corporations*. 400 p.

Volume Seven: *Governments and Transnational Corporations*. 352 p.

Volume Eight: *Transnational Corporations and International Trade and Payments*. 320 p.

Set C (Boxed set of 4 volumes. ISBN 0-415-08556-X. £350):

Volume Nine: *Transnational Corporations and Regional Economic Integration*. 331 p.

Volume Ten: *Transnational Corporations and the Exploitation of Natural Resources*. 397 p.

Volume Eleven: *Transnational Corporations and Industrialization*. 425 p.

Volume Twelve: *Transnational Corporations in Services*. 437 p.

Set D (Boxed set of 4 volumes. ISBN 0-415-08557-8. £350):

Volume Thirteen: ***Cooperative Forms of Transnational Corporation Activity***. 419 p.

Volume Fourteen: ***Transnational Corporations: Transfer Pricing and Taxation***. 330 p.

Volume Fifteen: ***Transnational Corporations: Market Structure and Industrial Performance***. 383 p.

Volume Sixteen: ***Transnational Corporations and Human Resources***. 429 p.

Set E (Boxed set of 4 volumes. ISBN 0-415-08558-6. £350):

Volume Seventeen: ***Transnational Corporations and Innovatory Activities***. 447 p.

Volume Eighteen: ***Transnational Corporations and Technology Transfer to Developing Countries***. 486 p.

Volume Nineteen: ***Transnational Corporations and National Law***. 322 p.

Volume Twenty: ***Transnational Corporations: The International Legal Framework***. 545 p.

Transnational Corporations (formerly ***The CTC Reporter***).

Published three times a year. Annual subscription price: $35; individual issues $15.

Transnationals, a quarterly newsletter, is available free of charge.

United Nations publications may be obtained from bookstores and distributors throughout the world. Please consult your bookstore or write to:

United Nations Publications

Sales Section
Room DC2-0853
United Nations Secretariat
New York, N.Y. 10017
U.S.A.
Tel: (1-212) 963-8302 or (800) 253-9646
Fax: (1-212) 963-3489
E-mail: publications@un.org

OR

Sales Section
United Nations Office at Geneva
Palais des Nations
CH-1211 Geneva 10
Switzerland
Tel: (41-22) 917-1234
Fax: (41-22) 917-0123
E-mail: unpubli@unog.ch

All prices are quoted in United States dollars.

QUESTIONNAIRE

World Investment Report 1998: Trends and Determinants

Sales No. E.98.II.D.5

In order to improve the quality and relevance of the work of the UNCTAD Division on Investment, Technology and Enterprise Development, it would be useful to receive the views of readers on this and other similar publications. It would therefore be greatly appreciated if you could complete the following questionnaire and return to:

Readership Survey
UNCTAD Division on Investment, Technology and Enterprise Development
United Nations Office in Geneva
Palais des Nations
Room E-9123
CH-1211 Geneva 10
Switzerland

1. Name and address of respondent (optional):

____
____
____
____

2. Which of the following best describes your area of work?

Government	☐	Public enterprise	☐
Private enterprise institution	☐	Academic or research	☐
International organization	☐	Media	☐
Not-for-profit organization	☐	Other (specify)	__________

3. In which country do you work? ____________________

4. What is your assessment of the contents of this publication?

Excellent	☐	Adequate	☐
Good	☐	Poor	☐

5. How useful is this publication to your work?

Very useful ☐ Of some use ☐ Irrelevant ☐

6. Please indicate the three things you liked best about this publication:

____

____

____

7. Please indicate the three things you liked least about this publication:

____

____

____

8. If you have read more than the present publication of the UNCTAD Division on Investment, Enterprise Development and Technology, what is your overall assessment of them?

Consistently good ☐ Usually good, but with some exceptions ☐

Generally mediocre ☐ Poor ☐

9. On the average, how useful are these publications to you in your work?

Very useful ☐ Of some use ☐ Irrelevant ☐

10. Are you a regular recipient of ***Transnational Corporations*** (formerly ***The CTC Reporter***), the Division's tri-annual refereed journal?

Yes ☐ No ☐

If not, please check here if you would like to receive a sample copy sent to the name and address you have given above ☐